Lecture Notes in Computer Science   10143

Commenced Publication in 1973
Founding and Former Series Editors:
Gerhard Goos, Juris Hartmanis, and Jan van Leeuwen

More information about this series at http://www.springer.com/series/7410

Kefei Chen · Dongdai Lin
Moti Yung (Eds.)

Information Security and Cryptology

12th International Conference, Inscrypt 2016
Beijing, China, November 4–6, 2016
Revised Selected Papers

 Springer

Editors
Kefei Chen
School of Science
Hangzhou Normal University
Hangzhou
China

Moti Yung
Snapchat Inc.
Columbia University
New York, NY
USA

Dongdai Lin
Institute of Information Engineering
SKLOIS
Beijing
China

ISSN 0302-9743   ISSN 1611-3349   (electronic)
Lecture Notes in Computer Science
ISBN 978-3-319-54704-6   ISBN 978-3-319-54705-3   (eBook)
DOI 10.1007/978-3-319-54705-3

Library of Congress Control Number: 2017930645

LNCS Sublibrary: SL4 – Security and Cryptology

Printed on acid-free paper

This Springer imprint is published by Springer Nature
The registered company is Springer International Publishing AG
The registered company address is: Gewerbestrasse 11, 6330 Cham, Switzerland

Preface

This volume contains the papers presented at Inscrypt 2016: the 12th China International Conference on Information Security and Cryptology held during November 4–6, 2016, in Beijing, China. Inscrypt is a well-recognized annual international forum for security researchers and cryptographers to exchange ideas and present their work, and is held every year in China.

The conference received 93 submissions. Each submission was reviewed by two to four Program Committee members. The Program Committee, after some deliberation, decided to accept 32 papers. The overall acceptance rate is, therefore, about 34.4%.

Inscrypt 2016 was held in cooperation with the International Association of Cryptologic Research (IACR), and was co-organized by the State Key Laboratory of Information Security (SKLOIS) of the Chinese Academy of Sciences (CAS) and the Chinese Association for Cryptologic Research (CACR). The conference could not have been a success without the support of these organizations, and we sincerely thank them for their continued assistance and help.

We would also like to thank the authors who submitted their papers to Inscrypt 2016, and the conference attendees for their interest and support. We thank the Organizing Committee for their time and effort dedicated to arranging the conference. This allowed us to focus on selecting papers and dealing with the scientific program. We thank the Program Committee members and the external reviewers for their hard work in reviewing the submissions; the conference would not have been possible without their expert reviews. Finally, we thank the EasyChair system and its operators, for making the entire process of managing the conference convenient.

November 2016

Kefei Chen
Dongdai Lin
Moti Yung

Inscrypt 2016

12th China International Conference on Information Security and Cryptology

Beijing, China
November 4–6, 2016

Sponsored and organized by

State Key Laboratory of Information Security
(Chinese Academy of Sciences)
Chinese Association for Cryptologic Research

in cooperation with

International Association for Cryptologic Research

General Chair

Dongdai Lin — Institute of Information Engineering, CAS, China

Steering Committee

Feng Bao	Huawei International, Singapore
Kefei Chen	Hangzhou Normal University, China
Dawu Gu	Shanghai Jiao Tong University, China
Xinyi Huang	Fujian Normal University, China
Hui Li	Xidian University, China
Dongdai Lin	Chinese Academy of Sciences, China
Peng Liu	Pennsylvania State University, USA
Wen-feng Qi	National Digital Switching System Engineering and Technological Research Center, China
Meiqin Wang	Shandong University, China
Xiaofeng Wang	Indiana University at Bloomington, USA
Xiaoyun Wang	Tsinghua University, China
Jian Weng	Jinan University, China
Moti Yung	Snapchat Inc. and Columbia University, USA
Fangguo Zhang	Sun Yat-Sen University, China
Huanguo Zhang	Wuhan University, China

Technical Program Committee

Xianfeng Zhao	Institute of Information Engineering, CAS, China
Hong-Sheng Zhou	Virginia Commonwealth University, USA
Cliff Zou	University of Central Florida, USA

Local Organizing Committee

| Yi Deng | Institute of Information Engineering, CAS, China |
| Yanping Yu | Chinese Association for Cryptologic Research, China |

External Reviewers

Abhishek Kumar Chauhan	Lei Wang
Adekemi Adedokun	Lei Zhang
Aidan Collins	Li Lin
Akinori Kawachi	Lingchen Li
Amit Kumar Chauhan	Long Chen
Bin Zhao	Maria Eichlseder
Boyang Wang	Mario Werner
Bo-Yin Yang	Ming Tang
Chang'An Zhao	Ming-Shing Chen
Chengfang Fang	Nalla Anand Kumar
Cheng-Kang Chu	Qiao Liu
Christoph Dobraunig	Qingju Wang
Chunhua Su	Ralph A.C. Coon
Dong Li	Raymond K.H. Tai
Haihua Gu	Russell W.F. Lai
Haoyang Jia	Shaohao Xie
Harry W.H. Wong	Shi-Feng Sun
Huang Zhang	Shujie Cui
Huige Li	Siang Meng Sim
Huiling Zhang	Sisi Li
Jack P.K. Ma	Sun Bing
James Bowman	Tao Huang
Jeroen Delvaux	Thao Tran Phuong
Jianfeng Wang	Tuyet Duong
Jianghua Liu	Wenhai Sun
Jiapeng Zhang	Xiaoyang Dong
Jingyuan Zhao	Xiong Fan
Jose Mireles	Xuyun Nie
Joshua Lampkins	Ya Liu
Junqing Gong	Yanjiang Yang
Kamel Ammour	Yi Chen
Kang Yang	Yongbin Zhou
Kazumasa Omote	Yongjun Zhao

Contents

Signature and Authentication

Homomorphic Encryption

Leakage-Resilient

Post-quantum Cryptography

Symmetric Ciphers

Biclique Attack of Block Cipher SKINNY

Yafei Zheng[1,2(✉)] and Wenling Wu[1]

[1] Institute of Software, Chinese Academy of Sciences, Beijing 100190, China
{zhengyafei,wwl}@tca.iscas.ac.cn
[2] State Key Laboratory of Cryptology, Beijing 100190, China

Abstract. SKINNY is a lightweight tweakable block cipher, which was proposed at CRYPTO 2016. This paper presents an optimized brute force attack on full SKINNY using biclique attack with partial matching and precomputation. The results show that full round SKINNY64/64 is not secure against balanced biclique attack, the data complexity is 2^{48}, and the time complexity is $2^{62.92}$. That is a very tiny advantage against brute force attack. Furthermore, an unbalanced biclique attack is considered, which improves the time complexity to $2^{62.82}$. Moreover, in order to be immune to biclique attack, the round of SKINNY64/64 needs to be increased by 4 rounds to 36 rounds. Other versions of SKINNY do not have full round biclique attack owing to more encryption rounds.

Keywords: Block cipher · SKINNY · Biclique attack · Partial match

1 Introduction

With the widespread appliance of sensor nodes, RFID tags and other low resource devices, lightweight block cipher has been designed to satisfy the new ubiquitous but constraint cryptography environment. A number of lightweight block ciphers have been proposed in recent years, like PRESENT [1], KATAN & KTANTAN [2], LBlock [3], SIMON, SPECK [4] etc.

SKINNY [5] is a family of lightweight tweakable block ciphers, whose goal is to compete with NSA's recent design SIMON in terms of hardware/software performances, while providing in addition much stronger security guarantees with regards to differential/linear attacks. The designers gave a basic security evaluation of SKINNY against traditional block cipher cryptanalysis, including differential cryptanalysis, linear cryptanalysis, meet-in-the-middle (MITM) attack and so on. In the part of MITM attack, the designers claim that they do not think improving brute force attack by a small factor will turn into serious vulnerability in future. However, for SKINNY64/64 with a short key size of 64 bits, it will be not secure enough as a result of the enhanced computing. Therefore, optimized brute force attack will surely has a non-ignorable impact on the security of full round SKINNY64/64.

MITM attack, which is introduced by Diffie and Hellman in 1977 [6], is a typical method in the cryptanalysis of block cipher. MITM attack has been

K. Chen et al. (Eds.): Inscrypt 2016, LNCS 10143, pp. 3–17, 2017.
DOI: 10.1007/978-3-319-54705-3_1

improved with many techniques, including splice-and-cut, initial structure, partial matching etc. Biclique attack is an optimized brute force attack using MITM attack and initial structure named biclique. Biclique attack has been applied to many block ciphers for full round security evaluation including the first single key attack on full AES [7], and its results can be important references for choosing the number of encryption round during the design of block ciphers.

Our Contributions. In this paper, we study the security of SKINNY against biclique attack. We perform a computer-based algorithm to evaluate the computational and data complexity of different attacks with different choices of original key difference. Based on the chosen key differential trails, we give the following results:

(1) With the balanced biclique, key recovery of full round SKINNY64/64 is presented, with data complexity 2^{48}, and time complexity $2^{62.92}$.

(2) For larger improvement of the time complexity, we introduce unbalanced biclique, which improves the time complexity to $2^{62.82}$ with data complexity 2^{52}, and to $2^{62.86}$ with data complexity 2^{48}. In fact, the encryption round of SKINNY64/64 should be increased by 4 rounds to 36 rounds, so as to be secure against biclique attack.

(3) Results of reduced round biclique attacks on other versions of SKINNY are also presented.

It is worth noting that, in our attack, we suppose that, in the tweakey schedule, the tweak will not affect the influence of key difference.

Organization. The paper is organized as follows. Section 2 provides a brief description of SKINNY and the notations used throughout this paper. Section 3 presents the general biclique attack. Key recovery attacks on full round SKINNY64/64 under balanced biclique and unbalanced biclique are shown in Sects. 4 and 5 respectively. Section 6 presents the results of other versions of SKINNY. Section 7 summarizes this paper.

2   Description of SKINNY

We introduce the notations and give a brief description of SKINNY.

2.1   Notations

K: master key of block cipher
tk: the initial tweakey
$tk[i]$: the i-th cell of tk
X_r: 64-bit input of the r-th round function
$X_r^{i,j}$: the i-th and j-th cell of X_r.

2.2   Description of SKINNY

The lightweight block ciphers of the SKINNY family have 64-bit and 128-bit block versions. The internal state is viewed as a 4×4 square array of cells, where each cell is a nibble (in the $n = 64$ case) or a byte (in the $n = 128$ case). We denote $IS_{i,j}$ the cell of the internal state located at Row i and Column j, and s the size of a cell.

SKINNY follows the TWEAKEY framework form [8] and thus takes a tweakey input instead of a key or a pair key/tweak. For block size n, there are versions with tweakey size $t = n, t = 2n$ and $t = 3n$, and the numbers of rounds are 32,36,40 for $n = 64$, and 40,48,56 for $n = 128$. $z = t/n$ is the tweakey size to block size ratio, and the initialization of the tweakey state is performed by simply setting for $0 \leq i \leq 15 : TK1[i] = tk[i]$ when $z = 1$, $TK1[i] = tk[i]$ and $TK2[i] = tk[16 + i]$ when $z = 2$, and $TK1[i] = tk[i]$, $TK2[i] = tk[16 + i]$ and $TK3[i] = tk[32 + i]$ when $z = 3$. $tk = tk[0]||tk[1]|| \cdots ||tk[16z - 1]$ is the tweakey input and $tk[i]$ is an s-bit cell.

The round encryption of SKINNY is depicted in Fig. 1.

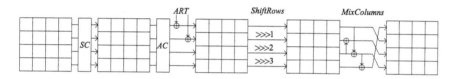

Fig. 1. The encryption of block cipher SKINNY.

Subcells. An s-bit S-box is applied to every cell of the cipher internal state.
AddConstants. Round constants are combined with the state.
AddRoundTweakey. For $i = \{0, 1\}, j = \{0, 1, 2, 3\}$:
$IS_{i,j} = IS_{i,j} \oplus TK1_{i,j}$ when $z = 1$,
$IS_{i,j} = IS_{i,j} \oplus TK1_{i,j} \oplus TK2_{i,j}$ when $z = 2$,
$IS_{i,j} = IS_{i,j} \oplus TK1_{i,j} \oplus TK2_{i,j} \oplus TK3_{i,j}$ when $z = 3$.
Then the tweakey arrays are updated as Fig. 2.

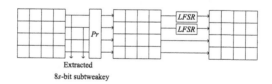

Fig. 2. The tweakey schedule in SKINNY.

$Pr = [9, 15, 8, 13, 10, 14, 12, 11, 0, 1, 2, 3, 4, 5, 6, 7]$.

Because the LFSR operation is cell-wise and has no influence in our attack, we omit it here.

ShiftRows. The rows of the cipher state cell array are rotated to the right by 0,1,2,3, respectively.

MixColumns. The state array is multiplied by a binary matrix M:

$$M = \begin{pmatrix} 1 & 0 & 1 & 1 \\ 1 & 0 & 0 & 0 \\ 0 & 1 & 1 & 0 \\ 1 & 0 & 1 & 0 \end{pmatrix}$$

3   Biclique Attack of Block Cipher

We introduce the notations of balanced biclique and unbalanced biclique, and present the general structure of biclique attack.

3.1   Definition of Biclique

Let f be a subcipher connects 2^d plaintexts $\{P_i\}$ to 2^d states $\{S_j\}$ with 2^{2d} keys:

$$\{K[i,j]\} = \left\{ \begin{matrix} K[0,0] & K[0,1] & \cdots & K[0,2^d-1] \\ K[1,0] & K[1,1] & \cdots & K[1,2^d-1] \\ \vdots & \vdots & \vdots & \vdots \\ K[2^d-1,0] & K[2^d-1,1] & \cdots & K[2^d-1,2^d-1] \end{matrix} \right\}$$

If for all $i,j \in \{0,\cdots,2^d-1\}$, $S_j = f_{K[i,j]}(P_i)$, the 3-tuple $[\{P_i\},\{S_j\}, \{K[i,j]\}]$ is called a balanced $d \times d$–dimensional biclique (Fig. 3).

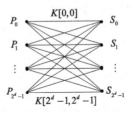

Fig. 3. $d \times d$-dimensional biclique.

If f is a subcipher that connects 2^d plaintexts to $2^{d'}$ states with $2^{d+d'}$ keys $(d \neq d')$, we define the corresponding structure an unbalanced $d \times d'$ - dimensional biclique. Take the $d \times 2d$ -dimensional biclique we use later for example: f is a subcipher that connects 2^d plaintexts $\{P_i\}$ to 2^{2d} states $\{S_{j_1,j_2}\}$ with keys $\{K[i,j_1,j_2]\}$. If $S_{j_1,j_2} = f_{K[i,j_1,j_2]}(P_i)$ for all $i,j_1,j_2 \in \{0,\cdots,2^d-1\}$, 3-tuple $[\{P_i\},\{S_{j_1,j_2}\},\{K[i,j_1,j_2]\}]$ is called an unbalanced biclique.

Besides dimension, the length, defined as the number of rounds f covers, is the other important parameter of a biclique.

3.2   Biclique Attack of Block Cipher

Biclique attack combines initial structure called biclique with MITM attack. During the MITM phase, techniques of precomputaion and partial matching are introduced. Figure 4 describes the general structure of biclique attack of block cipher.

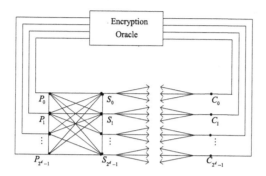

Fig. 4. Structure of biclique attack against block cipher.

The attack procedure is as follows:

Step 1. Divide the full key space into disjoint groups.

Step 2. Construct a biclique of appropriate dimension for each key group.

Step 3. For each biclique:

1. Choose the internal matching variable v.

2. Ask for the encryption of plaintexts P_i obtained during Step 2, get the corresponding ciphertexts C_i.

3. Compute $S_j \rightarrow v$ in the forward direction and $v \leftarrow C_i$ in the backward direction. If one of the tested keys $K[i, j]$ is the correct key, it will match $S_j \rightarrow v \leftarrow C_i$. Delete the keys that do not match in the internal matching variable.

Step 4. Exhaustively test the remaining key candidates until the correct key is found.

The procedure for unbalanced biclique is exactly the same, while j will stand for two positions j_1, j_2.

In order to avoid full codebook, the attacks afterwards only keep the bicliques whose plaintexts belong to a set of cardinality smaller than 2^{64}. We exhaustively search the choices of related-key differential trails. Based on the optimal related-key differentials, we construct 6-round balanced bicliques of dimension 4×4 and unbalanced bicliques of dimension 4×8 for SKINNY64/64 in Sects. 4 and 5.

4   Key Recovery for SKINNY64/64 with Balanced Bicliques

In this section, we show the procedure of key recovery attack of full round SKINNY64/64 with balanced 4×4-dimensional bicliques. Table 1 summarizes the attack parameters.

Table 1. Parameters for key recovery for SKINNY64/64(balanced bicliques)

Rounds	Blen	Bdim	v	Forward rounds	Backward rounds
32	6(0–5)	4×4	$X_{19}^{0,10}$	6–18	19–31

† Blen: Length of Biclique;
† Bdim: Dimension of Biclique.

Considering the time complexity of the whole attack, we choose cell $tk[2]$ and $tk[10]$ as original positions of key difference, which is optimal for the attack.

4.1   Key Partitioning

We define the key groups with respect to the master key and enumerate the groups by 2^{56} base keys. We divide the key space into 2^{56} groups of 2^8 keys each. The base keys of these groups are all possible 64-bit values with the $\{2\}$-th and $\{10\}$-th cell fixed to 0 and the remaining 56 bits running over all values. For each key group, the following steps are applied.

We denote the 2^8 keys in one group by $tk[i, j](i, j \in \{0, 1\}^4)$ and the different values are distinguished as: $tk[i, j]\{2\} = i, tk[i, j]\{10\} = j$.

For a fixed i, the keys $tk[i, j](j \in \{0, 1\}^4)$ share common 60 bits and are only different in the $\{10\}$-th cell. Similarly, the keys $tk[i, j](i \in \{0, 1\}^4)$ are only different in the $\{2\}$-th cell. In the sequel, the difference will be called active. As Table 2 shows, round subkeys computed during the key schedule share common values in parts noted 0, and subkeys noted with **1** are influenced active.

Then we construct a biclique covering 2^8 keys.

4.2   6-Round Biclique of Dimension 4 × 4

We construct a 6-round (0-th to 5-th round) biclique of dimension 4×4 for each key group.

P is plaintext of the encryption algorithm and state S is defined as X_6, which is the output of the 5-th round encryption. The procedure of computing the plaintexts and states is depicted in Fig. 5 and are described as follows:

Step 1. Fix $P_0 = 0_{(64)}$ and derive $S_0 = f_{tk[0,0]}(P_0)$. The process is called basic computation.

Step 2. Encrypt P_0 with different keys $tk[0, j](0 < j < 2^4)$ and the corresponding states are denoted by S_j (Fig. 5, Left). Because of the same starting with basic computation, the time complexity of this procedure is determined by the influence of difference between $tk[0, j]$ and $tk[0, 0]$. Keys $\{tk[0, j](0 < j < 2^4)\}$ are only different in the $\{10\}$-th cell and the round subkeys are different in parts noted with **1** (Table 2). So the process share common values with basic computation in white parts and different parts are marked with red color. Altogether, the red parts need to be computed 2^4 times because there are 2^4 keys in $\{tk[0, j]\}$.

Table 2. Key schedule of SKINNY64/64 influenced by key difference

Round	Active cell:{2}								Active cell:{10}							
0	0	0	1	0	0	0	0	0	0	0	0	0	0	0	0	0
1	0	0	0	0	0	0	0	0	0	0	0	0	1	0	0	0
2	0	0	0	0	1	0	0	0	0	0	0	0	0	0	0	0
3	0	0	0	0	0	0	0	0	0	0	0	0	0	0	1	0
4	0	0	0	0	0	0	1	0	0	0	0	0	0	0	0	0
5	0	0	0	0	0	0	0	0	0	0	0	0	0	1	0	0
6	0	0	0	0	0	1	0	0	0	0	0	0	0	0	0	0
7	0	0	0	0	0	0	0	0	0	0	0	1	0	0	0	0
8	0	0	0	1	0	0	0	0	0	0	0	0	0	0	0	0
9	0	0	0	0	0	0	0	0	0	0	0	0	0	0	0	1
10	0	0	0	0	0	0	0	1	0	0	0	0	0	0	0	0
11	0	0	0	0	0	0	0	0	0	1	0	0	0	0	0	0
12	0	1	0	0	0	0	0	0	0	0	0	0	0	0	0	0
13	0	0	0	0	0	0	0	0	1	0	0	0	0	0	0	0
14	1	0	0	0	0	0	0	0	0	0	0	0	0	0	0	0
15	0	0	0	0	0	0	0	0	0	0	1	0	0	0	0	0
16	0	0	1	0	0	0	0	0	0	0	0	0	0	0	0	0
17	0	0	0	0	0	0	0	0	0	0	0	0	1	0	0	0
18	0	0	0	0	1	0	0	0	0	0	0	0	0	0	0	0
19	0	0	0	0	0	0	0	0	0	0	0	0	0	0	1	0
20	0	0	0	0	0	0	1	0	0	0	0	0	0	0	0	0
21	0	0	0	0	0	0	0	0	0	0	0	0	0	1	0	0
22	0	0	0	0	0	1	0	0	0	0	0	0	0	0	0	0
23	0	0	0	0	0	0	0	0	0	0	0	1	0	0	0	0
24	0	0	0	1	0	0	0	0	0	0	0	0	0	0	0	0
25	0	0	0	0	0	0	0	0	0	0	0	0	0	0	0	1
26	0	0	0	0	0	0	0	1	0	0	0	0	0	0	0	0
27	0	0	0	0	0	0	0	0	0	1	0	0	0	0	0	0
28	0	1	0	0	0	0	0	0	0	0	0	0	0	0	0	0
29	0	0	0	0	0	0	0	0	1	0	0	0	0	0	0	0
30	1	0	0	0	0	0	0	0	0	0	0	0	0	0	0	0
31	0	0	0	0	0	0	0	0	0	0	1	0	0	0	0	0

Step 3. Decrypt S_0 under different keys $tk[i,0](0 < i < 2^4)$ and let P_i be the corresponding plaintexts (Fig. 5, Right). This process shares common starting with the inverse basic computation. Similarly, keys $\{tk[i,0](0 < i < 2^4)\}$ are only different in the {2}-th cell and the influence of the keys difference is marked with red color.

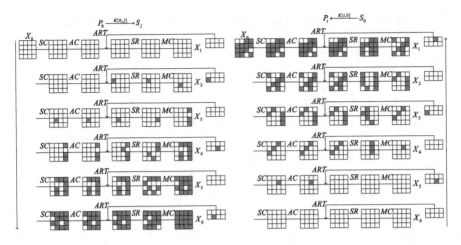

Fig. 5. Construction of 6-round biclique with 4×4 dimension (Color figure online).

Now, we have two differential trails $P_0 \xrightarrow{tk[0,j]} S_j$ $(j \in \{0,1\}^4)$ and $P_i \xrightarrow{tk[i,0]} S_0$ $(i \in \{0,1\}^4)$. Owing to the low diffusion of the key schedule and encryption algorithm, these two differential trails share no active S-boxes as demonstrated in Fig. 5.

We obtain a 4×4 -dimensional biclique for each key group: $P_i \xrightarrow{tk[i,j]} S_j$ $(i, j \in \{0,1\}^4)$.

4.3   Matching over 26 Rounds

For best time complexity, we choose $X_{19}^{0,10}$, which is an 8-bit output of 18-th round as the internal matching variable. There are 7 choices equivalent to this position: $X_{19}^{1,11}, X_{19}^{2,8}, X_{19}^{3,9}, X_{19}^{4,12}, X_{19}^{5,13}, X_{19}^{6,14}, X_{19}^{7,15}$. The value of the matching variable is computed in both forward and backward directions and keys do not match will be deleted.

S-boxes are the major contributor to the time complexity, so we count the number of S-boxes need to be computed to evaluate the time complexity.

Forward computation. We aim to get the values of corresponding internal matching variable from the encrypt direction. Let S_j be fixed and use keys $tk[i,j](i \in \{0,1\}^4)$ to partially encrypt S_j to $X_{19}^{0,10}$. We first precomputed $S_j \xrightarrow{tk[0,j]} V_{0,j}$. When encrypting the same S_j with keys $tk[i,j](i \in \{0,1\}^4, i \neq 0)$, we only need to compute the different parts compared to the process under $tk[0,j]$. Because of the same starting, the computational complexity is determined by the influence of differences between $tk[i,j](i \neq 0)$ and $tk[0,j]$. These keys are only different in the $\{2\}$-th cell and the round subkeys are different in parts noted with **1** in Table 2. As demonstrated in the left of Fig. 6, it makes no difference between the S-boxes marked with blue color, while the red parts represent active parts. The parts without color can be skipped because they are

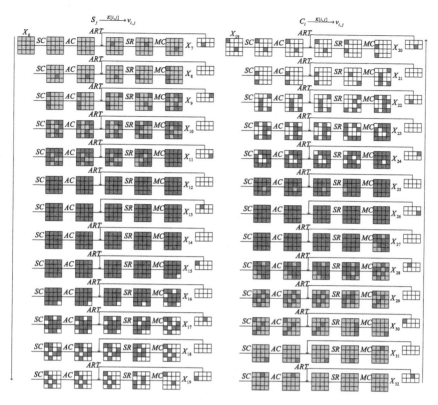

Fig. 6. Process of partial matching over 26 rounds (balanced biclique) (Color figure online).

not involved in the computation of matching variable. Altogether, for a single S_j, the matching values can be obtained after computing 129 S-boxes 2^4 times and 55 S-boxes once.

Backward computation. Now we evaluate the amount of S-boxes in backward direction. First of all, ask for the encryptions of plaintexts P_i $(i \in \{0,1\}^4)$ and get 2^4 ciphertexts C_i. Then decrypt the ciphertexts C_i with the keys $tk[i,j](j \in \{0,1\}^4)$ to $X_{19}^{0,10}$. We know the keys are only different in the $\{10\}$-th cell and the round subkeys are different in parts noted with **1** in Table 2. Taking a fixed C_i for example, the process of backward matching can be described as right part of Fig. 6. There is no difference between the S-boxes marked by blue color and the parts without color can be skipped. Altogether, for a single C_i, the matching values can be obtained after computing 101 S-boxes 2^4 times and 55 S-boxes once.

4.4   Search Candidates

We test 2^8 keys under 8-bit matching, so the number of remaining key candidates should be 2^{56}. Exhaustively test the remaining key candidates in each key group until the correct key is found.

4.5   Complexity

Now we evaluate the complexity of the whole attack. The construction of biclique and the process of matching are applied to 2^{56} key groups successively and each key group only includes 2^8 keys. So the memory complexity will not exceed 2^8 full-round SKINNY64/64 states.

Data Complexity. We fix $P_0 = 0_{(64)}$ for every biclique and all the plaintexts are same in $X_0^{0,1,11,14}$, so the data complexity will not exceed 2^{48} chosen plaintexts.

Time Complexity. The basic computation costs 16 S-boxes for each round, 96 S-boxes in total. Computing $P_i(0 < i < 2^4)$, 29 S-boxes need to be computed 2^4 times. Similarly, computing $S_j(0 < j < 2^4)$ involves 25 S-boxes 2^4 times. As a result, a biclique is constructed with complexity of 960 S-boxes.

In the matching part, we compute the 8-bit matching variable from two directions. It needs $2^4 \times (55 + 2^4 \times 129)$ S-boxes in the forward direction and $2^4 \times (55 + 2^4 \times 101)$ S-boxes in the backward direction. In total, it costs 60640 S-boxes per biclique.

The whole computational complexity is:

$$TC = 2^{56}(\frac{960 + 60640}{512}) + 2^{56} \approx 2^{62.92}$$

We exhaustively searched each key group, so the success probability is 1.

5   Key Recovery for SKINNY64/64 with Unbalanced Bicliques

In this section, we show the process of key recovery attack with unbalanced 4×8-dimensional bicliques on full round SKINNY64/64 in detail. This process follows the basic strategy in Sect. 4 but differs in the way of S-boxes counting.

We choose cell $tk[6]$ and $tk[8,11]$ as original positions of key difference.

5.1   Key Partitioning

We divide the key space into 2^{52} groups of 2^{12} keys each. The base keys of these groups are all possible 64-bit values with the $\{6\}$-th, $\{8\}$-th and $\{10\}$-th cell fixed to 0, and the remaining 52 bits running over all values.

There are 2^{12} keys in one group and they share common 52 bits except $\{6\}$-th, $\{8\}$-th and $\{10\}$-th cells. We denote them by $tk[i, j_1, j_2](i, j_1, j_2 \in \{0,1\}^4)$

and the different values are distinguished as: $tk[i, j_1, j_2]\{6\} = i, tk[i, j_1, j_2]\{8\} = j_1, tk[i, j_1, j_2]\{11\} = j_2$.

Round subkeys share common values and are influenced active during key schedule should be computed. Due to the similarity with Table 2 and limitation in paper space, we will not list it here.

5.2 6-Round Biclique of Dimension 4×8

We need to determine 2^4 plaintexts and 2^8 states that satisfy the definition of biclique. The procedure is depicted in Fig. 7 and can be described as follows:

Step 1. Fix $P_0 = 0_{(64)}$ and derive $S_0 = f_{tk[0,0,0]}(P_0)$.

Step 2. Encrypt P_0 with different keys $tk[0, j_1, j_2](0 < j_1, j_2 < 2^4)$ and the corresponding states are denoted by S_{j_1, j_2} (Fig. 7, Left). Because of the same starting with basic computation, the time complexity of this procedure is determined by the influence of difference between $tk[0, j_1, j_2]$ and $tk[0, 0, 0]$. As the definition, keys $\{tk[0, j_1, 0](0 < j_1 < 2^4)\}$ are only different in the $\{8\}$-th cell, and $\{tk[0, 0, j_2](0 < j_2 < 2^4)$ are only different in the $\{11\}$-th cell. So the process share common values with basic computation in white parts. The red parts are influenced by the difference between $tk[0, j_1, 0]$ and $tk[0, 0, 0]$ only so need to be computed 2^4 times. The blue parts are influenced by the difference between $tk[0, 0, j_2]$ and $tk[0, 0, 0]$ only, so need to be computed 2^4 times. The yellow parts are influenced by both two differences, so need to be computed 2^8 times.

Step 3. Decrypt S_0 with different keys $tk[i, 0, 0](0 < i < 2^4)$ and let P_i be the corresponding plaintexts (Fig. 7, Right). This process shares common starting point with the inverse basic computation. The influence of the keys difference is marked with red color, which parts need to be computed 2^4 times.

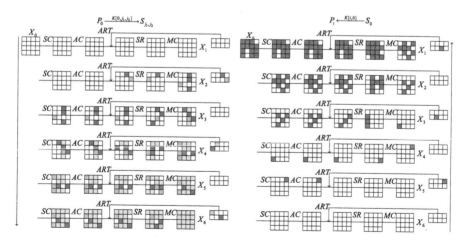

Fig. 7. Construction of 6-round biclique with 4×8 dimension (Color figure online).

These two differential trails share no active S-boxes during first 6 rounds as demonstrated in Fig. 7. It is obvious that $P_i \xrightarrow{tk[i,j_1,j_2]} S_{j_1,j_2}$ $(i, j_1, j_2 \in \{0,1\}^4)$.

5.3 Matching over 26 Rounds

We still choose $X_{19}^{0,10}$ as the internal matching variable.

Forward computation. Let S_{j_1,j_2} be fixed and use keys $tk[i,j_1,j_2](i \in \{0,1\}^4)$ to partially encrypt S_{j_1,j_2} to derive the values of $X_{19}^{0,10}$, which is corresponding denoted by v_{i,j_1,j_2}. We first compute and store the process of $S_{j_1,j_2} \xrightarrow{tk[0,j_1,j_2]} V_{0,j_1,j_2}$. When encrypting the same S_{j_1,j_2} with keys $tk[i,j_1,j_2](i \in \{0,1\}^4)$, we only compute the different parts compared to that process with $tk[0,j_1,j_2]$. Because of the same starting, the time complexity is determined by the influence of differences between $tk[i,j_1,j_2](i \neq 0)$ and $tk[0,j_1,j_2]$. We know the keys are only different in the $\{6\}$-th cell. As demonstrated in the left of Fig. 8, it makes no difference between the S-boxes marked with blue color, while the red parts

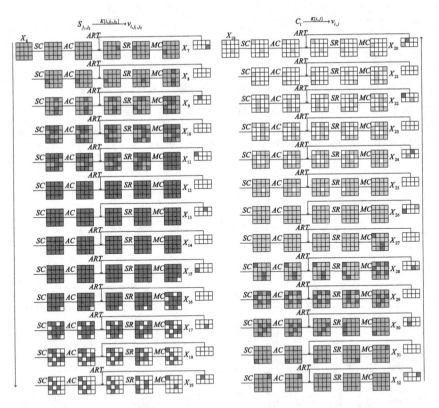

Fig. 8. Process of partial matching over 26 rounds (unbalanced biclique) (Color figure online).

represent active parts. Altogether, for a single S_{j_1,j_2}, the matching values can be obtained after computing 129 S-boxes 2^4 times and 55 S-boxes once.

Backward computation. Now we evaluate the amount of S-boxes in backward direction. First of all, ask for the encryptions of plaintexts P_i ($i \in \{0,1\}^4$) and get 2^4 ciphertexts C_i. Decrypt ciphertexts C_i with the keys $tk[i,j_1,j_2]$ ($j_1,j_2 \in \{0,1\}^4$) to $X_{19}^{0,10}$. Taking a fixed C_i for example, the process of backward matching can be described as right part of Fig. 8. There is no difference between the S-boxes marked by blue color and we can skip the computation of the states without color. The green parts are influenced by the difference between $tk[i,j_1,0]$ and $tk[i,0,0]$ only, so need to be computed 2^4 times. The red parts are influenced by the difference between $tk[i,0,j_2]$ and $tk[i,0,0]$ only, so need to be computed 2^4 times. The yellow parts are influenced by both the above two differences, so need to be computed 2^8 times. Altogether, for a single C_i, the matching values can be obtained after computing 89 S-boxes 2^8 times, 28 S-boxes 2^4 times and 39 S-boxes once.

5.4 Search Candidates

The number of remaining key candidates in each key group is 2^4 on average. Exhaustively test the remaining key candidates in each key group until the correct key is found.

5.5 Complexity

The construction of biclique and the process of matching are applied to 2^{52} key groups exhaustively and each key group only includes 2^{12} keys. So the memory complexity will not exceed 2^{12} full-round SKINNY64/64 states.

Data Complexity. We fix $P_0 = 0_{(64)}$ for every biclique and all the plaintexts share the same values in $X_0^{3,9,13}$, so the data complexity will not exceed 2^{52} chosen plaintexts.

Time Complexity. As before, in order to get $P_i (0 < i < 2^4)$, we need to compute 27 S-boxes 2^4 times. Similarly, computing $S_{j_1,j_2}(0 < j_1, j_2 < 2^4)$ involves 17 S-boxes 2^4 times and 18 S-boxes 2^8 times. Thus, a biclique is constructed with complexity of $96 + 432 + 4880 = 5408$ S-boxes.

In the matching part, it spends $2^8 \times (55 + 2^4 \times 129) = 542464$ S-boxes in forward direction and $2^4 \times (39 + 2^4 \times 28 + 2^8 \times 89) = 372336$ S-boxes in backward direction.

The whole computational complexity is:

$$TC = 2^{52}(\frac{5408 + 542464 + 372336}{512}) + 2^{56} \approx 2^{62.82}$$

If we choose $tk[i,j_1,j_2]\{1\} = i, tk[i,j_1,j_2]\{12\} = j_1, tk[i,j_1,j_2]\{15\} = j_2$, the data complexity will be 2^{48}, and the time complexity will be $2^{62.86}$, which is still better than $2^{62.92}$ as in balanced biclique attack.

6   Other Results

Due to the simple tweakey schedule, the biclique with dimension $d \times d'$ when $z = 1$ can be easily extended to biclique with dimension $2d \times 2d'$ when $z = 2$, and to biclique with dimension $3d \times 3d'$ when $z = 3$. The key recovery attack will be similar with the attack of SKINNY64/64. Here, we give our parameters and results in Table 3.

Table 3. Results summary

Cipher	Round	Blen	Bdim	Active cell	v	DC	TC
64/64	32	0–5	4×4	{2},{10}	$X_{19}^{0,10}$	2^{48}	$2^{62.92}$
	32	0–5	4×8	{6},{8,11}	$X_{19}^{0,10}$	2^{52}	$2^{62.82}$
	32	0–5	4×8	{1},{12,15}	$X_{19}^{0,10}$	2^{48}	$2^{62.86}$
64/128	35	0–5	8×16	{6,22},{8,11,24,27}	$X_{19}^{0,10}$	2^{52}	$2^{126.86}$
64/192	37	0–5	12×24	{1,17,33},{12,15,28,31,44,47}	$X_{19}^{0,10}$	2^{48}	$2^{190.95}$
128/128	37	0–5	8×16	{1},{12,15}	$X_{19}^{0,10}$	2^{48}	$2^{126.95}$
128/256	37	0–5	16×32	{6,22},{8,11,24,27}	$X_{19}^{0,10}$	2^{48}	$2^{254.95}$
128/384	37	0–5	24×48	{1,17,33},{12,15,28,31,44,47}	$X_{19}^{0,10}$	2^{48}	$2^{382.95}$

7   Conclusion

Our results are summarized in Table 3. Moreover, we find that the number of encryption round of SKINNY64/64 needs to be increased by 4 rounds to 36 rounds, so as to be secure against full round biclique attack.

Whether the sieve-in-the-middle technique proposed by Anne Canteaut etc. at CRYPTO 2013 can be introduced to improve the complexity, especially the time complexity of SKINNY64/64, will be the future work.

Acknowledgments. We would like to thank anonymous referees for their helpful comments and suggestions. The research presented in this paper is supported by the National Basic Research Program of China (No. 2013CB338002) and National Natural Science Foundation of China (No. 61272476, 61672509 and 61232009).

References

1. Bogdanov, A., Knudsen, L.R., Leander, G., Paar, C., Poschmann, A., Robshaw, M.J.B., Seurin, Y., Vikkelsoe, C.: PRESENT: an ultra-lightweight block cipher. In: Paillier, P., Verbauwhede, I. (eds.) CHES 2007. LNCS, vol. 4727, pp. 450–466. Springer, Heidelberg (2007). doi:10.1007/978-3-540-74735-2_31
2. De Cannière, C., Dunkelman, O., Knežević, M.: KATAN and KTANTAN a family of small and efficient hardware-oriented block ciphers. In: Clavier, C., Gaj, K. (eds.) CHES 2009. LNCS, vol. 5747, pp. 272–288. Springer, Heidelberg (2009)

3. Wu, W., Zhang, L.: LBlock: a lightweight block cipher. In: Lopez, J., Tsudik, G. (eds.) ACNS 2011. LNCS, vol. 6715, pp. 327–344. Springer, Heidelberg (2011). doi:10.1007/978-3-642-21554-4_19

4. Beaulieu, R., Shors, D., Smith, J., Treatman-Clark, S., Weeks, B., Wingers, L.: The SIMON and SPECK block ciphers on AVR 8-bit microcontrollers. In: Eisenbarth, T., Öztürk, E. (eds.) LightSec 2014. LNCS, vol. 8898, pp. 3–20. Springer, Cham (2015). doi:10.1007/978-3-319-16363-5_1

5. Beierle, C., et al.: The SKINNY family of block ciphers and its low-latency variant MANTIS. In: Robshaw, M., Katz, J. (eds.) CRYPTO 2016. LNCS, vol. 9815, pp. 123–153. Springer, Heidelberg (2016). doi:10.1007/978-3-662-53008-5_5

6. Diffie, W., Hellman, M.E.: Special feature exhaustive cryptanalysis of the NBS data encryption standard. Computer **10**(6), 74–84 (1977)

7. Bogdanov, A., Khovratovich, D., Rechberger, C.: Biclique cryptanalysis of the full AES. In: Lee, D.H., Wang, X. (eds.) ASIACRYPT 2011. LNCS, vol. 7073, pp. 344–371. Springer, Heidelberg (2011). doi:10.1007/978-3-642-25385-0_19

8. Jean, J., Nikolić, I., Peyrin, T.: Tweaks and keys for block ciphers: the TWEAKEY framework. In: Sarkar, P., Iwata, T. (eds.) ASIACRYPT 2014. LNCS, vol. 8874, pp. 274–288. Springer, Heidelberg (2014). doi:10.1007/978-3-662-45608-8_15

Improved Differential Cryptanalysis of CAST-128 and CAST-256

Shaomei Wang, Tingting Cui, and Meiqin Wang[✉]

Key Laboratory of Cryptologic Technology and Information Security,
Ministry of Education, Shandong University, Jinan 250100, China
mqwang@sdu.edu.cn

Abstract. CAST-128 and CAST-256 are two symmetric algorithms designed by Adams in 1990s. Both of them adopt the CAST design procedure which makes them process a number of desirable cryptographic. CAST-128 is notably used as the default cipher in some versions of GNU Privacy Guard (GPG) and Pretty Good Privacy (PGP) systems. As an extension of CAST-128, CAST-256 was submitted as a candidate for the Advanced Encryption Standard (AES). Since they are widely used, there are many different attacks on them. Differential cryptanalysis is one of the most powerful tools. In this paper, we achieve improved differential cryptanalysis of both CAST-128 and CAST-256 based on the technique of accessing differential tables. Firstly, we propose a differential attack on 9-round CAST-128 with 2^{73} encryptions and 2^{58} chosen plaintexts. Although we cannot improve the number of attacked rounds, the time complexity is significantly reduced. Then we mount an improved differential attack on 10 quad-rounds of modified CAST-256 which increase one quad-round than previous attack. The time complexity of this attack is 2^{217} encryptions, and the data complexity is 2^{123} chosen plaintexts. As far as we know, these are the best known attacks on CAST-128 and CAST-256 under weak key assumption.

Keywords: Differential analysis · CAST-128 · CAST-256 · Weak key assumption

1 Introduction

In 1997, Adams proposed the CAST design procedure for constructing a family of DES-like Substitution-Permutation Network (SPN) cryptosystems in [1]. The ciphers, known as CAST family, appear to have good resistance to differential [7], linear [12] and related-key cryptanalysis [5]. CAST-128 [2] and CAST-256 [3] both adopt the CAST design procedure. CAST-128 is notably used as the default cipher in some versions of GNU Privacy Guard (GPG) and Pretty Good Privacy (PGP) systems. It has also been approved for Canadian government being used by the Communications Security Establishments. As an extension of CAST-128, CAST-256 was submitted as a candidate for the Advanced Encryption Standard (AES) [13] in June 1998.

© Springer International Publishing AG 2017
K. Chen et al. (Eds.): Inscrypt 2016, LNCS 10143, pp. 18–32, 2017.
DOI: 10.1007/978-3-319-54705-3_2

Since CAST-128 and CAST-256 were proposed, they have been wildly attacked by differential attack, linear attack, boomerang attack [17] and multidimensional zero-correlation linear attack [8]. Adams *et al.* firstly investigated the resistance of CAST-256 to linear and differential cryptanalysis, but they did not give any concrete attack [4]. Then at FSE 1999, Wagner presented a boomerang attack on 16-round CAST-256 [17]. The first concrete linear cryptanalysis of 3-round CAST-128 and 12-round CAST-256 was presented in [14]. Then at SAC 2008, Wang *et al.* improved the results of [14] and mounted linear attacks on 6-round CAST-128 and 24-round CAST-256 [19]. Zhao *et al.* also mounted a linear cryptanalysis of 32 rounds of CAST-256, and they recovered partial key information of round 32 of CAST-256.

In [16], Seki *et al.* presented a differential attack on 9 quad-rounds of modified CAST-256 with a differential characteristic of 8 quad-rounds which remove the rotation keys of f_2 functions. Then in [18], Wang *et al.* presented a 6-round differential characteristic of CAST-128. With this characteristic, they recovered at less 104-bit subkey of 9-round CAST-128. These are the well known differential cryptanalysis of CAST-128 and CAST-256.

It is also worth mentioning that Bogdanov *et al.* mounted a multidimensional zero-correlation attack on 28-round CAST-256 at ASIACRYPT 2012 [8]. And in [9], Cui *et al.* proposed a statistical attack on 29-round CAST-256 by exploiting the statistical integral distinguisher. This is the best attack on CAST-256 in the single-key model without weak key (i.e. key which makes the cipher behave in some undesirable way [10]) assumption.

Our Contribution. In this paper, we use the known technique of the "Looking up Differential Tables" [11] and mount improved differential attacks on CAST-128 and CAST-256. We improve the previous attacks and achieve the best known attacks on both CAST-128 and CAST-256 under the weak key assumption.

- For CAST-128, We append three rounds to the end of the 6-round differential characteristic proposed by Wang *et al.* in [18] and recover all subkeys of the reduced 9-round CAST-128. In [18], Wang *et al.* recovered at less 104-bit subkey of 9-round CAST-128 with 2^{57} chosen plaintexts and $2^{101.8}$ encryptions. In our attack, we reduce the time complexity to 2^{73} encryptions while the data complexity is also 2^{58} chosen plaintexts. This is the best known attack on CAST-128 under the weak key assumption.
- For CAST-256, Seki *et al.* proposed a differential characteristic of 8 quad-rounds in [16], and they recovered 74-bit subkey of a 9 quad-rounds of modified CAST-256 under 2^{123} chosen plaintexts and 2^{95} encryptions. With the same differential characteristic, we recover 222 bits of subkeys including 148-bit subkey in the 10-th quad-round and 74-bit subkey in the 9-th quad-round with 2^{123} chosen plaintexts and 2^{217} encryptions which increases one more quad-round than previous result in [16]. As far as we known, it is also the best known attack on CAST-256 with regard to the attack rounds under weak key assumption.

In order to make a more accurate comparison, we summarise the related attacks on CAST-128 and CAST-256 in Table 1.

Table 1. Summary of attacks on CAST-128 and CAST-256

Target	Rounds	Attack type	Data(KP/CP)[a]	Time	Source	Rate of weak key
CAST-128	3	Linear	2^{37}KP	$2^{72.5}$	[14]	
	6	Linear	$2^{53.96}$KP	$2^{88.51}$	[19]	
	9	Differential	2^{58}CP	$2^{101.8}$	[18]	$2^{-23.8}$
	9	Differential	2^{58}CP	2^{73}	Sect. 3	$2^{-23.8}$
CAST-256	12	Linear	2^{101}KP	2^{101}	[14]	
	16	Boomerang	$2^{49.3}$CP	$2^{49.3}$	[17]	
	24	Linear	$2^{124.10}$KP	$2^{156.20}$	[19]	
	28	Multidimensional ZC[b]	$2^{98.8}$KP	$2^{246.9}$	[8]	
	29	Statistic integral	$2^{96.8}$CP	$2^{219.4}$	[9]	
	32	Linear	$2^{126.8}$KP	2^{250}	[20]	
	36	Differential	2^{123}CP	2^{95}	[16]	2^{-35}
	40	Differential	2^{123}CP	2^{217}	Sect. 4	2^{-35}

[a]KP: Known Plaintext; CP: Chosen Plaintext.
[b]Multi ZC: Multidimensional Zero-Linear.

Overview of This Paper. In Sect. 2, we give a brief description of CAST-128 and CAST-256. Then the improved differential attacks on CAST-128 and CAST-256 are proposed in Sects. 3 and 4 respectively. Finally, we conclude in Sect. 5.

2   Brief Description of CAST-128 and CAST-256

2.1   Brief Description of CAST-128

CAST-128 [2] is a DES-like Substitution-Permutation Network (SPN) cryptosystem. It is Feistel network encryption algorithm with 64-bit block size and key size of 40 to 128 bits (in 8-bit increments). When key size is no more than 80 bits, the algorithm use 12 rounds, and when key size is greater than 80 bits, the algorithm uses the full 16 rounds.

CAST-128 adopts three different round functions f_1, f_2, f_3. Different round functions share the same operations but different order of the these operations. f_1, f_2 and f_3 are described as following and shown in Fig. 1.

$$f_1: \quad I = ((K_{m_i} + D) \lll K_{r_i})$$
$$f = ((S_1[I_a] \oplus S_2[I_b]) - S_3[I_c]) + S_4[I_d]$$

$$f_2: \quad I = ((K_{m_i} \oplus D) \lll K_{r_i})$$
$$f = ((S_1[I_a] - S_2[I_b]) + S_3[I_c]) \oplus S_4[I_d]$$

$$f_3: \quad I = ((K_{m_i} - D) \lll K_{r_i})$$
$$f = ((S_1[I_a] + S_2[I_b]) \oplus S_3[I_c]) - S_4[I_d]$$

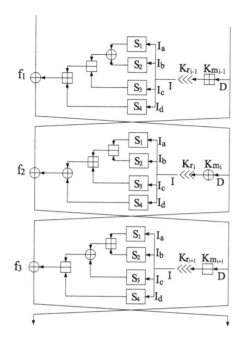

Fig. 1. Encryption procedure of CAST-128

where D is the data input to the round function. K_{r_i} is 5-bit "rotation key" of round i, and K_{m_i} is 32-bit "masking key" of round i. $I = (I_a, I_b, I_c, I_d)$ is the state after rotation key operation. S_1, S_2, S_3 and S_4 are four 8×8 bits S-boxes. $\lll, \oplus, +$ and $-$ denote circular left-shift operation, bitwise XOR, addition modulo 2^{32} and subtraction modulo 2^{32} respectively.

Note that the round number starts from 1 in this paper, so for CAST-128, rounds 1, 4, 7, 10, 13 and 16 use f_1 as round function, round 2, 5, 8, 11 and 14 use f_2 as round function, and rounds 3, 6, 9, 12, and 15 use f_3 as round function. The consecutive 3-round encryption procedure is described in Fig. 1.

Since in our attacks, we do not care for the key schedule. We assume that all subkeys are independent. So we will not describe it in more details. For more details about the key schedule, please refer to [2].

2.2 Brief Description of CAST-256

CAST-256 [3] was published in June 1998 adopting CAST design procedure. It is the extension of CAST-128 and was submitted as a candidate for the Advanced Encryption Standard (AES). Its block size and key size are 128 bits and 256 bits respectively. The whole construction adopts a generalized Feistel network including four 32-bit branches. Between two adjacent branches there are three different functions f_1, f_2 and f_3 which are same as the ones used in CAST-128.

Specially, CAST-256 consists of two types of round function: forward quad-round and reverse quad-round, which are described as following:

$$forward\ quad - round:\quad C = C \oplus f_1(D, K_{r_0}^i, K_{m_0}^i)$$
$$B = B \oplus f_2(C, K_{r_1}^i, K_{m_1}^i)$$
$$A = A \oplus f_3(B, K_{r_2}^i, K_{m_2}^i)$$
$$D = D \oplus f_1(A, K_{r_3}^i, K_{m_3}^i)$$

$$reverse\ quad - round:\quad D = D \oplus f_1(A, K_{r_3}^i, K_{m_3}^i)$$
$$A = A \oplus f_3(B, K_{r_2}^i, K_{m_2}^i)$$
$$B = B \oplus f_2(C, K_{r_1}^i, K_{m_1}^i)$$
$$C = C \oplus f_1(D, K_{r_0}^i, K_{m_0}^i)$$

where $K_{r_j}^i, K_{m_j}^i$ $(j = 0, 1, 2, 3)$ are "rotation key" and "masking key" of the i-th quad-round respectively. A, B, C, D together denotes a 128-bit block, and each one of them is a 32-bit word.

The overall encryption procedure is composed of 12 quad-rounds including 6 forward quad-rounds then 6 reverse quad-rounds, which is described in Fig. 2.

Similar to CAST-128, we do not care about the key schedule and assume that all subkeys are independent. So we ignore it here. For more details, please refer to [3].

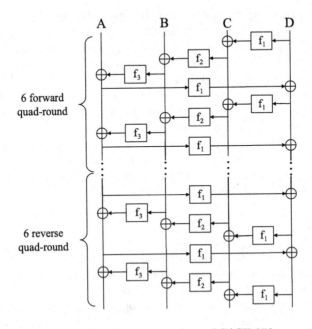

Fig. 2. Encryption procedure of CAST-256

3   Improved Differential Attack on 9-Round CAST-128

In this section, we will propose an improved differential attack on 9-round CAST-128. Firstly in Sect. 3.1, we recall a 6-round differential characteristic proposed by Wang $et\ al.$ in [18]. Based on this characteristic, we present the detailed attack in Sect. 3.2. In this attack, we append three rounds to the end of the differential characteristic and recover all subkeys of 9-round CAST-128, which needs 2^{58} chosen plaintexts and 2^{73} encryptions under about $2^{106.2}$ weak keys.

3.1   6-Round Differential Characteristic of CAST-128

In this subsection, we recall the 6-round differential characteristic of CAST-128 presented by Wang $et\ al.$ in [18]. Its probability is 2^{-53}, and it can be satisfied under $2^{-23.8}$ of the total key space, i.e., $2^{104.2}$ weak keys for CAST-128, which was found by studying the properties of round function f_1 and f_3. The form of such 6-round differential characteristic is $(f7e00000 \ggg K_{r_2}||00000000) \rightarrow (f7e00000 \ggg K_{r_2}||00000000)$, which is listed in the Fig. 3.

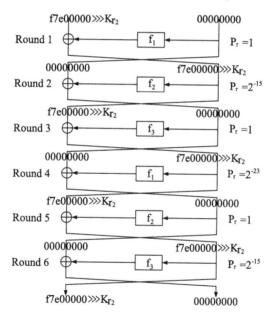

Fig. 3. 6-Round differential characteristic of CAST-128

Note that in the Fig. 3, K_{r_2} is the "rotation key" of the round 2. For each of 2^5 values of K_{r_2}, the differential characteristic is feasible.

3.2   Key Recovery Attack on CAST-128

In order to make the attack faster, we perform a precomputation: we compute the Differential Distribution Tables (called as DDT) for part of f_2 and f_3 functions, which means that we build a table according to all combinations of input and output differences, then store all possible input-output pairs into the corresponding cells of the table that have the same input and output differences.

For f_3 function, we exclude the modular subtraction operation with K_{m_i} and compute the $DDTs$ for remained part according to the value of K_{r_i}. Since there are 2^5 values of K_{r_i}, we need to compute 32 tables. Without loss of generality, we denote them as $DDT_j^3 (j = 0, 1, \ldots, 31)$. However, it is worth noting that the input differences are subtractive differences (modulo 2^{32}) and the output differences are xor differences in these $DDTs$.

For example, if let $K_{r_i} = j$, and suppose a, b are two 32-bit inputs, then the input difference is $\Delta In = (a - b)$ (modulo 2^{32}), and the output difference is $\Delta Out = f_3'(a) \oplus f_3'(b)$, where f_3' denotes the remaining part of f_3 by excluding the modular subtraction operation with K_{m_i}. Then we need to store $(a, f'(a))$ into the cell satisfying the $\Delta In \rightarrow \Delta Out$ of DDT_j^3.

For f_2 function, we build a DDT for the part of f_2 without mixing subkeys operations (renamed as f_2'), which means we only consider the part from the state before S-boxes layer to the end of f_2 function. Without loss of generality, we denote this DDT as DDT^2, and its input and output differences are both xor differences. Until now, we build 33 $DDTs$.

As the sizes of input and output of f_3' and f_2' functions are both 32 bits, there are 2^{64} different pairs and $2^{32} \times 2^{32}$ items (called cells as well) at each DDT. For fixed input and output differences, one input-output pair can be found on average.

In the precomputation phase, we need to build 33 $DDTs$. For each DDT, all possible input pairs should be traversed, so the total time complexity is $(33 \times 2^{32} \times 2^{32} \times 2)/9 \approx 2^{66.9}$ 9-round encryptions. We can only store one input-output pair instead of the input pair and output pair into the DDT because of the fixed input and output difference, the memory complexity is about $33 \times 2^{64} \times 8 \approx 2^{72.0}$ bytes.

Next, we will use these $DDTs$ to implement the key recovery phase step by step. Before giving the detailed attack, we need to define some notations. As illustrated in Fig. 4, (I_{L_i}, I_{R_i}) and (O_{L_i}, O_{R_i}) are the input and output values of round i respectively. D_i is input value of round function, and I_i is input value of S-boxes layer. X_i is the result of different operations on D_i and K_{m_i}. And Y_i is the output value of round function.

The overall key recovery phase is shown in Fig. 4, and the detailed attack is as follows:

- **Step 1.** Loop for all possible values of K_{r_2}. In data collection phase, we choose 2^n structures. Each of structures involves 2^{32} plaintexts with the same value of the right half I_r. To satisfy the special difference $f7e00000 \ggg K_{r_2}||00000000$, each structure can produce 2^{31} plaintext pairs, so in total we can obtain 2^{n+31} pairs. Ask for encryption of the pairs, and we can obtain 2^{n+31} ciphertext pairs as well.

- **Step 2.** Guess 5-bit value of K_{r_9} and 5-bit value of K_{r_8}. Then create a vector counter V of size 2^{64}, and initialize all its elements to zero.

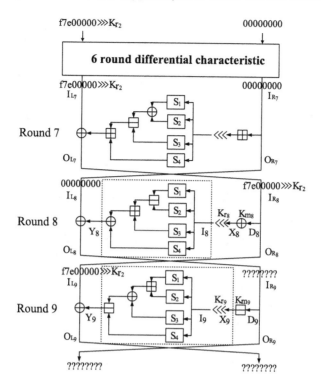

Fig. 4. Key recovery procedure of CAST-128

– **Step 3.** Loop for 2^{n+31} ciphertext pairs, and we can compute the output xor difference $\Delta Y_9 = (C_{L_9} \oplus C'_{L_9}) \oplus (f7e00000 \gg K_{r_2})$ and the input substractive difference $\Delta X_9 = (C_{R_9} - C'_{R_9}) mod \ 2^{32}$ of f'_3 in round 9 since we already knew the output values of round 9 (i.e. ciphertexts). Then through accessing the corresponding DDT, we can get input-output pairs (X_9, Y_9) and (X'_9, Y'_9) of f'_3 in round 9. Note that $X_9 = (K_{m_9} - C_{R_9}) mod \ 2^{32}$, we can further compute the value of K_{m_9}.

Since the input xor difference ΔI_8 of f'_2 in round 8 equals $(f7e00000 \gg K_{r_2}) \lll K_{r_8}$ and the output xor difference ΔY_8 equals $C_{R_9} \oplus C'_{R_9}$, we can get the input-output pairs (I_8, Y_8) and (I'_8, Y'_8) through accessing DDT^2. Further, we can compute $K_{m_8} = (I_8 \gg K_{r_8}) \oplus I_{L_9}$.

Then the corresponding $K_{m_8} || K_{m_9}$ counter are increased by 1. When all the ciphertext pairs are utilized, the maximum entry in the counter and the corresponding $(K_{r_2}, K_{r_9}, K_{r_8}, K_{m_9}, K_{m_8})$ are stored. In the end, there are 2^{15} candidates as there are 2^{15} values of $K_{r_2} || K_{r_9} || K_{r_8}$, and we consider the sub-key with the most happen times as the right key.

– **Step 4.** We have obtained the subkeys of round 8, round 9 and K_{r_2}. In order to recover the remaining subkeys from round 1 to round 7, we truncate the first 5 rounds from the 6-round differential characteristic, and decrypt ciphertexts in the last two rounds. Then we use a very similar way to recover the subkeys

Algorithm 1. Key Recovery Procedure of 9-round CAST-128

1 **for** 2^5 *values of* K_{r_2} **do**
2   Collect 2^{57} plaintext pairs whose differences equal
    $f7e00000 \lll K_{r_2}||00000000$.
3   Ask for encryption of these pairs and get their ciphertext pairs.
4   **for** 2^{10} *values of* K_{r_9} *and* K_{r_8} **do**
5   Allocate a vector counter $V[2^{64}]$, and initialize it to zero.
6   **for** 2^{57} *ciphertext pairs* **do**
7   Compute $\Delta X_9 = (C_{R_9} - C'_{R_9}) mod\ 2^{32}$.
8   Compute $\Delta Y_9 = (C_{L_9} \oplus C'_{L_9}) \oplus (f7e00000 \lll K_{r_2})$.
9   Look up the corresponding DDT, and get (X_9, Y_9) and (X'_9, Y'_9).
10   Compute K_{m_9} with $X_9 = (K_{m_9} - C_{R_9}) mod\ 2^{32}$.
11   Compute $\Delta I_8 = (f7e00000 \ggg K_{r_2}) \lll K_{r_8}$.
12   Compute $\Delta Y_8 = C_{R_9} \oplus C'_{R_9}$ where $C_{R_8} = C_{L_9} \oplus Y_9$ and
           $C'_{R_8} = C'_{L_9} \oplus Y'_9$.
13   Look up corresponding DDT, and get (I_8, Y_8) and (I'_8, Y'_8).
14   Compute K_{m_8} with $K_{m_8} = (I_8 \ggg K_{r_8}) \oplus C_{R_8}$.
15            $V[K_{m_9}||K_{m_8}] + +$.
16   Store the maximum value of counter V and corresponding
        $(K_{r_2}, K_{m_8}, K_{r_8}, K_{m_9}, K_{r_9})$.

17 $(K_{r_2}, K_{m_8}, K_{r_8}, K_{m_9}, K_{r_9})$ with the maximum happen times is considered as
the right key.

of round 6 and round 7. The complexity is smaller than what we need to recover $K_{m_8}, K_{r_8}, K_{m_9}, K_{r_9}$ and K_{r_2}, which can be ignored. Subkeys of the first 5 rounds also can be recovered with similar way.

In order to illustrate the key recovery phase more succinctly, the whole key recovery phase is summarized in Algorithm 1.

3.3 Complexity Evaluation

The ratio of signal to noise is proposed by Selçuk *et al.* in [15], which is calculated as follows:

$$S/N = \frac{p \times 2^k}{\alpha \times \beta} \tag{1}$$

where α is the average count of keys per analyzed pair, β is the ratio of analyzed pairs to all the pairs, k is the number of key bits we are searching and p is the probability of the differential characteristic.

In our attack, $p = 2^{-53}$. Since we can not filter the ciphertext pairs by the known condition, $\beta = 1$. The number of the all subkeys in round 8, round 9 and K_{r_2} is 79, so $k = 79$. For every analyzed pair, if we fix the value of $(K_{r_2}, K_{r_9}, K_{r_8})$, one possible value of $K_{m_8}||K_{m_9}$ can be deduced on average.

There are 2^{15} values of K_{r_2}, K_{r_9} and K_{r_8} in total, so we can get that $\alpha = 2^{15}$. Consequently

$$S/N = \frac{p \times 2^k}{\alpha \times \beta} = \frac{2^{-53} \times 2^{79}}{2^{15} \times 1} = 2^{11}. \tag{2}$$

The success probability in [20] is calculated as follows:

$$Ps = \int_{-\frac{\sqrt{\mu S_N} - \Phi^{-1}(1-2^{-k})}{\sqrt{S_N+1}}}^{\infty} \Phi(x)dx \tag{3}$$

where μ is the number of the right pairs (i.e. the pairs that satisfy the differential characteristic). In our attack, $\mu = 2^{n-22}$.

In order to attack the 9-round CAST-128 with the success rate 0.999, we choose $n = 26$. Consequently the data complexity of the attack is $2^{26} \times 2^{32} = 2^{58}$ chosen plaintexts.

The time complexity of Step 1 is $2^5 \times 2^{57} \times 2 = 2^{63}$ 9-round encryptions. Step 2 and Step 3 need about $2^5 \times 2^{10} \times 2^{57} \times 2 = 2^{73}$ memory access. The time complexity of Step 4 is not the domain term, so it can be ignored. We assume one access to the DDT (memory access) equals one 9-round encryption. Consequently the time complexity of the key recovery phase is about $2^{63} + 2^{73} \approx 2^{73}$ 9-round encryptions. And we also need $2^{64.2}$ bytes of memory in the key recovery phase. Besides, in the precomputation stage, we need $2^{66.9}$ encryptions an $2^{72.0}$ bytes of memory, so the complexity of the overall attack is about $2^{74} + 2^{66.9} \approx 2^{74}$ encryptions, and the memory complexity is about $2^{64.2} + 2^{72.0} \approx 2^{72.0}$ bytes of memory.

4   Improved Differential Attack on 10 Quad-Rounds of Modified CAST-256

In this section, we will mount an improved differential attack on 10 quad-rounds of modified CAST-256. In Sect. 4.1, we recall a differential characteristic of 8 quad-rounds proposed by Seki et al. [16] firstly. Then in Sect. 4.2, we will give the detailed attack. In this attack, We append two quad-rounds to the end of the differential characteristic and recover 148-bit subkey including all subkeys of round 10 and 74-bit subkey of $K_{r_0}^9$, $K_{m_0}^9$, $K_{r_1}^9$, $K_{m_1}^9$, which needs 2^{123} chosen plaintexts and 2^{217} encryptions under about 2^{221} weak keys.

4.1   A Differential Characteristic of 8 Quad-Rounds for CAST-256

In [16], Seki et al. proposed a differential characteristic of 8 quad-rounds for the modified CAST-256, which removed the rotation keys of all f_2 functions. The form of the characteristic is $(00000000||00000000||0000e0f7||00000000) \rightarrow (00000000||00000000||0000e0f7||00000000)$ (see Fig. 5). Its probability is 2^{-120}, and it is satisfied under 2^{-35} of the total key space, i.e. 2^{221} weak keys. With this characteristic, Seki et al. gave a differential attack on 9 quad-rounds of modified CAST-256. In Sect. 4.2, we will improve their attack and propose a differential attack on 10 quad-rounds of modified CAST-256.

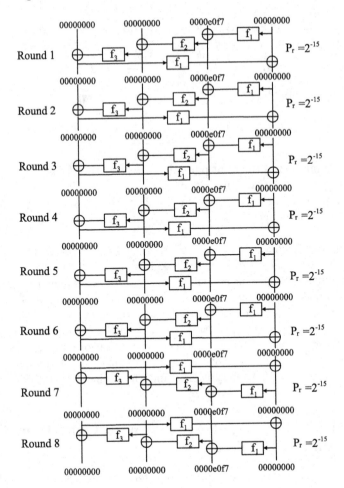

Fig. 5. A differential characteristic of 8 Quad-Rounds for CAST-256

4.2 Key Recovery Attack on CAST-256

In the attack on CAST-256, we also need the "differential distribution tables" of f_2' and f_3' functions. The procedure to produce these $DDTs$ is the same as before. The precomputation stage requires about $(33 \times 2^{32} \times 2^{32} \times 2)/40 \approx 2^{64.6}$ encryptions and $33 \times 2^{64} \times 8 \approx 2^{72.0}$ bytes.

In this attack, we append two quad-rounds to the end of the differential characteristic of 8 quad-rounds. Before giving concrete attack, we define some notations. As described in Fig. 6, $A_i\|B_i\|C_i\|D_i$ is the input of round i, which also is the output of round $(i-1)$, so in our new attack the ciphertext is $A_{11}\|B_{11}\|C_{11}\|D_{11}$. There are four round functions in one quad-round, then we use $D_i^j, X_i^j, I_i^j, Y_i^j (j = 0, 1, 2, 3)$ to denote corresponding values in the j-th round function of the i-th quad-round, which are similar with D_i, X_i, I_i, Y_i in the attack on CAST-128.

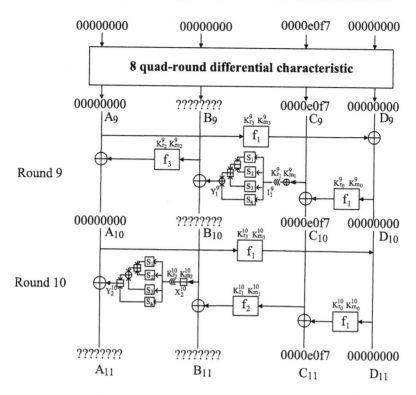

Fig. 6. Key recovery procedure of CAST-256

The overall key recovery phase is shown in Fig. 6, and the detailed attack is as follows:

- **Step 1.** We need to choose 2^n structures. Each of structures involves 2^{32} plaintexts with the same value in the A, B and D parts which can produce 2^{31} plaintext pairs satisfying the special input difference $00000000||00000000||0000e0f7||00000000$. So there are 2^{n+31} pairs in total. Ask for encryption of the plaintext pairs, then choose pairs whose ciphertext differences satisfy $C_{11} = 0000e0f7$ and $D_{11} = 00000000$. About $2^{n+31} \times 2^{-64} = 2^{n-33}$ pairs are reserved.

- **Step 2.** Guess 74-bit $K_{r_0}^{10}$, $K_{m_0}^{10}$, $K_{r_1}^{10}$, $K_{m_1}^{10}$. By decrypting the last round, we can get the second and the third part of the input values of round 10. $C_{10} = C_{11} \oplus f_1(D_{11}, K_{r_0}^{10}, K_{m_0}^{10})$, $C_{10}' = C_{11}' \oplus f_1(D_{11}', K_{r_0}^{10}, K_{m_0}^{10})$, $B_{10} = B_{11} \oplus f_2(C_{10}, K_{r_1}^{10}, K_{m_1}^{10})$, $B_{10}' = B_{11}' \oplus f_2(C_{10}', K_{r_1}^{10}, K_{m_1}^{10})$. Store $A_{11}||B_{10}||C_{10}||D_{11}$ and $A_{11}'||B_{10}'||C_{10}'||D_{11}'$ instead of ciphertext pairs.

- **Step 3.** Guess the 5-bit value of $K_{r_2}^{10}$, 74-bit value of $K_{r_3}^{10}$, $K_{m_3}^{10}$, $K_{r_0}^9$, $K_{m_0}^9$ and 5-bit value of $K_{r_1}^9$. Then create a vector counter of size 2^{64}, and initialize all elements of it to zero.

– **Step 4.** Loop for the remaining pairs. Compute input and output differences of f_3' in round 10 with $\Delta X_2^{10} = (B_{10} - B_{10}') \bmod 2^{32}$ and $\Delta Y_2^{10} = A_{11} \oplus A_{11}'$. Access the corresponding DDT of f_3', then get the input-output pairs (X_2^{10}, Y_2^{10}) and $(X_2^{10'}, Y_2^{10'})$ of f_3'. And compute $K_{m_2}^{10}$ with $X_2^{10} = (K_{m_2}^{10} - B_{10}) \bmod 2^{32}$.
Compute the forth part of the input of round 10 and the third part of the input of round 9 with $D_{10} = D_{11} \oplus f_1(A_{10}, K_{r3}^{10}, K_{m3}^{10})$ and $C_9 = C_{10} \oplus f_1(D_{10}, K_{r_0}^9, K_{m_0}^9)$ where A_{10} and D_{10} can be computed by the obtained values. Then compute the input and output difference of f_2' in round 9 with $\Delta I_1^9 = 0000e0f7 \lll K_{r_1}^9$, $\Delta Y_1^9 = B_{10} \oplus B_{10}'$, and get the input-output pairs (I_1^9, Y_1^9) and $(I_1^{9'}, Y_1^{9'})$ through looking up DDT^2 of f_2'. Then compute $K_{m_1}^9$ with $K_{m_1}^9 = (I_1^9 \ggg K_{r_1}^9) \oplus C_9$.
The corresponding $K_{m_2}^{10} \| K_{m_1}^9$ counter is increased by 1. When all the remaining pairs are utilized, store the maximum value of the counter and corresponding $(K_{r_2}^{10}, K_{r_3}^{10}, K_{m_3}^{10}, K_{r_0}^9, K_{m_0}^9, K_{r_1}^9, K_{r_0}^{10}, K_{m_0}^{10}, K_{r_1}^{10}, K_{m_1}^{10})$. Compare the selected value with the previous stored one, and preserve the larger one and corresponding subkeys. However, no comparison is needed in the first storage.

In order to illustrate the key recovery phase more succinctly, the key recovery phase can be performed like Algorithm 2.

4.3   Complexity Evaluation

In order to calculate the ratio of signal to noise, $p = 2^{-120}$ and $\beta = 2^{-64}$ in our attack. k is number of the total subkeys in round 10 and partial subkeys in round 9 which equals 222. For fixed value of $K_{r_0}^{10}$, $K_{m_0}^{10}$, $K_{r_1}^{10}$, $K_{m_1}^{10}$, $K_{r_2}^{10}$, $K_{r_3}^{10}$, $K_{m_3}^{10}$, $K_{r_0}^9$, $K_{m_0}^9$, $K_{r_1}^9$, one possible value of $K_{m_2}^{10} \| K_{m_1}^9$ can be deduced on average. There are 2^{158} values of $K_{r_0}^{10}$, $K_{m_0}^{10}$, $K_{r_1}^{10}$, $K_{m_1}^{10}$, $K_{r_2}^{10}$, $K_{m_2}^{10}$, $K_{r_3}^{10}$, $K_{m_3}^{10}$, $K_{r_0}^9$, $K_{r_1}^9$ in total, so $\alpha = 2^{158}$. Consequently

$$S/N = \frac{p \times 2^k}{\alpha \times \beta} = \frac{2^{-120} \times 2^{222}}{2^{158} \times 2^{-64}} = 2^8. \tag{4}$$

In the formula of success probability, we need to know the number of the right pairs, which $\mu = 2^{n-89}$ in our attack. In order to let the success rate be close to 1, we choose $n = 91$. Consequently the data complexity of the attack is $2^{91} \times 2^{31} \times 2 = 2^{123}$ chosen plaintexts.

The time complexity of Step 1 is 2^{123} 10 quad-rounds of encryptions. The time complexity of Step 2 is $2^{58} \times 2^{74} \times 2 = 2^{133}$ half quad-round of encryptions. Then Step 3 and Step 4 need about $2^{58} \times 2^{74} \times 2^{84} \times 2 = 2^{217}$ memory accesses. Consequently the overall complexity of the key recovery phase is about $2^{123} + 2^{133}/20 + 2^{217} \approx 2^{217}$ encryptions. And we need $2^{58} \times 16 + 2^{64} = 2^{64.3}$ bytes of memory in this phase. What's more, in the precomputation stage, we need $2^{64.6}$ encryptions and $2^{72.0}$ bytes of memory. So the overall time complexity of this attack is about $2^{217} + 2^{64.6} \approx 2^{217}$ encryptions, and the memory complexity is about $2^{64.3} + 2^{72.0} \approx 2^{72.0}$ bytes of memory.

Algorithm 2. Key Recovery Procedure of 10 Quad-Rounds CAST-256

---

1 Collect 2^{122} plaintext pairs whose difference equal
   $00000000||00000000||0000e0f7||00000000$.

2 Ask for ciphertext pairs, and filter them with ciphertext difference. //About
   2^{58} pairs remained.

3 **for** 2^{74} *values of* $K_{r_0}^{10}, K_{m_0}^{10}, K_{r_1}^{10}, K_{m_1}^{10}$ **do**

4   Decrypt ciphertext pairs in the last round, and get C_{10}, C_{10}' and B_{10}, B_{10}'.
   Store $(A_{11}||B_{10}||C_{10}||D_{11})$ and $(A_{11}'||B_{10}'||C_{10}'||D_{11}')$ instead of ciphertext
   pairs.

5   **for** 2^5 *values of* $K_{r_2}^{10}$, 2^{74} *values of* $K_{r_3}^{10}, K_{m_3}^{10}, K_{r_0}^{9}, K_{m_0}^{9}$ *and* 2^5 *values of*
   $K_{r_1}^9$ **do**

6   Allocate a vector counter $V[2^{64}]$, and initialize it to zero.

7   **for** 2^{58} *remained pairs* **do**

8   Compute $\Delta X_2^{10} = (B_{10} - B_{10}') mod\ 2^{32}$.

9   Compute $\Delta Y_2^{10} = A_{11} \oplus A_{11}'$.

10   Look up the corresponding DDT, and get (X_2^{10}, Y_2^{10}) and
   $(X_2^{10'}, Y_2^{10'})$.

11   Compute $K_{m_2}^{10}$ with $X_2^{10} = (K_{m_2}^{10} - B_{10}) mod\ 2^{32}$.

12   Compute $D_{10} = D_{11} \oplus f_1(A_{10}, K_{r_3}^{10}, K_{m_3}^{10})$.

13   Compute $C_9 = C_{10} \oplus f_1(D_{10}, K_{r_0}^9, K_{m_0}^9)$.

14   Compute $\Delta I_1^9 = 0000e0f7 \lll K_{r_1}^9$.

15   Compute $\Delta Y_1^9 = B_{10} \oplus B_{10}'$.

16   Look up the corresponding DDT, and get (I_1^9, Y_1^9) and $(I_1^{9'}, Y_1^{9'})$.

17   Compute $K_{m_1}^9$ where $K_{m_1}^9 = (I_1^9 \ggg K_{r_1}^9) \oplus C_9$.

18       $V[K_{m_2}^{10}||K_{m_1}^9]++$.

19   Find the maximum value of the counter and the corresponding
   $(K_{r_2}^{10}, K_{r_3}^{10}, K_{m_3}^{10}, K_{r_0}^9, K_{m_0}^9, K_{r_1}^9, K_{r_0}^{10}, K_{m_0}^{10}, K_{r_1}^{10}, K_{m_1}^{10})$.

20   Compare the maximum value of the counter with the previous stored
   one, and preserve the larger one. //No comparison is needed in the
   first storage.

21 The subkey corresponding to the final maximum entry is considered as the right
   key.

---

5 Conclusion

In this paper, we have proposed an improved differential attack on reduced
9-round CAST-128 cipher which needs 2^{58} chosen plaintexts and 2^{73} 9-round
encryptions based on the known 6-round differential characteristic. Besides, we
also proposed a differential attack on 10 quad-rounds of modified CAST-256.
The data and time complexity of the attack are 2^{123} chosen plaintexts and 2^{217}
encryptions respectively. Our attacks on CAST-128 and CAST-256 are the best
known ones under the weak key assumption.

References

1. Adams, C.: Constructing symmetric ciphers using the CAST design procedure. Des. Codes Crypt. **9**, 283–316 (1997)
2. Adams, C.: The CAST-128 Encryption Algorithm. RFC 2144 (1997)
3. Adams, C., Cilchist, J.: The CAST-256 Encryption Algorithm. RFC 2612 (1997)
4. Adams, C., Heys, H.: An analysis of the CAST-256 cipher. In: IEEE Canadian Conference on Electrical and Computer Engineering, pp. 9–12. IEEE Press, Canada (1999)
5. Biham, E.: New types of cryptanalytic attacks using related keys. In: Helleseth, T. (ed.) EUROCRYPT 1993. LNCS, vol. 765, pp. 398–409. Springer, Heidelberg (1994). doi:10.1007/3-540-48285-7_34
6. Biham, E., Shamir, A.: Differential cryptanalysis of DES-like cryptosystems. In: Menezes, A.J., Vanstone, S.A. (eds.) CRYPTO 1990. LNCS, vol. 537, pp. 2–21. Springer, Heidelberg (1991). doi:10.1007/3-540-38424-3_1
7. Biham, E., Shamir, A.: Differential Cryptanalysis of the Data Encryption Standard. Springer New York, New York (1993)
8. Bogdanov, A., Leander, G., Nyberg, K., Wang, M.: Integral and multidimensional linear distinguishers with correlation zero. In: Wang, X., Sako, K. (eds.) ASIACRYPT 2012. LNCS, vol. 7658, pp. 244–261. Springer, Heidelberg (2012). doi:10.1007/978-3-642-34961-4_16
9. Cui, T., Chen, H., Wen, L., Wang, M.: Statistic integral attack on CAST-256 and IDEA. In: ArcticCrypt 2016, Longyearbyen (2016)
10. Fluhrer, S., Mantin, I., Shamir, A.: Weaknesses in the key scheduling algorithm of RC4. In: Vaudenay, S., Youssef, A.M. (eds.) SAC 2001. LNCS, vol. 2259, pp. 1–24. Springer, Heidelberg (2001). doi:10.1007/3-540-45537-X_1
11. Mala, H., Dakhilalian, M., Rijmen, V., Modarres-Hashemi, M.: Improved impossible differential cryptanalysis of 7-Round AES-128. In: Gong, G., Gupta, K.C. (eds.) INDOCRYPT 2010. LNCS, vol. 6498, pp. 282–291. Springer, Heidelberg (2010). doi:10.1007/978-3-642-17401-8_20
12. Matsui, M., Yamagishi, A.: A new method for known plaintext attack of FEAL cipher. In: Rueppel, R.A. (ed.) EUROCRYPT 1992. LNCS, vol. 658, pp. 81–91. Springer, Heidelberg (1993). doi:10.1007/3-540-47555-9_7
13. National Institute of Standards and Technology: Advanced Encryption Standard(AES). crsc.nist.gov/encryption/aes
14. Nakahara, J., Rasmussen, M.: Linear analysis of reduced-round CAST-128 and CAST-256. In: SBSEG2007, pp. 45–55. Brazil (2007)
15. Selçuk, A., Bicak, A.: On probability of success in linear and differential cryptanalysis. J. Crypt. **21**, 131–147 (2008)
16. Seki, H., Kaneko, T.: Differential cryptanalysis of CAST-256 reduced to nine quadrounds. IEICE Trans. Fundam. **E84–A**, 913–918 (2001)
17. Wagner, D.: The boomerang attack. In: Knudsen, L. (ed.) FSE 1999. LNCS, vol. 1636, pp. 156–170. Springer, Heidelberg (1999). doi:10.1007/3-540-48519-8_12
18. Wang, M., Wang, X., Chow, K.: New differential cryptanalysis results for reduced-round CAST-128. IEICE Trans. Fundam. Electron. Commun. Comput. Sci. **E93–A**, 2744–2754 (2010)
19. Wang, M., Wang, X., Hu, C.: New linear cryptanalytic results of reduced-round of CAST-128 and CAST-256. In: Avanzi, R.M., Keliher, L., Sica, F. (eds.) SAC 2008. LNCS, vol. 5381, pp. 429–441. Springer, Heidelberg (2009). doi:10.1007/978-3-642-04159-4_28
20. Zhao, J., Wang, M., Wen, L.: Improved linear cryptanalysis of CAST-256. J. Comput. Sci. Technol. **537**, 2–21 (2001)

Improved Integral and Zero-correlation Linear Cryptanalysis of CLEFIA Block Cipher

Wentan Yi[1,2]($\boxtimes$), Baofeng Wu[2], Shaozhen Chen[1], and Dongdai Lin[2]

[1] State Key Laboratory of Mathematical Engineering and Advanced Computing,
Zhengzhou 450001, People's Republic of China
nlwt8988@gmail.com, chenshaozhen@vip.sina.com
[2] State Key Laboratory of Information Security, Institute of Information Engineering,
Chinese Academy of Sciences, Beijing 100049, People's Republic of China
wubaofeng@iie.ac.cn, ddlin@iie.ac.cn

Abstract. CLEFIA is a block cipher developed by Sony Corporation in 2007. It is a recommended cipher of CRYPTREC, and has been adopted as ISO/IEC international standard in lightweight cryptography. In this paper, some new 9-round zero-correlation linear distinguishers of CLEFIA are constructed with independent input masks and output masks, which admit multiple zero-correlation linear attacks on 14/15-round CLEAIA-192/256 about 79 times faster than results of the SAC paper with one-eighth of data. Furthermore, some new integral distinguishers over 9 rounds are derived by the relations between integral distinguishers and zero-correlation linear approximations. By using these integral distinguishers, the previous integral attacks on CLEFIA are improved with the partial sum technique. Our results have either one more rounds or lower time complexity than previous attack results with integral and zero-correlation linear cryptanalysis.

Keywords: Cryptography · Block cipher · CLEFIA · Integral attack · Zero-correlation linear cryptanalysis

1 Introduction

The block cipher CLEFIA [11] was proposed in 2007 by Sony Corporation. It was submitted to IETF (Internet Engineering Task Force) and is on the Candidate Recommended Ciphers List of CRYPTREC. Besides, it is one of the only two lightweight block ciphers recommended by the ISO/IEC standard. CLEFIA performs well in both software and hardware, and it is claimed to be highly secure. The efficiency comes from the generalized Feistel structure and the byte orientation, while the security is based on the novel technique called DSM (Diffusion Switching Mechanism), which increases resistance against linear and differential attacks.

A great deal of attention has been paid to CLEFIA and many cryptanalytic methods have been used to evaluate its security, such as integral attack [8,10,17], truncated differential attack [7], impossible differential attack

© Springer International Publishing AG 2017
K. Chen et al. (Eds.): Inscrypt 2016, LNCS 10143, pp. 33–46, 2017.
DOI: 10.1007/978-3-319-54705-3_3

Table 1. Summary of the attacks on CLEFIA

Attack type	Key size	Rounds	Data	Time	Reference
Impossible differential	192	13	$2^{119.8}$CPs	2^{146}Enc	[16]
Impossible differential	256	14	$2^{120.3}$CPs	2^{212}Enc	[16]
Improbable differential	192	14	$2^{118.9}$CPs	$2^{177.6}$Enc	[15]
Improbable differential	256	15	$2^{119.3}$CPs	$2^{242.1}$Enc	[15]
Truncated differential	256	15	2^{100}CPs	2^{203}Enc	[7]
Truncated differential	192	14	2^{100}CPs	2^{135}Enc	[7]
Integral	192	13	2^{113}CPs	$2^{180.5}$ Enc	[8]
Integral	192	14	2^{128}CPs	$2^{166.7}$ Enc	Sect. 4.2
Integral	256	14	2^{113}CPs	$2^{244.5}$ Enc	[8]
Integral	256	15	2^{128}CPs	$2^{230.7}$ Enc	Sect. 4.2
Multidimensional zero-correlation	192	14	$2^{127.5}$KPs	$2^{180.2}$ Enc	[5]
Multiple zero-correlation	192	14	$2^{124.5}$KPs	$2^{173.9}$ Enc	Sect. 3.2
Multidimensional zero-correlation	256	15	$2^{127.5}$KPs	$2^{244.2}$ Enc	[5]
Multiple zero-correlation	256	15	$2^{124.5}$KPs	$2^{237.9}$ Enc	Sect. 3.2

CPs refer to the number of chosen plaintexts, KPs refer to the number of known plaintexts, Enc refers to the number of encryptions.

[6,9,13,16], improbable differential attack [1,14,15] and zero-correlation linear cryptanalysis [5]. Since CLEFIA adopts a 4-branch generalized Feistel structure as the fundamental structure, in which there are two 4-byte F-functions per round, the designers [11] showed that there are 9-round impossible differentials in CLEFIA, that is, $(0, \alpha, 0, 0) \nrightarrow (0, \alpha, 0, 0)$ and $(0, 0, 0, \alpha) \nrightarrow (0, 0, 0, \alpha)$, where α is any 32-bit nonzero value. Note that the plaintext and ciphertext differences must be the same. By observing the inner structure of F-functions, where the branch numbers of the linear transformations are 5, Tsunoo et al. [16] presented some new 9-round impossible differentials, that is, $(0, \alpha 000, 0, 0) \nrightarrow (0, 0\beta 00, 0, 0)$, where α, β are any nonzero 8-bit values. Although the length of those parts is 8 bits, it is not necessary for the plaintext and ciphertext differences to be the same. Later, Sun et al. [12] found 9-round impossible differentials with the form $(0, \alpha \beta 00, 0, 0) \nrightarrow (0, \gamma 000, 0, 0)$, where α, β, γ are any nonzero 8-bit values. With respect to linear distinguishers with zero-correlation of CLEFIA, the only known are of the forms $(\alpha, 0, 0, 0) \nrightarrow (\alpha, 0, 0, 0)$ and $(0, 0, \alpha, 0) \nrightarrow (0, 0, \alpha, 0)$ over 9 rounds, where α is any 32-bit nonzero value. Note that the input masks and output masks are the same. So, it is a natural question whether there are any zero-correlation linear distinguishers whose nonzero parts of the input masks and output masks are different. This is part of the motivations of our work.

The links between integral and zero-correlation distinguishers were established by Bogdanov et al. in [2]. They proved that an integral distinguisher implies a zero-correlation distinguisher and vise versa under some independent conditions. For a vectorial Boolean function F, if the input mask α and output mask $\beta \neq 0$ are independent, then the approximation $(\alpha, 0) \rightarrow (\beta, 0)$ of F has correlation zero if and only for any λ, $\lambda \cdot F(x_0, x_1)$ is balanced with any fixed x_0. In a more general case, if the approximation $(M' \cdot \alpha, 0) \rightarrow (M'' \cdot \beta, 0)$ has correlation zero, then there also exist corresponding integral distinguishers, where M', M'' are two matrices and α, β are two independent values.

In this paper, we investigate the propagation characteristics of the linear masks on the matrices of F-functions, and propose some independent zero correlation linear distinguishers over 9-round CLEFIA. Some integral distinguishers are also deduced. Furthermore, key recovery attacks on 14/15-round CLEFIA-192/256 are conducted with integral and multiple zero-correlation cryptanalysis. Our contributions are summarized as follows.

1. The matrices M_0, M_1 adopted by CLEFIA in the linear transformations of F-functions are MDS (Maximum Distance Separable) matrices, that is, their branch numbers are 5. Let $\alpha = (\alpha_0, 0, 0, 0)$ and $\beta = (\beta_0, \beta_1, 0, 0)$ be 32-bit values with $(M_0 M_1)^T \cdot \beta = (\gamma_0, \gamma_1, \gamma_2, 0)$, where α_0, β_0, β_1 are any nonzero 8-bit values and γ_0, γ_1, γ_2 are any 8-bit values. Then, by the propagation characteristics of linear masks, the linear approximation $(((M_0)^T)^{-1} \cdot \alpha, 0, 0, 0) \rightarrow (((M_1)^T)^{-1} \cdot \beta, 0, 0, 0)$ is zero correlation linear approximation over 9-round CLEFIA. These new linear approximations are 9-round ones, the same with the existing approximations. However, the input masks and output masks are not required to be independent, which can be seen as the dual work of Tsunoo et al. [16]. Further, we propose the first multiple zero correlation linear cryptanalysis of 14/15-round CLEFIA-192/256 with those new linear approximations.

2. We study the relations between integral and zero-correlation distinguishers in detail, which can be improved to more general cases. For the zero correlation linear approximations with linear transformations operated on independent input masks and output masks, there exist corresponding integral distinguishers. Then, some integral distinguishers over 9-round CLEFIA are derived from the zero correlation linear approximations, which have much stronger ability to distinguish the right keys from wrong keys, because the phenomenons of the integral properties emerge in an extremely low probability in the case of wrong keys. With the new integral distinguishers, we present key recovery attacks on 14/15-round CLEFIA-192/256. The comparison of our results and known attack results on CLEFIA are summarized in Table 1.

The paper is organized as follows. In Sect. 2, we give some necessary notations, a brief description of CLEFIA and concise explanation of zero-correlation linear cryptanalysis. Some zero-correlation linear distinguishers over 9-round CLEFIA are presented in Sect. 3, and multiple zero correlation linear attacks on 14/15-round CLEFIA-192/256 are proposed in Sect. 4. The relations between integral and zero-correlation linear distinguishers are discussed in Sect. 5, with some 9-round integral distinguishers derived, and key recovery attacks on 14/15-round CLEFIA-192/256 are given. Finally, we summarize our work in Sect. 6.

2   Preliminaries

2.1   Notations

$\mathbb{F}_2$: the binary finite field $\{0,1\}$;
$\mathbb{F}_2^n$: the n-dimensional vector space over $\mathbb{F}_2$;
$|A|$: the cardinality of the set A;
$\oplus$: bitwise XOR;
$a \cdot b$: the scalar product of binary vectors, i.e., $a \cdot b := \oplus_{i=1}^n a_i b_i$;
M^{-1}: the inverse matrix of a non-singular matrix M;
M^T: the transposition of the matrix M;
$M \cdot a$: the multiplication of the matrix M and vector a^T;
$z[i]$: the i-th byte of z, and '0' is the most significant byte;
P, C: the plaintexts and ciphertexts of CLEFIA;
C_j^i: the j-th byte of the $i+1$-round with $j = 0,1,2,3$;
rk_i: the subkeys in the round functions of CLEFIA;
wk_i: the 32-bit whitening keys with $i = 0,1,2,3$;
$s_i(\cdot)$: the S-box of CLEFIA with $i = 0,1$;
$F_i(\cdot)$: the round function of CLEFIA with $i = 0,1$;
$X\|Y$: the concatenation of X and Y;

2.2   Description of CLEFIA

CLEFIA is a 128-bit block cipher with variable key lengths of 128, 192 and 256 bits, which takes a 4-branch generalized Feistel network with two parallel F-functions (F_0, F_1) per round. See Fig. 1(a). The number of rounds are 18/22/26

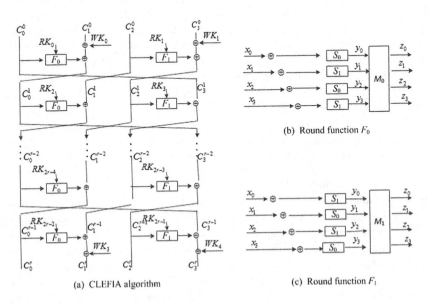

(a) CLEFIA algorithm   (b) Round function F_0

(c) Round function F_1

Fig. 1. The structure and building blocks of CLEFIA

for CLEFIA-128/192/256, respectively. Firstly, a 128-bit plaintext P is split up into four 32-bit words P_0, P_1, P_2 and P_3. The input state of the first round is $(C_0^0, C_1^0, C_2^0, C_3^0) = (P_0, P_1 \oplus wk_0, P_2, P_3 \oplus wk_1)$. For i from 1 to r, the states are computed in the following steps:

$$C_0^i = C_1^{i-1} \oplus F_0(C_0^{i-1}, C_1^{i-1}, rk_{2i-2}), \ C_1^i = C_2^{i-1},$$

$$C_2^i = C^{i-1} \oplus F_1(C_1^{i-1}, C_2^{i-1}, rk_{2i-1}), \ C_3^i = C_0^{i-1}.$$

Finally, the 128-bit ciphertext C is computed as $C = (C_0^r, C_1^r \oplus wk_2, C_2^r, C_3^r \oplus wk_3)$.

The round functions F_0 and F_1 take the SP structure; see Fig. 1(b), (c). There are two types of byte orientation S-boxes in the substitution layer, behaving in different orders in the two round functions. More precisely,

$$S_0(x_0, x_1, x_2, x_3) = (s_0(x_0), s_1(x_1), s_0(x_2), s_1(x_3)),$$

$$S_1(x_0, x_1, x_2, x_3) = (s_1(x_0), s_0(x_1), s_1(x_2), s_0(x_3)).$$

The diffusion layer uses two different MDS matrices M_0 and M_1 in the functions F_0 and F_1, respectively, where

$$M_0 = \begin{pmatrix} 0x01 & 0x02 & 0x04 & 0x06 \\ 0x02 & 0x01 & 0x06 & 0x04 \\ 0x04 & 0x06 & 0x01 & 0x02 \\ 0x06 & 0x04 & 0x02 & 0x01 \end{pmatrix}, \ M_1 = \begin{pmatrix} 0x01 & 0x08 & 0x02 & 0x0a \\ 0x08 & 0x01 & 0x0a & 0x02 \\ 0x02 & 0x0a & 0x01 & 0x08 \\ 0x0a & 0x02 & 0x08 & 0x01 \end{pmatrix}.$$

These are the so-called 4×4 Hadamard type matrices. We remark that the multiplications between these matrices and vectors are performed in $\mathbb{F}_{2^8}$ defined by the primitive polynomial $x^8 + x^4 + x^3 + x^2 + 1$.

Since the relations between the round subkeys will not help in our attacks, we omit the key scheduling algorithm here. The interested readers can refer to [11].

2.3   Multiple Zero-correlation Cryptanalysis

Consider a function $f : \mathbb{F}_2^n \to \mathbb{F}_2^n$. The correlation of the linear approximation $x \mapsto \beta \cdot f(x) \oplus \alpha \cdot x$, with input mask α and output mask β is defined as

$$Cor_x(\beta \cdot f(x) \oplus \alpha \cdot x) = 2Pr_x(\beta \cdot f(x) \oplus \alpha \cdot x = 0) - 1.$$

In zero-correlation linear cryptanalysis, the distinguishers use linear approximations with zero correlation. To reduce the data complexity, Bogdanov et al. [3] proposed the multiple zero-correlation linear distinguishers, which use ℓ zero-correlation linear approximations and requires $O(2^n/\sqrt{\ell})$ known plaintexts, where n is the block size of a cipher. Denote by N, ℓ the number of required known plaintexts and zero-correlation linear approximations for an n-bit block cipher. For each of the given linear approximations, compute the number T_i of times that the i-th linear approximation is fulfilled on N plaintexts and ciphertexts, $i \in \{1, 2, ...\ell\}$. Each T_i suggests an empirical correlation value $\hat{c}_i = 2T_i/N - 1$. Then, evaluate the statistic

$$T = \sum_{i=0}^{\ell} \hat{c}_i^2 = \sum_{i=0}^{\ell} (2\frac{T_i}{N} - 1)^2. \tag{1}$$

Under a statistical independency assumption, the statistic T follows a χ^2-distribution with mean $\mu_0 = \ell/N$ and variance $\sigma_0^2 = 2\ell/N^2$ for the right key guess, while for the wrong key guess, it follows a χ^2-distribution with mean $\mu_1 = \ell/N + \ell/2^n$ and variance $\sigma_1^2 = 2\ell/N^2 + 2\ell/2^{2n} + 2\ell/N2^{n-1}$.

If the probabilities of the type-I error and the type-II error to distinguish a wrong key with a right key are denoted as β_0 and β_1, respectively, considering the decision threshold $\tau = \mu_0 + \sigma_0 z_{1-\beta_0} = \mu_1 - \sigma_1 z_{1-\beta_1}$, the number of known plaintexts N should be about

$$N \approx \frac{2^n(z_{1-\beta_0} + z_{1-\beta_1})}{\sqrt{\ell/2} - z_{1-\beta_1}}, \tag{2}$$

where $z_{1-\beta_0}$ and $z_{1-\beta_1}$ are the respective quantiles of the standard normal distribution. More details are described in [3].

3   New Zero-correlation Linear Approximations for CLFEIA

To construct the zero-correlation linear approximations, one adopts the miss-in-the-middle techniques just like to find impossible differentials. Firstly, we give some properties of the matrices M_0 and M_1, which are used in the diffusion layers of the functions F_0 and F_1, respectively.

Lemma 31. $M_0^{-1} = M_0$, $M_1^{-1} = M_1$.

Lemma 32. $M_0M_1 = M_1M_0$ and they are MDS matrices.

Proof. It can be computed that

$$M_1M_0 = M_0M_1 = \begin{pmatrix} 0x37 & 0x46 & 0x34 & 0x40 \\ 0x46 & 0x37 & 0x40 & 0x34 \\ 0x34 & 0x40 & 0x37 & 0x46 \\ 0x40 & 0x34 & 0x46 & 0x37 \end{pmatrix}.$$

In addition we have $(M_0M_1)^{-1} = M_1^{-1}M_0^{-1} = M_1M_0 = M_0M_1$ by Lemma 31. Recall that a matrix is MDS if and only if all of its sub-matrices are invertible. It was proved in [12] that all of the two-order sub-matrices of M_0M_1 are invertible. Besides, by the definition of inverse matrix by adjugate matrix, we know that the determinants of all 3×3 sub-matrices of M_0M_1 are in one-to-one correspondence

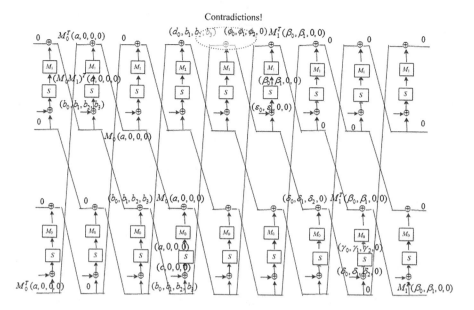

Fig. 2. Zero-correlation linear approximations of 9-round CLEFIA

with elements of $(M_0 M_1)^{-1} = M_0 M_1$, which are all non-zero. Therefore, $M_0 M_1$ is MDS.

We assert the linear approximations over 9-round CLEFIA (covering rounds 1–9, see Fig. 2).

$$\left(M_0^T \cdot (\alpha_0, 0, 0, 0), 0, 0, 0 \right) \rightarrow \left(M_1^T \cdot (\beta_0, \beta_1, 0, 0), 0, 0, 0 \right)$$

have zero-correlation, where $(M_0 M_1)^T \cdot (\beta_0, \beta_1, 0, 0) = (\gamma_0, \gamma_1, \gamma_2, 0)$, that is $0x40^T \cdot \beta_0 \oplus 0x34^T \cdot \beta_1 = 0$, $\alpha_0, \beta_0, \beta_1 \in \mathbb{F}_2^8 / \{0\}$ and $\gamma_0, \gamma_1, \gamma_2 \in \mathbb{F}_2^8$, $0x34^T$ denotes the transposition of matrix $0x34$ in finite field.

Along the encryption direction: We consider the linear trail with non-zero correlation. Given the mask $\left(M_0^T \cdot (\alpha_0, 0, 0, 0), 0, 0, 0 \right)$, the mask of the 4-th branch after 5 rounds must have the form (d_0, b_1, b_2, b_3) if the corresponding 5-round linear trail has non-zero correlation, where $b_1, b_2, b_3 \in \mathbb{F}_2^8$ are unknown non-zero values by Lemma 32.

Along the decryption direction: Given the mask $\left(M_1^T \cdot (\beta_0, \beta_1, 0, 0), 0, 0, 0 \right)$, the mask of the 4-th branch after 4 rounds must have the form $(\phi_0, \phi_1, \phi_2, 0)$ if the corresponding 4-round linear trail has non-zero correlation, because $(M_0 M_1)^T \cdot (\beta_0, \beta_1, 0, 0) = (\gamma_0, \gamma_1, \gamma_2, 0)$, where $\gamma_0, \gamma_1, \gamma_2, \phi_0, \phi_1, \phi_2$ are unknown values.

Contradiction: We just focus on the linear masks of the 4-th branch of the 5-th round function. From the encryption direction, the input masks are (d_0, b_1, b_2, b_3) under the condition that the corresponding linear trail has non-zero correlation, where b_1, b_2, b_3 are unknown non-zero values. Similarly, from the decryption direction, the output masks are $(\phi_0, \phi_1, \phi_2, 0)$, where ϕ_0, ϕ_1, ϕ_2 are unknown non-zero values, which is in contradiction with $b_3 \neq 0$. Thus, the linear hull is a zero-correlation linear hull. See Fig. 2.

4   Zero-correlation Linear Cryptanalysis of CLEFIA

In this section, we will attack 14-round CLFEIA-192. We mount the 9-round linear approximations from round 4 to round 12, and extend 3 rounds forward and 2 rounds backward respectively; see Fig. 3(a). The key-recovery attacks on 14-round CLEFIA-192 are proceeded with the partial-sum technique as follows.

Step 1. Collect all the N plaintext-ciphertext pairs (P, C). Allocate 8-bit counters $N_1[y_1]$ for 2^{160} possible values of

$$y_1 = P_0\|P_1\|P_2\|M_0 \cdot P_3[0]\|C_0\|C_1[0,1]\|M^1,$$

and initialize them to zero, where M^1 is a 8-bit value with

$$M^1 = 0x34^T \cdot (M_1 \cdot C_2[0]) \oplus 0x40^T \cdot (M_1 \cdot C_2[1]).$$

For every (P, C) pair, extract the value of y_1 and increase the corresponding counter $N_1[y_1]$.

Step 2. Allocate 8-bit counters $N_2[y_2]$ for 2^{120} possible values of

$$y_2 = P_0\|P_1\|P_2\|M_0 P_3[0]\|C_1[1]\|M^1,$$

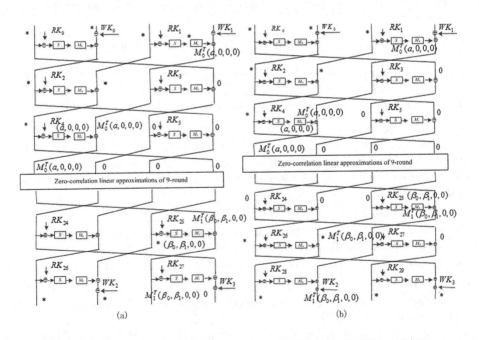

(a)   (b)

Fig. 3. Zero-correlations linear attacks on 14/15-round CLEFIA-192/256

and initialize them to zero. Guess rk_{26} and $wk_2[0] \oplus rk_{25}[0]$, and partially decrypt y_1 to get the value of y_2, that is,

$$M^1 = M^1 \oplus 0x34^T \cdot s_1\big(F_0(C_0, rk_{26})[0] \oplus C_1[0] \oplus wk_2[0] \oplus rk_{25}[0]\big).$$

Then update the corresponding counter by $N_2[y_2] + = N_1[y_1]$.

Step 3. Allocate a counter $N_3[y_3]$ for 2^{112} possible values of

$$y_3 = P_0 \| P_1 \| P_2 \| M_0 \cdot P_3[0] \| M^1,$$

and initialize them to zero. Guess $wk_2[1] \oplus rk_{25}[1]$, and partially decrypt y_2 to get the value of y_3, that is,

$$M^1 = M^1 \oplus 0x40^T \cdot s_0\big(F_0(C_0, rk_{26})[1] \oplus C_1[1] \oplus wk_2[1] \oplus rk_{25}[1]\big).$$

Then update the corresponding counter by $N_3[y_3] + = N_2[y_2]$.

The following steps in the partial encryption and decryption phase are similar to Step 3. Thus, to be consistent, we use Table 2 to show the details of Step 4 to Step 16 of the partial encryption and decryption.

Step 17. Compute the statistic T according to Eq. (1). If $T < \tau$, the guessed key value is a right key candidate. After Step 16, 152 key bits have been guessed,

Table 2. Partial encryption and decryption of the attack on 14-round CLEFIA.

Guess keys	Counters	Computed states
$rk_0[0]$	$y_4 = P_0[1,2,3] \| P_1 \| P_2 \| M_0 \cdot P_3[0] \| M^1$	$P_1[0] + = 0x01 \cdot s_0(P_0[0] \oplus rk_0[0]),$
		$P_1[1] + = 0x02 \cdot s_0(P_0[0] \oplus rk_0[0]);$
		$P_1[2] + = 0x04 \cdot s_0(P_0[0] \oplus rk_0[0]),$
		$P_1[3] + = 0x06 \cdot s_0(P_0[0] \oplus rk_0[0]);$
$rk_0[1]$	$y_5 = P_0[2,3] \| P_1 \| P_2 \| M_0 \cdot P_3[0] \| M^1$	$P_1[0] + = 0x02 \cdot s_1(P_0[1] \oplus rk_0[1]),$
		$P_1[1] + = 0x01 \cdot s_1(P_0[1] \oplus rk_0[1]);$
		$P_1[2] + = 0x06 \cdot s_1(P_0[1] \oplus rk_0[1]),$
		$P_1[3] + = 0x04 \cdot s_1(P_0[1] \oplus rk_0[1]);$
$rk_0[2]$	$y_6 = P_0[3] \| P_1 \| P_2 \| M_0 \cdot P_3[0] \| M^1$	$P_1[0] + = 0x04 \cdot s_0(P_0[2] \oplus rk_0[2]),$
		$P_1[1] + = 0x06 \cdot s_0(P_0[2] \oplus rk_0[2]);$
		$P_1[2] + = 0x02 \cdot s_0(P_0[2] \oplus rk_0[2]),$
		$P_1[3] + = 0x01 \cdot s_0(P_0[2] \oplus rk_0[2]);$
$rk_0[3]$	$y_7 = P_1 \| P_2 \| M_0 \cdot P_3[0] \| M^1$	$P_1[0] + = 0x06 \cdot s_1(P_0[3] \oplus rk_0[3]),$
		$P_1[1] + = 0x04 \cdot s_1(P_0[3] \oplus rk_0[3]);$
		$P_1[2] + = 0x02 \cdot s_1(P_0[3] \oplus rk_0[3]),$
		$P_1[3] + = 0x01 \cdot s_1(P_0[3] \oplus rk_0[3]);$
$rk_1[1]$	$y_8 = P_1 \| P_2[0,2,3] \| M_0 \cdot P_3[0] \| M^1$	$M_0 P_3[0] + = 0x08 \cdot s_0(P_2[1] \oplus rk_1[1]);$
$rk_1[2]$	$y_9 = P_1 \| P_2[0,3] \| M_0 \cdot P_3[0] \| M^1$	$M_0 P_3[0] + = 0x02 \cdot s_1(P_2[2] \oplus rk_1[2]);$
$rk_1[3]$	$y_{10} = P_1 \| P_2[0] \| M_0 \cdot P_3[0] \| M^1$	$M_0 P_3[0] + = 0x0a \cdot s_0(P_2[3] \oplus rk_1[3]);$
$rk_1[0]$	$y_{11} = P_1 \| P_2[0] \| M_0 \cdot P_3[0] \| M^1$	$M_0 P_3[0] + = 0x01 \cdot s_1(P_2[0] \oplus rk_1[0]);$
$rk_2[0] \oplus wk_0[0]$	$y_{12} = P_1[1,2,3] \| P_2[0] \| M_0 \cdot P_3[0] \| M^1$	$P_2[0] + = 0x01 \cdot s_0(P_1[0] \oplus rk_2[0] \oplus wk_0[0]);$
$rk_2[1] \oplus wk_0[1]$	$y_{13} = P_1[2,3] \| P_2[0] \| M_0 \cdot P_3[0] \| M^1$	$P_2[0] + = 0x02 \cdot s_1(P_1[1] \oplus rk_2[1] \oplus wk_0[1]);$
$rk_2[2] \oplus wk_0[2]$	$y_{14} = P_1[3] \| P_2[0] \| M_0 \cdot P_3[0] \| M^1$	$P_2[0] + = 0x04 \cdot s_0(P_1[2] \oplus rk_2[2] \oplus wk_0[2]);$
$rk_2[3] \oplus wk_0[3]$	$y_{15} = P_2[0] \| M_0 \cdot P_3[0] \| M^1$	$P_2[0] + = 0x06 \cdot s_1(P_1[3] \oplus rk_2[3] \oplus wk_0[3]);$
$rk_4[0]$	$y_{16} = M_0 \cdot P_3[0] \| M^1$	$M_0 \cdot P_3[0] + = 0x01 \cdot s_0(P_2[0] \oplus rk_4[0]);$

then there are 40 master key bits that we have not guessed. We do exhaustive search for all keys conforming to this possible key candidate.

Complexity of the Attack. In this attack, we set the type-I error probability $\beta_0 = 2^{-2.7}$ and the type-II error probability $\beta_1 = 2^{-20}$. We have $z_{1-\beta_0} = 1$, $z_{1-\beta_1} = 4.2$, $n = 128$, $\ell = 2^{16}$. The data complexity N is about $2^{124.5}$ by formula (2), and the decision threshold $\tau \approx 2^{6.23}$. The time complexity of steps 1–17 in the described attack is as follows:

1. Step 1 requires $2^{124.5}$ memory accesses;
2. Step 2 requires $2^{124.5} \times 2^{40} = 2^{164.5}$ memory accesses, because we should guess 40 bits rk_{26} and $wk_2[0] \oplus rk_{27}[0]$;
3. Step 3–11 require 9×2^{168} memory accesses;
4. Step 12–16 require 5×2^{176} memory accesses;
5. Step 17 requires $2^{152} \times 2^{20}$ 14-round CLEFIA encryption, because only the right key candidates can survive in the wrong key filtration.

If we assume that processing each memory accesses is equivalent to half round encryption, then the total time complexity is about $1/2 \times 5/14 \times 2^{176} \approx 2^{173.9}$ 14-round encryptions. In total, the data complexity is $2^{124.5}$ KPs, the time complexity is about $2^{173.9}$ 14-round encryptions and the memory requirement is 2^{160} bytes for counters.

For the attack on 15-round CLEFIA-256, we mount the 9-round zero-correlation linear approximations from round 4 to round 12, and extend 3 rounds forward and 3 rounds backward; see Fig. 3(b). We proceed similar steps to attack 14-round CLEFIA-192. The data complexity of the attack is $2^{124.5}$ KPs, the total time complexity is $2^{237.9}$ encryptions and the memory complexity is about 2^{224} bytes.

5 Integral Cryptanalysis of CLEFIA

In this section, the relations between integral and zero-correlation linear distinguishers are discussed. Some 9-round integral distinguishers are deduced, and then key recovery attacks on 14/15-round CLEFIA-192/256 are given with integral cryptanalysis.

5.1 Some New Integral Distinguishers over 9-round CLEFIA

Bogdanov et al. [2] showed that an integral implies a zero-correlation distinguisher and vise versa under some independent conditions.

Theorem 51 (See [2]). *Let m, m_1, m_2 be integers. For the vectorial Boolean function $f : \mathbb{F}_2^{m_1} \times \mathbb{F}_2^{m_2} \to \mathbb{F}_2^m$, the following are equivalent:*

(i) $Cor_{x_{m_2}}((b_q, 0) \cdot f(x_{m_1}, x_{m_2})) = 0$, for all $b_q \in \mathbb{F}_2^q \setminus \{0\}$;
(ii) $Cor_{x_{m_1}, x_{m_2}}((d_{m_1}, 0) \cdot x \oplus (b_q, 0) \cdot f(x_{m_1}, x_{m_2})) = 0$, for all $d_{m_1} \in \mathbb{F}_2^{m_1}$ and $b_q \in \mathbb{F}_2^q \setminus \{0\}$.

Let M_0, M_1 be two invertible matrices. For any $d_{m_1'} \in \mathbb{F}_2^{m_1'}$, $b_{q_1} \in \mathbb{F}_2^{q_1}$, and $M_0 \cdot (d_{m_1'}, 0, ..., 0) \in \mathbb{F}_2^{m_1}$, $M_1 \cdot (b_{q_1}, 0, ..., 0) \in \mathbb{F}_2^q$, we have the following result.

Corollary 51. *The following two conditions are equivalent.*

(i) $Cor_{x_{(d_{m_1} - d_{m_1'})}, x_{m_2}} \left(b_{q_1} \cdot M_1^T \cdot f((M_0^{-1})^T \cdot x)_{q_1} \right) = 0$, *for all* $b_{q_1} \in \mathbb{F}_2^{q_1} \setminus \{0\}$;

(ii) $Cor_x \left((M_0 \cdot (d_{m_1'}, 0, ..., 0), 0) \cdot (x_{d_{m_1'}}, x_{(d_{m_1} - d_{m_1'})}, x_{m_2}) \oplus (M_1 \cdot (b_{q_1}, 0, ..., 0), 0) \cdot f(x) \right) = 0$, *for all* $d_{m_1'} \in \mathbb{F}_2^{m_1'}$ *and* $b_{q_1} \in \mathbb{F}_2^{q_1} \setminus \{0\}$.

The corollary can be proved by the fact that $((M \cdot a)^T \cdot x) = (a^T \cdot (M^T \cdot x))$, where M is a linear transformation, so we omit the proof here. By Corollary 51, an integral distinguisher covering 9 rounds of CLEFIA can be derived from zero-correlation linear approximations.

Proposition 51. *Choose a set of 2^{120} inputs of the r-th round, where the 32-bit values of C_0^r are set to the form $M_0^T \cdot (a, b, c, d)$, C_1^r, C_2^r, C_3^r range over $\mathbb{F}_2^{32}$, where a is fixed to be any 8-bit values, b, c, d range over $\mathbb{F}_2^8$. Encrypt the 2^{120} chosen values by 9 rounds. Then, each of the 2^8 possible values of $0x34^T \cdot (M_1 \cdot C_0^{r+9})[0] \oplus 0x40^T \cdot (M_1 \cdot C_0^{r+9})[1]$ occurs 2^{112} times.*

Let $F : \mathbb{F}_2^{120} \to \mathbb{F}_2^8$ be a random vectorial Boolean function and the sets $A_j = \{x_j \in \mathbb{F}_2^{120} | F(x_j) = y_j\}$, where $y_j \in \mathbb{F}_2^8$, $0 \leq j \leq 2^8 - 1$. Then the probability of the random vectorial Boolean function satisfying $|A_j| = 2^{112}$ for each $0 \leq j \leq 2^8 - 1$ is

$$\left(C_{2^{120}}^{2^{112}} \times C_{2^{120} - 2^{112}}^{2^{112}} \times \cdots \times C_{2^{113}}^{2^{112}} \times C_{2^{112}}^{2^{112}} \right) / (2^8)^{2^{120}},$$

which is extremely small compared with 2^{-256}. Only under the case of the right keys, the phenomenons of the integral properties can emerge, that is, the integral distinguisher has much stronger ability to distinguish the right and wrong keys.

5.2   Key-Recovery Attacks on 14/15-round CLEFIA-192/256

In this section, the new integral distinguisher is applied to key-recovery attacks on 14/15-round CLEFIA-192/256. The 9-round integral distinguisher starts from round 3 and ends at round 11; see Fig. 4(a). In the attack process, we adopt the idea of subkey-dependent chosen plaintexts. We first construct a pre-computation table T.

Table T: For each of the 2^{160} possible sextuples $(P_0, P_1, P_2[1, 2, 3], P_3, rk_0, wk_0[0] \oplus rk_2[0])$, we calculate $P_2[0] = s_0(F_0(P_0, rk_0)[0] \oplus wk_0[0] \oplus rk_2[0]) \oplus 0x02 \cdot P_2[1] \oplus 0x04 \cdot P_2[2] \oplus 0x06 \cdot P_2[3]$. Store all the 2^{120} quadruples (P_0, P_1, P_3, P_4) in a hash table T indexed by 40-bit $(rk_0, wk_0[0] \oplus rk_2[0])$.

Attack Process. The key-recovery attacks on 14-round CLEFIA-192 are proceeded with the partial-sum technique as follows.

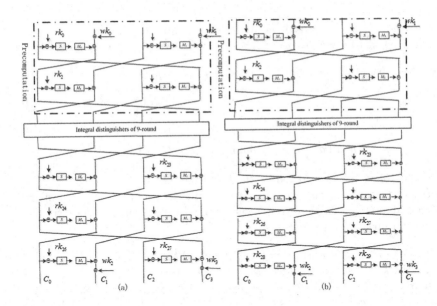

Fig. 4. Integral attacks on 14/15-round CLEFIA-192/256

Step 1. Guess the subkeys $rk_0, wk_0[0] \oplus rk_2[0]$ by the table T. Choose a set of 2^{120} plaintexts to obtain their cipertexts. Allocate a 32-bit counter $V_1[x_1]$ for each of the 2^{104} possible values of

$$x_1 = C_0 \| C_2 \| C_3 \| M^1,$$

and initialize them to zero, where M^1 is a 8-bit middle-value with

$$M^1 = 0x34^T \cdot (M_1 \cdot C_1[0]) \oplus 0x40^T \cdot (M_1 \cdot C_1[1]).$$

For each set of the chosen ciphertexts, extract the value of x_1 and increase the corresponding counter $V_1[x_1]$.

Step 2. Allocate 32-bit counters $V_2[x_2]$ for 2^8 possible values of

$$x_2 = C_0 \| C_2[1, 2, 3] \| C_3 \| M^1,$$

and set them zero. Guess $rk_{27}[0]$ and partially decrypt x_1 to get the value of x_2, then update the corresponding counter $V_2[x_2]+ = V_1[x_1]$.

Step 3. In the following partial decryption phase, guess $rk_{27}[1]$, $rk_{27}[2]$, $rk_{27}[3]$, $rk_{26}[0]$, $rk_{26}[1]$, $rk_{26}[2]$, $rk_{26}[3]$, $rk_{24}[0], rk_{24}[1], rk_{24}[2], rk_{24}[3]$, $rk_{23}[0]$, $rk_{23}[1]$, compute corresponding values and update the counters, and get $V_3[x_3]$, where

$$x_3 = 0x37^T \cdot (M_1 \cdot C_0^{11})[0] \oplus 0x40^T \cdot (M_1 \cdot C_0^{11})[1].$$

Step 4. After Step 3, 152 key bits have been guessed. If there exists $x_3 \in \mathbb{F}_2^8$ such that $V_3[x_3] \neq 2^{112}$, discard the guessed keys and guess another sub-key, until we get the correct sub-key. As there are 40 master key bits that we have not guessed, we do exhaustive search for all keys conforming to this possible key candidate.

Complexity of the Attack. In this attack, there are 152-bit key value guessed during the encryption phase, and only the right key candidates survive in the wrong key filtration.

(1) Step 1 requires about 2^{160} memory accesses;
(2) Step 2 requires about $2^{104} \times 2^{40} \times 2^8 = 2^{152}$ memory accesses;
(3) Step 3 requires about 10×2^{168} memory accesses;
(4) Step 4 requires 2^{40} 14-round CLEFIA encryption, because only the right key candidates can survive in the wrong key filtration.

If we assume that processing each memory accesses is equivalent to $1/2$ round encryption, then the total time complexity is about $2^{168} \times 1/2 \times 10/14 \approx 2^{166.7}$ 14-round encryptions. In total, the data complexity is 2^{128} CPs, the time complexity is about $2^{166.7}$ 14-round encryptions and the memory requirement is 2^{104} bytes for counters.

For the integral attack on 15-round CLEFIA-256, we mount the 9-round zero-correlation linear approximations from round 3 to round 12; see Fig. 4(b). We proceed similar steps to attack 14 rounds of CLEFIA-192. The data complexity of the attack is 2^{128} CPs, the total time complexity is $2^{230.7}$ encryptions and the memory complexity is about 2^{128} bytes.

6   Conclusion

In this paper, we have evaluated the security of CLEFIA by means of integral and zero-correlation linear cryptanalysis. Firstly, we investigate the propagation characteristics of the linear masks on the matrices of the F-functions, and propose some new linear distinguishers with zero correlation over 9-round CLE-FIA, where the input masks and output masks are independent. Then multiple zero-correlation linear attack are conducted on 14/15-round CLEFIA-192/256. Further, the relations between zero correlation and integral are improved, and some integral distinguishers are derived. Key recovery attacks on 14/15-round CLEFIA-192/256 are conducted by means of integral cryptanalysis. These results are not the best for CLEFIA compared with the truncated differential attack results. However, the multiple zero-correlation linear attacks are better compared with the multidimensional zero-correlation linear attacks in terms of both data and time complexities, and in addition, our integral cryptanalysis can attack one more round than previous integral cryptanalysis.

References

1. Blondeau, C.: Improbable differential from impossible differential: on the validity of the model. In: Paul, G., Vaudenay, S. (eds.) INDOCRYPT 2013. LNCS, vol. 8250, pp. 149–160. Springer, Heidelberg (2013). doi:10.1007/978-3-319-03515-4_10

2. Bogdanov, A., Leander, G., Nyberg, K., Wang, M.: Integral and multidimensional linear distinguishers with correlation zero. In: Wang, X., Sako, K. (eds.) ASIACRYPT 2012. LNCS, vol. 7658, pp. 244–261. Springer, Heidelberg (2012). doi:10.1007/978-3-642-34961-4_16

3. Bogdanov, A., Wang, M.: Zero correlation linear cryptanalysis with reduced data complexity. In: Canteaut, A. (ed.) FSE 2012. LNCS, vol. 7549, pp. 29–48. Springer, Heidelberg (2012). doi:10.1007/978-3-642-34047-5_3

4. Bogdanov, A., Rijmen, V.: Linear hulls with correlation zero and linear cryptanalysis of block ciphers. Des. Codes Crypt. **70**(3), 369–383 (2014)

5. Bogdanov, A., Geng, H., Wang, M., Wen, L., Collard, B.: Zero-correlation linear cryptanalysis with FFT and improved attacks on ISO standards camellia and CLEFIA. In: Lange, T., Lauter, K., Lisoněk, P. (eds.) SAC 2013. LNCS, vol. 8282, pp. 306–323. Springer, Heidelberg (2014). doi:10.1007/978-3-662-43414-7_16

6. Boura, C., Naya-Plasencia, M., Suder, V.: Scrutinizing and improving impossible differential attacks: applications to CLEFIA, camellia, LBlock and SIMON. In: Sarkar, P., Iwata, T. (eds.) ASIACRYPT 2014. LNCS, vol. 8873, pp. 179–199. Springer, Heidelberg (2014). doi:10.1007/978-3-662-45611-8_10

7. Li, L., Jia, K., Wang, X., Dong, X.: Meet-in-the-middle technique for truncated differential and its applications to CLEFIA and camellia. In: Leander, G. (ed.) FSE 2015. LNCS, vol. 9054, pp. 48–70. Springer, Heidelberg (2015). doi:10.1007/978-3-662-48116-5_3

8. Li, Y., Wu, W., Zhang, L.: Improved integral attacks on reduced-round CLEFIA block cipher. In: Jung, S., Yung, M. (eds.) WISA 2011. LNCS, vol. 7115, pp. 28–39. Springer, Heidelberg (2012). doi:10.1007/978-3-642-27890-7_3

9. Mala, H., Dakhilalian, M., Shakiba, M.: Impossible differential attacks on 13-round CLEFIA-128. J. Comput. Sci. Technol. **26**(4), 744–750 (2011)

10. Sasaki, Y., Wang, L.: Meet-in-the-middle technique for integral attacks against feistel ciphers. In: Knudsen, L.R., Wu, H. (eds.) SAC 2012. LNCS, vol. 7707, pp. 234–251. Springer, Heidelberg (2013). doi:10.1007/978-3-642-35999-6_16

11. Shirai, T., Shibutani, K., Akishita, T., Moriai, S., Iwata, T.: The 128-bit blockcipher CLEFIA (Extended Abstract). In: Biryukov, A. (ed.) FSE 2007. LNCS, vol. 4593, pp. 181–195. Springer, Heidelberg (2007). doi:10.1007/978-3-540-74619-5_12

12. Sun, B., Li, R., Wang, M., Li, P., Li, C.: Impossible differential cryptanalysis of CLEFIA. In: ePrint 2008/151 (2008). http://eprint.iacr.org/2008/151

13. Tang, X., Sun, B., Li, R., Li, C.: Impossible differential cryptanalysis of 13-round CLEFIA-128. J. Syst. Softw. **84**(7), 1191–1196 (2011)

14. Tezcan, C.: The improbable differential attack: cryptanalysis of reduced round CLEFIA. In: Gong, G., Gupta, K.C. (eds.) INDOCRYPT 2010. LNCS, vol. 6498, pp. 197–209. Springer, Heidelberg (2010). doi:10.1007/978-3-642-17401-8_15

15. Tezcan, C., Selcuk, A.A.: Improved improbable differential attacks on ISO standard CLEFIA: expansion technique revisited. Inf. Process. Lett. **116**, 136–143 (2016)

16. Tsunoo, Y., Tsujihara, E., Shigeri, M., Saito, T., Suzaki, T., Kubo, H.: Impossible differential cryptanalysis of CLEFIA. In: Nyberg, K. (ed.) FSE 2008. LNCS, vol. 5086, pp. 398–411. Springer, Heidelberg (2008). doi:10.1007/978-3-540-71039-4_25

17. Wang, W., Wang, X.: Saturation cryptanalysis of CLEFIA. J. Commun. **29**(10), 88–92 (2008)

Impossible Differentials of SPN Ciphers

Xuan Shen[1,2], Guoqiang Liu[1(✉)], Bing Sun[1,2,3], and Chao Li[1(✉)]

[1] College of Science, National University of Defense Technology,
Changsha 410073, People's Republic of China
shenxuan_08@163.com, liuguoqiang87@hotmail.com,
happy_come@163.com, academic_lc@163.com
[2] State Key Laboratory of Cryptology,
P.O. Box 5159, Beijing 100878, People's Republic of China
[3] State Key Laboratory of Information Security, Institute of Information Engineering,
Chinese Academy of Sciences, Beijing 100093, People's Republic of China

Abstract. An upper bound of the length of impossible differentials for an SPN structure was presented at EUROCRYPT 2016. This paper mainly focuses on the lengths of impossible differentials for two specific SPN structures. The details of the S-boxes could be exploited to construct longer impossible differentials for ciphers adopting these structures. For Kuznyechik and the internal permutation of PHOTON, we can construct 3-round and 5-round impossible differentials, respectively. The lengths of impossible differentials of these two ciphers are 1 more round compared with the lengths of impossible differentials of the structures deduced from the corresponding ciphers.

Keywords: Structure · Impossible differential · Kuznyechik · PHOTON

1 Introduction

Block cipher is one of the most important symmetric cryptographic schemes and the security of these schemes in some sense depends on the resistance to known cryptanalytic techniques. Differential cryptanalysis [1] was developed to analyze the security of the Data Encryption Standard(DES). In differential cryptanalysis, one first tries to find some differential characteristics with high probability and then by some statistical methods we may recover the round keys. However, in impossible differential cryptanalysis, which was independently proposed by Knudsen [2] and Biham [3], it uses the differentials with probability zero which are called impossible differentials to discard the wrong keys. To our knowledge, impossible differential cryptanalysis has obtained much attention and been used to attack a large number of block ciphers [4–7].

The work in this paper is supported by the National Natural Science Foundation of China (No: 61672530, 61402515), the Foundation of Science and Technology on Information Assurance laboratory (No: KJ-14-003), and the Research Fund for the doctoral program of Higher Education of China (RFDP No: 2012150112004).

© Springer International Publishing AG 2017
K. Chen et al. (Eds.): Inscrypt 2016, LNCS 10143, pp. 47–63, 2017.
DOI: 10.1007/978-3-319-54705-3_4

In impossible differential cryptanalysis, it first constructs some impossible differentials which cover as many rounds as possible, then impossible differentials will be used to recover the right key. For any function $F : \mathbb{F}_{2^n} \to \mathbb{F}_{2^n}$, we can always find some α and β such that $\alpha \to \beta$ is an impossible differential of F. However, if the size of the block cipher is large and we do not know any algebraic structure of F, it can be very hard to determine whether $\alpha \to \beta$ is a possible differential or an impossible one. Furthermore, for a block cipher F, it is possible that for some key k, $\alpha \to \beta$ is a possible differential while for other k, it is impossible. From the practical view, we are interested in impossible differentials that are independent of the round keys. Note that in most cases, the non-linear complements applied to x can be described as $S(x \oplus k)$, we always detect impossible differentials that are independent of the S-boxes, which are called truncated impossible differentials, i.e., we do not care about the specific value of the difference when it is nonzero, and we are only interested in whether the value is zero or not.

Usually, the most popular method to construct an impossible differential is the miss-in-the-middle technique, i.e., trace the property of input difference α and output difference β, respectively, once some contradiction is detected in the middle, an impossible differential is constructed. Several automatic methods have been proposed to search truncated impossible differentials of a block cipher such as the $\mathcal{U}$-method [8], UID-method [9] and the linearized method [10].

Though there have already been 4-/4-/8-round impossible differentials for the AES, ARIA and Camellia without FL/FL^{-1} layers [11–16], finding longer length of impossible differentials has never stopped. Sun et al. proposed the concept of structure deduced by a block cipher at CRYPTO 2015 [17], based on which they proved at EUROCRYPT 2016 [18] that for an SPN structure, if $\alpha_1 \to \beta_1$ and $\alpha_2 \to \beta_2$ are possible differentials, $\alpha_1|\alpha_2 \to \beta_1|\beta_2$ is also a possible differential. They further showed that for an SPN structure, there exists an r-round impossible differential if and only if there exists an r-round impossible differential $\alpha \nrightarrow \beta$ where the Hamming weights of both α and β are 1 and that the length of impossible differentials of an SPN structure is upper bounded by the primitive index of the linear layers. As a result, there does not exist 5-round impossible differentials for the AES and ARIA unless the details of the S-boxes are considered.

There are also some literatures that concentrated on exploiting the details of the S-boxes to construct longer impossible differentials. In SAC 2011 [19], Bouillaguet et al. presented that if there exists $b \notin \Delta F^{(r)}(a)$ for MARS-like and CAST-like ciphers, where $\Delta F^{(r)}(a)$ denotes the all possible output differences that the input difference a can propagate through the round function F for successive r rounds, the length of impossible differentials can be r rounds longer than that of the case when the round function F is only viewed as bijective transformation. For lightweight block ciphers, due to the low confusion and diffusion, we can construct some impossible differentials of a cipher which is much longer than the length of the corresponding structure. For example, there are $(1100) \to (\ast\ast\ast0)$ and $(0100) \to (\ast1\ast\ast)$ for the 4-bit S-box and the inverse of the

S-box in RECTANGLE [20], respectively. Combined with the linear transformation, an 8-round impossible differential can be constructed for RECTANGLE.

In this paper, we attempt to find longer length of impossible differentials by investigating the details of the S-boxes for SPN ciphers. For an r-round SPN cipher which is defined as $(SP)^{r-1}S$, where $r = r_1 + r_2 + 1$, assume a and b be the input and output difference respectively, if we can test all differential characteristics of $a \to b$ being impossible differentials, $a \to b$ is an impossible differential. Otherwise, $a \to b$ is a possible differential. When $E = (SP)^{r-1}S = (SP)^{r_1+r_2}S = (SP)^{r_1}S(PS)^{r_2}$, $a \xrightarrow{E} b \Leftrightarrow E_1(a) \xrightarrow{S} E_2(b)$, where $E_1(a) = (P \circ S)^{r_1}(a)$, $E_2(b) = (P^{(-1)} \circ S^{(-1)})^{r_2}(b)$, $E_1(a)$ and $E_2(b)$ mean the differences which a and b can propagate from the forward and backward directions respectively. Therefore, if there is no element which belongs to $E_1(a)$ that can propagate to the element which belongs to $E_2(b)$, we call that $E_1(a)$ can not be matched with $E_2(b)$, and $a \to b$ is an r-round impossible differential for the SPN cipher. In the rebound attack, $E_1(a)$ can always be matched with $E_2(b)$. Furthermore, if we prove that $a \to b$ is an r-round impossible differential, $a \to b$ can not be an r-round rebound attack distinguisher. Given the computation complexity in the middle match phase, we only consider that the Hamming weights of input and output differences are 1 in this paper.

Our contributions. Nowadays, for many byte-oriented block ciphers, the lengths of impossible differentials are the same as those of the structures deduced by these ciphers. In this paper, we exploit the details of the S-boxes to construct longer impossible differentials than those of the structures. Note that considering impossible differential cryptanalysis on structure, the output differences can take all nonzero values for a given nonzero input difference. However, for a cipher, the S-box is fixed and there are at most half of the whole space of output difference values that can be taken for a given nonzero input difference. Therefore, we can exploit this property for a cipher to construct longer impossible differentials than those of the corresponding structure. Assume n, m, d denote the size of S-box, linear transformation and MixColumns respectively. The main results of this paper are as follows.

(1) For two structures $\varepsilon^{(1)}(n, m)$ and $\varepsilon^{(2)}(n, d)$ defined in our paper, we prove that the longest impossible differentials for these two structures are two rounds and four rounds when $m \leq 2^{n-1} - 1$ and $d \leq 2^{n-1} - 1$, respectively.
(2) For Kuznyechik, we construct 3-round impossible differentials and show all 3-round impossible differentials with the Hamming weights of the input and output differences being 1. Compared with the structure deduced by Kuznyechik which belongs to $\varepsilon^{(1)}(8, 16)$, the length of impossible differentials of Kuznyechik is one more round than that of the structure.
(3) For the internal permutation in PHOTON, 5-round impossible differentials for $n = 4, d = 6, 7$ can be constructed. Compared with the structure deduced by the internal permutation in PHOTON which belongs to $\varepsilon^{(2)}(4, d)(d = 6, 7)$, the length of impossible differentials of the internal permutation in PHOTON is one more round than that of the structure.

Organization. The rest of this paper is organized as follows. First, we introduce the notations and concepts used throughout the paper in Sect. 2. In Sect. 3, 3-round impossible differentials of Kuznyechik are constructed. Moreover, we construct 5-round impossible differentials of the internal permutation in PHOTON in Sect. 4. Section 5 concludes the paper.

2 Preliminary

2.1 Vectors and Matrices

Assume $X = (x_0, \ldots, x_{m-1}) \in \mathbb{F}_{2^n}^m$, the *Hamming weight* of X is defined as

$$H(X) = \#\{i | x_i \neq 0, i = 0, 1, \ldots, m - 1\}.$$

For $P = (p_{ij}) \in \mathbb{F}_{2^n}^{m \times m}$, denote $\mathbb{Z}$ the integer ring, the *characteristic matrix* of P is defined as $P^* = (p_{ij}^*) \in \mathbb{Z}^{m \times m}$, where

$$p_{ij}^* = \begin{cases} 0, & p_{ij} = 0, \\ 1, & p_{ij} \neq 0. \end{cases}$$

For a matrix $M \in \mathbb{Z}^{m \times m}$, $M \geq 0$ means that all elements of M are non-negative; $M > 0$ means that all elements of M are positive. Furthermore, the primitive index of P is defined as

$$\gamma(P) = \min\{t | (P^*)^t > 0, t \in \mathbb{Z}^+\}.$$

2.2 Some Parameters for the S-box

Given a function $G: \mathbb{F}_2^n \to \mathbb{F}_2^k$, let $\delta \in \mathbb{F}_2^n$ and $\Delta \in \mathbb{F}_2^k$. The differential probability $\delta \to \Delta$ is defined as

$$p(\delta \xrightarrow{G} \Delta) \triangleq \frac{\#\{x \in \mathbb{F}_2^n | G(x) \oplus G(x \oplus \delta) = \Delta\}}{2^n}.$$

If $p(\delta \xrightarrow{G} \Delta) = 0$, then $\delta \to \Delta$ is called an *impossible differential* of G.

For an S-box $S: \mathbb{F}_2^n \to \mathbb{F}_2^n$, let $a, b \in \mathbb{F}_2^n$, $p(a \xrightarrow{S} b) > 0$ means that the input difference a can propagate to the output difference b through the S-box, and we get that $a \xrightarrow{S} b$ is a possible differential. Moreover, we call that a can be matched with b through the S-box. We denote $V_S(a)$ all possible output differences through an S-box for the fixed input difference a, i.e.,

$$V_S(a) \triangleq \{b | p(a \xrightarrow{S} b) > 0\}.$$

Similarly, for the inverse of the S-box, $V_{S^{-1}}(a)$ is defined as

$$V_{S^{-1}}(a) \triangleq \{b | p(a \xrightarrow{S^{-1}} b) > 0\}.$$

Furthermore, we denote λ_S as the maximum number of nonzero output differences for any nonzero input difference in an S-box, i.e.,

$$\lambda_S \triangleq \max_{a \neq 0} \{\#V_S(a)\}.$$

Similarly, $\lambda_{S^{-1}}$ is defined as

$$\lambda_{S^{-1}} \triangleq \max_{a \neq 0} \{\#V_{S^{-1}}(a)\}.$$

Moreover, let μ_S denote the match probability of a nonzero input difference and a nonzero output difference selected in a random way for an S-box, i.e.,

$$\mu_S \triangleq \frac{\sum\limits_{a=1}^{2^n-1} \{\#V_S(a)\}}{(2^n - 1)^2}.$$

Note that since the number of "0" in *differential distribution table* (DDT) is larger than a half of all elements, we get that $\lambda_S \leq 2^{n-1}, \lambda_S^{-1} \leq 2^{n-1}, \mu_S < \frac{1}{2}$.

2.3   Two SPN Structures

SPN Ciphers. The SPN structure is one of the most popular structures used in constructing cryptographic primitives. It iterates some SP-type round functions to achieve confusion and diffusion. $\mathbb{F}_{2^n}$ denotes the finite field with 2^n elements. The SP-type function $f: \mathbb{F}_{2^n}^m \to \mathbb{F}_{2^n}^m$ used in this paper is defined as follows.

Assume the input $x = (x_0, \ldots, x_{m-1})$, where $x_i \in \mathbb{F}_{2^n}$ and $i = 0, 1, \ldots, m-1$. The output of f is defined as

$$f(x) = P \circ S(x),$$

where $S(x) \triangleq (s_0(x_0), \ldots, s_{m-1}(x_{m-1})) \in \mathbb{F}_{2^n}^m$, the bijective transformation $s_i: \mathbb{F}_{2^n} \to \mathbb{F}_{2^n}$, the linear transformation $P: \mathbb{F}_{2^n}^m \to \mathbb{F}_{2^n}^m$. Note that the linear transformation in the last round is omitted for an r-round SPN structure. Then, an r-round SPN cipher is simply denoted as $(SP)^{r-1}S$.

The linear transformation P in the SPN structure is vital against different kinds of cryptographic methods. One method to construct linear transformation is directly taking large branch number. Specifically, the linear transformation matrix can be maximum distance separable (MDS) matrix such as Kuznyechik [21]. Another popular method is combining the ShiftRows and MixColumns transformations together to construct the linear transformation, such as AES [11], LED [23], PHOTON [24]. In this paper, we mainly investigate two structures with these two kinds of linear transformations.

Note that the S-box is defined as $S: \mathbb{F}_2^n \to \mathbb{F}_2^n$ for the two structures. When the following condition is satisfied, the structure is defined as $\varepsilon^{(1)}(n, m)$.

– The linear transformation matrix $P = (p_{ij}) \in \mathbb{F}_{2^n}^{m \times m}$ is an $m \times m$ MDS matrix.

When the following condition is satisfied, the structure is defined as $\varepsilon^{(2)}(n, d)$.

- The linear transformation P consists of ShiftRows and MixColumns. Moreover, the ShiftRows transformation is a permutation of $\{0, 1, \ldots, d-1\}$, and the MixColumns transformation matrix is a $d \times d$ MDS matrix.

At CRYPTO 2015, Sun *et al.* proposed the definition of the structure:

Definition 1. [17] *Let $E: \mathbb{F}_2^k \to \mathbb{F}_2^k$ be a block cipher with bijective S-boxes as the basic nonlinear components.*

(1) A structure ε^E on $\mathbb{F}_2^k$ is defined as a set of block ciphers E' which is exactly the same as E except that the S-boxes can take all possible bijective transformation on the corresponding domains.
(2) Let $\alpha, \beta \in \mathbb{F}_2^k$. If for any $E' \in \varepsilon^E$, $\alpha \nrightarrow \beta$ is an impossible differential of E', $\alpha \nrightarrow \beta$ is called an impossible differential of ε^E.

From Definition 1, we learn that if $\alpha \to \beta$ is an impossible differential of ε^E, $\alpha \to \beta$ is always an impossible differential of the cipher E.

Furthermore, the structure $\varepsilon^{Kuznyechik}$ deduced by Kuznyechik in Sect. 3 belongs to $\varepsilon^{(1)}(8, 16)$, the structure ε^{PHOTON} deduced by the internal permutation of PHOTON in Sect. 4 belongs to $\varepsilon^{(2)}(n, d)$.

3 Impossible Differentials of Kuznyechik

3.1 Specification of Kuznyechik

Kuznyechik [21] is an SPN block cipher that has been recently chosen to be standardized by the Russian federation as a new GOST cipher. It updates a 128-bit state for 9 rounds with a 256-bit mask key. As depicted in Fig. 1, the round function consists of:

(1) SubBytes (S): A nonlinear byte bijective mapping.
(2) Linear Transformation (P): An optimal diffusion operation that operates on a 16-byte input and the branch number is 17. P and P^{-1} are shown in Appendix A.
(3) Xor layer (X): Mixing round keys with the encryption state.

Additionally, an initial XOR layer is applied to the first round. The full encryption process where the ciphertext C is updated by the plaintext M is given as:

$$C = (X[K_{10}] \circ P \circ S) \circ \cdots (X[K_2] \circ P \circ S) \circ (X[K_1])(M).$$

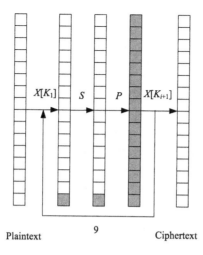

Plaintext   9   Ciphertext

Fig. 1. Encryption procedure of Kuznyechik

3.2   Impossible Differentials of Kuznyechik and Its Structure

Firstly, we consider the length of impossible differentials of the structure deduced by Kuznyechik which belongs to $\varepsilon^{(1)}(8, 16)$.

Since any submatrix of an MDS matrix is nonsingular [22], any element of the MDS matrix is nonzero. Therefore, we can get the following lemma.

Lemma 1. *Let $P \in \mathbb{F}_{2^n}^{m \times m}$ be an MDS matrix. Then $\gamma(P) = \gamma(P^{-1}) = 1$.*

Sun *et al.* showed that the upper bound of impossible differentials for an SPN structure is $\gamma(P) + \gamma(P^{-1})$ at EUROCRYTO 2016 [18], where P is the linear transformation and $m \leq 2^{n-1} - 1$. Moreover, when the input difference α and the output difference β satisfy $H(\alpha) + H(\beta) \leq m$ for $\varepsilon^{(1)}(n, m)$, 2-round impossible differentials can be constructed. Therefore, we have the following theorem.

Theorem 1. *If $m \leq 2^{n-1} - 1$, the longest impossible differentials of $\varepsilon^{(1)}(n, m)$ is 2-round.*

From Theorem 1, we can know the upper bound of the length of impossible differentials for the structure, i.e., the details of the S-boxes are not investigated. However, for Kuznyechik with specific an S-box, there may exist longer length of impossible differentials. In this section, we are going to construct 3-round impossible differentials considering the S-box and permutation of Kuznyechik.

For Kuznyechik, we only consider the input and output differences whose Hamming weights are 1 in this section. Instead of constructing 3-round impossible differentials, we are going to search all possible 3-round differentials with practical differential characteristics.

In Fig. 2, assume the 15-th position of Δ_{in} and Δ_{out} have nonzero differences, others have zero differences. If $\Omega = \emptyset$ after implementing Algorithm 1, it shows

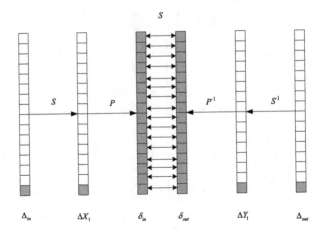

Fig. 2. 3 rounds of Kuznyechik

that not all positions of $P(\Delta X_1)$ and $P^{-1}(\Delta Y_1)$ can be matched through the 16 S-boxes, thus they are 3-round impossible differentials for any $\Delta_{in} \neq 0$ and $\Delta_{out} \neq 0$. If $\Omega \neq \emptyset$, when the differentials in Ω can not cover all possible differentials, there also exist 3-round impossible differentials.

Algorithm 1. The middle match phase for Kuznyechik

Input: the nonzero position of Δ_{in}, the nonzero position of Δ_{out}
output: the set Ω which contains all $V_{S^{-1}}(\Delta X_1) \to V_S(\Delta Y_1)$
1.   **for every** $\Delta X_1, \Delta Y_1$
2.   **if** δ_{in} can be matched with δ_{out} for all 16 S-boxes,
3.   put $V_{S^{-1}}(\Delta X_1) \to V_S(\Delta Y_1)$ into the set Ω
4.   **end if**
5.   **end for**

We have tested all possible nonzero input and output difference positions by implementing Algorithm 1, the results are listed as in Table 1 and Proposition 1 is obtained. Since all 3-round possible differentials are presented in Table 1, the remaining ones are 3-round impossible differentials.

Proposition 1. *For Kuznyechik, if $H(\Delta X_1) = H(\Delta Y_1) = 1$, there is at most one differential characteristic of $\Delta X_1 \xrightarrow{PSP} \Delta Y_1$.*

Remark 1. For Kuznyechik, we can search 3-round impossible differentials where the Hamming weights of the input and output differences are larger than 1. However, the larger the Hamming weights differences are, the higher the computation complexity is. Furthermore, 3-round impossible differentials searched in this paper are closely related to the S-box, if we change the S-box for another one, 3-round impossible differentials will be different.

Table 1. All 3-round possible differentials for Kuznyechik

Position	Input differences	Output differences
(0,15)	$V_{S^{-1}}(196)$	$V_S(75)$
(1,0)	$V_{S^{-1}}(221)$	$V_S(58)$
(5,9)	$V_{S^{-1}}(5)$	$V_S(81)$
(6,3)	$V_{S^{-1}}(169)$	$V_S(213)$
(8,12)	$V_{S^{-1}}(98)$	$V_S(28)$
(11,4)	$V_{S^{-1}}(110)$	$V_S(192)$
(11,13)	$V_{S^{-1}}(116)$	$V_S(45)$
(13,9)	$V_{S^{-1}}(41)$	$V_S(186)$
(14,1)	$V_{S^{-1}}(110)$	$V_S(231)$
(14,7)	$V_{S^{-1}}(68)$	$V_S(31)$
(14,8)	$V_{S^{-1}}(207)$	$V_S(121)$
(15,3)	$V_{S^{-1}}(95)$	$V_S(156)$
(15,7)	$V_{S^{-1}}(103)$	$V_S(84)$

3.3 Theoretical Analysis

For $\varepsilon^{(1)}(n, m)$, the length of impossible differentials is at most 2-round. In this paper, we denote N_Δ the number of differential characteristics for a pair of the input and output difference selected randomly. N_Δ can be used to estimate whether there are impossible differentials for a concrete cipher. When $N_\Delta < 1$, there probably exists an impossible differential for this concrete difference pair. Since we only consider the input and output differences where the Hamming weights of them are 1 in this section, we present the following proposition.

Proposition 2. *In a specific cipher of $\varepsilon^{(1)}(n, m)$, 3-round impossible differentials of this cipher can probably be constructed if the following estimation holds:*

$$N_\Delta \approx (\lambda_S \times \lambda_{S^{-1}}) \times \mu_S^m < 1.$$

Proposition 2 can give us some suggestions whether there exist 3-round impossible differentials before searching. For Kuznyechik, we find $\lambda_S = 114, \lambda_{S^{-1}} = 128, \mu_S = 0.42$, then

$$N_\Delta \approx (114 \times 128) \times 0.42^{-16} = 2^{-6.19} < 1.$$

Since $\lambda_S \leq 2^{n-1}, \lambda_{S^{-1}} \leq 2^{n-1}, \mu_S < \frac{1}{2}$, according to Proposition 2, $N_\Delta \approx (\lambda_S \times \lambda_{S^{-1}}) \times \mu_S^m < 2^{2(n-1)} \times 2^{-m} = 2^{2(n-1)-m}$, we obtain the following corollary.

Corollary 1. *In a specific cipher of $\varepsilon^{(1)}(n, m)$, 3-round impossible differentials of this cipher can probably be constructed if the following estimation holds:*

$$2(n - 1) < m.$$

For example, $n = 8, m = 16$ in Kuznyechik, $2 \times (8 - 1) < 16$.

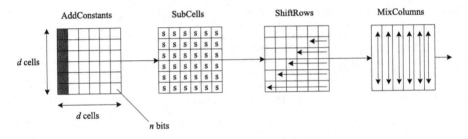

Fig. 3. One round function

4 Impossible Differentials of the Internal Permutation in PHOTON

4.1 Specification of the Internal Permutation in PHOTON

The PHOTON family were designed by Guo *et al.* at CRYPTO 2011 [24] and they take extended sponge function as the whole structure. The internal permutation in the sponge function is similar with AES and we view the internal permutation as a block cipher in this paper. Moreover, the round number of the internal permutation in PHOTON is 12. One round of the permutation consists of the following steps which is presented in Fig. 3.

(1) AddConstants(AC): The first column is mixed with constants.
(2) SubCells(S): Every sub-block is updated by S-box, where $n = 4, 8$.
(3) ShiftRows(SR): The i-th row is rotated by i positions to the left, where $i = 0, 1, \ldots, d - 1$.
(4) MixColumns(MC): The MixColumns matrix is a $d \times d$ MDS matrix, the number of branch is $d + 1$, where $d = 5, 6, 7, 8$. The MixColumns matrices for different d are shown in [24].

4.2 Impossible Differentials of the Internal Permutation in PHOTON and Its Structure

In the structure $\varepsilon^{(2)}(n, d)$, the linear transformation P consists of two parts: the ShiftRows and MixColumns, where the MixColumns can be represented by a $d \times d$ MDS matrix. Furthermore, Sun *et al.* showed that the upper bound of impossible differentials for an SPN structure is $\gamma(P) + \gamma(P^{-1})$. Note that when $P = MC \circ SR$, the restricted condition in [18] can be modified as $d \leq 2^{n-1} - 1$. Therefore, we have the following theorem.

Theorem 2. *If* $d \leq 2^{n-1} - 1$*, the longest impossible differentials of* $\varepsilon^{(2)}(n, d)$ *cover 4 rounds.*

The proof of this theorem is shown in Appendix B.

From Theorem 2, we know the upper bound of the length of impossible differentials for $\varepsilon^{(2)}(n, d)$. However, for the internal permutation in PHOTON, there

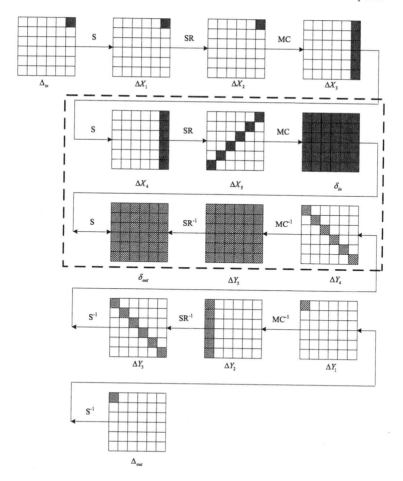

Fig. 4. 5 rounds of the internal permutation in PHOTON

may exist longer length of impossible differentials if we exploit the specific S-box. In this section, we are going to find 5-round impossible differentials considering the specific S-box in PHOTON. As in Sect. 3, we only consider that the Hamming weights of the input and output differences are 1, and we only search all possible differentials.

The procedure can be divided into three phases (see Fig. 4).

Middle match phase: In Fig. 4, this phase is between ΔX_4 and ΔY_4. Our method searches all possible ΔY_4 to match all possible ΔX_4. If we directly match each other by exhaustive search, the computation complex is $(2^n - 1)^{2d}$. However, we can take the *Early-Abort* [25] technique to reduce the computation complexity. If we run all possible ΔX_5 with one column by another to match ΔY_4, the computation complexity can reduce to at most $(2^n - 1)^{d+1} \times d$. If $\Theta = \emptyset$ after implementing Algorithm 2, all Δ_{in} and Δ_{out} which can propagate

---

Algorithm 2. The middle match phase($\Delta X_4 \rightarrow \Delta Y_4$)

Input: the nonzero position of ΔX_4, ΔY_4 and the size of MixColumns d
Output: the set Θ which contains all $\Delta X_4 \rightarrow \Delta Y_4$

1.   **for** every ΔY_4 **do**
2.   **for** the j-th column of ΔX_5 from 0 to $(d-1)$
3.   **if** all the j-th column of δ_{in} and δ_{out} can not be matched with each other
             for d S-boxes,
4.   **break**;
5.   **end if**
6.   **end for**
7.   put $\Delta X_4 \rightarrow \Delta Y_4$ into the set Θ
8.   **end for**

Algorithm 3. The backward match phase($\Delta X_1 \rightarrow \Delta X_4$)

Input: the nonzero position of ΔX_1, all ΔX_4 obtained by Algorithm 2 and
       the size of MixColumns d
Output: the set Φ which contains all $\Delta X_1 \rightarrow \Delta X_4$

1.   **for** every ΔX_1 **do**
2.   **if** ΔX_3 can be matched with ΔX_4 obtained by Algorithm 2 for d S-boxes,
3.   put $\Delta X_1 \rightarrow \Delta X_4$ into the set Φ
4.   **end if**
5.   **end for**

---

to ΔX_4 and ΔY_4 respectively are 5-round impossible differentials and we finish searching. Otherwise, we operate next match phase.

Backward match phase: In Fig. 4, this phase is between ΔX_1 and ΔX_4. After middle match phase, ΔX_4 are obtained. If $\Phi = \emptyset$ after implementing Algorithm 3, all Δ_{in} and Δ_{out} which can propagate to ΔX_4 and ΔY_4 respectively are 5-round impossible differentials. Then we finish searching. Otherwise, we operate next match phase.

Forward match phase: In Fig. 4, this phase is between ΔY_4 and ΔY_1. After backward match phases, we can get ΔX_1 and ΔY_4 which can match with ΔX_4 obtained in Algorithm 3. If $\Lambda = \emptyset$ after implementing Algorithm 4, all Δ_{in} and Δ_{out} which can propagate to ΔX_4 and ΔY_4 respectively are 5-round impossible differentials. Otherwise, ΔY_1 are obtained. Furthermore, all possible differentials $\Delta X_1 \rightarrow \Delta Y_1$ are searched. Therefore, $V_{S^{-1}}(\Delta X_1) = \Delta_{in} \rightarrow \Delta_{out} = V_S(\Delta Y_1)$ are all 5-round possible differentials for given the nonzero positions of ΔX_4 and ΔY_4. And the remaining differentials are 5-round impossible differentials. When all nonzero positions of ΔX_4 and ΔY_4 are searched, all 5-round impossible differentials with the Hamming weights of the input and output differences being 1 are obtained.

Example: When $n = 4, d = 6$ in PHOTON, let all the differences of the 5-th column of ΔX_4 and the diagonal of ΔY_4 be nonzero and other elements be zero(see Fig. 4), we implement Algorithm 2 and the results are listed in Table 2.

Since $\Theta \neq \emptyset$ after implementing Algorithm 2, we implement Algorithm 3 and the results are presented in Table 3.

Algorithm 4. The forward match phase($\Delta Y_4 \to \Delta Y_1$)

Input: all ΔY_4 which can propagate to ΔX_4 obtained in Algorithm 3,
the nonzero position of ΔY_1 and the size of MixColumns d
Output: the set Λ which contains all $\Delta Y_4 \to \Delta Y_1$
1.   for every ΔY_1 do
2.   if ΔY_1 can be matched with ΔY_4 obtained by Algorithm 2 for d S-boxes,
3.   put $\Delta Y_4 \to \Delta Y_1$ into the set Λ
4.   end if
5.   end for

Table 2. Results of Implementing Algorithm 2

The 5-th column of ΔX_4	Diagonal of ΔY_4
(12,8,7,13,3,5)	(5,13,3,6,2,6)
(2,10,11,5,4,3)	(3,12,4,5,4,6)
(7,7,8,8,8,3)	(8,7,9,15,13,8)
(13,12,1,15,4,4)	(3,4,4,5,12,9)
(13,4,10,15,4,4)	(7,4,4,5,12,9)
(11,3,4,11,2,12)	(1,5,1,4,4,15)

Since there are some results obtained after implementing Algorithms 2 and 3, we continue to implement Algorithm 4 and we find that there is no result obtained. Therefore, any difference of Δ_{in} and Δ_{out} with $H(\Delta_{in}) = H(\Delta_{out}) = 1$ which can propagate to ΔX_4 and ΔY_4 respectively in Fig. 4 are 5-round impossible differentials.

When we change the nonzero difference positions of ΔX_4 and ΔY_4, we can use above method to search 5-round impossible differentials. Similarly, if $n = 4$, $d = 7$, we can also search 5-round impossible differentials with our method.

4.3   Theoretical Analysis

For $\varepsilon^{(2)}(n, d)$, we have shown that the longest impossible differentials cover 4 rounds. In this section, we also use N_Δ to estimate whether there is an impossible differential. When $N_\Delta < 1$, it means that there probably exists an impossible differential. Moreover, we show the following proposition.

Table 3. Results of Implementing Algorithm 3

Row of the 5-th column of ΔX_1	Value of ΔX_1	The 5-th column of ΔX_4
1	2	12,8,7,13,3,5
2	2	11,3,4,11,2,12
4	3	11,3,4,11,2,12
5	7	13,12,1,15,4,4

Proposition 3. *In a specific cipher of $\varepsilon^{(2)}(n,d)$, 5-round impossible differentials of this cipher can probably be constructed if the following estimation holds:*

$$N_{\Delta} \approx (\lambda_S \times \lambda_{S^{-1}})^{d+1} \times \mu_S^{d^2} < 1.$$

Proposition 3 can give us some suggestions whether there are 5-round impossible differentials or not before searching. For the PHOTON with $n = 4, d = 6$, we find that $\lambda_S = 8, \lambda_{S^{-1}} = 8, \mu_S = 0.43$. Therefore,

$$N_{\Delta} \approx (8 \times 8)^7 \times 0.43^{-36} = 2^{-1.83} < 1.$$

Furthermore, when $n = 4, d = 7$, Proposition 3 holds.

Remark 2. For a specific cipher of $\varepsilon^{(2)}(n,d)$, if we attempt to search 5-round impossible differentials, we need to take small S-box and big $d \times d$ MixColumns for the cipher. Moreover, if the S-box is given, the bigger the value of d is, the higher of the probability to search 5-round impossible differentials is.

Since $\lambda_S \le 2^{n-1}, \lambda_{S^{-1}} \le 2^{n-1}, \mu_S < \dfrac{1}{2}$, according to Proposition 3, $N_{\Delta} \approx (\lambda_S \times \lambda_{S^{-1}})^{d+1} \times \mu_S^{d^2} < 2^{2(n-1)(d+1)-d^2}$. We obtain the following corollary.

Corollary 2. *In a specific cipher of $\varepsilon^{(2)}(n,d)$, 5-round impossible differentials of this cipher can probably be constructed if the following inequation holds:*

$$2(n - 1)(d + 1) < d^2.$$

Note that when $n = 4, d = 7$ in PHOTON, Corollary 2 holds.

5   Conclusion

For many byte-oriented ciphers, the lengths of impossible differentials for the ciphers are the same as those of the corresponding structures. In this paper, we find that the details of the S-boxes could be used to construct longer impossible differentials provided the sizes of the confusion and diffusion layers satisfy some special constraint. For Kuznyechik, 3-round impossible differentials have been constructed, specially, all of these differentials whose input and output Hamming weights are 1 have been found. For the internal permutation in the PHOTON family, we have constructed 5-round impossible differentials with the 4-bit S-box and $d \times d$ MixColumns where $d = 6, 7$. For these two ciphers, both the lengths of impossible differentials are 1 round more than those of their structures.

We have also tried to construct longer zero correlation linear hulls for these two ciphers. However, since most of the elements in the *Linear Approximation Table* (LAT) are nonzero rather than that more than half of the elements in the *Differential Distribution Table* are zero, the strategy shown in this paper does not work for these two ciphers. We leave the problem that whether these new impossible differentials could lead to better key-recovery attacks as an open problem.

A   The Linear Transformation Matrix P and the Inverse Transformation Matrix P^{-1} of Kuznyechik

$$P = \begin{pmatrix}
cf & 98 & 74 & bf & 93 & 8e & f2 & f3 & 0a & bf & f6 & a9 & ea & 8e & 4d & 6e \\
6e & 20 & c6 & da & 90 & 48 & 89 & 9c & c1 & 64 & b8 & 2d & 86 & 44 & d0 & a2 \\
a2 & c8 & 87 & 70 & 68 & 43 & 1c & 2b & a1 & 63 & 30 & 6b & 9f & 30 & e3 & 76 \\
76 & 33 & 10 & 0c & 1c & 11 & d6 & 6a & a6 & d7 & f6 & 49 & 07 & 14 & e8 & 72 \\
72 & f2 & 6b & ca & 20 & eb & 02 & a4 & 8d & d4 & c4 & 01 & 65 & dd & 4c & 6c \\
6c & 76 & ec & 0c & c5 & bc & af & 6e & a3 & e1 & 90 & 58 & 0e & 02 & c3 & 48 \\
48 & d5 & 62 & 17 & 06 & 2d & c4 & e7 & d5 & eb & 99 & 78 & 52 & f5 & 16 & 7a \\
7a & e6 & 4e & 1a & bb & 2e & f1 & be & d4 & af & 37 & b1 & d4 & 2a & 6e & b8 \\
b8 & 49 & 87 & 14 & cb & 8d & ab & 49 & 09 & 6c & 2a & 01 & 60 & 8e & 4b & 5d \\
5d & d4 & b8 & 2f & 8d & 12 & ee & f6 & 08 & 54 & 0f & f3 & 98 & c8 & 7f & 27 \\
27 & 9f & be & 68 & 1a & 7c & ad & c9 & 84 & 2f & eb & fe & c6 & 48 & a2 & bd \\
bd & 95 & 5e & 30 & e9 & 60 & bf & 10 & ef & 39 & ec & 91 & 7f & 48 & 89 & 10 \\
10 & e9 & d0 & d9 & f3 & 94 & 3d & af & 7b & ff & 64 & 91 & 52 & f8 & 0d & dd \\
dd & 99 & 75 & ca & 97 & 44 & 5a & e0 & 30 & a6 & 31 & d3 & df & 48 & 64 & 84 \\
84 & 2d & 74 & 96 & 5d & 77 & 6f & de & 54 & b4 & 8d & d1 & 44 & 3c & a5 & 94 \\
94 & 20 & 85 & 10 & c2 & c0 & 01 & fb & 01 & c0 & c2 & 10 & 85 & 20 & 94 & 01
\end{pmatrix}$$

$$P^{-1} = \begin{pmatrix}
01 & 94 & 20 & 85 & 10 & c2 & c0 & 01 & fb & 01 & c0 & c2 & 10 & 85 & 20 & 94 \\
94 & a5 & 3c & 44 & d1 & 8d & b4 & 54 & de & 6f & 77 & 5d & 96 & 74 & 2d & 84 \\
84 & 64 & 48 & df & d3 & 31 & a6 & 30 & e0 & 5a & 44 & 97 & ca & 75 & 99 & dd \\
dd & 0d & f8 & 52 & 91 & 64 & ff & 7b & af & 3d & 94 & f3 & d9 & d0 & e9 & 10 \\
10 & 89 & 48 & 7f & 91 & ec & 39 & ef & 10 & bf & 60 & e9 & 30 & 5e & 95 & bd \\
bd & a2 & 48 & c6 & fe & eb & 2f & 84 & c9 & ad & 7c & 1a & 68 & be & 9f & 27 \\
27 & 7f & c8 & 98 & f3 & 0f & 54 & 08 & f6 & ee & 12 & 8d & 2f & b8 & d4 & 5d \\
5d & 4b & 8e & 60 & 01 & 2a & 6c & 09 & 49 & ab & 8d & cb & 14 & 87 & 49 & b8 \\
b8 & 6e & 2a & d4 & b1 & 37 & af & d4 & be & f1 & 2e & bb & 1a & 4e & e6 & 7a \\
7a & 16 & f5 & 52 & 78 & 99 & eb & d5 & e7 & c4 & 2d & 06 & 17 & 62 & d5 & 48 \\
48 & c3 & 02 & 0e & 58 & 90 & e1 & a3 & 6e & af & bc & c5 & 0c & ec & 76 & 6c \\
6c & 4c & dd & 65 & 01 & c4 & d4 & 8d & a4 & 02 & eb & 20 & ca & 6b & f2 & 72 \\
72 & e8 & 14 & 07 & 49 & f6 & d7 & a6 & 6a & d6 & 11 & 1c & 0c & 10 & 33 & 76 \\
76 & e3 & 30 & 9f & 6b & 30 & 63 & a1 & 2b & 1c & 43 & 68 & 70 & 87 & c8 & a2 \\
a2 & d0 & 44 & 86 & 2d & b8 & 64 & c1 & 9c & 89 & 48 & 90 & da & c6 & 20 & 6e \\
6e & 4d & 8e & ea & a9 & f6 & bf & 0a & f3 & f2 & 8e & 93 & bf & 74 & 98 & cf
\end{pmatrix}$$

B   Proof of Theorem 2

To prove Theorem 2, we only need calculate $\gamma(P)$ and $\gamma(P^{-1})$. The linear transformation $P = MC \circ SR$, which is an $d^2 \times d^2$ matrix. According to the definition of $\gamma(P)$, we have $P^* \geq 0, \gamma(P) > 1$, where P^* is the characteristic matrix of P. Thus we consider whether $(P^*)^2 > 0$.

We denote $(P^*)^2 = (q_{ij})$, thus $q_{ij} = 0$ means that the i-th output byte of the 2-round SPN cipher is independent of the j-th input byte. Furthermore, when $Y = (P \circ S)^2(X)$, we denote $X = (x_0, x_1, \cdots, x_{d^2-1}), Y = (y_0, y_1, \cdots, y_{d^2-1})$, where $x_i, y_i \in \mathbb{F}_{2^n}$. If we can prove that any x_i is dependent on all y_j, then $(P^*)^2 > 0$.

Assume that $X_1 = \underbrace{(0, 0, \ldots, 0, x_i, 0, \ldots, 0)}_{i-1}, x_i \in \mathbb{F}_{2^n}^*$, $Y_1 = S(X_1)$, there is only one element of Y_1 related to x_i. We denote $Y_2 = P(Y_1) = MC \circ SR(Y_1)$, since the MC matrix is a $d \times d$ MDS matrix, there is one column of Y_2 which is viewed as a $d \times d$ matrix related to x_i. We denote $Y = P \circ S(Y_2)$, since the index transformation of ShiftRows is a permutation and the MC matrix is a $d \times d$ MDS matrix, all elements of Y are dependent on x_i.

Therefore, $\gamma(P) = 2$. Similarly, with the same method, we get $\gamma(P^{-1}) = 2$. Furthermore, $\gamma(P) + \gamma(P^{-1}) = 4$. Note that we can construct 4-round impossible differentials for $\varepsilon^{(2)}(n, d)$ when the input difference α and the output difference β such that $H(\alpha) = H(\beta) = 1$.

References

1. Biham, E., Shamir, A.: Differential Cryptanalysis of the Data Encryption Standard. Springer, New York (1993)
2. Knudsen, L.R.: DEAL – A 128-bit Block Cipher. Technical report, Department of Informatics, University of Bergen, Norway (1998)
3. Biham, E., Biryukov, A., Shamir, A.: Cryptanalysis of skipjack reduced to 31 rounds using impossible differentials. In: Stern, J. (ed.) EUROCRYPT 1999. LNCS, vol. 1592, pp. 12–23. Springer, Heidelberg (1999). doi:10.1007/3-540-48910-X_2
4. Blondeau, C.: Impossible differential attack on 13-round Camellia-192. Inf. Process. Lett. **115**(9), 660–666 (2015)
5. Boura, C., Naya-Plasencia, M., Suder, V.: Scrutinizing and improving impossible differential attacks: applications to CLEFIA, Camellia, LBlock and SIMON. In: Sarkar, P., Iwata, T. (eds.) ASIACRYPT 2014. LNCS, vol. 8873, pp. 179–199. Springer, Heidelberg (2014). doi:10.1007/978-3-662-45611-8_10
6. Li, R., Sun, B., Li, C.: Impossible differential cryptanalysis of SPN ciphers. IET Inf. Secur. **5**(2), 111–120 (2011)
7. Sun, B., Zhang, P., Li, C.: Impossible differential and integral cryptanalysis of zodiac. J. Softw. **22**(8), 1911–1917 (2011)
8. Kim, J., Hong, S., Lim, J.: Impossible differential cryptanalysis using matrix method. Discrete Math. **310**(5), 988–1002 (2010)
9. Luo, Y., Lai, X., Wu, Z., Gong, G.: A unified method for finding impossible differentials of block cipher structures. Inf. Sci. **263**, 211–220 (2014)
10. Wu, S., Wang, M.: Automatic search of truncated impossible differentials for word-oriented block ciphers. In: Galbraith, S., Nandi, M. (eds.) INDOCRYPT 2012. LNCS, vol. 7668, pp. 283–302. Springer, Heidelberg (2012). doi:10.1007/978-3-642-34931-7_17
11. Daemen, J., Rijmen, V.: The Design of Rijndael: AES - The Advanced Encryption Standard. Information Security and Cryptography. Springer, Berlin (2002)
12. Lu, J., Dunkelman, O., Keller, N., Kim, J.: New impossible differential attacks on AES. In: Chowdhury, D.R., Rijmen, V., Das, A. (eds.) INDOCRYPT 2008. LNCS, vol. 5365, pp. 279–293. Springer, Heidelberg (2008). doi:10.1007/978-3-540-89754-5_22

13. Mala, H., Dakhilalian, M., Rijmen, V., Modarres-Hashemi, M.: Improved impossible differential cryptanalysis of 7-round AES-128. In: Gong, G., Gupta, K.C. (eds.) INDOCRYPT 2010. LNCS, vol. 6498, pp. 282–291. Springer, Heidelberg (2010). doi:10.1007/978-3-642-17401-8_20

14. Kwon, D., Kim, J., Park, S., Sung, S.H., Sohn, Y., Song, J.H., Yeom, Y., Yoon, E.-J., Lee, S., Lee, J., Chee, S., Han, D., Hong, J.: New block cipher: ARIA. In: Lim, J.-I., Lee, D.-H. (eds.) ICISC 2003. LNCS, vol. 2971, pp. 432–445. Springer, Heidelberg (2004). doi:10.1007/978-3-540-24691-6_32

15. Wu, W., Zhang, W., Feng, D.: Impossible differential cryptanalysis of reduced round ARIA and Camellia. J. Comput. Sci. Technol. **22**(3), 449–456 (2007)

16. Aoki, K., Ichikawa, T., Kanda, M., Matsui, M., Moriai, S., Nakajima, J., Tokita, T.: Camellia: a 128-Bit block cipher suitable for multiple platforms-design and analysis. In: Stinson, D.R., Tavares, S.E. (eds.) SAC 2000. LNCS, vol. 2012, pp. 39–56. Springer, Heidelberg (2001)

17. Sun, B., Liu, Z., Rijmen, V., Li, R., Cheng, L., Wang, Q., Alkhzaimi, H., Li, C.: Links among impossible differential, integral and zero correlation linear cryptanalysis. In: Gennaro, R., Robshaw, M. (eds.) CRYPTO 2015. LNCS, vol. 9215, pp. 95–115. Springer, Heidelberg (2015). doi:10.1007/978-3-662-47989-6_5

18. Sun, B., Liu, M., Guo, J., Rijmen, V., Li, R.: Provable security evaluation of structures against impossible differential and zero correlation linear cryptanalysis. In: Fischlin, M., Coron, J.-S. (eds.) EUROCRYPT 2016. LNCS, vol. 9665, pp. 196–213. Springer, Heidelberg (2016). doi:10.1007/978-3-662-49890-3_8

19. Bouillaguet, C., Dunkelman, O., Fouque, P.-A., Leurent, G.: New insights on impossible differential cryptanalysis. In: Miri, A., Vaudenay, S. (eds.) SAC 2011. LNCS, vol. 7118, pp. 243–259. Springer, Heidelberg (2012). doi:10.1007/978-3-642-28496-0_15

20. Zhang, W., Bao, Z., Lin, D., Rijmen, V., Yang, B., Verbauwhede, I.: RECTANGLE: a bit-slice ultra-lightweight block cipher suitable for multiple platforms. Sci. China Inf. Sci. **58**(12), 1–15 (2015). Springer, Heidelberg

21. Shishkin, V., Dygin, D., Lavrikov, I., Marshalko, G., Rudskoy, V., Trifonov, D.: Low-weight and Hi-End: draft Russian encryption standard. In: CTCrypt, vol. 2014, pp. 183–188 (2014)

22. MacWilliams, F.J., Sloane, N.J.A.: The Theory of Error-Correcting Codes, 2nd edn. North-Holland Publishing Company, Amsterdam (1986)

23. Guo, J., Peyrin, T., Poschmann, A., Robshaw, M.: The LED block cipher. In: Preneel, B., Takagi, T. (eds.) CHES 2011. LNCS, vol. 6917, pp. 326–341. Springer, Heidelberg (2011). doi:10.1007/978-3-642-23951-9_22

24. Guo, J., Peyrin, T., Poschmann, A.: The PHOTON family of lightweight hash functions. In: Rogaway, P. (ed.) CRYPTO 2011. LNCS, vol. 6841, pp. 222–239. Springer, Heidelberg (2011). doi:10.1007/978-3-642-22792-9_13

25. Lu, J., Kim, J., Keller, N., Dunkelman, O.: Improving the efficiency of impossible differential cryptannalysis of reduced Camellia and MISTY1. In: Malkin, T. (ed.) CT-RSA 2008. LNCS, vol. 4964, pp. 370–386. Springer, Heidelberg (2008)

SPF: A New Family of Efficient Format-Preserving Encryption Algorithms

Donghoon Chang[1], Mohona Ghosh[1], Kishan Chand Gupta[2], Arpan Jati[1],
Abhishek Kumar[1(✉)], Dukjae Moon[3], Indranil Ghosh Ray[2],
and Somitra Kumar Sanadhya[1]

[1] Indraprastha Institute of Information Technology, Delhi, India
{donghoon,mohonag,arpanj,abhishekk,somitra}@iiitd.ac.in
[2] ASU, ISI, Kolkata, India
kish_gupta@yahoo.com, indranilgray@gmail.com
[3] Security Research Group, Samsung SDS, Inc., Seoul, Republic of Korea
dukjae.moon@samsung.com

Abstract. Commonly used encryption methods treat the plaintext merely as a stream of bits, disregarding any specific format that the data might have. In many situations, it is desirable and essential to have the ciphertext follow the same format as the plaintext. Moreover, ciphertext length expansion is also not allowed in these situations. Encryption of credit card numbers and social security numbers are the two most common examples of this requirement. Format-Preserving Encryption (FPE) is a symmetric key cryptographic primitive that is used to achieve this functionality. Initiated by the work of Black and Rogaway (CT-RSA 2002), many academic solutions have been proposed in literature that have focused on designing efficient FPE schemes. However, almost all the existing FPE schemes are based on Feistel construction and have efficiency issues.

In this work, we propose a new family of efficient FPE schemes that are Substitution-Permutation (SP) based constructions at their core. We term it as **SPF** family of FPE schemes. All the underlying SP transformations in these constructions have been defined such that they preserve the format of the data. We then demonstrate an instance of our construction applicable for digits. We show that our scheme is at least 5 times more efficient than existing FPE designs for most of the practical applications.

Keywords: Format-Preserving Encryption · SPN · MDS matrix · Binary matrix · Active S-boxes

1 Introduction

1.1 Format-Preserving Encryption

Block ciphers such as AES [13] and DES [11] are the most popular and widely used cryptographic primitives to maintain confidentiality of messages. Traditionally,

© Springer International Publishing AG 2017
K. Chen et al. (Eds.): Inscrypt 2016, LNCS 10143, pp. 64–83, 2017.
DOI: 10.1007/978-3-319-54705-3_5

block ciphers handle binary data of specific sizes, for example 128-bit for AES [13]. Various modes of operations are used to encrypt data of size other than the block size. In many practical applications, such as encryption of Credit Card Number (CCN) or Social Security Number (SSN), it is desirable to encrypt messages from an arbitrarily sized set onto the same set. Unfortunately, the conventional block ciphers and their modes such as ECB, CBC, or CTR are not suitable for this purpose.

Format-Preserving Encryption (FPE) refers to transformation of data that is formatted as a sequence of the symbols in such a way that the encrypted form of the data has the same format and length as the original data. Thus, a format-preserving encrypted CCN also "looks like" a CCN. Many financial or e-commerce databases contain credit card numbers or social security numbers and for both practical and legal reasons, encryption of these values are important. However, these fields that need to be encrypted have fixed formats and a plain use of conventional block cipher will produce ciphertexts violating the specified format.

1.2   Existing Work

The problem of encryption over fixed formats was first investigated in the database community by Brightwell and Smith [10]. They mention that when a traditional block cipher is used to encrypt a plaintext of a specific format, it produces a ciphertext which "bears roughly the same resemblance to plaintext . . . as a hamburger does to a T-bone steak". Schoroeppel and Orman proposed the Hasty Pudding Cipher which first demonstrated an encryption scheme that worked for arbitrary domain [34]. A few years later, Black and Rogaway [8] made the first systematic study of this problem and suggested some approaches to achieve the desired functionality. They proposed three methods: Prefix cipher, Cyclic walking and a Feistel based construction. However, all these methods have some serious efficiency or security issues. The Prefix cipher is suitable only for small domain messages, say when it contains $\leq 2^{30}$ elements. Cycle walking scheme is expensive when the message set is significantly smaller than the block size of the underlying encryption algorithm. The Feistel based construction only achieves birthday bound security and is not suitable for domains of intermediate size (say, domain size between 2^{30} to 2^{60}, which covers most of the real world use-cases such as SSN or CCN).

In 2008, Terence Spices proposed Feistel Finite Set Encryption Mode (FFSEM) [37], which combines cycle walking and an AES based balanced Feistel network. An year later, Bellare et al. [3] studied the problem of FPE in its full generality. They provided rigorous treatment of "rank-then-encipher" approach to encrypt over arbitrary domains. In [31], a method to construct a format-preserving block cipher using maximally unbalanced Feistel network was proposed. Based on the theoretical analysis of [3], Bellare et al. [30] proposed a concrete design based on Feistel network and submitted the same to NIST. This design was named FFX as an abbreviation of "Format-preserving Feistel-based encryption". FFX uses 10 or more rounds thus requiring at least ten invocations of the underlying cipher. Thus, for most of the motivating applications of FPE (such as CCN or SSN) at least 10 invocation of the underlying cipher are required.

BPS [9] is another Feistel based scheme submitted to NIST and very similar to FFX. BPS consists of 8 rounds and is more efficient than FFX, although still much slower than many block ciphers. Visa Format Preserving Encryption (VFPE) [36] is an FPE scheme by Visa Inc. which uses AES in counter mode and uses the resulting stream to encrypt the plaintext data. A special publication of NIST SP800-38G [20] specifies three modes of operation for format-preserving encryption, submitted to NIST earlier under the names FFX[Radix] [1], VAES3 [38] and BPS-BC [9]. The mode FE2 was shown to be insecure [21]. Recently, new message recovery attacks on FF1 and FF3 have been shown by Rogaway *et al.* [2]. A method to construct FPE scheme using tweakable block ciphers was proposed in [26].

Our Contribution: In this work, we present a new FPE construction SPF and a concrete instance of SPF for digits. This is the first known SPN based FPE construction. The key idea is to use only format-preserving transformations to ensure that the format of message and ciphertext are always same. Considering the domain size of the practical applications of FPE schemes, we add tweak in the proposed construction. To handle long length messages, we propose the adoption of well-known counter mode. We estimate a lower bound on the number of active S-boxes for different number of rounds of the proposed construction. The security of our design is then analyzed against differential, linear, square, multiset, related tweak and key scheduling attacks. Finally, we compare the efficiency of a concrete instance of the proposed construction for the most popular and widely used format - 'digit', with FFX and show that the proposed design is almost 5 times efficient.

The rest of the paper is organized as follows. In Sect. 2, the important preliminaries are described. The proposed SPF construction is presented in Sect. 3. The concrete instance of SPF for digits and security analysis of the proposed scheme against conventional attacks is presented in Sects. 4 and 5 respectively. We then analyze the performance of the proposed design in Sect. 6. Finally, we conclude our work in Sect. 7.

2   Preliminaries

Let $\Sigma = \{0, 1, 2, \ldots, N - 1\}$ be the alphabet set, where $N \geq 2$. The size N of the set Σ is referred to as the 'format size' and the elements of Σ are referred to as 'symbols', for example for digits, $N = 10$. Σ^* denotes the set of strings with elements from Σ. We assume that the plaintext contains symbols only from Σ. If this is not the case, suitable encoding and decoding functions could be used and then one can apply the "rank-then-encipher" approach [3] to use the methods described in this work.

2.1 Notations

$|\Sigma|$: The number of elements of a set Σ containing symbols
$\boxplus_N$: Symbol wise addition modulo N
$\lceil x \rceil$: Smallest integer just greater than the real number x
$S[i]$: i^{th} symbol of the string S from the left
$S \parallel T$: Concatenation of two strings S and T
$|S|_N$: Length of the string S in base N
$\mathbb{F}_{2^b}$: Galois Field GF(2^b).

3   The SPF Construction

In this section, we describe a new approach to design an efficient FPE algorithm for substitution-permutation network (SPN) based constructions termed as SPF format-preserving encryption.

3.1 Specification

The SPF is an example of SPN based iterated block cipher. Specifically SPF$_r^N$ denotes a member of SPF family consisting of r-rounds that can be used to realize FPE for the format set Σ, where $|\Sigma| = N$. The input/output of each intermediate round is denoted as $state$ [13]. Each state consists of $n = 16$ symbols. For ease of representation and discussion, we represent each $state$ as a 4×4 two-dimensional array of symbols.

The transformation of an input string of length n over symbol set Σ to $state$ is described by the function STATE(X) (Algorithm 1); while the inverse transformation of a $state$ to produce a string over Σ^n is described by the function STRING$(state)$ (Algorithm 2).

Algorithm 1. STATE(X)

input : string X
output: $state$

1 **for** $i \leftarrow 0$ to $(n-1)$ **do**
2 $\quad$ $j \leftarrow i \bmod 4$;
3 $\quad$ $k \leftarrow \lfloor i/4 \rfloor$;
4 $\quad$ $state[j,k] \leftarrow X[i]$;
5 **return** $state$

Algorithm 2. STRING$(state)$

input : $state$
output: string X

1 **for** $i \leftarrow 0$ to 3 **do**
2 $\quad$ **for** $j \leftarrow 0$ to 3 **do**
3 $\quad\quad$ $n \leftarrow (i + j \times 4)$;
4 $\quad\quad$ $X[n] \leftarrow state[i,j]$;
5 **return** X

3.2 The Round Transformations

Each round of SPF construction consists of these basic transformations: (1) Format-Preserving SubBytes (FPSB), (2) ShiftRows, (3) Format-Preserving MixColumns (FPMC) (4) Format-Preserving Key Addition (FPKA) and (5) Format-Preserving Tweak Addition (FPTA).

Format-Preserving SubBytes Transformation (S-layer): By substitution, we refer to a non-linear transformation that is used to create confusion. The S-box used here is a bijective mapping of Σ over Σ, i.e., $S : \Sigma \rightarrow \Sigma$. Since, each symbol of the *state* is going to be substituted by a symbol of Σ, this transformation ensures that the each symbol of resulting *state* is an element of Σ. As choice of S-box is critical to the security of the block cipher, proper characterization and selection of the same is of utmost importance. Apart from the criteria to thwart differential and linear attacks, hardware implementation cost should be considered as the final metric to choose the S-box. For smaller formats it is possible to exhaustively search for all possible S-boxes and choose the optimal one.

ShiftRows Transformation: The ShiftRows transformation is same as described for AES [13] and will always preserve the format of the message in its current description.

Format-Preserving MixColumns Transformation (P-layer): Permutation layer is used to introduce diffusion in the cipher and is also called the diffusion layer. This layer ensures that the local differences of an internal *state* before P-layer propagates to the larger area of the *state* after this layer. Selection of a linear diffusion layer P is very crucial from the view point of efficiency as well as security. The P-layer of popular ciphers like AES [13] is realized by using MDS matrix [23].

The branch number of a permutation function represents the diffusion rate and measures the security of the design against differential [6] and linear [29] cryptanalysis. The weight $wt(X)$ can be defined as the number of non-zero components in X, where $X = (x_1, x_2, \ldots, x_n)^T$. The branch number (β) of a matrix M is defined as:

$$\beta(M) = min\{wt(X) + wt(M \times X) | X \neq 0\}$$

While determining the format-preserving permutation layer, the main criteria for us was that it should preserve the format like other transformations and have maximum branch number, i.e., an MDS matrix for every format size. However, we could not find a suitable MDS-matrix satisfying our requirements. This is explained through Lemma 1 which shows the non-existence of such matrices under some reasonable restrictions.

Lemma 1. *Let $M = (m_{i,j})$ be a $d \times d$ MDS matrix over a field $\mathbb{F}_{2^b}$. Let S be a set of v elements such that $S = \{0, 1, \ldots, v - 1\}$. Further, let S be a subset of $\mathbb{F}_{2^b}$ such that $\{0, 1\} \subset S$ and $\forall X \in S^d$, $Y = M \times X^T \in S^d$. Then:*

1. $m_{i,j} \in S^*, \forall\ 0 \leq i, j \leq d$,
2. $S^* = m_{i,j}S^*, \forall\ 0 \leq i, j \leq d$,

3. For any $i, j \in \{0, \ldots, d-1\}$, the cyclic group generated by $m_{i,j}$ with respect to multiplication is subset of S^*, i.e., $\langle m_{i,j} \rangle \subseteq S^*$,
4. S is an additive subgroup of $\mathbb{F}_{2^b}$.

Proof. Let $|S| = v$ and $S^* = S \setminus \{0\}$. So $|S^*| = v - 1$.

1. Let $M = (C_0, C-1, \ldots, C_{d-1})$, where C_i denotes the i-th column. Then for $X = (1, 0, 0, \ldots, 0) \in S^d, Y = M \times X^T = C_0$ and from the property of M and S, $C_0 = Y \in S^d$. Since $M = (m_{i,j})$ is MDS, $m_{i,j}$ can not be 0 for any $i, j \in \{0, \ldots, d-1\}$. So $C_0 = Y \in S^{*d}$. Similarly it can be shown that $C_i \in S^{*d}$. Thus $m_{i,j} \in S^*$, $\forall\, 0 \le i, j \le d$.
2. Whenever $m_{i,j} = 1$, the statement is true. Let $m_{d-1,d-1} \ne 1$. Let $X_i = (0, \ldots, 0, s_i) \in S^d$. So $Y_i = M \times X^T = s_i C_{d-1} \in S^d$. For all $s_i \in S^*$, let us consider the codes of the form $(X_i | Y_i)$. For all these $v - 1$ codes, the first $d - 1$ components of X_i's are 0. Since M is MDS, following points are easy to observe:
   (i) d components of all Y_i's are non-zero i.e. $Y_i \in S^{*d}$.
   (ii) For all $d - 1 \le i \le 2d - 1$, the i-th component for all these $v - 1$ codes should be different.
   Note that $(2d - 1)$-th component of any of these $v - 1$ codes, is of the form xs_j, where $s_j \in S^*$. From the second observation it is clear that $|\{xs_j | s_j \in S^*\}| = v - 1$. Also form the property of M and S, $\{xs_j | s_j \in S^*\} \subseteq S^*$. Thus $S^* = \{xs_j | s_j \in S^*\}$ i.e. $S^* = xS^*$.
3. Since $1 \in S^*$, using 2 we get
   $m_{i,j}^k = m_{i,j}^k \times 1 = (m_{i,j} \times m_{i,j} \times m_{i,j} \times \ldots \times (m_{i,j} \times 1)))) \ldots) \in S^*$
   for any integer k. Thus $\langle m_{i,j} \rangle \subseteq S^*$.
4. Let $s_0, s_1 \in S_*$. From 2, it is easy to check that $m_{0,0}^{-1} s_0 \in S^*$. Similarly $m_{0,1}^{-1} s_1 \in S^*$. Let $X = (m_{0,0}^{-1} s_0, m_{0,1}^{-1} s_1, 0, \ldots, 0) \in S^d$. Then $Y = M \times X^t \in S^d$. Note that the first component of Y is $m_{0,0} \times m_{0,0}^{-1} s_0 + m_{0,1} \times m_{0,1}^{-1} s_1 = s_0 + s_1$. So, $s_0 + s_1 \in S$. Also $0 \in S$. Since $S \subset \mathbb{F}_{2^b}$, elements of S itself are their additive inverses and also the associative property is inherited. So S is an additive subgroup of $\mathbb{F}_{2^b}$. $\qquad \square$

Remark: From result 4 of *Lemma 1*, a $d \times d$ format-preserving MDS matrix exists if $|S| = v$ is of the form 2^b.

The linear diffusion layer of SPF can be instead realized by 4×4 binary matrix with addition modulo N.

Format-Preserving Key Addition Transformation: Given a round key K_i and current *state* S_i, the key addition operation is symbol wise addition modulo N.

$$S_i' \leftarrow (K_i + S_i) \bmod N$$

The modular addition of each symbol of K_i and S_i ensures that each symbol of S_i' is over Σ. Given the secret key K, the round keys K_i will be generated through a key scheduling algorithm (KSA).

Format-Preserving Tweak Addition Transformation: Similar to key addition step, given a subtweak Tw_i, and the current state S_i', the tweak addition is a symbol wise addition modulo N.

$$S_{i+1} \leftarrow (Tw_i + S_i') \bmod N$$

The modular addition of each symbol of K_i and S_i' ensures that each symbol of S_{i+1} is over Σ. Given the public tweak Tw (tweak value is known to the attacker), the subtweaks Tw_i will be generated through a tweak scheduling algorithm (TSA).

The Operating Mode of SPF: We adopt the Counter Mode [19] of operation using SPF_r^N routine internally to handle large messages. For a large message M, let us suppose j plaintext blocks are generated, i.e., $M = M_1||M_2||\dots||M_j$ such that $\forall i, 1 \le i < (j-1)$, $|M_i|_N = n$ symbols and $|M_j|_N \le n$. Given a sequence of counters $T_1, T_2, \dots, T_j$, the SPF_r^N cipher is invoked for each counter block to generate output blocks $O_1, O_2, \dots, O_j$ respectively. These output blocks are then added modulo N with corresponding plaintext blocks to produce the respective ciphertext blocks $C_1, C_2, \dots, C_j$. The ciphertext C is then formed by concatenating these ciphertext blocks together, i.e., $C = C_1||C_2||\dots||C_j$. The overall process is defined as follows:

$$C_i \leftarrow \mathsf{SPF}_r^N(K, M_i, T_i) \qquad \text{for } i = 1, \dots, j.$$
$$C \leftarrow C_1||C_2||\dots||C_j.$$

For decryption, the same scheme is used, except that the received ciphertext block is now subtracted modulo N with the output block to produce the corresponding plaintext block. The same SPF_r^N routine is used internally for both encryption and decryption processes.

We choose counter mode primarily for two reasons. Firstly, this mode allows us to convert the SPF_r^N block cipher into a stream cipher, i.e., it eliminates the need to pad a message to be a multiple of block length. Thus, it allows operation in real time. Secondly, it has many attractive properties like it allows random access during decryption and supports parallel encryption of message blocks. On the other hand, this mode suffers from one major limitation of *malleability*, i.e., by changing one symbol in ciphertext the corresponding plaintext symbol can be changed without affecting the rest of the symbols in the plaintext. This limitation is inherently translated to our SPF scheme as well. However, this constraint is applicable to other block cipher modes like CBC, OFB etc. as well [32]. To mitigate this flaw, one can follow the standard practice of incorporating some additional message authentication protocol in our SPF_r^N scheme, the design and analysis of which is currently beyond the scope of this work.

Algorithms 3 and 4, show the encryption and decryption process of SPF construction respectively.

Algorithm 3. EncSPF$_r^N$ (K, M, T, Tw)
input : Key K, Message M, Counter T, Tweak Tw
output: Ciphertext C
1   Initialize a string Q=NULL and $\ell \leftarrow |M|_N$;
2   $state \leftarrow$ STATE(T);
3   FPKA$(state, K)$;
4   FPTA$(state, Tw)$;
5   **for** $j \leftarrow 1$ **to** $r-1$ **do**
6   FPSB$(state)$;
7   ShiftRow$(state)$;
8   FPMC$(state)$;
9   FPKA$(state, K_j)$;
10   FPTA$(state, Tw)$;
11   FPSB$(state)$;
12   ShiftRow$(state)$;
13   FPKA$(state, K_j)$;
14   FPTA$(state, Tw)$;
15   string $Q \leftarrow$ STRING$(state)$;
16   **for** $i \leftarrow 0$ **to** $(\ell - 1)$ **do**
17    $C[i] \leftarrow (M[i] \boxplus_N Q[i])$;
18   **return** C;

Algorithm 4. DecSPF$_r^N$ (K, C, T, Tw)
input : Key K, Ciphertext C, Counter T, Tweak Tw
output: Message M
1   Initialize a string Q=NULL and $\ell \leftarrow |M|_N$;
2   $state \leftarrow$ STATE(T);
3   FPKA$(state, K)$;
4   FPTA$(state, Tw)$;
5   **for** $j \leftarrow 1$ **to** $r-1$ **do**
6   FPSB$(state)$;
7   ShiftRow$(state)$;
8   FPMC$(state)$;
9   FPKA$(state, K_j)$;
10   FPTA$(state, Tw)$;
11   FPSB$(state)$;
12   ShiftRow$(state)$;
13   FPKA$(state, K_j)$;
14   FPTA$(state, Tw)$;
15   string $Q \leftarrow$ STRING$(state)$;
16   **for** $i \leftarrow 0$ **to** $(\ell - 1)$ **do**
17    $M[i] \leftarrow (C[i] \boxminus_N Q[i])$;
18   **return** M;

4   SPF for Digits

The motivating applications of FPE are CCN and SSN, i.e., string of digits. In this section, we present an instance of SPF construction for digits. Our design rationales are motivated by efficiency and security on target applications. Since, SPF is a family of format-preserving encryption schemes, the actual number of rounds for a scheme depends upon different parameters: format size, available plaintext/ciphertext, number of rounds that can be attacked using existing cryptanalytic techniques and security margin.

4.1   The S-box Layer

We use a single S-box $S : \Sigma \rightarrow \Sigma$, where $|\Sigma| = 10$. We first analyzed all possible 10! mapping of S exhaustively and picked up mappings that have good differential and linear probabilities. In our next step, we applied the same criteria for mapping $S \circ S$. Finally, we used hardware implementation cost as the final metric to choose the S-box for digits shown in Table 1. The selected S-box is implemented as a 4-bit to 4-bit lookup table. For better space efficiency, we can use Boolean logic to implement the same. The S-box can be represented as $y_n = S[x_n]$. An optimal implementation with logic gates is as follows:

$$y_0 = \{x_2 x_3 + x_1 \bar{x_3} + x_0 \bar{x_3}\} \quad y_1 = \{\bar{x_1}\bar{x_2}\bar{x_3} + \bar{x_0}\bar{x_1}\bar{x_3}\}$$
$$y_2 = \{\bar{x_0}x_3\} \quad y_3 = \{x_2\bar{x_3}\}$$

The maximum differential probability and the maximum correlation for this S-box are $2^{-2.32}$ and $2^{-1.32}$ respectively. We will discuss this in detail in Sect. 5.1.

Table 1. Representation of S-box for digits.

x	0	1	2	3	4	5	6	7	8	9
$S[x]$	2	6	8	7	1	4	9	5	3	0

4.2 The ShiftRow Layer

As discussed earlier, the ShiftRows operation in our construction will work like AES.

4.3 The Permutation Layer

The linear diffusion layer of our SPF construction is realized by the following 4×4 binary matrix with addition modulo N.

$$M = \begin{pmatrix} 1 & 1 & 1 & 0 \\ 0 & 1 & 1 & 1 \\ 1 & 0 & 1 & 1 \\ 1 & 1 & 0 & 1 \end{pmatrix}$$

The binary matrix M used for the presented scheme has a branch number of 4. The usage of such binary matrix also results in a fast implementation in the hardware setup. The transformation of a column of *state* through our MixColumn matrix is represented as:

$$\begin{bmatrix} b_{r,0} \\ b_{r,1} \\ b_{r,2} \\ b_{r,3} \end{bmatrix} = \begin{pmatrix} 1 & 1 & 1 & 0 \\ 0 & 1 & 1 & 1 \\ 1 & 0 & 1 & 1 \\ 1 & 1 & 0 & 1 \end{pmatrix} \times \begin{bmatrix} a_{r,0} \\ a_{r,1} \\ a_{r,2} \\ a_{r,3} \end{bmatrix} \mod N$$

4.4 Key Schedule

We propose a new format preserving key scheduling algorithm (KSA) for the SPF cipher. Simplicity, performance and security are the main design rationals behind determining the structure of the proposed KSA. The key schedule algorithm takes the 128-bit cipher key K and the format size $(N = 10)$ as inputs and generates $(r+1)$ round subkeys as outputs. Let the cipher key K be represented as $k_{127}k_{126}\ldots k_2 k_1 k_0$. We first divide the cipher key K into two bit string of equal size and find $K_0 = \text{STATE}(K \mod 10^{16})$. We iterate Step 5 to Step 9 of the Algorithm 5 to extract remaining r subkeys. In [3] Bellare *et al.* estimated the lower bound of statistical distance between the uniform distribution on Z_p and the distribution obtained by $b \mod p$ after picking b randomly in Z_a as p/a where $a > p$. We estimate 2^{-75} ($a = 2^{128}$, $p = 10^{16} \approx 2^{53}$) as the statistical distance for digits. This bound suggests that the mod 10^{16} operation does not impact distributions dramatically.

Algorithm 5. KSA(K)
input : Key K
output: Round Keys
$\qquad K_0, K_1, \ldots, K_r$
1 $x_1 \leftarrow k_{127}k_{126} \ldots k_{65}k_{64}$;
2 $y_1 \leftarrow k_{63}k_{62} \ldots k_1 k_0$;
3 $K_0 \leftarrow \text{STATE}(K \bmod 10^{16})$
4 **for** $i \leftarrow 1$ **to** r **do**
5 $\quad y_i \leftarrow ((y_i \lll 15) + x_i) \oplus i$;
6 $\quad x_i \leftarrow (x_i \ggg 31) \oplus y_i$;
7 $\quad K_i \leftarrow$
$\qquad \text{STATE}((x_i \| y_i) \bmod 10^{16})$;
8 $\quad x_{i+1} \leftarrow x_i$;
9 $\quad y_{i+1} \leftarrow y_i$;
10 **return** $(K_0, K_1, \ldots, K_r)$;

Algorithm 6. TSA(Tw)
input : Tweak Tw
output: Round tweaks
$\qquad Tw0, Tw1$
1 $Tw_0 \leftarrow \text{STATE}(Tw \bmod 10^8)$;
2 $Tw \leftarrow (Tw \lll 32)$;
3 $Tw_1 \leftarrow \text{STATE}(Tw \bmod 10^8)$;
4 **return** $(Tw0, Tw1)$;

4.5 Tweak Addition

Liskov et al. [28] formalized the concept of tweakable block cipher and showed that tweakable block ciphers are an important construction if changing the tweak is efficient than changing the key. The tweak is supposed to be completely public data and is used to randomize the instance of block cipher, i.e., different values of tweak corresponds to different families of permutations. In [25], Jean et al. presented the generic TWEAKEY framework that can be built using any key alternating block cipher and proposed three instantiations - Deoxys-BC, JoltiK-BC and KIASU-BC that were the first ad-hoc tweakable block ciphers based on AES.

Considering the domain size (in between 2^{30} to 2^{60}) of traditional FPE applications and birthday bound security ($2^{b/2}$ for b-bit block cipher), we introduce an additional parameter tweak in our construction. Choice of tweak addition of SPF construction is motivated by the tweak addition of KIASU-BC cipher [25]. A 64-bit Tw will be used to generate two subtweaks $Tw0$ and $Tw1$ (Algorithm 6) and will be added to the first two rows of the state for each even and odd numbered rounds correspondingly. As discussed in [3], the statistical distance between choosing random subtweaks and subtweaks generated by TSA is upper bounded by 2^{-37}. This bound suggests that the mod 10^8 operation (as shown in Algorithm 6) does not impact the distributions dramatically.

5 Security Analysis

In this section, we evaluate the security of the SPF construction against conventional differential [6] and linear attacks [29]. However, there are many other dedicated and effective attacks against AES type structure. We provide preliminary analysis of our construction against these dedicated attacks.

5.1 Differential and Linear Cryptanalysis

Differential and linear cryptanalysis are two of the most powerful techniques to analyze symmetric-key primitives. An S-box is called active if the given input pattern is non-zero for this particular S-box. In order to provide security analysis of proposed design against linear and differential cryptanalysis, we use the results of the seminal work done by Daemen and Rijmen [14] to provide lower bound on active S-boxes for different rounds of SPF.

Theorem 1 [14]. *For a key-alternating block cipher with a $\gamma\lambda$ round structure the number of active S-boxes of any two-round is lower bounded by the branch number of λ.*

Theorem 2 [14]. *For a key-iterated block cipher with a $\gamma\pi\theta$ round transformation and diffusion optimal π, the number of active S-boxes in a four-round is lower bounded by the square of branch number of θ.*

Note that, the notation γ and λ used in Theorem 1 refer to a local non-linear transformation (S-box layer) and a linear mixing transformation (P-layer) respectively. The notations γ, π and θ of Theorem 2 refers Substitution transformation, Shift Row transformation and Permutation transformation respectively.

Number of Active S-boxes for SPF: The permutation layer of SPF uses a 4×4 binary M matrix with branch number 4. Hence, any two round differential/linear characteristic of SPF has a minimum of 4 active S-boxes and any four round differential/linear characteristic of SPF has a minimum of 16 active S-boxes. Table 2 contains number of rounds (r) and minimum number of active S-boxes (A_r) for SPF. In FSE 2006, Granboulan et al. [22] presented a general framework for differential and linear cryptanalysis of block cipher when the block is not a bitstring. A $N \times N$ matrix Δ simulates the behavior of S-box S over differences by $\Delta(S)_{a,b} = \#\{x|S(x+a) - S(x) = b\}$. The maximum entry of the matrix $D(S)$ is defined as:

$$D(S) = \max_{(a,b)\neq\{0,0\}} \Delta(S)_{a,b}.$$

The corresponding maximum propagation probability is defined as $DP(S) = D(S)/N$. The $D(S)$ is equal to 2 for SPF_r^{10} and the corresponding maximum differential probability $(DP(S))$ is equal to $2^{-2.32}$ ($\frac{2}{10} \approx 2^{-2.32}$).

Table 2. Minimum number of active S-boxes A_r for r rounds of SPF.

r	1	2	3	4	5	6	8	10	12	16	20
A_r	1	4	5	16	17	20	32	36	48	64	80

In order to investigate the security against linear cryptanalysis of the S-box $S : \Sigma \rightarrow \Sigma$, firstly we calculate the distribution vector $\Lambda_0(S)_{\{a,b\}} = (\#\{x \in \Sigma|\langle a, b|x, S(x)\rangle = u\})_{u\in\{Z\}}$, where $\langle a, b|x, y\rangle = \langle a|x\rangle - \langle b|y\rangle$ and $\langle a, x\rangle$ is scalar product of a and x. The distribution vector represents the behavior of the considered S-box. The random behavior can be defined as:

$f_{a,b;u} = \frac{1}{N}\#(x,y) \in \Sigma \times \Sigma |\langle a,b|x,y\rangle = u$. The bias of the S-box represents the difference of behavior of S-box S and random case and defined as $\Lambda_S(S)_{a,b;u} = \Lambda_0(S)_{a,b;u} - f_{a,b;u}$. The highest bias measures the non linearity of the S-box. The maximal bias is equal to $\frac{2}{10}$, i.e., $2^{-2.32}$. The maximum correlation for this S-box is $2^{-1.32}$ respectively.

The probability of a single 8-round differential characteristic is upper bounded by 2^{-72} and the maximum correlation of a 8-round linear trial is 2^{-42}. These bounds ensure that the data requirement to mount these attacks will exceed the available data $2^{54} (10^{16} \approx 2^{53.2})$ for 8 rounds.

5.2   Square Attack

The SQUARE attack was first proposed by Daemen *et al.* in [12] for block cipher SQUARE, a forerunner of AES. It was shown to be applicable to AES as well. This attack consists of choosing a special set of plaintexts and studying its propagation through the block cipher. This attack is very powerful against AES type ciphers.

In this section, we describe a 8-round square attack against SPF. This attack is similar to that described in [17]. For our 8-round attack, we first construct a 5-round distinguisher. Consider a set of 10 plaintexts in which the first symbol takes all possible 10 values (active symbol) and the remaining symbols take any constant value that remains same throughout the set. We call such a set of plaintexts as Λ-set. Since, our construction involves tweak addition, in this attack, let us suppose that the attacker uses Λ-sets for the two subtweaks as well, i.e., one symbol of both the subtweaks are active. Considering these, Fig. 1 shows the five round transformations of SPF construction. Let x_j, y_j, z_j, w_j denote the symbol values in round j after *SubBytes*, *ShiftRows*, *MixColumns* and *Key/Tweak Addition* stage respectively. Let A[p] denote the pth symbol (column wise) in any intermediate state A where, $0 \leq p \leq 15$. Similarly, $A^i_j[p]$ denotes the pth symbol of ith state A in round j where, (where, $0 \leq i \leq 9$).

In the pre-whitening stage, since Λ-sets of plaintexts and subtweaks are in control of the attacker, he chooses the plaintexts P^i and subtweaks TW^i_0 (where, $0 \leq i \leq 9$) such that for each i the sum $(P^i + Tw^i_0)$ mod 10 is a constant. The state remains constant until S_1 where the first symbol becomes active again due to addition of the second sub-tweak Tw_1. In, round 2 consider state $S_2[0]$. Due to sub-tweak addition of $Tw_1[0]$, we have:

$$w^i_2[0] = (z^i_2[0] + Tw^i_1[0]) \mod 10$$

Since the tweak symbol as well as the state symbol are active, if we add all the values in $w_2[0]$, it follows that the addition sum mod 10 is always 0:

$$w^0_2[0] + w^1_2[0] + \ldots w^9_2[0] = (z^0_2[0] + Tw^0_1[0]) \mod 10 +$$
$$(z^1_2[0] + Tw^2_1[0]) \mod 10 +$$
$$\vdots$$
$$(z^9_2[0] + Tw^9_1[0]) \mod 10$$

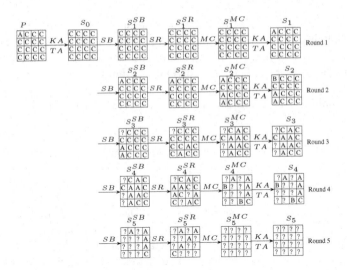

Fig. 1. A five round distinguisher for SPF. Here 'A' denotes an active symbol, 'B' denotes that mod 10 sum of all values in that symbol is 0 and '?' denotes unknown symbol.

This can be re-written as[1]:

$$w_2^0[0] + w_2^1[0] + \ldots w_2^9[0] = \left(\sum_{i=0}^{9} z_2^i + \sum_{i=0}^{9} Tw_1^i\right) \bmod 10$$
$$= (45 + 45) \bmod 10$$
$$= 0$$

This shows that the set of values in the first symbol position after second round tweak addition forms a *balanced* set with probability 1. After *SubBytes* operation in round 3, the balanced set property is destroyed. Similar explanation can be given till state transformation after *ShiftRows* in round 5. After *MixColumns* operation in round 5, we get a completely unknown state as shown in Fig. 1. However, at state S_5^{MC}, consider the second column. Then, we have:

$$\sum_{i=0}^{9} z_5^i[1] + \sum_{i=0}^{9} z_5^i[3] = \sum_{i=0}^{9} y_5^i[1] + \sum_{i=0}^{9} y_5^i[2] + \sum_{i=0}^{9} y_5^i[3] + \sum_{i=0}^{9} y_5^i[0] + \sum_{i=0}^{9} y_5^i[1] + \sum_{i=0}^{9} y_5^i[3]$$
$$= 2\left(\sum_{i=0}^{9} y_5^i[1] + \sum_{i=0}^{9} y_5^i[3]\right) + \sum_{i=0}^{9} y_5^i[0] + \sum_{i=0}^{9} y_5^i[2]$$
$$= 2\left(\sum_{i=0}^{9} y_5^i[1] + \sum_{i=0}^{9} y_5^i[3]\right) + 0$$
$$= \text{Even number}$$

---

[1] Sum of first 10 numbers is $\frac{10 \times 9}{2}$.

In the right hand side of the above equation, since $y_5[0]$ and $y_5[2]$ bytes are active bytes their sum over all 10 states is always going to be zero as discussed above. As such the additive sum of $Z_5[1] + Z_5[3]$ over all 10 states will always be an even number with probability 1. This property will hold true even after tweak addition in round 5 (since $(10 \times C) \bmod 10 = 0$). In random case, the output will be even with a probability half. Hence, a valid distinguisher is constructed. This five round attack can be extended up to eight rounds by adding one round in backward and 2 rounds in the forward directions to recover the secret key.

5.3 Impossible Differential Cryptanalysis

Impossible Differential Cryptanalysis (IDC) [5] uses impossible differential characteristics to eliminate the incorrect keys. We propagated 16 input truncated differential and 16 output different truncated differential with encryption and decryption function respectively. Then, we used miss-in-the-middle technique to found impossible differential characteristics for our SPF construction. We searched for truncated input characteristics and output characteristics contradicting with probability one and found 5 rounds impossible characteristics for proposed construction. The input and output characteristics for 5 rounds impossible characteristics is as follows:

$$(0,0,1,0,0,0,0,0,0,0,0,0,0,0,0,0) \xrightarrow{5R} (0,0,0,0,0,0,0,0,0,0,0,1,0,0,0,0)$$

More rounds can be appended before and after the 5 rounds impossible characteristics depending upon the block size and the key size. We found up to 9 rounds characteristics, which can be used for key-recovery attacks, but no such characteristics could be found when the number of round is greater than 9.

5.4 Key Related Attacks

Slide attacks [7] and related-key attacks [4] are the two most important types of key scheduling attacks. Our key scheduling algorithm (KSA) for SPF discussed in Sect. 4.4 adds a round dependent counter in each round to prevent sliding of subkeys. For related key attack to work, the attacker should be able to identify meaningful relationships between the different subkeys so that a related key differential can be constructed over certain rounds. However, the non-linear addition operation and the modular function in our key scheduling algorithm does not allow an adversary to deduce all the other round keys (and the master key) from one round key by working through the key schedule. The modular function in particular also makes it very hard for an attacker to control the difference propagation through different round keys. Moreover, we also analyzed that each bit of the secret key K is used by the fourth round for all format size 10 or more. Hence, we believe that these features of the proposed KSA are sufficient to resist related key attacks.

5.5   Related Tweak Attack

Unlike the related key attack where the master key is unknown to the attacker and it is difficult for him to control the difference propagation in the various round keys, launching a related tweak attack to recover the secret key is easier for him. This is because the tweak value is a public entity and can be chosen by the attacker himself. This allows him to insert differences in the tweak input of the block cipher and construct related tweak differentials. Thus, it is imperative to assess the security of our SPF scheme in this stronger related tweak setting.

We developed an automated program to count the number of active S-boxes and return an upper bound on the probability of the best related tweak differentials. To keep the search space from exploding, we consider the differential trails in a truncated manner, i.e., either a symbol is active or it is not active.

The best related tweak differentials for 3 and 4 rounds of SPF have 1 and 4 active S-boxes respectively. For 6-rounds, SPF has 26 active S-boxes and for 7-rounds the count is 40.[2] Table 3 lists the number of active S-boxes for the first 8-rounds of SPF. Thus, the probability of any characteristic on more than 6 rounds is not higher than $2^{-26 \times 2.32} = 2^{-60.32}$. This bound ensures that the amount of data required to launch the attack will exceed the data available to an attacker (i.e., $10^{16} \approx 2^{53.2}$). Hence, our SPF construction can resist any related tweak attack of practical complexity if the number of rounds is ≥ 6.

Table 3. Count of active S-box (A_r) and corresponding differential probability ($P_r 0$) over different rounds of SPF for related tweak differentials.

Rounds	1	2	3	4	5	6	7	8
A_r	0	0	1	4	12	26	40	55
P_r	0	0	$2^{-2.32}$	$2^{-9.28}$	$2^{-27.84}$	$2^{-60.32}$	$2^{-92.8}$	$2^{-127.6}$

5.6   Multiset Attack

Multiset attack on AES was first proposed by Dunkelman *et al.* in [18]. This attack which is a variant of meet-in-the-middle attack on AES presented by Demirci *et al.* in [15], involves constructing a set of functions which maps an ordered 256-byte sequence in one active byte in the first round to an unordered 256-byte sequence (a multiset) in one byte of the output after 4-rounds of AES to recover the key. The current best multiset attacks can reach 7-rounds of AES-128 [16], 9-rounds of AES-192 [27] and 10-rounds of AES-256 [33].

Since our FPE scheme has structural similarity with AES, therefore it was imperative for us to test this attack against our scheme. Our key schedule algorithm (described in Sect. 4.4 does not allow recovery of all round keys (and the secret key) from the knowledge of only one round key. Hence, attacks discussed

---

[2] These active S-box counts are the lower bounds and the actual count might be larger.

in [27,33] will not work for our construction (since they exploit dependencies between round keys). Our preliminary analysis shows that the number of rounds attacked in our scheme is same as that for AES-128, i.e., a maximum of 7-rounds can be attacked. This is because addition of sub-tweaks to each round key just changes their values to some new constant C' and thus does not provide any extra degrees of freedom to exploit with.

By considering the attacks above discussed, performance and security margin, we recommend $r = 14$.

6   Performance

In this section, we provide performance analysis of SPF construction for digit. We present efficiency comparison of FFX, BPS, VFPE and SPF for digits.

The existing popular design FFX and BPS [20] requires minimum 11 and 8 invocations of AES respectively to encrypt messages containing 16 symbols, i.e., approximately 110 and 80 substitutions and permutations for FFX and BPS respectively. On the other hand SPF achieves the same goal by using 14 substitution and permutation. Table 4 shows that the SPF is almost 7 and 5 times more efficient than FFX and BPS respectively for most practical uses of FPE.

Table 4. Efficiency comparison of FFX, BPS and VFPE with SPF_{14}^{10} for digits. The table shows an analysis of numbers of symbols vs number of substitution and permutation required [35] (an entry corresponding to FPE schemes (in row) and number of symbols (in column) represents number of substitution and permutation required).

FPE schemes	No. of symbols			
	16	32	64	128
SPF	14	28	56	112
FFX	110	110	310	410
BPS	80	80	160	240
VFPE	10	10	20	40

VFPE [36] outperforms all three constructions including SPF construction for digits. However it is a patented design and has few security concerns [26,35]. For large format size messages, the SPF construction will outperform VFPE.

6.1   Implementations

SPF is suitable for efficient implementation on a wide range of devices. Considering the practical uses of FPE, we implemented SPF_{14}^{10} on 64-bit platforms and compared the performance with FFX. Similar to AES, table lookups in SPF can be used to combine different round transforms, leading to very fast implementations. Interestingly, the lookup tables are much smaller compared to AES. Apart from making such implementations more interesting for resource constrained environments, the small lookup tables also reduce timing attacks. Unlike AES, SPF uses a binary matrix for the FPMC operation, as a result the implementation can be much more efficient on constrained devices. Some of the major uses of FPE algorithms are in encrypting large databases on high performance processors, as a result we tested our implementation on two high performance platforms as well as one mobile and one server platform, the experimental results are shown in Table 5.

Table 5. Experimental results on various 64-bit processors.

Processor	Clock	Speed for SPF_{14}^{10}	
	Speed	Symbols/s	Cycles/Symbol
Intel Core i7 6700	3.4 GHz	132.4×10^6	25.6
Intel Core i7 4770	3.4 GHz	117.2×10^6	29.0
Intel Core i5 5200	2.2 GHz	26.8×10^6	82.0
Intel Xeon E5 2630	2.3 GHz	52.9×10^6	43.4

We implemented SPF_{14}^{10} using a table based implementation, similar to AES implementations in C using assembly intrinsics wherever necessary. The MOD operations were implemented using a table look-up in conjunction with PDEP and PEXT instructions, added in the new BMI2 instruction set, significantly improving the overall performance. BMI2 instruction set was introduced in the Haswell Micro-architecture.

We performed comparisons with reference implementations of FF2 and found out that the performance ratios with SPF_{14}^{10} are in agreement with the values in Table 4.

7   Conclusion

In this work, we presented a new efficient format-preserving encryption construction based on substitution-permutation networks. The construction uses only format-preserving basic transformations. We present a concrete instance of proposed construction for format size 10, which is the most practical use of FPE. For the security analysis of the presented design, we consider conventional cryptanalytic techniques as well as dedicated attacks. We estimated the number of rounds of constructions considering security and efficiency. Finally, we compared the efficiency of the presented construction with existing schemes. The construction is approximately five times more efficient than existing popular designs such as FFX and BPS for all practical uses of FPE. A similar construction for other popular format size is an interesting open problem. Another interesting research direction would be to design an efficient format preserving encryption scheme that can handle long messages and solve the problem of malleability.

References

1. Bellare, M., Rogaway, P., Spies, T.: Addendum to "The FFX Mode of Operation for Format-Preserving Encryption": a parameter collection for enciphering strings of arbitary radix and length, Draft 1.0, Natl. Inst. Stand. Technol. (2010). http://csrc.nist.gov/groups/ST/toolkit/BCM/documents/proposedmodes/ffx/ffx-spec2.pdf
2. Bellare, M., Hoang, V.T., Tessaro, S.: Message-recovery attacks on feistel-based format preserving encryption. Cryptology ePrint Archive, Report 2016/794 (2016). http://eprint.iacr.org/2016/794
3. Bellare, M., Ristenpart, T., Rogaway, P., Stegers, T.: Format-preserving encryption. In: Jacobson, M.J., Rijmen, V., Safavi-Naini, R. (eds.) SAC 2009. LNCS, vol. 5867, pp. 295–312. Springer, Heidelberg (2009). doi:10.1007/978-3-642-05445-7_19
4. Biham, E.: New types of cryptanalytic attacks using related keys (extended abstract). In: Helleseth [24], pp. 398–409
5. Biham, E., Biryukov, A., Shamir, A.: Cryptanalysis of skipjack reduced to 31 rounds using impossible differentials. In: Stern, J. (ed.) EUROCRYPT 1999. LNCS, vol. 1592, pp. 12–23. Springer, Heidelberg (1999). doi:10.1007/3-540-48910-X_2
6. Biham, E., Shamir, A.: Differential cryptanalysis of DES-like cryptosystems. In: Menezes, A.J., Vanstone, S.A. (eds.) CRYPTO 1990. LNCS, vol. 537, pp. 2–21. Springer, Heidelberg (1991). doi:10.1007/3-540-38424-3_1
7. Biryukov, A., Wagner, D.: Advanced slide attacks. In: Preneel, B. (ed.) EUROCRYPT 2000. LNCS, vol. 1807, pp. 589–606. Springer, Heidelberg (2000). doi:10.1007/3-540-45539-6_41
8. Black, J., Rogaway, P.: Ciphers with arbitrary finite domains. In: Preneel, B. (ed.) CT-RSA 2002. LNCS, vol. 2271, pp. 114–130. Springer, Heidelberg (2002). doi:10.1007/3-540-45760-7_9
9. Brier, E., Peyrin, T., Stern, J.: BPS: a format-preserving encryption proposal, NIST. http://csrc.nist.gov/groups/ST/toolkit/BCM/documents/proposedmodes/bps/bps-spec.pdf
10. Brightwell, M., Smith, H.: Using datatype-preserving encryption to enhance data warehouse security
11. Coppersmith, D., Holloway, C., Matyas, S.M., Zunic, N.: The data encryption standard. Inf. Secur. Tech. Rep. 2(2), 22–24 (1997)
12. Daemen, J., Knudsen, L., Rijmen, V.: The block cipher Square. In: Biham, E. (ed.) FSE 1997. LNCS, vol. 1267, pp. 149–165. Springer, Heidelberg (1997). doi:10.1007/BFb0052343
13. Daemen, J., Rijmen, V.: Rijndael for AES. In: AES Candidate Conference, pp. 343–348 (2000)
14. Daemen, J., Rijmen, V.: The wide trail design strategy. In: Honary, B. (ed.) Cryptography and Coding 2001. LNCS, vol. 2260, pp. 222–238. Springer, Heidelberg (2001). doi:10.1007/3-540-45325-3_20
15. Demirci, H., Selçuk, A.A.: A meet-in-the-middle attack on 8-round AES. In: Nyberg, K. (ed.) FSE 2008. LNCS, vol. 5086, pp. 116–126. Springer, Heidelberg (2008). doi:10.1007/978-3-540-71039-4_7

16. Derbez, P., Fouque, P.-A., Jean, J.: Improved key recovery attacks on reduced-round AES in the single-key setting. In: Johansson, T., Nguyen, P.Q. (eds.) EURO-CRYPT 2013. LNCS, vol. 7881, pp. 371–387. Springer, Heidelberg (2013). doi:10. 1007/978-3-642-38348-9_23

17. Dobraunig, C., Eichlseder, M., Mendel, F.: Square attack on 7-round Kiasu-BC. In: Manulis, M., Sadeghi, A.-R., Schneider, S. (eds.) ACNS 2016. LNCS, vol. 9696, pp. 500–517. Springer, Heidelberg (2016). doi:10.1007/978-3-319-39555-5_27

18. Dunkelman, O., Keller, N., Shamir, A.: Improved single-key attacks on 8-round AES-192 and AES-256. J. Cryptol. 28(3), 397–422 (2015)

19. Dworkin, M.: NIST Special Publication 800-38A: Recommendation for Block Cipher Modes of Operation-Methods and Techniques, December 2001

20. Dworkin, M.: Recommendation for block cipher modes of operation: methods for format-preserving encryption. NIST Special Publication, 800:38G

21. Dworkin, M., Perlner, R.A.: Analysis of VAES3 (FF2). IACR Cryptology ePrint Archive, 2015:306 (2015)

22. Granboulan, L., Levieil, É., Piret, G.: Pseudorandom permutation families over abelian groups. In: Robshaw, M. (ed.) FSE 2006. LNCS, vol. 4047, pp. 57–77. Springer, Heidelberg (2006). doi:10.1007/11799313_5

23. Chand Gupta, K., Ghosh Ray, I.: On constructions of involutory MDS matrices. In: Youssef, A., Nitaj, A., Hassanien, A.E. (eds.) AFRICACRYPT 2013. LNCS, vol. 7918, pp. 43–60. Springer, Heidelberg (2013). doi:10.1007/978-3-642-38553-7_3

24. Helleseth, T. (ed.): EUROCRYPT 1993. LNCS, vol. 765. Springer, Heidelberg (1994)

25. Jean, J., Nikolić, I., Peyrin, T.: Tweaks and keys for block ciphers: the TWEAKEY framework. In: Sarkar, P., Iwata, T. (eds.) ASIACRYPT 2014. LNCS, vol. 8874, pp. 274–288. Springer, Heidelberg (2014). doi:10.1007/978-3-662-45608-8_15

26. Lee, J.-K., Koo, B., Roh, D., Kim, W.-H., Kwon, D.: Format-preserving encryption algorithms using families of tweakable blockciphers. In: Lee, J., Kim, J. (eds.) ICISC 2014. LNCS, vol. 8949, pp. 132–159. Springer, Heidelberg (2015). doi:10. 1007/978-3-319-15943-0_9

27. Li, L., Jia, K., Wang, X.: Improved single-key attacks on 9-round AES-192/256. In: Cid, C., Rechberger, C. (eds.) FSE 2014. LNCS, vol. 8540, pp. 127–146. Springer, Heidelberg (2015). doi:10.1007/978-3-662-46706-0_7

28. Liskov, M., Rivest, R.L., Wagner, D.: Tweakable block ciphers. In: Yung, M. (ed.) CRYPTO 2002. LNCS, vol. 2442, pp. 31–46. Springer, Heidelberg (2002). doi:10. 1007/3-540-45708-9_3

29. Matsui, M.: Linear cryptoanalysis method for DES cipher. In: Helleseth [24], pp. 386–397

30. Rogaway, P., Bellare, M., Spies, T.: The ffx mode of operation for format-preserving encryption. NIST submission (2010). http://csrc.nist.gov/groups/ST/ toolkit/BCM/documents/proposedmodes/ffx/ffx-spec2.pdf

31. Morris, B., Rogaway, P., Stegers, T.: How to encipher messages on a small domain. In: Halevi, S. (ed.) CRYPTO 2009. LNCS, vol. 5677, pp. 286–302. Springer, Heidelberg (2009). doi:10.1007/978-3-642-03356-8_17

32. Rogaway, P.: Evaluation of some blockcipher modes of operation. http://www. cryptrec.go.jp/estimation/techrep_id2012_2.pdf

33. Rongjia, L., Chenhui, J.: Meet-in-the-middle attacks on 10-round AES-256. Des. Codes Crypt., 1–13 (2015)

34. Schroeppel, R., Orman, H.: The hasty pudding cipher. In: AES Candidate Submitted to NIST, p. M1 (1998)

35. Scott, M.: A note on the implemention of format preserving encryption modes. http://cdn2.hubspot.net/hub/230906/file-20129878/certivox_labs_fpe.pdff
36. Sheets, J., Wagner, K.R.: Visa Format Preserving Encryption (VFPE), NIST submission (2011)
37. Spies, T.: Feistel Finite Set Encryption. NIST submission, February 2008. http://csrc.nist.gov/groups/ST/toolkit/BCM/modes-development.html
38. Vance, J.: VAES3 scheme for: An addendum to "The FFX Mode of Operation for Format-Preserving Encryption", Draft 1.0, 20 May 2011. http://csrc.nist.gov/groups/ST/toolkit/BCM/documents/proposedmodes/ffx/ffx-ad-VAES3.pdf

Transposition of AES Key Schedule

Jialin Huang[1], Hailun Yan[2], and Xuejia Lai[2(✉)]

[1] TU Darmstadt, Darmstadt, Germany
jlhuang.cn@gmail.com
[2] Cryptography and Information Security Lab, Department of Computer Science,
Shanghai Jiao Tong University, Shanghai, China
helenyan@sjtu.edu.cn, lai-xj@cs.sjtu.edu.cn

Abstract. In this paper, we target the poor diffusion pattern in the key schedule of AES. More specifically, the column-by-column word-wise property in the key schedule matches closely with the MixColumns operation in the round diffusion, which leads to several attacks in both single-key and related-key model. Therefore, we propose a new key schedule by switching the interaction from between different columns to between different rows, which offers stronger security than the original AES key schedule and better efficiency than other key schedule proposals. First, our proposal reduces the number of rounds of several single-key attacks, such as popular SQUARE attacks and meet-in-the-middle attacks, e.g. Derbez *et al.*, EUROCYRPT 2013 and Li *et al.*, FSE 2014. Meanwhile, it increases the security margin for AES in the related-key model, namely making the related-key differential attacks with local collisions which broke the full rounds of AES impossible.

Compared with the original key schedule, our modification is slight and just does a transposition on the output matrix of the subkeys. Compared with other AES key schedule variants, no extra non-linear operations, no complicated diffusion method, and no complicated iteration process of generating subkeys exist in our modification.

Keywords: AES · Key schedule · Meet-in-the-middle · Related-key · Differentials · MixColumns

1 Introduction

In 2000, Rijndael was chosen by NIST as the Advanced Encryption Standard (AES), as a replacement of DES for the US government. This new standard encryption algorithm has become one of the most widely used block ciphers in the last decade. There has been a lot of cryptanalysis against it, such as SQUARE attacks, differential attacks, impossible differential attacks, differential-linear attacks, and meet-in-the-middle attacks. A considerable number of these attacks exploit the weaknesses of the AES key schedule. In the single-key setting, the weakness in the key schedule can be exploited in the SQUARE and meet-in-the-middle attacks. This assists the attacker to gain free bytes of subkeys for extending the targeted rounds of an attack. Moreover, almost all the differential-type

© Springer International Publishing AG 2017
K. Chen et al. (Eds.): Inscrypt 2016, LNCS 10143, pp. 84–102, 2017.
DOI: 10.1007/978-3-319-54705-3_6

attacks can be put in a related-key model with a lower time and data complexity than in a single-key model by using such weaknesses. Since most current attacks focus on maximizing the number of rounds that can be broken and on minimizing the time and data complexity, these security vulnerabilities caused by the key schedule are worthy of more study.

There are many modified variants of AES, especially modifications of the key schedule, which aim to patch the security flaw. In 2002, May et al. studied the defects of the AES key schedule [5]. By taking frequency test and SAC test they found that the original AES key schedule has a problem of bit leakage and does not satisfy a one-way function property. The authors then proposed a new design of key schedule, applying a three-round AES cipher function, which has good bit diffusion and confusion, to derive the subkeys. In 2010, Nikolic presented a tweak for the key schedule of AES, which is called xAES [9]. The author added several rotation operations and extra S-boxes, which would not change the overall structure of the original key schedule. After checking by an automatic search tool developed by [1], the author showed that xAES can resist related-key differential attacks. In 2011, Choy et al. [8] proved that there are a number of equivalent key pairs in May et al.'s key schedule, which should be avoided in a block cipher design. Then they improved this key schedule by eliminating these weak keys. Moreover, they emphasized that the improved key schedule can defend against the related-key differential attacks in [2] and the related-key boomerang attacks in [3]. All of these modifications to the AES key schedule introduce extra operations leading to a reduction of execution speed and making the new key schedule totally inconsistent with the old one.

Our contribution. This paper starts with an interesting observation of the AES key schedule. That is, the column-based diffusion pattern is poor. Not only the widely studied properties of slow diffusion and high linearity, but also this poor diffusion pattern is responsible for the existing attacks using weaknesses of the key schedule. We propose a new key schedule almost the same as the original one, without bringing any additional operations, e.g., no non-linear operations (S-boxes) and no complicated diffusion course (adding rotation or XOR operations to involve more bits). So it is significantly faster than other AES variants. All we have done is just to transpose the output matrix of the subkeys by changing the subscripts before it enters the round encryption. Our simple change affects the positions of the diffusion pattern of the key schedule, instead of altering the branch number. We demonstrate that with our key schedule, the threat of SQUARE attacks, meet-in-the-middle attacks and related-key differential attacks has been eased.

Although our key schedule does not eliminate the two important weaknesses—slow diffusion and high linearity—it is interesting that the minor change can bring much higher security for both related-key attacks and single-key attacks, while most of other modifications to the AES key schedule only impact related-key attacks.

Organization. This paper is organized as follows. In Sect. 2, we present the AES block cipher, especially its key schedule. Then we introduce several major pieces of analysis as well as modifications proposed in previous work. In Sect. 3, the new key schedule is described. In Sect. 4, we focus on the single-key attacks for AES, and show why exploiting our key schedule is more resistant against these attacks. In Sect. 5, we revisit the related-key differential attacks for AES, and explain why applying our key schedule can avoid the relate-key differential attacks. In Sect. 6 we summarize this paper and give some discussions.

2 Description and Security Analysis of the AES Key Schedule

2.1 A Short Description of AES

AES has a 128-bit state and supports three key sizes: 128, 192, and 256 bits [7]. It is a byte-oriented cipher, and has 10 rounds for 128-bit, 12 rounds for 192-bit and 14 rounds for 256-bit keys. In each round of AES, the internal state can be seen as a 4×4 matrix of bytes, which undergoes the following basic transformations:

- SubBytes(SB): byte-wise application of S-boxes.
- ShiftRows(SR): cyclic shift of each row of the state matrix by some amount.
- MixColumns(MC): column-wise matrix multiplication.
- AddRoundKey(AK): XOR of the subkey to the state.

An additional AddRoundKey operation is performed before the first round (the whitening key) and the MixColumns is omitted in the last round. The state byte in the i'th row and j'th column of round r is $S_{i,j}^r$.

The key schedule is required to produce 11, 13 or 15 128-bit subkeys from master keys of size 128, 192 or 256-bit respectively. Each 128-bit subkey contains four words (a word is a 32-bit quantity which is denoted by $W[\cdot]$). Call the number of rounds N_r, and the number of 32-bit words in the master key N_k(e.g., for AES-128, $N_r = 10$, $N_k = 4$). The key schedule is shown in Algorithm 1 below: $K[\cdot]$ is a word of the master key, $RCON[\cdot]$ are round constants, and RotWord($\cdot$) rotates four bytes by one byte position to the left. The subkey used in the AddRoundKey of round r is denoted by K^r. The whitening key is K^0. Each subkey is represented as a byte matrix of size 4×4 (corresponding to the state matrix), and the j'th byte in the i'th row of the matrix is denoted by $K_{i,j}^r(0 < i, j < 4)$. The "equivalent" key obtained when the MixColumns and AddRoundKey operations are interchanged is denoted as $\widehat{K}^r = MC^{-1}(K^r)$.

2.2 Previous Analysis of the AES Key Schedule

Partial key guessing property and key splitting property of the AES key schedule were discussed in [4]. Partial key guessing describes the situation where knowledge of parts of the subkeys allows the attacker to calculate many other subkey (or even master key) bits. Key splitting describes the following phenomenon:

Algorithm 1. Key schedule of AES

---

for $i = 0, ..., N_k - 1$ **do**
    $W[i] = K[i];$
end for
for $i = N_k, ..., 4(N_r + 1) - 1$ **do**
    temp $\longleftarrow W[i-1];$
    if $i \bmod N_k == 0$ **then**
        temp $\longleftarrow$ SB(RotWord(temp)) $\oplus RCON[i/N_k];$
    end if
    if $N_k = 8$ and $i \bmod 8 == 4$ **then**
        temp $\longleftarrow$ SB(temp);
    end if
    $W[i] \longleftarrow W[i - N_k] \oplus$ temp;
end for

---

the two topmost rows interact with the two bottommost rows through only 14 bytes (for AES-256) and if we guess these 14 bytes, the rest of the key has been split into two independent halves controlling half of the expanded key bytes.

The authors in [5] proposed the following three properties to strengthen the key schedule of AES:

1. be a collision-resistant one-way function;
2. has minimal mutual information between all subkey bits and master key bits;
3. has an efficient implementation.

The authors measured property 1 with Shannon's concepts of bit confusion and bit diffusion. They also used the frequency test to judge the bit confusion of AES key schedule, and the Strict Avalanche Criterion (SAC) test to measure its bit diffusion. According to the results, they pointed out that the majority of subkeys do not attain complete bit confusion, and none of them pass the SAC test. This poor performance suggests that the AES key schedule suffers a serious bit leakage and is not one-way.

The linear relationship between subkey values were described in [6]. The authors studied the propagation of (known) key differences in the key schedule for all three key sizes of AES, which is supposed to be useful for related-key attacks. However, the authors pointed out that for any key sizes, no such relationship exists which covers the entire key schedule (i.e., which involves the first subkey and the last subkey, but no subkeys in between), so there is no straightforward way to exploit the finding to mount a related-key attack against the full AES.

A breakthrough in the related-key cryptanalysis of AES has been made in [2,3]. In [2], a related-key attack on all 14 rounds of AES-256 was presented. And [3] mounted boomerang attacks on full-round AES-192/256 soon afterwards. The authors in [2] analyzed two features of the AES key schedule. One is the slow diffusion which has already been discussed widely in the related-key cryptanalysis. Another feature is that the shift operation in the internal state is preserved by the key schedule. Based on these features and the existence of local collisions, they constructed the best related-key differential trails for 9–14 rounds.

2.3   Previous Modifications to the AES Key Schedule

Increasing the number of rounds is a straightforward and effective way to avoid many kinds of attacks. The current key schedule of AES can easily produce a few more subkeys without any substantial change. This enhances the security of AES to a large extent, and is also what the designer has done for different versions of AES [7]. However, this method affects the speed of not only the key schedule but also the actual cipher, reducing the execution speed by a factor that cannot be ignored. So most of the designers seek to modify the key schedule itself.

The key schedule proposed in [5] generates each 128-bit subkey after the execution of three rounds of the cipher function, using the XOR of master key and different round constants as both the data input and the key input. The only difference among the three versions of the key schedule is the initialization of the data input and the key input. The authors aimed to apply the elegant and succinct AES round function to the key schedule, and claimed that his key schedule has much better performance than the old one by measuring with the frequency test and the SAC test. However, this key schedule has a relatively large change compared to the original one, and also has low efficiency due to the large number of S-boxes, especially in a hash mode. Moreover, 2^{271} equivalent key pairs exist in this key schedule [8], which produce the same encryption output and could be taken as an attack point. Two AES variants to protect against the related-key attacks of [2,3] are also designed in [8]. One is a revision of [5]'s key schedule that eliminates the equivalent key pairs. The authors simplify the initialization of the data input and the key input so that each byte of them only depends on one instead of two bytes of the master key. This prevents an adversary from forcing the inputs to have zero differences by choosing an appropriate pair of related master keys. Another is a new on-the-fly key schedule required in the hardware implementation.

Both of the key schedules mentioned in [5,8] have irreversibility for subkey, which may make an attack more difficult to a certain extent. However, the irreversibility is likely to result in a lot of equivalent keys. Moreover, these key schedules increase the security by bringing more nonlinearity that reduces the efficiency greatly.

A tweaking AES called xAES is presented in [9] by adding a certain number of rotations and additional S-boxes in the key schedule. A subkey word is rotated by one byte before participating in the generation of next subkey word. The other operations are the same as the original AES key schedule. After exploiting an automatic search tool, the author claimed that the number of active S-boxes in the best round-reduced related-key differential characteristics has increased, so xAES is resistant against related-key differential attacks. However, xAES cannot defend against any single-key attacks, such as recent meet-in-the-middle attacks [12,14], and also suffers a reduced efficiency.

The key schedules in [8,9] protect mainly against the recent related-key differential attacks. Hashing the master key before passing it through the key scheduling can also achieve this purpose, since it is hard for an adversary to control the key differences at the beginning [15].

3 A New AES Key Schedule Proposal

When it comes to the key schedule design of block ciphers, there still have been less practical and necessary principles. It is generally believed that, which is often the case, the design of the key schedule is independent of the design of the round function. However, in [10], Huang and Lai pointed out that the interaction between the diffusion of the round function and the diffusion of the key schedule should get more attention.

Indeed, previous results only focus on the amount of leaked key bits and the speed of diffusion. Even with the same amount of leaked key bits and the same speed of diffusion, *poor leaked positions and inappropriate diffusion pattern* will lead to

- a calculation dependency path with less actual key information, which is usually used in the single-key attacks,
- a related-key differential path with high probability, which is exploited in the related-key attacks.

Therefore, we reconsider the AES key schedule. We find that the position of leaked subkey materials and the pattern of the diffusion are also responsible for a number of existing attacks. The major reason is that the AES key schedule has a column-by-column word-wise property, which matches nicely with the MixColumns operation in the round diffusion layer.

We propose a new key schedule that only has a minor modification to the original one but offers stronger security in both single-key attacks and related-key differential attacks, that is, after the execution of original key scheduling, we transpose the output matrix of each subkey. More specifically, we rearrange the position of the subkey bytes, by taking the $K_{j,i}^r$ as subkeys, instead of $K_{i,j}^r$, just as Fig. 1. The pseudocode is shown in Algorithm 2. Note that ExpandedKey denotes the output matrix of the original key schedule.

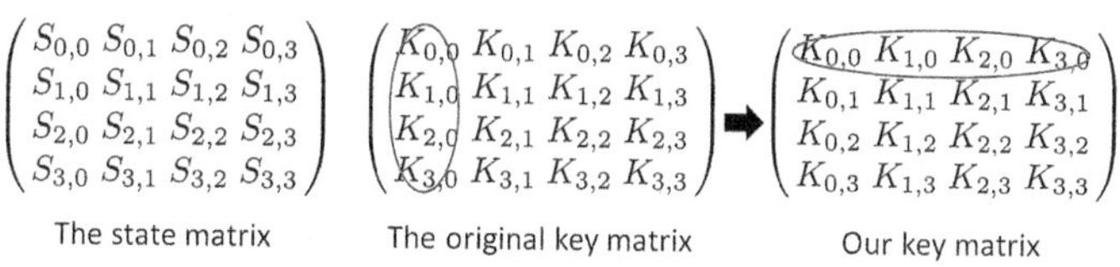

$$\begin{pmatrix} S_{0,0} & S_{0,1} & S_{0,2} & S_{0,3} \\ S_{1,0} & S_{1,1} & S_{1,2} & S_{1,3} \\ S_{2,0} & S_{2,1} & S_{2,2} & S_{2,3} \\ S_{3,0} & S_{3,1} & S_{3,2} & S_{3,3} \end{pmatrix} \quad \begin{pmatrix} K_{0,0} & K_{0,1} & K_{0,2} & K_{0,3} \\ K_{1,0} & K_{1,1} & K_{1,2} & K_{1,3} \\ K_{2,0} & K_{2,1} & K_{2,2} & K_{2,3} \\ K_{3,0} & K_{3,1} & K_{3,2} & K_{3,3} \end{pmatrix} \Rightarrow \begin{pmatrix} K_{0,0} & K_{1,0} & K_{2,0} & K_{3,0} \\ K_{0,1} & K_{1,1} & K_{2,1} & K_{3,1} \\ K_{0,2} & K_{1,2} & K_{2,2} & K_{3,2} \\ K_{0,3} & K_{1,3} & K_{2,3} & K_{3,3} \end{pmatrix}$$

The state matrix   The original key matrix   Our key matrix

Fig. 1. Transposition on subkey matrix

Algorithm 2. AddRoundKey (State, ExpandedKey)

---
for $i = 0$ **to** 3 **do**
    for $j = 0$ **to** 3 **do**
        $State[i, j] = State[i, j]$ **XOR** $ExpandedKey[j, i]$;
    end for
end for

Efficiency. Our key schedule is almost as efficient as the original one on byte level. This is especially important for Smart Cards applications. We just need to change the subscripts of the subkey matrices before they are XORed with the internal state bytes. Other parts of the implementation are the same as AES. Also, in hardware the transposition of output only costs negligible time.

Security. After this transposition, the route of subkey generation is changed and the weakness is removed. Therefore, our new proposal offers stronger security in both single-key and related-key model. We will give detailed explanations in Sects. 4 and 5 respectively.

For the convenience of illustrating, hereafter we denote AES with our new key schedule as tAES.

4   Security Comparison of AES and tAES for Single-Key Attacks

In the standard single-key model, the block cipher cryptanalysis mainly includes two aspects: how to find a distinguisher to distinguish the block cipher from a random permutation and how to recover the key. The cryptanalysts first construct a distinguisher for the reduced-round block cipher, then mount a key-recovery attack by appending several rounds after the distinguisher. As for the first aspect, the property of a distinguisher in the single-key setting usually depends on the construction of the round function rather than the design of the key schedule. However, in the key-recovery phase, the weakness of the key schedule can be exploited to improve the overall complexity. Therefore, we only focus on the key-recovery phase when we compare the security of tAES with AES in the single-key attacks, since our proposal does not change the round function and tAES can always deduce the same effective distinguisher as AES.

In this section, we first analyse the security of tAES in the single-key setting by evaluating the actual key information, which was introduced by Huang and Lai [10] to measure the minimal number of key bits in an attack path when recover the secret key. Further more, we revisit the SQUARE attacks and Meet-in-the-middle attacks on AES and demonstrate how tAES can effectively resist such attacks.

4.1   Actual Key Information of AES and tAES

Actual key information(AKI) was proposed by Huang and Lai in [10], which can be used to evaluate the time complexity in the key-recovery phase of the single-key attack, as long as the distinguisher is determined. For simplicity, here we directly introduce AKI by taking AES and tAES as an example. Refer to [10] for more details.

First consider the case that there is only one active byte at the end of the internal state in the $(r\text{-}3)$-th round (out of r rounds). When we do a partial

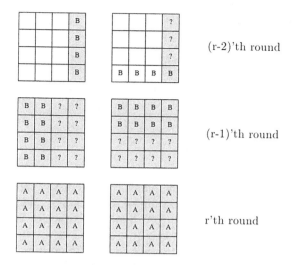

Fig. 2. Left is the key schedule of AES, and right is that of tAES. the gray boxes are the involved key bytes; the "A" mark the key bytes having been guessed; the "B" mark the leaked key bytes, which can derive from "A"; the "?" mark the unknown key bytes.

decryption in the last three rounds, $S^r \to S^{r-1} \to (S_{1,4}^{r-2}, S_{2,4}^{r-2}, S_{3,4}^{r-2}, S_{4,4}^{r-2})$ $\to S_{1,4}^{r-3}$ forms a *calculation dependency path* [10]. See Fig. 2. All bytes of the subkey in the last two rounds and four subkey bytes in the $(r-2)$-th round need to be guessed. Note that when four bytes in the same column are obtained by MixColumns from one active byte (This occurs in the last two rounds), one byte of the equivalent key $\widehat{K}_j$ is guessed, instead of guessing four bytes of K_j. That is to say, there are 21 bytes key bits involved in this path: K^r, $\widehat{K}_{1,4}^{r-1}$, $\widehat{K}_{2,3}^{r-1}$, $\widehat{K}_{3,2}^{r-1}$, $\widehat{K}_{4,1}^{r-1}$, $\widehat{K}_{1,4}^{r-2}$.

Now we revisit the AES-192 key schedule. In the key schedule of AES-192, knowledge of columns 0, 1, 2, 3 of the subkey K^r allows an attacker to deduce two columns of the subkey K^{r-1}, and one column of the subkey K^{r-2}. See the left part of Fig. 2. Therefore, $\widehat{K}_{3,2}^{r-1}$, $\widehat{K}_{4,1}^{r-1}$, $\widehat{K}_{1,4}^{r-2}$ can be derived from K^r, in which case the *actual key information* [10] is K^r, $\widehat{K}_{1,4}^{r-1}$ and $\widehat{K}_{2,3}^{r-1}$, 18 bytes in total.

However, in the key schedule of tAES-192, knowledge of rows 0, 1, 2, 3 of the subkey K^r allows an attacker to deduce two rows of the subkey K^{r-1}, and one row of the subkey K^{r-2}. See the right part of Fig. 2. Obviously it is not sufficient for any one column to compute $\widehat{K}_j$ unless the remaining two (or three) unknown bytes in K_j are also guessed, which leads to a heavier workload than guessing just one byte of $\widehat{K}_j$ directly. The AKI now is 21 bytes, which is larger than that of AES. In this situation, although the *calculation dependency path* and the involved key bits are the same in tAES as that in AES due to the unchanged round function, the attacker cannot gain any free bytes to reduce the overall complexity.

Table 1. Actual key information of AES and tAES

Path length/ rounds	Key bits involved on the path/bytes	Actual key information/bytes					
		AES-128	AES-128	AES-192	tAES-192	AES-256	tAES-256
1	1	1	1	1	1	1	1
2	5	5	5	5	5	5	5
3	21	–	–	18	21	20	21
4	–	–	–	–	–	–	–

A similar analysis can also be applied to AES-128 and AES-256. For all the *calculation dependency pathes* of 1–4 rounds, we calculated the number of key bits involved on the path (theoretical value of key guessing) and the AKI (actual value of key guessing) of all versions of AES and tAES, which is summarized in Table 1.

Since the total number of key bytes that we need to guess in an key-recovery phase depends mainly on actual key information, tAES increases the attacking difficulty in the single-key setting, as we will see in Sect. 4.2.

4.2   SQUARE Attacks and MITM Attacks on AES and tAES

In this section, we compare the security of tAES against SQUARE attacks and Meet-in-the-middle (MITM) attacks with AES. First we review the well-known observation on the AES-192 key schedule, which has also been mentioned above.

Observation 1. In the key schedule of AES-192, knowledge of the subkey K^r allows an attacker to deduce columns 0 and 1 of the subkey K^{r-1}, and column 3 of the subkey K^{r-2}.

This weakness of the AES key schedule makes it possible to extend the last three rounds in the single-key attacks, such as SQUARE attacks and MITM attacks.

In [11], a generic 7-round SQUARE attack extended from a 6-round SQUARE attack is proposed, with complexity of 2^{208}. This running time should not have been suitable for AES-192. But by using Observation 1, three useful key bytes are gained for free, so 2^{184} encryption is needed actually, which is lower than exhaustive search of AES-192. For tAES, Observation 1 turns out to be "In the key schedule of tAES-192, knowledge of the subkey K^r allows an attacker to deduce rows 0 and 1 of the subkey K^{r-1}, and rows 3 of the subkey K^{r-2}". In this case, there are no bytes gained for free any more. Therefore the total time complexity is 2^{208}, which is computationally infeasible.

In [4], an improved 6-round SQUARE attack is mentioned, whose complexity is comparable to 2^{72} encryptions. After extending to 7 rounds by adding 128 bits of key guessing in the last round, a total workload of 2^{200} is required. However, guessing the last round key K^7 gives us two of the four bytes from $\widehat{K}^6$, plus one byte from $\widehat{K}^5$, which saves us three bytes of key guessing. Two improvements are also given in [4] to generate a 7-round attack, which make an extension to 8 rounds possible. This 8-round attack has a complexity of 2^{204}. Again, fixing K^8

determines two useful key bytes of $\widehat{K}^7$, which gives a 2^{188} complexity. For tAES, just as mentioned above, we could not get any extra advantage even if we take the key schedule into consider.

In [13], a new multiset variant of the SQUARE-type attack mentioned in [12] is presented. Then the authors show that for AES-192, the time complexity of the 8-round attack can be reduced by a factor of 2^{32} using key schedule weaknesses. A factor of 2^{24} in this reduction is due to Observation 1. Later, a 8-round MITM attack on AES-192 in [14] has a dramatically smaller data complexity of 2^{41} chosen plaintexts. And Observation 1 also contributes to a reduction of the time complexity in this attack. Again, for tAES, such attacks fails since the time complexity has increased by a factor of 2^{24}.

In recent years, the meet-in-the-middle attack combined with subkey relations has shown to be a very powerful form of cryptanalysis against 7-round AES-128 [22], 9-round AES-192 [23] and 10-round AES-256 [24], which are the best single-key attacks on all versions of AES so far.

In [22], Derbez et al. presented the best attack on 7 rounds of AES-128 with data/time/memory complexities lower than 2^{100}. They further extended the attack to an 8-round attack for AES-192 with a data complexity of 2^{107} chosen-plaintexts, a memory complexity of 2^{96} and a time complexity of 2^{172}. Thanks to the above weakness of the AES key schedule, they can get 3 bytes of subkey for free, which is the key point to make the attack successful. However, for tAES, the time complexity should be 2^{196}.

Above single-key attacks exploit the fact that the actual key information is insufficient in a 3-round calculation path. As for tAES, the actual key information on the calculation path is exactly all the key bits involved. The attacker cannot gain any free bytes to reduce the overall complexity, thereby fail in all the attacks. We summarized these attack results on both AES and tAES in Table 5.

In [23], Li et al. proposed a MITM attack on AES-192 combined with a new technique named key-dependent sieve. On one hand, by using Observation 1 of the AES-192 key schedule, two bytes (namely 0,7) of the equivalent subkey $\widehat{K}^2$ can be deduced from K^3. On the other hand, the two bytes of $\widehat{K}^2$ have already been computed by the intermediate parameters in the MITM distinguisher. Thus there exists a contradiction between $\widehat{K}^2[0,7]$ and K^3 with probability 2^{-16}. And the size of the lookup table is improved by a factor of 2^{16}, which should have been 2^{208}. Finally, with a data-time-memory trade-off, the total time complexity is approximately $2^{187.5}$, which includes the precomputation phase. When it comes to tAES, without the key schedule weakness in Observation 1, there is no such contradiction to filter values in the precomputation table, thereby the key-dependent sieve technique becomes invalid and the time complexity in the precomputation phase increases to $2^{210.8}$. Even though the time complexity online is still lower than the exhaustive search, tAES offers stronger security since the complexity in the precomputation phase becomes the bottleneck of the MITM attack on tAES-192. We also summarized the attack results in Table 5.

5 Security Comparison of AES and tAES for Related-Key Attacks

In this section we discuss the related-key differential attacks on AES, and demonstrate that tAES has better resistance against this type of attacks, as the transposition in the key schedule brings more active S-boxes in the related-key differential trails.

5.1 Related-Key Differential Attacks on AES

High probability differential trails (characteristics) play the most important role in the related-key differential attacks. We give some descriptions about differential trails first. $E_K(P)$ is the block cipher with master key K, and $e_{K_i}()$ is one round of the cipher. The key schedule $KS(K)$ produces a set of subkeys K_i. S_i is the state at the beginning of round i, and $S_0 = P$. $p^{\Delta K, \Delta K_i}$ is the probability that a given difference ΔK of K produces a set of differences ΔK_i of K_i, $i = 0, ..., r$:

$$p^{\Delta K, \Delta K_i} = P(KS(K) \oplus KS(K \oplus \Delta K) = (\Delta K_0, ..., \Delta K_r)).$$

$p_i^{\Delta K_i, \Delta S_i, \Delta S_{i+1}}$ is the probability that the differences ΔS_i of state S_i and ΔK_i produce the difference ΔS_{i+1}:

$$p_i^{\Delta K_i, \Delta S_i, \Delta S_{i+1}} = P(e_{K_i}(S_i) \oplus e_{K_i \oplus \Delta K_i}(S_i \oplus \Delta S_i) = \Delta S_{i+1}).$$

An r-round related-key differential trail is composed of a set $(\Delta S_i, \Delta K_i, p^{\Delta K, \Delta K_i}, p_i^{\Delta K_i, \Delta S_i, \Delta S_{i+1}})$, with the probability that

$$p = p^{\Delta K, \Delta K_i} \cdot \prod_{0 \leq i \leq r} p_i^{\Delta K_i, \Delta S_i, \Delta S_{i+1}}.$$

As a useful cryptanalysis tool for AES, related-key differential attacks have been widely studies, especially its variants of related-key boomerang and rectangle attacks [18–20]. None of these attacks could break any version of full rounds AES, until in [2,3]. In [2], the author identified certain differential trails in the key schedule of AES-256 which match nicely with the differential properties of the cipher round function. Based on this discovery he constructed the local collision, which is a specific pattern of differences. The method is to inject a difference into the internal state from the key schedule, causing a disturbance, and then to correct it with the next injections, which also come from the key schedule. Using the found related-key differential trail, the author developed the first full round related-key attack for AES-256 for one out of 2^{35} key pairs, with 2^{131} time complexity and 2^{65} memory. The result was further improved in [3], where a related-key boomerang attack covers the full AES-256 with $2^{99.5}$ time and data complexity for all the keys. The first related-key amplified-boomerang attack for full AES-192, whose key schedule has better diffusion which leads to more active S-boxes in subkeys, was also presented in [3].

Following [2,3], a tool for systematically searching optimal related-key differential trails was proposed [1]. The best results for AES-128 now are a 4-round trail with 13 active S-boxes and a 5-round trail with 17 active S-boxes [1]. No 6-round related-key trail with less than 21 ($\lfloor\frac{128}{6}\rfloor$) active S-boxes is found. The authors proposed a related-key boomerang attack on 7-round AES-128 based on the found trails. For AES-192, differential trails up to 11 rounds are found. Our following analysis focuses on AES-128, as AES-128 is a representative example of explaining the advantage of tAES over AES, regarding these related-key differential attacks.

5.2   Best 2-Round and 3-Round Related-Key Differential Trails

We compare the number of active S-boxes for the best 2-round and 3-round trails for AES-128 and tAES-128, and show that tAES-128 has more active S-boxes. For sake of clarity, here we follow the methodology of [1] and assume that *there is no whitening key*. That is to say, in order to draw a more general conclusion, we consider an input state at the beginning of any internal round rather than limiting the inputs to the plaintexts.

Proposition 1. *For AES-128, the best 2-round related-key differential trail has 1 active S-box. For tAES-128, the best 2-round related-key differential trail has 2 active S-boxes.*

Note that one round in Proposition 1 means one *complete* round, namely including SubBytes, ShiftRows, MixColumns and Key Addition step. Now we give the proof of Proposition 1.

Proof. For AES-128 if a non-zero byte is introduced in the internal state of the first round, it can be cancel at the end of this round. Then there is no active S-boxes in the second round. See the left part of Fig. 3, with the dark grey box denoting the active S-box.

For tAES-128 there are two cases. Once the first round has one non-zero byte, four non-zero bytes in some row of the key schedule are needed to cancel the MC-column derived from this byte. The last one byte in the four bytes key differences has to pass an S-box, 2 active S-boxes totally. Once the last non-zero byte in the row of key schedule is avoid, which means that the last byte is zero for an MC-column, then the number of active bytes of the internal state before MixColumns is at least 2 (the branch number of MixColumns is 5). See the middle and right part of Fig. 3. The two active S-boxes are marked in dark grey.   □

The authors in [1] proposed a tool for systematically searching the best related-key differential trails in byte-oriented block ciphers. By this tool the authors searched for the best possible (in terms of the number of rounds) related-key differential trails in AES, byte-Camellia, Khazad, FOX, and Anubis. According to different kinds of key schedules, the authors gave three variants of the tool. Since the key schedule of tAES is almost the same as the one in AES, we use the same variant as did the authors when analyzing AES, which is the variant

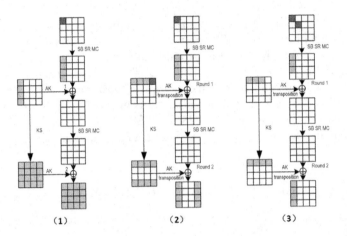

Fig. 3. Best 2-round Related-key Differential Trails of AES-128 (1) and tAES-128 (2 and 3).

2 of the tool. We implement this tool in practice and for the pseudocode please refer to the Algorithm 1.2 of [2].

Due to the limit of computation, we search for the best related-key differential trail on 3-round tAES-128 and believe that the situations in tAES-192 and tAES-256 are the same because of the similar structure. The result shows that the number of active S-boxes for the best trail is ≥ 9 for tAES, while for AES is 5. This means lower related-key differential probability for tAES and proves better resistance of tAES against related-key differential attacks. As mentioned before, in terms of one round, we mean one complete round without involving the whitening key at the beginning.

5.3 Comparison Between tAES and AES

For related-key differential trails which are longer than 3 rounds, we compare AES and tAES based on the analysis of their structure. As we know, the resistance is usually measured by the number of active in the differential trails, both in the internal state and in the key schedule. If the attacker is able to find a differential trail with fewer S-boxes, the cipher will have poorer resistance against related-key differential attacks.

Traditional related-key differential trails. Early used trails focus on minimizing the number of disturbance differences, which usually take the same value in one trail until they are spread out. This is because of the shift and XOR operations. The shift operation in the internal state is preserved by the XOR in the key schedule, both changing the value of one byte into zero or the same $(a \oplus a = 0, a \oplus 0 = a)$. Therefore, using the same disturbance value pays the minimum cost for active S-boxes. Another reason why the same disturbance value is often used is because if we choose different values of disturbance differences and take the maximal differential propagation of each S-box, after passing the S-boxes the differences become more divergent and irregular. However, even the differences introduced to the state are as few as possible, they will be diffused very quickly due to the wide trail strategy of the round function. So the targeted rounds of attacks are limited, and cannot reach the full rounds. Both AES and tAES have similar security margins for this kind of related-key differentials.

Related-key differential trails with local collisions. The related-key differential trails with the pattern of local collisions are much more threatening, since they cancel the diffused differences at the end of each round so that the trails can last more rounds. So far the best results of related-key differential attacks are constructed from this type of differential trails. The disturbance differences are again required to be the same in these trails to guarantee the fewest active S-boxes. The search results in [1] also show that the best trail disturbs each active byte of the state with the same difference and then corrects the differences diffused from this disturbance difference. Our analysis target the attacks using differentials with local collisions in general, with demonstration specially on AES-128.

The existence of MC-columns is a necessary condition that the related-key differentials with local collisions in AES are able to last longer rounds, while tAES breaks this condition. In order to demonstrate the difference propagation, we first recall the MixColumns and stress the operations it uses.

MixColumns. The MixColumns step is a linear transformation which makes every input byte influence four output bytes. Each 4-byte column is considered as a vector and multiplied by a fixed 4×4 matrix. The matrix MC contains constant entries, as follows (1). The vector-matrix multiplication and addition are done in $GF(2^8)$. Each byte element is represented as polynomials with coefficients in $GF(2)$. The addition in $GF(2^8)$ is simple bitwise XOR of the respective bytes.

$$MC = \begin{pmatrix} 02 & 03 & 01 & 01 \\ 01 & 02 & 03 & 01 \\ 01 & 01 & 02 & 03 \\ 03 & 01 & 01 & 02 \end{pmatrix} \tag{1}$$

For the constants in the matrix a hexadecimal notation is used: "01" refers to the $GF(2^8)$ polynomial with the coefficients (00000001), i.e., it is the element 1 of the Galois field; "02" refers to the polynomial with the bit vector (00000010), i.e., to the polynomial x; and "03" refers to the polynomial with the bit vector (00000011), i.e., the Galois field element $x + 1$. Multiplication by 02 is implemented as a multiplication by x, which is a left shift by one bit, and a modular reduction with $P(x) = x^8 + x^4 + x^3 + x + 1$. Similarly, multiplication by 03 can be implemented by a left shift by one bit and addition of the original value followed by a modular reduction with $P(x)$. When the degree of the polynomials represented by $02 \cdot b$ and $03 \cdot b$ is less than 8, there are the following relations: $(02 \cdot b) \oplus b = 03 \cdot b, (03 \cdot b) \oplus b = 02 \cdot b, (02 \cdot b) \oplus (03 \cdot b) = b$.

Table 2. Differences states and their corresponding MC-columns

Index	Differences	MC-columns
1	$(b,0,0,0)^T$	$(2b,b,b,3b)^T$
2	$(0,b,0,0)^T$	$(3b,2b,b,b)^T$
3	$(b,b,0,0)^T$	$(b,3b,0,2b)^T$
4	$(0,0,b,0)^T$	$(b,3b,2b,b)^T$
5	$(b,0,b,0)^T$	$(3b,2b,3b,2b)^T$
6	$(0,b,b,0)^T$	$(2b,b,3b,0)^T$
7	$(b,b,b,0)^T$	$(0,0,2b,3b)^T$
8	$(0,0,0,b)^T$	$(b,b,3b,2b)^T$
9	$(b,0,0,b)^T$	$(3b,0,2b,b)^T$
10	$(0,b,0,b)^T$	$(2b,3b,2b,3b)^T$
11	$(b,b,0,b)^T$	$(0,2b,3b,0)^T$
12	$(0,0,b,b)^T$	$(0,2b,b,3b)^T$
13	$(b,0,b,b)^T$	$(2b,3b,0,0)^T$
14	$(0,b,b,b)^T$	$(3b,0,0,2b)^T$
15	$(b,b,b,b)^T$	$(b,b,b,b)^T$

When an one-byte difference a injected to $s_{0,0}$, it is expanded by MixColumns to a four-byte difference in column 0, which is of special form: it is the result of multiplying a vector $(b,0,0,0)^T$ by the MixColumns matrix (where b equals S-box(a) with the highest probability). In [2] the resulting vectors are called MC-columns. We consider all possible MC-columns here. e.g. When the column difference before MixColumns is $(0,b,b,0)^T$, it turns to be $(2b,b,3b,0)^T$ after MixColumns. There are 15 types of MC-columns, as in Table 2.

State Transition between MixColumns. For AES-128, the best related-key differential trail shown by [1] demonstrates that the most probable one-round transition differentials correspond to two values of each column in the internal state, namely $(0,0,0,0)^T$, $(0,a,0,0)^T$, and four values of each column in the subkey, namely $(0,0,0,0)^T$, $(0,a,0,0)^T$, $MC \cdot (0,b,0,0)^T$, $(0,a,0,0)^T \oplus MC \cdot (0,b,0,0)^T$. So the number of all possible states is $2^4 \times 4^4 = 2^{12}$.

In order to check the (most probably) best trail, we study the state space corresponding to all 15 MC-columns in Table 2. Compare with the key schedule of AES, for tAES we consider the MC-columns by row. We consider the state transition regarding all possible difference values in MC-columns. The resulted matrix (probability transition matrix) is too large and too sparse to be included here, so we focus on the possible paths in it according to the non-zero probability and show that no path longer than 4 rounds even in the key schedule (the paths corresponding to both key and internal state transform will not be longer) exists for tAES. For each row of the key schedule, the state transition from one MC-column to another MC-column only possibly occurs in the cases listed in Table 3, meaning that they have a non-zero probability.

Table 3. The possible state transition from one MC-column to another MC-column

$(b, 3b, 0, 2b) \rightarrow (2b, b, b, 3b)$	$(b, 3b, 0, 2b) \rightarrow (3b, 0, 0, 2b)$
$(3b, 2b, 3b, 2b) \rightarrow (0, 2b, b, 3b)$	$(3b, 2b, 3b, 2b) \rightarrow (b, 3b, 0, 2b)$
$(2b, b, 3b, 0) \rightarrow (2b, 3b, 0, 0)$	$(2b, b, 3b, 0) \rightarrow (3b, 2b, b, b)$
$(3b, 0, 2b, b) \rightarrow (0, 0, 2b, 3b)$	$(3b, 0, 2b, b) \rightarrow (b, b, 3b, 2b)$
$(2b, 3b, 2b, 3b) \rightarrow (2b, b, 3b, 0)$	$(2b, 3b, 2b, 3b) \rightarrow (3b, 0, 2b, b)$
$(0, 2b, b, 3b) \rightarrow (0, 2b, 3b, 0)$	$(0, 2b, b, 3b) \rightarrow (b, 3b, 2b, b)$
$(b, b, b, b) \rightarrow (2b, 3b, 2b, 3b)$	$(b, b, b, b) \rightarrow (3b, 2b, 3b, 2b)$

Table 4. All possible 4-round paths for key states transition

$(b, b, b, b) \rightarrow (3b, 2b, 3b, 2b) \rightarrow (b, 3b, 0, 2b) \rightarrow (2b, b, b, 3b)$
$(b, b, b, b) \rightarrow (3b, 2b, 3b, 2b) \rightarrow (b, 3b, 0, 2b) \rightarrow (3b, 0, 0, 2b)$
$(b, b, b, b) \rightarrow (3b, 2b, 3b, 2b) \rightarrow (0, 2b, b, 3b) \rightarrow (0, 2b, 3b, 0)$
$(b, b, b, b) \rightarrow (3b, 2b, 3b, 2b) \rightarrow (0, 2b, b, 3b) \rightarrow (b, 3b, 2b, b)$
$(b, b, b, b) \rightarrow (2b, 3b, 2b, 3b) \rightarrow (2b, b, 3b, 0) \rightarrow (3b, 2b, b, b)$
$(b, b, b, b) \rightarrow (2b, 3b, 2b, 3b) \rightarrow (2b, b, 3b, 0) \rightarrow (2b, 3b, 0, 0)$
$(b, b, b, b) \rightarrow (2b, 3b, 2b, 3b) \rightarrow (3b, 0, 2b, b) \rightarrow (0, 0, 2b, 3b)$
$(b, b, b, b) \rightarrow (2b, 3b, 2b, 3b) \rightarrow (3b, 0, 2b, b) \rightarrow (b, b, 3b, 2b)$

Longest MixColumns Propagation. As mentioned before, for each state of the subkey, there should be at least one row possessing MC-column values (for canceling the differences diffused by MixColumns). For any row of the subkeys, MC-column states continue 4 rounds at most. e.g., $(b, b, b, b) \rightarrow (2b, 3b, 2b, 3b) \rightarrow (2b, b, 3b, 0) \rightarrow (2b, 3b, 0, 0)$. So even considering all non-zero probabilities in the state transition matrix, the existing paths are 4 rounds at most. Since a transition path with non-zero probability is necessary for a related-key differential path (trail) with non-zero probability. In this case the related-key differential trails of tAES with non-zero probabilities are 4-round at most. Not to mention that they may not satisfy the requirement for an available differential trail, which is with a probability large than 2^{-128}. Due to the rotation operation in the key schedule, the path corresponding to one row also relates to non-zero bytes in other rows. All 4-round paths for key states are shown in Table 4. No 5-round path exists, and this indicates the upper bound of targeted rounds of related-key differential trails in tAES.

6   Summary and Other Discussions

In this paper, we analyze the security of AES after doing a transposition on the output matrix of subkeys, while other conditions are totally the same as the original key schedule. We point out that by this slight change, we obtain a higher

Table 5. A comparison of attack results on AES and transposition-AES

Attack type and rounds	Time complexity AES-192	Time complexity tAES-192
7-round SQUARE [4]	2^{176}	2^{200}(failed)
8-round SQUARE [4]	2^{188}	2^{204}(failed)
8-round multiset variant [13]	2^{172}	2^{196}(failed)
8-round meet-in-the-middle [14]	$2^{187.63}$	$2^{211.63}$(failed)
8-round meet-in-the-middle [22]	2^{172}	2^{196}(failed)
9-round meet-in-the-middle [23]	$2^{187.5}$(trade-off, total)	$2^{210.8}$(offline)
	Rounds	Rounds
Attack type	AES-256	tAES-256
Related-key multicollisions for weak keys [2]	full	no full
Related-key boomerang [3]	full	no full
Attack type	AES-192	tAES-192
Related-key amplified-boomerang [3]	full	no full

security level for AES. In that, first, tAES can prevent from gaining free bytes of needed subkeys during the procedure of an attack, so the number of targeted rounds is reduced. Second, we do not adopt the traditional idea of adding more non-linear operations, to avoid related-key differential attacks. By just changing the diffusion pattern in the key schedule without speeding up the diffusion, we stop potential local collisions found in AES that may generate long related-key differential trails.

Some attack results on AES and tAES are compared in Table 5. For the same attack, tAES needs higher time complexity than AES, which makes the original attack fail or the number of targeted rounds reduce.

We discuss the resistance of tAES against other attacks. The round function of tAES is the same as that of AES. Therefore other single-key attacks only based on vulnerabilities of the round function have the same security margin as in AES. That is, the number of attacked rounds cannot be increased in tAES. The biclique attacks, which penetrate full rounds of all three versions of AES in a single-key scenario by exploiting related-key properties, could still be applied on tAES. This is principally because the rounds of related-key differential trails needed for constructing biclique are small: 3 rounds for AES-128, and 4 rounds for AES-192 and AES-256, which cannot be avoid even in tAES. The round transformation of AES (so as tAES) is not designed to have strong resistance against several classes of attacks for a smaller number of rounds. So the biclique attacks can still split up the cipher into three parts (other two parts are for MITM matching). Actually, biclique attacks go through the whole key space and the total complexity depends on the average computation of each guess.

There is no indication that tAES has a lower computation complexity so we think that it has a similar security level for this attack.

The analysis in this paper also shows that as well as the speed of the diffusion and the amount of non-linearity, the route, or position of diffusion propagation should get more attention.

Acknowledgments. This work was supported by the National Natural Science Foundation of China (61272440, 61472251, U1536101), China Postdoctoral Science Foundation (2013M531174, 2014T70417), and Science and Technology on Communication Security Laboratory.

References

1. Biryukov, A., Nikolić, I.: Automatic search for related-key differential characteristics in byte-oriented block ciphers: application to AES, Camellia, Khazad and others. In: Gilbert, H. (ed.) EUROCRYPT 2010. LNCS, vol. 6110, pp. 322–344. Springer, Heidelberg (2010). doi:10.1007/978-3-642-13190-5_17
2. Biryukov, A., Khovratovich, D., Nikolić, I.: Distinguisher and related-key attack on the full AES-256. In: Halevi, S. (ed.) CRYPTO 2009. LNCS, vol. 5677, pp. 231–249. Springer, Heidelberg (2009). doi:10.1007/978-3-642-03356-8_14
3. Biryukov, A., Khovratovich, D.: Related-key cryptanalysis of the full AES-192 and AES-256. In: Matsui, M. (ed.) ASIACRYPT 2009. LNCS, vol. 5912, pp. 1–18. Springer, Heidelberg (2009). doi:10.1007/978-3-642-10366-7_1
4. Ferguson, N., Kelsey, J., Lucks, S., Schneier, B., Stay, M., Wagner, D., Whiting, D.: Improved cryptanalysis of Rijndael. In: Goos, G., Hartmanis, J., Leeuwen, J., Schneier, B. (eds.) FSE 2000. LNCS, vol. 1978, pp. 213–230. Springer, Heidelberg (2001). doi:10.1007/3-540-44706-7_15
5. May, L., Henricksen, M., Millan, W., Carter, G., Dawson, E.: Strengthening the key schedule of the AES. In: Batten, L., Seberry, J. (eds.) ACISP 2002. LNCS, vol. 2384, pp. 226–240. Springer, Heidelberg (2002). doi:10.1007/3-540-45450-0_19
6. Armknecht, F., Lucks, S.: Linearity of the AES key schedule. In: Dobbertin, H., Rijmen, V., Sowa, A. (eds.) AES 2004. LNCS, vol. 3373, pp. 159–169. Springer, Heidelberg (2005). doi:10.1007/11506447_14
7. Daemen, J., Rijmen, V.: AES proposal: Rijndael. In: The First AES Candidate Conference (1998)
8. Choy, J., Zhang, A., Khoo, K., Henricksen, M., Poschmann, A.: AES variants secure against related-key differential and boomerang attacks. In: Ardagna, C.A., Zhou, J. (eds.) WISTP 2011. LNCS, vol. 6633, pp. 191–207. Springer, Heidelberg (2011). doi:10.1007/978-3-642-21040-2_13
9. Nikolić, I.: Tweaking AES. In: Biryukov, A., Gong, G., Stinson, D.R. (eds.) SAC 2010. LNCS, vol. 6544, pp. 198–210. Springer, Heidelberg (2011). doi:10.1007/978-3-642-19574-7_14
10. Huang, J., Lai, X.: Revisiting key schedule's diffusion in relation with round function's diffusion. Des. Codes Crypt. **73**(1), 85–103 (2014)
11. Lucks, S.: Attacking seven rounds of Rijndael under 192-bit and 256-bit Keys. In: The Third AES Candidate Conference, pp. 215–229 (2000)
12. Demirci, H., Selçuk, A.A.: A meet-in-the-middle attack on 8-round AES. In: Nyberg, K. (ed.) FSE 2008. LNCS, vol. 5086, pp. 116–126. Springer, Heidelberg (2008). doi:10.1007/978-3-540-71039-4_7

13. Dunkelman, O., Keller, N., Shamir, A.: Improved single-key attacks on 8-round AES-192 and AES-256. In: Abe, M. (ed.) ASIACRYPT 2010. LNCS, vol. 6477, pp. 158–176. Springer, Heidelberg (2010). doi:10.1007/978-3-642-17373-8_10

14. Wei, Y., Lu, J., Hu, Y.: Meet-in-the-middle attack on 8 rounds of the AES block cipher under 192 key bits. In: Bao, F., Weng, J. (eds.) ISPEC 2011. LNCS, vol. 6672, pp. 222–232. Springer, Heidelberg (2011). doi:10.1007/978-3-642-21031-0_17

15. Kelsey, J., Schneier, B., Wagner, D.: Key-schedule cryptanalysis of IDEA, G-DES, GOST, SAFER, and Triple-DES. In: Koblitz, N. (ed.) CRYPTO 1996. LNCS, vol. 1109, pp. 237–251. Springer, Heidelberg (1996). doi:10.1007/3-540-68697-5_19

16. Data Encryption Standard (DES), FIPS PUB 46-2. http://www.itl.nist.gov/fipspubs/fip46-2.htm

17. Lai, X., Massey, J.L., Murphy, S.: Markov ciphers and differential cryptanalysis. In: Davies, D.W. (ed.) EUROCRYPT 1991. LNCS, vol. 547, pp. 17–38. Springer, Heidelberg (1991). doi:10.1007/3-540-46416-6_2

18. Fleischmann, E., Gorski, M., Lucks, S.: Attacking 9 and 10 rounds of AES-256. In: Boyd, C., González Nieto, J. (eds.) ACISP 2009. LNCS, vol. 5594, pp. 60–72. Springer, Heidelberg (2009). doi:10.1007/978-3-642-02620-1_5

19. Biham, E., Dunkelman, O., Keller, N.: Related-key boomerang and rectangle attacks. In: Cramer, R. (ed.) EUROCRYPT 2005. LNCS, vol. 3494, pp. 507–525. Springer, Heidelberg (2005). doi:10.1007/11426639_30

20. Kim, J., Hong, S., Preneel, B.: Related-key rectangle attacks on reduced AES-192 and AES-256. In: Biryukov, A. (ed.) FSE 2007. LNCS, vol. 4593, pp. 225–241. Springer, Heidelberg (2007). doi:10.1007/978-3-540-74619-5_15

21. Jakimoski, G., Desmedt, Y.: Related-key differential cryptanalysis of 192-bit key AES variants. In: Matsui, M., Zuccherato, R.J. (eds.) SAC 2003. LNCS, vol. 3006, pp. 208–221. Springer, Heidelberg (2004). doi:10.1007/978-3-540-24654-1_15

22. Derbez, P., Fouque, P.-A., Jean, J.: Improved key recovery attacks on reduced-round AES in the single-key setting. In: Johansson, T., Nguyen, P.Q. (eds.) EUROCRYPT 2013. LNCS, vol. 7881, pp. 371–387. Springer, Heidelberg (2013). doi:10.1007/978-3-642-38348-9_23

23. Li, L., Jia, K., Wang, X.: Improved single-key attacks on 9-round AES-192/256. In: Cid, C., Rechberger, C. (eds.) FSE 2014. LNCS, vol. 8540, pp. 127–146. Springer, Heidelberg (2015). doi:10.1007/978-3-662-46706-0_7

24. Li, R., Jin, C.: Meet-in-the-middle attacks on 10-round AES-256. Des. Codes Crypt., 1–13 (2015)

Revisiting the Security Proof of QUAD Stream Cipher: Some Corrections and Tighter Bounds

Goutam Paul[1]([⊠]) and Abhiroop Sanyal[2]

[1] Cryptology and Security Research Unit,
R.C. Bose Centre for Cryptology and Security, Indian Statistical Institute,
Kolkata 700108, India
goutam.paul@isical.ac.in
[2] Chennai Mathematical Institute, Kelambakkam, Chennai 603103, India
abhiroop.sanyal@gmail.com

Abstract. In EUROCRYPT 2006, Berbain et al. proposed a provably secure stream cipher named QUAD based on the hardness of solving multivariate quadratic equations. The authors also mentioned that whether the security bound can be made tighter or not is an open problem. Through the last decade, there have been some works on the analysis of QUAD as well as design extensions of QUAD, but to our knowledge no work has addressed the existence of tighter bounds. In this paper, we revisit the proof technique by the authors and correct some bugs in their proof. Further, we derive tighter security bounds using two approaches.

Keywords: Multivariate quadratic · Provably secure stream cipher · Pseudo-random generator · QUAD · Stream cipher

1 Introduction

Stream ciphers are important primitives in symmetric-key cryptography, especially for fast encryption and decryption. A stream cipher is basically a pseudo-random number generator (PRNG) that takes as input a secret key and produces as output a pseudo-random sequence called the keystream. For encryption of a message, the sender performs bitwise XOR of the message and the keystream. For decryption, the receiver uses the same secret key and the same PRNG algorithm to generate the same keystream, which when bitwise XOR-ed with the ciphertext, restores the plaintext.

Formally, a deterministic function $G : \{0,1\}^* \to \{0,1\}^*$ is called a PRNG, if the following three conditions hold:

1. *Efficiency:* G is computable in polynomial time.
2. *Expansion:* $\exists$ a polynomial $l : \mathbb{N} \to \mathbb{N}$ such that $l(n) > n, \forall n \in \mathbb{N}$ and $|G(x)| = l(|x|) \quad \forall x \in \{0,1\}^*$.

© Springer International Publishing AG 2017
K. Chen et al. (Eds.): Inscrypt 2016, LNCS 10143, pp. 103–116, 2017.
DOI: 10.1007/978-3-319-54705-3_7

3. *Pseudo-randomness*: for any probabilistic polynomial-time (PPT) algorithm D, for any positive polynomial p, and for all sufficiently large n's, it holds that

$$|\Pr[D(G(U_n)) = 1] - \Pr[D(U_{l(n)}) = 1]| < \frac{1}{p(n)}, \qquad (1)$$

where U_k denotes the uniform distribution over $\{0,1\}^k$ and the probability is taken over all choices of inputs of D as well as over the internal coin tosses of D. The left hand side of Eq. (1) is called the *advantage* of the distinguisher algorithm D and is denoted by $Adv(D)$.

Traditionally, stream ciphers for hardware applications have been designed using linear feedback shift registers (LFSR), non-linear feedback shift registers (NFSR), Boolean functions with good cryptographic properties and possibly with some memory elements. On the other hand, stream ciphers for software applications have been designed using arrays with mathematical operations that can be performed very fast in software, e.g., swaps, modular additions, rotations, XOR's etc. For almost all of these designs, the security of the stream cipher is a conjecture. It is based on the assumption that the underlying generator is indeed a PRNG. However, often such PRNG assumption is subsequently invalidated by showing an event whose probability in the output keystream of the stream cipher is non-negligibly away from the probability of the same event in a uniformly random stream. The procedure of testing such an event is a *distinguisher* algorithm D, that violates the third condition of the definition of PRNG above.

Possibility of distinguishers for stream ciphers designed in an ad-hoc manner provides motivation for the *provable security* paradigm in designing a stream cipher. Such stream ciphers come with a proof of security which typically relies on the one-wayness of some number-theoretic functions, i.e., computing the function given an element of its domain is easy, but computing the inverse function given an element of its range is hard. In other words, the proof establishes that if there exists a distinguisher D for the stream cipher, then this distinguisher can be used as a subroutine to solve the underlying inverse problem that is known (or believed) to be hard.

Earliest provably secure PRNG was proposed by Blum and Micali [9] and was based on the fact that exponentiation modulo a prime number is essentially one-way. Another provably secure PRNG introduced by L. Blum, M. Blum and Shub [10], called the BBS generator relies upon the one-wayness of quadratic residuosity modulo large Blum integers. Fisher and Stern [11] proposed a PRNG construction relying on the intractability of the subset-sum problem. In the same year, Impagliazzo and Naor [12] suggested exploiting the difficulty of the syndrome decoding problem to build a secure PRNG.

1.1 Motivation and Contributions

The QUAD stream cipher was proposed at EUROCRYPT 2006 by Berbain, Gilbert and Patarin [1] and is based on the result that if an over-determined generic random multivariate quadratic map over $\mathbb{F}_2$ is a probabilistically one-way function, then it gives rise to a provably secure pseudo-random generator. This idea was further extended by Liu et al. [3], when they proposed the stream cipher SPONGE based on the hardness of sparse multivariate polynomial class of inversion problems. However, Yang et al. [2] argued that the lack of tightness on the time bound in the proof of security renders many practical instances of QUAD "unproven". It was shown in [2] that instances such as QUAD(256, 20, 20) can be broken in approximately 2^{66} Opteron cycles and the underlying hard problem can be broken in approximately 2^{45} Opteron cycles. In fact, all the QUAD instances presented at EUROCRYPT 2006 were shown to be "unproven", i.e., they were either not secure or would never be proven secure under the current bound. Hence, it is necessary to provide a stronger bound for making the QUAD instances secure. In this paper, we improve the security bound of QUAD using two different approaches. Our contribution also includes correcting a bug in the security proof of QUAD by its original designers in [1, Theorem 2].

2   The QUAD Stream Cipher

In this section, we review the design of the QUAD cipher in brief. Before we give its short description, we need to introduce some notations and equations.

A multivariate quadratic form in n variables over a finite field $\mathbb{F}_q$ is a polynomial of maximal degree 2 in n variables as follows:

$$Q(x) = \sum_{1 \leq i \leq j \leq n} a_{ij} x_i x_j + \sum_{1 \leq i \leq n} b_i x_i + c,$$

where the coefficients a_{ij}, b_i and $c \in \mathbb{F}_q$.

Choosing a random multivariate quadratic form in n unknowns is the same as choosing an N-tuple with each co-ordinate being chosen uniformly and independently from the underlying field $\mathbb{F}_q$, where $N = \frac{n(n+1)}{2} + 1$ for $q = 2$; otherwise $N = \frac{n(n+3)}{2} + 1$.

The multivariate quadratic (MQ) problem, which forms the basis of the QUAD stream cipher, is based on the fact that for general values of m and n, solving a system of m multivariate quadratic equations in n variables is NP-hard, whether it is over any finite field [6] or restricted to equations over $\mathbb{F}_2$. This problem is perhaps the most difficult when $|m - n|$ is small. For $m = n$, the complexity of the best known attack is $2^{n-O(\sqrt{n})}$, which is nearly as bad as exhaustive search. Another advantage of the MQ problem is that the MQ is NP-hard, whereas problems such as discrete log is in NP $\cap$ co-NP. Some well known algorithms that are dedicated to solving multivariate quadratic systems are XL [7] and Faugere's [8] F_4 and F_5.

The QUAD stream cipher is a parameterized family of stream ciphers with three parameters: q (prime), n and r. QUAD(q, n, r) is an instance of QUAD with the underlying field size being a power of q, where n is the number of variables, and r is the number of outputs per round. The total number of maps used is $kn = n + r$, so that $r = (k - 1)n$.

For the key and IV setup, two randomly chosen multivariate quadratic systems of n equations in n unknowns are considered. Let us call them S_0 and S_1. For keystream generation, we need separate kn randomly chosen multivariate quadratic equations in n unknowns. Let us denote them by $S = (Q_1, \ldots, Q_{kn})$.

Let us denote the key as K and the initialization vector as IV, both of size n bits. Also let IV_i be the i-th bit of the initialization vector, $1 \leq i \leq n$. The state initialization using the secret key is described in Algorithm 1.

Algorithm 1. Initialization of Internal State

Input: Secret key K and initialization vector IV, each of size n bits
Output: Initial internal state x
Choose two random MQ systems S_0 and S_1 of n variables over n unknowns;
Let $x = K$;
for $i = 1$ *to* n **do**
$\quad$ **if** $IV_i = 0$ **then**
$\quad\quad$ | Set $x = S_0(x)$;
$\quad$ **else**
$\quad\quad$ | Set $x = S_1(x)$;

Run Algorithm 2 for n iterations, without generating output;

In the keystream generation phase, we shall update the internal state using the equations $Q_1, Q_2, \ldots, Q_n$ and generate keystream using the equations $Q_{n+1}, Q_{n+2}, \ldots, Q_{kn}$. We illustrate the keystream generation procedure in Algorithm 2.

Algorithm 2. Keystream Generation

Input: Initial internal state x
Output: Keystream sequence
for *As many $(k-1)n$ tuples of keystream words needed* **do**
$\quad$ Output the sequence $S_{out}(x) = (Q_{n+1}(x), \ldots, Q_{kn}(x))$;
$\quad$ Update the internal state x by $S_{it}(x) = (Q_1(x), \ldots, Q_n(x))$;

---

3   Revisiting the Security Proof of QUAD as in [1] and Our Corrections

The security proof of QUAD consists of 3 major theorems which are combined into the final result. We state each result exactly as in [1] and show a sketch of the security proof for each.

Theorem 1. *Let $L = \lambda(k-1)n$ be the number of keystream bits produced in time λT_S, using λ iterations of QUAD. Suppose there is an algorithm A that distinguishes the L-bit keystream sequence associated with a known randomly chosen system S and an unknown randomly chosen initial internal state $x \in \{0,1\}^n$*

from a random L-bit sequence, in time T with advantage ϵ. Then there exists an algorithm B that, for a randomly chosen S, distinguishes $S(x)$ corresponding to an unknown random input x, from a random value of size kn in time $T' = T + \lambda T_S$ with advantage $\frac{\epsilon}{\lambda}$.

Proof sketch: The proof introduces hybrid probability distributions $D^i(S)$ over $\{0, 1\}^L$ for the random variables

$$t^i(S, x) = (p_1, p_2, \ldots, p_i, S_{out}(x), S_{out}(S_{it}(x)), \ldots, S_{out}(S_{it}^{\lambda - i - 1}(x)),$$

where p_j and x are uniformly random over $\in \{0, 1\}^n$. As per this notation, $D^0(S)$ is the distribution of the keystream and $D^\lambda(S)$ is the uniform probability distribution over $\{0, 1\}^n$.

Algorithm B is constructed by considering an input (x_1, x_2) over $\{0, 1\}^{kn}$ such that $x_1 \in \{0, 1\}^n$ and $x_2 \in \{0, 1\}^{(k-1)n}$ and choosing a random i where $0 \le i \le \lambda - 1$, thereby constructing the L-bit vector

$$t(S, x_1, x_2) = (p_1, p_2, \ldots, p_i, x_2, S_{out}(x_1), S_{out}(S_{it}(x_1)), \ldots S_{out}(S_{it}^{\lambda - i - 2}(x_1))).$$

Then B calls algorithm A with inputs $(S, t(S, x_1, x_2))$ and returns the value returned by A. Now, if (x_1, x_2) is distributed as per the distribution of the L-bit keystream, then $t(S, x_1, x_2)$ is distributed as per $D^i(S)$; and if (x_1, x_2) is distributed uniformly over $\{0, 1\}^L$, then $t(S, x_1, x_2)$ is distributed as per $D^{i+1}(S)$.

Let P^i be the probability that the Algorithm B accepts an L-bit keystream averaged over the vector space of quadratic systems S. Now, it can be shown that

$$Adv(B) = |\frac{1}{\lambda} \sum_{i=0}^{\lambda-1} P^i - \frac{1}{\lambda} \sum_{i=1}^{\lambda} P^i| = \frac{1}{\lambda} |P^0 - P^\lambda| \ge \frac{\epsilon}{\lambda}.$$

$\square$

We state the second theorem in the series.

Theorem 2. *Suppose there is an algorithm A that, given a randomly chosen known multivariate quadratic system S of kn equations in n unknowns, distinguishes $S(x)$, where x is an unknown random input value, from a random string of length kn with advantage at least ϵ and in time T. Then there is an algorithm B that, given a randomly chosen quadratic system S of kn equations in n unknowns, any n-bit to 1-bit quadratic form R, and $y = S(x)$ where x is a random input value, predicts $R(x)$ with success probability at least $\frac{1}{2} + \frac{\epsilon}{4}$ using at most $T' = T + 2T_S$ operations.*

We noticed an error in the proof of this theorem as presented in [1]. The Theorem along with the corrected proof has been presented in Sect. 3.1.

The third theorem as in [1] is stated below. Before we state the third theorem, we shall state a lemma used in [1] to prove the third theorem.

Lemma 1. *Let x be a fixed unknown n-bit value and f be a fixed n-bit to m-bit function. Suppose there exists an algorithm B that given the value of $f(x)$ allows to predict the value of any linear equation R over n unknowns with probability*

$\frac{1}{2} + \epsilon$ *over* R, *using at most* T *operations. Then there exists an algorithm* C, *which given* $f(x)$ *produces in time at most* T' *a list of at most* $4n^2\epsilon^{-2}$ *values such that the probability that* x *appears in the list is at least* $\frac{1}{2}$ *where*

$$T' = \frac{2n^2}{\epsilon^2}\left(T + \log\left(\frac{2n}{\epsilon^2}\right) + 2\right) + \frac{2n}{\epsilon^2}T_f.$$

Theorem 3. *Suppose there is an algorithm* B, *that given a randomly chosen quadratic system* S *of* m *quadratic equations, a randomly chosen* n-bit to 1-bit quadratic form R and the image $S(x)$ of a randomly chosen (unknown) n-bit value x, predicts the value of $R(x)$ with probability at least $\frac{1}{2} + \epsilon$ over all possible (x, S, R) triplets using T operations. Then there is an algorithm C, which given the image $S(x)$ of a randomly chosen (unknown) n-bit value x produces a preimage of $S(x)$ with probability at least $\frac{\epsilon}{2}$ (over all possible values of x and S) in time*

$$T' = \frac{8n^2}{\epsilon^2}\left(T + \log\left(\frac{8n}{\epsilon^2}\right) + 2\right) + \frac{8n}{\epsilon^2}T_f.$$

Proof sketch: We shall first provide a proof sketch of Lemma 1 stated above and then use it to prove the theorem. The proof of Lemma 1 is essentially similar to the proof of Goldreich-Levine's theorem and uses t n-bit to 1-bit linear forms R_i to randomize requests to algorithm B. For each bit, a voting procedure is conducted in which algorithm B is called 2^t times using all possible linear combinations of the chosen linear forms. For each possible combination, for each call, the value returned by $C(i, \alpha) = B(\sum_{j=1}^{2^t} \alpha_i R_j \oplus L_i, f(x)) \oplus \sum_{j=1}^{2^t} \alpha_i R_j(x)$ at x (here $L_i(x) = x_i$ is the i-th bit of the n-bit value x) is considered a vote for x_i. The value of x_i is chosen same as that of the majority of the result of this vote. The efficiency of the algorithm C is a direct consequence of the efficiency of the algorithm B. Here, a fast Walsh transform is used in order to simultaneously compute the results of the votes on the $C(i, \alpha)$ values rather than an independent computation. This proves the lemma.

   Now, one can show by a simple method of contradiction that for a fraction of at least ϵ of all the (x, S) pairs, the conditions of Lemma 1 are met and algorithm C of the lemma provides a preimage of $S(x)$ with probability at least $\frac{1}{2}$.   □

   Theorems 1, 2 and 3 of [1] are naturally combined to obtain the final theorem in the security proof which shows that if MQ is intractable, then for general m and n, most instances of QUAD are secure.

Theorem 4. *Let* $L = \lambda(k - 1)n$ *be the number of keystream bits produced by QUAD in time* λT_S *using* λ *iterations of the QUAD construction. Suppose there exists an algorithm* A *that distinguishes the* L-bit keystream sequence associated with a known randomly chosen system S and an unknown randomly chosen initial internal state $x \in \{0, 1\}^n$ from a random L-bit sequence in time T with advantage ϵ. Then there exists an algorithm C, which given the image $S(x)$ of a randomly chosen unknown n-bit value x of a randomly chosen n-bit to m-bit quadratic* *system S, produces a preimage of $S(x)$ with probability at least $\frac{\epsilon}{2^3 \lambda}$ over all possible values of x and S in time upper bounded by*

$$T' = \frac{2^7 n^2 \lambda^2}{\epsilon^2} \left(T + (\lambda + 2)T_S + \log\left(\frac{2^7 n\lambda^2}{\epsilon^2}\right) + 2 \right) + \frac{2^7 n\lambda^2}{\epsilon^2}T_S.$$

3.1   Corrections in the QUAD Security Proof

We first present an error in the proof of Theorem 2 proposed in [1] and then propose suitable corrections.

Error in the proof of Theorem 2 of [1]: The last step of algorithm B claimed: "B returns what A' returns". But our calculations show that this would result in $\Pr(B((S, S(x)), R) = R(x)) \geq \frac{1}{2}$, which does not prove the theorem.

Corrected proof: We use the same idea as in [1] to produce an algorithm A' which returns 1 on input $(S, S(x))$ with probability at least $\frac{1}{2} + \frac{\epsilon}{2}$ and returns 1 on input (S, r) for some random r with probability $\frac{1}{2}$. Algorithm B is designed as follows:

Algorithm 3. Algorithm B

Input: An n-bit to 1-bit quadratic form R, a kn-bit value y, and a system
     $S = (Q_1, Q_2, \ldots, Q_{kn})$ of kn multivariate quadratic systems
Output: Predicted value of $R(x)$
Select a random kn-bit vector $v=(v_1, v_2, \ldots, v_{kn})$ and a random bit b;
for $i = 1$ **to** kn **do**
    $P_i = Q_i + (v_i \cdot R)$;
Set $S' = (P_1, P_2, \ldots P_{kn})$;
Compute $A'(S', y + (b \cdot v))$;
if A' *returns 1* **then**
    return b;
else
    return $1-b$;

Case 1: If $b = R(x)$.

If this is the case then, $S'(x) = y + (b \cdot v)$. So, A' has input S' and $S'(x)$. Hence, $\Pr(B((S, S(x)), R) = R(x)) = \Pr(A'(S', S'(x)) = 1) \geq \frac{1}{2} + \frac{\epsilon}{2}$.

Case 2: If $b \neq R(x)$.

So, A' has input S' and $S'(x) + v$. As v is a randomly chosen kn-bit vector, $S'(x) + v$ can also be assumed to be random kn-bit vector. We have

$$\Pr(B((S, S(x)), R) = R(x)) = \Pr(A'(S', S'(x)+v) = 0) = \Pr(A'(S', r) = 0) \geq \tfrac{1}{2},$$

where r is a random kn-bit vector. Hence,

$$\Pr(B((S, S(x)), R) = R(x)) \geq \tfrac{1}{2}(\tfrac{1}{2} + \tfrac{\epsilon}{2}) + \tfrac{1}{2} \cdot \tfrac{1}{2} = \tfrac{1}{2} + \tfrac{\epsilon}{4}.$$

$\square$

4   Improving the Tightness of the Security Bound

Concerns were expressed in [2] about the lack of tightness in the security proof of QUAD leading to the use of larger values of $n+r$, resulting in a slower performance of QUAD. Also, as a result of the lack of tightness in the security proof, the most popular QUAD instance QUAD(2,160,160) was shown to be unproven. In fact, all instances of QUAD reported in [2] were shown to be "unproven", i.e., they will never be proven secure due to the "looseness factor" in the current security proof. Theorem 4 in [1] states that if λn bits of output of QUAD(2, n, r) can be distinguished from uniform with advantage ϵ in time T, then a random MQ system of $n+r$ equations in n variables over $\mathbb{F}_2$ can be solved with probability at least $\frac{2^{-3}\epsilon}{\lambda}$ in at most time $T' = \frac{2^7 n^2 \lambda^2}{\epsilon^2}(T + (\lambda+2)T_S + \log(\frac{2^7 n \lambda^2}{\epsilon^2}) + 2) + \frac{2^7 n \lambda^2}{\epsilon^2} T_S$, where T_S is the time necessary to run one block of QUAD. This statement does not conclude $T \geq 2^{80}$ without assuming that the corresponding $T' \geq \frac{2^{230}}{n}$. We shall improve the bound in the security proof considerably using Chernoff bound and Hoeffding's bound/inequality.

4.1   A Short Note on Chernoff Bound and Hoeffding's Inequaliy

The Chernoff and Hoeffding's bounds are two important *concentration inequalities* in probability theory.

4.1.1   Chernoff Bound

The Chernoff bound [5], named after Herman Chernoff, gives exponentially decreasing bounds on tail distributions of sums of independent random variables. The statement in its most general form as stated in [5] is as follows.

Theorem 5. *Let $M(t)$ denote the moment-generating function of the random variable X. Then $\Pr(X \geq a) \leq e^{-ta}M(t)$, $\forall t > 0$ and $\Pr(X \leq a) \leq e^{-ta}M(t)$, $\forall t < 0$.*

However, we will not use this most general form. We will use the multiplicative form of the Chernoff bound and we will show how to derive the form that we use from the multiplicative form of the Chernoff bound. A form of the multiplicative bound for Poisson random variables can be found in [13]. Here we prove a version for Bernoulli variables.

Theorem 6. *Let $X = \sum_{i=1}^{n} X_i$, where X_i's are independent Bernoulli random variables. Let $\mu = E(X)$. Then for any $\delta > 0$ we have,*

$$\Pr\left(X \geq (1+\delta)\mu\right) < \left(\frac{e^\delta}{(1+\delta)^{1+\delta}}\right)^\mu.$$

Proof. We have $\Pr\left(X \geq (1+\delta)\mu\right) = \Pr\left(e^{tX} \geq e^{t(1+\delta)\mu}\right)$ $\forall t > 0$. By Markov's inequality, we obtain the following bound:

$$\Pr\left(e^{tX} \geq e^{t(1+\delta)\mu}\right) \leq \frac{E\left(e^{tX}\right)}{e^{t(1+\delta)\mu}}. \tag{2}$$

As the X_i's are independent and they are Bernoulli random variables with $p_i = \Pr(X_i = 1)$, we must have the follows (using the moment generating function for such random variables):

$$E(e^{tX}) = \prod_{i=1}^{n} E\left(e^{tX_i}\right) = \prod_{i=1}^{n} \left(1 + p_i\left(e^t - 1\right)\right).$$

We shall now use the well-known result that $e^x > 1 + x \ \ \forall x > 0$. Hence, if $p_i > 0$, for at least one i, we must have the follows:

$$E\left(e^{tX}\right) < \prod_{i=1}^{n} e^{p_i\left(e^t - 1\right)} = e^{\left(e^t - 1\right)\mu}.$$

Now, using this result in Eq. (2), we get

$$\Pr\left(X \geq (1+\delta)\mu\right) < \frac{e^{\left(e^t - 1\right)\mu}}{e^{t(1+\delta)\mu}}.$$

Now, differentiating the right hand side and plugging in the t for which it is minimum, we get the desired result. $\qquad\square$

From the above result, one can derive the following corollary which we shall use to obtain our improvements in the next section.

Corollary 1. For $0 < \delta \leq 1$, $\Pr(|X - \mu| \geq \delta\mu) \leq 2e^{\frac{-\mu\delta^2}{3}}$.

Proof. Note that $\Pr(|X - \mu| \geq \delta\mu) = \Pr\left(X \geq (1+\delta)\mu\right) + \Pr\left(X \leq (1-\delta)\mu\right)$.

We will show that each term in the above sum is $\leq e^{-\frac{\mu\delta^2}{3}}$. First, lets work with the first term. From Theorem 6, it is clear that we just need to show that for $0 < \delta \leq 1$:

$$\frac{e^\delta}{(1+\delta)^{1+\delta}} \leq e^{-\frac{\delta^2}{3}}. \tag{3}$$

Taking logarithm on both sides, and rearranging, we obtain the following,

$$f(\delta) := \delta - (1+\delta)\ln(1+\delta) + \frac{\delta^2}{3} \leq 0.$$

We now get, by differentiating $f(\delta)$:

$$f'(\delta) = -\ln(1+\delta) + \frac{2}{3}\delta.$$

$$f''(\delta) = -\frac{1}{1+\delta} + \frac{2}{3}.$$

From the above equations, it is clear that $f'' < 0$ for $0 \leq \delta < \frac{1}{2}$ and $f''(\delta) > 0$ for $\delta > \frac{1}{2}$. It is clear that as $f'(0) = 0$ and $f'(1) < 0$ and f' is first decreasing and then increasing over the interval $[0, 1]$, we also must have $f'(\delta) \leq 0$ in the interval $[0, 1]$. As $f(0) = 0$, we must have $f(\delta) \leq 0$ in that interval, which proves Eq. (3) and in turn proves

$$\Pr\left(X \geq (1+\delta)\mu\right) \leq e^{-\frac{\mu\delta^2}{3}}. \tag{4}$$

Imitating the above proof technique, one can obtain the following bound as well.

$$\Pr\left(X \leq (1-\delta)\mu\right) \leq e^{-\frac{\mu\delta^2}{2}}. \tag{5}$$

Combining Eqs. (4) and (5), we obtain the result.   □

4.1.2   Hoeffding's Inequality

Hoeffding's inequality, proved by Wassily Hoeffding in 1963 [4], provides an upper bound on the probability that the sum of random variables deviates from its expected value. The statement of Hoeffding's inequality is as follows.

Theorem 7. *Let $X_1, X_2, \ldots, X_n$ be independent random variables bounded by the interval $[a_i, b_i]$. Let $S_n = \sum\limits_{i=1}^{n} X_i$. Then we have,*

$$\Pr(|S_n - E(S_n)| \geq t \leq 2e^{-\frac{2t^2}{\sum\limits_{i=1}^{n}(b_i - a_i)^2}}.$$

4.2   Improving Tightness Using the Chernoff Bound

We shall modify the proof of Lemma 1 in [1] using the above concentration inequalities, and in doing so will provide a tighter security bound. We first state the lemma with the improved bound.

Lemma 2. *If x is a fixed unknown n-bit value and f be a fixed n-bit to m-bit function. Suppose there exists an algorithm B that given the value of $f(x)$ allows to predict the value of any linear equation R over n unknowns with probability $\frac{1}{2} + \epsilon$ over R, using at most T operations. Then there exists an algorithm C, which given $f(x)$ produces in time at most T' a list of at most $4n^2\epsilon^{-2}$ values such that the probability that x appears in the list is at least $\frac{1}{2}$, where*

$$T' = \frac{3 \cdot (\frac{1}{2} + \epsilon)\, n \ln(4n)}{\epsilon^2}\left(T + \log\left(\frac{3 \cdot (\frac{1}{2} + \epsilon)\ln(4n)}{\epsilon^2}\right) + 2\right) + \frac{3 \cdot (\frac{1}{2} + \epsilon)\ln(4n)}{\epsilon^2}T_f.$$

Proof. Proceed as in [1] to produce the necessary algorithm C. Then we will try to upper bound the failure probability of C. Let X_i for $1 \leq i \leq 2^t$ be the random variables that count the number of correct votes for a given voting round for a particular output bit. Let p_j be the probability that the j-th round fails to produce the correct bit value. Let the average of $\sum X_i$ be μ. We know,

$\mu = 2^t(\frac{1}{2} + \epsilon)$ due to the dependance of C on B. So, we have, by applying Chernoff bound (under the assumption of independent samples)

$$p_i = \Pr(\sum_{i=1}^{2^t} X_i < 2^{t-1}) = \Pr(\sum_{i=1}^{2^t} X_i - \mu < -2^t \cdot \epsilon)$$

$$\leq \Pr(|\sum_{i=1}^{2^t} X_i - \mu| > 2^t \cdot \epsilon) \leq 2 \cdot e^{-\frac{2^t \cdot \epsilon^2}{3(\frac{1}{2}+\epsilon)}}$$

Hence, the failure probability of C is upper bounded by $2ne^{-\frac{2^t \cdot \epsilon^2}{3(\frac{1}{2}+\epsilon)}}$. From this, we get 2^t as $\frac{3 \cdot (\frac{1}{2}+\epsilon)\ln(4n)}{\epsilon^2}$. From [1], we have that the run-time of algorithm C is $n2^t(T+t+2) + 2^t T_f$. Substituting, we get the required bound. $\qquad\square$

The bound provided in Theorem 4 of [1] is very closely related to the bound provided in Lemma 1 and hence our tighter bound in Lemma 2 gives us a tighter bound of Theorem 4 as:

$$T'_{cher} = \frac{3 \cdot 2^6(\frac{1}{2} + \epsilon)n \ln(4n)\lambda^2}{\epsilon^2}\left(T + (\lambda + 2)T_S + \log\left(\frac{3 \cdot 2^6(\frac{1}{2} + \epsilon)\ln(4n)\lambda^2}{\epsilon^2}\right) + 2\right)$$
$$+ \frac{3 \cdot 2^6(\frac{1}{2} + \epsilon)\ln(4n)\lambda^2}{\epsilon^2}T_S.$$

4.3   Improving Tightness Using the Hoeffding's Inequality

We now use the Hoeffding's inequality to obtain an even tighter bound than the one in the previous subsection. We state the Lemma again with the improved bound.

Lemma 3. *If x is a fixed unknown n-bit value and f be a fixed n-bit to m-bit function. Suppose there exists an algorithm B that given the value of $f(x)$ allows to predict the value of any linear equation R over n unknowns with probability $\frac{1}{2} + \epsilon$ over R, using at most T operations. Then there exists an algorithm C, which given $f(x)$ produces in time at most T' a list of at most $4n^2\epsilon^{-2}$ values such that the probability that x appears in the list is at least $\frac{1}{2}$ where*

$$T' = \frac{n \cdot \ln(2\sqrt{n})}{\epsilon^2} \cdot \left(T + \log\left(\frac{\ln(2\sqrt{n})}{\epsilon^2}\right) + 2\right) + \frac{\ln(2\sqrt{n})}{\epsilon^2} \cdot T_f.$$

Proof. We proceed exactly as in the above subsection and use the same terminology and notations. In this case, we have, by applying Hoeffding's inequality (under the assumption of independent samples)

$$p_i = \Pr(\sum_{i=1}^{2^t} X_i < 2^{t-1}) = \Pr(\sum_{i=1}^{2^t} X_i - \mu < -2^t \cdot \epsilon)$$

$$\leq \Pr(|\sum_{i=1}^{2^t} X_i - \mu| > 2^t \cdot \epsilon) \leq 2 \cdot e^{-2^{t+1} \cdot \epsilon^2}$$

Hence, the failure probability of C is upper bounded by $2ne^{-2^{t+1}\cdot\epsilon^2}$. From this, we get 2^t as $\frac{\ln(2\sqrt{n})}{\epsilon^2}$. From [1], we have that the run-time of algorithm C is $n2^t(T+t+2)+2^tT_f$. Substituting, we get the required bound.   □

Our tighter bound in Lemma 3 results in the following tighter bound on Theorem 4 of [1]

$$T'_{hoeff} = \frac{2^6 n \ln(2\sqrt{n})\lambda^2}{\epsilon^2}(T + (\lambda+2)T_S + \log(\frac{2^6\ln(2\sqrt{n})\lambda^2}{\epsilon^2}) + 2) + \frac{2^6\ln(2\sqrt{n})\lambda^2}{\epsilon^2} \cdot T_S$$

This bound is even stronger than the bound we have presented in the previous subsection and is a further improvement over the bound in [1].

4.4   Comparison of Our Results with the Existing Bound

To compare the bounds, in the expression of T' of Theorem 4 in [1], let $\alpha_n = \frac{2^7 n^2 \lambda^2}{\epsilon^2}$, $\beta_n = \log(\frac{2^7 n\lambda^2}{\epsilon^2})$ and $\gamma_n = \frac{2^7 n\lambda^2}{\epsilon^2}$.

In the expression of T'_{cher}, let $\alpha'_n = \frac{3\cdot2^6(\frac{1}{2}+\epsilon)n\ln(4n)\lambda^2}{\epsilon^2}$, $\beta'_n = \log(\frac{3\cdot2^6(\frac{1}{2}+\epsilon)n\ln(4n)\lambda^2}{\epsilon^2})$ and $\gamma'_n = \frac{3\cdot2^6(\frac{1}{2}+\epsilon)\ln(4n)\lambda^2}{\epsilon^2}$.

In the expression of T'_{hoeff}, let α_n, β_n and γ_n are as explained above while $\alpha''_n = \frac{2^6 n\ln(2\sqrt{n})\lambda^2}{\epsilon^2}$, $\beta''_n = \log(\frac{2^6\ln(2\sqrt{n})\lambda^2}{\epsilon^2})$ and $\gamma''_n = \frac{2^6\ln(2\sqrt{n})\lambda^2}{\epsilon^2}$.

Then we can write

$$T' = \alpha_n(T + (\lambda+2)T_S + \beta_n + 2) + \gamma_n T_S.$$

$$T'_{cher} = \alpha'_n(T + (\lambda+2)T_S + \beta'_n + 2) + \gamma'_n T_S.$$

$$T'_{hoef} = \alpha''_n(T + (\lambda+2)T_S + \beta''_n + 2) + \gamma''_n T_S.$$

In Table 1, we compare the ratios α_n/α'_n, α_n/α''_n, β_n/β'_n, β_n/β''_n, γ_n/γ'_n and γ_n/γ''_n, by taking $\lambda = 2^{40}$ and $\epsilon = 0.01$. This shows that Chernoff bound gives tighter security than [1] and Hoeffding's inequality gives even tighter security than that provided by Chernoff bound.

Table 1. Comparison between existing results and our bounds

n	$\frac{\alpha_n}{\alpha'_n}$	$\frac{\beta_n}{\beta'_n}$	$\frac{\gamma_n}{\gamma'_n}$	$\frac{\alpha_n}{\alpha''_n}$	$\frac{\beta_n}{\beta''_n}$	$\frac{\gamma_n}{\gamma''_n}$
20	5.9661	1.0276	5.9661	18.2564	1.0303	18.2564
40	10.3026	1.0367	10.3026	31.5260	1.0358	31.5260
160	32.3689	1.0570	32.3689	99.0487	1.0483	99.0487
256	48.2784	1.0645	48.2784	147.7320	1.0528	147.7320
350	63.1559	1.0696	63.1559	193.2573	1.0559	193.2573

We have used these specific values of n, as these are the most frequently used values for use in QUAD instances. Also, the proof of QUAD guarantees security for $n > 350$. Beyond $n > 350$ there is no 2^{80} distinguishing attack, as long as no better MQ attacks are discovered.

5   Conclusion

In this paper, we have presented techniques to tighten the security proof of the QUAD stream cipher. Similar technique may be used to increase the tightness of security proof of SPONGE [3]. However, we believe that $QUAD(2, 160, 160)$ still remains "unproven" and the tight-most bound remains open, which can be established by deriving the bound and showing a matching attack.

Acknowledgments. Part of this work was done while the second author was visiting R. C. Bose Centre for Cryptology and Security, Indian Statistical Institute, Kolkata during the Summer of 2016 for internship under the supervision of the first author. Both the authors are grateful to the Project CoEC (Centre of Excellence in Cryptology), Indian Statistical Institute, Kolkata, funded by the Government of India, for partial support towards this project.

References

1. Berbain, C., Gilbert, H., Patarin, J.: QUAD: a practical stream cipher with provable security. In: Vaudenay, S. (ed.) EUROCRYPT 2006. LNCS, vol. 4004, pp. 109–128. Springer, Heidelberg (2006). doi:10.1007/11761679_8
2. Yang, B.-Y., Chen, O.C.-H., Bernstein, D.J., Chen, J.-M.: Analysis of QUAD. In: Biryukov, A. (ed.) FSE 2007. LNCS, vol. 4593, pp. 290–308. Springer, Heidelberg (2007). doi:10.1007/978-3-540-74619-5_19
3. Liu, F.-H., Lu, C.-J., Yang, B.-Y.: Secure PRNGs from specialized polynomial maps over any $\mathbb{F}_q$. In: Buchmann, J., Ding, J. (eds.) PQCrypto 2008. LNCS, vol. 5299, pp. 181–202. Springer, Heidelberg (2008). doi:10.1007/978-3-540-88403-3_13
4. Hoeffding, W.: Probability inequalities for the sum of bounded random variables. J. Am. Stat. Assoc. **58**(301), 13–30 (1963)
5. Chernoff, H.: A measure of asymptotic efficiency for tests of a hypothesis based on the sum of observations. Ann. Math. Stat. **23**(4), 493–507 (1952)
6. Patarin, J., Goubin, L.: Asymmetric cryptography with S-Boxes is it easier than expected to design efficient asymmetric cryptosystems? In: Han, Y., Okamoto, T., Qing, S. (eds.) ICICS 1997. LNCS, vol. 1334, pp. 369–380. Springer, Heidelberg (1997). doi:10.1007/BFb0028492
7. Courtois, N., Klimov, A., Patarin, J., Shamir, A.: Efficient algorithms for solving overdefined systems of multivariate polynomial equations. In: Preneel, B. (ed.) EUROCRYPT 2000. LNCS, vol. 1807, pp. 392–407. Springer, Heidelberg (2000). doi:10.1007/3-540-45539-6_27
8. Ars, G., Faugère, J.-C., Imai, H., Kawazoe, M., Sugita, M.: Comparison between XL and Gröbner basis algorithms. In: Lee, P.J. (ed.) ASIACRYPT 2004. LNCS, vol. 3329, pp. 338–353. Springer, Heidelberg (2004). doi:10.1007/978-3-540-30539-2_24
9. Blum, M., Micali, S.: How to generate cryptographically strong sequences of pseudo-random bits. SIAM J. Comput. **13**(4), 850–864 (1984)
10. Blum, L., Blum, M., Shub, M.: A simple unpredictable pseudo-random number generator. SIAM J. Comput. **15**(2), 364–383 (1986)

11. Fischer, J.-B., Stern, J.: An efficient pseudo-random generator provably as secure as syndrome decoding. In: Maurer, U. (ed.) EUROCRYPT 1996. LNCS, vol. 1070, pp. 245–255. Springer, Heidelberg (1996). doi:10.1007/3-540-68339-9_22
12. Impagliazzo, R., Naor, M.: Efficient cryptographic schemes provably as secure as subset sum. J. Cryptology **9**(4), 199–216 (1996)
13. Mitzenmacher, M., Upfal, E.: Probability and Computing: Randomized Algorithms and Probability Analysis. Cambridge University Press, Cambridge (2005)

Public-Key Cryptosystems

Achieving IND-CCA Security for Functional Encryption for Inner Products

Shiwei Zhang$^{(\boxtimes)}$, Yi Mu$^{(\boxtimes)}$, and Guomin Yang$^{(\boxtimes)}$

School of Computing and Information Technology,
Centre for Computer and Information Security Research,
University of Wollongong, Wollongong, Australia
{sz653,ymu,gyang}@uow.edu.au

Abstract. Functional encryption allows the authorised parties to reveal partial information of the plaintext hidden in a ciphertext while in conventional encryption decryption is all-or-nothing. Focusing on the functionality of inner product evaluation (i.e. given vectors x and y, calculate $\langle x, y \rangle$), Abdalla et al. (PKC 2015) proposed a functional encryption scheme for inner product functionality (FE-IP) with s-IND-CPA security. In some recent works by Abdalla et al. (eprint: Report 2016/11) and Agrawal et al. (CRYPTO 2016), IND-CPA secure FE-IP schemes have also been proposed. In order to achieve Indistinguishable under Chosen Ciphertext Attacks (IND-CCA security) for FE-IP, in this paper, we propose a generic construction of FE-IP from hash proof systems. We prove the constructed FE-IP is IND-CCA secure, assuming the hardness of the subset membership problem. In addition, we give an instantiation of our generic construction from the DDH assumption.

Keywords: IND-CCA · Functional encryption · Inner product · Hash proof system

1 Introduction

Encryption provides information confidentiality such that messages are hidden and can only be revealed by authorised parties. In traditional encryption, accessing to the plaintext is in an all-or-nothing manner. Precisely, Alice encrypts a message using Bob's encryption key and sends the ciphertext to Bob. Later, Bob can decrypt the ciphertext to read the message using his decryption key while a malicious interceptor Eve gets no information about the encrypted message. Whereas in functional encryption, it is possible for different authorised parties to reveal different partial information of the plaintext from a ciphertext by granting them different secret keys. It is also possible to control the information leaked from the ciphertexts. In detail, a functional encryption enables the authorised receivers to reveal the output of a functionality $F(k, x)$ from a ciphertext containing the plaintext x and a secret key associated with a function key value k.

In this paper, we focus on the functional encryption for the functionality of inner product evaluation where $F(x, y) = \langle x, y \rangle$. A direct application of

© Springer International Publishing AG 2017
K. Chen et al. (Eds.): Inscrypt 2016, LNCS 10143, pp. 119–139, 2017.
DOI: 10.1007/978-3-319-54705-3_8

such a functional encryption scheme is privacy-preserving descriptive statistics such as calculating the weighted mean or sum of a list of integers. For instance, suppose in a high school the subject grades of each student are stored in a vector y which is encrypted under the school manager Alice's public key. As a university admission officer, Bob wants to offer scholarship to those students who are excellent at mathematics, physics, English, and good at other subjects. To ensure good students can get the scholarship, Alice decides to assist Bob in identifying the candidates. At the same time, Alice does not want to reveal the grades of all the students to Bob for privacy reasons. With functional encryption for inner-products, Alice can generate a secret key for Bob, which is associated with a vector $x = (10, 8, 8, 5, 5)$ that represents the weight for different subjects (i.e. 10 for mathematics, 8 for physics and English, and 5 for other subjects). Later, Bob can run the decryption algorithm to get the weighted sum of each student's subject grades, and nothing else. For example, Charlie has a grade vector $y = (90, 70, 80, 50, 60)$. The function $F(x, y)$ gives $\langle x, y \rangle = 10 \times 90 + 8 \times 70 + 8 \times 80 + 5 \times 50 + 5 \times 60 = 2650$. In this case, Bob can only learn the result 2650 but nothing else about y.

The security of functional encryption for inner products is defined by the notion of IND-CPA in [2]. However, such a security notion is not strong enough to cover the following variation of the above scenario. In order to restrict Bob's ability to calculate the weighted sum of each student, Alice gives the security key for the vector x to her colleague David instead of directly giving it to Bob. Consequently, Bob can only get the result of $F(x, y)$ from David by sending the ciphertext to him, and David can reject any queries related to those students whose grades are below a threshold. If the scheme is malleable, then Bob can modify a rejected ciphertext such that it can pass the threshold.

In this paper, we aim to build functional encryption for inner products with IND-CCA security, which is stronger than IND-CPA and can withstand the attack described above.

1.1   Related Work

The notion of *functional encryption* is introduced by Lewko et al. [14] and later formally defined by Boneh et al. [7]. In [7], the security of functional encryption is naturally defined via *indistinguishability*-based security (IND-security) where an adversary cannot distinguish which message x_0 or x_1 is encrypted in the ciphertext with oracles provided according to the attacking model. However, the IND-security is not sufficient for the general functional encryption [7,16], and thus simulation-based security (SIM-security) has been proposed. However, the SIM-security is only achievable in the programmable random oracle model.

For generic functionality, Goldwasser et al. [12] proposed a function encryption scheme for circuits. Later in [11], the functionality is further extended to accept multiple inputs such that it is able to compute $F(k, x_1, \ldots, x_n)$ instead of $F(k, x)$. Since the construction for generic functionalities is very inefficient for practical use, the construction for specific functionality has been the main focus. It is worth noting there is a subclass of functional encryption named *Predicate*

Encryption [13]. Its message space X consists of two subspaces, index space I and payload space M. For a predicate $P : K \times I \to \{0,1\}$, the functionality $F : K \times X \to M \cup \{\bot\}$ is defined as $F(k,(ind,m)) = m$ if $P(k,ind) = 1$ or $F(k,(ind,m)) = \bot$ otherwise. More subclasses of the functionalities can be derived from the Predicate Encryption class, including but not limited to Identity-Based Encryption [6], Attribute-Based Encryption [15,18], Hidden Vector Encryption [8], Inner Product Encryption [14,15], and Deterministic Finite Automata (DFA) Based Encryption (Functional Encryption for Regular Languages) [19]. Another notable functional encryption is searchable encryption [5] where $F(k,x) = 1$ if $k = x$ or $F(k,x) = 0$ otherwise where k and x are the keywords embedded in the trapdoor and ciphertext, respectively.

Recently, Abdalla et al. [2] investigated a new functionality $F(\boldsymbol{x}, \boldsymbol{y}) = \langle \boldsymbol{x}, \boldsymbol{y} \rangle$, i.e. to calculate the inner product of two vectors $\boldsymbol{x}$ and $\boldsymbol{y}$ where $\boldsymbol{x}$ is embedded in the secret key and $\boldsymbol{y}$ is embedded in the ciphertext. Unlike Inner Product Encryption [14,15] where inner product is used for access control, the new functionality here is to compute the actual inner product value. In [2], Abdalla et al. proposed a functional encryption for inner products scheme, which is selectively secure against chosen-plaintext attacks (s-IND-CPA). The scheme is generic as it can be constructed from any s-IND-CPA secure public key encryption, which is secure under randomness reuse and has linear key homomorphism and linear ciphertext homomorphism under shared randomness. Based on the generic construction, two instantiations are given from Decisional Diffie-Hellman (DDH) assumption and Learning With Error (LWE) assumption respectively. In some recent works [1,3], FE-IP schemes with IND-CPA security were also proposed. Specifically, Abdalla et al. [1] proposed another generic construction with IND-CPA security from any s-IND-CPA secure public key encryption with the same requirements as in [2]. They also showed that the IND-CPA security and Non-Adaptive Simulation (NA-SIM) security are equivalent for inner product functionality. Furthermore, an instantiation from Decisional Composite Residuosity (DCR) assumption is also proposed in [1].

In addition to the confidentiality, a notion called *function privacy* [4] has also been investigated for functional encryption which means an adversary should not be able to distinguish k (or F_k as $F(k,x) = F_k(x)$) from a secret key sk_k. However, the scheme [4] with function privacy is proposed in the private key setting while normal functional encryption schemes [1,2,19] are in the public key setting.

1.2   Our Contribution

In this paper, we define the notion of *Indistinguishablilty under adaptive Chosen Ciphertext Attacks* (i.e. IND-CCA, or more precisely IND-CCA2 security) for the general functional encryption. We also present the precise definition of functional encryption for the inner product functionality. In particular, we show that the secret keys for the functions $\langle \boldsymbol{x}_1, \cdot \rangle, \cdots, \langle \boldsymbol{x}_n, \cdot \rangle$ implies the secret key for the function $\langle \boldsymbol{x}', \cdot \rangle$ where $\boldsymbol{x}' \in \mathrm{span}(\boldsymbol{x}_1, \ldots, \boldsymbol{x}_n)$.

As the main contribution of this paper, we propose under certain conditions an IND-CCA secure functional encryption for inner products (FE-IP) scheme from hash proof systems, assuming the hardness of the subset membership problem. In the generic construction, we require two hash proof systems Ξ_1 and Ξ_2 with some special properties as the building blocks. In detail, Ξ_1 is required to be *diverse* (Definition 10) and have *key linearity* (Definition 8) and *hash linearity* (Definition 9). For Ξ_2, we require it to be *universal$_2$* (Definition 7) and have *hash linearity*. We show that those special properties are not hard to achieve. In [10], Cramer and Shoup constructed hash proof systems from a diverse group system $\mathbf{G} = (\mathcal{H}, X, L, \Pi)$. We show that their constructions have the key linearity and the hash linearity. If the hash codomain Π of the underlying diverse group system has prime order, the constructed hash proof system has the property of *diversity*. In other words, we can generically construct an IND-CCA secure FE-IP scheme from a diverse group system $\mathbf{G} = (\mathcal{H}, X, L, \Pi)$ when $|\Pi|$ is prime.

In addition, we propose a concrete IND-CCA secure FE-IP scheme from DDH assumption as an instantiation of our generic construction. Note that if we remove the NIZK proof part of Definition 5, the resulting scheme is exactly the same as the schemes in [1,3]. Thus the efficiency is the same as [1,3].

1.3 Paper Organisation

The rest of this paper is organised as follows. Beginning with Sect. 2, we review the subset membership problem, the definition and the security model of the functional encryption, and introduce the IND-CCA security model. In Sect. 3, we review the hash proof system and its construction, define new properties of HPS, and show that the existing construction has the new defined properties. After that, we give out a precise definition of FE-IP and a generic construction of IND-CCA secure FE-IP with security proof in Sect. 4. In addition, an instantiation of our generic construction from DDH assumption is provided in Sect. 5. Finally, the conclusion is addressed in Sect. 6.

2   Preliminaries

2.1   Subset Membership Problems

In this subsection, we review a problem class named *Subset Membership Problems* (SMP) defined by Cramer and Shoup [10]. Some standard problems such as Quadratic Residuosity and Decisional Diffie-Hellman problems belong to the SMP problem class.

Definition 1 (Subset Membership Problem). *Let X, L, W be three non-empty sets, and $R \subset X \times W$ be a binary relation such that $L \subset X$ and $\forall x \in X, \exists w \in W, (x, w) \in R \iff x \in L$. In other words, w is a witness of x if $x \in L$. Let $\Lambda = (X, L, W, R)$, $x \in_R L$, and $x' \in_R X \setminus L$ where $x \in_R L$ means that x is randomly chosen from L. Giving two probability distributions $\mathcal{D}_L = \{(\Lambda, x)\}$*

and $\mathcal{D}_{X \setminus L} = \{(\Lambda, x')\}$, there is an algorithm $\mathcal{A}$ can distinguish $\mathcal{D}_L$ and $\mathcal{D}_{X \setminus L}$ with advantage:

$$\mathsf{Adv}_{\mathcal{A}}^{SMP} = \left| \Pr[1 \leftarrow \mathcal{A}(D \in_R \mathcal{D}_L)] - \Pr[1 \leftarrow \mathcal{A}(D \in_R \mathcal{D}_{X \setminus L})] \right|$$

A subset membership problem is computational hard if and only if the advantage $\mathsf{Adv}_{\mathcal{A}}^{SMP}$ is negligible.

2.2 Functional Encryption

In this subsection, we review the definition of functional encryption in [7].

Definition 2 (Functional Encryption). *Let $F : K \times X \rightarrow \{0,1\}^*$ be a function where K is the function key space and X is the message space. A functional encryption (FE) for a functionality F consists of the following four polynomial time algorithms:*

- *(PK, MSK) $\leftarrow$ Setup(1^λ): The randomised system setup algorithm takes a security parameter 1^λ as input, and generates system-wide parameters and a key pair of the master secret key MSK and the public key PK.*
- *SK $\leftarrow$ KeyGen(MSK, k): The randomised secret key generation algorithm takes a master secret key MSK and a function key $k \in K$ as input, and generates a secret key SK for the functionality F_k.*
- *$C \leftarrow$ Encrypt(PK, x): The randomised encryption algorithm takes a public key PK and a plaintext x as input, and calculates a ciphertext for it.*
- *$D \leftarrow$ Decrypt(SK, C): The (probably) deterministic decryption algorithm takes a secret key SK of the functionality F_k and a ciphertext containing x. It outputs a value D, which is equivalent to the output of $F(k, x)$.*

In this paper, we consider the indistinguishability-based security and enhance the IND-CPA security model defined in [7] to the *Indistinguishability under adaptive Chosen Ciphertext Attacks* (IND-CCA) as the generalisation of the IND-CCA2 security [17] for public key encryption schemes [9]. The difference is that the decryption oracle $\mathcal{O}_{\mathsf{Decrypt}}$ is not allowed in the IND-CPA game at any stage. The IND-CCA game (Game 1) is defined as follows where an adaptive adversary $\mathcal{A}$ tries to distinguish a ciphertext from two chosen plaintexts x_0 and x_1.

$$
\begin{array}{ll}
\mathsf{Game}_{\mathrm{IND\text{-}CCA}}^\lambda : & \mathcal{O}_{\mathsf{KeyGen}} : \\
\quad (\mathsf{PK}, \mathsf{MSK}) \leftarrow \mathsf{Setup}(1^\lambda) & \quad \mathcal{K} \leftarrow \mathcal{K} \cup \{k\} \\
\quad (x_0, x_1) \leftarrow \mathcal{A}^{\mathcal{O}_{\mathsf{KeyGen}}, \mathcal{O}_{\mathsf{Decrypt}}}(\mathsf{PK}) & \quad \text{return } \mathsf{SK} \leftarrow \mathsf{KeyGen}(\mathsf{MSK}, k) \\
\quad b \in_R \{0, 1\} & \mathcal{O}_{\mathsf{Decrypt}} : \\
\quad C \leftarrow \mathsf{Encrypt}(\mathsf{PK}, x_b) & \quad \mathcal{C} \leftarrow \mathcal{C} \cup \{C'\} \\
\quad b' \leftarrow \mathcal{A}^{\mathcal{O}_{\mathsf{KeyGen}}, \mathcal{O}_{\mathsf{Decrypt}}}(C) & \quad \mathsf{SK} \leftarrow \mathsf{KeyGen}(\mathsf{MSK}, k) \\
& \quad \text{return } D \leftarrow \mathsf{Decrypt}(\mathsf{SK}, C')
\end{array}
$$

Game 1: IND-CCA

1. The challenger S runs $\mathsf{Setup}(1^\lambda)$ to generate a key pair $(\mathsf{MSK}, \mathsf{PK})$, and passes the public key PK to the adversary $\mathcal{A}$.
2. The adversary $\mathcal{A}$ can adaptively query the key generation oracle $\mathcal{O}_{\mathsf{KeyGen}}$ for the secret key SK of a function F_k from the challenger S. The restriction is that $\mathcal{A}$ can only query the secret keys for the functionality F_k such that $F(k, x_0) = F(k, x_1)$ where x_0 and x_1 are the target plaintexts in the next step. Otherwise, the game is trivial since $\mathcal{A}$ can simply win the game by testing $\mathsf{Decrypt}(\mathsf{SK}_k, C) \overset{?}{=} F(k, x_0)$. Besides that, the adversary $\mathcal{A}$ can also ask the challenger S for decrypting a ciphertext C' of x to obtain the output of $F(k, x)$ for any $k \in K$ via the decryption oracle $\mathcal{O}_{\mathsf{Decrypt}}$.
3. At some point, the adversary $\mathcal{A}$ outputs two target plaintexts x_0 and x_1.
4. The challenger S randomly selects a bit $b \in_R \{0, 1\}$, and generates a target ciphertext $C \leftarrow \mathsf{Encrypt}(\mathsf{PK}, x_b)$. Then S passes C to the adversary $\mathcal{A}$.
5. The adversary $\mathcal{A}$ can continue to query the oracle $\mathcal{O}_{\mathsf{KeyGen}}$ with the same restriction as before, and the oracle $\mathcal{O}_{\mathsf{Decrypt}}$ with the restriction that $\mathcal{A}$ cannot query the target ciphertext C since $\mathcal{A}$ can win the game trivially by testing $\mathcal{O}_{\mathsf{Decrypt}}(k, C) \overset{?}{=} F(k, x_0)$ for some $k \in K$ such that $F(k, x_0) \neq F(k, x_1)$.
6. Eventually, the adversary $\mathcal{A}$ outputs a bit b', and $\mathcal{A}$ wins if $b = b'$.

The advantage of $\mathcal{A}$ winning the Game 1 is

$$\mathsf{Adv}_{\mathcal{A}}^{\mathrm{IND\text{-}CCA}} = \left| \Pr\left[b = b' \,\middle|\, C \notin \mathcal{C} \wedge \left(\forall k \in \mathcal{K}, F(k, x_0) = F(k, x_1)\right) \right] - \frac{1}{2} \right|$$

Definition 3 (IND-CCA Security). *A FE scheme is Indistinguishable under adaptive Chosen Ciphertext Attacks (IND-CCA) if* $\mathsf{Adv}_{\mathcal{A}}^{IND\text{-}CCA}$ *is a negligible function for all adversary $\mathcal{A}$ winning the Game 1 in polynomial time.*

3 Hash Proof System

In this section, we review the *hash proof system* (HPS) introduced by Cramer and Shoup [10]. We also extend their HPS with some extra properties so that we can use it to construct our scheme.

3.1 Definition

Definition 4 (Hash Proof System). *Let X be a non-empty set, and L be a $\mathcal{NP}$ language with a witness space W and a binary relation R such that $L = \{x \in X \mid \exists w : (x, w) \in R\}$. A hash proof system (HPS) consists of the following five polynomial time algorithms:*

- param $\leftarrow \mathsf{Setup}(1^\lambda)$: *The randomised system setup algorithm takes a security parameter 1^λ as input, and specifies an instance of X, L, W and R, using X as the hash domain. It also defines a secret hash key space K, a public hash key space S, and a hash codomain Π. After that, it packs all descriptions as the system public parameter* param $= (X, L, W, R, K, S, \Pi)$.

- SK $\leftarrow$ SKGen(param): *The randomised secret hash key generation algorithm takes system parameter* param *as input, and outputs a randomly chosen hash key* SK $\in_R K$.
- PK $\leftarrow$ PKGen(SK): *The deterministic public hash key generation algorithm takes a secret key* SK $\in K$ *as input, and maps it to a public hash key* PK $\in S$.
- $\pi \leftarrow$ Hash(SK, x): *The deterministic private evaluation algorithm takes a secret hash key* SK $\in K$ *and a value* $x \in X$, *and outputs a hash value* $\pi \in \Pi$ *of* x.
- $\pi \leftarrow$ PHash(PK, x, w): *The deterministic public evaluation algorithm takes a public key* $PK \in S$, *a value* $x \in L$ *and its witness* $w \in W$ *as input, and generate an equivalent hash value* $\pi =$ Hash(SK, x) $\in \Pi$ *of* x *such that* PK $=$ PKGen(SK).

As a basic property, a HPS should be correct.

Definition 5 (Correctness). *A hash proof system is correct if the following statement is always true.*

$$\forall \text{param} \leftarrow \text{Setup}(1^\lambda), \quad \forall \text{SK} \leftarrow \text{SKGen}(\text{param}), \quad \text{PK} \leftarrow \text{PKGen}(\text{SK}),$$
$$\forall (x, w) \in R, \quad \text{Hash}(\text{SK}, x) = \text{PHash}(\text{PK}, x, w).$$

Furthermore, some useful security properties of a HPS are required.

Definition 6 (Universal). *A hash proof system is universal if the following probability is negligible for all* PK $\in S$, $x \in X \setminus L$ *and* $\pi \in \Pi$.

$$\text{Adv}^{Universal} = \Pr[\text{Hash}(\text{SK}, x) = \pi \mid \text{PKGen}(\text{SK}) = \text{PK}]$$

Definition 7 (Universal$_2$). *A hash proof system is universal$_2$ if the following probability is negligible for all* PK $\in S$, $x^* \in X$, $x \in X \setminus (L \cup \{x^*\})$ *and* $\pi^*, \pi \in \Pi$.

$$\text{Adv}^{Universal_2} = \Pr[\text{Hash}(\text{SK}, x) = \pi \mid \text{Hash}(\text{SK}, x^*) = \pi^* \wedge \text{PKGen}(\text{SK}) = \text{PK}]$$

If a hash proof system is universal$_2$ and $|X| > 1$, it is also universal. Besides all above properties defined in [10], we require three extra properties to construct our schemes.

Definition 8 (Key Linearity). *A hash proof system has linear key homomorphism if* K *and* S *are abelian groups and*

$$\forall \text{SK}_1, \text{SK}_2 \in K, \quad \text{PKGen}(\text{SK}_1) + \text{PKGen}(\text{SK}_2) = \text{PKGen}(\text{SK}_1 + \text{SK}_2) \in S.$$

Particularly, if a HPS has key linearity, we have $\mu \cdot \text{PKGen}(\text{SK}) = \text{PKGen}(\mu \cdot \text{SK})$ for all SK $\in K$ and $\mu \in \mathbb{Z}$.

Definition 9 (Hash Linearity). *A hash proof system has linear hash homomorphism if* K *and* Π *are abelian groups and*

$$\forall \text{SK}_1, \text{SK}_2 \in K, \forall x \in X, \text{Hash}(\text{SK}_1, x) + \text{Hash}(\text{SK}_2, x) = \text{Hash}(\text{SK}_1 + \text{SK}_2, x) \in \Pi.$$

Similar to the key linearity, we have $\mu \cdot \mathsf{Hash}(\mathsf{SK}, x) = \mathsf{Hash}(\mu \cdot \mathsf{SK}, x)$ for all $\mathsf{SK} \in K$, $x \in X$, and $\mu \in \mathbb{Z}$.

Definition 10 (Diversity). *A hash proof system is diverse if there exists $\pi \in \Pi$ such that $\pi \neq 0$ and for all $x \in X \setminus L$, there exists $\mathsf{SK} \in K$ such that $\mathsf{Hash}(\mathsf{SK}, x) = \pi$ and $\mathsf{PKGen}(\mathsf{SK}) = 0$. Formally,*

$$\exists \pi \in \Pi, \pi \neq 0 \wedge (\forall x \in X \setminus L, \exists \mathsf{SK} \in K, \mathsf{Hash}(\mathsf{SK}, x) = \pi \wedge \mathsf{PKGen}(\mathsf{SK}) = 0)$$

3.2   Construction

In this subsection, we review the Cramer-Shoup constructions of HPS from universal projective hashing derived from diverse group systems [10]. We start with the definition of the group system, then the constructions of the universal projective hashing. In the end, we show that the reviewed constructions have *key linearity*, *hash linearity*, and *diversity*. For notational convenience, we use addition for the group operations.

Definition 11 (Group System). *Let X, Π be two finite abelian groups, and L be a $\mathcal{NP}$ language with a witness space W and a binary relation R such that $L = \{x \in X \mid \exists w : (x, w) \in R\}$. Let Φ be a finite abelian group of homomorphism $\phi : X \to \Pi$ such that for all $\phi, \phi' \in \Phi$, $x \in X$, and $a \in \mathbb{Z}$, we have $(\phi \pm \phi')(x) = \phi(x) \pm \phi'(x)$ and $(a\phi)(x) = a\phi(x) = \phi(ax)$. If $\phi = 0 \in \Phi$, we have $\phi(x) = 0 \in \Pi$ for all $x \in X$. Let $\mathcal{H}$ be a subgroup of Φ. Then $\mathbf{G} = (\mathcal{H}, X, L, \Pi)$ is a group system.*

Definition 12 (Diverse Group System). *A group system $\mathbf{G}$ is diverse if there exists $\phi \in \Phi$ such that $\phi(L) = \langle 0 \rangle$ and $\phi(x) \neq 0$ for all $x \in X \setminus L$.*

Construction 1 (Projective Hash Families from Group Systems). *Let $\mathbf{G} = (\mathcal{H}, X, L, \Pi)$ be a group system and $(g_1, \ldots, g_d) \in L$ be a generator of L. A projective hash family $\mathbf{H} = (H, K, X, L, \Pi, S, \alpha)$ defined in [10] can be constructed from $\mathbf{G}$ by setting $\{\phi = H_k \mid k \in K\} = \mathcal{H}$ with uniform distribution, $S = \Pi^d$, and $\alpha : K \to S$ that $\alpha(k) = (\phi(g_1), \ldots, \phi(g_d)) = (H_k(g_1), \ldots, H_k(g_d))$. To hash $x \in X$, it simply calculates $H_k(x) = \phi(x) \in \Pi$. If $x \in L$ that $x = \sum_{i=1}^{d} w_i g_i$ where $(w_1, \ldots, w_d) \in W$ is the witnesses of x, it can alternatively calculates $H_k(x) = \phi(\sum_{i=1}^{d} w_i g_i) = \sum_{i=1}^{d} w_i \phi(g_i) \in \Pi$, using $\alpha(k)$ and $(w_1, \ldots, w_d)$.*

Construction 2 (HPS from Projective Hash Families). *Let $\mathbf{H} = (H, K, X, L, \Pi, S, \alpha)$ be a projective hash family where L is a $\mathcal{NP}$ language with a witness space W and a binary relation R such that $L = \{x \in X \mid \exists w : (x, w) \in R\}$. A hash proof system $\Xi = (\mathsf{Setup}, \mathsf{SKGen}, \mathsf{PKGen}, \mathsf{Hash}, \mathsf{PHash})$ can be constructed as follows.*

- param $\leftarrow$ Setup(1^λ): *return* param $= (X, L, W, R, K, S, \Pi)$.
- SK $\leftarrow$ SKGen(param): *return* $k \in_R K$.
- PK $\leftarrow$ PKGen(SK): *return* $\alpha(k)$.

- $\pi \leftarrow \mathsf{Hash}(\mathsf{SK}, x)$: *return* $H_k(x)$.
- $\pi \leftarrow \mathsf{PHash}(\mathsf{PK}, x, w)$: *return* $H_k(x)$ *computed using* $\alpha(k)$ *and a witness* w *of* x *without the actual* k.

Let Ξ be a hash proof system constructed from a group system $\mathbf{G}$ by combining Constructions 1 and 2. From [10], Ξ is *universal* if $\mathbf{G}$ is *diverse*. Furthermore, we need a universal$_2$ HPS, which can be derived from a universal projective hash family.

Construction 3 (Universal$_2$ Projective Hash Families). *Let* $\mathbf{H} = (H, K, X, L, \Pi, S, \alpha)$ *be a universal projective hash family,* p *be the smallest prime dividing* $|X \setminus L|$, *and* $\Gamma : X \times E \to \mathbb{Z}_p^n$ *be an injective map. A universal$_2$ projective hash family* $\hat{\mathbf{H}} = (\hat{H}, K^{n+1}, X \times E, L \times E, \Pi, S^{n+1}, \hat{\alpha})$ *can be constructed that* $\hat{k} = (k_0, \ldots, k_n) \in K^{n+1}$, $\hat{\alpha}(k) = (\alpha(k_0), \ldots, \alpha(k_n)) \in S^{n+1}$, *and* $\hat{H}_{\hat{k}} = H_{k_0}(x) + \langle \Gamma(x, e), (H_{k_1}(x), \ldots, H_{k_n}(x)) \rangle$ *for all* $x \in X$ *and* $e \in E$.

Let Ξ_2 be a hash proof system constructed from a group system $\mathbf{G}$ by combining Constructions 1, 3 and 2 in sequence. From [10], Ξ_2 is *universal$_2$* if $\mathbf{G}$ is *diverse*.

Besides the above security properties, we find that HPS from a group system $\mathbf{G} = (\mathcal{H}, X, L, \Pi)$ has some extra properties. Let K be a finite abelian group of order $|\mathcal{H}|$. Since H_k is uniformly distributed over $\mathcal{H}$ by randomly choosing $k \in K$ in Construction 1, we have that H is a bijection for K and $\mathcal{H}$. Thus we have $H_{k_1} + H_{k_2} = H_{k_1+k_2} \in \mathcal{H}$ for all $k_1, k_2 \in K$.

Theorem 1 (Key Linearity). *Let* Ξ *be a universal HPS and* Ξ_2 *be a universal$_2$ HPS as constructed above from a group system* $\mathbf{G}$. *The HPSs* Ξ *and* Ξ_2 *have key linearity.*

Proof As Ξ and Ξ_2 share the same mapping $\alpha : K \to \Pi^d$, we show the linearity of α that for all $k_1, k_2 \in K$,

$$
\begin{aligned}
\alpha(k_1) + \alpha(k_2) &= (H_{k_1}(g_1), \ldots, H_{k_1}(g_d)) + (H_{k_2}(g_1), \ldots, H_{k_2}(g_d)) \\
&= (H_{k_1}(g_1) + H_{k_2}(g_1), \ldots, H_{k_1}(g_d) + H_{k_2}(g_d)) \\
&= ((H_{k_1} + H_{k_2})(g_1), \ldots, (H_{k_1} + H_{k_2})(g_d)) \\
&= (H_{k_1+k_2}(g_1), \ldots, H_{k_1+k_2}(g_d)) = \alpha(k_1 + k_2)
\end{aligned}
$$

From the linearity of α, we directly have the key linearity of Ξ.

$$
\begin{aligned}
&\mathsf{PKGen}(\mathsf{SK}_1) + \mathsf{PKGen}(\mathsf{SK}_2) \\
&= \alpha(\mathsf{SK}_1) + \alpha(\mathsf{SK}_2) = \alpha(\mathsf{SK}_1 + \mathsf{SK}_2) = \mathsf{PKGen}(\mathsf{SK}_1 + \mathsf{SK}_2)
\end{aligned}
$$

For Ξ_2, we show the key linearity as follows where $\mathsf{SK}_1 = (k_{1,0}, \ldots, k_{1,n})$, $\mathsf{SK}_2 = (k_{2,0}, \ldots, k_{2,n}) \in K^{n+1}$.

$$
\begin{aligned}
&\mathsf{PKGen}(\mathsf{SK}_1) + \mathsf{PKGen}(\mathsf{SK}_2) \\
&= (a(k_{1,0}), \ldots, a(k_{1,n})) + (a(k_{2,0}), \ldots, a(k_{2,n})) \\
&= (a(k_{1,0}) + a(k_{2,0}), \ldots, a(k_{1,n}) + a(k_{2,n}))) \\
&= (a(k_{1,0} + k_{2,0}), \ldots, a(k_{1,n} + k_{2,n})) = \mathsf{PKGen}(\mathsf{SK}_1 + \mathsf{SK}_2)
\end{aligned}
$$

Theorem 2 (Hash Linearity). *Let Ξ be a universal HPS and Ξ_2 be a universal$_2$ HPS as constructed above from a group system* **G**. *The HPSs Ξ and Ξ_2 have hash linearity.*

Proof. Starting from Ξ, we show the hash linearity that

$$\mathsf{Hash}(SK_1, x) + \mathsf{Hash}(SK_2, x)$$
$$= H_{\mathsf{SK}_1}(x) + H_{\mathsf{SK}_2}(x) = H_{\mathsf{SK}_1 + \mathsf{SK}_2}(x) = \mathsf{Hash}(\mathsf{SK}_1 + \mathsf{SK}_2, x)$$

Then we show the hash linearity of Ξ_2 as follows where $\mathsf{SK}_1 = (k_{1,0}, \ldots, k_{1,n})$ and $\mathsf{SK}_2 = (k_{2,0}, \ldots, k_{2,n}) \in K^{n+1}$.

$$\mathsf{Hash}(\mathsf{SK}_1, (x, e)) + \mathsf{Hash}(\mathsf{SK}_2, (x, e))$$
$$= H_{k_{1,0}}(x) + \langle \Gamma(x, e), (H_{k_{1,1}}(x), \ldots, H_{k_{1,n}}(x)) \rangle$$
$$+ H_{k_{2,0}}(x) + \langle \Gamma(x, e), (H_{k_{2,1}}(x), \ldots, H_{k_{2,n}}(x)) \rangle$$
$$= (H_{k_{1,0}}(x) + H_{k_{2,0}}(x)) + \langle \Gamma(x, e), (H_{k_{1,1}}(x) + H_{k_{2,1}}(x), \ldots, H_{k_{1,n}}(x) + H_{k_{2,n}}(x)) \rangle$$
$$= H_{k_{1,0}+k_{2,0}}(x) + \langle \Gamma(x, e), (H_{k_{1,1}+k_{2,1}}(x), \ldots, H_{k_{1,n}+k_{2,n}}(x)) \rangle$$
$$= \mathsf{Hash}(\mathsf{SK}_1 + \mathsf{SK}_2, (x, e))$$

Theorem 3 (Diversity). *Let Ξ be a universal HPS as constructed above from a group system* **G**. *The HPS Ξ is diverse if $|\Pi|$ is prime and* **G** *is diverse.*

Proof Since **G** is diverse, we have that there exists $k \in K$ such that $\mathsf{Hash}(k, x) = 0$ for all $x \in L$ and $\mathsf{Hash}(k, x^*) \neq 0$ for all $x^* \in X \setminus L$. Let $\pi = \mathsf{Hash}(k, x^*) \neq 0$. Since Π is a prime order cyclic group, π is a generator of Π and thus for all $\pi' \in \Pi$, $\pi' = \mu \cdot \pi$ for some $\mu \in \mathbb{Z}_{|\Pi|}$. By Theorem 2, we have that for all $x' \in X \setminus L$,

$$\pi' = \mathsf{Hash}(k, x') \iff \mu \cdot \pi = \mathsf{Hash}(k, x')$$
$$\iff \pi = \mu^{-1} \cdot \mathsf{Hash}(k, x') \iff \pi = \mathsf{Hash}(\mu^{-1} \cdot k, x')$$

Hence, for a fixed π, there exists a secret key $\mu^{-1} \cdot k$ that hashes x' to π for all $x' \in X$. Let w be a witness of $x \in L$. Recall the construction of Ξ that $\mathsf{Hash}(k, x) = H_k(x)$ and $\mathsf{PKGen}(k) = \alpha(k) = (H_k(g_1), \ldots, H_k(g_d))$. Since $g_1, \ldots, g_d \in L$ and $H_k(x) = 0$ for all $x \in L$, we have $\mathsf{PKGen}(k) = 0$. Therefore, by Theorem 1, we have $\mathsf{PKGen}(\mu^{-1} \cdot k) = \mu^{-1} \cdot \mathsf{PKGen}(k) = 0$ and complete the proof.

4   Functional Encryption for Inner Products

4.1   Definition

Let $\mathbb{G}_x$, $\mathbb{G}_y$, $\mathbb{G}_z$ be three abelian groups where there exists an efficient inner product computation $\langle \cdot, \cdot \rangle : \mathbb{G}_x \times \mathbb{G}_y \to \mathbb{G}_z$. The functional encryption for inner products is associated with a functionality $F : \mathbb{G}_x^\delta \times \mathbb{G}_y^\delta \to \mathbb{G}_z$, mapping two δ-dimension vectors into a single group $\mathbb{G}_z$ such that $F(\boldsymbol{x}, \boldsymbol{y}) = \langle \boldsymbol{x}, \boldsymbol{y} \rangle = \sum_{i=1}^\delta \langle x_i, y_i \rangle$ for all $\boldsymbol{x} = (x_1, \ldots, x_\delta) \in \mathbb{G}_x^\delta$ and $\boldsymbol{y} = (y_1, \ldots, y_\delta) \in \mathbb{G}_y^\delta$. Based on the functionality F, we derive the syntax of the functional encryption from Definition 2.

Definition 13 (Functional Encryption for Inner Products). *A functional encryption for inner products (FE-IP) scheme for a functionality* $F : \mathbb{G}_x^\delta \times \mathbb{G}_y^\delta \rightarrow \mathbb{G}_z$ *consists of the following four polynomial time algorithms:*

- $(\mathsf{PK}, \mathsf{MSK}) \leftarrow \mathsf{Setup}(1^\lambda, 1^\delta)$: *The randomised system setup algorithm takes a security parameter* 1^λ *and a unary value* 1^δ *that specifies the maximum vector dimension as input. Then it generates system-wide parameters and a key pair* $(\mathsf{PK}, \mathsf{MSK})$.
- $\mathsf{SK} \leftarrow \mathsf{KeyGen}(\mathsf{MSK}, \boldsymbol{x})$: *The randomised secret key generation algorithm takes a master secret key* MSK *and a vector* $\boldsymbol{x} \in \mathbb{G}_x^d$ *with dimension* d. *If* $d > \delta$, *the extra dimensions of* $\boldsymbol{x}$ *is discarded. If* $d < \delta$, *the vector* $\boldsymbol{x}$ *is reconstructed to the dimension* δ *by filling an additive identity element* 0 *(i.e.* $\boldsymbol{x}' = (\boldsymbol{x}, \underbrace{0, \ldots, 0}_{\delta-d})$*).*

  After that, the algorithm generates a secret key SK *for the (modified) vector* $\boldsymbol{x}$ *with dimension* δ.
- $C \leftarrow \mathsf{Encrypt}(\mathsf{PK}, \boldsymbol{y})$: *The randomised encryption takes a public key* PK *and a vector* $\boldsymbol{y} \in \mathbb{G}_y^d$ *with dimension* d. *If* $d \neq \delta$, *the ciphertext may still be constructed. However, it may not be decrypted properly. Hence, the same modification to* $\boldsymbol{x}$ *in the algorithm* KeyGen *is applied to* $\boldsymbol{y}$. *After that, the algorithm generates a ciphertext* C *for the (modified) vector* $\boldsymbol{y}$ *with dimension* δ.
- $D \leftarrow \mathsf{Decrypt}(\mathsf{SK}, C)$: *The deterministic decryption algorithm takes a secret key* SK *for* $\boldsymbol{x}$ *and a ciphertext* C *of* $\boldsymbol{y}$, *and computes* $D = \langle \boldsymbol{x}, \boldsymbol{y} \rangle \in \mathbb{G}_z$. *If the decryption fails, the algorithm outputs a special symbol* $\perp$.

Before introducing the security model of FE-IP, we review the inner product functionality along with the vector space first.

Due to the linearity that $\langle x_0 + x_1, y \rangle = \langle x_0, y \rangle + \langle x_1, y \rangle$ for all $x_0, x_1 \in \mathbb{G}_x$ and $y \in \mathbb{G}_y$, we have $\mu \langle \boldsymbol{x}, \boldsymbol{y} \rangle = \langle \mu \boldsymbol{x}, \boldsymbol{y} \rangle$ for all $\mu \in \mathbb{Z}$, $\boldsymbol{x} \in \mathbb{G}_x^\delta$, and $\boldsymbol{y} \in \mathbb{G}_y^\delta$. Thus the ability of the secret key for a vector $\boldsymbol{x}$ is not only to calculate $F(\boldsymbol{x}, \boldsymbol{y})$ but also to compute $F(\mu \boldsymbol{x}, \boldsymbol{y}) = \langle \mu \boldsymbol{x}, \boldsymbol{y} \rangle = \mu \langle \boldsymbol{x}, \boldsymbol{y} \rangle = \mu F(\boldsymbol{x}, \boldsymbol{y})$, which is equivalent to the ability of the secret key for the vector $\mu \boldsymbol{x}$ for all $\mu \in \mathbb{Z}$. In other words, the key generation algorithm KeyGen actually generates a secret key for a vector space $\mathrm{span}(\boldsymbol{x})$ linearly spanned by $\boldsymbol{x}$ instead of a single vector $\boldsymbol{x}$. Generally, given multiple secret keys for a vector set $S = \{\boldsymbol{x}_1, \ldots, \boldsymbol{x}_n\}$, we are able to compute $F(\boldsymbol{x}, \boldsymbol{y})$ for all $\boldsymbol{x} \in \mathrm{span}(S)$. It is possible since $F(\boldsymbol{x}, \boldsymbol{y}) = \sum_{i=1}^n \mu_i F(\boldsymbol{x}_i, \boldsymbol{y})$ where $\boldsymbol{x} = \sum_{i=1}^n \mu_i \boldsymbol{x}_i$. Notably, if we obtain secret keys for a vector set S such that $\mathrm{span}(S) = \mathbb{G}_x$ (e.g. S contains δ linearly dependent vectors), we have the same ability of the master secret key without compromising it.

Since δ secret keys for linearly independent vectors are equivalent to the master secret key, the function key space K (recall Definition 2) is reduced to the size of δ, which is polynomial bounded. Let $\boldsymbol{v}_1, \ldots, \boldsymbol{v}_\delta$ be a basis of $\mathbb{G}_x$. Intuitively, one may think that the "brute force" construction in [7] becomes practical by encrypting the output of $F(\boldsymbol{v}_1, \boldsymbol{y}), \ldots, F(\boldsymbol{v}_\delta, \boldsymbol{y})$ instead of the vector $\boldsymbol{y}$ where the resulting ciphertext size is $\Theta(\delta)$. However, it is not true since $\mathrm{span}(\boldsymbol{v}_1 + \boldsymbol{v}_2) \neq \mathrm{span}(\boldsymbol{v}_1, \boldsymbol{v}_2)$ where $\boldsymbol{v}_1$ and $\boldsymbol{v}_2$ are independent. Hence, a proper construction is still required.

Besides that, if $\mathbb{G}_x = \mathbb{G}_y = \mathbb{G}_z = \mathbb{F}$ are the same field, it is impossible to hide x in the public key setting, given the secret key for the vector x. Since it is in the public key setting, δ linearly independent vectors $y_1, \ldots, y_\delta$ can be chosen and encrypted freely. By decrypting the above ciphertexts with the secret key for the vector $x = (x_1, \ldots, x_\delta)$, we can obtain the results $\{D_i = F(x, y_i)\}_{i=1\ldots\delta}$. After that, we can calculate x by solving the following matrix equation in polynomial time.

$$\begin{bmatrix} y_1 \\ \vdots \\ y_\delta \end{bmatrix} x^\top = \begin{bmatrix} D_1 \\ \vdots \\ D_\delta \end{bmatrix}$$

Hence, it is impossible to achieve *function privacy*. As a side effect, it is "safe" to provide x along with the secret key in the key generation algorithm KeyGen.

For the security model, the definition of the IND-CPA security and the IND-CCA security can be derived from the security model of the general functional encryption. The difference is that the setup algorithm is required to take an additional parameter 1^δ.

4.2 Generic Construction from Hash Proof Systems

In this subsection, we describe the key ideas to construct an IND-CCA secure FE-IP scheme. Then we present our FE-IP scheme from Hash Proof Systems.

In a FE-IP scheme, the plaintext vector y should be encrypted in a raw form that can be recovered instead of being encrypted as the output of the function $F(x, y)$ so that it can be manipulated by arbitrary x to compute $F(x, y)$. In order to achieve the IND-CCA security, the sender who encrypts the message shall provide a non-interactive zero knowledge (NIZK) proof that it knows the decryption in terms of the raw form of the plaintext vector y [17]. This is the essential idea of achieving the IND-CCA security. On the other hand, the decryption of a functional encryption involves two parts: the function evaluation and the authorisation to that function evaluation. Obviously, we have to do manipulation first then decryption instead of decryption first then manipulation since the receiver should only be able to compute $F(x, y)$ but not y itself. For inner product functionality, the ciphertext of the plaintext vector y is manipulated into the ciphertext of $F(x, y) = \langle x, y \rangle$ by using the vector x and the ciphertext homomorphism. Later, the receiver can decrypt the resulted ciphertext to obtain $F(x, y)$, given the authorisation to $F(x, \cdot)$. Before decryption, the receiver also needs to verify the NIZK proof attached to the ciphertext. Using the hash proof system as the NIZK proof system (with auxiliary input), the receiver is required to use the secret key of the HPS to verify the proof. If we consider attacks from outsiders only, it is safe to give the secret key to the end users. However, from the Game 1, we allow attacks from insiders. Therefore, we cannot give the secret key directly to the users. Otherwise, they can generate the proofs without knowing the witnesses. To solve this problem, we limit the scheme to serve at most η users and generate a vector β of secret keys for the proof system with dimension η. For each user, we randomly pick a vector s and compute the inner product

$\langle s, \beta \rangle$ as the secret key for the end user. When encrypting, the sender generates the proof using the individual public keys directly derived for β as η proof parts. To verify, the receiver assembles the proof parts using s and checks with its secret key $\langle s, \beta \rangle$. Since both β and s have the dimension η, it is impossible to compute β with $\eta - 1$ pairs of $(s, \langle s, \beta \rangle)$ (i.e. β is statistically indistinguishable with a random vector). If all η users collude together, they can obtain β and generate proofs without witnesses but it is meaningless to launch attacks against themselves.

Unfortunately, we are not able to construct a generic FP-IP scheme for arbitrary $\mathbb{G}_x$, $\mathbb{G}_y$, and $\mathbb{G}_z$. Due to the definition of hash linearity (Definition 9) of HPS, we have to make $\mathbb{G}_x = \mathbb{G}_y = \mathbb{G}_z = \mathbb{Z}_\rho \subset \mathbb{Z}$. To build our FE-IP scheme, we need a diverse HPS with key linearity and hash linearity, a universal$_2$ HPS with hash linearity. Note that the key linearity is used in the proof only. Formally, we present our construction as follows.

Construction 4 (FE-IP from HPS). *Let $\Xi_1 = (\mathsf{Setup}, \mathsf{SKGen}, \mathsf{PKGen}, \mathsf{Hash},$ $\mathsf{PHash})$ be a diverse HPS associated with spaces (X, L, W, R, K, S, Π) and $\Xi_2 = (\mathsf{Setup}, \mathsf{SKGen}, \mathsf{PKGen}, \mathsf{Hash}, \mathsf{PHash})$ be a universal$_2$ HPS associated with space $(X \times \Pi^\delta, L \times \Pi^\delta, W, R, K', S', \Pi')$ where δ is passed as the input of the algorithm Setup. Both Ξ_1 and Ξ_2 are required to have the hash linearity. Ξ_1 is required to have the key linearity for the security proof. Let $\chi \in \Pi$ derived from the diversity property of Ξ_1 that $\chi \neq 0$ and $\forall x \in X \setminus L, \exists \mathsf{SK} \in K, \Xi_1.\mathsf{Hash}(\mathsf{SK}, x) = \chi \wedge \Xi_1.\mathsf{PKGen}(\mathsf{SK}) = 0$. We use $\mu = \chi^{-1}(\pi)$ to denote the calculation of $\mu \in \mathbb{Z}_\rho$ such that $\mu \cdot \chi = \pi \in \Pi$. Our functional encryption scheme for the functionality $F : \mathbb{Z}_\rho^\delta \times \mathbb{Z}_\rho^\delta \to \mathbb{Z}_\rho$ works as follows.*

- (PK, MSK) $\leftarrow$ Setup($1^\lambda, 1^\delta, 1^\eta$): *Given a security parameter 1^λ, a maximum vector size 1^δ and a maximum user size 1^η, the algorithm generates system-wide parameters $\mathsf{param}_1 \leftarrow \Xi_1.\mathsf{Setup}(1^\lambda)$ and $\mathsf{param}_2 \leftarrow \Xi_2.\mathsf{Setup}(1^\lambda)$. The algorithm generates two secret key vectors $\alpha = (\alpha_1, \ldots, \alpha_\delta) \in K^\delta$ and $\beta = (\beta_1, \ldots, \beta_\eta) \in K'^\eta$ where $\alpha_i \leftarrow \Xi_1.\mathsf{SKGen}(\mathsf{param}_1)$, $\beta_i \leftarrow \Xi_2.\mathsf{SKGen}(\mathsf{param}_2)$. After that, it generates corresponding public keys $A = (A_1, \ldots, A_\delta) \in S^\delta$ and $B = (B_1, \ldots, B_\eta) \in S'^\eta$ where $A_i = \Xi_1.\mathsf{PKGen}(\alpha_i)$, $B_i = \Xi_2.\mathsf{PKGen}(\beta_i)$. Next, the algorithm packs the public key $PK = (A, B)$ and the master secret key $MSK = (\alpha, \beta)$. Finally, the algorithm publishes PK and keeps MSK private.*

$$\mathsf{param}_1 \leftarrow \Xi_1.\mathsf{Setup}(1^\lambda), \quad \mathsf{param}_2 \leftarrow \Xi_2.\mathsf{Setup}(1^\lambda)$$
$$For \; i = 1 \ldots \delta, \quad \alpha_i \leftarrow \Xi_1.\mathsf{SKGen}(\mathsf{param}_1), \quad A_i = \Xi_1.\mathsf{PKGen}(\alpha_i)$$
$$For \; i = 1 \ldots \eta, \quad \beta_i \leftarrow \Xi_2.\mathsf{SKGen}(\mathsf{param}_2), \quad B_i = \Xi_2.\mathsf{PKGen}(\beta_i)$$

return (PK, MSK) $= ((A, B), (\alpha, \beta))$.

- SK $\leftarrow$ KeyGen(MSK, x): *To generate a secret key for the vector x, the algorithm randomly selects a vector $s = (s_1, \ldots, s_\eta) \in_R \mathbb{Z}_\rho^\eta$ and calculates K_1 and K_2 as follows.*

$$s \in_R \mathbb{Z}_\rho^\eta, \quad K_1 = \langle x, \alpha \rangle, \quad K_2 = \langle s, \beta \rangle.$$

return SK $= (x, s, K_1, K_2)$.

$-\ C \leftarrow$ Encrypt(PK, $\boldsymbol{y}$): *To encrypt a vector $\boldsymbol{y}$, the algorithm randomly samples a word $l \in L$ with a witness $w \in W$. Then the algorithm computes the ciphertext part $C = (C_1, \ldots, C_\delta)$ where $C_i = y_i \chi + \Xi_1.$PHash(A_i, l, w). After that, the algorithm computes the proof part $\boldsymbol{\pi} = (\pi_1, \ldots, \pi_\eta)$ where $\pi_i = \Xi_2.$PHash$(B_i, (l, C), w)$. Finally, the algorithm packs the word, the ciphertext part, and the proof part as one single ciphertext.*

$$(l, w) \in_R R$$
$$For\ i = 1 \ldots \delta, \quad C_i = y_i \chi + \Xi_1.\text{PHash}(A_i, l, w)$$
$$For\ i = 1 \ldots \eta, \quad \pi_i = \Xi_2.\text{PHash}(B_i, (l, C), w)$$

return $C = (l, C, \boldsymbol{\pi})$.

$-\ D \leftarrow$ Decrypt(SK, C): *To decrypt, the algorithm assembles the proof parts $D_2 = \langle \boldsymbol{s}, \boldsymbol{\pi} \rangle$. If $D_2 \neq \Xi_2.$Hash$(K_2, (l, C))$, the algorithm outputs $D = \perp$ to reject the ciphertext. Otherwise, the algorithm assembles the ciphertext part $D_1 = \langle \boldsymbol{x}, C \rangle$. Then the algorithm decrypts the resulted ciphertext $D^* = D_1 - \Xi_1.$Hash(K_1, l). Finally, the algorithm extracts the result $D = \chi^{-1}(D^*)$.*

$$D_2 = \langle \boldsymbol{s}, \boldsymbol{\pi} \rangle, \quad D_2 \overset{?}{=} \Xi_2.\text{Hash}(K_2, (l, C)),$$
$$D_1 = \langle \boldsymbol{x}, C \rangle, \quad D^* = D_1 - \Xi_1.\text{Hash}(K_1, l).$$

return $D = \chi^{-1}(D^*)$.

Theorem 4. *The Construction 4 is correct.*

Proof. We verify the correctness by verifying the decryption algorithm.

$$D_2 = \langle \boldsymbol{s}, \boldsymbol{\pi} \rangle = \sum_{i=1}^{\eta} s_i \pi_i = \sum_{i=1}^{\eta} s_i \Xi_2.\text{PHash}(B_i, (l, C), w) = \sum_{i=1}^{\eta} s_i \Xi_2.\text{Hash}(\beta_i, (l, C))$$

$$= \Xi_2.\text{Hash}(\sum_{i=1}^{\eta} s_i \beta_i, (l, C)) = \Xi_2.\text{Hash}(\langle \boldsymbol{s}, \boldsymbol{\beta} \rangle, (l, C)) = \Xi_2.\text{Hash}(K_2, (l, C)).$$

$$D_1 = \langle \boldsymbol{x}, C \rangle = \sum_{i=1}^{\delta} x_i C_i = \sum_{i=1}^{\delta} x_i (y_i \chi + \Xi_1.\text{PHash}(A_i, l, w))$$

$$= \sum_{i=1}^{\delta} x_i y_i \chi + \sum_{i=1}^{\delta} x_i \Xi_1.\text{Hash}(\alpha_i, l) = \langle \boldsymbol{x}, \boldsymbol{y} \rangle \chi + \Xi_1.\text{Hash}(\sum_{i=1}^{\delta} x_i \alpha_i, l)$$

$$= \langle \boldsymbol{x}, \boldsymbol{y} \rangle \chi + \Xi_1.\text{Hash}(\langle \boldsymbol{x}, \boldsymbol{\alpha} \rangle, l) = \langle \boldsymbol{x}, \boldsymbol{y} \rangle \chi + \Xi_1.\text{Hash}(K_1, l).$$

After verifying D_2 and computing D_1, we compute D as follows and complete the verification.

$$D^* = D_1 - \Xi_1.\text{Hash}(K_1, l) = \langle \boldsymbol{x}, \boldsymbol{y} \rangle \chi, \quad D = \chi^{-1}(D^*) = \chi^{-1}(\langle \boldsymbol{x}, \boldsymbol{y} \rangle \chi) = \langle \boldsymbol{x}, \boldsymbol{y} \rangle.$$

In Construction 4, we require the calculation of χ^{-1}, which may not be computed in polynomial time. If the decryption space $|\{\langle \boldsymbol{x}, \boldsymbol{y} \rangle\}|$ is polynomial bounded, we can do decryption in an alternative way. In this variation, D_1, D_2, and D^* are computed and checked as normal. To calculate D, we check $D\chi \stackrel{?}{=} D^*$ for each possible $D \in |\{\langle \boldsymbol{x}, \boldsymbol{y}\rangle\}|$. Since $|\{\langle \boldsymbol{x}, \boldsymbol{y}\rangle\}|$ is polynomial-sized, the checking algorithm can be done in polynomial time.

In terms of the maximum number η of users, it is not a defect and the IND-CCA model is still suitable for Construction 4. Since the number of users is polynomial sized, the value of η is also polynomial sized. By observing Construction 4, we have the following size table.

Item	PK	MSK	SK	C	D
Size	$\delta\|S\| + \eta\|S'\|$	$\delta\|K\| + \eta\|K'\|$	$(\delta + \eta)\|\mathbb{Z}_\rho\| + \|K\| + \|K'\|$	$\|L\| + \delta\|\Pi\| + \eta\|\Pi'\|$	$\|\mathbb{Z}_\rho\|$

As long as the value of η is polynomial sized, all the elements in Construction 4 are polynomial sized. Hence, the limitation on the maximum user number is no longer an issue.

4.3 Security Proof

Theorem 5. *The proposed FE-IP scheme (Construction 4), allowing at most η users, is IND-CCA secure (Definition 3) if the language (X, L, W, R) associated with both the underlying diverse HPS Ξ_1 and universal$_2$ HPS Ξ_2 satisfies a hard subset membership problem (Definition 1).*

Proof. Having a glance at the security proof, we leverage the diversity property of the HPS Ξ_1 to prove the ciphertext indistinguishability of our construction. At the same time, we exploit the universal$_2$ property of the HPS Ξ_2 to finalise the IND-CCA security in terms of dealing the decryption oracle.

In detail, we show that an algorithm $\mathcal{S}$ (i.e. simulator) can be constructed to solve subset membership problems in polynomial time with non-negligible probability if an adversary $\mathcal{A}$ can win the Game 1 with non-negligible probability, querying the key generation oracle $\mathcal{O}_{\mathsf{KeyGen}}$ at most $\eta-1$ times and the decryption oracle $\mathcal{O}_{\mathsf{Decrypt}}$ for at most q times. As explained in Sect. 4.2, it is meaningless to obtain all secret keys of η users and this is the reason why we let the adversary $\mathcal{A}$ query the key generation oracle at most $\eta - 1$ times. Although we limit the maximum number of the key generation queries, we do not limit the maximum number of the decryption queries to a function of η. Therefore, the proof is still in a valid IND-CCA model.

Let $(\Lambda = (X, L, W, R), x^*)$ be an instance of subset membership problems challenged to the simulator $\mathcal{S}$ for distinguishing whether $x^* \in L$ or $x^* \in X \setminus L$ where x^* is sampled from L or $X \setminus L$ with equal probability. To simulate the Game 1, the simulator $\mathcal{S}$ runs the algorithm Setup as normal to generate a key pair $(\mathsf{PK}, \mathsf{MSK}) = ((\boldsymbol{A}, \boldsymbol{B}), (\boldsymbol{\alpha}, \boldsymbol{\beta}))$, and passes the public key PK to the adversary $\mathcal{A}$. Since the simulator $\mathcal{S}$ has the master secret key MSK, it can answer the oracles $\mathcal{O}_{\mathsf{KeyGen}}$ and $\mathcal{O}_{\mathsf{Decrypt}}$ as normal using the master secret key MSK.

The adversary $\mathcal{A}$ is restricted to query the secret keys for $\boldsymbol{x}$ to $\mathcal{O}_{\mathsf{KeyGen}}$ such that $\langle \boldsymbol{x}, \boldsymbol{y}_0 \rangle \neq \langle \boldsymbol{x}, \boldsymbol{y}_1 \rangle$ where $\boldsymbol{y}_0$ and $\boldsymbol{y}_1$ are the target vectors output by the adversary $\mathcal{A}$ in the next phase. In other words, the adversary $\mathcal{A}$ can only ask the secret keys for $\boldsymbol{x}$ such that $\langle \boldsymbol{x}, \boldsymbol{y}_0 - \boldsymbol{y}_1 \rangle = 0$.

At some point, the adversary $\mathcal{A}$ outputs two target vectors $\boldsymbol{y}_0$ and $\boldsymbol{y}_1$. Then the simulator $\mathcal{S}$ randomly chooses $b \in_R \{0, 1\}$. After that, the simulator $\mathcal{S}$ computes the target ciphertext $C^* = (x^*, \boldsymbol{C}^*, \boldsymbol{\pi}^*)$ where

$$C_i^* = y_{b,i}\chi + \Xi_1.\mathsf{Hash}(\alpha_i, x^*), \quad \pi_i^* = \Xi_2.\mathsf{Hash}(\beta_i, (x^*, \boldsymbol{C}^*)).$$

After receiving the target ciphertext C^*, the adversary $\mathcal{A}$ can continue to query provided oracles as before with the restriction that $\mathcal{A}$ cannot query C^* to the decryption oracle $\mathcal{O}_{\mathsf{Decrypt}}$. Eventually, the adversary $\mathcal{A}$ outputs a bit b'. If $b = b'$, the simulator $\mathcal{S}$ outputs 1, indicating that $\mathcal{A}$ wins the Game 1. Otherwise, the simulator $\mathcal{S}$ outputs 0. After that, the simulator $\mathcal{S}$ halts in order to complete the simulation.

Let E_L be the event that $\mathcal{S}$ outputs 1 conditioned on $x^* \in L$, and $E_{X \setminus L}$ be the event that $\mathcal{S}$ outputs 1 conditioned on $x^* \in X \setminus L$. Thus we have the advantage $\mathsf{Adv}_{\mathcal{S}}^{\mathsf{SMP}}$ of solving the subset membership problem.

$$\begin{aligned} \mathsf{Adv}_{\mathcal{S}}^{\mathsf{SMP}} &= |\Pr[1 \leftarrow \mathcal{S} \mid x^* \in L] - \Pr[1 \leftarrow \mathcal{S} \mid x^* \in X \setminus L]| \\ &= |\Pr[E_L] - \Pr[E_{X \setminus L}]| \end{aligned} \tag{1}$$

For the case of $x^* \in L$, the simulation is perfect since the algorithms $(\Xi_1.\mathsf{PHash}, \Xi_2.\mathsf{PHash})$ and $(\Xi_1.\mathsf{Hash}, \Xi_2.\mathsf{Hash})$ are equivalent. Thus we have

$$\left| \Pr[E_L] - \frac{1}{2} \right| = \mathsf{Adv}_{\mathcal{A}}^{\mathsf{IND\text{-}CCA}}. \tag{2}$$

For the case of $x^* \in X \setminus L$, we modify the game to a new game such that the simulator $\mathcal{S}$ rejects all ciphertexts $C = (l, \boldsymbol{C}, \boldsymbol{\pi})$ where $l \in X \setminus L$ in the decryption oracle $\mathcal{O}_{\mathsf{Decrypt}}$ in addition to those words, which cannot pass the proof verification. Let E_m be the event that $\mathcal{S}$ outputs 1 conditioned on $x^* \in X \setminus L$ in this modified game, and $E_\perp$ be the event that $l \in X \setminus L$ and $\langle \boldsymbol{s}, \boldsymbol{\pi} \rangle = \Xi_2.Hash(K_2, (l, \boldsymbol{C}))$. In other words, $E_\perp$ is the event that a ciphertext is rejected in the modified game but accepted in the original game. Since the original game and the modified game are identical until event $E_\perp$ occurs, we have

$$|\Pr[E_m] - \Pr[E_{X \setminus L}]| \le \Pr[E_\perp]. \tag{3}$$

Lemma 1. *The event $E_\perp$ occurs in negligible probability as long as Ξ_2 is a universal$_2$ HPS. More precisely, letting $\mathcal{A}$ query $\mathcal{O}_{\mathsf{Decrypt}}$ for at most q times, we have a upper bound of the probability that $E_\perp$ occurs.*

$$\Pr[E_\perp] \le q \cdot \mathsf{Adv}^{Universal_2} \tag{4}$$

Proof. Let $C = (l, \boldsymbol{C}, \boldsymbol{\pi})$ be a ciphertext submitted to the decryption oracle $\mathcal{O}_{\mathsf{Decrypt}}$.

- Suppose that $(l, \boldsymbol{C}) = (x^*, \boldsymbol{C}^*)$, the adversary $\mathcal{A}$ tries to find a $\boldsymbol{\pi} \ne \boldsymbol{\pi}^*$ such that $\langle \boldsymbol{s}, \boldsymbol{\pi} \rangle = \langle \boldsymbol{s}, \boldsymbol{\pi}^* \rangle$. Let $\hat{\boldsymbol{\pi}} = \boldsymbol{\pi} - \boldsymbol{\pi}^* \ne \boldsymbol{0}$. Since $\boldsymbol{s}$ is independent from $\mathcal{A}$'s view, it is impossible to find a $\hat{\boldsymbol{\pi}}$ such that $\langle \boldsymbol{s}, \hat{\boldsymbol{\pi}} \rangle = 0$.

– Suppose that $(l, C) \neq (x^*, C^*)$, the adversary $\mathcal{A}$ tries to find a π such that $\langle s, \pi \rangle = \Xi_2.\mathsf{Hash}(K_2, (l, C))$. Let $\hat{\pi}_i = \Xi_2.\mathsf{Hash}(\beta_i, (l, C))$. Since

$$\langle s, \pi \rangle = \Xi_2.\mathsf{Hash}(K_2, (l, C)) = \Xi_2.\mathsf{Hash}(\langle s, \beta \rangle, (l, C))$$

$$= \sum_{i=1}^{\eta} s_i \Xi_2.\mathsf{Hash}(\beta_i, (l, C)) = \langle s, \hat{\pi} \rangle$$

and s is independent from $\mathcal{A}$'s view, we have $\langle s, \pi \rangle = \langle s, \hat{\pi} \rangle \iff \pi = \hat{\pi}$. As the scheme allows at most η users (i.e. $\mathcal{A}$ can query $\mathcal{O}_{\mathsf{KeyGen}}$ for at most $\eta - 1$ times), the adversary can get at most $\eta - 1$ pairs of $(s, \langle s, \beta \rangle)$ where all s are linearly independent. In the worst case, the vector β is collapsed into a space of dimension 1 with size $|K'|$ but β is still uniformly distributed over that space. Let $\hat{s} \in \mathbb{Z}_\rho^\eta$ such that $\hat{s}$ is linearly independent with all s obtained by $\mathcal{A}$. Thus $k = \langle \hat{s}, \beta \rangle$ is independent from $\mathcal{A}$'s view and uniformly distributed over K'. If $\mathcal{A}$ find a π such that $\pi = \hat{\pi}$, we immediately have attacked the universal$_2$ property of Ξ_2 that $\langle \hat{s}, \pi \rangle = \Xi_2.\mathsf{Hash}(k, (l, C))$. This completes the proof of Eq. (4).

Lemma 2. *The hidden bit b is independent from $\mathcal{A}$'s view that*

$$\Pr[E_m] = \frac{1}{2} \tag{5}$$

Proof. Thanks to the diversity property of Ξ_1, there exists a $r \in K$ such that $\Xi_1.\mathsf{Hash}(r, x) = \chi$ and $\Xi_1.\mathsf{PKGen}(r) = 0$. Note that we do not need to calculate r. Since $\chi \neq 0$, we have $r \neq 0$. Let $\gamma = r \cdot (y_b - y_{1-b}) \in K^\delta$. Thus we have $\Xi_1.\mathsf{Hash}(\gamma_i, x^*) = (y_{b,i} - y_{1-b,i}) \cdot \Xi_1.\mathsf{Hash}(r, x^*) = y_{b,i}\chi - y_{1-b,i}\chi$. Recall the target ciphertext C^* where $C_i^* = y_{b,i}\chi + \Xi_1.\mathsf{Hash}(\alpha_i, x^*)$. Although C^* is a ciphertext for y_b, it can also be a ciphertext for y_{1-b} that

C_i^*
$$= y_{1-b,i}\chi + \Xi_1.\mathsf{Hash}(\alpha_i + \gamma_i, x^*) = y_{1-b,i}\chi + \Xi_1.\mathsf{Hash}(\alpha_i, x^*) + \Xi_1.\mathsf{Hash}(\gamma_i, x^*)$$
$$= y_{1-b,i}\chi + \Xi_1.\mathsf{Hash}(\alpha_i, x^*) + y_{b,i}\chi - y_{1-b,i}\chi = y_{b,i}\chi + \Xi_1.\mathsf{Hash}(\alpha_i, x^*).$$

Thus C^* is a ciphertext of y_b for α or y_{1-b} for $\alpha + \gamma$ where $\alpha \neq \alpha + \gamma$. Since the adversary $\mathcal{A}$ can only request the secret keys for x such that $\langle x, y_0 \rangle = \langle x, y_1 \rangle$, we have

$$\langle x, \alpha + \gamma \rangle = \langle x, \alpha \rangle + \langle x, \gamma \rangle = \langle x, \alpha \rangle + \langle x, r \cdot (y_b - y_{1-b}) \rangle = \langle x, \alpha \rangle$$

Hence, the adversary $\mathcal{A}$ cannot distinguish α and $\alpha + \gamma$ from generated keys. Since $\mathsf{PKGen}(\alpha_i + \gamma_i) = \mathsf{PKGen}(\alpha_i) + (y_{b,i} - y_{1-b,i}) \cdot \mathsf{PKGen}(r) = \mathsf{PKGen}(\alpha_i)$, the adversary $\mathcal{A}$ cannot distinguish α and $\alpha + \gamma$ from public keys. Therefore, the hidden bit b is independent from $\mathcal{A}$'s view.

Combining Eqs. (3)–(5), we have

$$\left| \Pr[E_{X \setminus L}] - \frac{1}{2} \right| \leq q \cdot \mathsf{Adv}^{\mathsf{Universal}_2}. \tag{6}$$

Combining Eqs. (1), (2) and (6), we have

$$\mathsf{Adv}_{\mathcal{A}}^{\text{IND-CCA}} \leq \mathsf{Adv}_{\mathcal{S}}^{\text{SMP}} + q \cdot \mathsf{Adv}^{\text{Universal}_2}. \tag{7}$$

From Eq. (7), we immediately have the theorem.

5   Instantiation from DDH

Definition 14 (Decisional Diffie-Hellman problem). *Let $\mathbb{G}$ be a cyclic group of prime order p, $a, b \in_R \mathbb{Z}_p$, and $g, T \in_R \mathbb{G}$. Giving two probability distributions $\mathcal{D}_{DDH} = \{(g, g^a, g^b, g^{ab})\}$ and $\mathcal{D}_{rand} = \{(g, g^a, g^b, T)\}$, there is an algorithm $\mathcal{A}$ can distinguish $\mathcal{D}_{DDH}$ and $\mathcal{D}_{rand}$ with advantage:*

$$\mathsf{Adv}_{\mathcal{A}}^{DDH} = |\Pr[1 \leftarrow \mathcal{A}(D \in_R \mathcal{D}_{DDH})] - \Pr[1 \leftarrow \mathcal{A}(D \in_R \mathcal{D}_{rand})]|$$

Let $g_1 = g$ and $g_2 = g^a$. The Decisional Diffie-Hellman (DDH) problem is to distinguish $\mathcal{D}_{DDH} = \{(g_1, g_2, g_1^b, g_2^b)\}$ and $\mathcal{D}_{rand} = \{(g_1, g_2, g_1^b, T)\}$. In other words, the problem is to decide whether $\log_{g_1} X_1 = \log_{g_2} X_2$ where $X_1, X_2 \in \mathbb{G}$. Obviously, the DDH problem is a subset membership problem where $X = \mathbb{G}^2$, $L = (g_1^r, g_2^r) \subset X$ and $r \in \mathbb{Z}_p$. We assume the DDH problem is hard. That is, the advantage $\mathsf{Adv}_{\mathcal{A}}^{DDH}$ is negligible.

We recall the universal projective hash family proposed by Cramer and Shoup [10] derived from a diverse group system based on the DDH problem. The key space is $K = \mathbb{Z}_p^2$. For the hash key $k = (s_1, s_2) \in K$, the projection key generation is $\alpha(k) = g_1^{s_1} g_2^{s_2} \in S = \Pi = \mathbb{G}$. To compute the hash value of $x = (X_1, X_2) \in X = \mathbb{G}^2$ with the hash key k, it computes $H_k(x) = X_1^{s_1} X_2^{s_2} \in \Pi$. To compute the have value of $x = (g_1^w, g_2^w) \in L$ with the projection key $\alpha(k)$ and a witness $w \in W = \mathbb{Z}_p$, it computes $H_k(x) = \alpha(k)^w \in \Pi$.

By applying Construction 2, we obtain a HPS Ξ_1. From Theorems 1–3 and $|\Pi| = |\mathbb{Z}_p| = p$, we have that Ξ_1 has key linearity and hash linearity, and is diverse. To ensure that the underlying group system is diverse, we show the existence of ϕ (or equivalent secret key k). Let $r \in \mathbb{Z}_p^+$ and $k = (r, -r \log_{g_2} g_1)$. For all $x = (g_1^w, g_2^w) \in L$, we have $H_k(x) = (g_1^w)^r (g_2^w)^{-r \log_{g_2} g_1} = g_1^0$. For all $x = (g_1^{w_1}, g_2^{w_2}) \in X \setminus L$, we have $H_k(x) = (g_1^{w_1})^r (g_2^{w_2})^{-r \log_{g_2} g_1} = g_1^{r(w_1-w_2)}$. To simplify our instantiation, we choose $r = 1$ and $x = (g_1^2, g_2)$, and computes $\chi = \Xi_1.\mathsf{Hash}(k, x) = g_1$. By applying Constructions 2 and 3 we obtain another HPS Ξ_2, which is universal$_2$. From Theorem 2, we have that Ξ_2 has hash linearity. Note that we use a collision resistant hash function (CRHF) $H : \mathbb{G}^2 \times \mathbb{G}^\delta \to \mathbb{Z}_p$ instead of an injective map Γ when applying Construction 3.

With Ξ_1 and Ξ_2, we apply Construction 4 to construct a functional encryption scheme for the inner product functionality $F : \mathbb{Z}_p^\delta \times \mathbb{Z}_p^\delta \to \mathbb{Z}_p$.

Construction 5. *Our instantiation works as follows.*

- $(\mathsf{PK}, \mathsf{MSK}) \leftarrow \mathsf{Setup}(1^\lambda, 1^\delta, 1^\eta)$:

$$H : \mathbb{G}^2 \times \mathbb{G}^\delta \to \mathbb{Z}_p, \quad g_1, g_2 \in_R \mathbb{G}.$$
$$\text{For } i = 1 \ldots \delta, \quad \alpha_i = (\alpha_{i,1}, \alpha_{i,2}) \in_R \mathbb{Z}_p^2, \quad A_i = g_1^{\alpha_{i,1}} g_2^{\alpha_{i,2}}.$$
$$\text{For } i = 1 \ldots \eta, \quad \beta_i = (\beta_{i,1}, \beta_{i,2}, \beta_{i,3}, \beta_{i,4}) \in_R \mathbb{Z}_p^4,$$
$$B_i = (B_{i,1}, B_{i,2}) = (g_1^{\beta_{i,1}} g_2^{\beta_{i,2}}, g_1^{\beta_{i,3}} g_2^{\beta_{i,4}}).$$

return $(\mathsf{PK}, \mathsf{MSK}) = ((\boldsymbol{A}, \boldsymbol{B}), (\boldsymbol{\alpha}, \boldsymbol{\beta}))$.

- $\mathsf{SK} \leftarrow \mathsf{KeyGen}(\mathsf{MSK}, \boldsymbol{x})$:

$$\boldsymbol{s} \in_R \mathbb{Z}_p^\eta, \quad K_1 = (K_{1,1}, K_{1,2}) = \left(\sum_{i=1}^{\delta} x_i \alpha_{i,1}, \sum_{i=1}^{\delta} x_i \alpha_{i,2} \right)$$

$$K_2 = (K_{2,1}, K_{2,2}, K_{2,3}, K_{2,4}) = \left(\sum_{i=1}^{\eta} s_i \beta_{i,1}, \sum_{i=1}^{\eta} s_i \beta_{i,2}, \sum_{i=1}^{\eta} s_i \beta_{i,3}, \sum_{i=1}^{\eta} s_i \beta_{i,4} \right)$$

return $\mathsf{SK} = (\boldsymbol{x}, \boldsymbol{s}, K_1, K_2)$.

- $C \leftarrow \mathsf{Encrypt}(\mathsf{PK}, \boldsymbol{y})$:

$$r \in_R \mathbb{Z}_p, \quad l = (u_1, u_2) = (g_1^r, g_2^r), \quad \text{For } i = 1 \ldots \delta, \quad C_i = g_1^{y_i} \cdot A_i^r$$
$$h = H(u_1, u_2, C_1, \ldots, C_\delta), \quad \text{For } i = 1 \ldots \eta, \quad \pi_i = (B_{i,1} \cdot B_{i,2}^h)^r$$

return $C = (l, \boldsymbol{C}, \boldsymbol{\pi})$.

- $D \leftarrow \mathsf{Decrypt}(\mathsf{SK}, C)$:

$$h = H(u_1, u_2, C_1, \ldots, C_\delta),$$

$$\prod_{i=1}^{\eta} \pi_i^{s_i} \stackrel{?}{=} u_1^{K_{2,1} + h \cdot K_{2,3}} u_2^{K_{2,2} + h \cdot K_{2,4}}, \quad D^* = \frac{\prod_{i=1}^{\delta} C_i^{x_i}}{u_1^{K_{1,1}} u_2^{K_{1,2}}}$$

return $D = \log_{g_1} D^*$.

As mentioned in Sect. 4.2, we can decrypt D in an alternative manner instead of calculating $\log_{g_1} D^*$ if $|\{D\}|$ is polynomial-sized.

6 Conclusion

In this paper, we reviewed the hash proof system (HPS) introduced by [10] and defined new properties of HPS. We found that the existing HPS constructions by [10] have those new properties. As the main contribution of this paper, we proposed an IND-CCA secure functional encryption for inner products, which can be generically constructed from a diverse HPS with key linearity and hash linearity, and a universal$_2$ HPS with hash linearity. Moreover, we constructed a concrete scheme from DDH assumption via our proposed generic construction.

One of our future work will be relaxing the scheme without limiting the number of user who can decrypt. Another future work will be finding new HPS, which has our defined properties, from other subset membership problems so that we can construct new functional encryption schemes under new assumptions.

References

1. Abdalla, M., Bourse, F., Caro, A.D., Pointcheval, D.: Better security for functional encryption for inner product evaluations. Cryptology ePrint Archive, Report 2016/011 (2016). http://eprint.iacr.org/
2. Abdalla, M., Bourse, F., Caro, A., Pointcheval, D.: Simple functional encryption schemes for inner products. In: Katz, J. (ed.) PKC 2015. LNCS, vol. 9020, pp. 733–751. Springer, Heidelberg (2015). doi:10.1007/978-3-662-46447-2_33
3. Agrawal, S., Libert, B., Stehlé, D.: Fully secure functional encryption for inner products, from standard assumptions. In: Robshaw, M., Katz, J. (eds.) CRYPTO 2016. LNCS, vol. 9816, pp. 333–362. Springer, Heidelberg (2016). doi:10.1007/978-3-662-53015-3_12
4. Bishop, A., Jain, A., Kowalczyk, L.: Function-hiding inner product encryption. In: Iwata, T., Cheon, J.H. (eds.) ASIACRYPT 2015. LNCS, vol. 9452, pp. 470–491. Springer, Heidelberg (2015). doi:10.1007/978-3-662-48797-6_20
5. Boneh, D., Crescenzo, G., Ostrovsky, R., Persiano, G.: Public key encryption with keyword search. In: Cachin, C., Camenisch, J.L. (eds.) EUROCRYPT 2004. LNCS, vol. 3027, pp. 506–522. Springer, Heidelberg (2004). doi:10.1007/978-3-540-24676-3_30
6. Boneh, D., Franklin, M.: Identity-based encryption from the weil pairing. In: Kilian, J. (ed.) CRYPTO 2001. LNCS, vol. 2139, pp. 213–229. Springer, Heidelberg (2001). doi:10.1007/3-540-44647-8_13
7. Boneh, D., Sahai, A., Waters, B.: Functional encryption: definitions and challenges. In: Ishai, Y. (ed.) TCC 2011. LNCS, vol. 6597, pp. 253–273. Springer, Heidelberg (2011). doi:10.1007/978-3-642-19571-6_16
8. Boneh, D., Waters, B.: Conjunctive, subset, and range queries on encrypted data. In: Vadhan, S.P. (ed.) TCC 2007. LNCS, vol. 4392, pp. 535–554. Springer, Heidelberg (2007). doi:10.1007/978-3-540-70936-7_29
9. Cramer, R., Shoup, V.: A practical public key cryptosystem provably secure against adaptive chosen ciphertext attack. In: Krawczyk, H. (ed.) CRYPTO 1998. LNCS, vol. 1462, pp. 13–25. Springer, Heidelberg (1998). doi:10.1007/BFb0055717
10. Cramer, R., Shoup, V.: Universal hash proofs and a paradigm for adaptive chosen ciphertext secure public-key encryption. In: Knudsen, L.R. (ed.) EUROCRYPT 2002. LNCS, vol. 2332, pp. 45–64. Springer, Heidelberg (2002). doi:10.1007/3-540-46035-7_4
11. Goldwasser, S., Gordon, S.D., Goyal, V., Jain, A., Katz, J., Liu, F.-H., Sahai, A., Shi, E., Zhou, H.-S.: Multi-input functional encryption. In: Nguyen, P.Q., Oswald, E. (eds.) EUROCRYPT 2014. LNCS, vol. 8441, pp. 578–602. Springer, Heidelberg (2014). doi:10.1007/978-3-642-55220-5_32
12. Goldwasser, S., Kalai, Y., Popa, R.A., Vaikuntanathan, V., Zeldovich, N.: Reusable garbled circuits and succinct functional encryption. In: Proceedings of the Forty-Fifth Annual ACM Symposium on Theory of Computing, pp. 555–564 (2013)
13. Katz, J., Sahai, A., Waters, B.: Predicate encryption supporting disjunctions, polynomial equations, and inner products. In: Smart, N. (ed.) EUROCRYPT 2008. LNCS, vol. 4965, pp. 146–162. Springer, Heidelberg (2008). doi:10.1007/978-3-540-78967-3_9
14. Lewko, A., Okamoto, T., Sahai, A., Takashima, K., Waters, B.: Fully secure functional encryption: attribute-based encryption and (hierarchical) inner product encryption. In: Gilbert, H. (ed.) EUROCRYPT 2010. LNCS, vol. 6110, pp. 62–91. Springer, Heidelberg (2010). doi:10.1007/978-3-642-13190-5_4

15. Okamoto, T., Takashima, K.: Fully secure unbounded inner-product and attribute-based encryption. In: Wang, X., Sako, K. (eds.) ASIACRYPT 2012. LNCS, vol. 7658, pp. 349–366. Springer, Heidelberg (2012). doi:10.1007/978-3-642-34961-4_22
16. O'Neill, A.: Definitional issues in functional encryption. Cryptology ePrint Archive, Report 2010/556 (2010). http://eprint.iacr.org/
17. Rackoff, C., Simon, D.R.: Non-interactive zero-knowledge proof of knowledge and chosen ciphertext attack. In: Feigenbaum, J. (ed.) CRYPTO 1991. LNCS, vol. 576, pp. 433–444. Springer, Heidelberg (1992). doi:10.1007/3-540-46766-1_35
18. Sahai, A., Waters, B.: Fuzzy identity-based encryption. In: Cramer, R. (ed.) EUROCRYPT 2005. LNCS, vol. 3494, pp. 457–473. Springer, Heidelberg (2005). doi:10.1007/11426639_27
19. Waters, B.: Functional encryption for regular languages. In: Safavi-Naini, R., Canetti, R. (eds.) CRYPTO 2012. LNCS, vol. 7417, pp. 218–235. Springer, Heidelberg (2012). doi:10.1007/978-3-642-32009-5_14

An Improved Analysis on Three Variants of the RSA Cryptosystem

Liqiang Peng[1,2], Lei Hu[1,2], Yao Lu[3(✉)], and Hongyun Wei[4]

[1] State Key Laboratory of Information Security,
Institute of Information Engineering, Chinese Academy of Sciences,
Beijing 100093, China
pengliqiang@iie.ac.cn, hu@is.ac.cn
[2] Data Assurance and Communication Security Research Center,
Chinese Academy of Sciences, Beijing 100093, China
[3] The University of Tokyo, Tokyo, Japan
lywhhit@gmail.com
[4] Department of Cyber Security and Law Enforcement,
Peoples Public Security University of China, Beijing, China

Abstract. Recently, Bunder, Nitaj, Susilo and Tonien utilized the continued fraction method to solve for the unknowns of a modular equation which has been applied in three variants of RSA cryptosystem, where the modular equation can be expressed as $ed \equiv 1 \bmod (p^2 - 1)(q^2 - 1)$ and $N = pq$ is an RSA modulus. According to their work, when the private key $d \simeq N^\delta$ satisfies that $\delta < \frac{3-\alpha}{2}$ for $\alpha \geq 1$, where $e \simeq N^\alpha$, the modulus N can be factored in polynomial time. In this paper, we revisit their work and improve the previous bound to $\delta < 2 - \sqrt{\alpha}$ for $\alpha \geq 1$. More specifically, by utilizing Coppersmith's method to solve for the unknowns of a modular equation and using unravelled linearization technique in the lattice construction, we can successfully improve their result. Our attack are verified by experiments.

Keywords: RSA · Cryptanalysis · Coppersmith's method

1 Introduction

In 1978, the RSA scheme, a new method to efficiently realize digital signature and authentication in data transmission was put forwarded by Rivest, Shamir and Adleman [16]. Due to its simplicity and efficiency, the RSA scheme has become the most popular public key cryptosystem and also has been widely used in practical applications since its concept was proposed. The key generation algorithm of the original RSA scheme can be described as follows:

Key Generation of RSA: For an RSA modulus $N = pq$, where p and q are primes of the same bitlength. Randomly choose an integer e such that $\gcd(e, \varphi(N)) = 1$, where $\varphi(N) = (p - 1)(q - 1)$ and calculate d such that $ed \equiv 1 \,(\bmod \varphi(N))$ by the Extended Euclidean Algorithm. The public key is (N, e) and the private key is (p, q, d).

© Springer International Publishing AG 2017
K. Chen et al. (Eds.): Inscrypt 2016, LNCS 10143, pp. 140–149, 2017.
DOI: 10.1007/978-3-319-54705-3_9

In addition, several variants of RSA have been proposed to obtain higher efficiency or security, like CRT-RSA [20], Prime Power RSA [19] and so on. Because of the widespread application, the security of the RSA scheme and its variants is one of important hot spots of cryptanalysis.

Small Private Exponent Attacks on RSA: In 1990, Wiener [20] utilized the continued fraction method to show that the original RSA scheme can be broken when the private key d is smaller than $N^{0.25}$. Later, Boneh and Durfee [1] used latticed based Coppersmith's method [5] which can solve for small root of integer or modular equation in polynomial time to improve the previous bound to $N^{0.292}$. Then, Herrmann and May [7] used unravelled linearization technique in the lattice construction to simplify the Boneh-Durfee's proof and obtained same bound as [1]. Along this direction, for the variants of RSA scheme, there are also many attacks [10,13,14,17] are proposed under small private exponents.

1.1   Background

In 1995, Kuwakado, Koyama and Tsuruoka [11] proposed a system based on singular cubic curves with equation modular $y^2 \equiv x^3 + bx^2 \pmod{N}$, where N is an RSA-type modulus. Compared with the original RSA scheme and its variants, the public key e and private key d of Kuwakado-Koyama-Tsuruoka scheme satisfy $ed \equiv 1 \pmod{(p^2 - 1)(q^2 - 1)}$. Later, in 2002, Elkamchouchi, Elshenawy and Shaban [6] extended the RSA scheme to the ring of Gaussian integers. Similarly, as the Kuwakado-Koyama-Tsuruoka scheme [11], the public key e and the private d of Elkamchouchi-Elshenawy-Shaban scheme [6] also satisfy $ed \equiv 1 \pmod{(p^2 - 1)(q^2 - 1)}$. Moreover, a probabilistic scheme based on the RSA scheme which was proposed by Castagnos [4] includes the same modular equation as [4,6]. Therefore, how to solve for the unknowns d, p, q from the modular equation $ed \equiv 1 \pmod{(p^2 - 1)(q^2 - 1)}$ is a question that is worth studying.

Recently, Bunder, Nitaj, Susilo and Tonien [3] utilized the continued fraction method to propose small private key attack on the above three schemes [4,6,11] and obtained the following theorem:

Theorem 1. *Let (N, e) be a public key in the Kuwakado-Koyama-Tsuruoka cryptosystem or in the RSA cryptosystem with Gaussian integer or in the Castagnos scheme with $N = pq$ and $q < p < 2q$. If $e < (p^2 - 1)(q^2 - 1)$ satisfies an equation $ed - k(p^2 - 1)(q^2 - 1) = 1$ with*

$$d < \sqrt{\frac{2N^3 - 18N^2}{e}},$$

then one can factor N in polynomial time.

Note that, for the above theorem, we assume that e, d have the roughly same bit-size as N^α and N^δ respectively, where $0 < \alpha, \delta < 2$. Then the result of Theorem 1 can be rewritten as

$$d < N^{\frac{3-\alpha}{2}},$$

or equivalently,

$$\delta < \frac{3-\alpha}{2},$$

neglecting any small constant since N is relatively large.

Moreover, we have that $ed \geq N^2$, otherwise, we have that

$$0 < 1 = ed - k(p^2 - 1)(q^2 - 1) < N^2 - kN^2 + k(p^2 + q^2 - 1).$$

Then since $q < p < 2q$, we have $p^2 + q^2 - 1 < N(\frac{p}{q} + \frac{q}{p}) < 3N$. Then the above inequation becomes $(k-1)N < 3k$ which contradicts the assumption N is a relatively large RSA modulus. Hence, for more accuracy, another condition $ed \geq N^2$ should be added in Bunder et al.'s theorem, so one can obtain that

$$N^2 d \leq ed^2 < 2N^3 - 18N^2 < 2N^3$$

which means their result should be written as

$$d < \sqrt{\frac{2N^3 - 18N^2}{e}}, \text{ for } e > \frac{N}{2},$$

or equivalently,

$$\delta < \frac{3-\alpha}{2}, \text{ for } \alpha \geq 1.$$

When $e \leq \frac{N}{2}$, namely $\alpha < 1$, one can not obtain Bunder et al.'s theorem.

1.2   Our Result

In this paper, we reconsider the small private key attack on the variants of RSA cryptosystem [4, 6, 11] and improve Bunder et al.'s work [3] to

$$\delta < 2 - \sqrt{\alpha},$$

where $\alpha \geq 1$.

More specifically, since e and d satisfy an equation $ed - k(p^2 - 1)(q^2 - 1) = 1$, the problem can be transformed into solving for the small solutions of modular equation $k(p^2 - 1)(q^2 - 1) + 1 \equiv 0 \mod e$. By utilizing Coppersmith's method to select polynomials and using unravelled linearization technique to simplify the lattice construction, we finally improve Bunder et al.'s result. For comparison with the previous work [3], an explicit picture on our improvement is illustrated in Fig. 1.

The rest of this paper is organized as follows. Section 2 is the preliminary knowledge on lattice and Coppersmith's method. Section 3 presents an improved analysis of Bunder et al.'s result [3]. Finally, Sect. 4 is the conclusion.

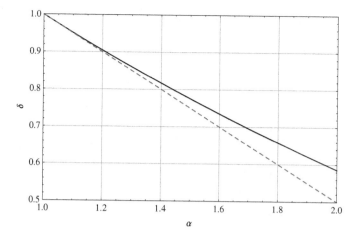

Fig. 1. Comparison on the ranges of δ with respect to α. Here the dashed line denotes the lower bound on δ in [3] and the thin solid line denotes that in this paper.

2   Preliminaries on Lattice

Let $\mathcal{L}$ be a lattice which is spanned by k linear independent vectors $w_1, w_2, \cdots, w_k \in \mathbb{R}^n$. The lattice $\mathcal{L}$ can be represented as $c_1 w_1 + \cdots + c_k w_k$, where $c_1, \cdots, c_k \in \mathbb{Z}$, which means $\mathcal{L}$ is the set of all integer linear combinations of $w_1, \cdots, w_k$. The set of vectors $w_1, \cdots, w_k$ is called as a lattice basis of $\mathcal{L}$ and k is the dimension of $\mathcal{L}$. Moreover, when the dimension of lattice is greater than 1, the lattice basis is not unique, one can obtain another lattice basis by a simple multiplication with some integral matrix with determinant ± 1, it means that any lattice of dimension larger than 1 has infinitely many bases. Hence, same with searching for the shortest vector of a lattice, how to obtain a lattice basis with good properties is also an important issue in the study of lattice. More details about lattice and related problems can be referred to [15].

In [12], Lenstra et al. proposed the famous L^3 lattice basis reduction algorithm. Based on their algorithm, for any lattice, one can always obtain a relatively short and nearly orthogonal lattice basis in polynomial time. More specifically, the L^3 lattice basis reduction algorithm can be described as follows:

Lemma 1. (L^3, [12]) Let $\mathcal{L}$ be a lattice of dimension k. Applying the L^3 algorithm to $\mathcal{L}$, the outputted reduced basis vectors $v_1, \cdots, v_k$ satisfy that

$$\|v_i\| \leq 2^{\frac{k(k-i)}{4(k+1-i)}} \det(\mathcal{L})^{\frac{1}{k+1-i}}, \text{ for any } 1 \leq i \leq k.$$

Coppersmith's method: Since the appearance of the L^3 lattice basis reduction algorithm, with restriction of the length of lattice basis, more and more researchers has begun to utilize lattice as a tool in the cryptanalysis. In 1996, Coppersmith applied the L^3 lattice basis reduction algorithm to find small root of univariate modular equations and bivariate equations [5] and this technique is now usually called as Coppersmith's method. Later, Jochemsz and May extended Coppersmith's method and gave a general strategy to solve for the small root of multivariate polynomials [9]. Since then, the Coppersmith's method has become an important technique in cryptanalysis of RSA scheme and its variants [1,10,13,14,17,18].

Note that, the following lemma due to Howgrave-Graham [8] gives a sufficient condition under which root of a modular equation also satisfy an integer equation. Note that, for a given polynomial $g(x_1, \cdots, x_k) = \sum\limits_{(i_1, \cdots, i_k)} a_{i_1, \cdots, i_k} x_1^{i_1} \cdots x_k^{i_k}$, we define the norm of g as

$$\|g(x_1, \cdots, x_k)\| = \left(\sum_{(i_1, \cdots, i_k)} a_{i_1, \cdots, i_k}^2 \right)^{\frac{1}{2}}.$$

Lemma 2. *(Howgrave-Graham, [8]) Let $g(x_1, \cdots, x_k) \in \mathbb{Z}[x_1, \cdots, x_k]$ be an integer polynomial with at most w monomials. Suppose that*

$$g(y_1, \cdots, y_k) \equiv 0 \pmod{p^m} \text{ for } |y_1| \leq X_1, \cdots, |y_k| \leq X_k, \text{ and}$$

$$\|g(x_1 X_1, \cdots, x_k X_k)\| < \frac{p^m}{\sqrt{w}}.$$

Then $g(y_1, \cdots, y_k) = 0$ holds over the integers.

According to the above Lemmas 1 and 2, we can give a brief description of Coppersmith's method. For a modular equation

$$f(x_1, \cdots, x_n) \equiv 0 \bmod p,$$

where $(y_1, \cdots, y_n)$ is the desired root. Firstly, we choose polynomials $h_i(x_1, \cdots, x_n)$ as many as possible and all the selected polynomials have the same root $(y_1, \cdots, y_n)$ modulo p^m, where m is an integer. Then we construct a lattice $\mathcal{L}$ whose row vectors correspond to the coefficients of the selected polynomials $h_i(x_1 X_1, \cdots, x_n X_n)$, where $|y_1| \leq X_1, \cdots, |y_n| \leq X_n$. For the convenience of the calculation of determinant of the constructed lattice, we usually select polynomials to make the lattice basis triangular. Then by applying L^3 lattice basis reduction algorithm to the lattice $\mathcal{L}$, we can obtain n polynomials $v_1(x_1, \ldots, x_n), \cdots, v_n(x_1, \ldots, x_n)$ corresponding to the first n reduced basis vectors with sufficiently small norm. Based on Lemma 1, we have that

$$\|v_1(x_1 X_1, \ldots, x_n X_n)\| \leq \cdots \leq \|v_n(x_1 X_1, \ldots, x_n X_n)\| \leq 2^{\frac{k(k-1)}{4(k+1-n)}} \det(\mathcal{L})^{\frac{1}{k+1-n}},$$

where k is the dimension of $\mathcal{L}$.

Moreover, since the obtained polynomials $v_1(x_1, \ldots, x_n), \ldots, v_n(x_1, \ldots, x_n)$ are some integer combinations of the polynomials $h_i(x_1, \cdots, x_n)$, $v_1(x_1, \ldots, x_n), \ldots, v_n(x_1, \ldots, x_n)$ have the same root $(y_1, \cdots, y_n)$ modulo p^m.

Then if the norm of $v_1(x_1, \ldots, x_n), \ldots, v_n(x_1, \ldots, x_n)$ satisfy the second condition of Lemma 2, namely if

$$2^{\frac{k(k-1)}{4(k+1-n)}} \det(\mathcal{L})^{\frac{1}{k+1-n}} < \frac{p^m}{\sqrt{k}},$$

we have that $v_1(y_1, \cdots, y_n) = 0, \ldots, v_n(y_1, \cdots, y_n) = 0$ hold over the integers.

Similarly as other lattice-based attacks, we ignore small terms that do not depend on p since p is relatively large, and only check whether $\det(\mathcal{L}) < p^{mk}$ does hold or not.

Then based on the following heuristic assumption, we can solve for the root $y_1, \cdots, y_n$ from the polynomials $v_1(y_1, \cdots, y_n) = 0, \ldots, v_n(y_1, \cdots, y_n) = 0$. In practical experiments, the following heuristic assumption usually holds. For the experiments in this paper, we always successfully collected the roots by using Gröbner basis technique and there was no experimental result to contradict this assumption. However, it seems very difficult to prove or demonstrate its validity.

Assumption 1. *Our lattice-based method yields algebraically independent polynomials. The common solutions of these polynomials can be efficiently computed by using numerical or symbolic methods.*

3   Our Improvement

In this section, we use Coppersmith's method to improve previous result and obtain the following theorem.

Theorem 2. *Let (N, e) be a public key in the Kuwakado-Koyama-Tsuruoka cryptosystem or in the RSA cryptosystem with Gaussian integer or in the Castagnos scheme with $N = pq$ and $q < p < 2q$. Let e be the public key and d be the private key. Assume that e and d have the roughly same bit-size as N^α and N^δ, respectively, where $0 < \alpha, \delta < 2$. Then under Assumption 1, one can factor N in polynomial time when*

$$\delta < 2 - \sqrt{\alpha}, \text{ for } \alpha \geq 1.$$

Proof. Since $ed = k(p^2 - 1)(q^2 - 1) + 1 = k(N^2 - p^2 - q^2 + 1) + 1$, for the unknowns $(k, p^2 + q^2)$, we have the following modular equation,

$$f(x, y) = x(N^2 - y) + 1. \tag{1}$$

Then following the Herrmann and May's [7] analysis, we use linearization $u = -xy + 1$ and the Eq. (1) can be transformed into

$$\hat{f}(x, u) = N^2 x + u.$$

In order to recover the unknowns, we select polynomials as follows:

$$g_{i,k}(u, x, y) = x^i \hat{f}^k(x, u) e^{m-k}, \text{ for } k = 0, \cdots, m, \text{ and } i = 0, \cdots, m - k,$$

and

$$h_{j,k}(u,x,y) = y^j \hat{f}^k(x,u)e^{m-k}, \text{for } j = 1, \cdots, t, \text{and } k = \lfloor \frac{m}{t} \rfloor j, \cdots, m.$$

where m and t are integers which will be chosen later, and each occurrence of monomial xy is replaced by $-u + 1$. Below we let $t \le m$ and $\tau = \frac{t}{m} \in [0,1]$.

Obviously, all the above polynomials have the same root which are desired unknowns $(-k(p^2+q^2)+1, k, p^2+q^2)$ modulo e^m and the solutions can be roughly estimated by $|k| \simeq X(:= N^{\alpha+\delta-2})$, $|p^2+q^2| \simeq Y(:= N)$ and $|-k(p^2+q^2)+1| \simeq U(:= XY = N^{\alpha+\delta-1})$, neglecting any small constant because N is relatively large.

Then we construct a matrix, whose row vectors are the coefficient vectors of $g_{i,k}(uU, xX, yY)$ and $h_{j,k}(uU, xX, yY)$ with respect to the monomials on u, x, y. It is easy to check that it is a triangular matrix, and its diagonal entries are

$$U^k X^i e^{m-k}, \text{ for } k = 0, \cdots, m, \text{and } i = 0, \cdots, m-k,$$

and

$$U^k Y^j e^{m-k}, \text{ for } j = 1, \cdots, t, \text{and } k = \lfloor \frac{m}{t} \rfloor j, \cdots, m.$$

Let the row vectors of this matrix span a lattice $\mathcal{L}$.

By construction, its determinant can be easily determined as

$$\det(\mathcal{L}) = U^{S_u} X^{S_x} Y^{S_y} e^{S_e},$$

where the exponents S_u, S_x, S_y, S_N are calculated as follows:

$$S_u = \sum_{k=0}^{m} \sum_{i=0}^{m-k} k + \sum_{j=1}^{t} \sum_{k=\lfloor \frac{m}{t} \rfloor j}^{m} k = (\frac{1}{6} + \frac{\tau}{3})m^3 + o(m^3),$$

$$S_x = \sum_{k=0}^{m} \sum_{i=0}^{m-k} i = \frac{1}{6}m^3 + o(m^3),$$

$$S_y = \sum_{j=1}^{t} \sum_{k=\lfloor \frac{m}{t} \rfloor j}^{m} j = \frac{\tau^2}{6}m^3 + o(m^3),$$

$$S_e = \sum_{k=0}^{m} \sum_{i=0}^{m-k} (m-k) + \sum_{j=1}^{t} \sum_{k=\lfloor \frac{m}{t} \rfloor j}^{m} (m-k) = (\frac{1}{3} + \frac{\tau}{6})m^3 + o(m^3).$$

On the other hand, the dimension of $\mathcal{L}$ is,

$$\dim(\mathcal{L}) = \sum_{k=0}^{m} \sum_{i=0}^{m-k} 1 + \sum_{j=1}^{t} \sum_{k=\lfloor \frac{m}{t} \rfloor j}^{m} 1 = \frac{1+\tau}{2}m^2 + o(m^2).$$

According to Lemmas 1 and 2, one can use the L^3 lattice basis reduction algorithm to $\mathcal{L}$ and obtain polynomial equations which share the root $(-k(p^2+q^2)+1, k, p^2+q^2)$ over integers if

$$\det(\mathcal{L}) < e^{m \dim(\mathcal{L})},$$

or equivalently,

$$U^{(\frac{1}{6}+\frac{\tau}{3})m^3+o(m^3)}X^{\frac{1}{6}m^3+o(m^3)}Y^{\frac{\tau^2}{6}m^3+o(m^3)}e^{(\frac{1}{3}+\frac{\tau}{6})m^3+o(m^3)} < e^{\frac{1+\tau}{2}m^3+o(m^3)}.$$

To obtain an asymptotic bound, we assume m goes to infinite and ignore the small terms $o(m^3)$. Putting the bounds U, X, Y into the above inequality, we obtain that

$$(\frac{1}{6}+\frac{\tau}{3})(\alpha+\delta-1)+\frac{1}{6}(\alpha+\delta-2)+\frac{\tau^2}{6}+(\frac{1}{3}+\frac{\tau}{6})\alpha < \frac{1+\tau}{2}\alpha.$$

Then the inequation becomes

$$\delta < \frac{3-\alpha+2\tau-\tau^2}{2+2\tau}.$$

When $\alpha \geq 1$, we set the parameter $\tau = \sqrt{\alpha}-1$, and obtain the bound $\delta < 2-\sqrt{\alpha}$.

When $\alpha < 1$, we set the parameter $\tau = 0$, and obtain the bound $\delta < \frac{3-\alpha}{2}$. Moreover, since $ed - k(p^2-1)(q^2-1) = 1$, we have that $ed > N^2$, namely, $\alpha+\delta > 1$, which contradicts our conditions $\alpha < 1$ and $\delta < \frac{3-\alpha}{2}$.

In a conclusion, we obtain the following bound on δ:

$$\delta < 2-\sqrt{\alpha}, \text{ for } \alpha \geq 1.$$

Then we can obtain several polynomial equations which share the root $(-k(p^2+q^2)+1, k, p^2+q^2)$ over integers. Under Assumption 1, we can successfully collect the desired solutions. This concludes the proof of our theorem.

Experimental Results. We have implemented the experiment program in Magma 2.11 computer algebra system [2] on a PC with Intel(R) Core(TM) CPU(3.30 GHz, 4.0 GB RAM Windows 7). In all experiments, we obtained several integer polynomials which satisfied the Howgrave-Graham's Lemma and successfully solved for the desired solutions $(-k(p^2+q^2)+1, k, p^2+q^2)$ over $\mathbb{Z}$ by using Gröbner basis of these polynomials. In [3], Bunder et al. presented an example to proof their method. For the 92-bit RSA modulus,

$$N = 2617939220553315302745462091,$$

Bunder et al. successfully recovered the 41-bit private key. Namely, the 92-bit RSA modulus can be factored in polynomial time by Bunder et al.'s method, when the bitlength of private key d is smaller than 41. Based on our method, for the same RSA modulus as Bunder et al.'s example, we construct a 60-dimensional lattice with parameters $m = 8, t = 3$ and successfully factor the RSA modulus when the bitlength of private key d is smaller than 48.

The following Table 1 lists some theoretical and experimental results on factoring RSA moduli with small private key d, where the bitlength of public key e is roughly same as N^2.

Table 1. Theoretical and experimental results of small private key attack on variants of RSA cryptosystem

Bitsize of N, i.e., $\log_2 N$	The theoretical value of $\log_2 d$ [3]	The value of $\log_2 d$ (Sect. 3)			
		theo.	expt.	$(m, t, \dim(\mathcal{L}))$	time of L^3(in sec.)
1000	500	585	537	(6,2,33)	45.630
1500	750	878	808	(6,2,33)	113.584
2000	1000	1171	1077	(6,2,33)	212.037

4 Conclusion

In this paper, we revisited the problem of Bunder et al.'s small private key attack on three variants of RSA cryptosystem, where the private key d and public key e satisfy $ed \equiv 1 \bmod (p^2-1)(q^2-1)$. By utilizing Coppersmith's method, we firstly transform the problem into solving for the unknowns of a modular equation and selected polynomials that have the same desired root. Then we use unravelled linearization technique to construct lattice which is composed of the selected polynomials and obtain integer equations by L^3 lattice basis reduction algorithm. Finally, we can successfully improve both theoretical bound and experimental result.

Acknowledgements. The authors would like to thank anonymous reviewers for their helpful comments and suggestions. The work of this paper was supported by the National Key Basic Research Program of China (Grants 2013CB834203 and 2011CB302400), the National Natural Science Foundation of China (Grants 61472417, 61402469, 61472416, 61502488 and 61272478), the Strategic Priority Research Program of Chinese Academy of Sciences under Grant XDA06010702 and XDA06010703, and the State Key Laboratory of Information Security, Chinese Academy of Sciences. Y. Lu is supported by Project CREST, JST.

References

1. Boneh, D., Durfee, G.: Cryptanalysis of RSA with private key d less than $N^{0.292}$. IEEE Trans. Inf. Theory **46**(4), 1339–1349 (2000)
2. Bosma, W., Cannon, J.J., Playoust, C.: The magma algebra system I: the user language. J. Symbolic Comput. **24**(3–4), 235–265 (1997)
3. Bunder, M., Nitaj, A., Susilo, W., Tonien, J.: A new attack on three variants of the RSA cryptosystem. In: Liu, J.K., Steinfeld, R. (eds.) ACISP 2016. LNCS, vol. 9723, pp. 258–268. Springer, Cham (2016). doi:10.1007/978-3-319-40367-0_16
4. Castagnos, G.: An efficient probabilistic public-key cryptosystem over quadratic fields quotients. Finite Fields Appl. **13**(3), 563–576 (2007)
5. Coppersmith, D.: Small solutions to polynomial equations, and low exponent RSA vulnerabilities. J. Cryptology **10**(4), 233–260 (1997)
6. Elkamchouchi, H., Elshenawy, K., Shaban, H.: Extended RSA cryptosystem and digital signature schemes in the domain of gaussian integers. In: The International Conference on Communication Systems, vol. 1, pp. 91–95 (2002)

7. Herrmann, M., May, A.: Maximizing small root bounds by linearization and applications to small secret exponent RSA. In: Nguyen, P.Q., Pointcheval, D. (eds.) PKC 2010. LNCS, vol. 6056, pp. 53–69. Springer, Heidelberg (2010). doi:10.1007/978-3-642-13013-7_4

8. Howgrave-Graham, N.: Finding small roots of univariate modular equations revisited. In: Darnell, M. (ed.) Cryptography and Coding 1997. LNCS, vol. 1355, pp. 131–142. Springer, Heidelberg (1997). doi:10.1007/BFb0024458

9. Jochemsz, E., May, A.: A strategy for finding roots of multivariate polynomials with new applications in attacking RSA variants. In: Lai, X., Chen, K. (eds.) ASIACRYPT 2006. LNCS, vol. 4284, pp. 267–282. Springer, Heidelberg (2006). doi:10.1007/11935230_18

10. Jochemsz, E., May, A.: A polynomial time attack on RSA with private CRT-exponents smaller than $N^{0.073}$. In: Menezes, A. (ed.) CRYPTO 2007. LNCS, vol. 4622, pp. 395–411. Springer, Heidelberg (2007). doi:10.1007/978-3-540-74143-5_22

11. Kuwakado, H., Koyama, K., Tsuruoka, Y.: A new RSA-type scheme based on singular cubic curves $y^2 \equiv x^3 + bx^2$ (n). IEICE Trans. Fundam. Electron. Commun. Comput. Sci. **78**(1), 27–33 (1995)

12. Lenstra, A.K., Lenstra, H.W., Lovász, L.: Factoring polynomials with rational coefficients. Math. Ann. **261**(4), 515–534 (1982)

13. Lu, Y., Zhang, R., Peng, L., Lin, D.: Solving linear equations modulo unknown divisors: revisited. In: Iwata, T., Cheon, J.H. (eds.) ASIACRYPT 2015. LNCS, vol. 9452, pp. 189–213. Springer, Heidelberg (2015). doi:10.1007/978-3-662-48797-6_9

14. May, A.: Secret exponent attacks on RSA-type schemes with moduli $N=p^r q$. In: Bao, F., Deng, R., Zhou, J. (eds.) PKC 2004. LNCS, vol. 2947, pp. 218–230. Springer, Heidelberg (2004). doi:10.1007/978-3-540-24632-9_16

15. Nguyen, P.Q., Vallée, B. (eds.): The LLL Algorithm - Survey and Applications. Series in Information Security and Cryptography. Springer, Heidelberg (2010)

16. Rivest, R.L., Shamir, A., Adleman, L.M.: A method for obtaining digital signatures and public-key cryptosystems. Commun. ACM **21**(2), 120–126 (1978)

17. Sarkar, S.: Small secret exponent attack on RSA variant with modulus $N = p^r q$. Des. Codes Crypt. **73**(2), 383–392 (2014)

18. Takayasu, A., Kunihiro, N.: How to generalize RSA cryptanalyses. In: Cheng, C.-M., Chung, K.-M., Persiano, G., Yang, B.-Y. (eds.) PKC 2016. LNCS, vol. 9615, pp. 67–97. Springer, Heidelberg (2016). doi:10.1007/978-3-662-49387-8_4

19. Takagi, T.: Fast RSA-type cryptosystem modulo $p^k q$. In: Krawczyk, H. (ed.) CRYPTO 1998. LNCS, vol. 1462, pp. 318–326. Springer, Heidelberg (1998). doi:10.1007/BFb0055738

20. Wiener, M.J.: Cryptanalysis of short RSA secret exponents. IEEE Trans. Inf. Theory **36**(3), 553–558 (1990)

How to Make the Cramer-Shoup Cryptosystem Secure Against Linear Related-Key Attacks

Baodong Qin[1,2(✉)], Shuai Han[3], Yu Chen[4], Shengli Liu[3], and Zhuo Wei[5]

[1] School of Computer Science and Technology,
Southwest University of Science and Technology, Mianyang 621010, China
qinbaodong@swust.edu.cn
[2] State Key Laboratory of Cryptology, P.O. Box 5159, Beijing 100878, China
[3] Department of Computer Science and Engineering,
Shanghai Jiao Tong University, Shanghai 200240, China
{dalen17,slliu}@sjtu.edu.cn
[4] State Key Laboratory of Information Security, Institute of Information
Engineering, Chinese Academy of Sciences, Beijing 100093, China
yuchen.prc@gmail.com
[5] Huawei Singapore Research Center, Singapore, Singapore
phdzwei@gmail.com

Abstract. Related-key attacks allow an adversary to change the key stored in the memory of a physical device via tampering or other means, and subsequently observe the outcomes of the cryptosystem under these modified keys. Cramer and Shoup (CRYPTO 1998) proposed the first practical public-key encryption scheme proven to be secure against adaptive chosen-ciphertext attacks in the standard model. The scheme (CS-PKE for short) has great influence since it embodies the paradigm of hash proof system. However, Wee (PKC 2012) showed that the CS-PKE scheme is not secure in the scenario of related-key attacks when the related-key derivation functions include linear functions. A fascinating problem left open is how to protect the classical CS-PKE scheme secure against linear related-key attacks. In this paper, we propose a simple method to make the Cramer-Shoup scheme secure against linear related-key attacks. The idea is to recompute the public key in the decryption algorithm from the secret key, so that any (dangerous) modification to the secret key could be detected during the decryption phase. The new scheme has the same efficiency as the original one, except for involving six exponentiations to fixed bases in the decryption algorithm. Fortunately, the computing time for one fixed-base exponentiation with precomputations is at least 5 times faster than that of one regular exponentiation.

Keywords: Related-key attacks · Public-key encryption · Cramer-Shoup cryptosystem

1 Introduction

Traditionally, security notions are defined in an ideal setting, where an adversary can only observe the input/output behavior to the setting, but can not access to

© Springer International Publishing AG 2017
K. Chen et al. (Eds.): Inscrypt 2016, LNCS 10143, pp. 150–165, 2017.
DOI: 10.1007/978-3-319-54705-3_10

or tamper with the internal states (such as the secret keys). In a real life, however, it may be far from this case. For example, related-key attacks (RKAs) allow an adversary to tamper with keys stored in the memory of a physical device and then observe the outcomes of the device under these modified keys. Numerous successful related-key attacks against blockciphers [5–9,28,33] indicate that such attacks might be a serious threat to the security of cryptographic algorithms in practice. Beyond block ciphers, related-key attacks may also be mounted on other cryptographic primitives, such as public-key encryption (PKE), identity-based encryption (IBE) and signatures.

The Cramer-Shoup Cryptosystem and Linear RKA Attacks. At Crypto 1998 [13], Cramer and Shoup proposed the first efficient public-key encryption scheme proven to be secure against adaptive chosen-ciphertext attacks (CCA) in the standard model. Here, we briefly review it from [15]. The scheme consists of a system parameter $sp = (G, p, g_1, g_2, \mathsf{TCR})$, where G is a prime order p group with two random generators g_1 and g_2, and TCR is a target collision resistant hash function. The system parameter can be shared between multiple users. Besides this, it also includes the following three (probabilistic) polynomial-time algorithms:

- **(Key Generation)** $\mathsf{Gen}(sp)$: It outputs a public key $pk = (h, u, v)$ and a secret key $sk = (x_1, x_2, \ldots, x_6)$, such that $h = g_1^{x_1} g_2^{x_2}$, $u = g_1^{x_3} g_2^{x_4}$ and $v = g_1^{x_5} g_2^{x_6}$.
- **(Encryption)** $\mathsf{Enc}(pk, m)$: It encrypts a message $m \in G$ to a ciphertext $C = (u_1, u_2, e, w)$, such that

$$u_1 = g_1^r, u_2 = g_2^r, e = m \cdot h^r, w = (uv^t)^r$$

where $r \in \mathbb{Z}_p$ and $t = \mathsf{TCR}(u_1 \| u_2 \| e)$.
- **(Decryption)** $\mathsf{Dec}(sk, C)$: It decrypts the ciphertext $C = (u_1, u_2, e, w)$ to a message $m = e/(u_1^{x_1} u_2^{x_2})$, unless $u_1^{x_3 + x_5 \cdot t} u_2^{x_4 + x_6 \cdot t} = w$, where $t = \mathsf{TCR}(u_1 \| u_2 \| e)$.

In the traditional CCA security model, the Cramer-Shoup public-key encryption scheme has been proven to be secure under the standard Decisional Diffie-Hellman (DDH) assumption. But, in the RKA security model (see Definition 1), there are two simple linear RKAs on it, pointed out by Wee [32]. Given a valid ciphertext (u_1, u_2, e, w) for some unknown message $m \in G$, for any $\Delta \in \mathbb{Z}_p$, the attacks work as follows:

- **Attack 1:** modifying x_3 to $x_3 + \Delta$, the ciphertext $(u_1, u_2, e, w \cdot u_1^{\Delta})$ is still a valid ciphertext and decrypts to the original message m.
- **Attack 2:** modifying x_1 to $x_1 + \Delta$, the ciphertext (u_1, u_2, e, w) will decrypt to the message $m \cdot u_1^{-\Delta}$ under the modified secret key.

Wee also proposed a general method to construct the RKA-secure PKE scheme from a tag-based CCA-secure encryption scheme that achieves both finger-printing and key-homomorphism, as well as an efficient strong one-time signature scheme. However, the Cramer-Shoup CCA-secure constructions [13,14] do not satisfy the finger-printing, as pointed out by Wee. We introduce shortly in the section of related work that there are some general methods available to make the CS-PKE scheme secure against RKAs. But, the obtained schemes are not efficient in terms of key sizes and/or computing cost. So, making the CS-PKE scheme secure against related-key attacks and preserve high efficiency is still a challenging problem.

OUR CONTRIBUTION. We propose a simple way to lift the Cramer-Shoup public-key encryption scheme from CCA security to linear-RKA security. The new scheme is the same as that of the original one, except for the following two modifications:

- In the encryption algorithm, we add the public key pk into the (target) collision resistant hash function, i.e., $t = \mathsf{CR}(u_1\|u_2\|e\|pk)$.
- In the decryption algorithm, we first use the secret key sk to recover the public key, i.e., $pk = (g_1^{x_1}g_2^{x_2}, g_1^{x_3}g_2^{x_4}, g_1^{x_5}g_2^{x_6})$, and then compute the tag $t = \mathsf{CR}(u_1\|u_2\|e\|pk)$.

We observe that the Cramer-Shoup scheme is compromised by the previous two linear RKA attacks, as the adversary can reuse the tag t to build other valid ciphertexts. Intuitively, these two attacks do not work in our scheme, as the tag may be changed if the adversary tampers with the secret key. Here, we note that the target collision resistant hash function in the original CS-PKE scheme is replaced by a normal collision resistant hash function. The reason is that if we use the TCR function, the simulator does not know the secret key from the TCR challenge tuple (u_1, u_2, e, pk), and hence cannot answer the adversary's RKA queries. In addition, we also do not know how to simulate the RKA queries directly (without the knowledge of the secret key) given only the challenge TCR tuple. If we replace it with a collision resistant hash function, our simulator can generate the secret key by himself, and then compute the corresponding public key and the CR tuple (for details, see the proof in game G_4). Finally, Theorem 1 shows that the linear-RKA security of our scheme can be reduced to the hardness of the DDH problem or the collision resistant hash function.

Clearly, the performance of our scheme is the same as that of the underlying CS-PKE scheme, except for the additional operations of six exponentiations to fixed bases over group G, when computing the public key in the decryption algorithm. To improve the efficiency of the decryption, a direct way is to reduce the number of exponentiations of the public key in the key generation algorithm. However, in the Cramer-Shoup type constructions [14], they rely on two hash proof systems (one is smoothness and the other is 2-universal), in which we need to generate two public keys corresponding to the two hash proof systems. This may be the bottleneck to improve the decryption efficiency using the direct method. Fortunately, the exponentiations to fixed bases can be sped up significantly with precomputations. Specifically, the relative time between one fixed-base exponentiation and one regular exponentiation is $\ll 0.2$ [10].

RELATED WORK. There are some basic RKA-secure primitives available for achieving RKA-secure PKE schemes. They include RKA-PRFs [1–3],

RKA-IBE [4,20], algebraic manipulation detection (AMD) codes [12] and (continuous) non-malleable codes/functions [11,19,21,29]. The framework of RKA-IBE relies on a normal one-time signature scheme. Compared to the underlying IBE scheme, it usually involves additional computational operations, including signing and verification, during the encryption and decryption phases. Moreover, it also extends the ciphertext sizes with the signing key and the signature. The other methods usually require to change the key generation algorithm of a normal CCA-secure PKE scheme and blows up the key sizes. There are also numerous concrete and efficient RKA-PKE schemes [16,17,20,22,23,32] based on specific number-theoretic assumptions, e.g., DDH and factoring. Specifically, to avoid the usage of one-time signature and pairing, Cui et al. [16] proposed an efficient PKE scheme based on the CS-PKE scheme. Jia et al. proposed two efficient RKA-secure PKE schemes [23] based on Kiltz et al.'s (normal) CCA-secure hybrid PKE schemes [24]. The two schemes almost have the same efficiency as that of the underlying CCA-PKE schemes. Later, Jia et al. [22] showed that their schemes can be generalized to constructing RKA secure hybrid PKE schemes from 1-universal hash proof systems (with some special properties).

ORGANIZATION. The rest of this paper is organized as follows. Section 2 reviews some basic cryptographic notations that will be used. We present our construction and show its security in Sect. 3. In Sect. 4, we compare the performance of our scheme with known RKA-PKE schemes. Section 5 is the summary of this paper.

2   Preliminary

NOTATIONS. Throughout this paper, $\kappa \in \mathbb{N}$ denotes the security parameter. If S is a finite set, then $s \leftarrow_R S$ denotes the operation of picking s from S uniformly at random. If $s \in S$ is an element, $|s|$ denotes its bit length. By $y \leftarrow A(x)$, we denote the operation of running algorithm A on input x, and letting y denote its output.

2.1   Public-Key Encryption and Related-Key Security

Public-Key Encryption. A public-key encryption scheme $\mathsf{PKE} = (\mathsf{Sys}, \mathsf{Gen}, \mathsf{Enc}, \mathsf{Dec})$ consists of four probabilistic polynomial-time (PPT) algorithms. $\mathsf{Sys}(1^\kappa)$ is the randomized public parameter generation algorithm, which takes as input a security parameter 1^κ, and outputs a global parameter sp. $\mathsf{Gen}(sp)$ is the randomized public key generation algorithm that takes as input the system parameter sp, and outputs a pair of public/secret keys (pk, sk). $\mathsf{Enc}(pk, m)$ is the randomized encryption algorithm, which takes as input a public pk and a message $m \in \mathcal{M}$, and outputs a ciphertext C. $\mathsf{Dec}(sk, C)$ is the deterministic decryption algorithm, which takes as input a secret key sk and a ciphertext C, and outputs a message m or the special symbol $\bot$ indicating that C is an invalid ciphertext. For consistence, we require that for all $\kappa \in \mathbb{N}$, all $sp \leftarrow \mathsf{Sys}(1^\kappa)$, $(pk, sk) \leftarrow \mathsf{Gen}(sp)$ and all message $m \in \mathcal{M}$, we have $\mathsf{Dec}(sk, \mathsf{Enc}(pk, m)) = m$.

Similar to the definition of IBE [4], in the above definition, we make a distinction between the system parameter and the public key. The former usually contains a description of a finite group which is independent of the secret key. While the later directly depends on the secret key. Without loss of generality, the system parameter is assumed to be fixed and available to all algorithms. We omit sp as input if the context is clear. We also assume that the system parameter sp implicitly specifies a secret key space $\mathcal{SK}$, a public key space $\mathcal{PK}$ and a message space $\mathcal{M}$.

CC-RKA Security. Informally, the Chosen-Ciphertext Related-Key Attack (CC-RKA) on a public-key encryption scheme is modeled by a class of related-key derivation (RKD) functions $\Phi = \{\phi : \mathcal{SK} \to \mathcal{SK}\}$ and an RKA (decryption) oracle $\mathcal{O}_{\mathsf{PKE},sk}^{\Phi\text{-RKA}}(\cdot,\cdot)$ parameterized by the secret key sk and the RKD function class Φ. The RKA-security allows an adversary to access the oracle with queries of the form $(\phi, C) \in \Phi \times \mathcal{C}$. The oracle responds to each query with $\mathsf{Dec}(\phi(sk), C)$, i.e., a decryption of C using a modified secret key $\phi(sk)$. If the adversary has seen the challenge ciphertext C^*, we naturally assume that the adversary never submits a decryption query of the form (ϕ, C) such that $C = C^*$ and $\phi(sk) = sk$. We assume that the RKD function class Φ contains the identity function id. The formal definition of CC-RKA security with respect to Φ is presented in Definition 1.

Definition 1 (CC-RKA Security). *A public-key encryption scheme* $\mathsf{PKE} = (\mathsf{Sys}, \mathsf{Gen}, \mathsf{Enc}, \mathsf{Dec})$ *is (semantically) secure against chosen-ciphertext related-key attacks (shorted as CC-RKA or RKA), if for any stateful PPT adversary* $\mathcal{A}$, *the advantage function defined as follows*

$$\mathsf{Adv}_{\mathsf{PKE},\mathcal{A}}^{\Phi\text{-CC-RKA}}(\kappa) := \left| \Pr \left[b = b' : \begin{array}{l} sp \leftarrow \mathsf{Sys}(1^\kappa); (pk, sk) \leftarrow \mathsf{Gen}(sp) \\ (m_0, m_1) \leftarrow \mathcal{A}^{\mathcal{O}_{\mathsf{PKE},sk}^{\Phi\text{-RKA}}(\cdot,\cdot)}(pk), |m_0| = |m_1| \\ b \leftarrow_R \{0,1\}, C^* \leftarrow \mathsf{Enc}(pk, m_b) \\ b' \leftarrow \mathcal{A}^{\mathcal{O}_{\mathsf{PKE},sk}^{\Phi\text{-RKA}}(\cdot,\cdot)}(C^*) \end{array} \right] - \frac{1}{2} \right|$$

is negligible in κ.

CCA Security [27]. The traditional CCA security is defined similarly to the above definition, with the restriction that the adversary cannot tamper with the secret key.

2.2 (Target) Collision Resistant Hash Functions

The notion of target collision resistant hash function is a special kind of universal one-way hash function. We recall it from [15].

Definition 2 (Target Collision Resistant Hash Functions). *Let* $\mathsf{TCR} : X \to Y$ *be a hash function. We say that* TCR *is a target collision resistant hash function, if for any PPT adversary* $\mathcal{A}$, *the following advantage*

$$\mathsf{Adv}_{\mathsf{TCR},\mathcal{A}}^{\mathsf{TCR}}(\kappa) := \Pr\left[x' \neq x \wedge \mathsf{TCR}(x') = \mathsf{TCR}(x) : x \leftarrow_R X, x' \leftarrow \mathcal{A}(x) \right]$$

is negligible in κ.

Similarly, we can give the definition of collision resistant hash functions. The key difference is that, the challenge value x in the above definition is also chosen by the adversary.

Definition 3 (Collision Resistant Hash Functions). *Let* $\mathsf{CR} : X \to Y$ *be a hash function. We say that* CR *is a collision resistant hash function, if for any PPT adversary* $\mathcal{A}$, *the following advantage*

$$\mathsf{Adv}^{\mathsf{CR}}_{\mathsf{CR},\mathcal{A}}(\kappa) := \Pr\left[x' \neq x \land \mathsf{CR}(x') = \mathsf{CR}(x) : (x, x') \leftarrow \mathcal{A}(X)\right]$$

is negligible in κ.

2.3 Intractability Assumptions

Let $\mathcal{G}(\kappa)$ be a group generation algorithm that takes as input a security parameter κ and outputs a finite group G with prime order p and generator g. The Discrete Logarithm (DL) assumption and the Decisional Diffie-Hellman (DDH) assumption over group G are respectively defined as follows.

Definition 4 (The DL Assumption). *The DL assumption for* G *states that for any PPT adversary* $\mathcal{A}$, *the following DL advantage*

$$\mathsf{Adv}^{\mathsf{DL}}_{G,\mathcal{A}}(\kappa) := \Pr\left[y = x : \begin{array}{c} (G, p, g) \leftarrow \mathcal{G}(\kappa), x \leftarrow_R \mathbb{Z}_p \\ y \leftarrow \mathcal{A}(g^x) \end{array}\right]$$

is negligible in κ.

Definition 5 (The DDH Assumption). *Let* $(G, p, g) \leftarrow \mathcal{G}(\kappa)$ *and let* $x, y, z \leftarrow_R \mathbb{Z}_p$. *The DDH assumption for* G *states that for any PPT adversary* $\mathcal{A}$, *the following DDH advantage*

$$\mathsf{Adv}^{\mathsf{DDH}}_{G,\mathcal{A}}(\kappa) := \left|\Pr\left[\mathcal{A}(g, g^x, g^y, g^{xy}) = 1\right] - \Pr\left[\mathcal{A}(g, g^x, g^y, g^z) = 1\right]\right|$$

is negligible in κ.

Clearly, the DDH problem is not harder than the DL problem.

3 The Construction

In this section, we present a public-key encryption scheme which is secure against chosen-ciphertext attacks and linear related-key attacks. Our scheme is described as follows.

- **(System Parameter)** $\mathsf{Sys}(1^\kappa)$: Run $\mathcal{G}(1^\kappa)$ to generate a finite group G of prime order p and randomly choose two distinct group elements $g_1, g_2 \in G$. It also chooses a collision resistant hash function $\mathsf{CR} : G^6 \to \mathbb{Z}_p$. The system parameter is $sp = (G, p, g_1, g_2, \mathsf{CR})$.

- **(Key Generation)** $\mathsf{Gen}(sp)$: Randomly choose $x_1, x_2, \ldots, x_6 \in \mathbb{Z}_p$, and then compute $h = g_1^{x_1} g_2^{x_2}$, $u = g_1^{x_3} g_2^{x_4}$ and $v = g_1^{x_5} g_2^{x_6}$. The public key is $pk = (h, u, v)$ and the secret key is $sk = (x_1, x_2, \ldots, x_6)$.
- **(Encryption)** $\mathsf{Enc}(pk, m)$: To encrypt a message $m \in G$, it first samples a random element $r \in \mathbb{Z}_p$ and then sets

$$u_1 = g_1^r, u_2 = g_2^r, e = m \cdot h^r, w = (uv^t)^r$$

where $t = \mathsf{CR}(u_1||u_2||e||h||u||v)$. The ciphertext is $C = (u_1, u_2, e, w)$.
- **(Decryption)** $\mathsf{Dec}(sk, C)$: To decrypt a ciphertext $C = (u_1, u_2, e, w)$, it first recomputes the public key $h = g_1^{x_1} g_2^{x_2}$, $u = g_1^{x_3} g_2^{x_4}$ and $v = g_1^{x_5} g_2^{x_6}$, and then
  - computes $t = \mathsf{CR}(u_1||u_2||e||h||u||v)$ and outputs $\perp$ if

$$u_1^{x_3 + x_5 \cdot t} u_2^{x_4 + x_6 \cdot t} \neq w.$$

  - otherwise outputs $m = e/(u_1^{x_1} u_2^{x_2})$.

Correctness. For any ciphertext $C = (u_1, u_2, e, w)$ that is correctly generated by the encryption algorithm, it clearly satisfies

$$u_1 = g_1^r, u_2 = g_2^r, e = m \cdot h^r, w = (uv^t)^r$$

for some (unknown) r and message m. Since

$$\mathsf{CR}(u_1||u_2||e||g_1^{x_1} g_2^{x_2}||g_1^{x_3} g_2^{x_4}||g_1^{x_5} g_2^{x_6}) = \mathsf{CR}(u_1||u_2||e||h||u||v) = t$$

and

$$u_1^{x_3 + x_5 \cdot t} u_2^{x_4 + x_6 \cdot t} = \left((g_1^{x_3} g_2^{x_4})(g_1^{x_5} g_2^{x_6})^t \right)^r = (uv^t)^r = w,$$

the decryption algorithm should output $e/(u_1^{x_1} u_2^{x_2}) = e/h^r = m$, which is just the message as in the ciphertext C.

The RKD Functions. As the secret key space is $\mathbb{Z}_p^6$, we define the class of linear related-key derivation functions as follows:

$$\Phi_{\mathsf{linear}} = \{\phi : (x_i)_{i=1}^6 \to (x_i + \Delta_i)_{i=1}^6\}$$

for any $(x_i)_{i=1}^6, (\Delta_i)_{i=1}^6 \in \mathbb{Z}_p^6$ and the operation "+" is defined over the additive group $\mathbb{Z}_p$.

Theorem 1. *If the DDH problem is hard in G and CR is a collision resistant hash function, then the above construction is a Φ_{linear}-CC-RKA secure public-key encryption scheme.*

Particularly, for any PPT adversary $\mathcal{A}$ against the Φ_{linear}-CC-RKA security of our scheme, there exist an adversary $\mathcal{B}_1$ against the DDH assumption for G, an adversary $\mathcal{B}_2$ against the collision-resistant hash function CR and an adversary $\mathcal{B}_3$ against the DL assumption for G such that

$$\mathsf{Adv}_{\mathcal{A},\mathsf{PKE}}^{\Phi_{\mathsf{linear}}\text{-CC-RKA}}(\kappa) \leq \mathsf{Adv}_{\mathcal{B}_1,G}^{\mathsf{DDH}}(\kappa) + \mathsf{Adv}_{\mathcal{B}_2,\mathsf{CR}}^{\mathsf{CR}}(\kappa) + \mathsf{Adv}_{\mathcal{B}_3,G}^{\mathsf{DL}}(\kappa) + \frac{Q(\kappa) + 1}{p - Q(\kappa)} + \frac{1}{p},$$

where $Q(\kappa)$ is the number of times $\mathcal{A}$ queried the decryption oracle.

Proof. We begin by defining a sequence of (CC-RKA security) games played between the challenger and an adversary $\mathcal{A}$. Let G_i denote the i-th game and let S_i denote the event that $\mathcal{A}$ succeeds in the i-th game. In each game, we denote by $C^* = (u_1^*, u_2^*, e^*, w^*)$ the challenge ciphertext and denote by $(\phi, C = (u_1, u_2, e, w))$ the decryption queries issued by the adversary $\mathcal{A}$. The challenge public key and its corresponding secret key are denoted by $pk^* = (h^*, u^*, v^*)$ and $sk^* = (x_1^*, x_2^*, \ldots, x_6^*)$ respectively.

G_0: This is the original CC-RKA experiment as defined in Definition 1. Thus,

$$\mathsf{Adv}_{\mathcal{A},\mathsf{PKE}}^{\Phi_{\mathsf{linear}}\text{-}\mathsf{CC}\text{-}\mathsf{RKA}}(\kappa) := \left| \Pr[S_0] - \frac{1}{2} \right|.$$

G_1: This game is the same as game G_0, except for a small modification to the challenge ciphertext. Concretely, G_1 computes e^* and v^* using the secret key rather than the public key, i.e.,

$$e^* = m_b \cdot (u_1^*)^{x_1^*} (u_2^*)^{x_2^*} \text{ and } w^* = (u_1^*)^{x_3^* + x_5^* \cdot t^*} (u_2^*)^{x_4^* + x_6^* \cdot t^*}.$$

Note that the values e^* and w^* have the same distributions in both games G_1 and G_0. So, the change made in game G_1 is purely conceptual and hence

$$\Pr[S_1] = \Pr[S_0].$$

G_2: In this game, we make a small modification to the decryption oracle. Instead of computing (h, u, v) using the modified secret key $\phi(sk^*) = \{x_i^* + \Delta_i\}_{i=1,2,\cdots,6}$, we compute these values just from the challenge public key pk^* and the RKD function ϕ. Particularly, we compute

$$h = h^* \cdot \left(g_1^{\Delta_1} g_2^{\Delta_2} \right) \qquad u = u^* \cdot \left(g_1^{\Delta_3} g_2^{\Delta_4} \right) \qquad v = v^* \cdot \left(g_1^{\Delta_5} g_2^{\Delta_6} \right)$$

for a decryption query (ϕ, C). As $h = (g_1)^{x_1^* + \Delta_1} (g_2)^{x_2^* + \Delta_2} = h^* \cdot \left(g_1^{\Delta_1} g_2^{\Delta_2} \right)$ (the same for u and v), the change made in game G_2 is purely conceptual. Therefore,

$$\Pr[S_2] = \Pr[S_1].$$

G_3: This game is the same as game G_2, except that we again make a small change to the encryption oracle. Instead of computing u_1^* and u_2^* using the same value r^*, we choose two random values $r_1^*, r_2^* \in \mathbb{Z}_p$ and compute

$$(u_1^*, u_2^*) = \left(g_1^{r_1^*}, g_2^{r_2^*} \right).$$

We now show that under the DDH assumption, the difference between games G_3 and G_2 is negligible in κ. Given a challenge tuple $T = (g_1, g_2, u_1^*, u_2^*)$, where T is either a DDH tuple or a random four tuple, we build a PPT algorithm (simulator) $\mathcal{B}_1$ to break the DDH assumption using the adversary $\mathcal{A}$ as a subroutine. The simulator first generates the challenge public key $pk^* = (h^*, u^*, v^*)$ and secret key $sk^* = (x_1^*, x_2^*, \ldots, x_6^*)$ as in game G_2. Since the simulator holds the decryption key, he can answer the adversary's decryption queries (ϕ, C) as in game G_2. To answer the adversary's encryption query for two equal-length messages m_0, m_1, the simulator first chooses a random bit $b \in \{0, 1\}$ and then computes

$$e^* = m_b \cdot (u_1^*)^{x_1^*} (u_2^*)^{x_2^*}$$
$$t^* = \mathsf{CR}(u_1^* \| u_2^* \| e^* \| h^* \| u^* \| v^*)$$
$$w^* = (u_1^*)^{x_3^* + x_5^* \cdot t^*} (u_2^*)^{x_4^* + x_6^* \cdot t^*}$$

and sends the challenge ciphertext $C^* = (u_1^*, u_2^*, e^*, w^*)$ to the adversary. Finally, the adversary will output a guess bit b'. The simulator outputs 1 if and only if $b = b'$. Observe that if T is a DDH-tuple, the simulator perfectly constructs the environment that the adversary communicates with in game G_2. Otherwise, the simulator perfectly constructs the environment of game G_3. So,

$$|\Pr[S_3] - \Pr[S_2]| \leq \mathsf{Adv}_{\mathcal{B}_1, \mathcal{G}}^{\mathrm{DDH}}(\kappa).$$

G_4: In this game, we reject all decryption queries (ϕ, C) such that

$$t = \mathsf{CR}(u_1 \| u_2 \| e \| h \| u \| v) = t^*.$$

We show that G_4 is indistinguishable from game G_3 under the hardness of the collision-resistant hash function and the hardness of the discrete logarithm problem over group G. We consider the following two cases:

- Case 1: $(u_1, u_2, e, h, u, v) \neq (u_1^*, u_2^*, e^*, h^*, u^*, v^*)$,
- Case 2: $(u_1, u_2, e, h, u, v) = (u_1^*, u_2^*, e^*, h^*, u^*, v^*)$.

We can prove that the first case implies a collision of the hash function CR. The proof is as follows. The simulator first chooses the secret key sk^* as in the previous game. Then, it computes the challenge public key pk^*. As the simulator knows the secret key, it can answer the adversary's RKA queries like in the previous game. Finally, the simulator computes the challenge ciphertext as in the previous game. So, if the adversary asks a query that satisfies the first case, the simulator actually find a collision of the hash function CR. Therefore, the first case occurs with probability at most $\mathsf{Adv}_{\mathcal{B}_2, \mathsf{CR}}^{\mathrm{CR}}(\kappa)$ for some PPT adversary $\mathcal{B}_2$ breaking the collision resistance of the hash function CR. Next, we show that the second case also occurs with a negligible probability.

For Case 2, if $\phi(sk^*) = sk^*$, we obtain that $w = w^*$. That is,

$$(\phi(sk^*), C) = (sk^*, C^*).$$

This case should be rejected by the decryption rule. If $\phi(sk^*) \neq sk^*$, without loss of generality, we have that $x_1 - x_1^* = \Delta_1 \neq 0 \pmod{p}$. Given a challenge discrete logarithm problem (G, p, g_1, g_2), we can choose the system parameter, the challenge public key pk^* and the secret key sk^* as in G_3. So, if the adversary submits a decryption query (ϕ, C) such that $\phi(sk^*) \neq sk^*$, but $(u_1, u_2, e, h, u, v) = (u_1^*, u_2^*, e^*, h^*, u^*, v^*)$, we have that

$$h = h^* \cdot (g_1^{\Delta_1} g_2^{\Delta_2}) = h^*.$$

As Δ_i are known, we solve the discrete logarithm problem between g_1 and g_2, i.e., $\log_{g_2} g_1 = -\Delta_2/\Delta_1 \pmod p$. By the hardness of the discrete logarithm problem over G, the above case occurs with a probability at most $\mathsf{Adv}^{\mathrm{DL}}_{\mathcal{B}_3, G}(\kappa)$ for some PPT adversary $\mathcal{B}_3$.

From the above analysis, we have that

$$|\Pr[S_4] - \Pr[S_3]| \leq \mathsf{Adv}^{\mathrm{CR}}_{\mathcal{B}_2, \mathrm{CR}}(\kappa) + \mathsf{Adv}^{\mathrm{DL}}_{\mathcal{B}_3, G}(\kappa).$$

G_5: In this game, we again change the random tuple $(g_1, g_2, u_1^* = g_1^{r_1^*}, u_2^* = g_2^{r_2^*})$ (in the challenge ciphertext) into a non-DDH tuple, i.e., $r_1^* \neq r_2^*$. As r_1^* and r_2^* are chosen uniformly at random from $\mathbb{Z}_p$ in the previous game, the probability that $r_1^* = r_2^*$ is at most $1/p$. Since game G_5 is the same as that of G_4 unless the event $r_1^* = r_2^*$ occurs in G_4, by the difference lemma [31], we have that

$$|\Pr[S_5] - \Pr[S_4]| \leq \frac{1}{p}.$$

G_6: This game is the same as game G_5, except that the decryption rejects all decryption queries $(\phi, C = (u_1 = g_1^{r_1}, u_2 = g_2^{r_2}, e, w))$, such that $r_1 \neq r_2$. For simplicity, we call such ciphertexts *invalid* ciphertexts. Let E denote the event that there exist invalid ciphertexts that are not rejected by the decryption rule in game G_5. Clearly, this game has the same distribution as that of G_5, unless the event E occurs. Again, by the difference lemma [31], we immediately have

$$|\Pr[S_6] - \Pr[S_5]| \leq \Pr[E].$$

We will show that all invalid ciphertexts have already been rejected by the decryption rule (in game G_5) with overwhelming probability.

First, we show that for all non-invalid ciphertexts (i.e., $r_1 = r_2 = r$), the decryption oracle does not reveal any additional information about the secret key to the adversary, besides the information leaked by the challenge public key pk^* and the challenge ciphertext C^*. As explained in game G_2, the public key (h, u, v) corresponding to the modified secret key $\phi(sk^*)$ is computed from the challenge public key (h^*, u^*, v^*) and the RKD function ϕ. So, the hash value $t = \mathsf{CR}(u_1||u_2||e||h||u||v)$ only depends on the challenge public key pk^* and the queried ciphertext $C = (u_1, u_2, e, w)$. In addition, we have the following two equations:

$$u_1^{x_3 + x_5 \cdot t} u_2^{x_4 + x_6 \cdot t} = (g_1^r)^{x_3^* + \Delta_3 + (x_5^* + \Delta_5) \cdot t} (g_2^r)^{x_4^* + \Delta_4 + (x_6^* + \Delta_6) \cdot t}$$
$$= (u^*)^r (v^*)^{r \cdot t} (u_1)^{\Delta_3 + \Delta_5 \cdot t} (u_2)^{\Delta_4 + \Delta_6 \cdot t}$$

and

$$\frac{e}{u_1^{x_1} u_2^{x_2}} = \frac{e}{(g_1^r)^{x_1^* + \Delta_1} (g_2^r)^{x_2^* + \Delta_2}}$$

$$= \frac{e}{(h^*)^r (u_1)^{\Delta_1} (u_2)^{\Delta_2}}.$$

So, the decryption result is only dependent on the challenge public key pk^*, the queried ciphertext C and the RKD function ϕ. Therefore, for valid ciphertexts, the adversary cannot obtain any additional information about the secret key sk^* from the decryption oracle.

Suppose that $(\phi, C) = (\{x_i^* + \Delta_i\}_{i \in 1,\ldots,6}, (u_1 = g_1^{r_1}, u_2 = g_2^{r_2}, e, w))$ is the first decryption query that contains an invalid ciphertext. We show that this query is rejected in game G_5 with overwhelming probability. Let $\alpha = \log_{g_1} g_2$. From the adversary's point of view, he may obtain the information of the secret key $(x_3^*, x_4^*, x_5^*, x_6^*)$ from the following values (over $\mathbb{Z}_p$):

$$\log_{g_1} u^* = x_3^* + \alpha \cdot x_4^*$$
$$\log_{g_1} v^* = x_5^* + \alpha \cdot x_6^*$$
$$\log_{g_1} w^* = (x_3^* + x_5^* \cdot t^*) \cdot r_1^* + (x_4^* + x_6^* \cdot t^*) \cdot \alpha \cdot r_2^*.$$

Let $w' = u_1^{x_3 + x_5 \cdot t} u_2^{x_4 + x_6 \cdot t}$. We now show that the value w' is unpredictable for the adversary, even given the above three values. It is sufficient to prove the following value be unpredictable:

$$\log_{g_1} w' = (x_3^* + \Delta_3 + (x_5^* + \Delta_5) \cdot t) \cdot r_1 + (x_4^* + \Delta_4 + (x_6^* + \Delta_6) \cdot t) \cdot \alpha \cdot r_2.$$

From the above four equations, we can derive the following system of linear equations with respect to variables $(x_3^*, x_4^*, x_5^*, x_6^*)$.

$$\begin{pmatrix} \log_{g_1} u^* \\ \log_{g_1} v^* \\ \log_{g_1} w^* \\ \log_{g_1} w' \end{pmatrix} = \underbrace{\begin{pmatrix} 1 & \alpha & 0 & 0 \\ 0 & 0 & 1 & \alpha \\ r_1^* & \alpha r_2^* & t^* r_1^* & t^* \alpha r_2^* \\ r_1 & \alpha r_2 & t r_1 & t \alpha r_2 \end{pmatrix}}_{A} \cdot \begin{pmatrix} x_3^* \\ x_4^* \\ x_5^* \\ x_6^* \end{pmatrix} + \begin{pmatrix} 0 \\ 0 \\ 0 \\ \Delta \end{pmatrix}$$

where $\Delta = (\Delta_3 + \Delta_5 t) r_1 + (\Delta_4 + \Delta_6 t) \alpha r_2$.

The determinant of A is $\det(A) = \alpha^2 (r_1^* - r_2^*)(r_1 - r_2)(t^* - t)$. Note that $r_1^* \neq r_2^*$, $r_1 \neq r_2$ and $t^* \neq t$. So, $\det(A) \neq 0$ and A is a full rank matrix. As x_3^*, x_4^*, x_5^* and x_6^* are chosen uniformly at random from $\mathbb{Z}_p$, $\log_{g_1} w'$ is still uniformly distributed over $\mathbb{Z}_p$, even fixing the other three values $\log_{g_1} u^*$, $\log_{g_1} v^*$ and $\log_{g_1} w^*$. So, the adversary can correctly guess the value w' with probability at most $1/p$. In other words, the decryption oracle will reject the first invalid ciphertext with probability at least $1 - 1/p$.

Similarly, we can discuss the rejection probability for the i-th invalid ciphertext. The only difference is that from each rejection, the adversary can rule out one solution. So, the decryption oracle rejects the i-th invalid ciphertext with probability at least $1 - 1/(p - i)$. Suppose that $\mathcal{A}$ makes at most $Q(\kappa)$ RKA queries (which is a polynomial in κ). We can calculate the following probability that the decryption oracle rejects all RKA queries with invalid ciphertexts in G_5.

$$\Pr[\overline{E}] \geq \prod_{i=1}^{Q(\kappa)} \left(1 - \frac{1}{p - i + 1}\right)$$

$$\geq 1 - \frac{Q(\kappa) + 1}{p - Q(\kappa)}.$$

So, $\Pr[E] \leq \frac{Q(\kappa)+1}{p-Q(\kappa)}$.

G_7: This game is the same as G_6, except that we make a small change to the challenge ciphertext. Specifically, we replace the vale $(u_1^*)^{x_1^*}(u_2^*)^{x_2^*}$ in the challenge ciphertext part e^* with a random element R^*. We show that the value $(u_1^*)^{x_1^*}(u_2^*)^{x_2^*}$ is already almost uniform over G. Note that in game G_6, the adversary cannot obtain any additional information about the challenge secret key from the RKA oracle. So, only the challenge public key part h^* may reveal some information of x_1^* and x_2^* and the leaked information is at most

$$\log_{g_1} h^* = x_1^* + \alpha \cdot x_2^*.$$

To show that $(u_1^*)^{x_1^*}(u_2^*)^{x_2^*}$ is distributed uniformly at random over G, it is sufficient to prove that $\log_{g_1}(u_1^*)^{x_1^*}(u_2^*)^{x_2^*}$ is uniform over $\mathbb{Z}_p$. Particularly, we have the following system of linear equations:

$$\begin{pmatrix} \log_{g_1} h^* \\ \log_{g_1}(u_1^*)^{x_1^*}(u_2^*)^{x_2^*} \end{pmatrix} = \underbrace{\begin{pmatrix} 1 & \alpha \\ r_1^* & \alpha r_2^* \end{pmatrix}}_{B} \cdot \begin{pmatrix} x_1^* \\ x_2^* \end{pmatrix}$$

Clearly, the determinant of the matrix B is $\det(B) = \alpha(r_2^* - r_1^*) \neq 0$. So, $\log_{g_1}(u_1^*)^{x_1^*}(u_2^*)^{x_2^*}$ is uniformly distributed over $\mathbb{Z}_p$. That is

$$\Pr[S_7] = \Pr[S_6].$$

Observe that, in game G_7, R^* is truly random. So, the challenge ciphertext part e^* is also uniformly distributed and does not leak any information about the message m_b. Therefore $\Pr[S_7] = 1/2$.

Taking all things together, Theorem 1 follows.   □

4   Comparison

In Table 1, we compare our scheme with previous CC-RKA secure PKE schemes, including Wee's DBDH-based PKE scheme [32, Sect. 5.2], Bellare et al.'s DBDH-based KEM scheme [4, Sect. 7.2 of the full version], Jia et al.'s DDH-based hybrid PKE scheme [23, Sect. 4], Cui et al.'s DDH-based PKE scheme [16, Sect. 4.2] and DBDH-based PKE scheme [18, Sect. 5.1], and Fujisaki et al.'s DBDH-based KEM

Table 1. Efficiency comparison of various CC-RKA secure PKE/KEM schemes

Scheme PKE/KEM	Ciphertext overhead	Encryption operations	Decryption operations	RKD functions	Assumption
		(#pairings, #[multi, reg, fix-base]-exps)			
CS04 [15][a]	$3\|p\|$	$0 + [0, 0, 5]$	$0 + [2, 0, 0]$	-	DDH
Wee12 [32]	$6\|p\|$	$1^{b} + [0, 0, 7]$	$3 + [1, 2, 1]$	Linear	DBDH
BPT12 [4]	$2\|p\|$	$0 + [0, 0, 4]$	$3 + [0, 0, 3]$	Affine	DBDH
JLLM13 [23]	$2\|p\|$+mac	$0 + [0, 0, 3]$	$0 + [1, 0, 0]$	Affine	DDH
CMA13 [16]	$4\|p\|$	$0 + [0, 0, 7]$	$0 + [2, 1, 0]$	Linear	DDH
CMA14 [17]	$9\|p\|$	$0 + [0, 0, 10]$	$1^{c} + [2, 0, 1]$	Linear	DBDH
FX15 [20]	$4\|p\|$	$0 + [0, 0, 4]$	$7 + [0, 0, 1]$	Invertible	DBDH
Ours	$3\|p\|$	$0 + [0, 0, 5]$	$0 + [2, 0, 6]$	Linear	DDH

[a] The Cramer-Shoup public-key encryption scheme is only CCA secure.
[b] This pairing operation can be replaced by a single fixed-base exponentiation, if the scheme adds the fixed-base into the system parameter.
[c] To check the correctness of the ciphertext, it actually requires more than 12 additional pairings. As they can be done by a third party [25], the authors do not count them in the computation cost.

scheme [20, Sect. 4]. In contrast to PKE, a KEM (key encapsulation mechanisms) scheme encrypts a random key rather than a real message. Bellare et al. [4] showed that a Φ-CC-RKA secure KEM scheme combined with a normal one-time CCA-secure symmetric key scheme can be used to build a Φ-CC-RKA secure hybrid PKE scheme.

In this table, $|p|$ is the bit-length of a group element. Ciphertext overhead denotes the difference between the ciphertext length and the message length. In counting numbers of operations, we make a distinction of exponentiation between multi-exponentiation, regular exponentiation, and exponentiation to a fixed base that allows pre-computations. We can use the following relative timings to compare the running times for the various operations: bilinear pairing ≈ 5 [30], multi-exponentiation ≥ 1.5, regular exponentiation $= 1$, fixed-base exponentiation $\ll 0.2$.

From the above table, our scheme has the same efficiency as that of the original Cramer-Shoup scheme, except for the six additional fixed-base exponentiations during decryption phase. Note that, one fixed-base exponentiation (allowing pre-computations) requires very less computing time compared with a regular exponentiation. So, these additional operations may have little effect on the total decryption cost in practice. Moreover, we can use three multi-exponentiations with fixed bases [26] to further speed up these six fixed base exponentiations.

Our ciphertext overhead contains just three group elements, which are shorter than the other RKA-secure schemes, with the exception of [4, 23]. Bellare et al.'s ciphertext contains only two group elements. Nevertheless, it is constructed over a bilinear group and its decryption requires three pairing operations, which are more expensive than exponentiations. Jia et al.'s scheme seems to be the nowadays most efficient scheme with a relative short ciphertexts. But, it needs to use groups with a sufficiently large order. For example, for a symmetric cipher with $\kappa = 80$ bits keys, the order of the group should be at least $|p| \geq 4\kappa = 320$ bits. The other schemes, including ours, do not have such restriction. The restriction may be avoided by increasing the cost of an additional exponentiation in the encryption algorithm [24]. We notice that, efficient RKA-secure schemes often suffer from small RKD function classes. Though Fujisaki and Xagawa's scheme [20] requires a heavy decryption operations, its RKD function class is very rich. It contains not only linear functions, but also non-linear functions (affine and polynomial functions).

5 Conclusion

In this paper, we proposed an efficient public-key encryption scheme resilient against linear related-key attacks, based on the well-known Cramer-Shoup PKE scheme. We made a very small modification to the encryption of the underlying scheme, just adding the public key into the hash function. The modification requires our decryption algorithm re-computing the public key using the secret key. Nevertheless, the additional operations do not cost expensively, compared with the other operations executed during the decryption phase. Our method may be applied to other non-RKA secure PKE scheme that cannot be made to RKA security using previous methods. In addition, we may generalize the scheme into Cramer and Shoup's general framework for constructing CCA-secure PKE using hash proof systems.

Acknowledgments. This work was supported by the National Natural Science Foundation of China (Grant No. 61502400, 61672346, 61402199, 61303257), the Science Foundation of Sichuan Educational Committee (Grant No. 16ZB0140), the Natural Science Foundation of Southwest University of Science and Technology (Grant No. 16zx7107), the Youth Innovation Promotion Association CAS and the Natural Science Funds of Guangdong (Grant No. 2015A030310017)

References

1. Abdalla, M., Benhamouda, F., Passelègue, A., Paterson, K.G.: Related-key security for pseudorandom functions beyond the linear barrier. In: Garay, J.A., Gennaro, R. (eds.) CRYPTO 2014. LNCS, vol. 8616, pp. 77–94. Springer, Heidelberg (2014). doi:10.1007/978-3-662-44371-2_5
2. Bellare, M., Cash, D.: Pseudorandom functions and permutations provably secure against related-key attacks. In: Rabin, T. (ed.) CRYPTO 2010. LNCS, vol. 6223, pp. 666–684. Springer, Heidelberg (2010). doi:10.1007/978-3-642-14623-7_36
3. Bellare, M., Cash, D., Miller, R.: Cryptography secure against related-key attacks and tampering. In: Lee, D.H., Wang, X. (eds.) ASIACRYPT 2011. LNCS, vol. 7073, pp. 486–503. Springer, Heidelberg (2011). doi:10.1007/978-3-642-25385-0_26

4. Bellare, M., Paterson, K.G., Thomson, S.: RKA security beyond the linear barrier: IBE, encryption and signatures. In: Wang, X., Sako, K. (eds.) ASIACRYPT 2012. LNCS, vol. 7658, pp. 331–348. Springer, Heidelberg (2012). doi:10.1007/978-3-642-34961-4_21

5. Biham, E.: New types of cryptanalytic attacks using related keys. J. Cryptology 7(4), 229–246 (1994)

6. Biham, E., Dunkelman, O., Keller, N.: A related-key rectangle attack on the full KASUMI. In: Roy, B. (ed.) ASIACRYPT 2005. LNCS, vol. 3788, pp. 443–461. Springer, Heidelberg (2005). doi:10.1007/11593447_24

7. Biham, E., Dunkelman, O., Keller, N.: A unified approach to related-key attacks. In: Nyberg, K. (ed.) FSE 2008. LNCS, vol. 5086, pp. 73–96. Springer, Heidelberg (2008). doi:10.1007/978-3-540-71039-4_5

8. Biryukov, A., Khovratovich, D.: Related-key cryptanalysis of the full AES-192 and AES-256. In: Matsui, M. (ed.) ASIACRYPT 2009. LNCS, vol. 5912, pp. 1–18. Springer, Heidelberg (2009). doi:10.1007/978-3-642-10366-7_1

9. Biryukov, A., Khovratovich, D., Nikolić, I.: Distinguisher and related-key attack on the full AES-256. In: Halevi, S. (ed.) CRYPTO 2009. LNCS, vol. 5677, pp. 231–249. Springer, Heidelberg (2009). doi:10.1007/978-3-642-03356-8_14

10. Boyen, X., Mei, Q., Waters, B.: Direct chosen ciphertext security from identity-based techniques. In: Atluri, V., Meadows, C., Juels, A. (eds.) CCS 2005, pp. 320–329. ACM (2005)

11. Chen, Y., Qin, B., Zhang, J., Deng, Y., Chow, S.S.M.: Non-malleable functions and their applications. In: Cheng, C., Chung, K., Persiano, G., Yang, B. (eds.) PKC 2016, Part II. LNCS, vol. 9615, pp. 386–416. Springer, Heidelberg (2016)

12. Cramer, R., Dodis, Y., Fehr, S., Padró, C., Wichs, D.: Detection of algebraic manipulation with applications to robust secret sharing and fuzzy extractors. In: Smart, N. (ed.) EUROCRYPT 2008. LNCS, vol. 4965, pp. 471–488. Springer, Heidelberg (2008). doi:10.1007/978-3-540-78967-3_27

13. Cramer, R., Shoup, V.: A practical public key cryptosystem provably secure against adaptive chosen ciphertext attack. In: Krawczyk, H. (ed.) CRYPTO 1998. LNCS, vol. 1462, pp. 13–25. Springer, Heidelberg (1998). doi:10.1007/BFb0055717

14. Cramer, R., Shoup, V.: Universal hash proofs and a paradigm for adaptive chosen ciphertext secure public-key encryption. In: Knudsen, L.R. (ed.) EUROCRYPT 2002. LNCS, vol. 2332, pp. 45–64. Springer, Heidelberg (2002). doi:10.1007/3-540-46035-7_4

15. Cramer, R., Shoup, V.: Design and analysis of practical public-key encryption schemes secure against adaptive chosen ciphertext attack. SIAM J. Comput. 33(1), 167–226 (2004)

16. Cui, H., Mu, Y., Au, M.H.: Public-key encryption resilient to linear related-key attacks. In: Zia, T., Zomaya, A., Varadharajan, V., Mao, M. (eds.) SecureComm 2013. LNICSSITE, vol. 127, pp. 182–196. Springer, Cham (2013). doi:10.1007/978-3-319-04283-1_12

17. Cui, H., Mu, Y., Au, M.H.: Public-key encryption resilient against linear related-key attacks revisited. In: TrustCom 2014, pp. 268–275. IEEE Computer Society (2014)

18. Cui, H., Mu, Y., Au, M.H.: Proof of retrievability with public verifiability resilient against related-key attacks. IET Inf. Secur. 9, 43–49 (2015)

19. Dziembowski, S., Pietrzak, K., Wichs, D.: Non-malleable codes. In: Yao, A.C. (ed.) Innovations in Computer Science - ICS 2010, pp. 434–452. Tsinghua University Press (2010)

20. Fujisaki, E., Xagawa, K.: Efficient RKA-secure KEM and IBE schemes against invertible functions. In: Lauter, K., Rodríguez-Henríquez, F. (eds.) LATIN-CRYPT 2015. LNCS, vol. 9230, pp. 3–20. Springer, Cham (2015). doi:10.1007/978-3-319-22174-8_1

21. Jafargholi, Z., Wichs, D.: Tamper detection and continuous non-malleable codes. In: Dodis, Y., Nielsen, J.B. (eds.) TCC 2015. LNCS, vol. 9014, pp. 451–480. Springer, Heidelberg (2015). doi:10.1007/978-3-662-46494-6_19

22. Jia, D., Li, B., Lu, X., Mei, Q.: Related key secure PKE from hash proof systems. In: Yoshida, M., Mouri, K. (eds.) IWSEC 2014. LNCS, vol. 8639, pp. 250–265. Springer, Cham (2014). doi:10.1007/978-3-319-09843-2_19

23. Jia, D., Lu, X., Li, B., Mei, Q.: RKA secure PKE based on the DDH and HR assumptions. In: Susilo, W., Reyhanitabar, R. (eds.) ProvSec 2013. LNCS, vol. 8209, pp. 271–287. Springer, Heidelberg (2013). doi:10.1007/978-3-642-41227-1_16

24. Kiltz, E., Pietrzak, K., Stam, M., Yung, M.: A new randomness extraction paradigm for hybrid encryption. In: Joux, A. (ed.) EUROCRYPT 2009. LNCS, vol. 5479, pp. 590–609. Springer, Heidelberg (2009). doi:10.1007/978-3-642-01001-9_34

25. Matsumoto, T., Kato, K., Imai, H.: Speeding up secret computations with insecure auxiliary devices. In: Goldwasser, S. (ed.) CRYPTO 1988. LNCS, vol. 403, pp. 497–506. Springer, New York (1990). doi:10.1007/0-387-34799-2_35

26. Möller, B.: Algorithms for multi-exponentiation. In: Vaudenay, S., Youssef, A.M. (eds.) SAC 2001. LNCS, vol. 2259, pp. 165–180. Springer, Heidelberg (2001). doi:10.1007/3-540-45537-X_13

27. Naor, M., Yung, M.: Public-key cryptosystems provably secure against chosen ciphertext attacks. In: Ortiz, H. (ed.) STOC 1990, pp. 427–437. ACM (1990)

28. Phan, R.C.-W.: Related-key attacks on triple-DES and DESX variants. In: Okamoto, T. (ed.) CT-RSA 2004. LNCS, vol. 2964, pp. 15–24. Springer, Heidelberg (2004). doi:10.1007/978-3-540-24660-2_2

29. Qin, B., Liu, S., Yuen, T.H., Deng, R.H., Chen, K.: Continuous non-malleable key derivation and its application to related-key security. In: Katz, J. (ed.) PKC 2015. LNCS, vol. 9020, pp. 557–578. Springer, Heidelberg (2015). doi:10.1007/978-3-662-46447-2_25

30. Scott, M.: Faster pairings using an elliptic curve with an efficient endomorphism. In: Maitra, S., Veni Madhavan, C.E., Venkatesan, R. (eds.) INDOCRYPT 2005. LNCS, vol. 3797, pp. 258–269. Springer, Heidelberg (2005). doi:10.1007/11596219_21

31. Shoup, V.: Sequences of games: a tool for taming complexity in security proofs. IACR Cryptology ePrint Archive 2004, 332 (2004)

32. Wee, H.: Public key encryption against related key attacks. In: Fischlin, M., Buchmann, J., Manulis, M. (eds.) PKC 2012. LNCS, vol. 7293, pp. 262–279. Springer, Heidelberg (2012). doi:10.1007/978-3-642-30057-8_16

33. Zhang, W., Wu, W., Zhang, L., Feng, D.: Improved related-key impossible differential attacks on reduced-round AES-192. In: Biham, E., Youssef, A.M. (eds.) SAC 2006. LNCS, vol. 4356, pp. 15–27. Springer, Heidelberg (2007). doi:10.1007/978-3-540-74462-7_2

Signature and Authentication

On Privacy-Preserving Biometric Authentication

Aysajan Abidin[(⊠)]

KU Leuven – COSIC and IMEC, Leuven, Belgium
aysajan.abidin@esat.kuleuven.be

Abstract. Biometric authentication is becoming increasingly popular as a convenient authentication method. However, the privacy and security issues associated with biometric authentication are very serious. Privacy-preserving biometric authentication addresses privacy concerns associated with the use of biometrics and offers a secure solution for user authentication. Given the tremendous expansion of wireless communications a new distributed architecture in biometric authentication is evolving. In this distributed setting, a resource constrained client may outsource part of the computations during the biometric authentication process to a more powerful device (cloud server). In this work, we consider one such distributed setting consisting of clients, a cloud server, and a service provider and make a case for the need for verifiable computation to achieve security against malicious, as opposed to an honest-but-curious, cloud server. In particular, we propose to use verifiable computation on top of an homomorphic encryption scheme to verify that the cloud server correctly performs the computations outsourced to it. A proof of security of a generic protocol in the presence of a malicious cloud server is also provided. Finally, we discuss how an XOR-linear message authentication code can be used to verify the correctness of the computation.

Keywords: Biometric authentication · Biometric template privacy · Homomorphic encryption · Verifiable computation · XOR-linear MAC

1 Introduction

The new era of ubiquitous computing has led to mobile biometric authentication in which resource constrained devices are involved in the authentication process. More precisely, in this setting the client gains access to the authentication system via a wireless resource constrained device (e.g., mobile phone) and part of computations involved in the authentication process are outsourced to more powerful devices (cloud servers). Although this distributed setting seems to be quite natural given the tremendous expansion of wireless communications and cloud computing, it also poses serious security and privacy concerns, since biometrics may reveal sensitive private information and could be used to profile and track individuals. In order to protect against such privacy threats, it is important to employ privacy-preserving techniques suitable for distributed settings such as secure multi-party computation techniques.

© Springer International Publishing AG 2017
K. Chen et al. (Eds.): Inscrypt 2016, LNCS 10143, pp. 169–186, 2017.
DOI: 10.1007/978-3-319-54705-3_11

By adopting a distributed model of internal entities in the biometric authentication process one can limit the amount of power each single protocol entity has at its disposal and consequently avoid single point of failure attacks [1]. Additionally, such separation of protocol entities ensures higher degree of privacy for the biometric data since not a single entity has access to all sensitive data (i.e., fresh biometric template, stored biometric template, user's identity). However, an important problem that rises when part of the computations of the biometric authentication process are outsourced to cloud servers is how to guarantee the confidentiality of the outsourced data as well as the correctness of the outsourced computation. A malicious cloud server could indeed modify the process in order to gain some advantages, for instance, to reduce the cost of computation or recover private information. In this paper, we treat such cases of malicious cloud server and make a case for the need for combining privacy-preserving biometric authentication with verifiable delegation of computation to protect the privacy of the biometric templates against the cloud.

Biometric authentication comprises of two phases: the *enrollment* phase and the *authentication* phase. In the enrollment phase, users provide their biometric templates derived from their biometrics (such as fingerprints, face recognition and iris scan) for storage in a database. In the *authentication* phase, users authenticate themselves by providing their fresh biometric templates, and they are authenticated if their fresh biometric template matches the reference biometric template stored in the database.

Following the previous work by [2,3], we consider the following setting for a biometric authentication system comprising three entities, namely, a client set $\mathcal{C}$ of clients $\mathcal{C}_i$, for $i = 1, \cdots, N$, one for each user $\mathcal{U}_i$, a computation (or a cloud) server $\mathcal{CS}$ with a database $\mathcal{DB}$, and a service provider $\mathcal{SP}$. The client $\mathcal{C}_i$ has a sensor that captures biometric templates from its owner (i.e., the user $\mathcal{U}_i$). The cloud server $\mathcal{CS}$ stores the reference biometric templates and performs computationally expensive calculations. The service provider $\mathcal{SP}$ takes the final decision depending on whether there is a match between the fresh and the reference biometric templates. This is a reasonable model considering the fast rise of cloud computing and storage services, and also the widespread use of smartphones with embedded biometric sensors.

A common cryptographic tool that is employed in building privacy-preserving biometric authentication is homomorphic encryption [1–7]. In such a scheme, encryption protects the privacy of the biometric templates while the matching of the fresh and reference biometric templates are performed over the encrypted data using the homomorphic property of the encryption. However, this requires the actor responsible for performing the delegated calculations on encrypted biometric templates to be trusted. Otherwise, by computing a function different than what the protocol specifies and using $\mathcal{SP}$ as an oracle, the computing actor (i.e., the $\mathcal{CS}$) can learn information about either the stored reference biometric template b_i or the fresh biometric template b_i'. Similar attacks on two recently proposed protocols employing ring-LWE and ideal lattice based somewhat homomorphic encryption schemes [2,3] are presented in [8]. Therefore, in addition to homomorphic encryption, a cryptographic scheme that allows the client/service provider to verify that the cloud server performed the correct computation. Schemes that allow verification of computations delegated to a computationally powerful third party (or the cloud server in our case) already exist and are known as verifiable computation [9–14] or signatures of correct computation [15]. In this paper, we study their employment in privacy-preserving biometric authentication.

1.1 Related Work

Over the years, quite a few proposals for privacy-preserving biometric authentication appeared in the literature. These are based upon cryptographic techniques, such as oblivious transfer [16,17], private information retrieval [18,19], and homomorphic encryption [20,21]. For example, Bringer *et al.* employed the Goldwasser-Micali cryptosystem [21] to protect the privacy of the biometric templates against *honest-but-curious* (or *passive*) adversaries in [1]. There are also other privacy-preserving biometric authentication protocols that are based on the additive HE by Paillier [20] and Damgård *et al.* [22] such as the protocols for face recognition in [5–7]. Oblivious transfer was used in SCiFi [23], a system for secure computation of face identification. Furthermore, somewhat HE schemes based on ideal lattices and ring learning with errors are also employed in designing privacy-preserving biometric authentication protocols in [2,3].

All of these protocols are designed to be secure against *honest-but-curious* adversaries, and their security and privacy properties are later analysed in [4,8,24–26]. In [24], Simoens *et al.* made a compelling case for the need for designing privacy-preserving biometric authentication protocols that are secure against *malicious* adversaries. They also presented a framework for analysing the security and privacy-preserving properties of biometric authentication protocols in the presence of such adversaries. In fact, the weaknesses of the protocols proposed in [1–3] that are identified in [8,25,26] can be attributed to the lack of verifiable computation. In other words, the attacks reported in [8,25,26] can also be mitigated using verifiable computation.

Since most biometric authentication schemes use binary biometric templates, the Hamming distance (or the normalised Hamming distance) is employed to check whether two biometric templates match each other. Therefore, protocols for secure Hamming distance computation based on oblivious transfer are proposed by Bringer, Chabanne and Patey in [27]. These protocols have potential applications in privacy-preserving biometric authentication. Recently Bringer *et al.* generalised their results for secure computation of other distances such as the Euclidean and the normalised Hamming distance in [28].

1.2 Our Contribution

In this paper, we propose to combine verifiable computation with homomorphic encryption in order to achieve security against malicious computing server (i.e., the cloud server) in the above mentioned distributed biometric authentication setting. To this end, we outline a generic biometric authentication protocol with enhanced security and privacy properties in the presence of a malicious cloud server, combining homomorphic encryption with a scheme for verifiable computation. We then prove the security of the generic protocol against malicious cloud server. Furthermore, we discuss how an XOR-linear message authentication code (MAC) can be used to verify the correctness of the outsourced computation in the studied biometric authentication setting.

Outline. The rest of the paper is organised as follows. Section 2 introduces the necessary background. Section 3 presents our threat model and communication model for the protocol. Next we propose a generic protocol combining a scheme for verifiable computation with HE, and show that the protocol has enhanced security and privacy properties even in the presence of a malicious cloud server in Sect. 4. Furthermore, we give a specific instantiation of our generic protocol using an XOR-linear MAC in Sect. 5. Finally, Sect. 6 concludes the paper.

2   Preliminaries

First, we introduce the notations used in this paper. Biometric templates are regarded as vectors in $\mathbb{Z}_{q\geqslant 2}^N$, where q is an integer. Let b_i and b'_i denote the reference and fresh biometric templates, respectively, of the i-th user $\mathcal{U}_i$ whose identity is denoted by ID_i, for $i = 1, \cdots, M$, where M is the total number of users. Let τ be the authentication threshold and $\mathsf{Dist} : \mathbb{Z}_q^M \times \mathbb{Z}_q^M \mapsto \mathbb{R}_{\geqslant 0}$ be a distance on $\mathbb{Z}_q^M$. Then we say that b_i and b'_i match each other and thus belong to the same user, if $\mathsf{Dist}(b_i, b'_i) \leqslant \tau$. In the case of binary templates, the Hamming distance between b_i and b'_i is denoted by $\mathsf{HD}(b_i, b'_i)$, which is also equal to the Hamming weight $\mathsf{HW}(b_i \oplus b'_i)$. Finally, PPT and IND-CPA refer to probabilistic polynomial time and indistinguishability against chosen plaintext attacks, respectively.

2.1   Homomorphic Encryption

We use an homomorphic encryption (HE) scheme, denoted by $\mathsf{HE} = (\mathsf{KeyGen}, \mathsf{Enc}, \mathsf{Dec})$, that allows, given $\mathsf{Enc}(b_i)$ and $\mathsf{Enc}(b'_i)$, to compute $\mathsf{Enc}(\mathsf{Dist}(b_i, b'_i))$ homomorphically. We require the employed HE scheme to have semantic security against chosen plaintext attacks, which is defined as follows. Let $(\mathsf{pk}, \mathsf{sk})$ be the public and private key pairs for the HE scheme and λ a security parameter. Consider the following game played between a PPT adversary $\mathcal{A}$ and a challenger

$$\boxed{\begin{aligned} &\mathsf{Exp}_{\mathsf{HE},\mathcal{A}}^{\mathsf{IND\text{-}CPA}}(\lambda): \\ &\quad (\mathsf{pk}, \mathsf{sk}), \leftarrow \mathsf{KeyGen}(\lambda); \quad (m_0, m_1), \; m_0 \neq m_1 \leftarrow \mathcal{A}(\lambda, \mathsf{pk}); \quad \beta \xleftarrow{R} \{0, 1\} \\ &\quad c \leftarrow \mathsf{Enc}(m_\beta, \mathsf{pk}); \quad \beta' \leftarrow \mathcal{A}(m_0, m_1, c, \mathsf{pk}) \\ &\quad \text{Return 1 if } \beta' = \beta, \, 0 \text{ otherwise} \end{aligned}}$$

and define the adversary's advantage in this game as $\mathsf{Adv}_{\mathsf{HE},\mathcal{A}}^{\mathsf{IND\text{-}CPA}}(\lambda) = |2\Pr\{\mathsf{Exp}_{\mathsf{HE},\mathcal{A}}^{\mathsf{IND\text{-}CPA}}(\lambda) = 1\} - 1|$.

Definition 1. *We say that HE is IND-CPA-secure if all PPT adversaries have a negligible advantage in the above game:* $\text{Adv}_{HE,\mathcal{A}}^{IND\text{-}CPA}(\lambda) \leqslant \text{negl}(\lambda)$.

Here, $\text{negl}(\lambda)$ is a negligible function defined as follows.

Definition 2. *We say that a function* $\text{negl} : \mathbb{N} \mapsto [0,1]$ *is negligible if for all positive polynomials* poly *and all sufficiently large* $\lambda \in \mathbb{N}$, *we have* $\text{negl}(\lambda) < 1/\text{poly}(\lambda)$.

2.2 Privacy-Preserving Biometric Authentication

At a high level, a privacy-preserving biometric authentication (PPBA) protocol employing HE can be defined by the following processes.

- Setup: In this step, the keys (pk, sk) for the HE scheme are generated and distributed to the relevant protocol actors by either one protocol actor or an external trusted third party.
- $\mathcal{DB} \leftarrow \text{Enroll}\big((\text{Enc}(b_i))_{i=1}^{M}, (\text{ID}_i)_{i=1}^{M}\big)$: This process collects the encrypted reference biometric template $\text{Enc}(b_i)$ and identity ID_i pair from all M users and stores them in the database $\mathcal{DB}$.
- $1 \cup 0 \leftarrow \text{Authen}(\text{Enc}(b_i'), \text{ID}_i)$: To authenticate a user $\mathcal{U}_i$, this process takes an encrypted fresh biometric template $\text{Enc}(b_i')$ and a claimed identity ID_i, retrieves $\text{Enc}(b_i)$ from the database $\mathcal{DB}$, and homomorphically computes $\text{Dist}(b_i, b_i')$ from $\text{Enc}(b_i)$ and $\text{Enc}(b_i')$. Finally, it outputs 1 if the authentication is successful, 0 otherwise.

A PPBA protocol must be both correct and secure.

Definition 3. *We say that a PPBA protocol is correct if, for all enrolled user identities* ID_i *with the corresponding reference biometric templates* b_i, *and for all fresh biometric templates* b_i' *with* $\text{Dist}(b_i, b_i') \leqslant \tau$, *it is always the case that* $1 \leftarrow \text{Authen}(\text{Enc}(b_i'), \text{ID}_i)$.

One may argue that one can set the Authen process to always return 1 and thus violate the correctness. However, the Authen process described here is just an abstraction for the verification process of a biometric authentication protocol, so for it to return 1, the fresh biometric template must match the reference biometric template.

Informally, a PPBA protocol is secure if a malicious adversary, which in our case is the cloud server, cannot learn more about the biometric templates than what is already revealed by the protocol transcripts. Formally, we define the security of against a malicious adversary $\mathcal{A}$ as follows. Consider the following game

$$
\begin{aligned}
&\text{Exp}_{\text{PPBA},\mathcal{A}}^{\text{Priv}}(\lambda): \\
&\quad (\text{pk}, \text{sk}) \leftarrow \text{KeyGen}(\lambda); \quad (\text{ID}_i, b_{i_0}', b_{i_1}'), \, b_{i_0}' \neq b_{i_1}' \leftarrow \mathcal{A}(\lambda, \text{pk}) \\
&\quad \beta \xleftarrow{R} \{0,1\}; \quad \text{Out} \leftarrow \text{Authen}\big(\text{ID}_i, \text{Enc}(b_{i_\beta}')\big) \\
&\quad \beta' \leftarrow \mathcal{A}\big(\text{ID}_i, b_{i_0}', b_{i_1}', \text{Enc}(b_{i_\beta}', \mathcal{DB}), \text{Out}\big) \\
&\quad \text{Return 1 if } \beta' = \beta, \, 0 \text{ otherwise}
\end{aligned}
$$

and define the adversary's advantage in this game as $Adv^{Priv}_{PPBA,\mathcal{A}}(\lambda) = |2\Pr\{Exp^{Priv}_{PPBA,\mathcal{A}}(\lambda) = 1\} - 1|$. Note, ID_i has to be an enrolled user identity.

Definition 4. *We say that a PPBA protocol is secure if all PPT adversaries have a negligible advantage in the above game: $Adv^{Priv}_{PPBA,\mathcal{A}}(\lambda) \leqslant negl(\lambda)$.*

We assume that the adversary is given an oracle access to Authen and is allowed to query it with user $ID_j (\neq ID_i)$ and b'_j polynomially many times (e.g., $poly(\lambda)$ times). The adversary is also given $Enc(b'_{i_\beta})$ and the database. If the adversary cannot distinguish whether it is (ID_i, b'_{i_0}) or (ID_i, b'_{i_1}) that is being used by Authen, then we say that the protocol preserves privacy of the biometric templates.

2.3   Verifiable Computation

A scheme for verifiable computation (VC) allows a computationally weak client to both outsource heavy computations to a computationally powerful cloud server and efficiently verify the output of the cloud server. In our case, we consider that the heavy computations outsourced by the client to the cloud server are performed over encrypted data. In particular, the cloud computes a function f on input $Enc(b_i)$ and $Enc(b'_i)$ so that $f(Enc(b_i), Enc(b'_i)) = Enc(Dist(b_i, b'_i))$.

Definition 5 (Verifiable computation [11]). *A VC scheme VC = (KeyGen, ProbGen, Com, Ver) comprises four algorithms defined as:*

- *$(PK, VK) \leftarrow KeyGen(\lambda, f)$: The (randomised) key generation algorithm KeyGen takes as input a security parameter λ and a function f, and outputs a public key PK and a verification key VK for the function f. The public key PK is provided to the cloud server, while the verification key VK is kept secret by the client.*
- *$(\sigma_x, \rho_x) \leftarrow ProbGen(x, VK)$: The problem generation algorithm ProbGen takes as input a function input x and a verification key VK, and outputs a public value σ_x and a secret value ρ_x. The public value σ_x is provided to the cloud, while the secret value ρ_x is kept secret by the client.*
- *$\sigma_y \leftarrow Com(\sigma_x, PK)$: The computation algorithm Com takes as input a public value σ_x and a public key PK for f, and outputs an encoded version σ_y of $y = f(x)$.*
- *$y \cup \perp \leftarrow Ver(\rho_x, \sigma_y, VK)$: The verification algorithm Ver takes as input a verification key VK, a secret value ρ_x, and the output from Com, and outputs y indicating that σ_y is a valid encoding of $y = f(x)$ or $\perp$ indicating that σ_y does not represent $f(x)$.*

A VC scheme is correct if the output of the problem generation algorithm ProbGen allows an honest cloud server to compute values that will be successfully verified and that correspond to the evaluation of f on the input values. Formally, correctness is defined as follows.

Definition 6. *A VC scheme* VC *is said to be correct if, for any function f and input x in the domain of f, it holds that $y \leftarrow \mathsf{Ver}(\rho_x, \sigma_y, \mathsf{VK})$ as long as* $(\mathsf{PK}, \mathsf{VK}) \leftarrow \mathsf{KeyGen}(\lambda, f)$, $(\sigma_x, \rho_x) \leftarrow \mathsf{ProbGen}(x, \mathsf{VK})$, *and* $\sigma_y \leftarrow \mathsf{Com}(\sigma_x, \mathsf{PK})$.

In order to be secure, a VC scheme VC must be such that, for any given function f and input x, a malicious cloud should not be able to make the verification algorithm accept y' such that $y' \neq f(x)$. Formally, the security of VC is defined as the advantage of an adversary in the following game $\mathsf{Exp}_{\mathsf{VC}, \mathcal{A}}(\lambda, f)$ which captures the intuitive argument above.

$$
\begin{aligned}
&\mathsf{Exp}_{\mathsf{VC}, \mathcal{A}}(\lambda, f): \\
&\quad (\mathsf{PK}, \mathsf{VK}) \leftarrow \mathsf{KeyGen}(\lambda, f) \\
&\quad x_1 \leftarrow \mathcal{A}(\lambda, \mathsf{PK}) \\
&\quad (\sigma_{x_1}, \rho_{x_1}) \leftarrow \mathsf{ProbGen}(x_1, \mathsf{VK}) \\
&\quad \sigma_{y_1} \leftarrow \mathcal{A}(\mathsf{PK}, x_1, \sigma_{x_1}) \\
&\quad \beta_1 \leftarrow \mathsf{Ver}(\rho_{x_1}, \sigma_{y_1}, \mathsf{VK}) \\
&\quad \text{For } i = 2, \cdots, \ell = \mathsf{poly}(\lambda) \\
&\qquad x_i \leftarrow \mathcal{A}(\mathsf{PK}, x_1, \sigma_{x_1}, \beta_1, \cdots, x_{i-1}, \sigma_{x_{i-1}}, \beta_{i-1}) \\
&\qquad (\sigma_{x_i}, \rho_{x_i}) \leftarrow \mathsf{ProbGen}(x_i, \mathsf{VK}) \\
&\qquad \sigma_{y_i} \leftarrow \mathcal{A}(\mathsf{PK}, x_1, \sigma_{x_1}, \beta_1, \cdots, x_{i-1}, \sigma_{x_{i-1}}, \beta_{i-1}, \sigma_{x_i}) \\
&\qquad \beta_i \leftarrow \mathsf{Ver}(\rho_{x_i}, \sigma_{y_i}, \mathsf{VK}) \\
&\quad x \leftarrow \mathcal{A}(\mathsf{PK}, x_1, \sigma_{x_1}, \beta_1, \cdots, x_\ell, \sigma_{x_\ell}, \beta_\ell) \\
&\quad (\sigma_x, \rho_x) \leftarrow \mathsf{ProbGen}(x, \mathsf{VK}) \\
&\quad \sigma'_y \leftarrow \mathcal{A}(\mathsf{PK}, x_1, \sigma_{x_1}, \beta_1, \cdots, x_\ell, \sigma_{x_\ell}, \beta_\ell, \sigma_x) \\
&\quad y' \leftarrow \mathsf{Ver}(\rho_x, \sigma'_y, \mathsf{VK}) \\
&\quad \text{Return 1 if } y' \neq f(x) \text{ and } y' \neq \perp, \text{ 0 otherwise}
\end{aligned}
$$

The adversary's advantage in this game is defined as $\mathsf{Adv}_{\mathsf{VC}, \mathcal{A}}(\lambda, f) = \Pr\{\mathsf{Exp}_{\mathsf{VC}, \mathcal{A}}(\lambda, f) = 1\}$. Note that the adversary is given an oracle access to ProbGen and Ver.

Definition 7 (Security of VC [11]**).** *We say that* VC *is secure if, for any function f, all* PPT *adversaries have a negligible advantage in the above game:* $\mathsf{Adv}_{\mathsf{VC}, \mathcal{A}}(\lambda, f) \leqslant \mathsf{negl}(\lambda)$.

3   Threat Model

When analysing the security of a protocol, there are two types of adversaries to consider: a *semi-honest* (also known as, *honest-but-curious* or *passive*) adversary and a *malicious* (or *active*) adversary. A *semi-honest* adversary follows the protocol correctly, but attempts to deduce as much information as possible about protected data from the protocol transcripts. A *malicious* adversary, on the other hand, can arbitrarily deviate from the protocol specifications. Both types of adversaries attempt to break either the correctness or the security property of the protocol. Here we focus on *malicious* adversaries.

We consider a three-party setting which comprises a client $\mathcal{C}_i$ (one for each user $\mathcal{U}_i$), a cloud server $\mathcal{CS}$, and a service provider $\mathcal{SP}$. The client $\mathcal{C}_i$ (e.g., a smartphone owned by the user $\mathcal{U}_i$) has a biometric sensor that extracts biometric templates from the user. We assume that each user's client device is not compromised. Since if a client $\mathcal{C}_i$ is compromised, then the reference biometric template of the owner $\mathcal{U}_i$ can be easily recovered using the fresh biometric template provided by the owner [29].

The service provider $\mathcal{SP}$ manages the keys for the employed encryption scheme and makes the authentication decision. Therefore, we consider the service provider $\mathcal{SP}$ as a trusted protocol actor. However, we do not entrust any biometric template to the service provider. The malicious actor is the cloud server $\mathcal{CS}$, which has a database storing the encrypted reference biometric templates and performs computations on the encrypted fresh and reference biometric templates. The result of the computation performed by $\mathcal{CS}$ will allow $\mathcal{SP}$ to make its decision. In this paper, we exclusively focus on biometric template privacy and template recovery attacks. Hence, denial-of-service type of attacks are outside the scope of this paper.

For the communication model, we assume that the communication channel between the protocol entities are both authentic and secure in the sense that messages exchanged between two parties cannot be modified or intercepted by an eavesdropper. This assumption is also necessary for avoiding replay attacks. Such a communication channel can be established by using TLS or IPsec between the protocol participants.

4   A Generic Protocol

This section presents a generic protocol that combines verifiable computation with an homomorphic encryption. The protocol also employs a collision resistant cryptographic hash function $H : \{0,1\}^* \mapsto \{0,1\}^n$ (in our security analysis, we regard H as a random oracle). To differentiate from the database $\mathcal{DB}$ on the cloud server side, we use db to denote the database on the service provider side. We call the generic protocol PPBA which comprises the following.

- Enroll: The user enrollment phase is depicted in Fig. 1. The service provider $\mathcal{SP}$ chooses a collision resistant cryptographic hash function H and runs the key generation algorithm KeyGen for the HE and VC schemes using a security parameter λ and the function f to be computed by the cloud as input: $(\mathsf{pk}, \mathsf{sk}) \leftarrow \mathsf{HE.KeyGen}(\lambda)$ and $(\mathsf{PK}, \mathsf{VK}) \leftarrow \mathsf{VC.KeyGen}(\lambda, f)$. The client $\mathcal{C}_i$ requests enrollment by sending its owner $\mathcal{U}_i$'s identity ID_i to $\mathcal{SP}$. $\mathcal{SP}$ then maps ID_i to an index i using a process known only to itself. The tuple $(i, H, \mathsf{pk}, \mathsf{VK})$ is sent to $\mathcal{C}_i$, and $(\mathsf{pk}, \mathsf{PK})$ to $\mathcal{CS}$. The function f is known to the protocol actors. After receiving (i, H, pk), $\mathcal{C}_i$ first obtains the reference biometric template b_i and encrypts the reference biometric template, $\mathsf{Enc}(b_i)$. $\mathcal{C}_i$ then provides $(i, \mathsf{Enc}(b_i))$ to the database $\mathcal{DB}$ on the cloud server side for storage. In addition, $\mathcal{C}_i$ sends the hash $\omega_i = H(\mathsf{Enc}(b_i))$ to $\mathcal{SP}$ which stores (i, ω_i) in its database db. Locally, $\mathcal{C}_i$ stores (i, VK). Since it is necessary for security, we assume that user enrollment is performed in a secure and controlled environment.
- Authen: In this phase, before the user $\mathcal{U}_i$ authenticates himself, the service provider $\mathcal{SP}$ authenticates itself to the client $\mathcal{C}_i$ and provides the public key pk for HE and the hash function H to $\mathcal{C}_i$. The authentication of $\mathcal{SP}$ is necessary to avoid sending sensitive information to a malicious party impersonating the legitimate $\mathcal{SP}$. After $\mathcal{SP}$ is authenticated, $\mathcal{C}_i$ obtains from its user

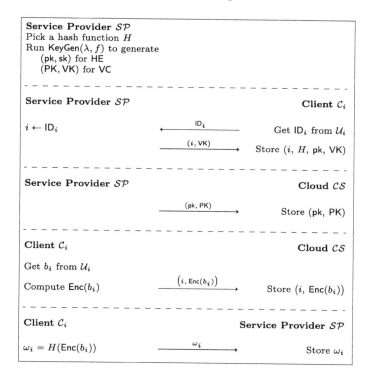

Fig. 1. The enrollment phase of PPBA.

$\mathcal{U}_i$ a fresh biometric template b_i' and an identity ID_i, and provides $\mathsf{Enc}(b_i')$ and the index i that it stored during enrollment to the cloud server $\mathcal{CS}$. The cloud then retrieves $\mathsf{Enc}(b_i)$ corresponding to i from its database $\mathcal{DB}$ and runs the computation algorithm $\sigma_{\mathsf{ct}_i} \leftarrow \mathsf{Com}(\mathsf{Enc}(b_i), \mathsf{Enc}(b_i'), \mathsf{pk}, \mathsf{PK})$ for the verifiable computation scheme VC. Note that pk is needed to evaluate the function f on $\mathsf{Enc}(b_i)$ and $\mathsf{Enc}(b_i')$. The output σ_{ct_i} is an encoded version of $\mathsf{ct}_i = f(\mathsf{Enc}(b_i), \mathsf{Enc}(b_i')) = \mathsf{Enc}(\mathsf{Dist}(b_i, b_i'))$. Then, $\mathcal{CS}$ sends $\mathsf{Enc}(b_i), \sigma_{\mathsf{ct}_i}$ back to the client $\mathcal{C}_i$, which runs the verification algorithm $\mathsf{ct}_i \leftarrow \mathsf{Ver}(\mathsf{Enc}(b_i), \mathsf{Enc}(b_i'), \sigma_{\mathsf{ct}_i}, \mathsf{VK})$. If $\mathsf{ct}_i \neq \perp$, then $\mathcal{C}_i$ computes $\widetilde{\omega}_i = H(\mathsf{Enc}(b_i))$ and sends $(\mathsf{ID}_i, \mathsf{ct}_i, \widetilde{\omega}_i)$ to $\mathcal{SP}$; otherwise, $\mathcal{C}_i$ aborts the protocol. Upon receiving $(\mathsf{ID}_i, \mathsf{ct}_i, \widetilde{\omega}_i)$ from $\mathcal{C}_i$, $\mathcal{SP}$ first extracts i from ID_i, retrieves ω_i from db and checks whether $\widetilde{\omega}_i = \omega_i$. Note here that the hash function is used to check whether the cloud used the correct input, i.e., $\mathsf{Enc}(b_i)$, to the function f. If $\widetilde{\omega}_i = \omega_i$, then $\mathcal{SP}$ decrypts ct_i, i.e., $\mathsf{Dec}(\mathsf{ct}_i) = \mathsf{Dec}\big(\mathsf{Enc}(\mathsf{Dist}(b_i, b_i'))\big) = \mathsf{Dist}(b_i, b_i')$. If $\mathsf{Dist}(b_i, b_i') \leqslant \tau$, then it outputs 1 (or YES) meaning that the client $\mathcal{C}_i$ (or the user $\mathcal{U}_i$) is authenticated; otherwise, it outputs 0 (or NO) meaning that the client $\mathcal{C}_i$ (or the user $\mathcal{U}_i$) is not authenticated.

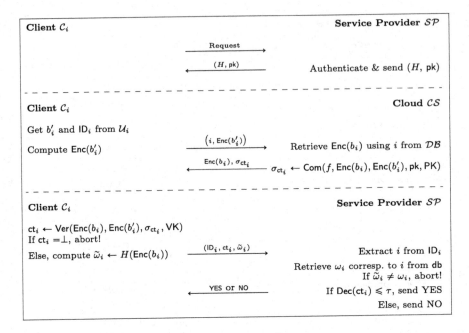

Fig. 2. The user authentication phase of PPBA.

Remark 1: We note that the problem generation algorithm ProbGen for the VC scheme is not used above since in our case the public and secret output of ProbGen algorithm are the same and equal to $(\mathsf{Enc}(b_i), \mathsf{Enc}(b'_i))$.

Remark 2: By requiring the correspondence between an identity and an index (e.g., $\mathsf{ID}_i \leftrightarrow i$) to be known only to the service provider, we can prevent a potentially malicious client $\mathcal{C}_i$ from impersonating another client $\mathcal{C}_j$, $j \neq i$. If this is not the case, then a misbehaving client, say $\mathcal{C}_i$, can initiate the authentication phase with an identity ID_j, $j \neq i$, and index j and obtain $\mathsf{Enc}(b_j)$ from the cloud $\mathcal{CS}$. Then, $\mathcal{C}_i$ aborts the current round and later authenticates itself as ID_j using $\mathsf{Enc}(b_j)$. Note that this also guarantees identity privacy against since $\mathcal{CS}$ does not know to which user identity a database entry belongs (Fig. 2).

It is straightforward to see that the correctness of the generic protocol readily follows. The following theorem summarises the security of the generic protocol PPBA against the malicious cloud server. The proof of the theorem is given in Appendix A.

Theorem 1 (Security of PPBA). *Let H be a random oracle. Let HE be an IND-CPA-secure HE scheme and VC a secure VC scheme as defined in Definition 7. Let $\mathcal{A}$ be a malicious cloud server that is PPT. Then the advantage of $\mathcal{A}$ in the game $\mathsf{Exp}_{PPBA,\mathcal{A}}^{Priv}(\lambda, f)$ (cf. Sect. 2.1) is negligible, i.e., $\mathsf{Adv}_{PPBA,\mathcal{A}}(\lambda, f) \leqslant \mathsf{negl}(\lambda)$.*

As mentioned in the previous work, the protocols previously proposed in [1–3] can be enhanced with a suitable verifiable computation scheme to mitigate the reported attacks in [8, 25, 26].

5   Instantiation

Here we discuss an instantiation of the generic protocol using an $\oplus$-linear message authentication code (MAC), where $\oplus$ is the XOR operation.

A MAC scheme consists of three algorithms (KeyGen, TAG, VRFY) (associated with a key space, a message space and a tag space). KeyGen, a key generation algorithm, takes a security parameter λ as input and outputs a key k (i.e., k $\leftarrow$ KeyGen(λ)). TAG, a tag generation algorithm, takes a message m and a key k as input, and outputs a tag (i.e., $t \leftarrow$ TAG(m, k)). VRFY, a verification algorithm, takes a message m, a tag t and a key k as input, and outputs a decision Out$_{MAC}$ (i.e., Out$_{MAC} \leftarrow$ VRFY(m, t, k)), which is 1 if the message-tag pair (m, t) is valid, and 0 otherwise.

A typical construction of a MAC scheme is via the use of Universal$_2$ (U$_2$) hash functions, see Appendix B for definitions and how U$_2$ hash functions can be used to construct a MAC scheme. There are constructions of U$_2$ hash functions that are $\oplus$-linear [30], from which one can construct an $\oplus$-linear MAC scheme. Note that a MAC scheme is called $\oplus$-linear if TAG($m_1 \oplus m_2$, k) = TAG(m_1, k) $\oplus$ TAG(m_2, k).

Using any HE scheme that enables the evaluation of XOR of two encrypted bitstrings (e.g., the Goldwasser-Micali encryption scheme [21] which supports this) and an $\oplus$-linear MAC to verify the correctness of the computation performed by $\mathcal{CS}$, we have the following variation of the generic protocol presented in the previous section.

- Enroll: The service provider $\mathcal{SP}$ runs the key generation algorithm KeyGen for the HE and MAC schemes using a security parameter λ: (pk, sk) $\leftarrow$ HE.KeyGen(λ) and k$_i$ $\leftarrow$ MAC.KeyGen(λ). The client $\mathcal{C}_i$ requests for enrollment by sending its owner $\mathcal{U}_i$'s identity ID$_i$ to $\mathcal{SP}$, which then maps ID$_i$ to an index i using a process known only to itself. The tuple $(i,$ pk, k$_i)$ is sent to $\mathcal{C}_i$, and pk to $\mathcal{CS}$. After receiving $(i,$ pk, k$_i)$, $\mathcal{C}_i$ first obtains the reference biometric template b_i and encrypts the reference biometric template, Enc(b_i). $\mathcal{C}_i$ then provides $(i,$ Enc(b_i)) to the database $\mathcal{DB}$ on the cloud server side for storage. In addition, $\mathcal{C}_i$ sends the tag $t_i =$ TAG(b_i, k$_i$) to $\mathcal{SP}$ which stores $(i,$ k$_i$, $t_i)$ in its database db. Locally, $\mathcal{C}_i$ stores $(i,$ k$_i)$. As before, we assume that user enrollment is performed in a secure and controlled environment.
- Authen: Again, before the user $\mathcal{U}_i$ authenticates himself, the service provider $\mathcal{SP}$ authenticates itself to the client $\mathcal{C}_i$. Then, $\mathcal{C}_i$ obtains from its user $\mathcal{U}_i$ a fresh biometric template b_i' and an identity ID$_i$, and provides Enc(b_i') and the index i to the cloud server $\mathcal{CS}$. In addition, $\mathcal{C}_i$ computes $t_i' =$ TAG(b_i', k$_i$) and sends (ID$_i$, t_i') to $\mathcal{SP}$. The cloud then retrieves Enc(b_i) corresponding to i from its database $\mathcal{DB}$ and computes $\gamma_i =$ Enc($b_i \oplus b_i'$) homomorphically from Enc(b_i)

and $\mathsf{Enc}(b'_i)$, and sends (i, γ_i) to $\mathcal{SP}$. The service provider then extracts i from ID_i and checks if the extracted i and the index received from $\mathcal{CS}$ match each other. If they match, $\mathcal{SP}$ continues to retrieves k_i and t_i corresponding to i from db, decrypts γ_i to obtain $\widetilde{b_i \oplus b'_i}$ (i.e., $\widetilde{b_i \oplus b'_i} \leftarrow \mathsf{Dec}(\gamma_i)$), and runs the MAC verification algorithm $\mathsf{VRFY}(\widetilde{b_i \oplus b'_i}, t_i \oplus t'_i, \mathsf{k}_i)$. If the output from VRFY is 0, $\mathcal{SP}$ rejects the user. Otherwise, $\mathcal{SP}$ checks if the Hamming weight $\mathsf{HW}(\widetilde{b_i \oplus b'_i}) \leqslant \tau$. Note that $\mathsf{HW}(b_i \oplus b'_i) = \mathsf{HD}(b_i, b'_i)$, where HD is the Hamming distance. If this is the case, $\mathcal{SP}$ authenticates the user $\mathcal{U}_i$, otherwise rejects.

5.1   Security Analysis

The instantiation is slightly different from the generic protocol in that the correctness of the computation is verified by $\mathcal{SP}$ in the instantiation, we will also present the security proof for the "instantiation" separately.

Definition 8. *A MAC scheme is called (Q_T, Q_V, t, ϵ)-secure (or, ϵ-secure, for short) if no PPT adversary $\mathcal{A}$ running in time at most t cannot generate a valid message-tag pair, even after making Q_T tag generation queries to TAG and Q_V verification queries to VRFY, except with probability ϵ.*

In any biometric template recovery attack that makes use of the side channel information (i.e., the authentication result), $\mathcal{CS}$ needs to be able to submit to $\mathcal{SP}$ a γ which encrypts a message that passes the MAC verification test performed by $\mathcal{SP}$. The ϵ-security of the employed MAC scheme does not allow this to happen. Furthermore, from a rejection response by $\mathcal{SP}$, $\mathcal{CS}$ does not know whether it is due the MAC verification failure or the mismatch between the fresh and reference biometric templates. Hence, our instantiation is robust and secure against the malicious $\mathcal{CS}$. Formally, the following summarises the security of the instantiation.

Theorem 2. *Let HE be an IND-CPA-secure HE scheme such that $HE.Enc(m_1, pk)HE.Enc(m_2, pk) = HE.Enc(m_1 \oplus m_2, pk)$ and MAC an ϵ-secure $\oplus$-linear MAC scheme. Then, the protocol that employs the HE and MAC schemes is secure against a malicious cloud server.*

The proof is given in Appendix C.

6   Summary

Privacy-preserving biometric authentication allows to authenticate users using their biometrics while preserving the biometric privacy. A natural approach to building a privacy-preserving biometric authentication protocol is the employment of an homomorphic encryption scheme that allows the computations and the matching process over encrypted biometric data. There are indeed multiple privacy-preserving biometric authentication protocols proposed in the literature over the years that rely on homomorphic encryption (cf. Sect. 1.1). In this work, we proposed to combine schemes for verifiable computation with homomorphic encryption to preserve the biometric privacy in a distributed remote biometric authentication setting comprising clients, a cloud server, and a service provider. A generic biometric authentication protocol which is secure against a malicious, as opposed to honest-but-curious, cloud server is presented. Moreover, an instantiation is also given using an XOR-linear MAC to verify the correctness of the computation performed by the cloud.

Acknowledgments. The author would like to thank the anonymous reviewers for their helpful comments. This work was supported by the European Commission through the SECURITY programme under FP7-SEC-2013-1-607049 EKSISTENZ.

A   Proof of Theorem 1

Before we proceed with the proof, let us first analyse the adversarial scenario in the case of the generic protocol PPBA. Note that by the attacker (or the adversary) $\mathcal{A}$, we refer to the malicious cloud server. We assume that the adversary $\mathcal{A}$ has oracle access to Authen, so $\mathcal{A}$ can query Authen with biometric templates and identity of its choice $\mathrm{poly}(\lambda)$ times, where λ is a security parameter. In addition, by the security of a privacy-preserving biometric authentication protocol, we mean the security of the biometric templates.

Again, we define the security of the protocol PPBA against a malicious adversary $\mathcal{A}$ via the following game played between $\mathcal{A}$ and PPBA.

$$\mathrm{Exp}_{\mathsf{PPBA},\mathcal{A}}^{\mathsf{Priv}}(\lambda, f):$$
$$(\mathsf{pk}, \mathsf{sk}), (\mathsf{PK}, \mathsf{VK}) \leftarrow \mathsf{KeyGen}(\lambda, f)$$
$$(\mathsf{ID}_i, b'_{i_0}, b'_{i_1}), b'_{i_0} \neq b'_{i_1} \leftarrow \mathcal{A}(\lambda, \mathsf{pk}, \mathsf{PK}, f)$$
$$\beta \xleftarrow{R} \{0,1\}; \quad \mathsf{Out} \leftarrow \mathsf{Authen}(\mathsf{ID}_i, i, \mathsf{Enc}(b'_{i_\beta}))$$
$$\beta' \leftarrow \mathcal{A}(\mathsf{ID}_i, b'_{i_0}, b'_{i_1}, \mathsf{Enc}(b'_{i_\beta}), \mathsf{Out})$$
$$\text{Return 1 if } \beta' = \beta, \text{ 0 otherwise}$$

The adversary's advantage at the end of this game is defined as $\mathsf{Adv}_{\mathsf{PPBA},\mathcal{A}}^{\mathsf{Priv}} = \left| 2 \Pr\{\mathsf{Exp}_{\mathsf{PPBA},\mathcal{A}}^{\mathsf{Priv}}(\lambda, f) = 1\} - 1 \right|$. We say that the protocol is secure (and preserves the privacy of biometric templates) against the malicious cloud server $\mathcal{CS}$, if $\mathsf{Adv}_{\mathsf{PPBA},\mathcal{A}}^{\mathsf{Priv}} \leqslant \mathsf{negl}(\lambda)$.

Let us write out the details of $\mathsf{Authen}(\mathsf{ID}_i, i, \mathsf{Enc}(b'_{i_\beta}))$ in the above experiment. Since the authentication process involves the client $\mathcal{C}_i$, the cloud server $\mathcal{CS}$, and the service provider $\mathcal{SP}$, in the description we write the entity name followed by a set of inputs it takes in a parenthesis to denote what that entity takes as input. For instance, $\mathcal{CS}(i, \mathsf{Enc}(b'_{i_\beta}), \mathsf{pk}, \mathsf{PK})$ denotes that $\mathcal{CS}$ takes i, $\mathsf{Enc}(b'_{i_\beta})$, and PK as input and performs the operations in the indented block underneath it.

$$\text{Authen}(\text{ID}_i, i, \text{Enc}(b'_{i_\beta})):$$

$\mathcal{C}_i$:	$\mathcal{SP}(\text{ID}_i, \text{ct}_i, \widetilde{\omega}_i, \text{sk})$:
$\quad$ Send $(i, \text{Enc}(b'_{i_\beta}))$ to $\mathcal{CS}$	$\quad i \leftarrow \text{ID}_i$
$\mathcal{CS}(i, \text{Enc}(b'_{i_\beta}), \text{pk}, \text{PK})$:	$\quad \omega_i \leftarrow \text{db}(i)$
$\quad \text{Enc}(b_i) \leftarrow \mathcal{DB}(i)$	$\quad$ if $\widetilde{\omega}_i \neq \omega_i$ then
$\quad \sigma_{\text{ct}_i} \leftarrow \text{Com}(\text{Enc}(b_i), \text{Enc}(b'_{i_\beta}), \text{pk}, \text{PK})$	$\quad\quad$ Return $\boxed{\text{Out}=0}$
$\quad$ Send $(\text{Enc}(b_i), \sigma_{\text{ct}_i})$ to $\mathcal{C}_i$	$\quad$ else
$\mathcal{C}_i(\text{Enc}(b'_{i_\beta}), \text{Enc}(b_i), \sigma_{\text{ct}_i})$:	$\quad\quad \text{Dist} \leftarrow \text{Dec}(\text{ct}_i)$
$\quad \text{ct}_i \leftarrow \text{Ver}(\text{Enc}(b_i), \text{Enc}(b'_{i_\beta}), \sigma_{\text{ct}_i}, \text{VK})$	$\quad\quad$ if $\text{Dist} \leqslant \tau$ then
$\quad$ if $\text{ct}_i = \perp$ then	$\quad\quad\quad$ Return $\boxed{\text{Out}=1}$
$\quad\quad$ Return $\boxed{\text{Out}=0}$	$\quad\quad$ else
$\quad$ else	$\quad\quad\quad$ Return $\boxed{\text{Out}=0}$
$\quad\quad \widetilde{\omega}_i \leftarrow H(\text{Enc}(b_i))$	
$\quad\quad$ Send $(\text{ID}_i, \text{ct}_i, \widetilde{\omega}_i)$ to $\mathcal{SP}$	

In the authentication process Authen, $\text{Out} = 1$ is returned in only one case (i.e., the case where the fresh and the reference biometric templates match each other), while $\text{Out} = 0$ is returned in three cases. The three cases are (1) $\mathcal{CS}$ does not perform the correct computation and the verification algorithm Ver outputs $\perp$, (2) $\mathcal{CS}$ performs the correct computation but uses a wrong input, so the integrity check fails, finally (3) there is no match between the fresh and the reference biometric templates.

Proof (of Theorem 1). We prove this theorem using two games.
game 0: This is the original game. Let S_0 be the event that $\beta' = \beta$.
game 1: This is the same as **game** 0, except that we now replace the output $(\text{Enc}(b_i), \sigma_{\text{ct}_i}) \leftarrow \mathcal{CS}(i, \text{Enc}(b'_{i_\beta}), \text{pk}, \text{PK})$ with the correct $\text{Enc}(b_i)$ corresponding to i and valid σ_{ct_i}. Let S_1 be the event that $\beta' = \beta$ in this game.

Claim 1: $|\Pr\{S_0\} - \Pr\{S_1\}|$ is negligible.

Proof (of Claim 1). The difference between **game** 0 and **game** 1 is that in **game** 0 it may happen that $\text{ct}_i = \perp$ and/or $\widetilde{\omega}_i \neq \omega_i$, while in **game** 1 these do not happen. While $\text{ct}_i = \perp$ means winning the game $\text{Exp}_{\text{VC}, \mathcal{A}}(\lambda, f)$, $\widetilde{\omega}_i \neq \omega_i$ means having a collision in H. So both of these happen with negligible probability because of the assumption that VC is secure (cf. Definition 7) and that H is a random oracle. Therefore, the difference between the winning probabilities in **game** 0 and **game** 1 is negligible.

Claim 2: $|2\Pr\{S_1\} - 1| \leqslant \text{negl}(\lambda)$.

Proof (of Claim 2). Suppose that the adversary's advantage is non-negligible, i.e., $|2\Pr\{S_1\} - 1| > \text{negl}(\lambda)$. Then we can construct an attacker $\mathcal{A}'$ that wins in the IND-CPA game against the underlying homomorphic encryption HE with non-negligible advantage as follows.

$$\text{Exp}_{\text{HE}, \mathcal{A}}^{\text{IND-CPA}}(\lambda):$$

$\quad (\text{pk}, \text{sk}) \leftarrow \text{KeyGen}(\lambda); \quad (m_0, m_1), m_0 \neq m_1 \leftarrow \mathcal{A}'(\lambda, \text{pk})$
$\quad \alpha \xleftarrow{R} \{0, 1\}; \quad c \leftarrow \text{Enc}(m_\alpha, \text{pk}); \quad \text{Simulate PPBA for } \mathcal{A}$
$\quad \alpha'(= \beta') \leftarrow \mathcal{A}'(\mathcal{A}(m_0, m_1, c, \text{pk}))$
Return 1 if $\alpha' = \alpha$, 0 otherwise

The attacker $\mathcal{A}'$ obtains the pk for HE, chooses two distinct messages $m_0, m_1 \in \mathbb{Z}_{q \geqslant 2}^N$, and rèceives a challenge $c = \mathsf{Enc}(m_\alpha)$, where $\alpha \xleftarrow{R} \{0, 1\}$. $\mathcal{A}'$ then simulates the protocol execution for PPBA. To simulate PPBA, $\mathcal{A}'$ uses pk to re-randomise $c = \mathsf{Enc}(m_\alpha)$ using the homomorphic property of the encryption, and registers the re-randomised c, let us call it c', along with an ID_i and a corresponding index i and a hash of c' in $\mathcal{DB}$ of $\mathcal{CS}$. For $\mathcal{CS}$, c and its randomised version c' are indistinguishable. This does faithfully simulate the protocol execution for the adversary $\mathcal{A}$, because $\mathcal{A}'$ knows the output of $\mathsf{Authen}(\mathsf{ID}_i, i, c)$. Now, if $\mathcal{A}$ outputs its guess β' for β, then $\mathcal{A}'$ outputs its guess $\alpha'(= \beta')$ for α. Thus, $\mathcal{A}'$ wins if $\mathcal{A}$ wins.

Hence, combining **Claim** 1 and 2, we have that $\mathsf{Adv}_{\mathsf{PPBA}, \mathcal{A}}^{\mathsf{Priv}}$ is negligible.

B   Universal Hash Functions

Universal hash functions were first proposed by Carter and Wegman [31] as, among others, a means to construct unconditionally secure MACs. Stinson formalised the definitions of Universal hash functions in [32]. Following these early works, there has been a considerable amount of research done on Universal hash functions to improve both the description length and computational performance, see e.g., [33] for a quick overview.

Definition 9 (ϵ-ASU$_2$ hash functions [32]). *Let $\mathcal{M}$ and $\mathcal{T}$ be finite sets. A family $\mathcal{F}$ of hash functions from $\mathcal{M}$ to $\mathcal{T}$ is ϵ-ASU$_2$ if the following two conditions are satisfied: (a) the number of hash functions in $\mathcal{F}$ that takes an arbitrary $m_1 \in \mathcal{M}$ to an arbitrary $t_1 \in \mathcal{T}$ is exactly $|\mathcal{F}|/|\mathcal{T}|$; (b) the fraction of those functions that also takes an arbitrary $m_2 \neq m_1$ in $\mathcal{M}$ to an arbitrary $t_2 \in \mathcal{T}$ (possibly equal to t_1) is at most ϵ. If $\epsilon = 1/|\mathcal{T}|$, then $\mathcal{F}$ is called SU$_2$.*

As can be seen from the definition, ϵ-ASU$_2$ hash functions can be used to construct a MAC scheme in a natural way. More specifically, in this case a pair of users, say Alice and Bob, share a secret key k which identifies a hash function h_k in a family of ϵ-ASU$_2$ hash functions. When Alice sends a message m to Bob, she also sends $t = h_k(m)$ along with m. Upon receiving (m, t), Bob checks the authenticity of m by comparing t with $h_k(m)$, which he himself computes using his share of the key k. If $h_k(m) = t$, then Bob accepts m as authentic; otherwise, he rejects it.

C   Proof of Theorem 2

Proof (of Theorem 2). Since the proof is similar to that of the Theorem 1, we just highlight the differences in the relevant hybrid security games and the claims. Let PPBA-HE-MAC denote the instantiation. The security against a malicious adversary $\mathcal{A}$ (e.g., $\mathcal{CS}$) is defined via the following game played between $\mathcal{A}$ and PPBA-HE-MAC.

$$\text{Exp}^{\text{Priv}}_{\text{PPBA-HE-MAC}, \mathcal{A}}(\lambda):$$
$$\quad (\text{pk}, \text{sk}), \ \text{MAC}.K \leftarrow \text{KeyGen}(\lambda)$$
$$\quad (\text{ID}_i, b'_{i_0}, b'_{i_1}), \ b'_{i_0} \neq b'_{i_1} \leftarrow \mathcal{A}(\lambda, \text{pk}, \text{MAC}.K)$$
$$\quad \beta \xleftarrow{R} \{0, 1\}; \quad \text{Out} \leftarrow \text{Authen}(\text{ID}_i, i, \text{Enc}(b'_{i_\beta}))$$
$$\quad \beta' \leftarrow \mathcal{A}(\text{ID}_i, b'_{i_0}, b'_{i_1}, \text{Enc}(b'_{i_\beta}), \text{Out})$$
$$\quad \text{Return 1 if } \beta' = \beta, \ 0 \text{ otherwise}$$

where $\text{MAC}.K$ is the key space for the employed MAC scheme (e.g., the set of U_2 hash functions). The adversary's advantage is defined as $\text{Adv}^{\text{Priv}}_{\text{PPBA-HE-MAC}, \mathcal{A}} = \left| 2 \Pr\{ \text{Exp}^{\text{Priv}}_{\text{PPBA-HE-MAC}, \mathcal{A}}(\lambda) = 1 \} - 1 \right|$. If $\text{Adv}^{\text{Priv}}_{\text{PPBA-HE-MAC}, \mathcal{A}} \leqslant \text{negl}(\lambda)$, we say that PPBA-HE-MAC is secure (and preserves the privacy of biometric templates) against $\mathcal{A}$.

The details of $\text{Authen}(\text{ID}_i, i, \text{Enc}(b'_{i_\beta}))$ are given below.

$$\textbf{Authen}(\text{ID}_i, i, \text{Enc}(b'_{i_\beta})):$$
$$\quad \mathcal{C}_i \text{ sends } (i, \text{Enc}(b'_{i_\beta})) \text{ to } \mathcal{CS}$$
$$\quad \mathcal{C}_i \text{ sends } (\text{ID}_i, t'_{i_\beta}) \text{ to } \mathcal{SP}$$
$$\quad \mathcal{CS}(i, \text{Enc}(b'_{i_\beta}), \text{pk}):$$
$$\qquad \text{Enc}(b_i) \leftarrow \mathcal{DB}(i)$$
$$\qquad \gamma_i \leftarrow \text{Enc}(b_i)\text{Enc}(b'_{i_\beta}) = \text{Enc}(b_i \oplus b'_{i_\beta})$$
$$\qquad \text{Send } (i, \gamma_i) \text{ to } \mathcal{SP}$$
$$\quad \mathcal{SP}(\text{ID}_i, i, \gamma_i, t'_{i_\beta}, \text{sk}):$$
$$\qquad \text{If } i \text{ is not the correct index for } \text{ID}_i \text{ then}$$
$$\qquad\qquad \text{Return } \boxed{\text{Out=0}}$$
$$\qquad (k_i, t_i) \leftarrow \text{db}(i)$$
$$\qquad \text{if } t_i \oplus t'_{i_\beta} \neq \text{TAG}(\text{Dec}(\gamma_i), k_i) \text{ then}$$
$$\qquad\qquad \text{Return } \boxed{\text{Out=0}}$$
$$\qquad \text{else}$$
$$\qquad\qquad \text{if } \text{HW}(\gamma_i) \leqslant \tau \text{ then}$$
$$\qquad\qquad\qquad \text{Return } \boxed{\text{Out=1}}$$
$$\qquad\qquad \text{else}$$
$$\qquad\qquad\qquad \text{Return } \boxed{\text{Out=0}}$$

The proof is based on the following two hybrid games.

game 0: This is the original game $\text{Exp}^{\text{Priv}}_{\text{PPBA-HE-MAC}, \mathcal{A}}(\lambda)$. Let S_0 be the event that $\beta' = \beta$ in **game** 0.

game 1: This is the same as **game** 0, except that now $\mathcal{CS}$ always performs the correct computation. Let S_1 be the event that $\beta' = \beta$ in **game** 1.

Claim 1: $| \Pr\{S_0\} - \Pr\{S_1\} |$ is negligible. This follows from the ϵ-security of the employed MAC scheme.

Claim 2: The adversary has negligible advantage in **game** 1, i.e., $\left| 2 \Pr\{S_1\} - 1 \right| \leqslant \text{negl}(\lambda)$. This follows from the IND-CPA-security of the HE scheme.

Hence, we have that $\text{Adv}^{\text{Priv}}_{\text{PPBA-HE-MAC}, \mathcal{A}}$ is negligible.

References

1. Bringer, J., Chabanne, H., Izabachène, M., Pointcheval, D., Tang, Q., Zimmer, S.: An application of the goldwasser-micali cryptosystem to biometric authentication. In: Pieprzyk, J., Ghodosi, H., Dawson, E. (eds.) ACISP 2007. LNCS, vol. 4586, pp. 96–106. Springer, Heidelberg (2007). doi:10.1007/978-3-540-73458-1_8

2. Yasuda, M., Shimoyama, T., Kogure, J., Yokoyama, K., Koshiba, T.: Packed homomorphic encryption based on ideal lattices and its application to biometrics. In: Cuzzocrea, A., Kittl, C., Simos, D.E., Weippl, E., Xu, L. (eds.) CD-ARES 2013. LNCS, vol. 8128, pp. 55–74. Springer, Heidelberg (2013). doi:10.1007/978-3-642-40588-4_5

3. Yasuda, M., Shimoyama, T., Kogure, J., Yokoyama, K., Koshiba, T.: Practical packing method in somewhat homomorphic encryption. In: Garcia-Alfaro, J., Lioudakis, G., Cuppens-Boulahia, N., Foley, S., Fitzgerald, W.M. (eds.) DPM/SETOP -2013. LNCS, vol. 8247, pp. 34–50. Springer, Heidelberg (2014). doi:10.1007/978-3-642-54568-9_3

4. Barbosa, M., Brouard, T., Cauchie, S., Sousa, S.M.: Secure biometric authentication with improved accuracy. In: Mu, Y., Susilo, W., Seberry, J. (eds.) ACISP 2008. LNCS, vol. 5107, pp. 21–36. Springer, Heidelberg (2008). doi:10.1007/978-3-540-70500-0_3

5. Erkin, Z., Franz, M., Guajardo, J., Katzenbeisser, S., Lagendijk, I., Toft, T.: Privacy-preserving face recognition. In: Goldberg, I., Atallah, M.J. (eds.) PETS 2009. LNCS, vol. 5672, pp. 235–253. Springer, Heidelberg (2009). doi:10.1007/978-3-642-03168-7_14

6. Sadeghi, A.-R., Schneider, T., Wehrenberg, I.: Efficient privacy-preserving face recognition. In: Lee, D., Hong, S. (eds.) ICISC 2009. LNCS, vol. 5984, pp. 229–244. Springer, Heidelberg (2010). doi:10.1007/978-3-642-14423-3_16

7. Huang, Y., Malka, L., Evans, D., Katz, J.: Efficient privacy-preserving biometric identification. In: NDSS (2011)

8. Abidin, A., Mitrokotsa, A.: Security aspects of privacy-preserving biometric authentication based on ideal lattices and ring-LWE. In: Proceedings of the IEEE Workshop on Information Forensics and Security, pp. 1653–1658 (2014)

9. Gennaro, R., Gentry, C., Parno, B.: Non-interactive verifiable computing: outsourcing computation to untrusted workers. In: Rabin, T. (ed.) CRYPTO 2010. LNCS, vol. 6223, pp. 465–482. Springer, Heidelberg (2010). doi:10.1007/978-3-642-14623-7_25

10. Chung, K.-M., Kalai, Y., Vadhan, S.: Improved delegation of computation using fully homomorphic encryption. In: Rabin, T. (ed.) CRYPTO 2010. LNCS, vol. 6223, pp. 483–501. Springer, Heidelberg (2010). doi:10.1007/978-3-642-14623-7_26

11. Benabbas, S., Gennaro, R., Vahlis, Y.: Verifiable delegation of computation over large datasets. In: Rogaway, P. (ed.) CRYPTO 2011. LNCS, vol. 6841, pp. 111–131. Springer, Heidelberg (2011). doi:10.1007/978-3-642-22792-9_7

12. Backes, M., Fiore, D., Reischuk, R.M.: Verifiable delegation of computation on outsourced data. In: ACM CCS 2013, pp. 863–874. ACM (2013)

13. Setty, S.T., McPherson, R., Blumberg, A.J., Walfish, M.: Making argument systems for outsourced computation practical (sometimes). In: NDSS 2012 (2012)

14. Zhang, L.F., Safavi-Naini, R.: Batch verifiable computation of outsourced functions. Des. Codes Crypt., 1–23 (2015)

15. Papamanthou, C., Shi, E., Tamassia, R.: Signatures of correct computation. In: Sahai, A. (ed.) TCC 2013. LNCS, vol. 7785, pp. 222–242. Springer, Heidelberg (2013). doi:10.1007/978-3-642-36594-2_13

16. Rabin, M.O.: How to exchange secrets with oblivious transfer. IACR Cryptology ePrint Archive 2005, 187 (2005)

17. Yao, A.C.C.: How to generate and exchange secrets. In: 27th Annual Symposium on Foundations of Computer Science, pp. 162–167. IEEE (1986)

18. Chor, B., Kushilevitz, E., Goldreich, O., Sudan, M.: Private information retrieval. J. ACM 45(6), 965–981 (1998)

19. Ostrovsky, R., Skeith, W.E.: A survey of single-database private information retrieval: techniques and applications. In: Okamoto, T., Wang, X. (eds.) PKC 2007. LNCS, vol. 4450, pp. 393–411. Springer, Heidelberg (2007). doi:10.1007/978-3-540-71677-8_26

20. Paillier, P.: Public-key cryptosystems based on composite degree residuosity classes. In: Stern, J. (ed.) EUROCRYPT 1999. LNCS, vol. 1592, pp. 223–238. springer, Heidelberg (1999). doi:10.1007/3-540-48910-X_16

21. Goldwasser, S., Micali, S.: Probabilistic encryption & how to play mental poker keeping secret all partial information. In: Proceedings of the Fourteenth Annual ACM Symposium on Theory of Computingm STOC 1982, pp. 365–377. ACM (1982)

22. Damgård, I., Geisler, M., Krøigaard, M.: Efficient and secure comparison for on-line auctions. In: Pieprzyk, J., Ghodosi, H., Dawson, E. (eds.) ACISP 2007. LNCS, vol. 4586, pp. 416–430. Springer, Heidelberg (2007). doi:10.1007/978-3-540-73458-1_30

23. Osadchy, M., Pinkas, B., Jarrous, A., Moskovich, B.: SCiFI - a system for secure face identification. In: IEEE S&P 2010, pp. 239–254, May 2010

24. Simoens, K., Bringer, J., Chabanne, H., Seys, S.: A framework for analyzing template security and privacy in biometric authentication systems. IEEE Trans. Inf. Forensics Secur. 7(2), 833–841 (2012)

25. Abidin, A., Matsuura, K., Mitrokotsa, A.: Security of a privacy-preserving biometric authentication protocol revisited. In: Gritzalis, D., Kiayias, A., Askoxylakis, I. (eds.) CANS 2014. LNCS, vol. 8813, pp. 290–304. Springer, Cham (2014). doi:10.1007/978-3-319-12280-9_19

26. Abidin, A., Pagnin, E., Mitrokotsa, A.: Attacks on privacy-preserving biometric authentication. In: Bernsmed, K., Fischer-Hübner, S. (eds.) NordSec 2014. LNCS, vol. 8788, pp. 293–294. Springer, Cham (2014)

27. Bringer, J., Chabanne, H., Patey, A.: SHADE: Secure hamming distance computation from oblivious transfer. In: Financial Cryptography Workshops, pp. 164–176 (2013)

28. Bringer, J., Chabanne, H., Favre, M., Patey, A., Schneider, T., Zohner, M.: GSHADE: faster privacy-preserving distance computation and biometric identification. In: Proceedings of the 2nd ACM Workshop on Information Hiding and Multimedia Security, pp. 187–198. ACM (2014)

29. Pagnin, E., Dimitrakakis, C., Abidin, A., Mitrokotsa, A.: On the leakage of information in biometric authentication. In: Meier, W., Mukhopadhyay, D. (eds.) INDOCRYPT 2014. LNCS, vol. 8885, pp. 265–280. Springer, Cham (2014). doi:10.1007/978-3-319-13039-2_16

30. Krawczyk, H.: LFSR-based hashing and authentication. In: Desmedt, Y.G. (ed.) CRYPTO 1994. LNCS, vol. 839, pp. 129–139. Springer, Heidelberg (1994). doi:10.1007/3-540-48658-5_15

31. Carter, L., Wegman, M.N.: Universal classes of hash functions. J. Comput. Syst. Sci. 18, 143–154 (1979)

32. Stinson, D.R.: Universal hashing and authentication codes. In: Feigenbaum, J. (ed.) CRYPTO 1991. LNCS, vol. 576, pp. 74–85. Springer, Heidelberg (1992). doi:10.1007/3-540-46766-1_5

33. Abidin, A., Larsson, J.Å.: New universal hash functions. In: Armknecht, F., Lucks, S. (eds.) WEWoRC 2011. LNCS, vol. 7242, pp. 99–108. Springer, Heidelberg (2012). doi:10.1007/978-3-642-34159-5_7

A Lightweight Authentication and Key Agreement Scheme for Mobile Satellite Communication Systems

Xinghua Wu, Aixin Zhang$^{(\boxtimes)}$, Jianhua Li, Weiwei Zhao,
and Yuchen Liu

School of Information Security Engineering, Shanghai Jiao Tong University,
Shanghai, China
{nervose,axzhang,lijh888,wendy_love3z,
yuchenchen}@sjtu.edu.cn

Abstract. Although many authentication and key agreement (AKA) schemes for the mobile satellite communication system have been proposed nowadays, the security performance of the existing schemes is still unable to satisfy the requirements of satellite communications. In 2015, Zhang et al. proposed an improved AKA scheme for satellite communication and they claimed that their scheme satisfied all the security requirements. However through a detailed analysis, in this paper we find that to some extent their scheme is vulnerable to replay attack, injection attack and verification table stolen attack. We further propose a new lightweight AKA scheme based on the synchronization mechanism of user's temporary identity. The SVO logic is used to provide a formal security analysis. We also give an overall comparison of computation overhead and security performance among several related AKA schemes. Meanwhile a Java program is developed to test the time delay caused by the scheme on the user and NCC's sides. All the results show that the proposed scheme has the advantages of high computation efficiency, good security performance and low time delay.

Keywords: Mobile satellite communication system · Verification table · Smart card · Security performance · Key agreement · Authentication

1 Introduction

With the developments of space information technology, the satellite communication is playing an increasingly important role now. A simple model of the satellite communication network is shown in Fig. 1. It is mainly composed of the network control center (NCC), gateways, LEO satellites and mobile users. The gateways preside over the communications between NCC and LEO satellites, and they are linked to NCC via a secure wired channel. The LEO satellites are responsible for forwarding the messages between mobile users and gateways through wireless channels and they can also be connected with each other by wireless channels. Compared with traditional ground network, the satellite network can provide communication service in a far greater scope. But the longer transmission delay, the time-varying network topology structure,

© Springer International Publishing AG 2017
K. Chen et al. (Eds.): Inscrypt 2016, LNCS 10143, pp. 187–204, 2017.
DOI: 10.1007/978-3-319-54705-3_12

the vulnerable transmission channel and the resource-constrained devices make the information security problems much more serious in the satellite communication system. In order to set up a safe mobile communication system, the security protocol should provide a comprehensive protection for the entities involved, such as mutual authentication, confidentiality, user's privacy protection, forward/backward secrecy, simple key management, low computation cost and so on [1–5].

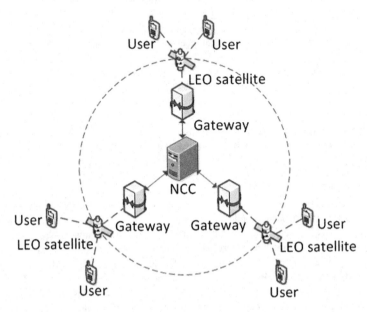

Fig. 1. A simple model of the satellite communication network.

Since Cruickshank first proposed a security scheme for the mobile satellite communication network in 1996 [6], a lot of authentication and key agreement (AKA) protocols have been proposed [7–16]. Most of the work focuses on the higher security and lower computation properties. Particularly in 2009, Chen et al. proposed a self-verification authentication scheme based on public key cryptography (PKC) and symmetric key cryptography (SKC) [9]. But the computation over head is too high due to the exponent operations adopted. Besides Lee et al. pointed out later that this scheme is unsecure since the attackers who have got NCC's verification table can work out NCC's long-term private key and then they proposed an improved scheme claimed to be much more secure [12]. However Zhang et al. pointed out that Lee et al.'s scheme couldn't resist smart card loss attack, denial of service attack and replay attack in 2015 [16]. They also proposed a new scheme and claimed that their scheme could meet all the security requirements of mobile satellite communication. Nevertheless, we find their scheme is not as secure as they claimed. In this paper, we will demonstrate the possible attacks against their scheme and propose an improved one.

The rest of the paper is organized as follows. In Sect. 2, a brief overview of Zhang et al.'s scheme is provided, along with the presentation of the details of three different kinds of attacks towards such scheme (replay, injection and verification table attack). Our improved AKA scheme and its security analysis is detailed in Sect. 3. The effectiveness of the mutual authentication and the session key negotiation between U and NCC are proved by SVO logic [17] specially. In Sect. 4, we compare the proposed scheme with some other typical AKA methods on the computation overhead and security performance. Also a simulation program is developed to test the time delay caused by the scheme on the user and NCC's sides. Finally, conclusions are given in Sect. 5.

2 Review and Cryptanalysis of Zhang et al.'s Scheme

In this section, we first review Zhang et al.'s scheme and then carry out a detailed analysis on its performance against replay attack, injection attack and verification table stolen attack. We also point out the information storage redundancy exists in Zhang et al.'s scheme.

In order to facilitate understanding, the commonly used notations in the scheme are listed in Table 1.

Table 1. Commonly used notations

Notation	Instruction
NCC	The network control center
U	The mobile user
U_{ID}	The permanent identity of the mobile user
T_{ID}	The temporary identity of the mobile user
LEO_{ID}	The identity of the LEO satellite
h(a)	The one-way hash function on a
$a \oplus b$	The bitwise XOR operation between a and b
$a \parallel b$	The string connection operation between a and b

2.1 The Review of Zhang et al.'s Scheme

There are three communication agents in Zhang et al.'s scheme, namely the mobile users, the LEO satellites and NCC. The scheme is divided into five phases: registration phase, login phase, authentication phase and two extra phases (smart card lost phase and password change phase).

During the registration phase, the mobile user U first chooses his permanent identity U_{ID} and password PW, and sends them to NCC via a secure channel. NCC issues the smart card containing $\{T_{ID}, R, k\}$ to U. (Here T_{ID} is generated by NCC randomly for U, $R = P \oplus h(U_{ID} \parallel k)$, $P = h(U_{ID} \parallel x)$, x is NCC's long term private key and k is a security parameter randomly chosen by NCC). NCC stores $\{U_{ID}, T_{ID}, PW\}$ in its verification table. During the login and authentication phases, U and NCC agree on a one-time used session key and update U's temporary identity T_{ID}. NCC stores not only $\{U_{ID}, T_{ID}, PW\}$ but also U's latest login message $\{Q, S, T_{ID}\}$. Detailed information of these two phases is illustrated in Fig. 2. Smart card lost phase and password change phase will be operated when the mobile users lose their smart cards or want to change their passwords respectively. Thorough description of Zhang et al.'s scheme can be found in [16].

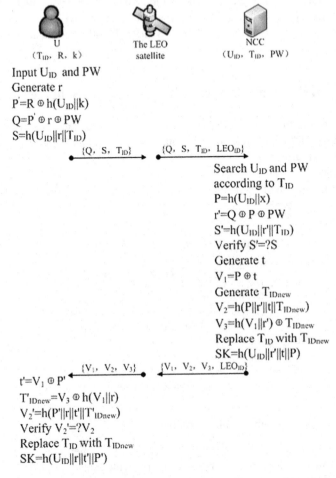

U
$(T_{ID},\ R,\ k)$

The LEO
satellite

NCC
$(U_{ID},\ T_{ID},\ PW)$

Input U_{ID} and PW
Generate r
$P'=R \oplus h(U_{ID}||k)$
$Q=P' \oplus r \oplus PW$
$S=h(U_{ID}||r||T_{ID})$

$\{Q,\ S,\ T_{ID}\}$ $\{Q,\ S,\ T_{ID},\ LEO_{ID}\}$

Search U_{ID} and PW
according to T_{ID}
$P=h(U_{ID}||x)$
$r'=Q \oplus P \oplus PW$
$S'=h(U_{ID}||r'||T_{ID})$
Verify $S'=?S$
Generate t
$V_1=P \oplus t$
Generate T_{IDnew}
$V_2=h(P||r'||t||T_{IDnew})$
$V_3=h(V_1||r') \oplus T_{IDnew}$
Replace T_{ID} with T_{IDnew}
$SK=h(U_{ID}||r'||t||P)$

$\{V_1,\ V_2,\ V_3\}$ $\{V_1,\ V_2,\ V_3,\ LEO_{ID}\}$

$t'=V_1 \oplus P'$
$T'_{IDnew}=V_3 \oplus h(V_1||r)$
$V_2'=h(P'||r||t'||T'_{IDnew})$
Verify $V_2'=?V_2$
Replace T_{ID} with T_{IDnew}
$SK=h(U_{ID}||r||t'||P')$

Fig. 2. The login and authentication phases of Zhang et al.'s scheme

2.2   The Security Analysis of Zhang et al.'s Scheme

In their scheme, in order to protect the privacy of mobile user U, U's permanent identity U_{ID} will never be transmitted in clear text via the unsecure wireless channel, and U's temporary identity T_{ID} which has been transmitted in clear text will be updated after each authentication phase. Furthermore to defense against the denial of service attack [11], NCC stores U's last login message in its verification table after the authentication phase, and U can re-login on NCC in case of losing the reply message. However, our analysis indicates that the re-login method makes it vulnerable to replay attack and the scheme cannot resist injection attack or the verification table stolen attack. In addition, it will occupy much more NCC's storage space to store the re-login information with the increasing of the mobile users involved.

Replay attack. To prevent attacker Z from taking advantage of the login message of the previous run, in Zhang et al.'s scheme the last login message $\{Q, S, T_{ID}\}$ is stored in NCC's verification table. Q and S are related to T_{ID} since they are computed with T_{ID} by $Q = P' \oplus r \oplus PW$ and $S = h(U_{ID} \parallel r \parallel T_{ID})$ respectively. However, we find that Z can still implement the replay attack. As is illustrated in Fig. 3, Z first intercepts the login message $\{Q, S, T_{ID}\}$ of U. Since U cannot receive the reply message from NCC, after a specific time, U will regenerate and send a new login message $\{Q', S', T_{ID}\}$ to NCC. After completing the check on S' by:

$$P = h(U_{ID} \parallel x) \tag{1}$$

$$r' = Q' \oplus P \oplus PW \tag{2}$$

$$S' = h(U_{ID} \parallel r' \parallel T_{ID}) \tag{3}$$

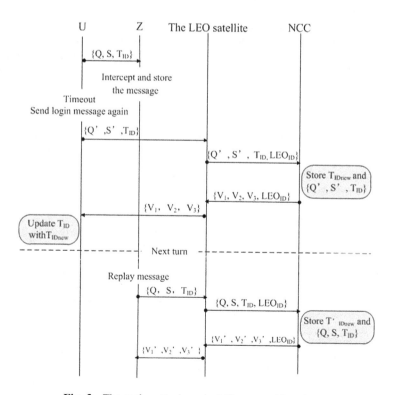

Fig. 3. The replay attack against Zhang et al.'s scheme

NCC stores $\{Q', S', T_{ID}\}$, generates T_{IDnew} and sends a reply message to U. And now the temporary identity stored in U's smart card is T_{IDnew} and the corresponding information stored in NCC's verification table is $\{U_{ID}, T_{IDnew}, PW\}$ and $\{Q', S', T_{ID}\}$. Then Z replays the previous intercepted message $\{Q, S, T_{ID}\}$ to NCC, and NCC will regard the replay message as U's re-login message. Similarly, NCC stores $\{Q, S, T_{ID}\}$, generates T'_{IDnew} and sends a reply message. Now the stored information of U in NCC's verification table becomes $\{U_{ID}, T'_{IDnew}, PW\}$ and $\{Q, S, T_{ID}\}$. During the next run, when the legal user U sends the login message $\{Q'', S'', T_{IDnew}\}$ to NCC, since T_{IDnew}mismatches T'_{IDnew} or T_{ID} in NCC's verification table, U's login request will always be denied by NCC.

Injection attack. The scheme provides U a method to change his password by adding an additional parameter Q_{new} in U's login message. But during the password change phase NCC identifies U by Eqs. (1) to (3). Therefore, the identification is related to $\{Q, S, T_{ID}\}$ instead of $\{Q, Q_{new}, S, T_{ID}\}$.

As is illustrated in Fig. 4, to implement injection attack, the attacker Z first intercepts the login message $\{Q, Q_{new}, S, T_{ID}\}$ sent by U to NCC in the password change phase. Then he generates a random data Q'_{new} which is in the same format as Q_{new}, and sends the altered message $\{Q, Q'_{new}, S, T_{ID}\}$ to NCC. After receiving the altered login request $\{Q, Q'_{new}, S, T_{ID}\}$, NCC obtains S' by Eqs. (1) to (3) and compares it with S. Obviously S' equals to S. Then NCC obtains PW_{new} by $PW_{new} = P \oplus r' \oplus Q_{new}$ and stores it in its verification table.

After that the PW_{new} which is owned by U is $P \oplus r \oplus Q_{new}$, while the stored one on the NCC side is $P \oplus r \oplus Q'_{new}$ ($Q_{new} \neq Q'_{new}$. Thus all the login requests during the subsequent runs of U will be rejected by NCC.

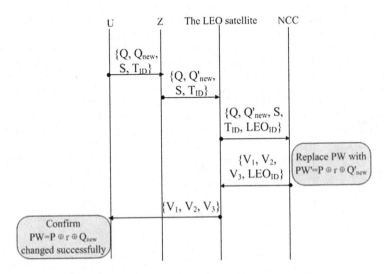

Fig. 4. The injection attack against Zhang et al.'s scheme

Furthermore, Z can also take a more simple way to realize such attack during the normal login phase. Z can directly alter the login request $\{Q, S, T_{ID}\}$ into a password changing request $\{Q, Q'_{new}, S, T_{ID}\}$ by intercepting the login request, injecting a random data Q'_{new} into it and then forwarding the altered one to NCC. As a result, U holds its original password while NCC is cheated to store a totally different one for U.

Verification table stolen attack. The verification table stolen attack is mainly based on the fact that U's permanent identity and the corresponding password are stored in clear text on NCC's side in Zhang et al.'s scheme. When the attacker Z steals NCC's verification table by some means, he can use $\{U_{ID}, PW\}$ to pretend himself as any legal users during the smart card lost phase. After receiving the message $\{U_{ID}, PW\}$ from Z via a secure channel, NCC regards that U has lost his own smart card. Then NCC sends a smart card with $\{T_{IDnew}, R', k'\}$ embedded to U and replaces T_{ID} with T_{IDnew} in its verification table. After receiving NCC's reply message, Z can forge as the legal user successfully, and U's login request will always be denied since the mismatch between T_{ID} and T_{IDnew}.

The redundant storage of information. As for the storage space analysis, NCC stores not only $\{U_{ID}, T_{ID}, PW\}$ but also user's last login request $\{Q, S, T_{IDold}\}$ in Zhang et al.'s scheme. But from above we can see that the storage of user's last login request still cannot resist the replay attack, which indicates that the $\{Q, S, T_{IDold}\}$ is redundant and useless in some sense. Besides, Zhang et al. claim that the use of U's password PW is necessary because the attacker may implement exhaustive attack to obtain U's permanent identity U_{ID} after stealing U's smart card. But when U_{ID} reaches a certain length such as 160 bits, a successful exhaustive attack requires more than 10^{47} hash operations on average, which is infeasible actually. So the use of U_{ID} with enough length has the same effect as the use of PW in defending against the exhaustive attack. From this point of view the use of PW is unnecessary.

3   Our Proposed Scheme

From above analysis, we can see Zhang et al.'s scheme is still unsecure to withstand replay attack, injection attack and verification table stolen attack. In this section we propose an improved AKA scheme which is powerful enough to defend against these attacks. The main idea is as follows. First, the synchronization mechanism of user's temporary identity T_{ID} is adopted to resist the replay attack, while the user's permanent identity U_{ID} is stored in NCC's verification table in cipher text to counteract the verification table stolen attack. Second, the mobile user do not need to choose a password in our scheme. Thus the chance for injection attack can be avoided without the password change phase. Finally the storage space of the proposed scheme is optimized by storing neither the last login request $\{Q, S, T_{IDold}\}$ nor the users' passwords.

3.1   The Process of the Proposed Scheme

There are three phases in our proposed scheme registration phase, login phase and authentication phase.

Registration phase

(R1) U → NCC: U_{ID}

U freely chooses his permanent identity U_{ID}, and then sends it to NCC via a secure channel.

(R2) NCC → U: T_{ID}, R, k

After receiving the message U_{ID} from U, NCC generates a random number k and calculates P, R with its long-term private key x:

$$P = h(U_{ID} \parallel x) \tag{4}$$

$$R = P \oplus h(U_{ID} \parallel k) \tag{5}$$

Then NCC generates U's initial temporary identity T_{ID}, calculates:

$$O = U_{ID} \oplus h(T_{ID} \parallel x) \tag{6}$$

and stores $\{O, T_{ID}, T_{IDold}\}$ in its verification table. T_{IDold} is initially blank. After that, NCC sends a smart card embedded with $\{T_{ID}, R, k\}$ to U via a secure channel.

Login phase

(L1) U → LEO: Q, S, T_{ID}

U inserts the smart card into his own device and inputs his permanent identity U_{ID}manually. Then the smart card automatically generates a secret random number r and calculates:

$$P' = R \oplus h(U_{ID} \parallel k) \tag{7}$$

$$Q = P' \oplus r \tag{8}$$

$$S = h(U_{ID} \parallel r \parallel T_{ID}) \tag{9}$$

Finally U sends the login message $\{Q, S, T_{ID}\}$ to the LEO satellite.

(L2) LEO → NCC: Q, S, T_{ID}, LEO_{ID}

Authentication phase

(A1) After receiving U's login request from the LEO satellite, NCC first decides whether T_{ID} exits in its verification table based on the second elements T_{ID}' of vector $\{O', T_{ID}', T_{IDold}'\}$.

(A1.1) If T_{ID} exists as the elements of T_{ID}', NCC calculates:

$$U_{ID} = O \oplus h(T_{ID} \parallel x) \tag{10}$$

$$P = h(U_{ID} \parallel x) \tag{11}$$

$$r' = Q \oplus P \tag{12}$$

$$S' = h(U_{ID} \| r' \| T_{ID}) \tag{13}$$

and verifies whether the calculated value S' equals to S which is received during L2. U will be authenticated if S' equals to S, and the authentication process will go to step (A2.1).

(A1.2) Else, NCC decides whether T_{ID} exists in its verification table based on the third elements T_{IDold}' of vector $\{O', T_{ID}', T_{IDold}'\}$. If it exists as the elements of T_{IDold}', NCC gets:

$$U_{ID} = O \oplus h(T_{ID}' \| x) \tag{14}$$

and calculates P, r', S' by Eqs. (11) to (13). If the calculated value S' equals to S, U is authenticated by NCC. Then NCC will start the synchronization mechanism and go to step (A2.2).

(A1.3) Otherwise, U's login request will be rejected.

(A2) NCC generates the replying messages at this step.

(A2.1) NCC chooses a secret random number t and U's new temporary identity T_{IDnew}, and calculates:

$$V_1 = P \oplus t \tag{15}$$

$$V_2 = h(P \| r' \| t \| T_{IDnew} \| tag) \tag{16}$$

$$V_3 = h(V_1 \| r') \oplus T_{IDnew} \tag{17}$$

$$O_{new} = U_{ID} \oplus h(T_{IDnew} \| x) \tag{18}$$

where tag = 1 indicates the communication is in a normal replying state. Then NCC replaces the stored message $\{O', T_{ID}', T_{IDold}'\}$ with $\{O_{new}, T_{IDnew}, T_{ID}\}$ in its verification table. Now NCC calculates the session key SK between U and itself and go to (A2.3).

$$SK = h(U_{ID} \| r' \| t \| P) \tag{19}$$

(A2.2) NCC generates a secret random number t and calculates V_1 by Eqs. (15), then gets:

$$V_2 = h(P \| r' \| t \| T_{ID}' \| tag) \tag{20}$$

$$V_3 = h(V_1 \| r') \oplus T_{ID}' \tag{21}$$

where tag = 0 suggests that the replying message is for synchronizing purpose.

(A2.3) NCC → LEO: V_1, V_2, V_3, tag, LEO_{ID}

(A3) LEO → U: V_1, V_2, V_3, tag

(A4) After receiving the message $\{V_1, V_2, V_3, \text{tag}\}$ from the LEO satellite, U calculates:

$$t' = V_1 \oplus P' \tag{22}$$

$$T'_{\text{IDnew}} = V_3 \oplus h(V_1 \| r) \tag{23}$$

$$V'_2 = h(P' \| r \| t' \| T'_{\text{IDnew}} \| \text{tag}) \tag{24}$$

Then U verifies whether the calculated value V_2' equals to V_2 it received. If it holds, NCC is authenticated successfully by U. Then U will replace T_{ID} with T'_{IDnew} in his smart card. Especially if tag = 1, U will go to step (A5). If tag = 0, U is aware that he is in the asynchronous state, and he will start a new run for login and authentication.

(A5) U calculates the session key SK between NCC and himself:

$$SK = h(U_{\text{ID}} \| r \| t' \| P') \tag{25}$$

Obviously the two session keys computed by NCC in Eq. (19) and obtained by U in Eq. (25) will be the same once NCC and U have been authenticated with each other. SK will be used as the symmetric encryption key to protect the session messages between U and NCC later.

3.2   The Security Analysis of Our Scheme

In this section, we will discuss the security performance of the proposed scheme by analyzing its ability to resist some commonly mentioned attacks. Then the formal security analysis based on SVO logic is given.

The ability to resist security attacks

Denial of service attack. Zhang et al. adopted re-login mechanism to prevent against DoS attack, but it makes the system become much more vulnerable to replay attack. The synchronization method of the user's temporary identity is used in the proposed scheme to resist DoS attack. For example, during the authentication process, both T_{ID} and T_{IDold} are stored in the verification table on the NCC's side. If the authentication replying message sent by NCC to U is intercepted, NCC can know that the mobile user has not received its last reply message according to user's login message containing T_{IDold}. And the system can still run properly after NCC sends a synchronizing message.

Replay attack. The synchronization of the user's temporary identity can also be used to defend against the replay attack. The attacker Z may attempt to intercept and replay user's login message $\{Q, S, T_{\text{IDold}}\}$ and NCC's reply message $\{V_1, V_2, V_3, \text{tag}\}$. In our scheme, if NCC receives user's login message containing his last temporary identity T_{IDold}, it will respond with the existing T_{ID} based on the synchronization mechanism, no matter whether the login message $\{Q, S, T_{\text{IDold}}\}$ is sent by user himself or not. Therefore, Z cannot cause the mismatch of user's temporary identity between the one stored in user's smart card and the one in NCC's verification table, and Z cannot obtain user's existing temporary identity T_{ID} from NCC's reply message $\{V_1, V_2, V_3, tag\}$ without r and P.

Injection attack. It is obviously that the chance for injection attack can be avoided in our scheme, since there is no password change phase at all.

Verification table stolen attack. In our scheme, if the attacker Z steals NCC's verification table, he can obtain parameter O, user's temporary identity T_{ID} and T_{IDold}. But he cannot obtain user's permanent identity U_{ID} without NCC's long-term private key x according to Eq. (10). Therefore, the verification table stolen attack can be resisted since there is no sensitive information stored in NCC's verification table.

Smart card loss attack. In the proposed scheme, Z cannot generate a valid login message even if he has got user's smart card due to the fact that user's permanent identity is not stored in the smart card. Moreover, based on the analysis in Sect. 2. B, Z cannot obtain user's permanent identity U_{ID} by exhaustive attack when the length of U_{ID} reaches a certain scale.

Impersonation attack. It is obviously that the login message of the proposed scheme is related to user's permanent identity U_{ID}. For example, Q and S in user's login message $\{Q, S, T_{ID}\}$ equals to $P \oplus r$ and $h(U_{ID}\|r\|T_{ID})$ respectively, and $P = h(U_{ID} \| x)$. Therefore, even if Z obtains user's temporary identity T_{ID}, he cannot generate a valid login message to impersonate a legal user without U_{ID}.

From above we can see the proposed scheme is secure enough to defend against the commonly used attacks. Next the formal analysis for the mutual authentication and session key negotiation will be given based on SVO logic.

The formal analysis based on SVO logic

The introduction of SVO logic. The notations used in SVO logic are listed in Table 2. There are two inference rules (MP, Nec) and twenty inference axioms in SVO. For detailed information please refer [17].

The formal analysis of our scheme. The analysis in SVO logic can be divided into four parts: protocol idealization, initial assumptions, goals setting and derivation procedure. In our protocol, NCC stores $\{O, T_{ID}, T_{IDold}\}$ in its verification table. The information $\{T_{ID}, R, k\}$ is stored in U's smart card. After omitting the satellite node which is only responsible for message forwarding, the description of the login and authentication phases can be described as follows:

$$U \rightarrow NCC : Q, S, T_{ID}$$

$$NCC \rightarrow U : V_1, V_2, V_3, tag$$

Table 2. Notations in SVO logic

Notation	Instruction
$\{*_1, \cdots, *_n\}$	The unrecognized message received by a participant
$\tilde{K}$	K's corresponding decryption key
$\{X^P\}_K$	The message X encrypted by K and sent by participant P
$[X]_K$	The message X signed by K
$\langle X^P \rangle_Y$	The message X compounded with Y and sent by participant P
$P \overset{K}{\leftrightarrow} Q$	A shared key K between participants P and Q
$PK_\psi(P, K)$	The public encryption key K of participant P
$PK_\sigma(P, K)$	The public signature verification key K of participant P
$PK_\delta(P, K)$	The public negotiation key K of participant P
$SV(X, K, Y)$	The message Y with a signature X verified by key K

For the detailed information of each message, please refer to Sect. 3.1.

The final negotiated session key between U and NCC is $SK = h(U_{ID} \parallel r \parallel t \parallel P)$.

(1) Protocol idealization

The protocol can be idealized as:

$$U \rightarrow NCC : \{r\}_P, h(U_{ID} \parallel r \parallel T_{ID}), T_{ID}$$

$$NCC \rightarrow U : \{t\}_P, \{T_{IDnew}\}_r, h(P \parallel r \parallel t \parallel T_{IDnew})$$

(2) Initial assumptions

The initial assumptions can be divided into four groups: the participant believes the freshness of the random number generated by itself, the participant believes that the trusted participants have jurisdiction over their shared key, the participant believes its own shared key and the assumptions obtained according to the idealization process of a security protocol.

The initial assumptions of the proposed scheme can be summarized as follows.

P_1:   U believes fresh(r)
      NCC believes fresh(t)
      NCC believes fresh(T_{ID})

P_2:   U sees (U_{ID}, T_{ID}, P, k, r)
      NCC sees (O, U_{ID}, T_{ID}, x, t)

P_3:   U believes NCC controls ($U \overset{t}{\leftrightarrow} NCC$)
      U believes NCC controls(T_{IDnew})
      NCC believes U controls ($U \overset{r}{\leftrightarrow} NCC$)

P_4:   U believes NCC controls fresh(t)
         U believes NCC controls fresh(T_{IDnew})
         NCC believes U controls fresh (r)

P_5:   U believes $U \overset{p}{\leftrightarrow} NCC$

         U believes $U \overset{r}{\leftrightarrow} NCC$

         NCC believes $U \overset{P}{\leftrightarrow} NCC$

         NCC believes $U \overset{t}{\leftrightarrow} NCC$

P_6:   NCC received $\{r\}_P, h(U_{ID} \parallel r \parallel T_{ID}), T_{ID}$
P_7:   U received $\{t\}_P, \{T_{IDnew}\}_r, h(P \parallel r \parallel t \parallel T_{IDnew})$
P_8:   NCC believes NCC received $\{*_1\}_{*2}, *_3, T_{ID}$
P_9:   NCC believes (NCC received $\{*_1\}_{*2}, *_3, T_{ID} \supset$
         NCC received $\left\{U \overset{r}{\leftrightarrow} NCC\right\}_P, h(U_{ID} \parallel r \parallel T_{ID}), T_{ID})$
P_{10}: U believes U received $\{*_4\}_P, \{*_5\}_r, *_6$
P_{11}:   U believes (U received $\{*_4\}_P, \{*_5\}_r, *_6 \supset$
         U received $\left\{U \overset{t}{\leftrightarrow} NCC\right\}_P, \{T_{IDnew}\}_r, h(P \parallel r \parallel t \parallel T_{IDnew}))$
P_{12}: U believes ($U \overset{r}{\leftrightarrow} NCC \wedge U \overset{t}{\leftrightarrow} NCC \supset U \overset{sk}{\leftrightarrow} NCC$)
P_{13}: NCC believes ($U \overset{r}{\leftrightarrow} NCC \wedge U \overset{t}{\leftrightarrow} NCC \supset U \overset{sk}{\leftrightarrow} NCC$)

(3) Goals setting

The goals of the proposed protocol are to achieve mutual authentication and session key negotiation between U and NCC. They can be described as:

G_1: NCC believes $U \overset{sk}{\leftrightarrow} NCC$

G_2: U believes $U \overset{sk}{\leftrightarrow} NCC$

G_3: NCC believes fresh(sk)

G_4: U believes fresh (sk)

G_5: U believes NCC sees $U \overset{sk}{\leftrightarrow} NCC$

Here G_1 and G_2 indicate that both NCC and U believe that SK is a proper shared session key, G_3 and G_4 mean that both NCC and U believe that SK is fresh while G_5 says that participant U believes that NCC owns SK.

(4) Derivation procedure

The derivation procedure is a process to obtain the security goals from the associated protocol idealization and assumptions by using the SVO inference rules. For simplicity, the inference rules are cited as 'Ax i', where Ax means axiom and i is the corresponding numbers of the SVO inference rules in [17].

The proving procedures of G1 are listed below:

$$\left. \begin{array}{l} P_8 \\ P_{10} \end{array} \right\} \overset{Ax1}{\rightarrow} \text{NCC believes NCC received } \left\{U \overset{r}{\leftrightarrow} NCC\right\}_P, h(U_{ID} \parallel r \parallel T_{ID}), T_{ID} \quad (M1)$$

$$M1\} \overset{Ax6}{\rightarrow} NCC \text{ believes } NCC \text{ received } \left\{U \overset{r}{\leftrightarrow} NCC\right\}_P \tag{M2}$$

$$\left.\begin{array}{l} M2 \\ P_5 \end{array}\right\} \overset{Ax1,Ax3}{\rightarrow} NCC \text{ believes } (U \text{ said } U \overset{r}{\leftrightarrow} NCC) \tag{M3}$$

$$P1\} \overset{Ax1,Ax17}{\rightarrow} NCC \text{ believes fresh } h(U_{ID} \parallel r \parallel T_{ID}) \tag{M4}$$

$$M4\} \overset{Ax1,Ax16}{\rightarrow} NCC \text{ believes fresh } (U \overset{r}{\leftrightarrow} NCC)) \tag{M5}$$

$$\left.\begin{array}{l} M3 \\ M5 \end{array}\right\} \overset{Ax1,Ax18}{\rightarrow} NCC \text{ believes } (U \text{ says } U \overset{r}{\leftrightarrow} NCC) \tag{M6}$$

$$\left.\begin{array}{l} M6 \\ P_3 \end{array}\right\} \overset{Ax1,Ax15}{\rightarrow} NCC \text{ believes } U \overset{r}{\leftrightarrow} NCC \tag{M7}$$

$$\left.\begin{array}{l} M7 \\ P_5 \\ P_{13} \end{array}\right\} \overset{Ax1,Ax5}{\rightarrow} NCC \text{ believes } U \overset{sk}{\leftrightarrow} NCC \ G_1 \text{ is proved.} \tag{M8}$$

$$\left.\begin{array}{l} P_9 \\ P_{11} \end{array}\right\} \overset{Ax1}{\rightarrow} U \text{ believes } U \text{ received } \left\{U \overset{t}{\leftrightarrow} NCC\right\}_{P'}$$

$$\{T_{IDnew}\}_r, h(P \parallel r \parallel t \parallel T_{IDnew}) \tag{M9}$$

$$M9\} \overset{Ax6}{\rightarrow} U \text{ believes } U \text{ received } \left\{U \overset{t}{\leftrightarrow} NCC\right\}_P \tag{M10}$$

$$\left.\begin{array}{l} M10 \\ P_5 \end{array}\right\} \overset{Ax1,Ax3}{\rightarrow} U \text{ believes } (NCC \text{ said } U \overset{t}{\leftrightarrow} NCC) \tag{M11}$$

$$M9\} \overset{Ax6}{\rightarrow} U \text{ believes } U \text{ received } \{T_{IDnew}\}_r \tag{M12}$$

$$\left.\begin{array}{l} M12 \\ P_5 \end{array}\right\} \overset{Ax1,Ax3}{\rightarrow} U \text{ believes } (NCC \text{ said } T_{IDnew}) \tag{M13}$$

$$\left.\begin{array}{l} M13 \\ P_1 \end{array}\right\} \overset{Ax17}{\rightarrow} U \text{ believes } (NCC \text{ says} T_{IDnew}) \tag{M14}$$

$$\left.\begin{array}{l} M14 \\ P_3 \end{array}\right\} \overset{Ax1,Ax15}{\rightarrow} U \text{ believes } T_{IDnew} \tag{M15}$$

$$P_1\} \overset{Ax1,Ax17}{\rightarrow} U \text{ believes fresh } h(P \parallel r \parallel t \parallel T_{IDnew}) \tag{M16}$$

$$M16\} \xrightarrow{Ax1,Ax16} U \text{ believes fresh } (U \overset{t}{\leftrightarrow} NCC) \tag{M17}$$

$$\left.\begin{array}{c} M11 \\ M17 \end{array}\right\} \xrightarrow{Ax1,Ax18} U \text{ believes } (NCC \text{ says } U \overset{t}{\leftrightarrow} NCC) \tag{M18}$$

$$\left.\begin{array}{c} M18 \\ P_3 \end{array}\right\} \xrightarrow{Ax1,Ax15} U \text{ believes } U \overset{t}{\leftrightarrow} NCC \tag{M19}$$

$$\left.\begin{array}{c} M19 \\ P_5 \\ P_{12} \end{array}\right\} \xrightarrow{Ax1,Ax5} U \text{ believes } U \overset{sk}{\leftrightarrow} NCC \ G_2 \text{is proved.} \tag{M20}$$

$$\left.\begin{array}{c} M5 \\ P_1 \end{array}\right\} \xrightarrow{Ax1,Ax17} NCC \text{ believes fresh(sk)} \ G_3 \text{is proved.} \tag{M21}$$

$$\left.\begin{array}{c} M17 \\ P_1 \end{array}\right\} \xrightarrow{Ax1,Ax17} U \text{ believes fresh(sk)} \ G_4 \text{is proved.} \tag{M22}$$

$$\left.\begin{array}{c} M12 \\ P_5 \end{array}\right\} \xrightarrow{Ax1} U \text{ believes } NCC \text{ sees } r \tag{M23}$$

$$\left.\begin{array}{c} M23 \\ P_2 \end{array}\right\} \xrightarrow{Ax10} U \text{ believes } NCC \text{ sees } U \overset{sk}{\leftrightarrow} NCC \ G_5 \text{is proved.} \tag{M24}$$

4 Comparison and Simulation

In this section, comparisons of the security properties and the computation overhead are made among the proposed scheme and several related schemes. From the comparison we can see that some schemes including Zhang's, Lee's, Lasc's, Chen's and ours can satisfy all the listed security requirements, while only the proposed scheme can resist all of the known attacks. As for the computation overhead, the proposed scheme only needs a certain amount of hash operations on both NCC and user's sides, which is comparable with that of Zhang's, Chang's and Lee's schemes. In Table 3, we summarizes the comparisons among these schemes. Here T_{sym} denotes a symmetric encryption operation and T_h a secure hash operation. Other lightweight operations such as bitwise XOR operation are omitted.

Also, we design a Java program to verify the effectiveness of our scheme by testing the time delay on the user and NCC's sides. The time delay that we have tested includes four parts, which are the time overhead of user to generate the login message after inputting his U_{ID} (T_1), the time overhead of user to authenticate NCC's reply message and generate the session key after receiving the reply message (T_2), the time overhead of NCC to authenticate the login message and generate the reply message after receiving user's login request (T_3) and the time overhead of NCC to authenticate

Table 3. Comparison of security and computation overheads among related schemes

Schemes	Chen's scheme [9]	Lasc's scheme [11]	Lee's scheme [12]	Zheng's scheme [13]	Chang's scheme [14]	Zhang's scheme [16]	Our Scheme
Mutual authentication	Yes	Yes	Yes	Yes	Yes	Yes	Yes
Confidentiality	Yes	Yes	Yes	Yes	Yes	Yes	Yes
User's privacy	Yes	Yes	Yes	No	Yes	Yes	Yes
Key independence	Yes	Yes	Yes	Yes	No	Yes	Yes
Denial of service attack	No	Yes	No	No	No	Yes	Yes
Replay attack	Yes	Yes	No	Yes	Yes	No	Yes
Injection attack	Yes	Yes	Yes	Yes	No	No	Yes
Verificationtablestolen attack	Yes	Yes	Yes	No	Yes	No	Yes
Smart card loss attack	No	No	Yes	Yes	Yes	Yes	Yes
Impersonation attack	Yes	Yes	Yes	Yes	No	Yes	Yes
User computation	$T_{sym} + 2T_h$	$T_{sym} + 2T_h$	$5T_h$	$(n\text{-}j + 5)\ T_h$	$3T_h$	$5T_h$	$5T_h$
NCC computation	$T_{sym} + 4T_h$	$T_{sym} + 4T_h$	$5T_h$	$4T_h$	$4T_h$	$5T_h$	$7T_h$

n, the total times which a user can access the services from NCC. j, the current number of a user's accession.

Table 4. Test results of time overhead

User scale	T_1	T_2	T_3	T_4
1000	0.2005 ms	0.3533 ms	0.5586 ms	0.5853 ms
10000	0.2095 ms	0.3768 ms	0.5897 ms	1.2658 ms

The results are the average value of 250 tests.

the login message and generate the synchronous message after receiving user's login request generated with T_{IDold} (T_4).

According to the test results in Table 4, the time overheads of the proposed scheme on both the user and NCC's sides are within milliseconds. While the transmission delay in satellite communication systems is normally within tens or hundreds of milliseconds. Furthermore, by comparing two groups of test results with different user scales, we can see that only T_4 has an obvious increase when the number of user increases from 1000 to 10000. It is because that the search time in the proposed scheme is mainly affected by the user scale. In the simulation, NCC stores user data in a hash table keyed by user's current temporary identity T_{ID}. So the time complexity for T_{ID} searching is O(1), but the time complexity for user's last temporary identity (T_{IDold}) searching is O(n), which ultimately results the obvious increase of T_4.

In a word, the time overhead of the mutual authentication and key agreement between user and NCC will not have an obvious effect on the system's overall time delay.

5   Conclusion

With the rapid development of satellite communication technology, the mobile satellite communication have brought great convenience to people, at the same time it also brings a huge challenge to the sensitive information protection during space transmission. The security protocol is the foundation to build a secure network environment. In this paper, we analyze Zhang et al.'s authentication and key agreement scheme in detail, and we find that the scheme is vulnerable to replay attack, injection attack and verification table stolen attack. Besides the storage redundancy exists in the scheme. Then, an improved AKA scheme based on the synchronization mechanism of user's temporary identity is proposed. The formal analysis with SVO logic and the simulation with a java program show that our scheme has the advantages of good security performance and high computation efficiency.

Acknowledgements. This work is funded by National Natural Science Foundation of China (61402287, 61431008) and Shanghai Municipal Science and Technology Commission (14YF1401900).

References

1. Min, S.: Discussion on space-based integrated information network. J. Space Int. **8**, 46–54 (2013)
2. Lee, W.: Research on Key Management of Space Information Networks. Doctoral Dissertation. PLA Information Engineering University, Zhengzhou (2009)
3. Zhong, Y.: Research on key issues of security in space information network. Doctoral Dissertation. Xidian University, Xian (2011)
4. CCSDS 350.1-G-2.: Security Threats against Space Missions (2015). https://public.ccsds. org/Pubs/350x1g2.pdf
5. CCSDS 713.5-B-1.: Space Communications Protocol Standards - Security Protocol (2015). https://public.ccsds.org/Pubs/713x5b1sc1.pdf
6. Cruickshank, H.S.: A security system for satellite networks. In: 5th International Conference on Satellite Systems for Mobile Communications and Navigation, pp. 187–190. IET (1996)
7. Hwang, M.S., Yang, C.C., Shiu, C.Y.: An authentication scheme for mobile satellite communication systems. J. ACM SIGOPS Operating Syst. Rev. **37**(4), 42–47 (2003)
8. Chang, Y.F., Chang, C.C.: An efficient authentication protocol for mobile satellite communication systems. J. ACM SIGOPS Operating Syst. Rev. **39**(1), 70–84 (2005)
9. Chen, T.H., Lee, W.B., Chen, H.B.: A self-verification authentication mechanism for mobile satellite communication systems. J. Comput. Electr. Eng. **35**(1), 41–48 (2009)
10. Yoon, E.J., Yoo, K.Y., Hong, J.W., Yoon, S.Y., Park, D.I., Choi, M.J.: An efficient and secure anonymous authentication scheme for mobile satellite communication systems. J. EURASIP J. Wirel. Commun. Network. **2011**(1), 1–10 (2011)
11. Lasc, I., Dojen, R., Coffey, T.: Countering jamming attacks against an authentication and key agreement protocol for mobile satellite communications. J. Comput. Electr. Eng. **37**(2), 160–168 (2011)
12. Lee, C.C., Li, C.T., Chang, R.X.: A simple and efficient authentication scheme for mobile satellite communication systems. J. Int. J. Satell. Commun. Network. **30**(1), 29–38 (2012)
13. Zheng, G., Ma, H.T., Cheng, C., Tu, Y.C.: Design and logical analysis on the access authentication scheme for satellite mobile communication networks. J. IET Inf. Secur. **6**(1), 6–13 (2012)
14. Chang, C.C., Cheng, T.F., Wu, H.L.: An authentication and key agreement protocol for satellite communications. J. Int. J. Commun. Syst. **27**(10), 1994–2006 (2014)

15. Zhang, Y., Chen, J., Huang, B.: Security analysis of an authentication and key agreement protocol for satellite communications. J. Int. J. Commun. Syst. **27**(12), 4300–4306 (2014)
16. Zhang, Y., Chen, J., Huang, B.: An improved authentication scheme for mobile satellite communication systems. J. Int. J. Satell. Commun. Network. **33**(2), 135–146 (2015)
17. Syverson, P.F., Van Oorschot, P.C.: On unifying some cryptographic protocol logics. In: IEEE Computer Society Symposium on Research in Security and Privacy, pp. 14–28. IEEE (1994)

Identity-Based Blind Signature from Lattices in Standard Model

Wen Gao[✉], Yupu Hu, Baocang Wang, and Jia Xie

School of Tele-Communications Engineering, Xidian University, Xi'an, China
gaowen0807@Outlook.com, yphu@mail.xidian.edu.cn,
bcwang@aliyun.com, xiejia199325@163.com

Abstract. Blind signature allows a user to get a signature of a signer on an arbitrary message, without leaking any information about the message. The verifier can check that whether the signature is indeed generated by the signer, and the signer cannot recall the signing situation. This property is essential when the signed message needs privacy protection for the user, like a bank bill or a trade secret. Lattice-based system is the most promising quantum-resistant primitive, and the first lattice-based blind signature is proposed by Rückert. For another, identity-based system is an alternative to public key infrastructure, as it can simplify the key management procedures in certificate-based public key systems. Illuminated by the demand of identity-based blind signature in the post-quantum circumstance, we consider the lattice-based identity based blind signature (IBBS) based on hard worst-case lattice problems. Besides, all existing lattice-based blind signatures are constructed and proved to be secure in the random oracle model. In this work, we construct an identity-based blind signature from lattices in the standard model. Our construction is proved to be one-more unforgeable under the selective identity and chosen message attacks (sID-CMA), and unconditionally blind in the standard model.

Keywords: Digital signature · Lattice-based cryptography · Blind signature

1 Introduction

1.1 Backgrounds

Digital signature can ensure the integrity of information transmission, identify the message sender, and avoid the repudiation in business deal. The signature is always created by the signer under his signing key, and the signer often knows the message signed. However, sometimes, the message signed may need privacy protection, and the owner of the message only needs a signature of a particular signer under the message without leaking its privacy.

Bind signature was first introduced by Chaum [1] in 1982 as a new type of signature with novel functionality, which enabled a user to get a signature from a signer S on an arbitrary message M without leaking any information about M, any verifier can check the signature whether it was indeed a signature on M signed by S. Blind signature is applicable in many situations, such as e-voting applications, anonymous Internet banking, and oblivious transfer.

© Springer International Publishing AG 2017
K. Chen et al. (Eds.): Inscrypt 2016, LNCS 10143, pp. 205–218, 2017.
DOI: 10.1007/978-3-319-54705-3_13

Shor's algorithms [2] show that the integer factoring and the discrete logarithm problems can be solved in polynomial time under quantum computers, on which the hardness of many existing blind signature schemes are based. Thus, these blind signatures become insecure once quantum computers become mature development, and quantum secure primitives are in urgent needs. Therefore, tremendous efforts have been made on the classical schemes that remain secure against a quantum adversary, which is called *post-quantum cryptosystems*. Lattice-based cryptography has become a hot research topic in post quantum cryptography, and many significant achievements have been obtained [3–10] in recent years.

A natural goal is to design blind signature from lattices. Rückert put forward the first lattice-based blind signature [11] at ASICRYPT'10 in the random oracle model. His signature protocol had 4 moves, and would fail with certain probability during generating signatures. Afterwards, Wang et al. constructed a lattice-based blind signature with random oracle [12] of 2 moves from pre-image sample function without failures in the signing procedure.

To simplify the key management procedures in certificate-based public key settings, the first identity-based signature was introduced by Shamir [13] in 1985. In an identity-based cryptosystem, the public key is the unique string that recognizes the user's identity, for instance, it can be an ID number, the email address, or the room number. A trusted-third-party generates the secret key by a specific algorithm and a private key. By identity-based cryptosystems, the existing problems in the public key infrastructure (PKI) can be well resolved, such as the public-key substitute problems, and the performance bottleneck of authentication center problems.

However, few literature studies on lattice-based IBBS, much less without random oracle. An interesting research topic is the design of lattice-based IBBS without random oracle. Therefore, we initiate the research on IBBS from lattices without random oracle in this research. A lattice-based IBBS scheme without random oracle is constructed based on hard worst-case lattice problems. Our construction is proved to be unconditionally blind and one-more sID-CMA unforgeable in the standard model (SM).

1.2   Related Works

Early IBBS schemes appeared in [14, 15] were designed with random oracles. The first secure construction of IBBS scheme in the standard model was constructed from the generic approach proposed by Galindo et al. [16] at ASIACRYPT 2006. The main approach was considerably straightforward and obvious: adding the authentication information of the signer to the general signature. But this led some disadvantages: the signature size was large because it includes two parts, and their scheme was inefficient as the computation and the verification needed double operations. Phong et al. [17] constructed an IBBS scheme based on bilinear parings with security based on the elliptic curve discrete logarithm problem.

All IBBS schemes were constructed based on classical number theories such as the integer factoring problem and the discrete logarithm problem, until Rückert made the first step in designing lattice-based blind signatures [11] at ASICRYPT 2010. But his schemes would fail with certain probability during generating signatures. Wang et al. [12]

put forward a lattice-based blind signature with random oracle of 2 moves from pre-image sample function without failures in the signing procedure. To the best of our knowledge, no literature studies on lattice-based IBBS scheme in standard model so far.

2 Preliminaries

2.1 Notations

$\mathbb{R}(\mathbb{Z})$ denotes the set of real numbers (integers). For a positive integer $d \in \mathbb{Z}$, $[d]$ denotes the set of integers $\{1, \cdots, d\}$. Vectors are denoted by bold lower-case letters in column form and matrices by bold capital letters. The l_2 and l_∞ norm are denoted by $||\cdot||$ and $||\cdot||_\infty$, respectively. A matrix $\mathbf{A} \in \mathbb{R}^{n \times m}$ is always viewed as the set of its column vectors $\mathbf{A} = \{\mathbf{a}_1, \cdots, \mathbf{a}_m\}$, and $\tilde{\mathbf{A}} = \{\tilde{\mathbf{a}}_1, \cdots, \tilde{\mathbf{a}}_m\}$ denotes the Gram-Schmidt orthogonalization of vectors $\mathbf{a}_1, \cdots, \mathbf{a}_m$ taken in that order. For matrix $\mathbf{B} \in \mathbb{R}^{n \times m'}$, the connection by columns of $\mathbf{A}$ and $\mathbf{B}$ is written as $[\mathbf{A}||\mathbf{B}] \in \mathbb{R}^{n \times (m+m')}$.

Let n be the security parameter, other quantities can be expressed by the functions of n. log denotes the natural logarithm, and $\Delta(X, Y) = \frac{1}{2}\sum_{a \in D} |Pr[X = a] - Pr[Y = a]|$ defines the statistical distance of two random variables (X and Y) over a domain D. The notations of O, ω are frequently used for describing the growth of function. For some constant c, $f(n) = \tilde{O}(g(n))$ denotes the function $f(n) = O(g(n) \cdot log^c(n))$ is denoted by $f(n) = \tilde{O}(g(n))$ and $f(n) = O(n^c)$ by $poly(n)$. A function is negligible in n if $f(n) = n^{-c}$ holds for sufficiently large n and positive c. An arbitrary such function is denoted by $negl(n)$, and a probability is overwhelming if it is $1 - negl(n)$.

2.2 Definitions

Definition 1(Lattices). Let $\mathbf{B} = \{\mathbf{b}_1, \cdots, \mathbf{b}_n\}$ be set of n linearly independent vectors over $\mathbb{R}^m$. The lattice generated by $\mathbf{B}$ is defined by

$$\mathcal{L}(\mathbf{B}) = \left\{ \sum_{i=1}^n x_i \mathbf{b}_i | x_i \in \mathbb{Z} \right\}.$$

Generally, $\lambda_1(\mathcal{L}(\mathbf{B}))$ denotes the shortest vector of the lattice $\mathcal{L}(\mathbf{B})$. For $i \in \{1, \cdots, n\}$, we denote the successive minima by $\lambda_i(\mathcal{L})$, which is the smallest value such that the sphere of radius $\lambda_i(\mathcal{L})$ of center the origin contains at least i linearly independent lattice vectors.

Definition 2 (SIS$_{q,n,m,\beta}$ problem). Given a random matrix $\mathbf{A} \in \mathbb{Z}_q^{n \times m}$, find a non-zero vector $\mathbf{v} \in \mathbb{Z}^m$ such that $\mathbf{A}\mathbf{v} = \mathbf{0} \in \mathbb{Z}_q^n$ and $||\mathbf{v}|| \leq \beta$.

2.3 Discrete Gaussian Distribution and Smoothing Parameter

Discrete Gaussian distribution and the smoothing parameter are important tools in analyzing integer lattices. For arbitrary $s > 0$, a Gaussian distribution with parameter s and c as its center is defined as $\forall x \in \mathbb{R}^n$, $\rho_{s,c}(x) = e^{-x\|x-c\|/s^2}$. The Gaussian distribution on lattice Λ is defined as $\forall x \in \Lambda$, $D_{\Lambda,s,c} = \rho_{s,c}(x)/\rho_{s,c}(\Lambda)$.

Theorem 1 ([7]). Given a trapdoor T for a lattice with dimension n, center $c \in \mathbb{R}^n$ and parameter $s \geq \|\tilde{T}\|\omega(\sqrt{\log n})$, there exists a probabilistic polynomial-time algorithm, whose outputs statistically close to the distribution $D_{\Lambda,s,c}$.

Theorem 2 ([7]). If the rows of a matrix $A \in \mathbb{Z}_q^{n \times m}$ generate the space $\mathbb{Z}_q^n$ with $m \geq 2n$, $\varepsilon \in (0, 1/2)$, and $s \geq \eta_\varepsilon(\Lambda^\perp(A))$, $u = A e \bmod q$ statistically close to the uniform distribution over $\mathbb{Z}_q^n$ when $e \sim D_{\mathbb{Z}^m,s}$.

2.4 Identity-Based Blind Signature

Syntax of IBBS. An IBBS scheme always consists of four algorithms (**Setup**, **Key-Extract**, **Sign**, **Verify**), where *Sign* is an interactive protocol between a signer S and a user U.

Setup. The KGC runs this algorithm to generate the security parameter and the master key pair (*mpk*, *msk*).

KeyExtract. Given the identity information *ID*, (*mpk*, *msk*), this algorithm generates the corresponding private key sk_{ID} for *ID*.

Sign. This algorithm describes the joint execution between S and U, it always consists of three algorithms.

   Blinding the message (executed by U): Takes the original message m and a randomness r as inputs, and outputs a blinded message m';
   Signing the blinded message (executed by S): Takes the blinded message m' and the secret signing key sk as inputs, outputs a blinded signature σ';
   Unblind the signature (executed by U): Takes the blinded signature σ', and the previous randomness r as inputs, this algorithm outputs the real signature for message m'.

Verify. Given m, *mpk*, *ID*, and σ, this algorithm outputs 1 to accept if σ is a valid signature of m under *ID* and otherwise 0 to reject.

Security Requirements for IBBS. *Blindness.* Assume that (μ_0, σ_0') and (μ_0, σ_0') are two blinded message/signature pairs. Given μ_b, σ_b' where $b \in \{0, 1\}$, an IBBS scheme meets the blindness if, any polynomial-time signer or distinguisher can output a bit $b' = b$ with a probability at most $1/2 + 1/n^c$, where n is enough large, and c is a constant. That is, (μ_0, σ_0') and (μ_0, σ_0') is indistinguishable for the signer and distinguisher.

One more unforgeable under sID-CMA. An **IBBS** scheme is sID-CMA one more unforgeable, if any polynomial-time adversary wins the following game with negligible probability of success.

Setup. The adversary claims the challenge ID^* in advance. Then, the challenger generates the security parameter and the master key pair (mpk, msk), and sends the mpk to the adversary with msk as his secret key.

Queries. The adversary is allowed to make two kinds of queries to the challenger.

Key-extract query. The adversary can query on any ID except ID^*. The challenger runs algorithm *KeyExtract* to return the corresponding sk_{ID}.
Signing query. The adversary adaptively chooses message m and ID, and gets the blinded signature σ' of the blinded message m' under ID.

Forge. After l key-extract and signing queries, the adversary outputs a bind signature σ^* of the $l+1$-th message m^* under ID^*. The adversary wins if the verifier outputs 1 when it checks the forgery (m^*, σ^*).

2.5 Key Algorithms

Algorithms TrapGen and SamplePre. Let $q = poly(n)$ be a prime, m be an arbitrary positive integer that $m > 5n \log q$.

With a security parameter n as input, algorithm **TrapGen** outputs the matrix $\mathbf{A} \in \mathbb{Z}_q^{n \times m}$ and $\mathbf{B} \in \mathbb{Z}^{m \times m}$. Here $\mathbf{B}$ is a good basis of lattice $\Lambda_q^\perp(\mathbf{A}) = \{\mathbf{v} \in \mathbb{Z}^m : \mathbf{A}\mathbf{v} = \mathbf{0} \bmod q\}$, and $||\tilde{\mathbf{B}}|| \leq O(\sqrt{n \log q})$.

With $\mathbf{A} \in \mathbb{Z}_q^{n \times m}$, $\mathbf{B} \in \mathbb{Z}^{m \times m}$, any $\sigma \geq ||\tilde{\mathbf{B}}|| \cdot \omega(\sqrt{\log n})$ and vector $\mathbf{y} \in \mathbb{Z}_q^n$ as inputs, algorithm **SamplePre** outputs a randomly nonzero vector $\mathbf{e} \in \{\mathbf{e} \in \mathbb{Z}^m : ||\mathbf{e}|| \leq \sigma\sqrt{m}\}$ such that $\mathbf{A}\mathbf{e} = \mathbf{y} \bmod q$ with overwhelming probability.

Algorithms ExtBasis, RandBasis and ExtRandBasis. Let $\mathbf{T} \in \mathbb{Z}^{m \times m}$ be an arbitrary basis of $\Lambda^\perp(\mathbf{A})$ for some $\mathbf{A} \in \mathbb{Z}_q^{n \times m}$ whose columns generate the entire group $\mathbb{Z}_q^n$, and let $\bar{\mathbf{A}} \in \mathbb{Z}_q^{n \times \bar{m}}$ be arbitrary.

There is a deterministic polynomial-time algorithm **ExtBasis**$(\mathbf{T}, \mathbf{A}' = \mathbf{A}||\bar{\mathbf{A}})$ that outputs a basis $\mathbf{T}'$ of $\Lambda^\perp(\mathbf{A}') \subseteq \mathbb{Z}^{m+\bar{m}}$ such that $||\tilde{\mathbf{T}}'|| = ||\tilde{\mathbf{T}}||$. See Lemma 3 in [5] for more details of **ExtBasis**.

Algorithm **RandBasis** is a probabilistic polynomial-time algorithm, which takes a basis $\mathbf{T}$ of an m-definitional integer lattice Λ and a parameter $s \geq ||\tilde{\mathbf{T}}|| \cdot \omega(\sqrt{\log n})$ as inputs, and outputs a basis $\mathbf{T}'$ of Λ that $||\tilde{\mathbf{T}}'|| \leq s\sqrt{m}$. See Lemma 4 in [5] for more details of **RandBasis**.

Algorithm **ExtRandBasis** can be implemented by algorithm **ExtBasis** and then algorithm **RandBasis**. It is a probabilistic algorithm that inputs an arbitrary basis $\mathbf{T}$ of $\Lambda^\perp(\mathbf{A})$ for some $\mathbf{A} \in \mathbb{Z}_q^{n \times m}$ whose columns generate the entire group $\mathbb{Z}_q^n$, a parameter

$s \geq ||\tilde{\mathbf{T}}|| \cdot \omega(\sqrt{\log n})$, an arbitrary $\bar{\mathbf{A}} \in \mathbb{Z}_q^{n \times \bar{m}}$, and outputs a basis $\mathbf{T'}$ of $\Lambda^\perp(\mathbf{A'} = \mathbf{A}||\bar{\mathbf{A}}) \subseteq \mathbb{Z}^{m+\bar{m}}$ such that $||\tilde{\mathbf{T}'}|| \leq s\sqrt{m}$.

Algorithms SampleLeft and SampleRight. Assume that $\mathbf{A}$, $\mathbf{B} \in \mathbb{Z}_q^{n \times m}$, $\mathbf{R} \in \{-1, 1\}^{m \times m}$, and the matrix $\mathbf{F}$ of form $\mathbf{F} = [\mathbf{A}||\mathbf{AR} + \mathbf{B}] \in \mathbb{Z}_q^{n \times 2m}$, algorithms **SampleLeft** and **SampleRight** can sample short vectors from $\Lambda_q^\perp(\mathbf{F})$ for some $\mathbf{u} \in \mathbb{Z}_q^n$ with either a trapdoor for $\Lambda_q^\perp(\mathbf{A})$ or a trapdoor for $\Lambda_q^\perp(\mathbf{B})$. We describe them briefly as follows, you can refer to [4] for more details.

SampleLeft. Given a rank n matrix $\mathbf{A} \in \mathbb{Z}_q^{n \times m}$ with a 'short' basis $\mathbf{T_A}$ for $\Lambda_q^\perp(\mathbf{A})$, a matrix $\mathbf{M}_1 \in \mathbb{Z}_q^{n \times m_1}$, a vector $\mathbf{u} \in \mathbb{Z}_q^n$, and a Gaussian parameter $\sigma \geq ||\tilde{\mathbf{T}}_\mathbf{A}|| \cdot \omega(\sqrt{\log(m + m_1)})$. The algorithm sets $\mathbf{F}_1 = [\mathbf{A}||\mathbf{M}_1]$, and outputs a vector $\mathbf{e} \in \mathbb{Z}^{m+m_1}$ sampled from a distribution statistically close to $D_{\Lambda_q^\mathbf{u}(F_1),\sigma}$. The vector $\mathbf{e}$ is generated as follows:

(a) Sample a random vector $\mathbf{e}_2 \in \mathbb{Z}^{m_1}$ distributed statistically close to $D_{\mathbb{Z}^{m_1},\sigma}$;
(b) Run $\mathbf{e}_1 \leftarrow \textbf{SamplePre}(\mathbf{A}, \mathbf{T_A}, \mathbf{y}, \sigma)$ where $\mathbf{y} = \mathbf{u} - (\mathbf{M}_1\mathbf{e}_2) \in \mathbb{Z}_q^n$;
(c) Output $\mathbf{e} \leftarrow (\mathbf{e}_1, \mathbf{e}_2) \in \mathbb{Z}^{m+m_1}$.

SampleRight. Given matrices $\mathbf{A} \in \mathbb{Z}_q^{n \times k}$ and $\mathbf{B} \in \mathbb{Z}_q^{n \times m}$ with a basis $\mathbf{T_B}$ for $\Lambda_q^\perp(\mathbf{B})$ where B is rank n, a matrix $\mathbf{R} \in \mathbb{Z}^{k \times m}$, $s_\mathbf{R} = ||\mathbf{R}|| = \sup_{||\mathbf{x}||=1} ||\mathbf{Rx}||$, a vector $\mathbf{u} \in \mathbb{Z}_q^n$, and a parameter $\sigma \geq ||\tilde{\mathbf{T}}_\mathbf{B}|| \cdot s_\mathbf{R}\omega(\sqrt{\log m})$, this algorithm sets $\mathbf{F}_2 = [\mathbf{A}||\mathbf{AR} + \mathbf{B}]$ and outputs a vector $\mathbf{e} \in \mathbb{Z}^{m+k}$ sampled from a distribution statistically close to $D_{\Lambda_q^\mathbf{u}(F_2),\sigma}$. The vector $\mathbf{e}$ is generated as follows:

(a) Construct a set $\mathbf{T}_{\mathbf{F}_2}$ of $(m+k)$ linearly independent vectors in $\Lambda_q^\perp(\mathbf{F}_2)$ where $||\tilde{\mathbf{T}}_{\mathbf{F}_2}|| < ||\tilde{\mathbf{T}}_\mathbf{B}||(s_\mathbf{R} + 1)$;
(b) if needed, by Lemma 7.1 in [17] to convert $\mathbf{T}_{\mathbf{F}_2}$ into a basis $\mathbf{T}'_{\mathbf{F}_2}$ of $\Lambda_q^\perp(\mathbf{F}_2)$ such that $||\tilde{\mathbf{T}}'_{\mathbf{F}_2}|| = ||\tilde{\mathbf{T}}_{\mathbf{F}_2}||$;
(c) invoke $\mathbf{e} \leftarrow \textbf{SamplePre}(\mathbf{F}_2, \mathbf{T}'_{\mathbf{F}_2}, \mathbf{u}, \sigma)$ to generate a vector $\mathbf{e} \in \Lambda_q^\mathbf{u}(\mathbf{F}_2)$ such that $\mathbf{e}$ is distributed close to $D_{\Lambda_q^\mathbf{u}(F_2),\sigma}$.

3 Our Construction

Assume that n is the system security parameter, other quantities are determined by n. q is a prime positive integer such that $q = poly(n)$, $m = O(2n \log q)$, $L = 8\sqrt{n \log q}$, $s' > L\omega(\sqrt{\log n})$.

Setup. Assume that the key generation center (KGC) has an n-dimensional lattice Λ with a trapdoor basis $\mathbf{B}$, we denote the check matrix of Λ by $\mathbf{A} \in \mathbb{Z}_q^{n \times m}$, and the

Gram-Schmidt orthogonal basis of $\mathbf{B}$ by $\tilde{\mathbf{B}}$. The smooth parameter of Λ is denoted as $\eta_\varepsilon(\Lambda)$. Set $s = ||\tilde{\mathbf{B}}||s'$, and $d = ||\tilde{\mathbf{B}}||/2$, L_M is the database of all signed blinded messages. The identity information of a signer is defined by $id \in \{0,1\}^k$, $H : \{0,1\}^k \to \mathbb{Z}_q^n$ and $H_0 : \{0,1\}^* \to \mathbb{Z}_q^n$ are secure collision-resistant hash functions, and $H_1 : \mathbb{Z}_q^n \to \mathbb{Z}_q^{n\times n}$ is an encoding with full-rank differences (FRD) function. The output of H is denoted as $\mathbf{v}_{id} = H(id) \in \mathbb{Z}_q^n$. The message is in $\{0,1\}^*$. The KGC operates as follows:

(a) Pick matrixes $\mathbf{C}_0, \mathbf{C}_1, \cdots, \mathbf{C}_k \in \mathbb{Z}_q^{n\times m}$.
(b) Uniformly choose random $\mathbf{A}_2, \mathbf{A}_3$ from $\mathbb{Z}_q^{n\times m}$.
(c) Output the system public parameters as $P = \{n, m, q, s', s, H, H_0, H_1\}$, the master secret key as $msk = \{\mathbf{B}\}$, and the master public key as $mpk = \{\mathbf{A}, \mathbf{A}_2, \mathbf{A}_3, \mathbf{C}_0, \cdots, \mathbf{C}_k\}$.

KeyExtract(id, P, msk, mpk). Take an identity id as input, the PKG generates the secret key for the identity as follows:

(a) Compute $\mathbf{A}_{id} = [\mathbf{A}||\mathbf{A}_2 + H_1(\mathbf{v}_{id})\mathbf{A}_3]$ where $H_1(\mathbf{v}_{id}) \in \mathbb{Z}_q^{n\times n}$;
(b) Extract a short basis $\mathbf{T}_{id} \leftarrow \textbf{ExtRandBasis}(\mathbf{B}, \mathbf{A}||\mathbf{A}_2 + H_1(\mathbf{v}_{id}), s')$ as the secret key for identity id, where $s' \geq max\{||\tilde{\mathbf{T}}_{id}||\omega(\sqrt{\log n})\}_{id\in\{0,1\}^k}$.

Figure 1 shows the key procedure of the IBBS scheme, the signature issue protocol. It has two moves between the signer and the user, and consists of three algorithms (**Blind, Sign, Unblind**).

Signer($id, \mathbf{A}, \mathbf{T}_{id}, \mu, P$)	**User**($M, \mathbf{A}, id, P$)
	$\mathbf{h} = H_0(M)$
	$\mathbf{v}_{id} = H(id)$, $\mathbf{A}_{id} = [\mathbf{A}||\mathbf{A}_2 + H_1(\mathbf{v}_{id})\mathbf{A}_3]$
If $\mu \in L_M$, return $\perp$. $\xleftarrow{\ \mu\ }$	$\mathbf{c} \leftarrow D_{\mathbb{Z}^m, s''}, t \in (1, d)$,
	$\bar{\mathbf{A}}_{id} = [\mathbf{A}||\mathbf{A}_2 + H_1(\mathbf{v}_{id})\mathbf{A}_3||\mathbf{C}_0 + \sum_{i\in[k]}(-1)^{id[i]}\mathbf{C}_i]$
	$\mu = (t^{-1}\mathbf{h} + \bar{\mathbf{A}}_{id}\mathbf{c}) \bmod q$
Else, $\mathbf{v}_{id} = H(id)$,	
$\bar{\mathbf{A}}_{id} = [\mathbf{A}||\mathbf{A}_2 + H_1(\mathbf{v}_{id})\mathbf{A}_3||\mathbf{C}_0 + \sum_{i\in[k]}(-1)^{id[i]}\mathbf{C}_i]$	
$\mathbf{v}' \leftarrow SamplePre(\bar{\mathbf{A}}_{id}, \mathbf{T}_{id}, s'\sqrt{m}, \mu)$	
Check $\bar{\mathbf{A}}_{id}\mathbf{v}' = \mu \bmod q$ and $||\mathbf{v}'|| \leq s'\sqrt{m}$	
If not, sample again.	
Else, $L_M \leftarrow L_M \cup \{\mu\}$. $\xrightarrow{\ \mathbf{v}'\ }$	$\mathbf{v} = t(\mathbf{v}' - \mathbf{c})$, output $(id, M, \mathbf{v})$

Fig. 1. Signature issue protocol of the IBBS scheme

Blind(*M*, *P*, *mpk*, *id*). Take the message $M \in \{0,1\}^*$ and the public parameters as inputs, the user blinds the message as follows:

(a) Compute $\mathbf{h} = H_0(M) \in \mathbb{Z}_q^n$,   and $\mathbf{A}_{id} = [\mathbf{A}||\mathbf{A}_2 + H_1(\mathbf{v}_{id})\mathbf{A}_3]$ where $\mathbf{v}_{id} = H(id) \in \mathbb{Z}_q^n$;

(b) Choose a random vector $\mathbf{c} = (c_1, c_2, \cdots, c_{3m}) \rightarrow D_{\mathbb{Z}^{3m}, s'}$ with the origin as its center, then $||c|| \leq s'\sqrt{3m}$ holds with overwhelming probability from Theorem 2. If not, repeat it.

(c) Compute $\bar{\mathbf{A}}_{id} = [\mathbf{A}||\mathbf{A}_2 + H_1(\mathbf{v}_{id})\mathbf{A}_3||\mathbf{C}_0 + \sum_{i\in[k]}(-1)^{id[i]}\mathbf{C}_i]$ for $id = (id[1], \cdots, id[k]) \in \{0,1\}^k$.

(d) From Theorem 2, $\bar{\mathbf{A}}_{id}\mathbf{c}$ is approximate uniform.

(e) Choose an arbitrary $t \in \mathbb{Z}_q$ such that $1 < t < d$.

(f) Compute the blinded message $\mu = (t^{-1}\mathbf{h} + \bar{\mathbf{A}}_{id}\mathbf{c})\bmod q$.

Finally, the user sends μ to the signer with identity *id*.

Sign($\mu, \mathbf{T}_{id}, P$, *mpk*, L_M). The signer with identity *id* signs the blinded message μ as follows:

(a) Search μ in L_M, if $\mu \in L_M$, output $\perp$; if not, go to **step 2**.

(b) For $id = (id[1], \cdots, id[k]) \in \{0,1\}^k$,   compute $\bar{\mathbf{A}}_{id} = [\mathbf{A}||\mathbf{A}_2 + H_1(\mathbf{v}_{id})\mathbf{A}_3|| \mathbf{C}_0 + \sum_{i\in[k]}(-1)^{id[i]}\mathbf{C}_i]$.

(c) Extract a basis $\bar{\mathbf{T}}_{id} \leftarrow ExtBasis(\bar{\mathbf{A}}_{id}, \mathbf{T}_{id}, s)$.

(d) Run $\mathbf{v}' \leftarrow SamplePre(\bar{\mathbf{A}}_{id}, \bar{\mathbf{T}}_{id}, s', \mu)$ to generate $\mathbf{v}'$,   then check   if $\bar{\mathbf{A}}_{id}\mathbf{v}' = \mu \bmod q$, and $||\mathbf{v}'|| \leq s'\sqrt{3m}$. If not, repeat it.

(e) Add μ into L_M.

Finally, the signer *id* outputs $\mathbf{v}'$ as his signature of the blinded message μ.

Unblind(*P*, *mpk*, $\mathbf{v}'$, $\mathbf{c}$, *t*, *id*). Upon receiving the signature $\mathbf{v}'$, the user computes $\mathbf{v} = t(\mathbf{v}' - \mathbf{c})$ as the signature of message *M* signed by the signer with *id*.

Verify (*P*,   *mpk*,   *id*,   *M*,   *v*).   The   verifier   computes $\bar{\mathbf{A}}_{id} = [\mathbf{A}||\mathbf{A}_2 + H_1(\mathbf{v}_{id})\mathbf{A}_3||\mathbf{C}_0 + \sum_{i\in[k]}(-1)^{id[i]}\mathbf{C}_i]$ and $\mathbf{h} = H_0(M)$, and then checks that: (1). $\bar{\mathbf{A}}_{id}\mathbf{v} = \mathbf{h} \bmod q$; (2). $||\mathbf{v}|| \leq s\sqrt{3m}$. The verifier outputs 1 if both the two conditions are satisfied, else output 0.

Correctness. As *n* is the security parameter, other parameters in the scheme allow the algorithms **SamplePre** and **ExtRandBasis** to operate correctly. In particular, the PKG can generate a trapdoor basis for larger dimension lattice $\Lambda_q^\perp(\bar{\mathbf{A}}_{id})$ as it has the trapdoor basis of $\Lambda_q^\perp(\mathbf{A})$. The signer can generate a short random vector for lattice $\Lambda_q^\perp(\bar{\mathbf{A}}_{id})$ with the trapdoor basis $\mathbf{T}_{id}$ as his secret key. Besides, $\mathbf{v}'$ is the output of algorithm *SamplePre*, $\bar{\mathbf{A}}_{id}\mathbf{v}' = \mu \bmod q$ and $||\mathbf{v}'|| \leq s'\sqrt{m}$ holds with overwhelming probability. So we have $\bar{\mathbf{A}}_{id}\mathbf{v}' = \mu = t^{-1}\mathbf{h} + \bar{\mathbf{A}}_{id}\mathbf{c}$, $t\bar{\mathbf{A}}_{id}\mathbf{v}' = \mathbf{h} + t\bar{\mathbf{A}}_{id}\mathbf{c}$, $\bar{\mathbf{A}}_{id}t(\mathbf{v}' - \mathbf{c}) = \mathbf{h}$, and $\bar{\mathbf{A}}_{id}\mathbf{v} = \mathbf{h}$.

On the other hand, we have $||\mathbf{v}|| = t||(\mathbf{v}' - \mathbf{c})|| \le ||\tilde{\mathbf{B}}||/2 \cdot 2s'\sqrt{3m} = s\sqrt{3m}$. Therefore, an honestly created signature will be accepted with overwhelming probability.

4 Security Analysis

In this section, we prove that our scheme is unconditionally blind, and one-more unforgeable under selective identity and chosen message attacks (sID-CMA) in the standard model.

Theorem 3 (Blindness). Our IBBS scheme is unconditionally blind.

Proof. From Theorem 2, $\bar{\mathbf{A}}_{id}\mathbf{c}$ is uniformly distributed. As the output of H_0 is approximate uniform, and t is randomly chosen, the blinded message $\boldsymbol{\mu} = (t^{-1}\mathbf{h} + \bar{\mathbf{A}}_{id}\mathbf{c}) \bmod q$ is indistinguishable from a uniform distribution over $\mathbb{Z}_q^n$. The signer chooses a random vector over $\mathbb{Z}_q^n$ and a random integer $t < d$, and then tries to recover the hash value of the real message from $t\boldsymbol{\mu} = \mathbf{h} + \bar{\mathbf{A}}_{id}\mathbf{c}$. Next, we show that the statistical distance of the resulting distribution of the signer is 0 from the uniform distribution, that is,

$$\Delta(t(\boldsymbol{\mu} - \mathbf{c}), \mathbf{h}) = \frac{1}{2}\sum\nolimits_{\mathbf{h} \in \mathbb{Z}_q^n, \mathbf{c}_1 \in \mathbb{Z}_q^m, t_1 \in \mathbb{Z}, t_1 < ||\tilde{\mathbf{B}}||/2} |\Pr[t_1(\boldsymbol{\mu} - \bar{\mathbf{A}}_{id}\mathbf{c}_1) = \mathbf{h})] - Pr[H_0(M) = \mathbf{h}]|$$
$$= \frac{1}{2}\sum\nolimits_{\mathbf{h} \in \mathbb{Z}_q^n, \mathbf{c}_1 \in \mathbb{Z}_q^m, t_1 \in \mathbb{Z}, t_1 < ||\tilde{\mathbf{B}}||/2} [(\tfrac{1}{q})^n - (\tfrac{1}{q})^n] = 0 \tag{1}$$

Therefore, they are indistinguishable, and our scheme is unconditionally blind.

Theorem 4 (One-more unforgeability against sID-CMA). Assume that the $SIS_{m,q,s\sqrt{m}}$ problem is hard, our IBBS scheme is one-more unforgeable against sID-CMA in the standard model.

Proof. Assume that there is a successful adversary $\mathcal{A}$ with the advantage of ε breaks one-more unforgeability of the proposed scheme, we can construct an algorithm $\mathcal{B}$ to solve the instance of the $SIS_{m,q,2s\sqrt{3m}}$ problem by employing $\mathcal{A}$ to be a subroutine.

Suppose that we get an instance of $SIS_{n,q,m,s\sqrt{m}} = (\hat{\mathbf{A}}, n, m, q, l, s)$, where $\hat{\mathbf{A}} \in \mathbb{Z}_q^{n \times m}$, l is the total query number that the adversary can make at most in the interactive game. Our goal is to find a vector such that $\hat{\mathbf{A}}\mathbf{e} = \mathbf{0} \bmod q$ and $||\mathbf{e}|| \le s\sqrt{m}$. The adversary outputs a challenge identity $id^* = (id^*[1], \cdots, id^*[k])$. Next, we simulate the circumstance to interact with $\mathcal{A}$, and solve the given instance using $\mathcal{A}$.

Setup. Assume that we receives the instance $\hat{\mathbf{A}} \in \mathbb{Z}_q^{n \times m}$. The system parameters are set as our scheme, we generate the public key $mpk = \{\mathbf{A}, \mathbf{A}_2, \mathbf{A}_3, \mathbf{C}_0, \cdots, \mathbf{C}_k\}$ as follows:

(a) Compute $(\mathbf{A}_3, \mathbf{T}) \leftarrow TrapGen(n, m, q)$, and then randomly choose $\mathbf{R}^* \in \{-1, 1\}^{m \times m}$.

(b) Set $\mathbf{A} = \hat{\mathbf{A}}$, and $\mathbf{A}_2 = \mathbf{A}\mathbf{R}^* - H_1(id^*)\mathbf{A}_3$.

(c) Run the trapdoor sampling algorithm to generate a random lattice $\Lambda_q^\perp(\mathbf{S}_0)$ with $\mathbf{S}_0 \in \mathbb{Z}_q^{n \times m}$ and its corresponding trapdoor basis $\mathbf{T}_0 \in \mathbb{Z}_q^{m \times m}$.

(d) Pick k short random matrices $\mathbf{R}_0, \mathbf{R}_1, \cdots, \mathbf{R}_k \in \mathbb{Z}^{m \times m}$. Fix $w_0 = 1 \in \mathbb{Z}_q$, uniformly pick random scalars $w_1, \cdots, w_k \in \mathbb{Z}_q$.

(e) Set $\mathbf{R}_{id_j} = \mathbf{R}_0 + \sum_{i \in [k]} (-1)^{id_j[i]} \mathbf{R}_i \in \mathbb{Z}^{m \times m}$, $w_{id_j} = 1 + \sum_{i \in [k]} (-1)^{id_j[i]} w_i \in \mathbb{Z}_q$.

(f) Send the public key $\{\mathbf{A}, \mathbf{A}_2, \mathbf{A}_3, \mathbf{C}_0, \cdots, \mathbf{C}_k\}$ to $\mathcal{A}$, where $\mathbf{C}_i = \mathbf{A}\mathbf{R}_i + w_i \mathbf{S}_0$ for $i = 0, 1, \cdots, k$.

$\mathcal{B}$ maintains two lists to store the extraction queries and the signing queries.

Extraction queries. For a fresh identity $id_j \neq id^*$, $j \in [l]$, $\mathcal{B}$ first computes $\mathbf{A}_{id_j} = [\mathbf{A}||\mathbf{A}_2 + H_1(\mathbf{v}_{id_j})\mathbf{A}_3] = [\mathbf{A}||\mathbf{A}\mathbf{R}^* + [H_1(\mathbf{v}_{id_j}) - H_1(\mathbf{v}_{id^*})]\mathbf{A}_3]$. By construction, we know that $[H_1(\mathbf{v}_{id_j}) - H_1(\mathbf{v}_{id^*})]$ is non-singular and therefore $\mathbf{T}$ is also a trapdoor for $\Lambda_q^\perp([H_1(\mathbf{v}_{id_j}) - H_1(\mathbf{v}_{id^*})]\mathbf{A}_3)$. Using the trapdoor basis $\mathbf{T}$, $\mathcal{B}$ first generates a random trapdoor basis $\mathbf{T}_{id_j}$ for $\Lambda_q^\perp(\mathbf{A}_{id_j})$, then adds $(id_j, \mathbf{T}_{id_j})$ into list L_1, and finally sends it to $\mathcal{A}$ as the response. If $\mathcal{A}$ sends an old identity id that has been queried before, $\mathcal{B}$ searches $(id_j, \mathbf{T}_{id_j})$ in L_1, and answers with $\mathbf{T}_{id_j}$.

Signing queries. On inputs a blinded message μ_j and an identity id_j for $j \in [l]$, algorithm $\mathcal{B}$ computes $\bar{\mathbf{A}}_{id_j} = [\mathbf{A}||\mathbf{A}\mathbf{R}^* + [H_1(\mathbf{v}_{id_j}) - H_1(\mathbf{v}_{id^*})]\mathbf{A}_3 || \mathbf{C}_0 + \sum_{i \in [k]} (-1)^{id_j[i]} \mathbf{C}_i]$, where $H_1(\mathbf{v}_{id_j}) \in \mathbb{Z}_q^{n \times n}$ and answers in two cases:

Case 1. $id_j \neq id^*$. $\mathcal{B}$ searches $(\mu_j, id_j, \mathbf{v}_j')$ in L_2. If it exists, $\mathcal{B}$ returns $\mathbf{v}_{j'}$. Otherwise, using $\mathbf{T}$ and the **SampleRight** algorithm, $\mathcal{B}$ first generates the trapdoor $\mathbf{T}_{id_j}$ for $\mathbf{F}_{id_j} = [\mathbf{A}||\mathbf{A}\mathbf{R}^* + [H_1(\mathbf{v}_{id_j}) - H_1(\mathbf{v}_{id^*})]\mathbf{A}_3]$, and then computes a random trapdoor $\bar{\mathbf{T}}_{id_j}$ for $\Lambda_q^\perp(\mathbf{F}_{id_j})$. With the trapdoor $\bar{\mathbf{T}}_{id_j}$ and the **SampleLeft** algorithm, $\mathcal{B}$ generates $\mathbf{v}_{j'} \leftarrow SamplePre(\bar{\mathbf{A}}_{id_j}, \bar{\mathbf{T}}_{id_j}, \mu_j, s)$ as a signature. Finally, $\mathcal{B}$ adds $(\mu_j, id_j, \mathbf{v}_j')$ into L_2 and returns $\mathbf{v}_{j'}$ as his response. $\mathcal{A}$ decodes (unblinds) $\mathbf{v}_{j'}$ to obtain the real signature.

Case 2. $id_j = id^*$. $\mathcal{B}$ searches $(\mu_j, id_j, \mathbf{v}_j')$ in L_2. If it exists, $\mathcal{B}$ returns $\mathbf{v}_{j'}$. Otherwise, using $\mathbf{T}_0$ and the **SampleRight** algorithm, $\mathcal{B}$ constructs the matrix $\mathbf{F}_{id^*}' = [\mathbf{A}||\mathbf{A}\mathbf{R}_{id^*} + w_{id^*}\mathbf{S}_0]$ and generates a random trapdoor $\mathbf{T}_{id^*}$ for $\Lambda_q^\perp(\mathbf{F}_{id^*}')$. Then, with the trapdoor $\mathbf{T}_{id^*}$ and the **SampleLeft** algorithm, $\mathcal{B}$ generates a random trapdoor $\bar{\mathbf{T}}_{id^*}$ for $\Lambda_q^\perp(\mathbf{F}_{id_j})$, where $\mathbf{F}_{id^*} = [\mathbf{F}_{id^*}'||\mathbf{A}\mathbf{R}^*] = [\mathbf{A}||\mathbf{A}\mathbf{R}_{id^*} + w_{id^*}\mathbf{S}_0||\mathbf{A}\mathbf{R}^*] \in \mathbb{Z}_q^{n \times 3m}$. $\mathcal{B}$ obtains a short random $\bar{\mathbf{v}}_*' \in \Lambda_q^\perp(\mathbf{F}_{id^*})$ with $||\bar{\mathbf{v}}_{l+1}^{*'}|| \leq s\sqrt{3m}$ by using the trapdoor $\bar{\mathbf{T}}_{id^*}$ and the **SamplePre** algorithm. Finally, $\mathcal{B}$ changes the order of the corresponding vectors of $\bar{\mathbf{v}}_*'$ to get a short random trapdoor $\tilde{\mathbf{v}}_*' \in \Lambda_q^\perp(\tilde{\mathbf{A}}_{id^*})$ for $\tilde{\mathbf{A}}_{id^*} = [\mathbf{A}||\mathbf{A}\mathbf{R}^*||\mathbf{A}\mathbf{R}_{id^*} + w_{id^*}\mathbf{S}_0]$. As $\mathbf{C}_0 + \sum_{i \in [k]} (-1)^{id_j[i]} \mathbf{C}_i = \mathbf{R}_{id} + w_{id}\mathbf{S}_0$ and $\bar{\mathbf{A}}_{id^*} = [\mathbf{A}||\mathbf{A}\mathbf{R}^* + [H_1(\mathbf{v}_{id_j}) - H_1(\mathbf{v}_{id^*})]\mathbf{A}_3||\mathbf{C}_0 + \sum_{i \in [k]} (-1)^{id_j[i]} \mathbf{C}_i]$, we have $\bar{\mathbf{A}}_{id^*} = \tilde{\mathbf{A}}_{id^*}$. So $\tilde{\mathbf{v}}_*'$ is also a short random vector in $\Lambda_q^\perp(\bar{\mathbf{A}}_{id^*})$ such that $||\tilde{\mathbf{v}}_{l+1}^{*'}|| \leq s\sqrt{3m}$. Finally, $\mathcal{B}$ adds $(\mu_j, id^*, \tilde{\mathbf{v}}_*')$ into L_2 and sends as his response. $\mathcal{A}$ decodes (unblinds) $\tilde{\mathbf{v}}_*'$ to obtain the real signature.

Challenge. After receiving l message-signature pairs, $\mathcal{A}$ outputs the $l+1$-th valid forgery $(\boldsymbol{\mu}_{l+1}^*, id^*, \mathbf{v}_{l+1}^{*\prime})$, such that $\bar{\mathbf{A}}_{id^*}\mathbf{v}_{l+1}^{*\prime} = \boldsymbol{\mu}_{l+1}^*$ and $\|\mathbf{v}_{l+1}^{*\prime}\| \leq s\sqrt{3m}$. $\mathcal{B}$ checks that $\boldsymbol{\mu}_{l+1}^* \neq \boldsymbol{\mu}_j$ for $j = 1, \cdots, l$, that is, $\boldsymbol{\mu}_{l+1}^*$ of a fresh message. Then, $\mathcal{B}$ generates a signature $\bar{\mathbf{v}}^{*\prime}$ for the blinded message $\boldsymbol{\mu}_{l+1}^*$ as in the signing queries, where $\bar{\mathbf{A}}_{id^*}\bar{\mathbf{v}}^{*\prime} = \boldsymbol{\mu}_{l+1}^*$ and $\|\bar{\mathbf{v}}^{*\prime}\| \leq s\sqrt{3m}$. If $\bar{\mathbf{v}}^{*\prime} = \mathbf{v}_{l+1}^{*\prime}$, $\mathcal{B}$ aborts (with negligible probability). Otherwise, $\mathcal{B}$ operates as follows:

(a) Compute $\mathbf{R}_{id^*} = \mathbf{R}_0 + \sum_{i \in [k]} (-1)^{id^*[i]}\mathbf{R}_i \in \mathbb{Z}^{m \times m}$ and $w_{id^*} = 1 + \sum_{i \in [k]} (-1)^{id^*[i]} w_i \in \mathbb{Z}_q$.

(b) If $w_{id^*} \neq 0 \bmod q$, abort the simulation (with a probability of about $1 - \frac{1}{q}$).

(c) Compute $\mathbf{e} = |\bar{\mathbf{v}}^{*\prime} - \mathbf{v}_{l+1}^{*\prime}|$, and parse $\mathbf{e} = (\mathbf{e}_1, \mathbf{e}_2, \mathbf{e}_3)^t$, where $\mathbf{e}_1, \mathbf{e}_2, \mathbf{e}_3 \in \mathbb{Z}^m$.

(d) Return $\mathbf{e}^* = \mathbf{e}_1 + \mathbf{R}^*\mathbf{e}_2 + \mathbf{R}_{id^*}\mathbf{e}_3 \in \mathbb{Z}^m$.

We show the success probability of $\mathcal{B}$ in solving $SIS_{m,n,q,2s\sqrt{3m}}$. From the above analysis, $\mathbf{R}_{id^*} = \mathbf{R}_0 + \sum_{i \in [k]} (-1)^{id^*[i]}\mathbf{R}_i \in \mathbb{Z}^{m \times m}$, and $w_{id^*} = 1 + \sum_{i \in [k]} (-1)^{id^*[i]} w_i \in \mathbb{Z}_q$, we have $\bar{\mathbf{A}}_{id^*}(|\mathbf{v}^{*\prime} - \mathbf{v}_{l+1}^{*\prime}|) = [\mathbf{A}\|\mathbf{A}\mathbf{R}^*\|\mathbf{A}\mathbf{R}_{id^*} + w_{id^*}\mathbf{S}_0]\mathbf{e} = \mathbf{0}$. If $w_{id^*} = 0 \bmod q$, we have $[\mathbf{A}\|\mathbf{A}\mathbf{R}^*\|\mathbf{A}\mathbf{R}_{id^*}](\mathbf{e}_1, \mathbf{e}_2, \mathbf{e}_3)^t = \mathbf{0} \bmod q$, that is, $[\mathbf{A}\|\mathbf{A}\|\mathbf{A}](\mathbf{e}_1, \mathbf{R}^*\mathbf{e}_2, \mathbf{R}_{id^*}\mathbf{e}_3)^t = \mathbf{0} \bmod q$. By the similar method as in Lemma 26 in [6], it can be obtained that $\mathbf{e}^*$ is a short non-zero vector as a solution to the given SIS instance with high probability. The probability of an abort in the above simulation is about $(1 - \frac{1}{q})$. The view of $\mathcal{A}$ in the game is identical to its view as provided by $\mathcal{B}$. Therefore, $\mathcal{B}$ can solve the SIS problem with probability at least $\frac{1}{q}\varepsilon$.

Table 1. Comparison of the related blind signature schemes

Schemes	[11]	[12]	Sect. 6
Moves number	4	2	2
Signature size	$O(n\log q)$	$O(n\log q)$	$O(n\log q)$
Without failure	✕	✓	✓
ID-based	✕	✕	✓
Security model	ROM	ROM	SM

Table 2. Bit length of concrete instances

Instances	1	2	3	4	5
n	284	284	284	284	284
q	2^{16}	2^{20}	2^{24}	2^{27}	2^{30}
m	9088	11360	13632	15336	17040
L	539	603	660	701	738
Secret key	$135s'$	$151s'$	$165s'$	$175s'$	$185s'$
Public key	$4.1k' \times 10^7$	$6.5k' \times 10^7$	$9.3k' \times 10^7$	$1.2k' \times 10^8$	$1.5k' \times 10^8$
Signature	$165s'$	$185s'$	$202s'$	$214s'$	$226s'$

5 Conclusions

Table 1 lists the comparison with the existing lattice-based schemes [11, 12], in terms of the interactive move numbers, failures in generating signatures, ID-based system, and security models. Here, the move number denotes the number of interactive moves in the issue protocol of the blind signature, without failure means there is no failures occur in the blind signing procedures. We use "ID-based" to denote if that scheme meets the requirement of identity-based cryptosystems, and "the security model" is to show the security model of that scheme, that is, in the random oracle model (ROM) or standard model (SM).

Many researchers still wonder whether a secure scheme constructed in the random oracle model keeps their security in practice, because the random oracles are replaced by hash functions when implemented. The highlight of our construction is that, it is designed without random oracle, while other schemes are constructed in the random oracle model.

Moreover, Table 2 shows the bit length of concrete instances of our scheme. During the experiments, we set $m = 2n \log q$ and $L = 8\sqrt{n \log q}$. s' is the smooth parameter that $s' > L\omega(\sqrt{\log n})$ with $L=8\sqrt{n \log q}$, $k'=k+4$ where k denotes the bit size of the identity. The secret key, public key, and signature sizes are tolerable when parameters are suitable set.

Comparing with the schemes designed in the random oracle model, the ones constructed without random oracles are much convincing in security and practical in engineering. From the above description, our construction has three additional advantages:

1. Similar to the scheme in [12], our scheme has 2 moves.
2. Our scheme has no failures in generating blind signatures.
3. Only our scheme is applicable to the ID-based system.

We conclude this work with a brief summary. This research studies on IBBS scheme from lattices. An identity-based blind signature scheme is put forward based on hard worst case lattice problem, which is considered to be the most promising one among the post quantum primitives. By the technique introduced in [18], our selectively secure constructions can be converted into adaptively secure ones by using chameleon hash functions. However, it needs more efforts to research on identity-based blind signature from lattices. For example, the verification matrix of the scheme in the standard model is three times of the master public key in dimension, and thus the signature sizes is increased. More exploration is needed for reducing the signature size of identity-based blind signature from lattices.

Acknowledgments. We thank the anonymous Inscrypt reviewers for their helpful comments. This work is supported by the National Natural Science Foundations of China (No.61472309 61572390, and 61672412), the 111 Project (No. B08038), and the Natural Science Foundation in Ningbo of China (No. 201601HJ-B01382).

References

1. Chaum, D.: Blind signatures for untraceable payments. In: Chaum, D., Rivest, R.L., Sherman, A.T. (eds.) Advances in Cryptology, pp. 199–203. Springer, Heidelberg (1982)
2. Shor, P.W.: Polynomial-time algorithms for prime factorization and discrete logarithms on a quantum computer. SIAM J. Comput. **26**(5), 1484–1509 (1997)
3. Gentry, C., Peikert, V., Vaikutanathan, V.: Trapdoors for hard lattices and new cryptographic construction. In: Proceedings of the 40th Annual ACM Symposium on Theory of Computing (STOC 2008), pp. 197–206. ACM, New York (2008)
4. Agrawal, S., Boneh, D., Boyen, X.: Efficient lattice (H)IBE in the standard model. In: Gilbert, H. (ed.) EUROCRYPT 2010. LNCS, vol. 6110, pp. 553–572. Springer, Heidelberg (2010). doi:10.1007/978-3-642-13190-5_28
5. Cash, D., Hofheinz, D., Kiltz, E., Peikert, C.: Bonsai trees, or how to delegate a lattice basis. In: Gilbert, H. (ed.) EUROCRYPT 2010. LNCS, vol. 6110, pp. 523–552. Springer, Heidelberg (2010). doi:10.1007/978-3-642-13190-5_27
6. Boyen, X.: Lattice mixing and vanishing trapdoors: a framework for fully secure short signatures and more. In: Nguyen, P.Q., Pointcheval, D. (eds.) PKC 2010. LNCS, vol. 6056, pp. 499–517. Springer, Heidelberg (2010). doi:10.1007/978-3-642-13013-7_29
7. Lyubashevsky, V., Micciancio, D.: Asymptotically efficient lattice-based digital signatures. In: Canetti, R. (ed.) TCC 2008. LNCS, vol. 4948, pp. 37–54. Springer, Heidelberg (2008). doi:10.1007/978-3-540-78524-8_3
8. Micciancio, D., Peikert, C.: Trapdoors for lattices: simpler, tighter, faster, smaller. In: Pointcheval, D., Johansson, T. (eds.) EUROCRYPT 2012. LNCS, vol. 7237, pp. 700–718. Springer, Heidelberg (2012). doi:10.1007/978-3-642-29011-4_41
9. Ducas, L., Lyubashevsky, V., Prest, T.: Efficient identity-based encryption over NTRU lattices. In: Sarkar, P., Iwata, T. (eds.) ASIACRYPT 2014. LNCS, vol. 8874, pp. 22–41. Springer, Heidelberg (2014). doi:10.1007/978-3-662-45608-8_2
10. Alperin-Sheriff, J.: Short signatures with short public keys from homomorphic trapdoor functions. In: Katz, J. (ed.) PKC 2015. LNCS, vol. 9020, pp. 236–255. Springer, Heidelberg (2015). doi:10.1007/978-3-662-46447-2_11
11. Rückert, M.: Lattice-based blind signatures. In: Abe, M. (ed.) ASIACRYPT 2010. LNCS, vol. 6477, pp. 413–430. Springer, Heidelberg (2010). doi:10.1007/978-3-642-17373-8_24
12. Wang, F., Hu, Y., Wang, C.: A lattice-based blind signature scheme. Geomatics Inf. Sci. Wuhan Univ. **35**(5), 550–553 (2010). (in Chinese)
13. Shamir, A.: Identity-based cryptosystems and signature schemes. In: Blakley, G.R., Chaum, D. (eds.) CRYPTO 1984. LNCS, vol. 196, pp. 47–53. Springer, Heidelberg (1985). doi:10.1007/3-540-39568-7_5
14. Zhang, F., Kim, K.: ID-based blind signature and ring signature from pairings. In: Zheng, Y. (ed.) ASIACRYPT 2002. LNCS, vol. 2501, pp. 533–547. Springer, Heidelberg (2002). doi:10.1007/3-540-36178-2_33
15. Zhang, F., Kim, K.: Efficient ID-based blind signature and proxy signature from bilinear pairings. In: Safavi-Naini, R., Seberry, J. (eds.) ACISP 2003. LNCS, vol. 2727, pp. 312–323. Springer, Heidelberg (2003). doi:10.1007/3-540-45067-X_27
16. Galindo, D., Herranz, J., Kiltz, E.: On the generic construction of identity-based signatures with additional properties. In: Lai, X., Chen, K. (eds.) ASIACRYPT 2006. LNCS, vol. 4284, pp. 178–193. Springer, Heidelberg (2006). doi:10.1007/11935230_12

17. Phong, L.T., Wakaha, O.: New identity-based blind signature and blind decryption scheme in the standard model. IEICE Trans. Fundam. Electron. Commun. Comput. Sci. **E92**(A(8)), 1822–1835 (2009)
18. Boneh, D., Boyen, X.: Efficient selective-ID secure identity-based encryption without random oracles. In: Cachin, C., Camenisch, J.L. (eds.) EUROCRYPT 2004. LNCS, vol. 3027, pp. 223–238. Springer, Heidelberg (2004). doi:10.1007/978-3-540-24676-3_14

Homomorphic Encryption

Multi-bit Leveled Homomorphic Encryption via **Dual.LWE**-Based

Zengpeng Li[1,2], Chunguang Ma[1,2(✉)], Eduardo Morais[3], and Gang Du[1,2]

[1] College of Computer Science and Technology, Harbin Engineering University,
Harbin 15001, China
{lizengpeng,machunguang,dugang}@hrbeu.edu.cn
[2] State Key Laboratory of Information Security,
Institute of Information Engineering, Chinese Academy of Sciences,
Beijing 100093, China
[3] Institute of Computing, University of Campinas, Campinas 13083-050, Brazil
eduardo.morais@gmail.com

Abstract. Fully Homomorphic Encryption (FHE) is a cryptographic primitive that allows computing over encrypted data without decrypting the corresponding ciphertexts. In general, existing FHE schemes can be achieved using standard Learning with Errors (LWE) assumption and most of the schemes are single-bit encryption. Hence, the construction of multi-bit FHE with high efficiency remains an open problem in cryptography. In this paper, we propose multi-bit versions of Public Key Encryption (PKE) via the dual LWE-based firstly proposed by Gentry, Peikert, and Vaikuntanathan at STOC 2008. We initially develop an universal construction derived from a general structure of the underlying combined public matrix for constructing the multi-bit version which increases the size of ciphertexts linearly. Then, utilizing multi-bit PKE scheme as building block, we propose a new multi-bit FHE scheme under the assumption of decisional LWE is hard and prove the scheme is IND-CPA-secure.

Keywords: Leveled homomorphic encryption · Dual LWE-based · First-is-errorless LWE · Multi-bit encryption

1 Introduction

The recent development of cloud computing allows users to outsource their data to cloud services. However, cloud computing raises new challenges with respect to the protection of user privacy. Fully Homomorphic Encryption (hereafter FHE) is one way to solve the problem. With homomorphic encryption, users send their data in encrypted form to the cloud, and the cloud still can perform computations on encrypted data. Since all data in the cloud can be stored in encrypted form, the confidentiality of user's data is preserved irrespective of any actions in the cloud. Owing to this attractive property, homomorphic encryption would give a powerful tool to break several barriers to the adoption of cloud services for security-critical usage.

© Springer International Publishing AG 2017
K. Chen et al. (Eds.): Inscrypt 2016, LNCS 10143, pp. 221–242, 2017.
DOI: 10.1007/978-3-319-54705-3_14

Actually, FHE is a public key encryption scheme supporting algebraic operations on encrypted data. Specially, FHE is a secure homomorphic mapping from plaintext space to ciphertext space, allowing us to evaluate directly any function over encrypted data by only using public information, and such that the output is a ciphertext of the equivalent function over the corresponding plaintexts.

The idea of homomorphic encryption can be traced back to 1978 by Rivest et al. [28]. It provides a construction of a cryptosystem such that an entity can carry out computations on encrypted data without decryption. However, the construction of FHE schemes remained an open problem in cryptography, until the breakthrough work by Gentry [12] in 2009. Since then, many candidate FHE schemes have been proposed following the Gentry's blueprint [5,7,8,20,23].

Up to now, there are two main computational problems that serve as security foundations of current fully homomorphic encryption schemes: Regev's Learning with Errors problem (LWE) over lattices and Howgrave-Graham's Approximate Greatest Common Divisor problem (AGCD) over the integers. However, most of constructions focus on single-bit encryption only. Once we have a single-bit encryption, then we can follow a straightforward composition to obtain a multi-bit FHE scheme. However, this straightforward construction for multi-bit FHE will not lead to better performance. Recently [4,9,15,24,29], many interesting new methods were proposed to construct multi-bit FHE schemes over the integers or over lattices, making FHE more efficient.

For multi-bit variants over the integers, we remark that Nuida and Kurosawa [24] suggested a scheme supporting homomorphic operations over vectors of plaintexts. Nuida and Kurosawa's scheme follows essentially the same ideas proposed by Cheon et al. [9], the only difference is that Cheon et al. gave a construction of batch FHE over the integers with message space restricted to $\mathbb{Z}_2$. Indeed, Smart and Vercauteren's work [29] was the first to describe how to achieve SIMD-like homomorphic operations for multi-bit variants, but the underlying lattice assumption was not the LWE problem, and since LWE-based constructions in general offer better performance, it would be interesting to have LWE-based schemes allowing SIMD-like operations. Brakerski, Gentry, and Halevi [4] used the method presented in [26], describing a way to extend packed Regev's encryption [27] to obtain FHE schemes [5,7,8]. In order to compute the key-switching procedure, using the encrypted secret key as input to reduce the dimension of fresh ciphertexts, Brakerski [3] utilized the tensoring technique. Hiromasa, Abe and Okamoto [15] proposed to pack multiple messages into a single ciphertext assuming an additional assumption, for instance, the circular security assumption. Their scheme is based on the Alperin-Sheriff and Peikert's [2] works, which encode messages into matrices, obtaining an optimized bootstrapping algorithm for any LWE-based FHE scheme.

Actually, all of these single-bit FHE schemes based on the hardness of LWE assumption have not satisfactory performance. Thus, in order to simultaneously encrypt t bits, we have that composing single-bit schemes is not a good strategy. This undesirable situation raises the question:

Can we construct a Dual.LWE-*based* FHE *scheme with one-time multi-bit encryption procedure?*

The state-of-the-art of homomorphic encryption construction, considering the asymptotic cost of the subjacent algorithms, is the LWE-based proposal by Gentry, Sahai, and Waters [14] (hereafter called GSW). Hence, in this paper we focus our attention on the GSW scheme, since it can achieve leveled homomorphic encryption without any key switching. However, regarding multi-bit encryption, a heavy computational cost would be required to evaluate a large number of ciphertexts. To overcome this issue, we propose a new composition for public key **A**, i.e. combining any number LWE distributions into a single public key matrix. Next we will sketch our main contribution.

1.1 Our Contributions and Techniques

The aim of this paper is to give a practical solution for multi-bit Dual.LWE-based cryptography and homomorphic encryption rather than by using a straightforward composition to obtain a multi-bit scheme. Before describing our contributions and results, we first briefly review some original motivation.

Regev originally constructed the so-called Primal.LWE-based PKE at STOC2005 [27] and Gentry, Peikert, and Vaikuntanathan constructed the Dual.LWE-based PKE at STOC2008 [13]. Our first observation is that FHE schemes are built in general over the perspective of Primal.LWE and the only FHE scheme based on Dual.LWE is the one proposed by Brakerski [3]. The main reason is that Dual.LWE-based encryption has larger parameters under the hardness of decisional LWE assumption. However, we observe that one can simultaneously encrypt polynomially-many bits using the LWE-based PKE without making the underlying assumption stronger [26], while simultaneously encrypting t bits in our scheme is still based on assumption of [26]. Hence, in order to solve the problem, the instantiations in the papers describing all the Dual.LWE-based public key and homomorphic encryption schemes cited above use Regev's proposal [13] as a building block.

Unlike the majority of previous works, we construct the public matrix **A** as a combination of many secret keys, each one protected by the LWE problem. The main ideas behind our method to compute the public matrix is described now. We define and construct the structure of the public matrix as follows:

$$\mathbf{A} = [\bar{\mathbf{A}} \mid \mathbf{u} - \bar{\mathbf{A}}\bar{\mathbf{e}}_1 \mid \cdots \mid \mathbf{u} - \bar{\mathbf{A}}\bar{\mathbf{e}}_l] \in \mathbb{Z}_q^{n \times m}$$

and construct t secret keys $\tilde{\mathbf{e}}_i = (1, \mathbf{e})^T = (1 \mid \bar{\mathbf{e}}_i \mid \mathbf{I}_i)^T$, $i \in [t]$ where the vector $\mathbf{I}_i$ in i-th position has value 1 and in other positions has value 0. Therefore, we can easily find integer matrices **A** modulo some small $q = poly(n)$, and evaluate simple linear (surjective) functions like $\mathbf{u} = f_{\mathbf{A}}(\mathbf{e}_i) = \mathbf{A} \cdot \mathbf{e}_i \pmod{q}$ on short integer vectors $\bar{\mathbf{e}}_i$ [22]. Utilizing the combined public matrix A, containing t secret keys (t bit each), we can construct multi-bit PKE and FHE scheme. Then, we will be able to give a detailed description in next sections.

1.2   Paper Organization

The remainder of this paper is organized as follows. In Sect. 2 we formally define the LWE problem, Ferr.LWE assumption and present notation that will be used throughout the paper. In Sect. 3 we describe our multi-bit encryption scheme. In Sect. 4 we show a multi-bit variant of the FHE scheme. Finally, we conclude in Sect. 5.

2   Preliminaries

In this section we introduce some notation and recall the Learning with Errors problem for both the search and decision variants. Finally, we give a formal definition and present the decisional version in detail.

2.1   Notation

For a natural number $n \in \mathbb{N}$, $[n]$ denotes the set $\{1, \cdots, n\}$. For a real number $x \in \mathbb{R}$, we let $\lfloor x \rfloor$ denote the largest integer not greater than x, and $\lfloor x \rceil = \lfloor x + \frac{1}{2} \rfloor$ denote the integer closest to x, with ties broken upward. We use bold lower-case letters like $\mathbf{x}$ to denote column vectors, while for row vectors we use the transpose $\mathbf{x}^T$. We use bold upper-case letters like $\mathbf{A}$ to denote matrices, and sometimes identify a matrix with its ordered set of column vectors. We denote the horizontal concatenation of vectors and/or matrices using a vertical bar, e.g., $[\mathbf{A} \mid \mathbf{Ax}]$.

We will be using norms in many of the inequalities in this work. For that reason, we will give two well known norms and inequalities related to norms that we will be using in the following sections. l_p-norm is: For every vector $\mathbf{v} = (v_1, \cdots, v_n)$ and $p \geq 1$, $||\mathbf{v}||_p = \sqrt[p]{\sum_{i=1}^{n} |v_i|^p}$, l_∞ norm is given by $||\mathbf{v}||_\infty = max\{|v_1|, \cdots, |v_n|\}$, l_1 norm is given by $||\mathbf{v}||_1 = \sum_{i=1}^{n} |v_i|$ and Euclidean norm defined as $||\mathbf{v}||_2 = \sqrt{\sum_{i=1}^{n} |v_i|^2}$. For the matrix norm, we adopt the [13] definition. For matrix $\mathbf{A} \in \mathbb{Z}^{k \times m}$, its i-th column vector is denoted $\mathbf{a}_i$. Let $\tilde{\mathbf{A}}$ be the result of applying Gram-Schmidt (GS) orthogonalization to the columns of $\mathbf{A}$. $||\mathbf{A}||$ denotes the l_2 norm of the longest column of $\mathbf{A}$. The length of a matrix is the norm of its longest column: $||\mathbf{A}|| = max_i ||\mathbf{a}_i||$, and, for notational convenience, we sometimes view a matrix as simply the set of its column vectors. Before we describe the GSW encryption, we state a useful fact from [22] which we heavily rely on in the construction.

Lemma 1 *([22, 23] Lemma 2.1). For any $m \geq n \lceil \log q \rceil$ there exists a fixed efficiently computable matrix $\mathbf{G} \in \mathbb{Z}_q^{n \times m}$ and an efficiently computable deterministic "short preimage" function $\mathbf{G}^{-1}(\cdot)$ satisfying the following. On input a matrix $\mathbf{M} \in \mathbb{Z}_q^{n \times m'}$ for any m'. The inverse function $\mathbf{G}^{-1}(\mathbf{M})$ outputs a bit matrix $\mathbf{G}^{-1}(\mathbf{M}) \in \{0,1\}^{m \times m'}$ such that $\mathbf{GG}^{-1}(\mathbf{M}) = \mathbf{M}$.*

2.2 Discrete Gaussian

Many works [25, 27] on lattice-based cryptography rely on Gaussian-like probability distributions. In our constructions, it is very convenient to analyze the behavior of error elements using the standard notion of Gaussian random variables. Here we recall the relevant definitions.

Definition 1 *([1] Definition 7). Let L be a subset of $\mathbb{Z}^m$. For a vector $\mathbf{c} \in \mathbb{R}^m$ and a positive parameter $\sigma \in \mathbb{R}$, we define*

$$\rho_{\sigma,c}(x) = exp\left(-\pi \cdot \frac{||x-c||^2}{\sigma^2}\right) \text{ and } \rho_{\sigma,\mathbf{c}}(L) = \sum_{x \in L} \rho_{\sigma,\mathbf{c}}(x).$$

The discrete Gaussian distribution over L with center c and parameter σ, $\forall y \in L$, is given by

$$D_{L,\sigma,c}(y) = \frac{\rho_{\sigma,c}(y)}{\rho_{\sigma,c}(L)}.$$

Lemma 2 *([13] Lemma 2.9). For any n-dimensional lattice Λ, $c \in span(\Lambda)$, real $\epsilon \in (0,1)$, and gaussian parameter $r \geq \eta_\epsilon(\Lambda)$:*

$$\Pr_{\mathbf{x} \leftarrow D_{\Lambda,r,c}}\left[||\mathbf{x} - \mathbf{c}|| > r \cdot \sqrt{n}\right] \leq \frac{1+\epsilon}{1-\epsilon} \cdot 2^{-n}$$

The final fact we need for certain applications is an upper bound on the probability of the mode (the most likely element) of a discrete Gaussian; equivalently, it is a lower bound on the min-entropy of the distribution.

Definition 2 *([7] Definition 2.1, B-bounded distributions). A distribution ensemble $\{\chi_n\}_{n \in \mathbb{N}}$, supported over the integers, is called B-bounded if:*

$$\Pr_{x \leftarrow \chi_n}[|x| \geq B] \leq 2^{-\tilde{\Omega}(n)}.$$

For a distribution ensemble $\chi = \chi(\lambda)$ over the integers, and integers bounded $B = B(\lambda)$, we say that χ is B-bounded if $Pr_{x \leftarrow \chi(\lambda)}[|x| \leq B(\lambda)] \leq 2^{-\tilde{\Omega}(\lambda)}$.

Throughout the paper, we use B instead of concrete size of some bounds and omit further details. The reader can find more details in [21] Lemma 4.4 (2).

Lemma 3 *([1] Lemma 12). Let vector $\mathbf{x}$ be some vector in $\mathbb{Z}^m$ and draw $\mathbf{e}$ from Gaussian distribution $D_{\mathbb{Z}^m,r}$. Then the quantity $|\mathbf{x}^T \cdot \mathbf{e}|$ when treated as an integer in $[0, \cdots, q-1]$ satisfies*

$$|\mathbf{x}^T \cdot \mathbf{e}| \leq ||\mathbf{x}||r\omega(\sqrt{\log m}) + ||\mathbf{x}||\sqrt{m}/2$$

with all but negligible probability in m. Where r is gaussian parameter and defined in Lemma 2.

We use the following variant of the leftover hash lemma [16].

Lemma 4 *(Matrix-vector Leftover Hash Lemma [7] Lemma 2.1). Let $\lambda \in \mathbb{Z}$, $n \in \mathbb{N}$, $q \in \mathbb{N}$, and $m \geq n \log q + 2\lambda$. Let $\mathbf{A} \xleftarrow{R} \mathbb{Z}_q^{m \times n}$ be a uniformly random matrix, let $\mathbf{r} \xleftarrow{R} \{0,1\}^m$ and $\mathbf{y} \xleftarrow{R} \mathbb{Z}_q^n$, then:*

$$\Delta((\mathbf{A}, \mathbf{A}^T \cdot \mathbf{r}), (\mathbf{A}, \mathbf{y})) \leq 2^{-\lambda} \tag{1}$$

where $\Delta(\mathbf{A}, \mathbf{B})$ denotes the statistical distance between the distributions $\mathbf{A}$ and $\mathbf{B}$.

2.3 Learning with Errors

We survey the main foundational works that directly underlie most modern lattice-based cryptographic schemes. Here we shortly describe LWE, its hardness, and the LWE-based cryptosystem in some detail.

Definition 3 *(Learning with errors distribution). For a vector $\mathbf{s} \in \mathbb{Z}_q^n$ called the secret, the LWE distribution $\mathcal{A}_{\mathbf{s},\chi}$ over $\mathbb{Z}_q^n \times \mathbb{Z}_q$ is sampled by choosing $\mathbf{a} \in \mathbb{Z}_q$ uniformly at random, choosing $\mathbf{e} \leftarrow \chi$, and outputting $(\mathbf{a}, b = \langle \mathbf{s}, \mathbf{a} \rangle + \mathbf{e} \pmod{q})$.*[1]

There are two main versions of the LWE problem: (i) the search version, which is to find the secret given LWE samples, and (ii) the decision version, which is to distinguish between LWE samples and uniformly random ones.

Definition 4 *(Seacrh.LWE$_{n,q,\chi,m}$). Given m independent samples $(\mathbf{a}_i, b_i) \in \mathbb{Z}_q^n \times \mathbb{Z}_q$ drawn from $\mathcal{A}_{\mathbf{s},\chi}$ for an uniformly random $\mathbf{s} \in \mathbb{Z}_q^n$, fixed for all samples, find $\mathbf{s}$.*

Definition 5 *(Decision.LWE$_{n,q,\chi,m}$). Given m independent samples $(\mathbf{a}_i, b_i) \in \mathbb{Z}_q^n \times \mathbb{Z}_q$, where every sample is distributed according to either: (1) $\mathcal{A}_{\mathbf{s},\chi}$ for an uniformly random $\mathbf{s} \in \mathbb{Z}_q^n$, fixed for all samples, or (2) the uniform distribution, then distinguish with non-negligible advantage which is the case.*

Without the error elements from χ, both problems are easy to solve, because we would be able to efficiently recover $\mathbf{s}$ from LWE samples by Gaussian elimination (in the uniform case of Decision.LWE, with high probability no solution $\mathbf{s}$ will exist).

Corollary 1 *([13] Corollary 5.4). Let n and q be positive integers with q prime, and let $m \geq 2n\lg q$. Then for all but a $2q^n$ fraction of all $\mathbf{A} \in \mathbb{Z}_q^{n \times m}$ and for any $r \geq \omega(\sqrt{\log m})$, the distribution of the syndrome $\mathbf{u} = \mathbf{A} \cdot \mathbf{e} \pmod{q}$ is statistically close to uniform over $\mathbb{Z}_q^n$, where $\mathbf{e} \leftarrow D_{\mathbb{Z}^m,r}$.*

---

[1] It is worth mentioning that LWE is a generalization of "learning parities with noise" (LPN) which is the special case where $q = 2$ and χ is a Bernoulli distribution over $\{0,1\}$.

2.4   First-Is-Errorless LWE

In this subsection, we show that the First-is-errorless LWE (hereafter Ferr.LWE) problem [6] is also hard in the case where we assume the error elements of Ferr.LWE problem follows a binary distribution $\{0,1\}^*$. We remark that the Ferr.LWE problem originally appeared in [6] and next definitions are based on the original work.

Definition 6 *([6] Definition 4.2). Consider a prime $q \geq 1$, positive integers n, m, an error distribution χ over $\mathbb{Z}$ and a $\mathcal{PPT}$ algorithm $\mathcal{A}$. The Ferr variant of the LWE problem is to distinguish between the following two scenarios:*

- *firstly, the sample is uniform over $\mathbb{Z}_q^n \times \mathbb{Z}_q$ and the rest are uniform over $\mathbb{Z}_q^n \times \mathbb{Z}$;*
- *secondly, there is an unknown uniformly distributed $\mathbf{s} \in \{0,\cdots,q-1\}^n$, the first sample we get is from $\mathcal{A}_{\mathbf{s},\{0\}}$, where $\{0\}$ denotes the distribution that is deterministically zero, and the remaining are from $\mathcal{A}_{\mathbf{s},\chi}$.*

Lemma 5 *([6] Lemma 4.3). For any $n \geq 2$, m, $q \geq 1$, and error distribution χ, there is an efficient reduction from $\mathsf{LWE}_{n-1,m,q,\chi}$ to the Ferr variant of $\mathsf{LWE}_{n,m,q,\chi}$ that reduces the advantage by at most $\sum_p p^{-n}$, with the sum going over all prime factors of q.*

As the name indicates, the first equation in the Ferr.LWE sample is given without error. Namely, Ferr.LWE$_{n,m,\chi}$ is defined analogously to LWE$_{n,m,\chi}$ except for the fact that the error $\mathbf{x}$ is sampled from $\{0\} \times \chi^m$ instead of χ^{m+1}, which captures the first-is-errorless notion. From [6], a tight efficient reduction from LWE to Ferr.LWE is known. This in return gives us an average to worst case reduction of the Ferr.LWE problem to a certain hard lattice problem.

2.5   Dual.LWE-Based Encryption (Dual-Regev Encryption)

Gentry, Peikert and Vaikuntanathan [13] have presented a "Dual" LWE-based encryption scheme at STOC2008, the main difference with Regev's scheme is that the roles of the key generation and the encryption procedure are reversed. Interestingly, Dual.LWE-based PKE's ciphertext takes the same form as in Regev's scheme (namely, $(\mathbf{a}, b = \langle \mathbf{a}, \mathbf{s} \rangle + 2e + m)$, albeit with higher dimensional vectors and different distribution of $\mathbf{a}$, $\mathbf{e}$) [7]. Unfortunately, Dual.LWE-based scheme with slightly longer parameters, but with an interesting property—there is non noise element in public key. Hence, in our paper, we will use the property to construct a combination public key $\mathbf{A}$.

2.6   Leveled Fully Homomorphic Encryption

In a public-key encryption, the encrypter holds a public key and encrypts a message such that the holder of the corresponding secret key is able to reconstruct the original plaintext message.

Definition 7. *Fix a function $L = L(\lambda)$. An L-homomorphic encryption scheme* HE *for a class of circuits $\{\mathcal{C}_\lambda\}_{\lambda \in N}$ consists of four polynomial-time algorithms* {KeyGen, Enc, Dec, Eval} *such that:*

- *key generation algorithm* KeyGen *is a randomized algorithm that takes the security parameter 1^λ as input and outputs a public key* pk *and secret key* sk;
- *encryption algorithm* Enc *is a randomized algorithm that takes a public key* pk *and a message $m \in \{0,1\}^*$ as input, and outputs a ciphertext c;*
- *decryption algorithm* Dec *is a deterministic algorithm that takes the secret key* sk *and a ciphertext c as input, and outputs a message $m \in \{0,1\}^*$;*
- *homomorphic evaluation algorithm* Eval *takes as input a public key* pk, *a circuit $C \in \mathcal{C}_\lambda$, and a list of ciphertexts $c_1, \cdots, c_\ell$, where ℓ is polynomial over λ, and it outputs a ciphertext $c^\star$.*

The following correctness properties are required to hold:

- for any λ, $m \in \{0,1\}^*$, and (pk, sk) output by $\mathsf{KeyGen}(1^\lambda)$, we have that

$$m = \mathsf{Dec}(\mathsf{sk}, (\mathsf{Enc}(\mathsf{pk}, m)));$$

- for any λ, any $m_1, \cdots, m_l \in \{0,1\}^*$, and $C \in \mathcal{C}_\lambda$, we have that

$$\mathcal{C}(m_1, \cdots, m_\ell) = \mathsf{Dec}(\mathsf{sk}, (\mathsf{Eval}(\mathsf{pk}, (C, \mathsf{Enc}(\mathsf{pk}, m_1), \cdots, \mathsf{Enc}(\mathsf{pk}, m_\ell))))).$$

We use the standard notion of security against *chosen-plaintext attacks*, also called CPA adversaries.

Definition 8. *A homomorphic encryption scheme is* IND-CPA-*secure if we have that for any polynomial-time adversary $\mathcal{A}$ the following is negligible in λ:*

$$|\Pr[\mathcal{A}(\mathsf{pk}, \mathsf{Enc}(\mathsf{pk}, m_0)) = 1] - \Pr[\mathcal{A}(\mathsf{pk}, \mathsf{Enc}(\mathsf{pk}, m_1)) = 1]|,$$

where $(\mathsf{pk}, \mathsf{sk}) \leftarrow \mathsf{KeyGen}(1^\lambda)$ *and m_0, m_1 are arbitrarily chosen from the plaintext space by the adversary.*

The security definition for multi-bit MBGSW is the same as that for single-bit GSW. Since in the public key setting, security for encryption of a single message implies security for encryption of multiple message. More details see [17] Chap. 11.

Definition 9 *(Compactness)([18] Definition 3). An L-homomorphic encryption for a class of circuits $\{\mathbf{C}_k\}_{k \in \mathbb{N}}$ is compact if there exists a polynomial $\alpha = \alpha(\lambda)$ such that ciphertexts output by* Eval *have length at most α. (For this to be non-trivial it should be the case that, for all λ, we have $\alpha(\lambda) \leq |C|$ for some $C \in \{\mathbf{C}\}_\lambda$).*

3   Multi-bit **PKE** Scheme

In this section we develop multi-bit public key encryption schemes based on Dual Regev scheme. Most notably, in order to conveniently analyze the magnitude of noise, we introduce Ferr.LWE assumption for the multi-bit **PKE** scheme.

3.1   Our Construction

We now describe our MBGPV construction and its properties. Roughly, it is a multi-bit PKE scheme via Dual.LWE-based under the hardness of LWE assumption. Given the security parameter λ, we sample random vector by Ferr.LWE distribution and set $t \in \mathbb{N}$ be the number of bits we want to encrypt, and it corresponds the number of secret keys.

– params ← MBGPV.Setup(1^λ):
  We receives as input the security parameter λ and we compute a positive integer $n = n(\lambda)$ and $q \geq 2$. Afterwards, we choose secondary parameters $\bar{m} = n \cdot \log q + 2\lambda$, $r \geq 2\sqrt{n}$ and $t \geq 1$ and $m = \bar{m} + t$.
– (pk, sk) ← MBGPV.KeyGen(params):
  – sk ← MBGPV.SecretKeyGen(params):
    For $1 \leq i \leq t$, we randomly sample vector $\bar{\mathbf{e}}_i \overset{R}{\leftarrow} D_{\mathbb{Z}_q^{\bar{m}}, r}$ rather than $\mathbf{e} \overset{R}{\leftarrow} D_{\mathbb{Z}_q^m, r}$, then we set $\mathbf{e}_i = [\bar{\mathbf{e}}_{i_{\bar{m} \times 1}} \mid \mathbf{I}_{t \times 1}]^T \in \mathbb{Z}_q^{m \times 1}$, where we have that $\mathbf{I}_{t \times 1} = [0, \cdots, 1_{\bar{m}+i}, \cdots, 0]$, i.e. the matrix whose $(\bar{m} + i)$-th value is 1 and other values are 0. The secret matrix is given by

    $$[\mathbf{e}_1, \cdots, \mathbf{e}_t] = \left[\begin{pmatrix} \bar{\mathbf{e}}_1 \\ \mathbf{I}_1 \end{pmatrix}, \cdots, \begin{pmatrix} \bar{\mathbf{e}}_t \\ \mathbf{I}_t \end{pmatrix} \right]$$

    and output t secret keys $\tilde{\mathbf{e}}_i = (1, \mathbf{e}_i)^T \in \mathbb{Z}_q^{(m+1) \times 1}$, where $i = 1, 2, \cdots, t$.
  – pk ← MBGPV.PublicKeyGen(params, sk):
    First, choose random matrix $\bar{\mathbf{A}} \in \mathbb{Z}_q^{n \times \bar{m}}$ rather than $\mathbf{A} \leftarrow \mathbb{Z}_q^{n \times m}$. Then generate matrix $\mathbf{A}$ such that $\mathbf{A} = [\bar{\mathbf{A}} \mid (\mathbf{u} - \bar{\mathbf{A}} \cdot \bar{\mathbf{e}}_1) \mid \cdots \mid (\mathbf{u} - \bar{\mathbf{A}} \cdot \bar{\mathbf{e}}_t)]$, where $\mathbf{u}$ sample from $\mathbb{Z}_q^{n \times 1}$ and $\mathbf{u} = \mathbf{A} \cdot \mathbf{e}_i$. Finally, output pk $= \mathbf{P} = [\mathbf{u} \mid -\mathbf{A}] \in \mathbb{Z}_q^{n \times (m+1)}$, where the size of pk is $\mathcal{O}(n \cdot \log^2 q)$. We remark that $\mathbf{P} \cdot \tilde{\mathbf{e}}_i = [\mathbf{u} \mid -\mathbf{A}] \cdot [1, \mathbf{e}_i]^T = 0$.
– c ← MBGPV.Enc(params, pk, m):
  1. set $\mathbf{m} = (0 \mid \underbrace{0, \cdots, 0}_{\bar{m}} \mid \underbrace{m_1, \cdots, m_t}_{t}) \in \mathbb{Z}_q^{1 \times (m+1)}$, $m_i \in \{0, 1\}$, then choose $\mathbf{s} \leftarrow \mathbb{Z}_q^{n \times 1}$;
  2. sample $\mathbf{x}^T = (x_0 \mid \mathbf{x}') = (x_0 \mid \underbrace{x_1, \cdots, x_{\bar{m}}}_{\bar{m}} \mid \underbrace{x_{\bar{m}+1}, \cdots, x_m}_{t}) = (x \leftarrow \{0\}, \mathbf{x}_1^T \leftarrow \chi^{1 \times \bar{m}}, \mathbf{x}_2^T \leftarrow \chi^{1 \times t}) \in D_{\mathbb{Z}^{1 \times (m+1)}}$;
  3. compute $\mathbf{c} = \mathbf{P}^T \cdot \mathbf{s} + \lfloor \frac{q}{2} \rfloor \cdot \mathbf{m} + \mathbf{x} \in \mathbb{Z}_q^{(m+1) \times 1}$, where the size of ciphertext is $\mathcal{O}((m+1) \log^2 q)$.
– m_i' ← MBGPV.bitDec(params, sk$_i$, c): We defined the bitDec($\cdot$) algorithm as the single-bit decryption algorithm. This program works as follows:
  1. firstly, let sk$_1$, sk$_2$, $\cdots$, sk$_t$ = $(1, \mathbf{e}_1)^T$, $(1, \mathbf{e}_2)^T$, $\cdots$, $(1, \mathbf{e}_t)^T$ and in order to decrypt the i-th bit of the ciphertext, it is convenient to choose the i-th secret key $\tilde{\mathbf{e}}_i = (1, \mathbf{e}_i)^T$;

2. then, compute and output

$$\langle \mathbf{c}, \tilde{\mathbf{e}}_i \rangle = \langle \mathbf{P}^T \cdot \mathbf{s} + \lfloor \frac{q}{2} \rfloor \cdot \mathbf{m} + \mathbf{x}, \tilde{\mathbf{e}}_i \rangle = \lfloor \frac{q}{2} \rfloor \cdot m_i + \text{small} \quad (\bmod\ q).$$

Considering that the single-bit decryption algorithm works as described above, we can get all of bits by the single-bit decryption algorithm with different secret keys. We now present the multi-bit decryption algorithm.

– $\mathbf{m}' \leftarrow$ MBGPV.Dec(params, $(\mathsf{sk}_1, \cdots, \mathsf{sk}_t), \mathbf{c}$):

   1. firstly, suppose the user with secret key matrix $\mathbf{S} = (\mathsf{sk}_1, \cdots, \mathsf{sk}_t)$ as follows:

$$\mathbf{S} = (\tilde{\mathbf{e}}_1, \cdots, \tilde{\mathbf{e}}_t) = \begin{pmatrix} 1 & \cdots & 1 \\ \hline \bar{\mathbf{e}}_1 & \cdots & \bar{\mathbf{e}}_1 \\ \vdots & \ddots & \vdots \\ \bar{\mathbf{e}}_{\bar{m}} & \cdots & \bar{\mathbf{e}}_{\bar{m}} \\ \hline 1 & \cdots & 0 \\ \vdots & \ddots & \vdots \\ 0 & \cdots & 1 \end{pmatrix} \in \{0,1\}^{(m+1) \times t};$$

2. then compute and output

$$\langle \mathbf{c}, \mathbf{S} \rangle = \langle \mathbf{P}^T \cdot \mathbf{s} + \lfloor \frac{q}{2} \rfloor \cdot \mathbf{m} + \mathbf{x}, \mathbf{S} \rangle = \lfloor \frac{q}{2} \rfloor \cdot \mathbf{m}^T \cdot \mathbf{S} + \mathbf{x}^T \cdot \mathbf{S}$$

$$= \lfloor \frac{q}{2} \rfloor \cdot \mathbf{m} + t \cdot \text{small} \quad (\bmod\ q).$$

Most notably, using single-bit decryption algorithm, we can decrypt the ciphertext bit-by-bit. i.e. repeating t times this step, we can get the message $\mathbf{m}$. However, we also can get the message $\mathbf{m}$ by one-time decryption. The only difference is that we need a secret key matrix $\mathbf{S}$ as input instead of i-th secret key sk_i. We have that the magnitude of multi-bit noise grows linearly with respect to t.

3.2 Correctness Analysis of MBGPV Scheme

We analyze the noise magnitude along the execution of encryption and decryption algorithms. We start with a lemma regarding the noise magnitude of properly encrypted ciphertexts.

Lemma 6 *(Correctness). Suppose that the following conditions are valid: $r = B \geq \omega(\sqrt{\log n}) \cdot \sqrt{n}$ (refer to [3,21]) and $\bar{m} \geq n \log q + 2\lambda$. Thus an E-noisy ciphertext, corresponding to some message $\mathbf{m} \in \{0,1\}^*$ under secret key sk is given by the vector $\mathbf{c} = \mathbf{P}^T \cdot \mathbf{s} + \lfloor \frac{q}{2} \rfloor \cdot \mathbf{m} + \mathbf{x} \pmod{q} \in \mathbb{Z}_q^{(m+1) \times 1}$, and for single-bit decryption with $\mathsf{sk}_i = \tilde{\mathbf{e}}_i \in \mathbb{Z}_q^{(m+1) \times 1}$, we have that*

$$\mathbf{c}^T \cdot \tilde{\mathbf{e}}_i = \lfloor \frac{q}{2} \rfloor \cdot m_i + x_0 + \mathbf{x}'^T \cdot \mathbf{e}_i = \lfloor \frac{q}{2} \rfloor \cdot m_i + \text{small} \quad (\bmod\ q),$$

with $|\text{small}| < E \leq \lfloor q/2 \rfloor / 2$.

For multi-bit decryption with $\mathsf{sk} = \mathbf{S} \in \mathbb{Z}_q^{(m+1) \times t}$, *we have that*

$$\mathbf{c}^T \cdot \mathbf{S} = \lfloor \frac{q}{2} \rfloor \cdot \mathbf{m} + \mathbf{x}^T \cdot \mathbf{S} = \lfloor \frac{q}{2} \rfloor \cdot \mathbf{m} + t \cdot \mathrm{small} \pmod{q},$$

with $|t \cdot \mathrm{small}| < t \cdot E \leq \lfloor q/2 \rfloor / 2$. *Therefore, we conclude that* $m_i \leftarrow$ MBGPV.Dec(sk, m).

Proof. For single-bit decryption, for $\mathbf{x} \leftarrow \{0\} \times \chi^m$ and $\forall x_i \leftarrow \chi, i \neq 1, |x_i| \leq B$ (where $B \ll q$ is a bound on the values of χ), $\mathbf{x}' \leftarrow \chi^m$. By definition, we get

$$\langle \mathbf{c}, \tilde{\mathbf{e}}_i \rangle = \mathbf{s}^T \cdot \mathbf{P} \cdot \tilde{\mathbf{e}}_i + \lfloor \frac{q}{2} \rfloor \cdot \mathbf{m} \cdot \tilde{\mathbf{e}}_i + \underbrace{x_0 + \mathbf{x}'^T \cdot \mathbf{e}}_{\mathrm{small}} \text{ (by Lemma 3)},$$

$$= 0 + \lfloor \frac{q}{2} \rfloor \cdot m_i + \underbrace{x_0 + \mathbf{x}_1 \cdot \bar{\mathbf{e}}_i + x_i}_{\mathrm{small}},$$

$$= 0 + \lfloor \frac{q}{2} \rfloor \cdot m_i + \underbrace{x_i + \mathbf{x}_1 \cdot \bar{\mathbf{e}}_i}_{\mathrm{small}} = \lfloor \frac{q}{2} \rfloor \cdot m_i + \mathrm{small} \pmod{q},$$

with $||\mathrm{small}|| \leq ||x|| + ||\mathbf{x}'^T \cdot \mathbf{e}|| = ||x|| + ||\mathbf{x}_1^T \cdot \bar{\mathbf{e}}|| \leq E$, the norm of the error elements $\mathbf{x}'^T \cdot \mathbf{e}$ is bounded by $B_\chi \cdot r \cdot \omega(\sqrt{\log \bar{m}}) + B_\chi \sqrt{\bar{m}}/2$, i.e. $||B + B_\chi \cdot r\omega(\sqrt{\log \bar{m}}) + B_\chi \sqrt{\bar{m}}/2|| < E$. For the sake of simplicity we denote the norm of error elements by E.

Similarly, for multi-bit decryption algorithm, we can easily get $\langle \mathbf{c}, \mathbf{S} \rangle = \lfloor \frac{q}{2} \rfloor \cdot \mathbf{m} + t \cdot \mathrm{small} \pmod{q}$ with $||t \cdot \mathrm{small}|| \leq t \cdot E$. □

3.3   Security Analysis of MBGPV Scheme

The following theorem formalizes the core result used to show MBGPV's security.

Theorem 1. *Let* $m \geq n \log q + 2\lambda$, $n \in \mathbb{N}$, *let* $q \in \mathbb{N}$ *and let* χ *be a discrete Gaussian distribution on* $\mathbb{Z}$ *such that the* LWE$_{n,q,\chi,m}$ *problem is hard. Let* t *be an integer such that* $t = \mathcal{O}(\log n)$. *Then we define two distribution* $\mathcal{X}$ *and* $\mathcal{Y}$ *as follows.*

– $\mathcal{X}$ *is the distribution on* $n \times m$ *matrices*

$$\mathcal{X} = \mathbf{A} = [\bar{\mathbf{A}} \mid \mathbf{b}_1 \mid \cdots \mid \mathbf{b}_t] = [\bar{\mathbf{A}} \mid \mathbf{u} - \bar{\mathbf{A}} \bar{\mathbf{e}}_1 \mid \cdots \mid \mathbf{u} - \bar{\mathbf{A}} \bar{\mathbf{e}}_t],$$

where $\bar{\mathbf{A}} \in \mathbb{Z}_q^{n \times \bar{m}}$ *is chosen uniformly at random and where, for all* $i \leq i \leq t$, *there exists* $\mathbf{b}_i = \mathbf{u} - \bar{\mathbf{A}} \bar{\mathbf{e}}_i \pmod{q} \in \mathbb{Z}_q^{n \times 1}$, *where* $\bar{\mathbf{e}}_i$ *is sampled from a discrete Gaussian distribution* $\chi^{\bar{m} \times 1}$;
– $\mathcal{Y}$ *is the uniform distribution on* $\mathbb{Z}_q^{n \times 1}$.

Then we have that distributions $\mathcal{X}$ *and* $\mathcal{Y}$ *are computationally indistinguishable.*

Proof. Suppose there exists a probability polynomial-time distinguisher $\mathcal{D}$ which can distinguish $\mathcal{X}$ from $\mathcal{Y}$ with non-negligible advantage ϵ. For $1 \leq i \leq t+1$ we introduce intermediate distribution $\mathcal{X}_i$ given by $[\bar{A} \mid \mathbf{b}'_1 \mid \cdots \mid \mathbf{b}'_{i-1} \mid \mathbf{b}_i \mid \cdots \mid \mathbf{b}_t]$, where $\mathbf{b}_i$ is as above and $\mathbf{b}'_i$ is uniformly sampled from $\mathbb{Z}_q^{n \times 1}$. Hence $\mathcal{X}_1 = \mathcal{X}$ and $\mathcal{X}_{t+1} = \mathcal{Y}$.

Since $\mathcal{D}$ can distinguish $\mathcal{X}_1$ from $\mathcal{X}_{t+1}$ with noticeable advantage ϵ, by a standard hybrid argument, there is some i such that $\mathcal{D}$ can distinguish $\mathcal{X}_i$ from $\mathcal{X}_{i+1}$ with some noticeable advantage at least ϵ/t.

It is straightforward that $\mathcal{D}$ gives an LWE distinguisher. Namely, given an LWE challenge $(\bar{A}, \mathbf{y})$ one samples $\mathbf{b}'_1, \cdots, \mathbf{b}'_{i-1}$ uniformly and samples $\mathbf{b}_{i+1}, \cdots, \mathbf{b}_t$ as specified above (such that they are sampled from an LWE distribution, for different choices of the secret vector) and then calls $\mathcal{D}$ on $[\bar{A} \mid \mathbf{b}'_1 \mid \cdots \mid \mathbf{b}'_{i-1} \mid \mathbf{y} \mid \mathbf{b}_{i+1} \mid \mathbf{b}_t]$. The theorem follows from the fact that, by assumption, no such distinguisher exists. $\square$

Next, we show the scheme is IND-CPA secure based on the LWE assumption by using Theorem 1 to show that the scheme is indistinguishable from the original GPV08 scheme [13].

Theorem 2. *Let* params $= (n, q, \chi, m, t)$ *be such that the* LWE$_{n,q,\chi,m}$ *assumption holds and* $m = \mathcal{O}(n \log q)$. *Then the* MBGPV *scheme is* IND-CPA-*secure.*

Proof. Below we present a sketch of the proof:

- firstly, we apply Theorem 1 to show that, under LWE assumption, the matrix $\mathbf{A}' = [\bar{A} \mid \mathbf{b}_1 \mid \cdots \mid \mathbf{b}_t] \in \mathbb{Z}_q^{n \times m}$ is computationally indistinguishable from a randomly chosen matrix;
- secondly, we show that $\mathbf{c}$ is computationally indistinguishable from uniform.

This concludes the proof of the theorem. $\square$

4   Multi-bit GSW13 Scheme

In this section we present our main contribution, we also use MBGPV as the building block to construct our variant of GSW FHE scheme. First we need to recall some terminology and tools from previous work [3, 5, 10].

4.1   Basic Tools

Fix $q, m \in \mathbb{N}$. Let $l_q = \lfloor \log q \rfloor + 1$ and $N = (m+1) \cdot l_q$.

Definition 10. *The algorithm* PowerOf2 *takes an* m-*dimensional vector* $\mathbf{v} \in \mathbb{Z}_q^m$ *and outputs an* N-*dimensional vector in* $\mathbb{Z}_q^N$, *in more detail*

$$\left(v_1, 2v_1, \cdots, 2^{l_q - 1} v_1, \cdots, v_m, 2v_m, \cdots, 2^{l_q - 1} v_m \right)$$

Definition 11. *The algorithm* BitDecomp *takes as input a vector* $\mathbf{v} \in \mathbb{Z}_q^m$ *and outputs an N-dimensional vector* $(v_{1,0}, \cdots, v_{1,l_q-1}, \cdots, v_{m,0}, \cdots, v_{m,l_q-1})$ *where $v_{i,j}$ is the j-th bit in v_i's binary representation (ordered from least significant to most significant.) In other words,*

$$v_i = \sum_{j=0}^{l_q-1} 2^j v_{i,j}.$$

Definition 12. *The algorithm* BitDecomp^{-1} *takes as input an N-dimensional vector* $\mathbf{v} = (v_{1,0}, \cdots, v_{1,l_q-1}, \cdots, v_{m,0}, \cdots, v_{m,l_q-1})$, *and outputs the m-dimensional vector* $(\sum_{j=0}^{l_q-1} 2^j \cdot v_{1,j}, \cdots, \sum_{j=0}^{l_q-1} 2^j \cdot v_{m,j})$. *Note that the input vectors $\mathbf{v}$ need not be binary, the algorithm is well-defined for any input vector in $\mathbb{Z}^N$.*

Definition 13. *The algorithm* Flatten *takes an N-dimensional vector* $\mathbf{v} \in \mathbb{Z}_q^N$ *and outputs an N-dimensional binary vector (i.e. an N-dimensional vector with $0/1$ coefficients). It is defined by* Flatten$(\mathbf{v}) =$ BitDecomp(BitDecomp$^{-1}(\mathbf{v})$).

The following straightforward facts are given in [14].

Proposition 1. *Let* $\mathbf{a}, \mathbf{b} \in \mathbb{Z}_q^m$ *be m-dimensional vectors, and let* $\mathbf{a}' \in \mathbb{Z}_q^N$ *be an N-dimensional vector, then* $\langle$BitDecomp$(\mathbf{a})$, PowerOf2$(\mathbf{b})\rangle = \langle \mathbf{a}, \mathbf{b} \rangle$ *and*

$$\langle \mathbf{a}', \text{PowerOf2}(\mathbf{b}) \rangle = \langle \text{BitDecomp}^{-1}(\mathbf{a}'), \mathbf{b} \rangle = \langle \text{Flatten}(\mathbf{a}'), \text{PowerOf2}(\mathbf{b}) \rangle.$$

4.2 Our Construction

Now we describe the details. Let $q = q(\lambda)$ be an integer function and let $\chi = \chi(\lambda)$ be a distribution ensemble over $\mathbb{Z}$. The various-GSW scheme is defined similarly to the cryptosystems proposed in [2,11,23] and is described as follows.

- params $\leftarrow$ MBGSW.Setup$(1^\lambda, 1^L)$:
  1. identical to MBGPV.Setup$(\cdot)$ algorithm. Specially, choose the modulus $q = q(\lambda)$, the lattice dimension parameter $n = n(\lambda, L)$, and the error distribution $\chi = \chi(\lambda, L)$, appropriately chosen in order to achieve at least 2^λ security against known LWE attacks. Finally, choose parameter $\bar{m} \geq n \log q + 2\lambda$ such that $m = m(\lambda, L, t) = n \log q + 2\lambda + t \approx \mathcal{O}(n \log q)$;
  2. let $l = \lfloor \log q \rfloor + 1$ and $N = (m+1) \cdot l$ and output params $= (n, q, \chi, m)$.
- (pk, sk) $\leftarrow$ MBGSW.KeyGen(params):
  - sk $\leftarrow$ MBGSW.SecretKeyGen(params):
    identical to sk $\leftarrow$ MBGPV.SecretKeyGen(params), and output sk$_i := \tilde{\mathbf{e}}_i = (1, \mathbf{e}_i) \in \mathbb{Z}_q^{1\times(m+1)}$, where $\mathbf{e}_i = (\bar{\mathbf{e}} \mid 0, \cdots, 1, \cdots, 0) \in \mathbb{Z}_q^{1\times m}$, i.e. i-th position is 1. Here it is important to remark that $\mathbf{v} = $ PowerOf2$(\tilde{\mathbf{e}})$;
  - pk $\leftarrow$ MBGSW.PublicKeyGen(sk):
    identical to pk $\leftarrow$ MBGPV.PublicKeyGen(s), and output pk $= \mathbf{P} = [\mathbf{u} \mid -\mathbf{A}] \in \mathbb{Z}_q^{n\times(m+1)}$, where the size of pk is $\mathcal{O}(nm \cdot \log q)$. Finally, we observe that $\mathbf{P} \cdot \tilde{\mathbf{e}}_i = [\mathbf{u} \mid -\mathbf{A}] \cdot (1, \mathbf{e}_i)^T = 0$).

- $\mathbf{C} \leftarrow$ MBGSW.Enc(params, pk, $\mathbf{M}$):
  1. sample a uniform matrix $\mathbf{R} \leftarrow \{0,1\}^{n \times N}$, $(\mathbf{R}' \leftarrow \{0,1\}^{n \times (m+1)})$ and sample $\mathbf{X} = \begin{pmatrix} \mathbf{x}_0 \leftarrow \{0\}^{1 \times N} \\ \mathbf{X}_1 \leftarrow \chi^{m \times N} \end{pmatrix} \in \mathbb{Z}_q^{(m+1) \times N}$. In order to encrypt t messages $m_i \in \{0,1\}$, compute

$$\mathbf{M} = \begin{pmatrix} \mathbf{E}_{(\bar{m}+1) \times (\bar{m}+1)} & \mathbf{0}_{(\bar{m}+1) \times t} \\ \hline \mathbf{0}_{t \times (\bar{m}+1)} & \mathbf{M}'_{t \times t} \end{pmatrix} \in \{0,1\}^{(m+1) \times (m+1)},$$

  where matrix $\mathbf{M}' \in \{0,1\}^{t \times t}$ and $\mathbf{E}$ is identity matrix. It is interesting to note that the $\mathsf{Dec}(\cdot)$ algorithm also can operate any length message when $\mathbf{M}' = \mathrm{diag}(m_1, \cdots, m_t)$ is a diagonal matrix, such that all diagonal positions are non-zero.
  2. compute and write $\mathbf{C} = \mathbf{M} \cdot \mathbf{G} + \mathbf{P}^T \cdot \mathbf{R} + \mathbf{X} \pmod{q} \in \mathbb{Z}_q^{(m+1) \times N}$, since we have that

$$\begin{aligned} \mathbf{C} &= \mathsf{Flatten}(\mathbf{M} \cdot \mathbf{I} + \mathsf{BitDecomp}(\mathbf{P}^T \mathbf{R}' + \mathbf{X})), \\ &= \mathsf{BitDecomp}(\mathsf{BitDecomp}^{-1}(\mathbf{M} \cdot \mathbf{I}) + \mathbf{P}^T \cdot \mathbf{R}' + \mathbf{X}), \\ &= \mathsf{BitDecomp}(\mathbf{M} \cdot \mathbf{G} + \mathbf{P}^T \cdot \mathbf{R}' + \mathbf{X}) \pmod{q}, \end{aligned}$$

  where $\mathbf{I}_{m+1}$ denotes the $(m+1)$-dimensional identity matrix and thus

$$g^T = [2^0, 2^1, \cdots, 2^{l-1}] \in \mathbb{Z}_q^l, l = \lceil \log q \rceil = \lfloor \log q \rfloor + 1,$$

  where $\mathbf{G} = \mathsf{BitDecomp}^{-1}(\mathbf{I}_{m+1}) = (g^T \otimes \mathbf{I}_{m+1}) \in \mathbb{Z}_q^{(m+1) \times N}, m \geq n\lceil \log q \rceil$, namely $m = \mathcal{O}(n(\log q))$.

- $m_i' \leftarrow$ MBGSW.bitDec(params, sk_i, $\mathbf{C}$):
  1. suppose we want to decrypt i-th bit, thus we let $\mathsf{sk}_i = \tilde{\mathbf{e}}_i \in \mathbb{Z}_q^{(m+1) \times 1}$, and then we define a vector $\mathbf{w} \in \mathbb{Z}_q^{1 \times (m+1)}$ such that

$$\mathbf{w}^T = [\underbrace{0, \cdots, 0}_{\bar{m}+1} \mid \underbrace{\lceil q/2 \rceil, \cdots, \lceil q/2 \rceil}_{t}];$$

  2. compute

$$\tilde{\mathbf{e}}_i^T \cdot \mathbf{C} = \underbrace{\tilde{\mathbf{e}}_i^T \cdot \mathbf{P}^T \cdot \mathbf{R}}_{equals\ 0} + \underbrace{\tilde{\mathbf{e}}_i^T \cdot \mathbf{X}}_{\mathbf{error}} + \tilde{\mathbf{e}}_i^T \cdot \mathbf{M} \cdot \mathbf{G} = \mathbf{error} + \tilde{\mathbf{e}}_i^T \cdot \mathbf{M} \cdot \mathbf{G}$$

  and $v_i = \tilde{\mathbf{e}}_i^T \cdot \mathbf{C} \cdot \mathbf{G}^{-1}(\mathbf{w}^T)$;
  3. finally, output the decryption message $m_i' = \left| \lfloor \frac{v_i}{q/2} \rceil \right|$, where $\lfloor \cdot \rceil$ denotes the operation of rounding to the nearest integer. Hence, by construction we have that the output belongs to $\{0,1\}$.

Considering that the single-bit decryption algorithm of MBGSW scheme works as described above, we can get each bit of the message using the single-bit decryption algorithm with the appropriate secret keys. We now present the multi-bit decryption algorithm of MBGSW scheme, which allows recovering all the bits of the message simultaneously.

$-\mathbf{m}' \leftarrow$ MBGSW.Dec(params, sk, $\mathbf{C}$):

1. define a vector $\mathbf{w} \in \mathbb{Z}_q^{1\times(m+1)}$ such that $\mathbf{w}^T = \underbrace{[0,\cdots,0}_{\bar{m}+1}$ |

   $\underbrace{\lceil q/2\rceil, \cdots, \lceil q/2\rceil]}_{t}$ and input a secret key matrix $\mathbf{S} \in \mathbb{Z}_q^{(m+1)\times t}$;

2. compute

$$\mathbf{S}^T \cdot \mathbf{C} = \underbrace{\mathbf{S}^T \cdot \mathbf{P}^T \cdot \mathbf{R}}_{equals\ 0} + \underbrace{\mathbf{S}^T \cdot \mathbf{X}}_{error} + \mathbf{S}^T \cdot \mathbf{M} \cdot \mathbf{G} = error + \mathbf{S}^T \cdot \mathbf{M} \cdot \mathbf{G}$$

   and $\mathbf{v}_i = \mathbf{S}^T \cdot \mathbf{C} \cdot \mathbf{G}^{-1}(\mathbf{w}^T)$;

3. output the decryption message $\mathbf{m}' = \left| \left\lfloor \frac{\mathbf{v}_i}{q/2} \right\rceil \right|$.

Normally, we can choose different secret keys sk_i to decrypt the ciphertext $\mathbf{c}$ bit-by-bit and get the i-th bit message corresponding to i-th secret key. But actually we can use secret key matrix $\mathbf{S}$ to recover the message using the one-time decryption algorithm described above. We compute $\mathbf{v}_i = \mathbf{S}^T\cdot\mathbf{C}\cdot\mathbf{G}^{-1}(\mathbf{w}^T)$ in order to get the result as follows:

$$\mathbf{v}_i = \mathbf{S}^T \cdot \mathbf{C} \cdot \mathbf{G}^{-1}(\mathbf{w}^T) = \lfloor \frac{q}{2} \rfloor \cdot \begin{pmatrix} m_1 \\ \vdots \\ m_t \end{pmatrix} + \begin{pmatrix} error_1 \\ \vdots \\ error_t \end{pmatrix} \cdot \mathbf{G}^{-1}(\mathbf{w}^T);$$

It is straightforward to compute the magnitude of noise and verify that it grows linearly when compared to the single-bit decryption algorithm. Next, we will show the analysis in detail in Subsect. 4.3.

$-$ MBGSW.Eval(params, $\mathbf{C}_1, \cdots, \mathbf{C}_l$):

  $-$ MBGSW.Add($\mathbf{C}_1, \mathbf{C}_2$): output

$$\mathbf{C}_1 + \mathbf{C}_2 = (\mathbf{M}_1 + \mathbf{M}_2)\mathbf{G} + \mathbf{P}^{\mathbf{T}}(\mathbf{R}_1 + \mathbf{R}_2) + (\mathbf{X}_1 + \mathbf{X}_2) \in \mathbb{Z}_q^{(m+1)\times N};$$

  $-$ MBGSW.Mult($\mathbf{C}_1, \mathbf{C}_2$): output the matrix product, because $\mathbf{C}_2 = \mu_2\cdot\mathbf{G} + \mathbf{P}^T \cdot \mathbf{R}_2 + \mathbf{X}_2$, then we have that

$$\begin{aligned}
\mathbf{C}_1\mathbf{G}^{-1}(\mathbf{C}_2) &= \left(\mathbf{M}_1 \cdot \mathbf{G} + \mathbf{P}^T \cdot \mathbf{R}_1 + \mathbf{X}_1\right) \cdot \mathbf{G}^{-1}(\mathbf{C}_2) \\
&= \mathbf{M}_1 \cdot \mathbf{M}_2 \cdot \mathbf{G} + \mathbf{P}^T \cdot \left(\mathbf{R}_1\mathbf{G}^{-1}(\mathbf{C}_2) + \mathbf{M}_1\mathbf{R}_2\right) \\
&\quad + \underbrace{\left(\mathbf{X}_1\mathbf{G}^{-1}(\mathbf{C}_2) + \mathbf{M}_1\mathbf{X}_2\right)}_{small^{mult}} \in \mathbb{Z}_q^{(m+1)\times N} \quad\quad (2)
\end{aligned}$$

This also allows us to compute a homomorphic NAND gate by outputting $\mathbf{G} - \mathbf{C}_1\mathbf{G}^{-1}(\mathbf{C}_2)$.

4.3 Homomorphic Operations Analysis

Below we will analyze the scheme's correctness and homomorphic operations.

Definition 14. *We say that a ciphertext $\mathbf{C}$ that is designed to encrypt $\mathbf{M}' \in \mathbb{Z}_q^{t \times t}$, under t different secret keys $\tilde{\mathbf{e}}_i$, for $i \in [t]$, it has error vector* error $\in \mathbb{Z}_q^{1 \times N}$, *if* $\tilde{\mathbf{e}}_i^T \cdot \mathbf{C} - \tilde{\mathbf{e}}_i^T \cdot \mathbf{M} \cdot \mathbf{G} = \tilde{\mathbf{e}}_i^T \cdot \mathbf{P}^T \cdot \mathbf{R} + \tilde{\mathbf{e}}_i^T \cdot \mathbf{X} =$ error *(mod q). Obviously, for secret key matrix $\mathbf{S} = [\tilde{\mathbf{e}}_1, \cdots, \tilde{\mathbf{e}}_t] \in \mathbb{Z}_q^{(m+1) \times t}$, it has error vector* Error $= ($error$_1, \cdots,$error$_t)^T \in \mathbb{Z}^{t \times N}$, *if* $\mathbf{S}^T \cdot \mathbf{C} - \mathbf{S}^T \cdot \mathbf{M} \cdot \mathbf{G} = \mathbf{S}^T \cdot \mathbf{P}^T \cdot \mathbf{R} + \mathbf{S}^T \cdot \mathbf{X} =$ Error *(mod q).*

In order to analyze correctness it is convenient to define the following notion of *noisy ciphertexts*.

Definition 15. *If there exists* $\mathbf{X} = \begin{pmatrix} \mathbf{x}_0 \leftarrow \{0\}^{1 \times N} \\ \mathbf{X}' \leftarrow \chi^{m \times N} \end{pmatrix} \in \mathbb{Z}_q^{(m+1) \times N}$, *where* $\mathbf{X}' = [\mathbf{X}_1 \leftarrow \chi^{\bar{m} \times N} \mid \mathbf{X}_2 \leftarrow \chi^{t \times N}]$, *for* $\forall x_{i,j} \leftarrow \chi$, *(denote $|\chi| \leq B$), $\mathbf{x}[j] \leftarrow \chi^{1 \times N}$, then $\|\mathbf{x}[j]\|_2 \leq B_\chi$ (which is equal to $\sqrt{N} \cdot B$) and $\|\mathbf{X}'\|_2 = max_i\|\mathbf{x}_i\| \leq B_\chi$.*

Lemma 7 *(E-noisy ciphertext). An E-noisy ciphertext, for a corresponding message $\mathbf{M}$, and under secret key* sk $= \tilde{\mathbf{e}} \in \mathbb{Z}_q^{(m+1) \times 1}$, *is a matrix $\mathbf{C} \in \mathbb{Z}_q^{(m+1) \times N}$ such that $\mathbf{C} = \tilde{\mathbf{e}}^T \cdot \mathbf{M} \cdot \mathbf{G} + \tilde{\mathbf{e}}^T \cdot \mathbf{X}$. Then, we set*

$$\text{error} = \tilde{\mathbf{e}}^T \mathbf{X} = (1, \mathbf{e}^T) \cdot [\mathbf{x}_0, \mathbf{X}']^T = \mathbf{x}_0 + \mathbf{e}^T \cdot \mathbf{X}' = \bar{\mathbf{e}}^T \cdot \mathbf{X}_1 + \mathbf{x},$$

with $\|\text{error}\| \leq \|\mathbf{x}\| + \|\bar{\mathbf{e}}^T\| \cdot \|\mathbf{X}_1\| \leq E = B_\chi \left(r \cdot \omega \sqrt{\log \bar{m}} + \sqrt{\bar{m}}/2 + 1 \right)$.

Furthermore, if we use the multi-bit decryption secret key matrix $\mathbf{S} \in \mathbb{Z}_q^{(m+1) \times t}$, we obtain

$$\text{Error} = \mathbf{S}^T \cdot \mathbf{X} = \begin{pmatrix} \mathbf{x}_0 + \mathbf{e}^T \cdot \mathbf{X}' \\ \vdots \\ \mathbf{x}_0 + \mathbf{e}^T \cdot \mathbf{X}' \end{pmatrix} = \begin{pmatrix} \bar{\mathbf{e}}^T \cdot \mathbf{X}_1 + \mathbf{x}_1 \\ \vdots \\ \bar{\mathbf{e}}^T \cdot \mathbf{X}_1 + \mathbf{x}_t \end{pmatrix}$$

with $\|\text{Error}\| \leq max_i\|\text{error}_i\| \leq E = B_\chi \left(r \cdot \omega \sqrt{\log \bar{m}} + \sqrt{\bar{m}}/2 + 1 \right)$.

Proof. Consider a fresh ciphertext $\mathbf{C} = \mathbf{P}^T \cdot \mathbf{R} + \mathbf{M} \cdot \mathbf{G} + \mathbf{X}$, which is generated by encrypting some message $\mathbf{M}$ under some public key $\mathbf{P}$ with corresponding secret key $\tilde{\mathbf{e}}$. First recall that $\mathbf{P} \cdot \tilde{\mathbf{e}} = 0$ and $\tilde{\mathbf{e}}^T \cdot \mathbf{C} = \tilde{\mathbf{e}}^T \cdot \mathbf{M} \cdot \mathbf{G} + \tilde{\mathbf{e}}^T \cdot \mathbf{X}$. Let error $= \tilde{\mathbf{e}}^T \cdot \mathbf{X}$ for $\mathbf{X} \leftarrow \{0\}^{1 \times N} \times \chi^{m \times N}$.[2] which implies $\|\text{error}\| \leq B_\chi \left(r \cdot \omega \sqrt{\log \bar{m}} + \sqrt{\bar{m}}/2 + 1 \right) \leq E$ by Lemma 3.

Similarly, the same procedure may be easily adapted to obtain the bound of **Error**, i.e. $\mathbf{S}^T \cdot \mathbf{C} = \mathbf{S}^T \cdot \mathbf{M} \cdot \mathbf{G} + \mathbf{S}^T \cdot \mathbf{X}$, where **Error** $= \mathbf{S}^T \cdot \mathbf{X}$ and $\|\text{Error}\| \leq E$ by Lemma 3. Hence $\mathbf{C}$ is an E-noisy encryption of $\mathbf{M}$ under $\mathbf{S}$ (or $\tilde{\mathbf{e}}_i$). We call this value the *initial noise* and we define

$$E_{init} = B_\chi \left(r \cdot \omega \sqrt{\log \bar{m}} + \sqrt{\bar{m}}/2 + 1 \right).$$

Next we analyze the correctness of decryption.

---

[2] If we choose Dual.LWE-based with binary secret, i.e. $\mathbf{e} \leftarrow \{0,1\}^m$, implying $\|\text{error}\| \leq \sqrt{m \cdot N} \cdot B_{\chi^m}$.

Lemma 8. *Let* $\mathbf{C}$ *be an* E-*noisy encryption of* $\mathbf{M}$, *if we want to decrypt* i-*th ciphertext, then there exists a secret key* $\tilde{\mathbf{e}}_i$ *such that* $\tilde{\mathbf{e}}^T \cdot \mathbf{C} = \mathbf{error} + \tilde{\mathbf{e}}^T.\mathbf{M} \cdot \mathbf{G}$, *where* $||\mathbf{error}^{dec}||_\infty \leq (m+1) \cdot E$, *by Lemma 7. Then we obtain*

$$v_i = \tilde{\mathbf{e}}^T \mathbf{C} \cdot \mathbf{G}^{-1}(\mathbf{w}^T) = (\tilde{\mathbf{e}}^T \cdot \mathbf{X} + \tilde{\mathbf{e}}^T \mathbf{M} \cdot \mathbf{G}) \cdot \mathbf{G}^{-1}(\mathbf{w}^T)$$

$$= \tilde{\mathbf{e}}^T \mathbf{X} \cdot \mathbf{G}^{-1}(\mathbf{w}^T) + \frac{q}{2} \cdot m_i = \mathbf{error}^{dec} + \frac{q}{2} \cdot m_i \pmod{q}.$$

Proof. Clearly, we have that

$$||\mathbf{error}^{dec}|| = ||\tilde{\mathbf{e}}^T \cdot \mathbf{X} \cdot \mathbf{G}^{-1}(\mathbf{w}^T)|| \leq ||\tilde{\mathbf{e}}^T \cdot \mathbf{X}|| \cdot ||\mathbf{G}^{-1}(\mathbf{w}^T)||_1 \leq (m+1) \cdot E.$$

Now one can observe that decryption works correctly as long as $||\mathbf{error}^{dec}||_\infty \leq \frac{q}{4}$, i.e. $E < \frac{q}{4(m+1)}$. We call this value $E_{\max} = \frac{q}{4(m+1)}$. $\square$

Lemma 9. *Let* $\mathbf{C}$ *be an* E-*noisy encryption of* $\mathbf{M}$, *if we want to decrypt ciphertext* $\mathbf{C}$, *then there exists a secret key matrix* $\mathbf{S}$ *such that* $\mathbf{S}^T \cdot \mathbf{C} = \mathbf{Error} + \mathbf{S}^T \cdot \mathbf{M} \cdot \mathbf{G}$, *where* $||\mathbf{Error}^{dec}||_\infty \leq (m+1) \cdot E$, *by Lemma 7. Then we obtain*

$$\mathbf{v}_i = \mathbf{S}^T \cdot \mathbf{C} \cdot \mathbf{G}^{-1}(\mathbf{w}^T) = \mathbf{S}^T \cdot \mathbf{X} \cdot \mathbf{G}^{-1}(\mathbf{w}^T) + \frac{q}{2} \cdot \mathbf{m}$$

$$= \mathbf{Error}^{dec} + \frac{q}{2} \cdot \mathbf{m} \pmod{q}.$$

Proof. We can easily prove Lemma 9 using Lemmas 7 and 8. We omit further details.

Homomorphic Addition Analysis. Let $\mathbf{C}_1$ or $\mathbf{C}_2$ be two ciphertexts which are E_1 or E_2 noisy encryption of $\mathbf{M}_1, \mathbf{M}_2 \in \{0,1\}^{(m+1)\times(m+1)}$ under the $\tilde{\mathbf{e}}$ respectively, such that $\tilde{\mathbf{e}}^T \cdot \mathbf{C}_1 = \tilde{\mathbf{e}}^T \cdot \mathbf{M}_1 \cdot \mathbf{G} + \mathbf{error}_1$ and $\tilde{\mathbf{e}}^T \cdot \mathbf{C}_2 = \tilde{\mathbf{e}}^T \cdot \mathbf{M}_1 \cdot \mathbf{G} + \mathbf{error}_2$ with $||\mathbf{error}_1||_\infty \leq E_1$ and $||\mathbf{error}_2||_\infty \leq E_2$ by Lemma 7. Furthermore, if $\mathbf{C}_1$ or $\mathbf{C}_2$ is under the $\mathbf{S}$ respectively, then $\mathbf{S}^T \cdot \mathbf{C}_1 = \mathbf{S}^T \cdot \mathbf{M}_1 \cdot \mathbf{G} + \mathbf{Error}_1$ and $\mathbf{S}^T \cdot \mathbf{C}_2 = \mathbf{S}^T \cdot \mathbf{M}_1 \cdot \mathbf{G} + \mathbf{Error}_2$ with $||\mathbf{Error}_1||_\infty \leq E_1$ and $||\mathbf{Error}_2||_\infty \leq E_2$ by Lemma 7.

Lemma 10. *If a ciphertext* $\mathbf{C}$ *is designed to encrypt message* $\mathbf{M} \in \{0,1\}^{(m+1)\times(m+1)}$ *under a secret key matrix* $\mathbf{S}$, *then ciphertext addition results in ciphertext* $\mathbf{C}^{Add} = \mathbf{C}_1 + \mathbf{C}_2$ *such that* $\mathbf{S}^T \cdot \mathbf{C}^{Add} = \mathbf{Error}^{Add} + \mathbf{S}^T \cdot (\mathbf{M}_1 + \mathbf{M}_2) \cdot \mathbf{G}$, *where* $\mathbf{C}_1, \mathbf{C}_2$ *are respectively designed to encrypt* $\mathbf{M}_1, \mathbf{M}_2 \in \{0,1\}^{(m+1)\times(m+1)}$, $\mathbf{M}^{Add} = \mathbf{M}_1 + \mathbf{M}_2$ *and* $\mathbf{Error}^{Add} = \mathbf{Error}_1 + \mathbf{Error}_2$. *Clearly, its is* $(E_1 + E_2)$-*noisy.*

Homomorphic Multiplication Analysis. Below we describe the multiplication.

Lemma 11. *Let* $\mathbf{S} \in \mathbb{Z}^{(m+1)\times t}$ *be a secret key matrix. Let* $\mathbf{C}_1 \in \mathbb{Z}_q^{(m+1)\times(m+1)\cdot l}$ *and* $\mathbf{C}_2 \in \mathbb{Z}_q^{(m+1)\times(m+1)\cdot l}$ *be ciphertexts that encrypt message* $\mathbf{M}_1 \in \{0,1\}^{(m+1)\times(m+1)}$ *and* $\mathbf{M}_2 \in \{0,1\}^{(m+1)\times(m+1)}$, *respectively. Thus ciphertext multiplication results in ciphertext* $\mathbf{C}^{Mult} = \mathbf{C}_1 \cdot \mathbf{G}^{-1}(\mathbf{C}_2)$ *such that* $\mathbf{C}^{Mult} = \mathbf{error}^{Mult} + \mathbf{M}_1 \cdot \mathbf{M}_2 \cdot \mathbf{G}$, *then the ciphertext* $\mathbf{C}^{Mult}$ *is* $((m+1)E_1 + E_2)$-*noisy.*

Proof. By Eq. 2, we have that $\mathbf{C}^{Mult} = \mathbf{C}_1 \cdot \mathbf{G}^{-1}(\mathbf{C}_2) = \text{error}^{Mult} + \mathbf{M}_1 \cdot \mathbf{M}_2 \cdot \mathbf{G}$, where $\text{error}^{Mult} = \mathbf{S}^T \cdot (\mathbf{P}^T \mathbf{R}_1 \mathbf{G}^{-1}(\mathbf{C}_2) + \mathbf{M}_1 \mathbf{P}^T \mathbf{R}_2 + \mathbf{X}_1 \mathbf{G}^{-1}(\mathbf{C}_2) + \mathbf{M}_1 \mathbf{X}_2) = \text{error}_1 \cdot \mathbf{G}^{-1}(\mathbf{C}_2) + \mathbf{M}_1 \cdot \text{error}_2$. Clearly, $||\text{error}^{Mult}|| \leq ||\text{error}_1 \cdot \mathbf{G}^{-1}(\mathbf{C}_2)|| + ||\mathbf{M}_1 \cdot \text{error}_2|| \leq ||\text{error}_1|| \cdot ||\mathbf{G}^{-1}(\mathbf{C}_2)|| + ||\mathbf{M}_1 \cdot \text{error}_2|| \leq ((m+1)E_1 + E_2)$ and the ciphertext $\mathbf{C}^{Mult}$ is $((m+1)E_1 + E_2)$-noisy.

The same calculation holds for NAND gates. Consider the evaluation of a Boolean circuit of depth L consisting of NAND gates. It takes as input fresh ciphertexts, i.e. E_{init}-noisy ciphertexts, and at each level the noise is multiplied by a factor of at most $(m+1)$, i.e. the norm of error elements is increased by a factor of at most $(m+1)$. Therefore, the error elements of final ciphertext has norm bounded by

$$E_{\text{final}} = (m+1)^L \cdot E_{init}.$$

To ensure correctness of decryption we need $E_{\text{final}} \leq E_{\max}$. In other words, we have that condition $(m+1)^L \cdot E < \lfloor \frac{q}{2} \rfloor / 4$ must hold, what is guaranteed by our choice of parameters. $\qquad\square$

4.4   Security Analysis

The security of the Dual.LWE-based MBGPV scheme is based on the hardness of DLWE assumption and is analogous to standard-LWE assumption. In fact, we show Dual.LWE-based MBGSW scheme is IND-CPA-secure based on DLWE assumption by using Theorem 1 to show that the scheme is indistinguishable from the original GSW13 scheme.

Theorem 3. *Suppose* MBGSW *scheme achieves circular-security and let* params $= (n, q, \chi, m, t)$ *be such that the* LWE$_{n,m,q,\chi}$ *assumption holds and* $m = \mathcal{O}(n \log q)$, *then the* MBGSW *scheme is* IND-CPA-*secure.*

Proof. The proof of security consists of two steps, as follows:

– firstly, we argue that if the public key ($\mathbf{P} = [\mathbf{u}, -\mathbf{A}]$) is sampled from the LWE distribution, then we are able to apply Theorem 1 to show that, under LWE assumption, the matrix $\mathbf{A} = [\bar{\mathbf{A}} \mid \mathbf{u} - \bar{\mathbf{A}}\bar{\mathbf{e}}_1 \mid \cdots \mid \mathbf{u} - \bar{\mathbf{A}}\bar{\mathbf{e}}_t] \in \mathbb{Z}_q^{n \times m}$ is computationally indistinguishable from a randomly chosen matrix and the vector $\mathbf{u}$ is statistically close to uniform by the Leftover Hash Lemma (Lemma 4), then the public key syndrome ($\mathbf{u} = f_{\mathbf{A}}(\mathbf{e}), -\mathbf{A}$) is statistically close to uniform, by Corollary 1;
– secondly, for the ciphertext $\mathbf{C} = \mathbf{P}^T \mathbf{R} + \mathbf{M}\mathbf{G} + \mathbf{X}$, we just focus on $\mathbf{P}^T \mathbf{R}$. The arguments we applied here are from proof of Theorem 2, i.e. $\mathbf{P}^T \mathbf{R}$ is indistinguishable from uniform assuming the hardness of LWE$_{n,q,\chi,m}$.

To sum up, the joint distribution $(\mathbf{P}, \mathbf{C})$ is indistinguishable from the uniform distribution $(\mathbb{Z}_q^{n \times (m+1)}, \mathbb{Z}_q^{(m+1) \times N})$.

Table 1. Comparison of LWE-based multi-bit PKE schemes

Scheme	PVW08 [26]	LP11 [19]	Ours-PKE
assumption	LWE-based	LWE-based	Dual.LWE-based
$\|$plaintext$\|$	t	t	t
$\|$pk$\|$	$\bar{m}(n+t)\log^2 q$	$(n_1 t)\log^2 q$	$mn\log^2 q$
$\|$sk$\|$	$(nt)\log^2 q$	$(n_2 t)\log^2 q$	$mt\log^2 q$
$\|$ciphertext$\|$	$(n+t)\log q$	$(n_2+t)\log q$	$m\log q$
key tools	packed ciphertext	error-tolerant encoder	combination **A**
flexibility dec	$\times$	$\times$	$\checkmark$

Table 2. Comparison of LWE-based multi-bit FHE schemes

Scheme	BGH13 [4]	HAO15 [15]	Ours-FHE
assumption	LWE-based	LWE-based	Dual.LWE-based
$\|$plaintext$\|$	t	$t \times t$	$[t, t \times t]$
$\|$pk$\|$	$(n+t)t\log^2 q$	$(n+t)\bar{m}\log^2 q$	$mn\log^2 q$
$\|$sk$\|$	$(n+t)t\log^2 q$	$(n+t)t\log^2 q$	$mt\log^2 q$
$\|$Eval key$\|$	$(n+t)^3\log^2 q$	$\times$	$\times$
$\|$ciphertext$\|$	$(n+t)\log q$	$(n+t)N'\log q$	$(mN)\log q$
key tools	packed ciphertext	packed message	combination **A**
flexibility dec	$\times$	$\times$	$\checkmark$

5 Conclusion

We summarize the concrete key sizes of lattice-based multi-bit encryption schemes via LWE-based and Dual.LWE-based in Tables 1,2, where $N' = (n+t)\cdot\lceil\log q\rceil$, $N = (m+t)\cdot\lceil\log q\rceil$, $m = \bar{m} + t$ and integer dimension $n, n_1, n_2 \geq 1$.

Compared with other schemes [4,15,19,26], we must point out that the main drawback of our scheme is that our parameters depend on m rather than on n. Then our parameters have large magnitude. However, Tables 1, 2 show that using the public key matrix **A** we have constructed, though it causes dimension expansion of public key and ciphertext, it doesn't affect the correctness of multi-bit scheme. Most notably, our FHE scheme can encrypt messages of arbitrary length, i.e. from t bits to $t \times t$ bits. Moreover, compared MBGSW's encryption with simple concatenation of single-bit ciphertexts, we construct MBGSW with improved efficiency, and with flexibility to decrypt target bit. We also think [15] can also achieve *any length message encryption* and *flexibility decrypt target bit* by simple modification.

The construction of a multi-bit FHE scheme with high efficiency is an open problem. Since most constructions focus on single bit encryption only, we showed a multi-bit construction that can be achieved by a straightforward bitwise composition, but unfortunately does not offer the best performance. Hence, in order to improve the performance of the multi-bit construction, we proposed to combine t elements chosen from Dual.LWE underlying distribution into the public key, where t is the number of bits we want to encrypt. Notably, utilizing the public key matrix $\mathbf{A}$, we obtained a variant of the GSW scheme which can achieve one-time encryption of arbitrary length messages.

Acknowledgements. We would like to thank all anonymous reviewers for their helpful advice and comments. This work was supported by the National Natural Science Foundation of China (Grant No. 61472097), Specialized Research Fund for the Doctoral Program of Higher Education of China (Grant No. 20132304110017).

References

1. Agrawal, S., Boneh, D., Boyen, X.: Efficient lattice (H)IBE in the standard model. In: Gilbert, H. (ed.) EUROCRYPT 2010. LNCS, vol. 6110, pp. 553–572. Springer, Heidelberg (2010). doi:10.1007/978-3-642-13190-5_28

2. Alperin-Sheriff, J., Peikert, C.: Faster bootstrapping with polynomial error. In: Garay, J.A., Gennaro, R. (eds.) CRYPTO 2014. LNCS, vol. 8616, pp. 297–314. Springer, Heidelberg (2014). doi:10.1007/978-3-662-44371-2_17

3. Brakerski, Z.: Fully homomorphic encryption without modulus switching from classical GapSVP. In: Safavi-Naini, R., Canetti, R. (eds.) CRYPTO 2012. LNCS, vol. 7417, pp. 868–886. Springer, Heidelberg (2012). doi:10.1007/978-3-642-32009-5_50

4. Brakerski, Z., Gentry, C., Halevi, S.: Packed ciphertexts in LWE-based homomorphic encryption. In: Kurosawa, K., Hanaoka, G. (eds.) PKC 2013. LNCS, vol. 7778, pp. 1–13. Springer, Heidelberg (2013). doi:10.1007/978-3-642-36362-7_1

5. Brakerski, Z., Gentry, C., Vaikuntanathan, V.: (leveled) fully homomorphic encryption without bootstrapping. In: Proceedings of the 3rd Innovations in Theoretical Computer Science Conference, pp. 309–325. ACM (2012)

6. Brakerski, Z., Langlois, A., Peikert, C., Regev, O., Stehlé, D.: Classical hardness of learning with errors. In: Proceedings of the Forty-Fifth Annual ACM Symposium on Theory of Computing, pp. 575–584. ACM (2013)

7. Brakerski, Z., Vaikuntanathan, V.: Efficient fully homomorphic encryption from (standard) LWE. In: 2011 IEEE 52nd Annual Symposium on Foundations of Computer Science, pp. 97–106. IEEE (2011)

8. Brakerski, Z., Vaikuntanathan, V.: Fully homomorphic encryption from ring-LWE and security for key dependent messages. In: Rogaway, P. (ed.) CRYPTO 2011. LNCS, vol. 6841, pp. 505–524. Springer, Heidelberg (2011). doi:10.1007/978-3-642-22792-9_29

9. Cheon, J.H., Coron, J.-S., Kim, J., Lee, M.S., Lepoint, T., Tibouchi, M., Yun, A.: Batch fully homomorphic encryption over the integers. In: Johansson, T., Nguyen, P.Q. (eds.) EUROCRYPT 2013. LNCS, vol. 7881, pp. 315–335. Springer, Heidelberg (2013). doi:10.1007/978-3-642-38348-9_20

10. Clear, M., McGoldrick, C.: Multi-identity and multi-key leveled FHE from learning with errors. In: Gennaro, R., Robshaw, M. (eds.) CRYPTO 2015. LNCS, vol. 9216, pp. 630–656. Springer, Heidelberg (2015). doi:10.1007/978-3-662-48000-7_31

11. Ducas, L., Micciancio, D.: FHEW: bootstrapping homomorphic encryption in less than a second. In: Oswald, E., Fischlin, M. (eds.) EUROCRYPT 2015. LNCS, vol. 9056, pp. 617–640. Springer, Heidelberg (2015). doi:10.1007/978-3-662-46800-5_24

12. Gentry, C., et al.: Fully homomorphic encryption using ideal lattices. STOC **9**, 169–178 (2009)

13. Gentry, C., Peikert, C., Vaikuntanathan, V.: Trapdoors for hard lattices and new cryptographic constructions. In: Proceedings of the Fortieth Annual ACM Symposium on Theory of Computing, pp. 197–206. ACM (2008)

14. Gentry, C., Sahai, A., Waters, B.: Homomorphic encryption from learning with errors: conceptually-simpler, asymptotically-faster, attribute-based. In: Canetti, R., Garay, J.A. (eds.) CRYPTO 2013. LNCS, vol. 8042, pp. 75–92. Springer, Heidelberg (2013). doi:10.1007/978-3-642-40041-4_5

15. Hiromasa, R., Abe, M., Okamoto, T.: Packing messages and optimizing bootstrapping in GSW-FHE. In: Katz, J. (ed.) PKC 2015. LNCS, vol. 9020, pp. 699–715. Springer, Heidelberg (2015). doi:10.1007/978-3-662-46447-2_31

16. Impagliazzo, R., Levin, L.A., Luby, M.: Pseudo-random generation from one-way functions. In: Proceedings of the Twenty-First Annual ACM Symposium on Theory of Computing, pp. 12–24. ACM (1989)

17. Katz, J., Lindell, Y.: Introduction to Modern Cryptography. CRC Press, Boca Raton (2014)

18. Katz, J., Thiruvengadam, A., Zhou, H.-S.: Feasibility and infeasibility of adaptively secure fully homomorphic encryption. In: Kurosawa, K., Hanaoka, G. (eds.) PKC 2013. LNCS, vol. 7778, pp. 14–31. Springer, Heidelberg (2013). doi:10.1007/978-3-642-36362-7_2

19. Lindner, R., Peikert, C.: Better key sizes (and attacks) for LWE-based encryption. In: Kiayias, A. (ed.) CT-RSA 2011. LNCS, vol. 6558, pp. 319–339. Springer, Heidelberg (2011). doi:10.1007/978-3-642-19074-2_21

20. López-Alt, A., Tromer, E., Vaikuntanathan, V.: On-the-fly multiparty computation on the cloud via multikey fully homomorphic encryption. In: Proceedings of the Forty-Fourth Annual ACM Symposium on Theory of Computing, pp. 1219–1234. ACM (2012)

21. Lyubashevsky, V.: Lattice signatures without trapdoors. In: Pointcheval, D., Johansson, T. (eds.) EUROCRYPT 2012. LNCS, vol. 7237, pp. 738–755. Springer, Heidelberg (2012). doi:10.1007/978-3-642-29011-4_43

22. Micciancio, D., Peikert, C.: Trapdoors for lattices: simpler, tighter, faster, smaller. In: Pointcheval, D., Johansson, T. (eds.) EUROCRYPT 2012. LNCS, vol. 7237, pp. 700–718. Springer, Heidelberg (2012). doi:10.1007/978-3-642-29011-4_41

23. Mukherjee, P., Wichs, D.: Two round multiparty computation via multi-key FHE. In: Fischlin, M., Coron, J.-S. (eds.) EUROCRYPT 2016. LNCS, vol. 9666, pp. 735–763. Springer, Heidelberg (2016). doi:10.1007/978-3-662-49896-5_26

24. Nuida, K., Kurosawa, K.: (Batch) Fully homomorphic encryption over integers for non-binary message spaces. In: Oswald, E., Fischlin, M. (eds.) EUROCRYPT 2015. LNCS, vol. 9056, pp. 537–555. Springer, Heidelberg (2015). doi:10.1007/978-3-662-46800-5_21

25. Peikert, C.: Public-key cryptosystems from the worst-case shortest vector problem. In: Proceedings of the Forty-First Annual ACM Symposium on Theory of Computing, pp. 333–342. ACM (2009)

26. Peikert, C., Vaikuntanathan, V., Waters, B.: A framework for efficient and composable oblivious transfer. In: Wagner, D. (ed.) CRYPTO 2008. LNCS, vol. 5157, pp. 554–571. Springer, Heidelberg (2008). doi:10.1007/978-3-540-85174-5_31

27. Regev, O.: On lattices, learning with errors, random linear codes, and cryptography. In: Proceedings of the Thirty-Seventh Annual ACM Symposium on Theory of Computing, pp. 84–93. ACM (2005)

28. Rivest, R.L., Adleman, L., Dertouzos, M.L.: On data banks and privacy homomorphisms. Found. Secure Comput. **4**(11), 169–180 (1978)

29. Smart, N.P., Vercauteren, F.: Fully homomorphic simd operations. Designs Codes Cryptography **71**(1), 57–81 (2014)

Cryptanalysis of a Homomorphic Encryption Scheme Over Integers

Jingguo Bi[1,2], Jiayang Liu[3], and Xiaoyun Wang[1,4(✉)]

[1] Institute for Advanced Study, Tsinghua University, Beijing 100084, China
{jingguobi,xiaoyunwang}@mail.tsinghua.edu.cn
[2] State Key Laboratory of Cryptology, P.O. Box 5159, Beijing 100878, China
[3] Department of Computer Science and Technology, Tsinghua University,
Beijing 100084, China
liujiaya14@mails.tsinghua.edu.cn
[4] Lab of Cryptographic Technology and Information Security, Shandong University,
Jinan 250100, People's Republic of China

Abstract. At Eurocrypt 2010, van Dijk et al. described a fully homomorphic encryption scheme (abbreviated as DGHV) over integers. It is conceptually simple but the public key size is large. After DGHV scheme was proposed, many variants of DGHV schemes with smaller public key size were proposed. In this paper, we present a multi-ciphertexts attack on a variant of the DGHV scheme with much smaller public key (abbreviated as HE^{RK}), which was proposed by Govinda Ramaiah and Vijaya Kumari at CNC 2012. Multi-ciphertexts attack considers the security of the schemes when the attacker captures a certain amount of ciphertexts. It is a common phenomena that the attacker can easily obtain enough ciphertexts in most of practical applications of fully homomorphic encryptions (even for public-key schemes). For all the four groups of the recommended parameters of HE^{RK}, we can recover the plaintexts successfully if we only capture five ciphertexts. Our attack only needs to apply LLL algorithm twice on two small dimension lattices, and the data show that the plaintexts can be recovered in seconds.

Keywords: Homomorphic encryption · LLL algorithm · Multi-ciphertexts attack · Lattice · Cryptanalysis

1 Introduction

Homomorphic encryption is an interesting concept to protect privacy and has been proposed by Rivest, Adleman and Dertouzos [22] in 1978. Since its publication, several homomorphic encryptions have been designed for the e-voting system, Private Information Retrieval Protocol and so on. Seven years ago, in a breakthrough work, Gentry proposed a *fully homomorphic* cryptosystem based on ideal lattice which allows arbitrary times additions and multiplications on encrypted data [13–15]. Recent works have shown how to implement existing fully homomorphic schemes [16,26], and how to construct new homomorphic

© Springer International Publishing AG 2017
K. Chen et al. (Eds.): Inscrypt 2016, LNCS 10143, pp. 243–252, 2017.
DOI: 10.1007/978-3-319-54705-3_15

encryption schemes based on other hard problems, such as approximate greatest common divisor problems [7,12] and Ring-LWE [1–3,17].

At Eurocrypt 2010, van Dijk, Gentry, Halevi and Vaikuntanathan described a fully homomorphic encryption scheme over the integers [12](abbreviated as DGHV). As in Gentry's scheme [13], the authors first propose a somewhat homomorphic scheme supporting a limited number of additions and multiplications over encrypted bits. Then they apply Gentry's squash decryption technique and ciphertext refresh procedure to obtain a fully homomorphic scheme. Compared with the original Gentry's scheme, the main appeal of the DGHV scheme is its conceptual simplicity: all operations are done over the integers instead of ideal lattices. However, the size of public-key is $O(n^{10})$ which is too large for any practical system, here n is the security parameter. The security of DGHV scheme relies on the hardness of sparse subset sum problem and the Approximate Greatest Common Divisor problem (AGCD). The AGCD problem which was firstly introduced by Howgrave-Graham in [18], is to recover a secret integer p from many approximate multiples $q_i \cdot p + r_i$ of p. The efficiency of the DGHV scheme has been improved in a series of works [4,6,7,9,11,23].

Compared with the booming development of the design side of the homomorphic encryptions, the cryptanalysis result of homomorphic encryptions seems scarce. Chen and Nguyen [8] presented a square-root attack to break the challenges announced in [7]. In [5], Cohn and Heninger constructed a lattice by generalizing the Howgrave-Graham's algorithm to search the approximate common divisor. Furthermore, they deduced that the scheme proposed in [12] can be broken by solving a $2^{\sqrt{n}}$-approximation SVP.

In most of practical applications of fully homomorphic encryptions, the attacker can easily obtain enough ciphertexts. In this paper, we consider the security of a variant of the DGHV scheme (called HE^{RK}) under this phenomena. The HE^{RK} scheme was proposed by Govinda Ramaiah and Vijaya Kumari at CNC 2012 [23], and has much smaller public key compared with DGHV scheme. For all the four groups of the recommended parameters of HE^{RK}, we can recover the plaintexts successfully if we only capture five ciphertexts. Our attack is based on orthogonal lattice which was firstly presented by Phong Nguyen and Stern at Crypto 1997 [20]. Our attack only needs to apply LLL algorithm twice on two small dimension lattices, and thus is very efficient. We implemented it and carried out our attack on the four groups of the parameters suggested in [24]. The data show that the plaintexts can be recovered in seconds on a single desktop computer.

The remainder of this paper is organized as follows. In Sect. 2, we review backgrounds of lattices. In Sect. 3, we describe the HE^{RK} fully homomorphic scheme based on integer. In Sect. 4, the orthogonal lattice attack is proposed. In Sect. 5, experimental results with our attack are given. Section 6 concludes the paper.

2 Preliminaries

2.1 Notations

We use row representation for matrices. Vectors are row vectors denoted by bold lowercase letters, matrices are denoted by uppercase letters, and their coefficients are denoted by lowercase letters. All logarithms are in base 2. Let $\|\|$ be the Euclidean norm. For a real number x, we denote by $\lceil x \rceil, \lfloor x \rfloor, \lceil x \rfloor$ the rounding of x up, down, or to the nearest integer. For integers z, p we denote the reduction of z modulo p by $[z]_p$ with $-p/2 < [z]_p \le p/2$. We write $f(\lambda) = \tilde{O}(g(\lambda))$ if $f(\lambda) = O(g(\lambda) \log^k(g(\lambda)))$ for some $k \in \mathbb{N}$.

2.2 Lattice

Let $\mathbb{R}^m$ be the m-dimensional Euclidean space. A lattice in $\mathbb{R}^m$ is the set $\mathcal{L}(\mathbf{b_1}, \ldots, \mathbf{b_n}) = \{\sum_{i=1}^n x_i \mathbf{b_i} : x_i \in \mathbb{Z}\}$ of all integral combinations of n linearly independent vectors $\mathbf{b_1}, \ldots, \mathbf{b_n} \in \mathbb{R}^m$. The integers n and m are called the rank and dimension of the lattice. A lattice can be conveniently represented by a matrix $\mathbf{B}$, where $\mathbf{b_1}, \ldots, \mathbf{b_n}$ are the row vectors. The determinant of the lattice $\mathcal{L}$ is defined as $\det(\mathcal{L}) = \det(\mathcal{L}(\mathbf{B})) = \sqrt{\det(\mathbf{BB}^T)}$. For any vectors $\mathbf{u}, \mathbf{v} \in \mathbb{Z}^m$, we say that $\mathbf{u}$ and $\mathbf{v}$ are orthogonal if $\langle \mathbf{u}, \mathbf{v} \rangle = 0$, and we denote it $\mathbf{u} \perp \mathbf{v}$. For any vector $\mathbf{u} \in \mathbb{Z}^m$, we denote $\mathbf{u}^\perp$ to be the set of vectors in $\mathbb{Z}^m$ orthogonal to $\mathbf{u}$. More generally, if $\mathcal{L}$ is a lattice in $\mathbb{Z}^m$, its orthogonal lattice $\mathcal{L}^\perp$ is defined as the set of vectors in Z^m orthogonal to the points in $\mathcal{L}$, i.e. $\mathcal{L}^\perp = \{\mathbf{v} \in \mathbb{Z}^m | \mathbf{u} \in \mathcal{L}, \langle \mathbf{u}, \mathbf{v} \rangle = 0\}$. For the properties of orthogonal lattice, we have the following theorems [20]:

Theorem 1. *If $\mathcal{L}$ is a lattice in $\mathbb{Z}^m$, then $rank(\mathcal{L}) + rank(\mathcal{L}^\perp) = m$.*

Theorem 2. *If $\mathcal{L}$ is a complete lattice in $\mathbb{Z}^m$, then $det(\mathcal{L}) = det(\mathcal{L}^\perp)$.*

Theorem 3. *There exists an algorithm which given any basis $\mathbf{b_1}, \cdots, \mathbf{b_n}$ of a lattice $\mathcal{L}$ in $\mathbb{Z}^m$ of dimension n, outputs an LLL-reduced basis of the orthogonal lattice $\mathcal{L}^\perp$, and whose running time is polynomial with respect to m, n and any upper bound on the bit-length of the $\| \mathbf{b_j} \|$.*

To calculate a LLL reduced base of $\mathcal{L}^\perp$, Phong Nguyen and Stern [20] presented a clever idea to construct a suitable lattice, and then a LLL reduced base of $\mathcal{L}^\perp$ can be obtained by invoking LLL algorithm [19] once on this new lattice. For more details, we refer the readers to [20]. In our attack, we will use this algorithm twice.

3   Description of the HE^{RK} Homomorphic Encryption Scheme

The main parameters:
The public key of HE^{RK} consists of only two big integers X_0 and X_1. X_0 is an exact multiple of the odd secret integer P and X_1 is an approximate multiple, i.e., multiple of P containing some additive error R. To encrypt a plaintext bit M, the erroneous integer X_1 of the public key is multiplied with a random even integer N, the result is added to the plaintext bit and the final sum is reduced modulo the error-free integer X_0 in the public key. For homomorphic evaluation of a function, the addition and multiplication operations in the corresponding arithmetic circuit are performed over ciphertexts, modulo the errorfree integer X_0 in the public key. The security of HE^{RK} is based on the two-element Partial Approximate Greatest Common Divisor (PAGCD) problem.

Given the security parameter n, the following parameters are used:

- e is the size of the secret key integer P, is taken as $e \geq d \cdot (n \log^2 n)$ to support homomorphism for evaluation of sufficiently deep circuits.
- r is the size of the noise in the public key integer X_1, is taken as $\omega(\log n)$ to foil the brute-force attack against the noise.
- g is the number of bits in each of the public key integers, is taken as $\omega(e \cdot \log n)$ to thwart lattice based attacks on the two-element PAGCD problem.
- d denotes the size of the even noise factor N used during the encryption. To avoid the brute-force attack against it, the size of this integer is taken as $2n$.

The theoretical parameter setting for HE^{RK} can be chosen as, $e = \tilde{O}(n^2)$, $r = n$, $d = 2n$, and $g = \tilde{O}(n^3)$. This setting results in a scheme with overall complexity of $\tilde{O}(n^3)$. The specific construction of HE^{RK} is as follows.

KeyGen(1^n): Generate a random odd integer P of size e bits. Choose a random r-bit integer R from the interval $(-2^r, 2^r)$. For $i = 0, 1$, Choose a random g-bit integer Q_i from $[0, 2^g/P)$. Calculate $X_0 = PQ_0, X_1 = PQ_1 + R$. Restart unless the integers X_0, X_1 are co-prime and $X_0 > X_1$. The public key is $pk = (X_0, X_1)$, and the secret key is $sk = P$.

Encrypt($pk, m \in \{0, 1\}$): For a plaintext bit $m \in \{0, 1\}$, choose a random even integer N from the interval $[2^{d-1}, 2^d)$. The ciphertext

$$c = [m + N \cdot X_1] \mod X_0.$$

Evaluate($pk, C, c_1, \cdots, c_t$): given the circuit C with t input bits, and t ciphertexts c_i, apply the addition and multiplication gates of C to the ciphertexts, performing all the additions and multiplications over the integers, and return the resulting integer.

Decrypt(sk, c): Output the plaintext $m = (c \mod P) \mod 2$.
The appealing feature of the scheme HE^{RK} is the relatively smaller public key with only two integers of size $O(n^3)$ each. Encryption method is also comparatively simple because, the product $N \cdot X_1$ corresponds to the operations of

choosing a random subset from the big set of public key elements in the DGHV Scheme [12].

4   Orthogonal Lattice Attack on Homomorphic Scheme

In this section, we give the details of our attack on HE^{RK} scheme. In some practical applications of homomorphic encryption schemes, the attacker can easily capture a certain amount of ciphertexts. Our attack is under this circumstances.

Let the vector $\mathbf{c} = (c_1, c_2, \cdots, c_t)^T \in \mathbb{Z}^t$ be the vector of ciphertext, such that

$$c_i = m_i + N_i \cdot X_1 + k_i \cdot X_0, 1 \leq i \leq t.$$

where the plaintext bit $m_i \in \{0, 1\}$, N_i is a random even integer from the interval $[2^{d-1}, 2^d)$, and k_i is the quotient in the division of $m_i + N_i \cdot X_1$ by X_0.

Therefore, let $\mathbf{m} = (m_1, m_2, \cdots, m_t)^T$, $\mathbf{N} = (N_1, N_2, \cdots, N_t)^T$, and $\mathbf{k} = (k_1, k_2, \cdots, k_t)^T$, we have

$$\mathbf{c} = \mathbf{m} + X_1 \cdot \mathbf{N} + X_0 \cdot \mathbf{k} \tag{1}$$

Consider short vectors $\mathbf{u}_1, \mathbf{u}_2, \cdots, \mathbf{u}_{t-3} \in \mathbb{Z}^t$ orthogonal to $\mathbf{c}$. For all $1 \leq i \leq t - 3$, we can obtain that

$$0 = \langle \mathbf{u}_i, \mathbf{c} \rangle = \langle \mathbf{u}_i, \mathbf{m} \rangle + X_1 \cdot \langle \mathbf{u}_i, \mathbf{N} \rangle + X_0 \cdot \langle \mathbf{u}_i, \mathbf{k} \rangle. \tag{2}$$

If $\|\mathbf{u}_i\|$ are sufficiently short, because of $(X_0, X_1) = 1$ and $\|\mathbf{m}\|, \|\mathbf{N}\|, \|\mathbf{k}\|$ are all short vector compared with X_0 and X_1.
Intuitively, for all $\mathbf{u}_i, 1 \leq i \leq t - 3$, we would have:

$$\langle \mathbf{u}_i, \mathbf{m} \rangle = 0, \langle \mathbf{u}_i, \mathbf{N} \rangle = 0, \text{ and } \langle \mathbf{u}_i, \mathbf{k} \rangle = 0.$$

Hence, the vectors $\mathbf{m}, \mathbf{N}$, and $\mathbf{k}$ are all belong to the orthogonal $\mathcal{L}^\perp$ of the lattice $\mathcal{L}$ spanned by the vectors $\mathbf{u}_1, \mathbf{u}_2, \cdots, \mathbf{u}_{t-3}$.

In particular, a simple observation is that a vector orthogonal to $\mathbf{c}$ is either large, or orthogonal to $\mathbf{m}, \mathbf{N}$, and $\mathbf{k}$.

Lemma 1. *Let $\mathbf{u} \in \mathbb{Z}^t$, and $\mathbf{u} \perp \mathbf{c}$, if $\|\mathbf{u}\| < X_0^{1/2}/(t^{1/2} \cdot 2^{d+1})$, then with the probability at least $1 - \frac{1}{2^{d-1}}$ that $\mathbf{u} \perp \mathbf{m}$, $\mathbf{u} \perp \mathbf{N}$, and $\mathbf{u} \perp \mathbf{k}$.*

Proof. Let $\mathbf{u} \in \mathbb{Z}^t$ such that $\mathbf{u} \perp \mathbf{c}$. From Eq. (1), we have

$$0 = \langle \mathbf{u}, \mathbf{c} \rangle = \langle \mathbf{u}, \mathbf{m} \rangle + X_1 \cdot \langle \mathbf{u}, \mathbf{N} \rangle + X_0 \cdot \langle \mathbf{u}, \mathbf{k} \rangle.$$

From $\|\mathbf{u}\| < X_0^{1/2}/(t^{1/2} \cdot 2^{d+1})$, we deduce that

$$|\langle \mathbf{u}, \mathbf{N} \rangle| \leq \|\mathbf{u}\| \cdot \|\mathbf{N}\| < X_0^{1/2},$$

and

$$|\langle \mathbf{u}, \mathbf{m} \rangle| \leq \|\mathbf{u}\| \cdot \|\mathbf{m}\| < X_0^{1/2}/2^{d+1}.$$

Now, we consider the probability P that $\mathbf{u} \perp \mathbf{m}$, $\mathbf{u} \perp \mathbf{N}$, and $\mathbf{u} \perp \mathbf{k}$ under the conditions $\|\mathbf{u}\| \leq X_0/(t^{1/2} \cdot 2^{d+1})$ and $\mathbf{u} \perp \mathbf{c}, \mathbf{u} \in \mathbb{Z}^t$.

$$P = Prob\left(\mathbf{u} \perp \mathbf{m}, \mathbf{u} \perp \mathbf{N}, \text{and } \mathbf{u} \perp \mathbf{k} \,\middle|\, \begin{array}{c} \|\mathbf{u}\| \leq X_0^{1/2}/(t^{1/2} \cdot 2^{d+1}), \\ \mathbf{u} \perp \mathbf{c}, \mathbf{u} \in \mathbb{Z}^t \end{array}\right)$$

$$= Prob\left(\mathbf{u} \perp \mathbf{m}, \mathbf{u} \perp \mathbf{N}, \text{and } \mathbf{u} \perp \mathbf{k} \,\middle|\, \begin{array}{c} \|\mathbf{u}\| \leq X_0^{1/2}/(t^{1/2} \cdot 2^{d+1}), \\ \langle \mathbf{u}, \mathbf{m}\rangle + X_1 \cdot \langle \mathbf{u}, \mathbf{N}\rangle + X_0 \cdot \langle \mathbf{u}, \mathbf{k}\rangle = 0 \end{array}\right)$$

$$= 1 - Prob\left(X_0 | \langle \mathbf{u}, \mathbf{m}\rangle + X_1 \cdot \langle \mathbf{u}, \mathbf{N}\rangle \,\middle|\, \begin{array}{c} \|\mathbf{u}\| \leq X_0^{1/2}/(t^{1/2} \cdot 2^{d+1}), \\ \langle \mathbf{u}, \mathbf{m}\rangle \neq 0, \langle \mathbf{u}, \mathbf{N}\rangle \neq 0, \langle \mathbf{u}, \mathbf{k}\rangle \neq 0 \end{array}\right)$$

$$\geq 1 - \frac{X_0^{1/2} \cdot X_0^{1/2}/2^{d+1}}{X_0} \geq 1 - \frac{1}{2^{d+1}}.$$

The third equality is because that if $\mathbf{u}$ is orthogonal to one of the three vectors $\mathbf{m}, \mathbf{N}$, and $\mathbf{k}$, then $\mathbf{u}$ must orthogonal to the other two vectors. Without loss of generality, if $\mathbf{u} \perp \mathbf{m}$, then we have

$$X_1 \cdot \langle \mathbf{u}, \mathbf{N}\rangle + X_0 \cdot \langle \mathbf{u}, \mathbf{k}\rangle = 0.$$

Because $(X_0, X_1) = 1$ and $|\langle \mathbf{u}, \mathbf{N}\rangle| \ll X_0$, this will yield that $\langle \mathbf{u}, \mathbf{N}\rangle = 0$, and thus, $\langle \mathbf{u}, \mathbf{k}\rangle = 0$.   □

Remark 1. *Lemma 1 tells us that if $\|\mathbf{u}\| < X_0^{1/2}/(t^{1/2} \cdot 2^{d+1})$ and $\mathbf{u} \perp \mathbf{c}$, then with overwhelming probability that $\mathbf{u} \perp \mathbf{m}$, $\mathbf{u} \perp \mathbf{N}$, and $\mathbf{u} \perp \mathbf{k}$. However, in practical experiments, the vector $\mathbf{u}$'s lengths are much shorter than $X_0^{1/2}/(t^{1/2} \cdot 2^{d+1})$, and thus the coefficients $\langle \mathbf{u}, \mathbf{m}\rangle, \langle \mathbf{u}, \mathbf{N}\rangle$ and $\langle \mathbf{u}, \mathbf{k}\rangle$ are much smaller. In this situation, $X_1 \cdot \langle \mathbf{u}, \mathbf{N}\rangle + X_0 \cdot \langle \mathbf{u}, \mathbf{k}\rangle$ cannot equal to a small value unless all the three coefficients are 0.*

From Theorem 3, it is easy to compute a LLL-reduced basis $\{\mathbf{u}_1, \mathbf{u}_2, \cdots, \mathbf{u}_{t-1}\}$ of $\mathbf{c}^\perp \in \mathbb{Z}^t$. From Lemma 1, we can get that for each $\mathbf{u}_i, 1 \leq i \leq t - 1$, there are two possibilities that either $\mathbf{u}_i$ is large, or orthogonal to $\mathbf{m}, \mathbf{N}$ and $\mathbf{k}$ with overwhelming probability. Since $\mathbf{m}, \mathbf{N}$ and $\mathbf{k}$ are heuristically linearly independent, the $t - 1$ vectors cannot be orthogonal to $\mathbf{m}, \mathbf{N}$ and $\mathbf{k}$.

Let rearrange these $t - 1$ vectors according to their lengths in the ascending order, then the last two vectors $\mathbf{u}_{t-2}, \mathbf{u}_{t-1}$, must satisfy

$$\|\mathbf{u}_{t-2}\| \geq X_0^{1/2}/(t^{1/2} \cdot 2^{d+1}), \|\mathbf{u}_{t-1}\| \geq X_0^{1/2}/(t^{1/2} \cdot 2^{d+1}).$$

The first $t - 3$ vectors form a lattice $\mathcal{L}_{new} = \mathbb{Z}\mathbf{u}_1 \oplus \cdots \oplus \mathbb{Z}\mathbf{u}_{t-3}$ of rank $t - 3$ and with the volume

$$V(\mathcal{L}_{new}) \approx \frac{vol(\mathbf{c}^\perp)}{\|\mathbf{u}_{t-2}\|\|\mathbf{u}_{t-1}\|} = \frac{\|\mathbf{c}\|}{\|\mathbf{u}_{t-2}\|\|\mathbf{u}_{t-1}\|} \leq t^{3/2} \cdot 2^{2d+2}.$$

Which can heuristically be expected to behave like a random lattice. In particular, we have

$$\|\mathbf{u}_i\| = \tilde{O}(\sqrt{t - 3}V(\mathcal{L}_{new})^{1/(t-3)}) = \tilde{O}(t^{1/2} \cdot V(\mathcal{L}_{new})^{1/(t-3)}), 1 \leq i \leq t - 3$$

Thus, the condition for $\mathbf{u}_1, \cdots, \mathbf{u}_{t-3}$ all being orthogonal to $\mathbf{m}, \mathbf{N}$, and $\mathbf{k}$ with overwhelming probability becomes:

$$\tilde{O}(\sqrt{t})(t^{3/2} \cdot 2^{2d+2})^{\frac{1}{t-3}} \ll \frac{X_0}{(t^{1/2} \cdot 2^{d+1})}.$$

Taking logarithms and ignoring logarithmic factors, we can choose

$$t \geq 3 + \frac{2d+2}{g-d-1}.$$

Assuming we choose the suitable t satisfy the above condition, then the vectors $\mathbf{m}, \mathbf{N}$ and $\mathbf{k}$ belong to $\mathcal{L}_{new}^{\perp}$ with overwhelming probability. From Theorem 3, we can recover the message vector $\mathbf{m}$ as long as we invoke LLL algorithm on the *doubly orthogonal* lattice,

To sum up, we formalize an algorithm to recover the plaintext vector in (Algorithm 1).

Algorithm 1. Recover the plaintexts

Input: The public key X_0 and X_1 and t ciphertexts $c_1, \cdots, c_t$ for the corresponding plaintexts $m_1 \cdots, m_t$.

1. Generate the lattice $\mathcal{L}_1$ in $\mathbb{Z}^{1+t}$ by the rows of the following $t \times (t+1)$ matrix:

$$\begin{pmatrix} \lambda \cdot c_1 & 1 & \cdots & 0 \\ \vdots & \vdots & \ddots & \vdots \\ \lambda \cdot c_t & 0 & \cdots & 1 \end{pmatrix}$$

   where λ is a large constant.
2. Apply LLL algorithm to $\mathcal{L}_1$ and keep only the t last coefficients of each resulting vector. Then, the first $t-1$ vectors $(\mathbf{u}_1, \cdots, \mathbf{u}_{t-1})$ is the LLL-reduced basis of the lattice $\mathbf{c}^{\perp} \in \mathbb{Z}^t$.
3. Generate the lattice $\mathcal{L}_2 \in \mathbb{Z}^{t-3+t}$ by the rows of the following $t \times (t-3+t)$ matrix

$$\begin{pmatrix} \lambda' u_{1,1} & \cdots & \lambda' u_{t-3,1} & 1 & \cdots & 0 \\ \vdots & & \vdots & & \ddots & \vdots \\ \lambda' u_{1,t} & \cdots & \lambda' u_{t-3,t} & 0 & \cdots & 1 \end{pmatrix}$$

   where λ' is a large constant.
4. Apply LLL algorithm to the lattice $\mathcal{L}_2$, and keep only the t last coefficients of each resulting vector. Then, the first 3 vectors $\mathbf{v}_1, \mathbf{v}_2, \mathbf{v}_3$ are the LLL-reduced basis of the lattice $\mathcal{L}_{new}^{\perp}$, which is orthogonal to the lattice $\mathcal{L}_{new} = \mathbb{Z}\mathbf{u}_1 \oplus \cdots \oplus \mathbb{Z}\mathbf{u}_{t-3} \in \mathbb{Z}^t$ of rank $t-3$.

Output: the plaintext vector $\mathbf{v}_1$.

5   Experiments Results

We implemented the homomorphic encryption scheme HE^{RK} and Algorithm 1 using Shoups NTL library [25]. However, for the LLL reduction in Algorithm 1, we used the fplll implementation [10] by Cad et al., which includes the L_2 algorithm [21]: fplll is much faster than NTL for some matrices with large coefficients. It should be stressed that fplll is a wrapper which actually implements several variants of LLL, together with several heuristics: L_2 is only used as a last resort when heuristic variants fail. This means that there might be a discrepancy between the practical running time and the theoretical complexity upper bound of LLL routines. Our test machine is a 2.93-GHz Intel Core 2 Duo processor E7500 running on Ubuntu. Running times are given in seconds.

Table 1. Values of parameters at different security levels

Level of security	n	e	r	d	g
Toy	32	1024	32	64	32768
Small	64	4096	64	128	262144
Medium	80	6400	80	160	512000
Large	128	16384	128	256	2097152

To assess our heuristical attack, we aim to the four groups of recommended parameters in [24], which corresponding to different security levels: Toy, Small, Medium, and Large (as shown in Table 1). We perform fifty experiments with $t = 5, 10, 15, 20, 25, 30$ for all the four groups of recommended parameters. In fact, our attack is successful for all the experiments even we choose $t = 5$, which means that our estimation of the parameter $t \geq 3 + \frac{2d+2}{g-d-1}$ is tight. This phenomenon also provides an evidence for the Lemma 1. The data of our attack is shown in Table 2. The last two columns data show the consuming time of LLL algorithm on lattice $\mathcal{L}_1$ and $\mathcal{L}_2$, independently.

Table 2. Efficiency of the attack

Level of security	n	t	Time of LLL on $\mathcal{L}_1$	Time of LLL on $\mathcal{L}_2$
Toy	32	5	70 ms	<1 ms
Small	64	5	3.91 s	<1 ms
Medium	80	5	17.6 s	10 ms
Large	128	5	180 s	40 ms

6   Conclusion

In this paper, we present an multi-ciphertexts attack on a variant of the DGHV scheme with much smaller public key, which was proposed by Govinda Ramaiah and Vijaya Kumari. More precisely, we show that one can recover the plaintexts by applying LLL algorithm twice on the lattices with small dimensions. We did experiments for all the four groups of the recommended parameters, the data show that the plaintexts can be recovered in seconds.

Acknowledgments. This paper is partially supported by: 973 Program grant 2013CB834205, NSF of China under grants No. 61502269 & 61133013 & 61272035.

References

1. Alperin-Sheriff, J., Peikert, C.: Faster bootstrapping with polynomial error. In: Garay, J.A., Gennaro, R. (eds.) CRYPTO 2014. LNCS, vol. 8616, pp. 297–314. Springer, Heidelberg (2014). doi:10.1007/978-3-662-44371-2_17
2. Brakerski, Z., Vaikuntanathan, V.: Efficient fully homomorphic encryption from (standard) LWE. In: FOCS 2011
3. Brakerski, Z., Vaikuntanathan, V.: Fully homomorphic encryption from ring-LWE and security for key dependent messages. In: Rogaway, P. (ed.) CRYPTO 2011. LNCS, vol. 6841, pp. 505–524. Springer, Heidelberg (2011). doi:10.1007/978-3-642-22792-9_29
4. Cheon, J.H., Coron, J.-S., Kim, J., Lee, M.S., Lepoint, T., Tibouchi, M., Yun, A.: Batch fully homomorphic encryption over the integers. In: Johansson, T., Nguyen, P.Q. (eds.) EUROCRYPT 2013. LNCS, vol. 7881, pp. 315–335. Springer, Heidelberg (2013). doi:10.1007/978-3-642-38348-9_20
5. Cohn, H., Heninger, N.: Approximate common divisors via lattices, Cryptology ePrint Archive, Report 2011/437 (2011). http://eprint.iacr.org/
6. Coron, J.-S., Lepoint, T., Tibouchi, M.: Scale-invariant fully homomorphic encryption over the integers. In: Krawczyk, H. (ed.) PKC 2014. LNCS, vol. 8383, pp. 311–328. Springer, Heidelberg (2014). doi:10.1007/978-3-642-54631-0_18
7. Coron, J.-S., Mandal, A., Naccache, D., Tibouchi, M.: Fully homomorphic encryption over the integers with shorter public keys. In: Rogaway, P. (ed.) CRYPTO 2011. LNCS, vol. 6841, pp. 487–504. Springer, Heidelberg (2011). doi:10.1007/978-3-642-22792-9_28
8. Chen, Y., Nguyen, P.Q.: Faster algorithms for approximate common divisors: breaking fully-homomorphic-encryption challenges over the integers. In: Pointcheval, D., Johansson, T. (eds.) EUROCRYPT 2012. LNCS, vol. 7237, pp. 502–519. Springer, Heidelberg (2012). doi:10.1007/978-3-642-29011-4_30
9. Coron, J.-S., Naccache, D., Tibouchi, M.: Public key compression and modulus switching for fully homomorphic encryption over the integers. In: Pointcheval, D., Johansson, T. (eds.) EUROCRYPT 2012. LNCS, vol. 7237, pp. 446–464. Springer, Heidelberg (2012). doi:10.1007/978-3-642-29011-4_27
10. Cadé, D., Pujol, X., Stehlé, D.: FPLLL library, version 3.0, Sep 2008. http://perso.ens-lyon.fr/damien.stehle
11. Cheon, J.H., Stehlé, D.: Fully homomophic encryption over the integers revisited. In: Oswald, E., Fischlin, M. (eds.) EUROCRYPT 2015. LNCS, vol. 9056, pp. 513–536. Springer, Heidelberg (2015). doi:10.1007/978-3-662-46800-5_20

12. Dijk, M., Gentry, C., Halevi, S., Vaikuntanathan, V.: Fully homomorphic encryption over the integers. In: Gilbert, H. (ed.) EUROCRYPT 2010. LNCS, vol. 6110, pp. 24–43. Springer, Heidelberg (2010). doi:10.1007/978-3-642-13190-5_2

13. Gentry, C.: A fully homomorphic encryption scheme. Ph.D. Thesis, Stanford University (2009). http://crypto.stanford.edu/craig

14. Gentry, C.: Fully homomorphic encryption using ideal lattices. In: Proceedings of the 41st ACM Symposium on Theory of Computing, STOC 2009, pp. 169–178. ACM, New York (2009)

15. Gentry, C.: Toward basing fully homomorphic encryption on worst-case hardness. In: Rabin, T. (ed.) CRYPTO 2010. LNCS, vol. 6223, pp. 116–137. Springer, Heidelberg (2010). doi:10.1007/978-3-642-14623-7_7

16. Gentry, C., Halevi, S.: Implementing gentry's fully-homomorphic encryption scheme. In: Paterson, K.G. (ed.) EUROCRYPT 2011. LNCS, vol. 6632, pp. 129–148. Springer, Heidelberg (2011). doi:10.1007/978-3-642-20465-4_9

17. Gentry, C., Sahai, A., Waters, B.: Homomorphic encryption from learning with errors: conceptually-simpler, asymptotically-faster, attribute-based. In: Canetti, R., Garay, J.A. (eds.) CRYPTO 2013. LNCS, vol. 8042, pp. 75–92. Springer, Heidelberg (2013). doi:10.1007/978-3-642-40041-4_5

18. Howgrave-Graham, N.: Approximate integer common divisors. In: Silverman, J.H. (ed.) CaLC 2001. LNCS, vol. 2146, pp. 51–66. Springer, Heidelberg (2001). doi:10.1007/3-540-44670-2_6

19. Lenstra, A.K., Lenstra Jr., H.W., Lovász, L.: Factoring polynomials with rational coefficients. Math. Ann. **261**(4), 515–534 (1982)

20. Nguyen, P., Stern, J.: Merkle-Hellman revisited: a cryptanalysis of the Qu-Vanstone cryptosystem based on group factorizations. In: Kaliski, B.S. (ed.) CRYPTO 1997. LNCS, vol. 1294, pp. 198–212. Springer, Heidelberg (1997). doi:10.1007/BFb0052236

21. Nguyen, P.Q., Stehlé, D.: An LLL algorithm with quadratic complexity. SIAM J. Comput. **39**(3), 874–903 (2009)

22. Rivest, R., Adleman, L., Dertouzos, M.: On data banks and privacy homomorphisms. In: Foundations of Secure Computation, pp. 169–180 (1978)

23. Ramaiah, Y.G., Kumari, G.V.: Efficient public key generation for homomorphic encryption over the integers. In: Das, V.V., Stephen, J. (eds.) CNC 2012. LNICSSITE, vol. 108, pp. 262–268. Springer, Heidelberg (2012). doi:10.1007/978-3-642-35615-5_40

24. Ramaiah, Y.G., Kumari, G.V.: Towards practical homomorphic encryption with efficient public key generation, pp. 10–17. ACEEE Int. J. Netw. Secur. **03**(04), 1–8 (2012)

25. Shoup, V.: NTL, Number Theory C++ Library. http://www.shoup.net/ntl/

26. Smart, N.P., Vercauteren, F.: Fully homomorphic encryption with relatively small key and ciphertext sizes. In: Nguyen, P.Q., Pointcheval, D. (eds.) PKC 2010. LNCS, vol. 6056, pp. 420–443. Springer, Heidelberg (2010). doi:10.1007/978-3-642-13013-7_25

Fully Homomorphic Encryption
for Point Numbers

Seiko Arita$^{(\boxtimes)}$ and Shota Nakasato

Graduate School of Information Security, Institute of Information Security,
Yokohama, Japan
arita@iisec.ac.jp, nakasatoshota@gmail.com

Abstract. Based on the FV scheme, we construct at first fully homomorphic encryption scheme **FX** that can homomorphically compute addition and multiplication of encrypted fixed point numbers without knowing the secret key. Then, we show that in the **FX** scheme one can efficiently and homomorphically compare magnitude of two encrypted numbers. That is, one can compute an encryption of the greater-than bit that indicates $x > x'$ or not, given two ciphertexts c and c' of x and x', respectively, without knowing the secret key. Finally we show that these properties of the **FX** scheme enables us to construct a fully homomorphic encryption scheme **FL** that can homomorphically compute addition and multiplication of encrypted floating point numbers.

Keywords: Fully Homomorphic Encryption $\cdot$ FV scheme $\cdot$ Fixed/floating point number $\cdot$ Greater-than bit

1 Introduction

Fully Homomorphic Encryption (FHE) scheme enables us to homomorphically compute an encrypted XORed bit $\mathsf{Enc}(b_1 \,\mathsf{XOR}\, b_2)$ and encrypted AND bit $\mathsf{Enc}(b_1 \,\mathsf{AND}\, b_2)$ of given encrypted bits $\mathsf{Enc}(b_1)$ and $\mathsf{Enc}(b_2)$ without knowing the secret key [9]. Since any function can be written using XOR and AND gates, this means that one can homomorphically compute any function of encrypted bits without knowing the secret key.

Practically, computation over bitwise encryptions is not efficient. It is a kind of "1-bit" processor. In schemes such as [3,4], one can encrypt congruent integers (i.e., $x \bmod n$) and can homomorphically compute addition $\mathsf{Enc}(x_1 + x_2 \bmod n)$ and multiplication $\mathsf{Enc}(x_1 \times x_2 \bmod n)$ of encrypted congruent integers $\mathsf{Enc}(x_1)$ and $\mathsf{Enc}(x_2)$ without knowing the secret key. Based on those schemes, various mining algorithms are experimentally and homomorphically evaluated against outsourced genomic, medical, or financial encrypted data [6,12–16].

However, the real world is not comprised of congruent integers. Real numbers have greater-than relation $x < y$, which requires computation of the most significant bit of $x - y$. Is it possible to efficiently compute $\mathsf{Enc}(\mathsf{MSb}(x - y))$ given $\mathsf{Enc}(x)$ and $\mathsf{Enc}(y)$ without knowing the secret key? Moreover, to compute real numbers, we must depend on some precision control mechanism, that enables

© Springer International Publishing AG 2017
K. Chen et al. (Eds.): Inscrypt 2016, LNCS 10143, pp. 253–270, 2017.
DOI: 10.1007/978-3-319-54705-3_16

computation of real numbers as fixed or floating point number computation. Is it possible to realize precision control against x only given its encryption $\mathsf{Enc}(x)$ without knowing the secret key? To make the theoretical universality of FHE schemes be of more practical interest, we need to resolve such problems. As we will see later, the two problems are tightly related to each other.

1.1 Our Contribution

FHE scheme FX for fixed point numbers. Our starting point is the FV scheme given by Fan and Vercauteren [8], which is an FHE scheme for congruent integers, instantiating the FHE scheme by Brakerski [2] based on the Ring LWE problem [18]. Let $R = \mathbb{Z}[X]/(\varPhi_m(X))$ be the m-th cyclotomic ring, where $\varPhi_m(X)$ denotes the m-th cyclotomic polynomial. Elements a of cyclotomic ring R are called cyclotomic integers and represented by integer coefficient polynomials $a(X) = \sum_{i=0}^{n-1} a_i X^i$ of degree less than $n = \phi(m)$. ($\phi(\cdot)$ denotes the Euler function.) Two cyclotomic integer a and b are added through polynomial addition: $(a + b)(X) = \sum_{i=0}^{n-1} (a_i + b_i) X^i$. Product of cyclotomic integer a and b is computed as polynomial multiplication followed by reduction via $\varPhi_m(X)$: $(a \cdot b)(X) = a(X)b(X) \bmod \varPhi_m(X)$.

Cyclotomic integers are reduced modulo an integer q, resulting elements of $R_q = \mathbb{Z}_q[X]/(\varPhi_m(X))$. A FV ciphertext is a pair $c = (c_0, c_1)$ $(\in R_q \times R_q)$ of cyclotomic integers modulo ciphertext modulus q. A plaintext is a cyclotomic integer x $(\in R_t)$ modulo plaintext modulus t. For simplicity we assume t divides q in this paper. A FV ciphertext $c = (c_0, c_1)$ of plaintext $x \in R_t$ satisfies the relation $c_0 + c_1 s = \frac{q}{t}x + v + q\alpha$ with some small noise v $(\in R_q)$ and some cyclotomic integer $\alpha \in R$. If one knows the secret key $s \in R$, by computing $\left\lfloor \frac{t}{q}(c_0 + c_1 s) \right\rceil \bmod t$, one can recover the plaintext x from the ciphertext c provided that coefficients of noise v are not too large relative to ratio $\frac{q}{t}$.

We modify the FV scheme so that we can treat fixed point numbers $\tilde{x} = 2^{-m}x$ $(x \in \mathbb{Z}_{2^{m+l}})$. Here, m is bit-length after point and l is bit-length before point of $\tilde{x}$ and so $x = 2^m \tilde{x}$ is an integer in $\mathbb{Z}_{2^{m+l}}$. We suppose that integer x represents a constant polynomial x (i.e., a polynomial whose unique non-zero term is its constant term) in the cyclotomic ring R. To enable homomorphic computation of $\tilde{x}$, we will use the relation: $c_0 + c_1 s = \frac{q}{t}2^{-m}x + v + q\alpha$ with $t = 2^{m+l}$. This is nothing but the relation for FV scheme with enlarged plaintext modulus $t' = t2^m$.

Let $c' = (c'_0, c'_1)$ be another ciphertext encrypting another fixed point number $\tilde{x}' = 2^{-m}x'$. Product of fixed point numbers $\tilde{x}$ and $\tilde{x}'$ is defined as $\tilde{x}\tilde{x}' = 2^{-m}\left\lfloor \left[2^{-m}xx'\right]_t \right\rfloor$. (Here, $[a]_t$ denotes the residue of a modulo t.) We want homomorphic version of this computation. By short calculation, we see that

$$\frac{t2^m}{q}(c_0 + c_1 s)(c'_0 + c'_1 s) = \frac{q}{t}(2^{-m}xx' + t(x'\alpha + x\alpha')) + v'' + 2^m q\alpha'' \quad (1)$$

for some small noise v'' and cyclotomic integer α''. By principle of division, we have $xx' = \left\lfloor 2^{-m}xx' \right\rfloor 2^m + \left[xx'\right]_{2^m}$. Substituting $2^{-m}xx' = \left\lfloor 2^{-m}xx' \right\rfloor + 2^{-m}\left[xx'\right]_{2^m}$ into Eq. (1), we get

$$\frac{t2^m}{q}(c_0 + c_1 s)(c_0' + c_1' s)$$

$$= \frac{q}{t}\left\{2^{-m}\left[xx'\right]_{2^m} + \left[\lfloor 2^{-m}xx'\rfloor\right]_t + \left(\lfloor 2^{-m}xx'\rfloor - \left[\lfloor 2^{-m}xx'\rfloor\right]_t\right)\right.$$
$$\left. + t(x'\alpha + x\alpha')\right\} + v'' + 2^m q\alpha''.$$

Thus, product of two ciphertexts c and c', as ciphertexts of the FV scheme with plaintext modulus $t' = t2^m$ (and ciphertext modulus q), is an encryption of

$$w = 2^{-m}\left[xx'\right]_{2^m} + \left[\lfloor 2^{-m}xx'\rfloor\right]_t + \left(\lfloor 2^{-m}xx'\rfloor - \left[\lfloor 2^{-m}xx'\rfloor\right]_t\right) + t(x'\alpha + x\alpha').$$

Here we see that w contains the wanted answer $2^m\tilde{x}\tilde{x}' = \left[\lfloor 2^{-m}xx'\rfloor\right]_t$ in the middle, but it also contains two annoying terms $LG = 2^{-m}\left[xx'\right]_{2^m}$ and $UG = \lfloor 2^{-m}xx'\rfloor - \left[\lfloor 2^{-m}xx'\rfloor\right]_t + t(x'\alpha + x\alpha')$. We call the former *lower garbage* and the latter *upper garbage*, since LG is the least significant m bits of w and UG is the most significant m bits of w. In order to realize homomorphic multiplication of encrypted fixed point numbers, we will implement some clearing methods of such two types of garbage LG and UG. Suppose here we had cleared LG and UG from (c_0, c_1) to get a new ciphertext (d_0, d_1), which will satisfy

$$\frac{t2^m}{q}(d_0 + d_1 s)(d_0' + d_1' s) = \frac{q}{t}\left[\lfloor 2^{-m}xx'\rfloor\right]_t + v'' + 2^m q\alpha''.$$

By dividing both sides by 2^m, we get

$$\frac{t}{q}(d_0 + d_1 s)(d_0' + d_1' s) = \frac{q}{t}2^{-m}\left[\lfloor 2^{-m}xx'\rfloor\right]_t + 2^{-m}v'' + q\alpha''$$

as desired.

As clearing methods of the lower and upper garbage, we introduce LowerClear and UpperClear algorithms. The algorithm LowerClear is a variant of arithmetic procedure for computing $\text{msb}_q : \mathbb{Z}_q \to \mathbb{Z}_2$ of [10,19]. Let $t = 2^{m+l}$ and let $w = x + 2^m z$ be an element of $\mathbb{Z}_{2^{2m+l}}$ with $x \in \mathbb{Z}_{2^m}$, $z \in \mathbb{Z}_t$. That is, x is the least significant m bits of $(2m + l)$-bit w (lower garbage). We want to clear $x \in \mathbb{Z}_{2^m}$ from w to get $2^m z$. The key observation is the following simple fact [10,19]: if w is equal to $b \in \{0, 1\}$ mod 2^i then w^2 is equal to the same $b \in \{0, 1\}$ mod 2^{i+1} for any integer $i \geq 1$. So, if w has bit decomposition $(b_{2m+l-1}, \ldots, b_0)_2$ then by repeating squaring $(2m + l - 1)$ times against w, we get an integer w_0 with bit decomposition $(0, \cdots, 0, b_0)_2$. LowerClear (w) repeats in this way to extract all lower m bits $b_0, b_1, \cdots, b_{m-1}$ of w in the form of integers $w_0 = (0, \cdots, 0, b_0)_2, w_1 = (0, \cdots, 0, b_1, 0)_2, \ldots, w_{m-1} = (0, \cdots, 0, b_{m-1}, 0, \cdots, 0)_2$ and gets the wanted $2^m z = w - \sum_{i=0}^{m-1} w_i$. UpperClear clears the upper garbage by a similar method.

Summarizing, we use the FV scheme with plaintext modulus $t' = 2^m t$ (with $t = 2^{m+l}$) to enable homomorphic evaluation on encrypted fixed point numbers $\tilde{x} = 2^{-m}x$ ($x \in \mathbb{Z}_{2^{m+l}}$). To clear lower and upper garbage involved in homomorphic multiplication of fixed point numbers, we use LowerClear and UpperClear arithmetic procedures homomorphically against the multiplied FV ciphertexts. We call our FHE scheme for fixed point numbers built in this way FX scheme. Since the FV scheme is semantically secure and fully homomorphic, our FX (which ciphertext is nothing but a FV ciphertext with enlarged plaintext modulus) is also semantically secure and fully homomorphic.

Greater-Than Bit Extraction. As an application of the FX scheme, we treat the problem of comparison of magnitude of two encrypted numbers. Suppose we have two encrypted numbers $\mathsf{Enc}(x_1)$ and $\mathsf{Enc}(x_2)$. Define a bit b to be 1 if $x_1 > x_2$ and 0 otherwise. We want to compute an encryption $\mathsf{Enc}(b)$ of the bit b given only ciphertexts $\mathsf{Enc}(x_1)$ and $\mathsf{Enc}(x_2)$ without knowing the secret key. In the literature [13,14] such problem is tackled by Greater-Than protocol based on (such as) the one given by Golle [11]. Let $D \subset \mathbb{Z}$ be a range that possible x_i's belong to. The protocol is based on the fact that if $x_1 > x_2$, there exists a positive integer i such that $x_1 = x_2 + i$. To establish security, it requires $O(|D|)$ encryptions and $O(|D|)$ homomorphic additions among them and needs interaction with secret key holder. By using the FX scheme, we show that one can compute the greater-than bit encryption $\mathsf{Enc}(b)$ given only $\mathsf{Enc}(x_1)$ and $\mathsf{Enc}(x_2)$ in polylogarithmic complexity of $|D|$, neither knowing the secret key nor interaction with secret key holder.

FHE scheme FL for floating point numbers. Using the method of greater-than bit extraction by FX, we will construct a fully homomorphic encryption scheme for floating point numbers, FL. The floating point number N is described as $N = (-1)^s f 2^e$, where $s \in \{0,1\}$ is the sign, $f \in [1,2)$ is the significant and e is the exponent of N. We will use three different (but related) FX schemes to encrypt each part of s, f and e into a ciphertext $([|s|]_s, [|f|]_f, [|e|]_e)$. In computation of floating point numbers $N = (-1)^s f 2^e$, different parts of s, f, e have influence to each other. For example, to add two floating point numbers $N = (-1)^s f 2^e$ and $N' = (-1)^{s'} f' 2^{e'}$, we need to compare e and e' to decide $e > e'$ or not. If so, we will compute $f'' = f + (0.5)^{e-e'} f'$ and if not we will compute $f'' = f' + (0.5)^{e'-e} f$. Since we can homomorphically compute a greater-than bit $e > e'$ as seen above, it is not difficult to evaluate such process homomorphically, given encryptions $([|s|]_s, [|f|]_f, [|e|]_e)$ and $([|s'|]_s, [|f'|]_f, [|e'|]_e)$ without knowing the secret key. Since the FX scheme is semantically secure and fully homomorphic, the FL scheme for floating point numbers is also semantically secure and fully homomorphic.

Related works. There are some different approaches to handle fixed-point arithmetic in homomorphic encryption schemes in the literatures. Costache, Smart, Vivek, and Waller [7] encodes fixed-point numbers as polynomials in cyclotomic rings, which enables a lower plaintext modulus. Although in contrast our method encodes point numbers only into constant terms of polynomials, our method can adapt to homomorphic SIMD operations using plaintext slots [20]. Chung and Kim [5] encodes rational numbers using continued fractions. They restrict their interest to linear multivariate polynomials.

Organization. Section 2 recalls the FV scheme as well as its basic properties. We construct the FX scheme for fixed point numbers in Sect. 3. After treating the problem of homomorphic greater-than bit extraction in Sect. 4, we construct the FL scheme for floating point numbers in Sect. 5.

2   Preliminaries

2.1   Homomorphic Encryption

A homomorphic encryption scheme is a quadruple $\mathsf{HE} = (\mathsf{Keygen}, \mathsf{Enc}, \mathsf{Dec}, \mathsf{Eval})$ of probabilistic polynomial time algorithms. Keygen generates a public key pk, a secret key sk and an evaluation key evk: $(\mathsf{pk}, \mathsf{sk}, \mathsf{evk}) \leftarrow \mathsf{Keygen}(1^n)$. Enc encrypts a plaintext $x \in \{0,1\}$ to a ciphertext c under a public key pk: $c \leftarrow \mathsf{Enc}(\mathsf{pk}, x)$. Decrypt decrypts a ciphertext c to a plaintext x by the secret key sk: $x \leftarrow \mathsf{Dec}(\mathsf{sk}, c)$. Eval applies a function $f : \{0,1\}^l \rightarrow \{0,1\}$ to given ciphertexts $c_1, \ldots, c_l$ and outputs a ciphertext c_f using the evaluation key evk: $c_f \leftarrow \mathsf{Eval}(\mathsf{evk}, f, c_1, \ldots, c_l)$.

A homomorphic encryption scheme HE is called *L-homomorphic* for $L = L(n)$ if for any function $f : \{0,1\}^l \rightarrow \{0,1\}$ given as a circuit of depth L and for any l bits $x_1, \ldots, x_l$, it holds that $\mathsf{Dec}_{\mathsf{sk}}(\mathsf{Eval}_{\mathsf{evk}}(f, c_1, \ldots, c_l)) = f(x_1, \ldots, x_l)$ for $c_i \leftarrow \mathsf{Enc}_{\mathsf{pk}}(x_i)$ $(i = 1, \ldots, l)$ except with a negligible probability. A homomorphic encryption scheme is called *fully homomorphic encryption* (FHE) scheme if it is L-homomorphic for any polynomial function $L = poly(n)$.

2.2   The FV Scheme

The FV scheme [8, 17] is an FHE scheme for congruent integers, instantiating the FHE scheme by Brakerski [2] based on the Ring LWE problem [18]. Let m be a positive integer and let $\Phi_m(X)$ be the m-th cyclotomic polynomial. The ring $R = \mathbb{Z}[X]/\Phi_m(X)$ is called the m-th cyclotomic ring. For cyclotomic integer $a = \sum_{i=0}^{n-1} a_i X^i \in R$, let $\|a\|_\infty = \max_{0 \le i < n}\{|a_i|\}$ be the infinity norm of a. Let δ be the expansion factor of R, i.e., $\delta = \sup_{a,b \in R}\{\|ab\|_\infty / (\|a\|_\infty \|b\|_\infty)\}$. The symbol $\lfloor a \rceil$ denotes the nearest cyclotomic integer (or the (coefficient wise) nearest integer coefficient polynomial) of a.

A ciphertext of FV scheme is a pair of cyclotomic integers in $R_q = \mathbb{Z}_q[X]/\Phi_m(X)$ for ciphertext modulus q and a plaintext is a cyclotomic integer in $R_t = \mathbb{Z}_t[X]/\Phi_m(X)$ for plaintext modulus t. Denote by $[\cdot]_q$ reduction modulo q into the interval $(-q/2, q/2]$. We fix an integer base w and let $l_w = \lfloor \log_w(q) \rfloor + 1$. Any cyclotomic integer $a \in R_q$ can be written as $a = \sum_{i=0}^{l_w-1} a_i w^i$ where $a_i \in R$ has coefficients in the interval $(-w/2, w/2]$. Define $\mathsf{WD}(a) = ([a_i]_w)_{i=0}^{l_w-1} \in R^{l_w}$ and $\mathsf{PO}(a) = ([aw^i]_q)_{i=0}^{l_w-1} \in R^{l_w}$. As easily verified, $\langle \mathsf{WD}(a), \mathsf{PO}(b) \rangle \equiv ab$ (mod q), where $\langle x, y \rangle = \sum_{i=0}^{l_w-1} x_i y_i$.

Keygen () :
$s \leftarrow \chi_{key}, e \leftarrow \chi_{err}, a \overset{u}{\leftarrow} R_q, b = \left[-(as + e)\right]_q$
$a \overset{u}{\leftarrow} R_q^{lw}, e \leftarrow \chi_{err}^{lw}, \boldsymbol{b} = \left[\mathsf{PO}(s^2) - (a s + e)\right]_q$
return sk $= s$, pk $= (a, b)$, evk $= (\boldsymbol{a}, \boldsymbol{b})$.
Enc $((a,b),\ x \in R_t)$:
$u \leftarrow \chi_{key}, e_1, e_2 \leftarrow \chi_{err}$, return $c = (c_0 = \left[\Delta x + bu + e_1\right]_q, c_1 = \left[au + e_2\right]_q)$
Dec $(s,\ c = (c_0, c_1))$:   return $\left[\left\lfloor \frac{t}{q}\left[c_0 + c_1 s\right]_q \right\rceil\right]_t$.
Add $(c = (c_0, c_1),\ c' = (c_0', c_1'))$: return $c_{add} = \left(\left[c_0 + c_0'\right]_q, \left[c_1 + c_1'\right]_q\right)$.
Mult $(c = (c_0, c_1),\ c' = (c_0', c_1'),\ \gamma = (\boldsymbol{a}, \boldsymbol{b}))$:
$d_0 = \left[\left\lfloor \frac{t}{q} c_0 c_0' \right\rceil\right]_q, d_1 = \left[\left\lfloor \frac{t}{q}(c_0 c_1' + c_1 c_0') \right\rceil\right]_q, d_2 = \left[\left\lfloor \frac{t}{q} c_1 c_1' \right\rceil\right]_q$
return $c_{mult} = \left(\left[d_0 + \langle \mathsf{WD}(d_2), \boldsymbol{b}\rangle\right]_q, \left[d_1 + \langle \mathsf{WD}(d_2), \boldsymbol{a}\rangle\right]_q\right)$.

Fig. 1. The FV scheme

Let χ_{key} and χ_{err} be two discrete, bounded probability distributions on R. Constants B_{key} and B_{err} denote the corresponding bounds: $\chi_{key} < B_{key}$, $\chi_{err} < B_{err}$. The symbol $x \leftarrow \chi$ denotes a random sampling of x according to distribution χ. For a finite set X, the symbol $x \overset{u}{\leftarrow} X$ denotes a uniformly random sampling of x from X.

Parameters. We parameterize FV schemes by two parameter q and t, denoting ciphertext modulus and plaintext modulus, respectively. In this paper we assume q is a power of two and t is a divisor of q for simplicity. Let integer $\Delta = q/t$ be a quotient of q by t.

Scheme Description. Figure 1 shows algorithms in the FV scheme. It is not difficult to see that the FV scheme is semantically secure under the ring-LWE assumption, that is, a pair $(a, b = -as + e) \in (R_q)^2$ sampled as in the Keygen algorithm is indistinguishable from uniformly random pair (a, b) in $(R_q)^2$. By standard hybrid argument a ciphertext (c_0, c_1) is also indistinguishable from uniformly random pair over $(R_q)^2$.

Definition 1. *The* inherent noise term v *of FV ciphertext* $c = (c_0, c_1)$ *designed for* $x \in R_t$ *is an element* $v \in R$ *of smallest norm* $\|v\|_\infty$ *satisfying* $c_0 + c_1 s = \Delta x + v + q\alpha$ *for some* $\alpha \in R$.

A fresh ciphertext (c_0, c_1) directly produced by $\mathsf{Enc}((a,b), x)$ satisfies $c_0 + c_1 s - \Delta x \equiv bu + e_1 + (au + e_2)s \equiv -eu + e_1 + e_2 \pmod q$. So, fresh ciphertexts have inherent noise terms $v = -eu + e_1 + e_2$ bounded as $\|v\|_\infty \leq V := B_{err}(1 + 2\delta B_{key})$.

Let $V_{max}^{\mathsf{FV}} = \frac{1}{2}\Delta = \frac{1}{2}\left(\frac{q}{t}\right)$. Following lemmas adapted from [1,8,17] show some basic properties of the FV scheme.

Lemma 1 (Correctness of FV scheme). *Let* v *be the inherent noise term of FV ciphertext* c *designed for* $x \in R_t$. *If* $\|v\|_\infty < V_{max}^{\mathsf{FV}}$, *then decryption works correctly, i.e.,* $\mathsf{Dec}(s, c) = [x]_t = x$.

Lemma 2 (Additive Noise of FV scheme). *Let v and v' be inherent noise terms of FV ciphertexts c and c', designed for x and $x' \in R_t$, respectively. Let v_{add} be the inherent noise term of $c_{add} = \mathsf{Add}(c, c')$ designed for $[x + x']_t \in R_t$. Then, $\|v_{add}\|_\infty \leq \|v\|_\infty + \|v'\|_\infty$.*

Lemma 3 (Multiplicative Noise of FV scheme). *Let v and v' be inherent noise terms of FV ciphertexts c and c', designed for x and $x' \in R_t$, respectively. Suppose $\|v\|_\infty, \|v'\|_\infty < V$ for some V $(< V_{max}^{\mathsf{FV}})$. Let v_{mult} be the inherent noise term of $c_{mult} \leftarrow \mathsf{Mult}(c, c')$ designed for $[xx']_t \in R_t$. Then, $\|v_{mult}\|_\infty \leq \delta t (2 + 4\delta B_{key}) V + \delta^2 B_{key}(2B_{key} + 4t^2) + 2^{-1}\delta l_w w B_{err}$.*

As a corollary of Lemmas 2 and 3, we have:

Corollary 1 (Homomorphic Noise of FV scheme). *Let f be an arithmetic circuit over R_t with L levels of multiplications. Let V be an upper bound of inherent noise terms of input FV ciphertexts c_i, designed for plaintexts x_i, for all i. Let v_f be the inherent noise term of homomorphically evaluated ciphertext $f(c_i)$ designed for $f(x_i) \in R_t$. Then, $\|v_f\|_\infty \leq C_1^L V + L C_1^{L-1} C_2$ where $C_1 \leq 2\delta t(1 + 2\delta B_{key})$, $C_2 \leq 2\delta^2 B_{key}(B_{key} + 2t^2) + 2^{-1}\delta l_w w B_{err}$.*

Let L_{dec} be the level of some circuit that evaluates decryption algorithm $\mathsf{Dec}(c, \cdot)$ with a FV ciphertext c built-in. By Lemma 1 and Corollary 1, if inequality $\Delta(= q/t) > 2(C_1^{L_{dec}} V + L_{dec} C_1^{L_{dec}-1} C_2)$ holds, we can homomorphically evaluate algorithm $\mathsf{Dec}(c, \cdot)$ using encrypted secret keys $\mathsf{Enc}(pk, s)$ and can recrypt the ciphertext c into a more noiseless new ciphertext (bootstrapping). By Lemma 4 of [2], we can implement algorithm $\mathsf{Dec}(c, \cdot)$ by some circuit of level $L_{dec} = O(\log n)$ which is independent of c. Hence the inequality can be satisfied by taking sufficiently large $q = O(n^{\log n})$ for any ciphertext c with $\delta = poly(n)$. Thus, the FV scheme will be fully homomorphic under circular security assumption (i.e., $\mathsf{Enc}(pk, \mathsf{sk} = s)$ does not leak any information about s) by taking sufficiently large $q = O(n^{\log n})$ for cyclotomic ring R with polynomial δ.

3 The Proposed Scheme FX

In this section we construct an FHE scheme that can homomorphically compute fixed point numbers, using the FV scheme as building blocks.

Let $\tilde{x}$ be a fixed point number that has l bits before point and m bits after point. We encode $\tilde{x}$ by an integer $x \in \mathbb{Z}_{2^{m+l}}$ as usual: $\tilde{x} = 2^{-m}x$. Let $t = 2^{m+l}$. Addition and multiplication of two fixed point numbers $\tilde{x} = 2^{-m}x$ and $\tilde{y} = 2^{-m}y$ are defined as

$$\tilde{x} + \tilde{y} = 2^{-m}[x + y]_t, \quad \tilde{x} \cdot \tilde{y} = 2^{-m}\left(\left[\lfloor 2^{-m}[x \cdot y]_{2^m t}\rfloor\right]_t\right).$$

We see that sum $\tilde{x} + \tilde{y}$ is encoded by integer $x + y \in \mathbb{Z}_t$. So, homomorphic addition of encrypted fixed point numbers is easy, just a homomorphic addition in underlying FV scheme. However, product $\tilde{x} \cdot \tilde{y}$ is more complicated. It is encoded by integer $\left[\left\lfloor 2^{-m}\left[x \cdot y\right]_{2^m t}\right\rfloor\right]_t$, that results from m-bit right shift of integer product $[x \cdot y]_{2^m t}$. Now our problem is distinguished: How can we homomorphically compute m-bit right shift of given encrypted $(2m + l)$-bit integers?

Let $\mathsf{FV}(2^m t)$ be the FV scheme of ciphertext modulus q and plaintext modulus $2^m t$. Using $\mathsf{FV}(2^m t)$, we construct a fully homomorphic encryption scheme for fixed point numbers, FX, that can homomorphically compute the m-bit right shift of encrypted encoding integers.

Parameters. The FX scheme is parameterized by three parameters q, m and l. The parameter q denotes ciphertext modulus. The parameter l denotes bit-length of fixed point number before point and the parameter m denotes bit-length of fixed point number after point. Let $t = 2^{m+l}$. We assume q, m and l are all powers of two and t is a divisor of q. Let integer $\Delta = q/t$ be a quotient of q by t.

Scheme Description. A fixed point number $\tilde{x} = 2^{-m}x$ to be encrypted is encoded by an integer $x \in \mathbb{Z}_t$ which we identify with a constant polynomial $x \in R_t$ in the cyclotomic ring. The FX scheme consists of the algorithms in Fig. 2. Note that FX ciphertexts of parameter (q, m, l) are nothing but the $\mathsf{FV}(2^m t)$ ciphertexts, and encryption/decryption algorithms are the same as corresponding algorithms of $\mathsf{FV}(2^m t)$ scheme. (More precisely, the decryption algorithm is slightly lighter than the original $\mathsf{FV}(2^m t)$ scheme, since $\mathsf{FX}(q, m, l)$ only recovers $(l + m)$-bit integers rather than $(l + 2m)$-bit integers in $\mathsf{FV}(2^m t)$.) Especially, the FX scheme is also semantically secure and fully homomorphic with suitable choice of parameters that makes the underlying $\mathsf{FV}(2^m t)$ scheme so. The difference is in the way of homomorphic evaluation.

Let c be a FX ciphertext of parameter (q, m, l). By definition of Enc, initially it is produced as an encryption of some constant polynomial $x \in R_t$ that encodes fixed point number $\tilde{x} = 2^{-m}x$ using $\mathsf{FV}(2^m t)$ scheme. Here note that bit length of plaintext integer x is only $l + m$ (l bits before point and m bits after point), but $\mathsf{FV}(2^m t)$ scheme treats much longer plaintext integer of $l + 2m$ bits. In fact, Dec algorithm only returns the least $l + m$ bits of recovered integer by $\mathsf{FV}(2^m t)$. That is, the FX scheme has m bits more in plaintext space than finally required for decryption. FX scheme uses this room of m bits in plaintext space in order to homomorphically compute the m-bit right-shift of encrypted integer.

To homomorphically compute such m-bit right-shift, algorithms LowerClear and UpperClear are useful. Let c be an $\mathsf{FV}(2^m t)$ ciphertext of some $(l + 2m)$-bit integer $w = x + 2^m z \in R_{2^m t}$ (x is the least m bits of w and z is the significant $(l + m)$-bit of w). Before m-bit right-shifting w homomorphically in the ciphertext c, we need to clear the least m-bit integer x of w, because without it the term $2^{-m}x$ should cause a significant noise in the resulting ciphertext. As verified in Lemma 5, the least m-bit x (lower garbage) of w will be cleared by LowerClearPlain algorithm in Fig. 3.

As directly verified, LowerClear (c) procedure (for c encrypting $w = x + 2^m z$) in Fig. 2 is a homomorphic version of LowerClearPlain (w) procedure, that computes $2^m z$ given $w = x + 2^m z$. Here we add some remark about this. Suppose

$$\begin{array}{|l|}
\hline
\textsf{Keygen ()} : \text{return } (\textsf{sk} = s, \textsf{pk} = (a,b), \textsf{evk} = (\boldsymbol{a},\boldsymbol{b})) \leftarrow \textsf{FV}(2^m t).\textsf{Keygen}() \\
\hline
\textsf{Enc } (\textsf{pk} = (a,b),\ x \in R_t) : \text{return } c = (c_0, c_1) \leftarrow \textsf{FV}(2^m t).\textsf{Enc}((a,b), x). \\
\hline
\textsf{Dec } (s,\ c) : \text{return } \left[\textsf{FV}(2^m t).\textsf{Dec}(s,c)\right]_t. \\
\hline
\textsf{Add } (c,\ c') : \text{return } c_{add} \leftarrow \textsf{FV}(2^m t).\textsf{Add}(c, c'). \\
\hline
\textsf{Mult } (c,\ c',\ \textsf{evk} = \gamma) : \\
\quad \tilde{c} \leftarrow \textsf{FV}(2^m t).\textsf{Mult}(c, c', \gamma),\ d = (d_0, d_1) \leftarrow \textsf{LowerClear}(\tilde{c}), \\
\quad e = \left(\left[\left\lfloor \frac{1}{2^m} d_0 \right\rceil\right]_q, \left[\left\lfloor \frac{1}{2^m} d_1 \right\rceil\right]_q\right) \\
\quad \text{return } c_{mult} \leftarrow \textsf{UpperClear}(e). \\
\hline
\textsf{LowerClear } (c) : \\
\quad d \leftarrow \textsf{FV}(2^m t).\textsf{Enc}_{\textsf{pk}}(0) \\
\quad \text{For } i \in [1..m]: \\
\quad\quad d_i \leftarrow \textsf{FV}(2^m t).\textsf{Add}(c, -d) \\
\quad\quad \text{For } j \in [1..(2m + l - i)]:\ d_i \leftarrow \textsf{FV}(\frac{2^m t}{2^{i-1}}).\textsf{Mult}(d_i, d_i) \\
\quad\quad d \leftarrow \textsf{FV}(2^m t).\textsf{Add}(d, d_i) \\
\quad \text{return } \textsf{FV}(2^m t).\textsf{Add}(c, -d). \\
\hline
\textsf{UpperClear } (c) : \\
\quad d \leftarrow \textsf{FV}(2^m t).\textsf{Enc}_{\textsf{pk}}(0) \\
\quad \text{For } i \in [1..(m + l)]: \\
\quad\quad d_i \leftarrow \textsf{FV}(2^m t).\textsf{Add}(c, -d) \\
\quad\quad \text{For } j \in [1..(2m + l - i)]:\ d_i \leftarrow \textsf{FV}(\frac{2^m t}{2^{i-1}}).\textsf{Mult}(d_i, d_i) \\
\quad\quad d \leftarrow \textsf{FV}(2^m t).\textsf{Add}(d, d_i) \\
\quad \text{return } d. \\
\hline
\end{array}$$

Fig. 2. The FX scheme

$$\begin{array}{|l|}
\hline
\textsf{LowerClearPlain } (w = x + 2^m z) : \\
\quad g \leftarrow 0 \\
\quad \text{For } i \in [1..m]: \\
\quad\quad w_i \leftarrow w - g,\ w_i = \left(\left(\tfrac{1}{2}\right)^{i-1} w_i\right)^{2^{2m+l-i}} \cdot 2^{i-1} \\
\quad\quad \{w_i \text{ is divisible by } 2^{i-1}\ (\text{See the proof of Lemma 5})\} \\
\quad\quad g = g + w_i \\
\quad \text{return } w - g. \quad \{= 2^m z\} \\
\hline
\end{array}$$

Fig. 3. The LowerClearPlain algorithm

a constant polynomial $x \in R_{2^m t}$ is divisible by 2^i ($i \geq 0$). Then, its encryption $c = (c_0, c_1)$ by $\textsf{FV}(2^m t)$ ($=\textsf{FX}(q, m, l)$) scheme will satisfy

$$c_0 + c_1 s = \frac{q}{2^m t} x + v + q\alpha = \frac{q}{2^{m-i}t} \frac{x}{2^i} + v + q\alpha$$

with some small noise $v \in R$ and $\alpha \in R$. This means that when plaintext integer x is divisible by 2^i, its ciphertext $c = (c_0, c_1)$ is nothing but the ciphertext of $\frac{x}{2^i}$ w.r.t. $\textsf{FV}(2^{m-i}t)$. So homomorphic version of the step:

$$- w_i = \left(\left(\tfrac{1}{2}\right)^{i-1} w_i\right)^{2^{2m+l-i}} \cdot 2^{i-1}$$

in Fig. 3 corresponds to the step:

– For $j \in [1..(2m + l - i)]$: $d_i \leftarrow \mathsf{FV}(\frac{2^m t}{2^{i-1}}).\mathsf{Mult}(d_i, d_i)$

in the LowerClear algorithm in Fig. 2. The resulting ciphertext d_i will be treated as a $\mathsf{FV}(2^m t)$ ciphertext.

Now we have cleared the lower garbage x from the ciphertext c that encrypts $w = x + 2^m z$, resulting a ciphertext d that encrypts $2^m z$. Then we simply divide each coefficients of d by 2^m and get a ciphertext e of $u = z + ty$ with some integer y. (Recall that our plaintext space is $2m + l$ bits. So the term $ty = 2^{2m+l}/2^m \cdot y$ should appear with some y due to the division by 2^m.) Note that y is the significant m bits of $z + ty$ (upper garbage). As in the case of LowerClear, we use UpperClear algorithm in Fig. 2 to clear the upper garbage y from $u = z + ty$, that is a homomorphic version of UpperClearPlain algorithm in Fig. 4.

UpperClearPlain $(u = z + ty)$:
  $r \leftarrow 0$
  For $i \in [1..(m + l)]$: $u_i \leftarrow u - r$, $u_i = \left(\left(\frac{1}{2} \right)^{i-1} u_i \right)^{2^{2m+l-i}} \cdot 2^{i-1}$, $r = r + u_i$.
  return r $\{= z\}$

Fig. 4. The UpperClearPlain algorithm

Now we turn to formal treatment.

Definition 2. *The* inherent noise term v *of* FX *ciphertext* $c = (c_0, c_1)$ *designed for* $x \in R_{2^m t}$ *is the term* v *of smallest norm* $\|v\|_\infty$ *satisfying* $c_0 + c_1 s = \Delta 2^{-m} x + v + q\alpha$ *for some* $\alpha \in R$.

Let $V_{max} = \frac{1}{2} \Delta 2^{-m} = \frac{1}{2} \left(\frac{q}{2^m t} \right)$. Immediately from Lemma 1,

Lemma 4. *Let* v *be the inherent noise term of* FX *ciphertext* c *designed for* $x \in R_t$. *If* $\|v\|_\infty < V_{max}$, *decryption works correctly, i.e.,* $\mathsf{Dec}(s, c) = [x]_t = x$.

Next we examine correctness of the LowerClear and UpperClear algorithms. For C_1 and C_2 given in Corollary 1, it holds that:

Lemma 5 (Lower Clear). *Let* $\tilde{v}$ *be the inherent noise term of* FX *ciphertext* $\tilde{c}$ *designed for constant polynomial* $w = x + 2^m z \in R_{2^m t}$ *with* $x \in R_{2^m}$ *and* $z \in R_t$. *Let* v *be the inherent noise term of the ciphertext* $c \leftarrow \mathsf{LowerClear}(\tilde{c})$ *designed for constant polynomial* $2^m z \in 2^m R_{2^m t}$. *Then,* $\|v\|_\infty \leq \|\tilde{v}\|_\infty + V_{\mathsf{LC}}$, *where* $V_{\mathsf{LC}} = C_1^{2m+l-1} V + LC_1^{2m+l-2} C_2$.

Proof. Since algorithm LowerClear is a homomorphic version of algorithm LowerClearPlain, first, we show that LowerClearPlain computes $2^m z$ given $w = x + 2^m z$. The key observation is the following simple fact [10, 19]: if w is equal to $b \in \{0,1\} \bmod 2^i$ then w^2 is equal to the same $b \bmod 2^{i+1}$ for any integer $i \geq 1$. So, if w has bit decomposition $(b_{2m+l-1}, \ldots, b_0)_2$ then by repeating squaring $(2m + l - 1)$ times against it, we get w_0 with bit decomposition $(0, \cdots, 0, b_0)_2$. By repeating the procedure for $w - w_0 = (b_{2m+l-1}, \cdots, b_1, 0)_2$, we get w_1 with bit decomposition $(0, \cdots, 0, b_1, 0)_2$: Multiply $w - w_0$ by $\frac{1}{2}$ to get $(0, b_{2m+l-1}, \cdots, b_2, b_1)_2$, repeat squaring $(2m + l - 2)$ times against it to get $(0, \cdots, 0, b_1)_2$, and multiply back it by 2 to get $(0, \cdots, 0, b_1, 0)_2$. LowerClearPlain (w) repeats in this way to extract all least m bits $b_0, b_1, \cdots, b_{m-1}$ of w in the form of integers $w_0 = (0, \cdots, 0, b_0)_2, w_1 = (0, \cdots, 0, b_1, 0)_2, \ldots, w_{m-1} = (0, \cdots, 0, b_{m-1}, 0, \cdots, 0)_2$ and gets the least m-bit x of w as $x = \sum_{i=0}^{m-1} w_i$. Then we get desired $2^m z = w - x$. Since LowerClearPlain has $2m + l - 1$ levels of nested multiplications, by Corollary 1 we get the claimed noise bound V_{LC} on the noise occurred by its homomorphic evaluation LowerClear. □

Similarly, we have:

Lemma 6 (Upper Clear). *Let $\tilde{v}$ be the inherent noise term of FX ciphertext $\tilde{c}$ designed for constant polynomial $u = z + ty \in R_{2^m t}$ with $z \in R_t$ and $y \in R_{2^m}$. Let v be the inherent noise term of the ciphertext $c \leftarrow \mathsf{UpperClear}(\tilde{c})$ designed for constant polynomial $z \in R_t$. Then, $\|v\|_\infty \leq \|\tilde{v}\|_\infty + V_{UC}$, where $V_{UC} = C_1^{2m+l-1} V + LC_1^{2m+l-2} C_2$.*

Proposition 1 (Additive Noise of FX scheme). *Let v and v' be inherent noise terms of FX ciphertexts c and c', designed for x and $x' \in R_t$, respectively. Let v_{add} be the inherent noise term of $c_{add} = \mathsf{Add}(c, c')$ designed for $[x + x']_t \in R_t$. Then, $\|v_{add}\|_\infty \leq \|v\|_\infty + \|v'\|_\infty$.*

Proof. This is a restatement of Lemma 2. □

Proposition 2 (Multiplicative Noise of FX scheme). *Let v and v' be inherent noise terms of FX ciphertexts c and c', designed for x and $x' \in R_{2^{m+l}}$, respectively. Suppose $\|v\|_\infty, \|v'\|_\infty < V$. Let v_{mult} be the inherent noise term of $c_{mult} \leftarrow \mathsf{Mult}(c, c', \mathsf{evk})$ designed for $\left[\lfloor 2^{-m} [xx']_{2^m t} \rceil\right]_t \in R_t$. Then, $\|v_{mult}\|_\infty \leq \delta t(2 + 4\delta B_{key})V + \delta^2 B_{key}(B_{key} + 4 \cdot 2^m t^2) + l_w \delta w B_{err} + 2^{-m} V_{LC} + V_{UC}$.*

Proof. We use notation in Fig. 2. For $\tilde{c} = \mathsf{FV}(2^m t).\mathsf{Mult}(c, c', \gamma)$ by Lemma 3 we have $\tilde{c}_0 + \tilde{c}_1 s = \Delta 2^{-m} [xx']_{2^m t} + v + q\alpha$ with $\|v\|_\infty \leq \delta 2^m t(2 + 4\delta B_{key})V + \delta^2 B_{key}(2B_{key} + 4 \cdot 2^{2m} t^2) + 2^{-1} \delta l_w w B_{err}$.

Then, by Lemma 5 for $d \leftarrow \mathsf{LowerClear}(\tilde{c})$ we have

$$d_0 + d_1 s = \Delta 2^{-m} \left(\lfloor \frac{[xx']_{2^m t}}{2^m} \rfloor 2^m \right) + v + w + q\alpha'$$

with $\|w\|_\infty \le V_{\mathsf{LC}}$. Dividing by 2^m,

$$\frac{1}{2^m}d_0 + \frac{1}{2^m}d_1 s = \Delta 2^{-m}\left(\left\lfloor \frac{[xx']_{2^m t}}{2^m}\right\rfloor\right) + \frac{v}{2^m} + \frac{w}{2^m} + \frac{q}{2^m}\alpha'$$

$$= \Delta 2^{-m}\left(\left\lfloor \frac{[xx']_{2^m t}}{2^m}\right\rfloor + t\alpha'\right) + \frac{v}{2^m} + \frac{w}{2^m}.$$

Hence, rounded $e = \left(\left[\left\lfloor \frac{1}{2^m}d_0\right\rfloor\right]_q, \left[\left\lfloor \frac{1}{2^m}d_1\right\rfloor\right]_q\right)$ must satisfy

$$e_0 + e_1 s = \Delta 2^{-m}\left(\left\lfloor \frac{[xx']_{2^m t}}{2^m}\right\rfloor + t\alpha'\right) + \frac{v}{2^m} + \frac{w}{2^m} + w'$$

with $\|w'\|_\infty \le \frac{1}{2}(1 + \delta B_{key})$. Lemma 6 shows for $c_{mult} = \mathsf{UpperClear}(e)$,

$$c_{mult,0} + c_{mult,1} s = \Delta 2^{-m}\cdot\left[\left\lfloor \frac{[xx']_{2^m t}}{2^m}\right\rfloor\right]_t + \frac{v}{2^m} + \frac{w}{2^m} + w' + w'' + q\beta \text{ with } \|w''\|_\infty \le V_{\mathsf{UC}}.$$

Accumulated noise $z = \frac{v}{2^m} + \frac{w}{2^m} + w' + w''$ satisfies

$$\|z\|_\infty \le 2^{-m}\left(\delta 2^m t(2 + 4\delta B_{key})V + \delta^2 B_{key}(2B_{key} + 4\cdot 2^{2m}t^2) + 2^{-1}\delta l_w w B_{err}\right)$$
$$+ 2^{-m}V_{\mathsf{LC}} + 2^{-1}(1 + \delta B_{key}) + V_{\mathsf{UC}}$$
$$\le \delta t(2 + 4\delta B_{key})V + \delta^2 B_{key}(B_{key} + 4\cdot 2^m t^2) + l_w \delta w B_{err} + 2^{-m}V_{\mathsf{LC}} + V_{\mathsf{UC}}$$

$\square$

By Propositions 1 and 2 we have

Theorem 1. *The* FX *scheme of parameter* q, l, m *can fully homomorphically compute additions and multiplications of encrypted fixed point numbers* $\tilde{x} = 2^{-m}x$ *for* $x \in \mathbb{Z}_{2^{m+l}}$ *with suitable choice of parameters that makes the underlying* FV *scheme (of parameter* $q, 2^{2m+l}$*) fully homomorphic. Here, addition of fixed point numbers* $\tilde{x} = 2^{-m}x$ *and* $\tilde{y} = 2^{-m}y$ *is such that* $\tilde{x} + \tilde{y} = 2^{-m}[x + y]_{2^{m+l}}$ *and their multiplication is such that* $\tilde{x}\cdot\tilde{y} = 2^{-m}\left(\left[\left\lfloor 2^{-m}[x\cdot y]_{2^{2m+l}}\right\rfloor\right]_{2^{m+l}}\right).$

Efficiency. We estimate efficiency of homomorphic operations of FX scheme of parameter q, l, m. Addition $\mathsf{Add}(c, c')$ is done by one addition of $\mathsf{FV}(q, 2^m t)$ scheme. We estimate complexity of multiplication $\mathsf{Mult}(c, c', \gamma)$ in terms of "multiplicative depth" and "multiplicative number". The multiplicative depth means the required depth of nested multiplications of the underlying FV scheme to perform the target operation. It determines noise growth due to the target operation and larger noise requires larger ciphertext modulus. Thus, the multiplicative depth dominates space complexity of the target operation. On a while, the multiplicative number means the required total number of multiplications of the underlying FV scheme to perform the target operation. It dominates time complexity of the target operation. By inspection, complexity of $\mathsf{Mult}(c, c', \gamma)$ operation is dominated by $\mathsf{UpperClear}(e)$. The multiplicative depth of $\mathsf{UpperClear}$ is $2m + l - 1$ and the multiplicative number of $\mathsf{UpperClear}$ is $(2m + l - 1) + \cdots + (m + l) = \frac{1}{2}(3m + 2l - 1)(m + l)$. Thus, roughly estimated, space and time complexity of multiplication $\mathsf{Mult}(c, c', \gamma)$ is linear and quadratic to the logarithmic of precision of fixed point numbers, respectively.

4   Greater-Than Bit Extraction

As an application of our FX scheme, we consider the problem of comparison of magnitude of two encrypted numbers. Suppose we have two encrypted numbers $\mathsf{Enc}(x_1)$ and $\mathsf{Enc}(x_2)$. Define a bit b to be 1 if $x_1 > x_2$ and 0 otherwise. We want to compute an encryption $\mathsf{Enc}(b)$ of the bit b given only ciphertexts $\mathsf{Enc}(x_1)$ and $\mathsf{Enc}(x_2)$ without knowing the secret key. In the literature [13,14] such problem is tackled by Greater-Than protocol based on (such as) the one given by Golle [11]. Let $D \subset \mathbb{Z}$ be a range that possible x_i's belong to. Their protocol is based on the fact that if $x_1 > x_2$, there exists a positive integer i such that $x_1 = x_2+i$. To establish security, the protocol requires $O(|D|)$ encryptions and $O(|D|)$ homomorphic additions among them and needs an interaction with secret key holder. We show that, by using the FX scheme, we can compute the greater-than bit encryption $\mathsf{Enc}(b)$ given only $\mathsf{Enc}(x_1)$ and $\mathsf{Enc}(x_2)$ in polylogarithmic complexity of $|D|$, neither knowing the secret key nor interaction with secret key holder.

First, we describe procedure $\mathsf{MSb}(c)$, that computes an encryption of the most significant bit of $x \in R_t$, given a $\mathsf{FX}(q,l,m)$ ciphertext c of some fixed point number $\tilde{x} = 2^{-m}x$. The point is that one can multiply any fixed point numbers by 0.5 in FX scheme. First it homomorphically extracts the msb b of x in the form $y = (b,0,\ldots,0)_2$ using similar method as $\mathsf{UpperClear}(c)$. Then, it repeats taking half of y homomorphically, i.e., computing $0.5 \times \mathsf{Enc}(y)$, until we get an encryption of $\mathsf{MSb}(x) = (0.5)^{l-1}y = (0,\ldots,0,b,0,\ldots,0)_2$ (here, 0 repeat m times after b) that encodes a fixed point number $b.0$, as desired. Figure 5 gives a description of MSb.

Using $\mathsf{MSb}(\cdot)$, it is straightforward to compute an encryption of greater-than bit b indicating $x_1 > x_2$, given $c_1 = \mathsf{Enc}(x_1)$ and $c_2 = \mathsf{Enc}(x_2)$. Basically it simply computes $\mathsf{MSb}(c_2 - c_1)$. If x_1 and x_2 represent signed numbers, we need

---

$\mathsf{MSb}\,(c, k = 0)$: {returns encryption of $b.0$ for the $(l+m-k)$-th bit b of x $(0 \leq k < l)$.}
 $d \leftarrow \mathsf{FV}(2^m t).\mathsf{Enc}_{\mathsf{pk}}(0)$
 For $i \in [1..(m+l-k)]$:
  $d_i \leftarrow \mathsf{FV}(2^m t).\mathsf{Add}(c, -d)$
  For $j \in [1..(2m+l-i)]$: $d_i \leftarrow \mathsf{FV}(\frac{2^m t}{2^{i-1}}).\mathsf{Mult}(d_i, d_i)$
  $d \leftarrow \mathsf{FV}(2^m t).\mathsf{Add}(d, d_i)$
 $d \leftarrow d_{m+l-k}, h \leftarrow \mathsf{FX}.\mathsf{Enc}(2^{m-1})$ {h encrypts "0.5"}
 Repeat $l - 1 - k$ times: $d \leftarrow h \cdot d$ {taking half of d}
 return d.

$\mathsf{GTb}\,(c_1, c_2)$: {returns an encryption of $b.0$ where a bit b is 1 if $x_1 > x_2$ or 0 otherwise}
 $one \leftarrow \mathsf{FX}.\mathsf{Enc}(2^m)$ {ciphertext one encrypts "1.0"}
 $d_1 \leftarrow \mathsf{MSb}(c_2 - c_1), d_2 \leftarrow \mathsf{MSb}(c_2), s_0 \leftarrow \mathsf{MSb}(c_1), s_1 = d_2$
 $same\_sign \leftarrow s_0 \cdot s_1 + (one - s_0) \cdot (one - s_1)$
 {$same\_sign$ encrypts 1.0 if x_1 and x_2 have the same sign, or encrypts 0.0 otherwise}
 return $d \leftarrow same\_sign \cdot d_1 + (one - same\_sign) \cdot d_2$.

Fig. 5. The MSb and GTb algorithms

also to take care of their signs. If x_1 and x_2 have the same sign, the greater-than bit b is equal to $\mathsf{MSb}(x_2 - x_1)$. Otherwise, $b = \mathsf{MSb}(x_2)$. Figure 5 gives also a description of GTb algorithm, in which $\mathsf{FX.Add}(c, c')$ (or $\mathsf{FX.Mult}(c, c')$) is simply written as $c + c'$ (or $c \cdot c'$, respectively).

$\mathsf{MSb}(c)$ needs $(m+l)^2$ Mult of the underlying FV scheme. So $\mathsf{GTb}(c_1, c_2)$ needs roughly $3(m + l)^2$ Mult of the FV scheme, that is polylogarithmic $\mathrm{polylog}(|D|)$ of the number of possible plaintexts $|D| = 2^{m+l}$.

5   The Proposed Scheme FL

In this section, we construct a fully homomorphic encryption scheme for floating point numbers, FL, using the GTb algorithm by FX. A floating point number N is written as $N = (-1)^s f 2^e$, where $s \in \{0, 1\}$ is the sign, $f \in [1, 2)$ is the significand and $e \in \mathbb{Z}$ is the exponent of N. Product $N'' = (-1)^{s''} f'' 2^{e''}$ of two floating point numbers $N = (-1)^s f 2^e$ and $N' = (-1)^{s'} f' 2^{e'}$ is computed as follows. The new sign s'' is XOR of signs s and s', i.e. $s'' = (1 - s)s' + (1 - s')s$. Significands are multiplied and exponents are added, $f'' = f f'$ and $e'' = e + e'$. If $f'' > 2$, we need to normalize the result as $f'' = f''/2$ and $e'' = e'' + 1$.

Computation of sum $N'' = (-1)^{s''} f'' 2^{e''}$ of two floating point numbers $N = (-1)^s f 2^e$ and $N' = (-1)^{s'} f' 2^{e'}$ is more complicated since we need to adjust the point position and to consider several cases as follows.

Add_{00}: If $s = s'$ and $e > e'$, let $s'' = s$, $f'' = f + 2^{e'-e} f'$, and $e'' = e$. If $f'' > 2$, let $f'' = f''/2$ and $e'' = e'' + 1$.

Add_{01}: If $s = s'$ and $e \leq e'$, let $s'' = s$, $f'' = 2^{e-e'} f + f'$, and $e'' = e'$. If $f'' > 2$, let $f'' = f''/2$ and $e'' = e'' + 1$.

Add_{11}: If $s \neq s'$ and $e > e'$, let $s'' = s$, $f'' = f - 2^{e'-e} f'$, and $e'' = e$. While $f'' < 1$, do $f'' = 2f''$, $e'' = e'' - 1$.

Add_{12}: If $s \neq s'$ and $e < e'$, let $s'' = s'$, $f'' = f' - 2^{e-e'} f$, and $e'' = e'$. While $f'' < 1$, do $f'' = 2f''$, $e'' = e'' - 1$.

Add_{101}: If $s \neq s'$, $e = e'$ and $f > f'$, let $s'' = s$, $f'' = f - f'$, $e'' = e$. While $f'' < 1$, do $f'' = 2f''$, $e'' = e'' - 1$.

Add_{102}: If $s \neq s'$, $e = e'$ and $f < f'$, let $s'' = s'$, $f'' = f' - f$, and $e'' = e'$. While $f'' < 1$, do $f'' = 2f''$, $e'' = e'' - 1$.

Add_{100}: If $s \neq s'$, $e = e'$ and $f = f'$, let $s'' = 0$, $f'' = 1.0$, $e'' = 0$.

5.1   The Scheme FL

Parameters. Consider a floating point number $N = (-1)^s f 2^e$. The FL scheme is parameterized by three parameters q, m and l. The parameter q is the ciphertext modulus. Parameters m and l are such that $1 + m$ is the bit-length of significand f and l is the bit-length of exponent e (excluding the sign-bit).

Building blocks. The scheme FL encrypts each part of sign s, significand f and exponent e of a floating point number N into a triple of ciphertexts $([|s|]_s, [|f|]_f, [|e|]_e)$, using three FX schemes FXs, FXf and FXe that share a same ciphertext modulus q and a same key pair $(\mathsf{pk}, \mathsf{sk})$.

- FXs : $\mathsf{FX}(q, 1, 0)$ scheme for the sign s
- FXf : $\mathsf{FX}(q, 2, m)$ scheme for the significand f
- FXe : $\mathsf{FX}(q, l + 1, 1)$ scheme for the exponent e

Although bit-length of the significand f is $1 + m$, we use $\mathsf{FX}(q, 2, m)$ scheme for f to take care of carries that occurs among addition $f + f'$. Similarly, we use $\mathsf{FX}(q, l + 1, 1)$ scheme for the exponent e of bit-length l, taking care of its sign.

Scheme Description. Figure 6 shows the first part, i.e. Keygen, Enc and Dec algorithms, of our FL scheme.

Keygen () : return $(\mathsf{sk} = s, \mathsf{pk} = (a, b), \mathsf{evk} = (a, b)) \leftarrow \mathsf{FXs.Keygen}()$.
{ The key $(\mathsf{sk}, \mathsf{pk}, \mathsf{evk})$ will be shared among the three schemes FXs, FXf and FXe. }
Enc (pk, $N = (s, f, e) \in R_2 \times R_{2^{2+m}} \times R_{2^{l+2}}$) :
$[|s|]_s \leftarrow \mathsf{FXs.Enc}(\mathsf{pk}, s), \quad [|f|]_f \leftarrow \mathsf{FXf.Enc}(\mathsf{pk}, f), \quad [|e|]_e \leftarrow \mathsf{FXe.Enc}(\mathsf{pk}, e)$
return $c = ([|s|]_s, [|f|]_f, [|e|]_e)$.
Dec (sk, $c = ([|s|]_s, [|f|]_f, [|e|]_e)$) :
$s \leftarrow \mathsf{FXs.Dec}(\mathsf{sk}, [|s|]_s), \quad f \leftarrow \mathsf{FXf.Dec}(\mathsf{sk}, [|f|]_f), \quad e \leftarrow \mathsf{FXe.Dec}(\mathsf{sk}, [|e|]_e)$
return $N = (s, f, e)$.

Fig. 6. The first part of FL algorithms

Conversion. Note that we can publicly and efficiently convert ciphertexts, keeping its underlying plaintext unchanged, between FX schemes that share a same ciphertext modulus q and a same key pair $(\mathsf{pk}, \mathsf{sk})$. In fact, suppose two schemes $\mathsf{FX}(q, l, m)$ and $\mathsf{FX}(q, l', m')$ share a same ciphertext modulus q and a same key pair $(\mathsf{pk}, \mathsf{sk})$. Let $c = (c_0, c_1)$ be a ciphertext in $\mathsf{FX}(q, l, m)$ scheme that encrypts $x \in R_t$: $c_0 + c_1 s \equiv \frac{q}{2^{2m+l}} x + v \pmod{q}$. Multiplying c by $2^{2(m-m')+(l-l')}$ homomorphically, we get a new ciphertext $d = (d_0, d_1)$ satisfying $d_0 + d_1 s \equiv \frac{q}{2^{2m'+l'}} x + v' \pmod{q}$ that encrypts $x \in R_{t'}$ as a ciphertext in $\mathsf{FX}(q, l', m')$ scheme. Here note that we can multiply c by $2^{2(m-m')+(l-l')}$ homomorphically, even if $2(m - m') + (l - l')$ is a negative integer, since we are using the FX scheme that can treat an encryption of "0.5".

Figure 7 shows the second part, i.e. Mult and Add algorithms, of FL scheme, in which conversions between, say $[|b|]_e$ and $[|b|]_f$, are implicit.

A ciphertext of the FL scheme of parameter (q, m, l) is just a triple of ciphertexts of three FX schemes that share a same ciphertext modulus q and a same key pair $(\mathsf{pk}, \mathsf{sk})$. Recall among those three FX schemes, ciphertexts in one scheme can be publicly converted into another scheme ciphertext, keeping its underlying plaintext unchanged. So, we can view the triple of ciphertexts just a set of

Mult $(c = ([|s|]_s, [|f|]_f, [|e|]_e), \ c' = ([|s'|]_s, [|f'|]_f, [|e'|]_e))$:
$[|s''|]_s \leftarrow [|1.0 - s|]_s \cdot [|s'|]_s + [|s|]_s \cdot [|1.0 - s'|]_s, \ [|f''|]_f \leftarrow [|f|]_f \cdot [|f'|]_f, \ [|e''|]_e \leftarrow [|e|]_e + [|e'|]_e$
$[|b|]_f \leftarrow \mathsf{MSb}([|f''|]_f) \quad \{\text{the } m{+}2\text{-th bit of } f''\}$
$[|f''|]_f \leftarrow [|b|]_f \cdot [|0.5|]_f \cdot [|f''|]_f + [|1.0 - b|]_f \cdot [|f''|]_f,$
$[|e''|]_e \leftarrow [|b|]_e \cdot [|e'' + 1.0|]_e + [|1.0 - b|]_e \cdot [|e''|]_e$
return $c'' = ([|s''|]_s, [|f''|]_f, [|e''|]_e)$.

Add $(c = ([|s|]_s, [|f|]_f, [|e|]_e), \ c' = ([|s'|]_s, [|f'|]_f, [|e'|]_e))$:
$[|s''|]_s \leftarrow [|s|]_s \cdot [|s'|]_s + [|1.0 - s|]_s \cdot [|1.0 - s'|]_s$, return $\mathsf{IfThenElse}([|s''|], \mathsf{Add}_0(c, c'), \mathsf{Add}_1(c, c'))$.

Add_0 $(c = ([|s|]_s, [|f|]_f, [|e|]_e), \ c' = ([|s'|]_s, [|f'|]_f, [|e'|]_e))$: $\quad \{s = s'\}$
$[|b|]_e \leftarrow \mathsf{GTb}([|e|]_e, [|e'|]_e), \ ([|s''|]_s, [|f''|]_f, [|e''|]_e) \leftarrow \mathsf{IfTenElse}([|b|], \mathsf{Add}_{00}(c, c'), \mathsf{Add}_{01}(c, c'))$
$[|d|]_f \leftarrow \mathsf{MSb}([|f''|]_f) \quad \{\text{the } m{+}2\text{-th bit of } f''\}$
$[|f''|]_f \leftarrow [|d|]_f \cdot [|0.5|]_f \cdot [|f''|]_f + [|1.0 - d|]_f \cdot [|f''|]_f,$
$[|e''|]_e \leftarrow [|d|]_e \cdot [|e'' + 1.0|]_e + [|1.0 - d|]_e \cdot [|e''|]_e$, return $c'' = ([|s''|]_s, [|f''|]_f, [|e''|]_e)$.

Add_{00} $(c = ([|s|]_s, [|f|]_f, [|e|]_e), \ c' = ([|s'|]_s, [|f'|]_f, [|e'|]_e))$: $\quad \{s = s', e > e'\}$
$[|s''|]_s \leftarrow [|s|]_s, \ [|e''|]_e \leftarrow [|e|]_e, \ [|f''|]_f \leftarrow [|f|]_f + \mathsf{RightShift}([|f'|]_f, [|e - e'|]_e)$
return $c'' = ([|s''|]_s, [|f''|]_f, [|e''|]_e)$.

Add_{01} $(c = ([|s|]_s, [|f|]_f, [|e|]_e), \ c' = ([|s'|]_s, [|f'|]_f, [|e'|]_e))$: $\quad \{s = s', e \leq e'\}$
$[|s''|]_s \leftarrow [|s|]_s, \ [|e''|]_e \leftarrow [|e'|]_e, \ [|f''|]_f \leftarrow [|f'|]_f + \mathsf{RightShift}([|f|]_f, [|e' - e|]_e)$
return $c'' = ([|s''|]_s, [|f''|]_f, [|e''|]_e)$.

Add_1 $(c = ([|s|]_s, [|f|]_f, [|e|]_e), \ c' = ([|s'|]_s, [|f'|]_f, [|e'|]_e))$: $\quad \{s \neq s'\}$
$[|b_e|]_e \leftarrow \mathsf{GTb}([|e|]_e, [|e'|]_e), \ c'' \leftarrow \mathsf{IfThenElse}([|b_e|], \mathsf{Add}_{11}(c, c'), \mathsf{Add}_{1a}(c, c'))$
return $\mathsf{Normalize}(c'')$.

Add_{11} $(c = ([|s|]_s, [|f|]_f, [|e|]_e), \ c' = ([|s'|]_s, [|f'|]_f, [|e'|]_e))$: $\quad \{s \neq s', e > e'\}$
$[|s''|]_s \leftarrow [|s|]_s, \ [|e''|]_e \leftarrow [|e|]_e, \ [|f''|]_f \leftarrow [|f|]_f - \mathsf{RightShift}([|f'|]_f, [|e - e'|]_e)$
return $c'' = ([|s''|]_s, [|f''|]_f, [|e''|]_e)$.

Add_{1a} $(c = ([|s|]_s, [|f|]_f, [|e|]_e), \ c' = ([|s'|]_s, [|f'|]_f, [|e'|]_e))$: $\quad \{s \neq s', e \leq e'\}$
$[|b'_e|]_e \leftarrow \mathsf{GTb}([|e'|]_e, [|e|]_e)$, return $\mathsf{IfThenElse}([|b'_e|], \mathsf{Add}_{12}(c, c'), \mathsf{Add}_{10}(c, c'))$

Add_{12} $(c = ([|s|]_s, [|f|]_f, [|e|]_e), \ c' = ([|s'|]_s, [|f'|]_f, [|e'|]_e))$: $\quad \{s \neq s', e < e'\}$
$[|s''|]_s \leftarrow [|s'|]_s, \ [|e''|]_e \leftarrow [|e'|]_e, \ [|f''|]_f \leftarrow [|f'|]_f - \mathsf{RightShift}([|f|]_f, [|e' - e|]_e)$
return $c'' = ([|s''|]_s, [|f''|]_f, [|e''|]_e)$.

Add_{10} $(c = ([|s|]_s, [|f|]_f, [|e|]_e), \ c' = ([|s'|]_s, [|f'|]_f, [|e'|]_e))$: $\quad \{s \neq s', e = e'\}$
$[|b_f|]_f \leftarrow \mathsf{GTb}([|f|]_f, [|f'|]_f)$, return $\mathsf{IfThenElse}([|b_f|], \mathsf{Add}_{101}(c, c'), \mathsf{Add}_{10a}(c, c'))$

Add_{101} $(c = ([|s|]_s, [|f|]_f, [|e|]_e), \ c' = ([|s'|]_s, [|f'|]_f, [|e'|]_e))$: $\quad \{s \neq s', e = e', f > f'\}$
$[|s''|]_s \leftarrow [|s|]_s, \ [|e''|]_e \leftarrow [|e|]_e, \ [|f''|]_f \leftarrow [|f|]_f - [|f'|]_f$, return $c'' = ([|s''|]_s, [|f''|]_f, [|e''|]_e)$.

Add_{10a} $(c = ([|s|]_s, [|f|]_f, [|e|]_e), \ c' = ([|s'|]_s, [|f'|]_f, [|e'|]_e))$: $\quad \{s \neq s', e = e', f \leq f'\}$
$[|b'_f|]_f \leftarrow \mathsf{GTb}([|f'|]_f, [|f|]_f)$, return $\mathsf{IfThenElse}([|b'_f|], \mathsf{Add}_{102}(c, c'), \mathsf{Add}_{100}(c, c'))$

Add_{102} $(c = ([|s|]_s, [|f|]_f, [|e|]_e), \ c' = ([|s'|]_s, [|f'|]_f, [|e'|]_e))$: $\quad \{s \neq s', e = e', f < f'\}$
$[|s''|]_s \leftarrow [|s'|]_s, \ [|e''|]_e \leftarrow [|e'|]_e, \ [|f''|]_f \leftarrow [|f'|]_f - [|f|]_f$, return $c'' = ([|s''|]_s, [|f''|]_f, [|e''|]_e)$.

Add_{100} (c, c') : return $c'' = ([|0|]_s, [|1.0|]_f, [|0.0|]_e)$. $\quad \{s \neq s', e = e', f = f\}$

Normalize $([|s|]_s, [|f|]_f, [|e|]_e)$:
Repeat m times:
$\quad [|b|]_f \leftarrow \mathsf{MSb}([|f|]_f, 1) \quad \{\text{the } m{+}1\text{-th bit of } f''\}$
$\quad [|f|]_f \leftarrow [|b|]_f \cdot [|f|]_f + [|1.0 - b|]_f \cdot [|2.0|]_f \cdot [|f|]_f$
$\quad [|e|]_e \leftarrow [|b|]_e \cdot [|e|]_e + [|1.0 - b|]_e \cdot [|e - 1.0|]_e$
return $([|s|]_s, [|f|]_f, [|e|]_e)$.

RightShift $([|a|]_f, [|e|]_e)$: $\quad \{e > 0\}$
$r \leftarrow [|1.0|]_f$
For i in $[1..(l-1)]$: $\quad \{l \text{ is the bit-length of } e\}$
$\quad r \leftarrow r \cdot r, \ [|b|]_e \leftarrow \mathsf{MSb}([|e|]_e, i), \ r \leftarrow [|b|]_f \cdot [|0.5|]_f \cdot r + [|1.0 - b|]_f \cdot r$
return $r \cdot [|a|]_f$.

IfThenElse $([|b|], ([|s|]_s, [|e|]_e, [|f|]_f), ([|s'|]_s, [|e'|]_e, [|f'|]_f))$:
$[|s''|]_s \leftarrow [|b|]_s \cdot [|s|]_s + [|1.0 - b|]_s \cdot [|s'|]_s$
$[|e''|]_e \leftarrow [|b|]_e \cdot [|e|]_e + [|1.0 - b|]_e \cdot [|e'|]_e$
$[|f''|]_f \leftarrow [|b|]_f \cdot [|f|]_f + [|1.0 - b|]_f \cdot [|f'|]_f$
return $([|s''|]_s, [|e''|]_e, [|f''|]_f)$.

Fig. 7. The second part of FL algorithms.

independent three ciphertexts under a single FXE4FX scheme. Especially, the FL scheme is also semantically secure and fully homomorphic with suitable choice of parameters that makes the underlying FX(q, m, l) scheme so.

Theorem 2. *The* FL *scheme of parameter* q, l, m *can fully homomorphically compute additions and multiplications of encrypted floating point numbers* $N = (-1)^s f 2^e$ *with suitable choice of parameters that makes the underlying* FX *scheme (of parameter* q, l, m) *fully homomorphic.*

Efficiency. Multiplicative depth, that is the depth of nested multiplications of the underlying FX scheme, of Mult(c, c') is $O(m)$, dominated by the complexity of MSb in it. Multiplicative depth of Add(c, c') is dominated by depth of Normalize and RightShift, which are $O(ml)$ and $O(l^2)$, respectively. Hence multiplicative depth of addition Add(c, c') is $O(ml + l^2)$.

Acknowledgements. This work was supported by CREST, JST.

References

1. Bos, J.W., Lauter, K., Loftus, J., Naehrig, M.: Improved security for a ring-based fully homomorphic encryption scheme. In: Stam, M. (ed.) IMACC 2013. LNCS, vol. 8308, pp. 45–64. Springer, Heidelberg (2013). doi:10.1007/978-3-642-45239-0_4
2. Brakerski, Z.: Fully homomorphic encryption without modulus switching from classical GapSVP. In: Safavi-Naini, R., Canetti, R. (eds.) CRYPTO 2012. LNCS, vol. 7417, pp. 868–886. Springer, Heidelberg (2012). doi:10.1007/978-3-642-32009-5_50
3. Brakerski, Z., Gentry, C., Vaikuntanathan, V.: (Leveled) fully homomorphic encryption without bootstrapping. In: Goldwasser, S. (ed.) ITCS, pp. 309–325. ACM (2012)
4. Cheon, J.H., Coron, J.-S., Kim, J., Lee, M.S., Lepoint, T., Tibouchi, M., Yun, A.: Batch fully homomorphic encryption over the integers. In: Johansson, T., Nguyen, P.Q. (eds.) EUROCRYPT 2013. LNCS, vol. 7881, pp. 315–335. Springer, Heidelberg (2013). doi:10.1007/978-3-642-38348-9_20
5. Chung, H.W., Kim, M.: Encoding rational numbers for FHE-based applications. IACR Cryptology ePrint Archive (2016/344)
6. Cheon, J.H., Kim, M., Lauter, K.: Homomorphic computation of edit distance. In: Brenner, M., Christin, N., Johnson, B., Rohloff, K. (eds.) FC 2015. LNCS, vol. 8976, pp. 194–212. Springer, Heidelberg (2015). doi:10.1007/978-3-662-48051-9_15
7. Costache, A., Smart, N.P., Vivek, S., Waller, A.: Fixed-point arithmetic in SHE schemes. IACR Cryptology ePrint Archive (2016/250)
8. Fan, J., Vercauteren, F.: Somewhat practical fully homomorphic encryption. IACR Cryptology ePrint Archive (2012/144)
9. Gentry, C.: Fully homomorphic encryption using ideal lattices. In: Mitzenmacher, M. (ed.) STOC, pp. 169–178. ACM (2009)
10. Gentry, C., Halevi, S., Smart, N.P.: Better bootstrapping in fully homomorphic encryption. In: Fischlin, M., Buchmann, J., Manulis, M. (eds.) PKC 2012. LNCS, vol. 7293, pp. 1–16. Springer, Heidelberg (2012). doi:10.1007/978-3-642-30057-8_1
11. Golle, P.: A private stable matching algorithm. In: Crescenzo, G., Rubin, A. (eds.) FC 2006. LNCS, vol. 4107, pp. 65–80. Springer, Heidelberg (2006). doi:10.1007/11889663_5

12. Graepel, T., Lauter, K., Naehrig, M.: ML confidential: machine learning on encrypted data. In: Kwon, T., Lee, M.-K., Kwon, D. (eds.) ICISC 2012. LNCS, vol. 7839, pp. 1–21. Springer, Heidelberg (2013). doi:10.1007/978-3-642-37682-5_1

13. Ishimaki, Y., Shimizu, K., Nuida, K., Yamana, H.: Faster privacy-preserving search for genome sequences using fully homomorphic encryption. In: SCIS 2016, Japan (2016)

14. Lu, W-J., Kawasaki, S., Sakuma, J.: Cryptographically-secure outsourcing of statistical data analysis I: descriptive statistics. In: CSS 2015, Japan (2015)

15. Lauter, K., López-Alt, A., Naehrig, M.: Private computation on encrypted genomic data. In: Aranha, D.F., Menezes, A. (eds.) LATINCRYPT 2014. LNCS, vol. 8895, pp. 3–27. Springer, Cham (2015). doi:10.1007/978-3-319-16295-9_1

16. Liu, J., Li, J., Xu, S., Fung, B.C.M.: Secure outsourced frequent pattern mining by fully homomorphic encryption. In: Madria, S., Hara, T. (eds.) DaWaK 2015. LNCS, vol. 9263, pp. 70–81. Springer, Cham (2015). doi:10.1007/978-3-319-22729-0_6

17. Lepoint, T., Naehrig, M.: A comparison of the homomorphic encryption schemes FV and YASHE. In: Pointcheval, D., Vergnaud, D. (eds.) AFRICACRYPT 2014. LNCS, vol. 8469, pp. 318–335. Springer, Cham (2014). doi:10.1007/978-3-319-06734-6_20

18. Lyubashevsky, V., Peikert, C., Regev, O.: On ideal lattices and learning with errors over rings. In: Gilbert, H. (ed.) EUROCRYPT 2010. LNCS, vol. 6110, pp. 1–23. Springer, Heidelberg (2010). doi:10.1007/978-3-642-13190-5_1

19. Alperin-Sheriff, J., Peikert, C.: Practical bootstrapping in quasilinear time. In: Canetti, R., Garay, J.A. (eds.) CRYPTO 2013. LNCS, vol. 8042, pp. 1–20. Springer, Heidelberg (2013). doi:10.1007/978-3-642-40041-4_1

20. Smart, N.P., Vercauteren, F.: Fully homomorphic SIMD operations. Des. Codes Crypt. 71(1), 57–81 (2014)

Leakage-Resilient

Bounded-Retrieval Model with Keys Derived from Private Data

Konrad Durnoga[1], Stefan Dziembowski[1], Tomasz Kazana[1],
Michał Zając[1,2(✉)], and Maciej Zdanowicz[1]

[1] University of Warsaw, Warsaw, Poland
mez@mimuw.edu.pl
[2] University of Tartu, Tartu, Estonia

Abstract. The *Bounded Retrieval Model (BRM)* was proposed at TCC 2006 (independently by Dziembowski and Di Crescenzo et al.). Essentially, the main idea of this model is to design cryptographic schemes with secret keys that are so large that it is infeasible for the adversary to steal them. One of the main technical problems of this idea is that it by definition requires the users to store large amounts of secret data on their disks.

In this paper we put forward a technique for dealing with the problem of this large space consumption for protocols in BRM. More precisely, we propose a method to derive keys for such protocols on-the-fly from weakly random private data (like text documents or photos, users keep on their disks anyway for non-cryptographic purposes) in such a way that no extra storage is needed. We prove that any leakage-resilient protocol (belonging to a certain, arguably quite broad class) when run with a key obtained this way retains a similar level of security as the original protocol had. Additionally, we guarantee privacy of the data the actual keys are derived from. In other words: the adversary obtains essentially no information about the private data that is used for the key derivation. Our techniques are based on the disperser graphs.

We have also implemented an experimental test of efficiency of our protocol. For arguably practical parameter settings the performance of the dispersing procedure is satisfactory.

1 Introduction

One of the biggest threats for the security of the real-life computer systems are the malicious software attacks (also called the *advanced persistent threats*). Obviously even very secure cryptographic schemes get completely broken if the machines on which they are executed get compromised by viruses, or Trojan horses. One of the reasons for this, is that the attacker can usually easily steal the secret key K used by the scheme, and hence create his own identical copy of the victims machine. One attractive solution for this problem is a technique called the *Bounded Retrieval Model (BRM)* [5,8], which is based on the following idea: design cryptosystems where the secret key K is so large that it is infeasible for the adversary to download it completely from the infected machine. Additionally,

K. Chen et al. (Eds.): Inscrypt 2016, LNCS 10143, pp. 273–290, 2017.
DOI: 10.1007/978-3-319-54705-3_17

it is required that the cryptosystems in the BRM remain secure even if a large amount of information about K leaks to the adversary. The term "amount of information" is usually understood as the number of bits the adversary can download from the machine on which K is stored. To be as realistic as possible, it is assumed that the adversary can use the computing power of the attacked machine and compute any (efficiently-computable) function Leak on K, and download only the output Leak(K), or, more generally, he can adaptively choose a number of functions $\text{Leak}_1, \ldots, \text{Leak}_k$ such that $|\text{Leak}_1(K)| + \cdots + |\text{Leak}_k(K)| \leq \lambda$, and learn $(\text{Leak}_1(K), \ldots, \text{Leak}_k(K))$.

Since its invention BRM has gained a noticeable attention in the research community. In particular, it has been shown how to construct the following cryptographic primitives in this model: the key-agreement [4,8], signature and identification schemes [2], public-key encryption schemes [1], and the secret-sharing schemes [9]. Despite their theoretical attractiveness, up to our knowledge, these techniques have never been used in the real-life. One of the reasons for this is that using them comes at a non-trivial price, namely the users need to store large random keys on their machines. Note that these keys need to be significantly larger than what the adversary is able to retrieve from the machine. Hence in practice, their sizes would probably be of an order of several gigabytes. This is prohibitively expensive for many real-life applications (for example a typical smart phone has memory of a size 32 GB at most). This means that computers running BRM protocols are clogged with huge blobs of random and otherwise useless data.

In this paper we propose a twist to the BRM that overcomes this problem. Our idea is to design schemes where the large key K is derived from the private data of the user. Moreover, this is done on-the-fly (that is, it is not necessary to keep them on disk, and they may be computed when a relevant portion of the key is requested) from data a user wants to store on his disk for any other reason. The private user data usable in this context may include: text documents, photos, audio files, or other media.

Several issues need to be addressed in this idea. Firstly, it is easy to see that such data, when viewed as a source of randomness, while being unpredictable, to a degree, for an adversary, is certainly not uniformly random (e.g., note that certain segments in some file formats may be fixed or come from a prescribed set of values). Secondly, some protocols assume that BRM keys are fully known to other trusted parties, e.g., a bank. This raises another problem with the idea of using randomness from private user data. We need to guarantee that if the user uses a key derived in this way, the privacy of his data will not be violated.

1.1 Overcoming Weak Expectations

A study of cryptographic applications that retain a comparable level of security when fed with weakly random sources instead of ones having uniform distributions was initiated by Barak et al. [3]. There, the authors explore the idea of applying universal hash functions to key derivation. The renowned Leftover Hash Lemma (LHL) [10] states that families of such functions constitute good randomness extractors. Specifically, when applied to a source of min-entropy k, an extractor of this form produces m bits which are δ-close (in terms of statistical distance) to uniform, as long as $k \geq m + 2\log(1/\delta)$. A key obtained this way can be then used in a cryptographic application. The min-entropy loss of magnitude $2\log(1/\delta)$ may be unacceptably large in some situations but, as shown by Radhakrishnan and Ta-Shma [13], it cannot be prevented in general. However, as argued by the authors, there exists a wide range of applications where the entropy loss can be cut down by the factor of 2 for a price of some security loss in the application using non-uniform keys. This line of research was continued by Dodis and Yu [7].

1.2 Sensitive Data

As already highlighted above building a cryptographic protocol on top of randomness derived from private data bears an obvious risk of compromising that data. One can, for example, imagine an artificial protocol that simply publishes all accessible randomness. Also, a protocol in the BRM does not necessarily guarantee protection of its key. Some fragments of a BRM key may be passed, as a part of normal operating procedure, to an honest party that did not possess the key in the first place. To give an example illustrating such a situation, one can conceive of an authentication protocol in the BRM, which itself appears to be folklore, based on Merkle tree [11]. There, a hash tree is built on an input BRM key and the resulting hash from the root is then forwarded to a verifier (say, a bank). This way a user can commit to his key which, in its entirety, is only stored on user's side for efficiency reasons. On the other hand, the verifier may learn parts of the key when the user attempts to authenticate himself. In order to do that, the verifier demands to be presented with hashes along some path of his choice in the Merkle tree. Such a path includes data from the initial BRM key and thus its fragment gets revealed to the verifier.

Now, if a BRM key used in this protocol is obtained from data stored on disk then, clearly, the key derivation procedure should enjoy some kind of a one-wayness property. If the procedure does not hide its input then a dishonest verifier may attempt to recover the underlying data or, at least, he may gain some partial knowledge. In this paper, we aim at a solution that allows a user to protect his private and possibly sensitive data in this scenario. Namely, we require that an adversary can hardly learn anything more about the data except that he could otherwise achieve via leakage. Below, we refer to it as the privacy requirement.

1.3 Our Contribution

In this paper, we give a new idea to overcome a problem with large space requirements in the BRM model. As a reminder: in the BRM one uses huge private keys for purpose of leakage-resiliency. Here we describe an idea to derive a secret key from private data (this could include text documents, videos, etc.). That content is supposed to have high enough min-entropy, however it raises a problem with privacy: we do not want to disclose any sensitive data. Our construction fulfills this expectation. So the private data remains secret even if the entire derived key is compromised.

The secret key is being computed on-the-fly from private data so that no extra memory is used to store the key. Access to the key is fast so one does need to read limited portion of private data to compute some part of the secret key.

The main result shows that any cryptographic protocol belonging to a well defined and quite broad class, that is: the class of game based protocols, is still secure if we use a key derived from private data in place of a random key.

Seemingly, the problem of extracting an almost random key from sufficiently random data can be easily solved, even in presence of leakage, using a well-known primitive – namely, an average-case strong randomness extractor. Its definition requires that for any two random variables X and I (where I can be viewed as side information about X, i.e., a leak) such that the (conditional) min-entropy of X given I (see (1) for a precise definition of conditional min-entropy) is high enough, then the output of the extractor $\text{Ext}(X, R)$ is statistically close to uniform even given a short random seed R and the side information I, in short: $\big(\text{Ext}(X, R), R, I\big) \approx (U, R, I)$. Dodis *et al.* [6] extend the LHL to show that universal hash functions constitute good average-case extractors retaining nearly the same parameters as in the original LHL.

To derive a random key using the above tool one could simply pick R and compute $\text{Ext}(X, R)$ on his data X. To ensure that the key can be recovered on demand in future it is also reasonable to store R on disk along with the regular data X. This, however, means that the seed is exposed to leakage and, since it is short, it can be fully learnt by the adversary issuing an appropriate leakage query. That said, we may as well assume that in our setting R is fixed and publicly known, which in turn severely hinders our attempt to directly apply extractors. This is because it enables the adversary to leak from X adaptively, depending on R. Note that such a possibility is not captured by the aforementioned definition of average-case extractor where I and X are independent of R. For the very same reason which precludes existence of seedless extractors in general, we can no longer expect that $\text{Ext}(X, R)$ is close to uniform when conditioned on $I = I_R$. On the other hand, one could hope that the conditioning does not degrade the min-entropy of extractor's output by more than the length of allowed leakage. This would still be acceptable for most BRM applications that do not crucially rely on full uniformity of their keys. In fact, in this aspect the definition of randomness extractor is even stronger than we actually require – we could resort to a weaker notion of *a condenser*. Either way, a simple argument leads to the conclusion that keys derived this way can replace original BRM keys without influencing security. However, when we move to discussing privacy of the underlying data in this solution, the reasoning breaks and one major setback becomes evident. One could argue that if $\text{Ext}(X, R)$ disclosed some information about the private data X then, by setting I to be this information, we would produce a correlation between $\text{Ext}(X, R)$ and I, thus violating the condition about $\text{Ext}(X, R)$ being close to uniform and independent of I. This is not valid. Namely, when R is known *a priori* then given $\text{Ext}(X, R)$ it may be possible to learn some non-trivial information about X. Even more so when we are additionally given a leak $I = I_R$ – this could, for instance, enable recovering X in full by "inverting" the function Ext. I_R would serve as a hint in guessing which of the possible preimages of $\text{Ext}(X, R)$ should be picked. Overall, randomness extractors do not guarantee that the privacy requirement is met.

Let us also observe that, for efficiency reasons, not every randomness extractor would be equally well suited for our application. It would certainly be disadvantageous if the derivation procedure required supplying the whole input X (or almost the whole) in order to compute even a small portion of the derived key on demand. And the ability to calculate a selected piece of the key efficiently on-the-fly seems to be a natural requirement in the BRM. To achieve it, we would need an extractor with the property that for *fixed R* every single bit of $\text{Ext}(X, R)$ depends only on a small number of input bits X. This is called *locality*. As shown by Vadhan [14] one can build locally computable extractors using a two-stage "sample-then-extract" technique where first a subset of input bits is selected and then an inner randomness extractor is applied to this subset. The validity of such an approach can be established using a far-reaching, yet intuitive, result by Nisan and Zuckerman [12] which asserts that a random sample of a sufficiently random (i.e., possessing high enough min-entropy) string of bits is likely to be sufficiently random (to have high min-entropy).

Another idea leading to an immediate solution of the problem we stated involves hashing the input data. Let us assume the existence of a random oracle computing a hash function $\mathcal{H}$ which outputs short random blocks. To produce a long random key, we need to invoke $\mathcal{H}$ multiple, say ℓ, times and collect the outputs into one string. This could be done by simply evaluating $\mathcal{H}(1, X), \mathcal{H}(2, X), \ldots, \mathcal{H}(\ell, X)$ for the same input data X. By the definition of a random oracle these values are uniformly random and independent.

To address the issue related to efficiency and locality, we propose a different way of deriving keys from private data. Our design is quite straightforward – it boils down to splitting all the data into consecutive blocks of the same fixed length n (say, $n = 4\,\text{kB}$). A block could naturally correspond to the smallest allocation unit in a filesystem present on a user's device. Then, we use hashing to extract randomness from blocks. A naïve method to implement it would be computing hashes block by block. This approach, albeit simple, has a significant drawback. The only assumption we make about the input data is that its joint min-entropy is not too small (this measures the *a priori* knowledge of the adversary about the private data, before leakage is taken into account). We do not demand however that the randomness is equidistributed across all the blocks. Therefore, it may happen that even for high overall min-entropy, e.g., $\frac{1}{2}\ell n$ where ℓ is the number of blocks, there exist $\ell/2$ blocks which, from the adversary's point of view, are constant. Consequently, the corresponding parts of a derived key carry no randomness at all and are known to the adversary.

To circumvent the problem caused by blocks with low min-entropy we increase the number of blocks a single block of the derived key depends on. That is, each hash is calculated by taking not one but d blocks of input. Additionally, we amplify the likelihood of the event that there is at least one high min-entropy block among the selected d-tuple. This step actually introduces a new flavor to the reasoning. Namely, we argue the assumption on joint min-entropy of the input blocks with large probability implies that there exists a large number of blocks each having high min-entropy. This statement may seem rather natural and intuitive yet it is somewhat tricky to prove. A related problem of extracting random blocks was considered before by Nisan and Zuckerman [12] and Alwen, Dodis, and Wichs [4].

The fact that there should be plenty of sufficiently random blocks in the input allows us to pick d-tuples of block randomly. However, to recreate portions of the derived on-the-fly one would have to store the auxiliary randomness used to select those tuples, which may not be acceptable. Instead, we suggest employing dispersers – d-regular bipartite graphs with the property that any sufficiently large set of vertices on the left side is connected to almost all vertices on the right side. Every disperser of this kind induces a selection of d-tuples.

Clearly, increasing the degree of regularity d of a disperser reduces locality of the key derivation method. This however comes as a trade-off. We use a simulation-based argument to prove that any protocol using the derived key can be simulated by a protocol operating on an original key with $O(n\ell/d)$ of additional leakage.

1.4   Implementation and Efficiency

As an evidence of reasonable efficiency of our solution we provided a C++ implementation of the disperse procedure. The results, which turned out to be promising in terms of practical application, are given in the full version of the paper. More precisely, we addressed the following practical issues:

(i) What is the efficiency of our protocol relative to the degree of the disperser graph?

(ii) What is the lower bound for the degree of the disperser graph necessary to preserve security of a leakage-resilient protocol executed on a key derived by our procedure?

2   Preliminaries

We assume the existence of a *random oracle*, i.e., perfectly random function

$$\mathcal{H}\colon \{0,1\}^* \to \{0,1\}^n$$

which can be evaluated only by querying a certain oracle $\mathcal{H}$. At the beginning, all values of $\mathcal{H}$ are uniformly distributed, in particular, unpredictable. Throughout the protocols operation, one can issue a query $\mathcal{H}(m)$ obtaining the value of $\mathcal{H}(m)$ and gaining no other information.

We say that a function f is $\mathcal{H}$-randomized (or simply randomized if no confusion can arise) if its result is dependent on a certain random oracle $\mathcal{H}$. We denote a $\mathcal{H}$-randomized function by $f(-, \mathcal{H})$.

The *min-entropy* $\mathbf{H}_\infty$ of a random variable X is defined as:

$$\mathbf{H}_\infty(X) \overset{\text{def}}{=} -\log(\max_x \Pr(X = x)).$$

For two random variables X, Y the conditional min-entropy $\widetilde{\mathbf{H}}_\infty(X|Y)$ [6] is given by the formula:

$$\widetilde{\mathbf{H}}_\infty(X|Y) \overset{\text{def}}{=} -\log\left(\mathbb{E}_y 2^{-\mathbf{H}_\infty(X|Y=y)}\right). \tag{1}$$

This definition turns out to preserve the natural interpretation of min-entropy as maximal probability of success in guessing X given Y, i.e., for any algorithm $\mathcal{A}$ we have:

$$\Pr(\mathcal{A}(Y) = X) = \mathbb{E}_y \Pr(\mathcal{A}(y) = X)$$
$$\leq \mathbb{E}_y 2^{-\mathbf{H}_\infty(X|Y=y)} = 2^{-\widetilde{\mathbf{H}}_\infty(X|Y)}.$$

For $R \in \{0, 1\}^*$ a *leakage oracle* Ω is machine that takes as input R and answers *leakage queries* – each ith of them consists of a description of a function $\text{Leak}_i : \{0, 1\}^M \to \{0, 1\}^{\lambda_i}$. Each such a query is answered with $\text{Leak}_i(R)$. We say that a machine $\mathcal{M}$, that interacts with Ω, has λ-*bounded* access to Ω (or is λ-*bounded*) if the total length of the outputs of the functions queried by $\mathcal{M}$, i.e. the sum of all the λ_i's, is bounded by λ.

We denote by $\mathbf{TM}_\lambda^{\Omega(D)}$ the class of all probabilistic Turing machines equipped with an adaptive access to a restricted leakage oracle Ω with the total leakage of at most λ bits. Moreover, by $\mathbf{TM}_{\lambda,q}^{\Omega(D,\mathcal{H}),\mathcal{H}}$ we mean the subclass of $\mathbf{TM}_\lambda^{\Omega(D)}$ equipped with an adaptive access to a leakage oracle $\Omega^{D,\mathcal{H}}$ together with additional q executions of $\mathcal{H}$.

3   Key Derivation Procedure Based on Sensitive Data

Let n be a security parameter and let $\mathcal{H} : \{0, 1\}^{2n} \to \{0, 1\}^n$ be a hash function modeled as a random oracle. A function $\text{kdf} : \mathbb{N} \times \{0, 1\}^N \to \{0, 1\}^M$ that depends on $\mathcal{H}$ (i.e. it is represented as a circuit that can make calls to $\mathcal{H}$) is called a *key-derivation function*. We now define, using the standard real-ideal paradigm, what it means for kdf to be a *secure*. Let $\mathcal{Z}$ be an interactive machine, called the *environment*, that takes as input a security parameter n and a string $Y \in \{0, 1\}^M$ and outputs 0 or 1. Informally, the goal of $\mathcal{Z}$ is to distinguish between the ideal and the real model.

In the *ideal model* the adversary is called the *simulator* and denoted $\mathcal{S}$. Assume $Y \leftarrow \{0, 1\}^M$ is chosen uniformly and given to the environment. The simulator receives n from $\mathcal{Z}$ and then interacts with $\mathcal{Z}$. The simulator has also access to a leakage oracle $\Omega(Y)$ (for some parameter λ). The output of $\mathcal{Z}$ at the end of this execution is denoted $\mathsf{ideal}_{\mathcal{Z},\mathcal{S}}(n,\lambda,M)$.

In the *real model* the adversary $\mathcal{A}$ has access to $\mathcal{H}$ and a leakage oracle $\Omega(X)$, where X is some (not necessarily uniform) random variable over $\{0,1\}^N$. The leakage queries to $\Omega(X)$ can depend on $\mathcal{H}$. The environment $\mathcal{Z}$ gets as input $Y := \mathsf{kdf}(X)$ (note: it does not directly learn X), and then interacts with $\mathcal{A}$. The output of $\mathcal{Z}$ is denoted as $\mathsf{real}_{\mathcal{Z},\mathcal{A}}(k,\mathsf{kdf},X)$.

Definition 1. *For a pair of functions (Λ,ε) we say that $\mathsf{kdf} : \mathbb{N} \times \{0,1\}^N \to \{0,1\}^M$ is a (Λ,ε)-secure key derivation function for sources of min-entropy κ if for every efficiently-sampleable random variable X (with alphabet $\{0,1\}^N$) such that $\mathbf{H}_\infty(X) \geq \kappa$, for every λ-bounded adversary $\mathcal{A}$ there exists a $\Lambda(\lambda)$-bounded simulator $\mathcal{S}$ such that*

$$|\Pr(\mathsf{real}_{\mathcal{Z},\mathcal{A}}(n,\mathsf{kdf},X) = 1) - \Pr(\mathsf{ideal}_{\mathcal{Z},\mathcal{S}}(n,M) = 1)| \leq \varepsilon(n).$$

We say that kdf is (Λ,ε)-private for sources of min-entropy κ if for variable X such that $\mathbf{H}_\infty(X) \geq \kappa$, and every λ-bounded machine $\mathcal{A}$ that gets as input k and $\mathsf{kdf}(k,X)$ and interacts with $\Omega(X)$ there exists a $\Lambda(\lambda)$-bounded machine $\mathcal{S}$ that interacts with $\Omega(X)$ such that

$$(Out(\mathcal{A}(n,\mathsf{kdf}(n,X)) \leftrightarrows \Omega(X)), X)$$
$$\approx_\varepsilon (Out(\mathcal{S}(n,\mathcal{A}) \leftrightarrows \Omega(X)), X)$$

4   Disperse as a Key Derivation Function

In this section we define a specific function Disperse. Then we prove that it is both secure and private key derivation function. Before the actual definition we will introduce *dispersers*: useful graph class that will be used later in our construction.

4.1   Disperser Graphs

Throughout the whole construction we shall make use of bipartite right M-regular graphs identified with functions $\sigma : [N_1] \times [M] \to [N_0]$ by the following recipe. By $\mathcal{G}_\sigma$ we denote a bipartite graph $\mathcal{G}$ with the sets of vertices equal to two disjoint sets $[N_0], [N_1]$ and with edges going from $n \in [N_1]$ to $\sigma_m^n \in [N_0]$ for any $m \in [M]$. The following definition is crucial:

Definition 2. *A bipartite graph $\mathcal{G} = (V^0 \sqcup V^1, E)$ is a right (K,L)-disperser if for every set $S \subset V^1$ such that $|S| = K$ the neighborhood $N(S)$ satisfies $|N(S)| \geq L$, i.e. the sets of size K expands into sets of size at least L.*

We often make use of explicit ℓ^d-regular $(\ell^e, (1-\eta)\ell)$-dispersers. We implicitly assume that the numbers d, e satisfy $d < 1, e < 1$ and $d + e > 1$, i.e., the degree of any vertex is non-trivially bounded by ℓ^d and moreover any set of vertices of cardinality at least ℓ^e expands to a set of almost full cardinality $(1-\eta)\ell$ (here we use the fact that $d + e > 1$). For the sake of completeness, we refer to those assumptions as *non-triviality of disperser*. Namely:

Non-triviality of Disperser. We say that a ℓ^d-regular $(\ell^e, (1 - \eta)\ell)$-disperser is *non-trivial* if the parameters d, e satisfy $d < 1, e < 1$ and $d + e > 1$.

For more details on dispersers and further definitions see full version of the paper.

In Fig. 1, we describe function Disperse explicitly. For the sake of simplicity, we identify vertices of graph with labels they contain. An exemplary Disperse function is shown in Fig. 2.

Implementation of Disperse$_{\mathcal{G}_\sigma}(D, \mathcal{H})$.

Input: a bitstring $D = D_1 \ldots D_\ell$ for $D_1, \ldots, D_\ell \in \{0, 1\}^n$; $\mathcal{G}_\sigma$ a d-regular biparite graph $(D \sqcup D', E)$, where $D = (D_1, \ldots, D_\ell)$ and $D' = (D'_1, \ldots, D'_\ell)$, such that $N(D'_i) = \{D_{\sigma_1^i}, \ldots, D_{\sigma_d^i}\}$; function $\mathcal{H}: \{0, 1\}^{dn + \log \ell} \to \{0, 1\}^n$

Output: a bitstring D'.

Execution:

1. Assign values to the "upper" vertices of $\mathcal{G}_\sigma$:
   $$D'_i \leftarrow \mathcal{H}\left(i, D_{\sigma_1^i}, \ldots, D_{\sigma_d^i}\right), \text{ for } i = 1, \ldots, \ell.$$
2. Return $D' = D'_1, \ldots, D'_\ell$.

Fig. 1. Operation of dispersion function.

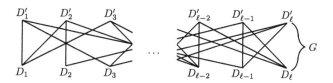

Fig. 2. An exemplary Disperse$_{\mathcal{G}_\sigma}(D, \mathcal{H})$

We now state our main result that for an appropriately chosen graph $\mathcal{G}_\sigma$ the function Disperse$_{\mathcal{G}_\sigma}$ is in fact private and secure for reasonable parameters.

Theorem 1. *Let $\mathcal{G}_\sigma$ be a non-trivial ℓ^d-regular $(\ell^e, (1 - \eta)\ell)$-right disperser and $\mathcal{H}$ be a random oracle. Then for any $\eta < p$ and $\kappa = pn\ell$ the function* Disperse$_{\mathcal{G}_\sigma}(-, \mathcal{H}): \{0, 1\}^{\ell n} \to \{0, 1\}^{\ell n}$ *is:*

- $\left(\lambda + \ell^e(\log q + \log \ell), 2^{-n((p - \eta - \lambda)\ell + \ell^e(\log q + \log \ell))}\right)$*-private* kdf,
- $\left(\lambda + \ell^e(\log q + n), 2^{-n((p - \eta - \lambda - \ell^e(\log q + n))\ell + \ell^e(\log q + n))}\right)$*-secure* kdf.

Since the proof of this theorem is long, it is divided into three parts – at the beginning it is shown that even under the presence of leakage, function Disperse effectively hides the data underneath; then, basing on this result, privacy property is proven; next security is shown.

Before proceeding to actual proofs we shortly elaborate about the bounds on the parameters.

Remark 1 (Efficiency of Disperse$_{\mathcal{G}_\sigma}$). It is important to note that in order to obtain a single bit of a derived key one need process ℓ^d blocks of disk data. This therefore constitutes a leakage-time trade-off for the operation of our function. Namely reduction of d allows to compute a single bit of key more efficiently with a cost of an increased parameter Δ_λ proportional to ℓ^e (recall that $d + e > 1$).

Remark 2 (Bounds on parameters). The bound $\eta \leqslant p$ express natural require-ments that the quality of disperser η should be superior to the entropy reserve represented by p. The bound on $q = 2^{o((\ell^{1-e})n)}$ corresponds to a robust, exponen-tial bound on the random oracle query-based complexity of an adversary.

4.2   One-Wayness of Disperse

The main reason for which the Disperse procedure is introduced is its certain *one-wayness* property, which states that given an output of Disperse, an adversary computes a large part of the input only with negligible probability. This property is expressed in the following lemma. We precede it with a necessary definitions and lemmata.

Definition 3 (Bad query). *Given a random variable D, a bipartite right d-regular graph $\mathcal{G}_\sigma$ and a random oracle $\mathcal{H}$ we say that a random oracle query $\mathcal{H}(b)$, submitted by some Turing machine $\mathcal{A}$, is* bad *if the argument b equals $(i, D_{\sigma_1^i} D_{\sigma_2^i} \ldots D_{\sigma_d^i})$ for some $i \in \{1, \ldots, \ell\}$, i.e., the argument of random oracle query equals one of the values defined by graph $\mathcal{G}_\sigma$ and a random variable D.*

By Bad$_{\mathcal{A}}$ we denote the set of all bad queries. By indices$_{\mathcal{A}}$ we denote a list of all pairs (k, i_k) of indices $k \in \{1, \ldots, q\}$ and $i_k \in \{1, \ldots, \ell\}$ such that k is the smallest index of a bad random oracle query of $\mathcal{A}$ which is equal to $(i_k, D_{\sigma_1^{i_k}} \ldots D_{\sigma_\delta^{i_k}})$. Since the total number of queries is q and $\mathcal{G}_\sigma$ has 2ℓ vertices, we can describe the list indices$_{\mathcal{A}}$ using $|\text{indices}_{\mathcal{A}}| \cdot (\log \ell + \log q)$ bits.

We start with the definition of a Guessing game which is tailored to be used in the proof of Lemma 2.

Definition 4. *Let $(X, \mathcal{H})$ be random variables. A* Guessing *game against adver-sary $\mathcal{A}$ consists of the steps described in* Fig. 3.

Lemma 1. *Let $(X_1, \ldots, X_\ell, \mathcal{H})$ be a random variable such that:*

1. *$(X_1, \ldots, X_\ell)$ and $\mathcal{H}$ are independent,*
2. *$\mathcal{H}$ is a vector of random independent $N = 2^{\delta n + \log \ell}$ blocks of length n,*
3. *each X_i is n bits long,*
4. *$\mathbf{H}_\infty(X_1, \ldots, X_\ell) = p\ell n$ for some $0 \leq p \leq 1$.*

Now let $\mathcal{A}$ be a randomized algorithm playing Guessing *game with λ. Then, the probability that $\mathcal{A}$ outputs all correct guesses (in both phases) is at most*

$$2^{-n(k_1 + k_2 - (1-p)\ell) + \lambda}$$

for $k_1 \geqslant (1 - p)\ell$.

Guessing game for adversary $\mathcal{A}$.

Input: random variables $(X, \mathcal{H})$, where $X = (X_1, \ldots, X_\ell)$ and $\mathcal{H} = (\mathcal{H}_{v_1}, \ldots, \mathcal{H}_{v_N})$ for some parameters ℓ, N and labels v_i. [a] Furthermore we declare k_1, k_2, leakage parameter λ_{Leak} and p such that X has min-entropy at least $p\ell n$.

Leakage phase:

1. $\mathcal{A}$ issues a leakage query $\text{Leak}(X_1, \ldots, X_\ell, \mathcal{H})$ of length λ_{Leak}.

First phase:

2. $\mathcal{A}$ adaptively queries $\mathcal{H}$ by submitting a label v and receiving $\mathcal{H}_v$.
3. $\mathcal{A}$ chooses a subset of indices $S_1 \subset [\ell]$ of size k_1 along with the guesses for all values $(X_j | j \in S_1)$.

Second phase:

4. $\mathcal{A}$ receives all values of $\{X_i | i \notin S_1\}$, i.e., all blocks that she did not try to guess.
5. $\mathcal{A}$ outputs a subset of labels $S_2 \subset \{v_i\}_{i=1..N}$ of size k_2 which were not previously (i.e., in the first phase) queried along with guesses for all values $(H_v | v \in S_2)$.

---

[a] The values of X_i should be considered as certain $\mathcal{H}$ labels.

Fig. 3. Definition of Guessing game

Proof. Suppose there exists algorithm winning the game with probability α. This implies that $\alpha \leqslant 2^\lambda \cdot \beta$, where β is a probability of winning for some non-leakage algorithm $\mathcal{B}$. The inequality holds since $\mathcal{B}$ can simply guess the leakage.

Say that β_1 is a probability of guessing k_1 values from S_1 for some non-leakage algorithm $\mathcal{B}$. Then the probability of guessing the whole X is at least $\beta_1 \cdot 2^{-(\ell-k_1)n}$, since $\mathcal{B}$ can guess the missing bits. On the other hand, this probability is not greater than $2^{-\mathbf{H}_\infty(X)}$, thus

$$\beta_1 \cdot 2^{-(\ell-k_1)n} \leqslant 2^{-pn\ell}$$
$$\beta_1 \leqslant 2^{-n(p\ell-\ell+k_1)}.$$

Probability β_2 of guessing the second phase of the game by an algorithm $\mathcal{B}$ can be bounded by the same inequality, so $\beta_2 \leqslant 2^{-nk_2}$. Since X and $\mathcal{H}$ are independent, the probability β that $\mathcal{B}$ wins both phases, is not greater than $2^{-n(p\ell-\ell+k_1+k_2)}$. As it was stated before, leakage λ can be simple guessed and $\alpha \leqslant 2^\lambda \cdot \beta$, hence

$$\alpha \leqslant 2^{-n(k_1+k_2-(1-p)\ell)+\lambda}.$$

Lemma 2 (One-wayness of Disperse). *Let $\mathcal{G}_\sigma$ be a ℓ^d-regular $(\ell^e, (1-\eta)\ell)$-right disperser and $D = (D_1, \ldots, D_\ell) \in \{0,1\}^{n\ell}$ be a random variable of min-entropy $p\ell n$. Then, the probability that an algorithm $\mathcal{A}(\text{Disperse}_{\mathcal{G}_\sigma}(D, \mathcal{H})) \in$ $\mathbf{TM}_{\lambda,q}^{\Omega(D,\mathcal{H}),\mathcal{H}}$ makes at least ℓ^e different bad queries satisfies:*

$$\Pr(|\text{indices}_\mathcal{A}| \geqslant \ell^e) \leqslant 2^{-n((p-\eta-\lambda)\ell)+\ell^e(\log q + \log \ell)}$$

for $\eta \leqslant p$ and $q = 2^{o(\ell^{1-e})n}$.

Proof. Given an adversary $\mathcal{A}$ such that its associated list indices$_\mathcal{A}$ is longer or equal to ℓ^e with probability ξ we construct a player $\mathcal{P_A}$ in game Guessing$_{\langle X_1,\ldots,X_\ell\rangle,\mathcal{H}}$ $(p, k_1, k_2, \lambda_{\text{Leak}})$ for

$$(X_1,\ldots,X_\ell) = (D_1,\ldots,D_\ell) \qquad k_2 = \ell$$
$$k_1 = (1-\eta)\ell \qquad\qquad \lambda_{\text{Leak}} = \lambda + \ell n + \ell^e(\log q + \log \ell)$$

winning with probability ξ. Therefore, we conclude that

$$\xi < 2^{-n((p-\eta-\lambda)\ell)+\ell^e(\log q + \log \ell)}$$

by Lemma 1. The detailed construction of $\mathcal{P_A}$ is described in Fig. 4.

Implementation of a player $\mathcal{P_A}$.

Learning phase:

1. Player $\mathcal{P_A}$ leaks ℓ values $(D'_1,\ldots,D'_\ell) = \left(\mathcal{H}(1, D_{\sigma^1_1}\ldots D_{\sigma^1_{\ell d}}),\ldots,\mathcal{H}(\ell, D_{\sigma^\ell_1}\ldots D_{\sigma^\ell_{\ell d}})\right)$ from a leakage oracle Ω;
2. initializes adversary $\mathcal{A} \in \mathbf{TM}^{\Omega(D,\mathcal{H}),\mathcal{H}}_{\lambda,q}$; feeds her with $D'_1,\ldots,D'_\ell$, then submits her to the leakage oracle Ω^a to get a hint Leak$(D,\mathcal{H})$ containing:
   - the results of all leakage queries by $\mathcal{A}$;
   - a list indices$'$ of at most ℓ^e first items of list indices$_\mathcal{A}$

Game phase:

The adversary $\mathcal{A}$ is now executed with the following recipe for answering to leakage and oracle queries:

1. The answers to leakage queries are obtained using Leak$(D,\mathcal{H})$.
2. The random oracle queries are obtained using $\mathcal{H}$ with an exception of elements $\mathcal{H}(j, D_{\sigma^j_1}\ldots D_{\sigma^j_{\ell d}})$ given in Leak$(D,\mathcal{H})$.

First phase 1. Everytime $\mathcal{A}$ issues a bad oracle query $(i_k, D_{\sigma^{i_k}_1},\ldots,D_{\sigma^{i_k}_{\ell d}})$ whose index k appears on the list indices$'$ the player $\mathcal{P_A}$ adds elements $D_{\sigma^{i_k}_j}$ to its list of guesses.

Second phase 1. $\mathcal{P_A}$ guesses random oracle queries leaked in the first item of Learning phase.

---
[a] submitting $\mathcal{A}(D'_1,\ldots,D'_\ell)$ to Ω means that Ω gets a description of Turing Machine realizing $\mathcal{A}$ along with input tape containing $D'_1,\ldots,D'_\ell$.

Fig. 4. Implementation of a player $\mathcal{P_A}$

The first step is to show that a player $\mathcal{P_A}$ follows the rules of the game:

$$\text{Guessing }_{\langle D_1,\ldots,D_\ell\rangle,\mathcal{H}} (p, (1-\eta)\cdot\ell, \ell, \lambda + \ell n + \ell^e(\log q + \log \ell)).$$

For this sake, we show that:

- Length of hint $\lambda_{\text{Leak}} = |\text{Leak}(D_1, \ldots, D_\ell, \mathcal{H})|$ is not greater than leakage λ of the adversary $\mathcal{A}$ along with $n\ell$ bits needed to feed the $\mathcal{A}$ and $\ell^e(\log q + \log \ell)$ to handle bad queries. Hence $\lambda_{\text{Leak}} = \lambda + \ell n + \ell^e(\log q + \log \ell)$.
- Rules of the game requires that $k_1 \geqslant p$, which follows from the assumptions.

Now, we need to show that $\mathcal{P}_\mathcal{A}$: (a) guesses at least k_1 elements in the first phase with probability ξ and (b) guesses $k_2 = \ell$ elements in the second phase. The claim (b) follows from directly from the definition of $\text{Leak}(D, \mathcal{H})$. Namely, $\text{Leak}(D, \mathcal{H})$ contains the values of $\mathcal{H}(i, D_{\sigma_1^i} \ldots D_{\sigma_{\ell d}^i})$ for $i = 1 \ldots \ell$ which are explicitly prohibited from being queried (Item 2 of the Game phase) and therefore can be guessed in the Second phase of operation of $\mathcal{P}_\mathcal{A}$. In order to prove (a) we use the fact that every bad query leads to the capability of guessing ℓ^d associated $D_{\sigma_j^i}$'s and apply the properties of disperser graphs. More precisely, by the assumptions on $\mathcal{A}$ the length of indices' is equal to ℓ^e with probability ξ. In this case, the neighborhood of vertices labeled with indices' $= \{i_1, \ldots, i_{\ell^e}\}$ consists of at least $(1 - \eta)\ell$ $(= k_1)$ elements (using basic property of disperser $\mathcal{G}_\sigma$) and therefore these k_1 elements $D_k^{i_j}$ for $j \in \{1, \ldots, \ell^e\}$ and $k \in \{1, \ldots, \ell^d\}$ can be guessed in the First phase of operation of $\mathcal{P}_\mathcal{A}$. We produced an adversary that wins the First phase of the Guessing game with probability ξ and Second phase with probability equals one. Thus, the whole game is won with probability ξ. Considering upper bound given by Lemma 1 we conclude that:

$$\xi < 2^{-n((p-\eta-\lambda)\ell) + \ell^e(\log q + \log \ell)},$$

which ends the proof.

4.3   Privacy of Disperse

In this section, we show that Disperse is in fact a private key-derivation procedure. The bottom line of the proof is an application of one-wayness together with a careful design of leakage query. It is important to note that we significantly use our computational model, where we can submit potentially non-polynomial queries.

Theorem 2 (Privacy). *Let $\mathcal{G}_\sigma$ be a ℓ^d-regular $(\ell^e, (1 - \eta)\ell)$-right disperser, $D = (D_1, \ldots, D_\ell) \in \{0, 1\}^{n\ell}$ be a random variable of min-entropy $p\ell n$ and $\eta \leqslant p$. Then Disperse is $(\lambda + \ell^e(\log q + \log \ell), 2^{-n((p-\eta-\lambda)\ell) + \ell^e(\log q + \log \ell)})$-private.*

In order to give a proof, we shall construct a machine $\mathcal{S}$ such that for any adversary $\mathcal{A}(\text{Disperse}_{\mathcal{G}_\sigma}(D, \mathcal{H})) \in \mathbf{TM}_{\lambda, q}^{\Omega(D, \mathcal{H}), \mathcal{H}}$ the result of $\mathcal{S}(\mathcal{A})$ is indistinguishable from $\mathcal{A}(K)$ conditioned on D. We precede the construction by an essential transformation of random oracles and leakage functions, which plays a role of random oracle re-programming.

Definition 5 (Twisted random oracle). *Let $\mathcal{H}$ be a random oracle and $L = \langle (\arg_1, v_1), \ldots, (\arg_k, v_k) \rangle$ be a list of pairs of an argument $\arg_i$ together with a potential value v_i. We define a twisted random oracle $\mathcal{H}\{L\}$ to be an oracle whose operation is described as follows:*

$$\mathcal{H}\{L\}(q) = \begin{cases} v_i & \text{if } q = \arg_i \text{ for some } i \\ \mathcal{H}(q) & \text{otherwise.} \end{cases}$$

In particular, given a random variable D, a random oracle $\mathcal{H}$ and a random variable $K = \langle K_1, \ldots, K_\ell \rangle \in \{0,1\}^{\ell n}$, by $\mathcal{H}\{D \xrightarrow{\mathcal{G}_\sigma} K\}$ we denote a random oracle $\mathcal{H}\{\langle (D_{\sigma_i^1} \ldots D_{\sigma_i^{\deg(G)}}, K_i) \rangle_{i=1\ldots\ell}\}$. Observe that if $K \sim U_{\ell n}$ is independent of $\mathcal{H}$ then the distributions of $\mathcal{H}\{D \xrightarrow{\mathcal{G}_\sigma} K\}$ and $\mathcal{H}$ are the same.

Construction of the Simulator. The operation of $\mathcal{S}(\mathcal{A})$, based on the description of $\mathcal{A}$, consists of the following steps described in Fig. 5.

Before giving a formal proof of statistical indistinguishability of output distributions, we give some clarifying remarks about consecutive steps of the construction. Firstly, we should emphasize that in Step (2) we crucially use the properties of our leakage model by querying leakage oracle with potentially non-polynomial function simulating whole behaviour of $\mathcal{A}$. Secondly, observe that in Step (2) the simulator leaks only the indices of queries, not their actual arguments as those can be observed during Step (3) of simulation. Thirdly, note that in Step (3a) we need not perform any additional leakage apart from the value of f, as $f\{D \xrightarrow{\mathcal{G}_\sigma} K\}$ can be obtained inside the leakage query as in Step (2). Therefore the leakage excess consists merely of the list $\text{indices}_\mathcal{A}$ and consequently $\Delta\lambda = |\text{indices}_\mathcal{A}|(\log q + \log \ell)$.

Proof (Proof of Theorem 2). We shall now argue that the simulator $\mathcal{S}$ constructed above satisfies the requirements of Theorem 2 for any adversary $\mathcal{A}$. Concretely, we prove that $\mathcal{S}$ perfectly simulates the execution of any adversary $\mathcal{A}$, unless $|\text{indices}_\mathcal{A}| \geqslant \ell^e$. Therefore, for any adversary $\mathcal{A}$ the output's distribution of $\mathcal{S}(\mathcal{A})$ satisfies:

$$(Out(\mathcal{A}(n, \text{kdf}(n, D)) \leftrightarrows \Omega(D)), D) \approx_\varepsilon (Out(\mathcal{S}(n, \mathcal{A}) \leftrightarrows \Omega(D)), D)$$

where $\varepsilon = \Pr(|\text{indices}_\mathcal{A}| \geqslant \ell^e)$. Firstly, note that the execution of $\mathcal{A}$ inside the leakage function ind_u (see Step (2)) is perfectly equivalent to an honest execution of $\mathcal{A}$ as $\mathcal{H}\{D \xrightarrow{\mathcal{G}_\sigma} K\}$ is distributed equally to $\mathcal{H}$. Consequently, the actual simulation given in Step (3) differs from a perfect simulation only by the condition on $|\text{indices}_\mathcal{A}|$, as its perfectly equivalent to the one performed during simulators leakage phase. This condition forces the return of $\perp$ instead of appropriate $\text{indices}_\mathcal{A}$ with probability $\Pr(|\text{indices}_\mathcal{A}| \geqslant \ell^e) = \varepsilon$. Consequently, we bound ε by a factor negligible (in a certain sense) in the security parameters. Directly by applying Lemma 2 for an adversary $\mathcal{A}$ we see that:

$$\varepsilon = \Pr(|\text{indices}_\mathcal{A}| \geqslant \ell^e) \leqslant 2^{-n((p-\eta-\lambda)\ell) + \ell^e(\log q + \log \ell)}.$$

This completes the proof.

Implementation of the simulator $\mathcal{S}$.

1. $\mathcal{S}$ initializes a random oracle $\mathcal{H}$, i.e., creates a table $\mathcal{H}$ of uniformly random values associated to all inputs of $\mathcal{H}$ (or use **OracleQueryList**). Moreover, it draws a random variable $K \leftarrow U_{\ell n}$.
2. $\mathcal{S}$ initializes the random tape of $\mathcal{A}$ to a fixed sequence of uniformly random bits and then queries the leakage oracle with the Turing machine $\mathsf{ind} : \{0,1\}^{|D|} \to \{0,1\}^*$ which operates as follows:

Operation of ind:

Description of the function Simulate the execution of $\mathcal{A}(K)$ step by step with random oracle queries $\mathcal{H}$ substituted with $\mathcal{H}\{D \xrightarrow{\mathcal{G}_\sigma} K\}$. Every time the adversary $\mathcal{A}$ issues a leakage oracle query given by a Turing machine f, the simulator $\mathcal{S}$ provides her with a result of a *twisted leakage function* $f\{D \xrightarrow{\mathcal{G}_\sigma} K\}$, i.e., a Turing machine with all random oracle queries substituted with $\mathcal{H}\{D \xrightarrow{\mathcal{G}_\sigma} K\}$.

Result The list $\mathsf{indices}_\mathcal{A}$. Returns $\mathsf{indices}_\mathcal{A}$ if its length satisfies $|\mathsf{indices}_\mathcal{A}| < \ell^e$, or $\perp$ otherwise.

Complexity Leakage: $|\mathsf{indices}_\mathcal{A}|(\log q + \log \ell)$

---

3. $\mathcal{S}$ executes $\mathcal{A}(K)$ with a previously initialized (see Step (2)) random tape and $\mathcal{H}$ sampled above (see Step (1)), and then runs it step by step with the following exceptions:

   (a) When $\mathcal{A}$ issues a leakage query given by a Turing machine f, the simulator $\mathcal{S}$ substitutes it with a twisted leakage function $f\{D \xrightarrow{\mathcal{G}_\sigma} K\}$.
   (b) $\mathcal{S}$ keeps track of the number k of random oracle queries issued to $\mathcal{H}$ and every time it appears in a pair $(k, i_k) \in \mathsf{indices}_\mathcal{A}$, replaces the value returned by $\mathcal{H}$ with K_{i_k}. Moreover, it stores the arguments a_k of queries appearing in the list $\mathsf{indices}_\mathcal{A}$ and substitutes the value of $\mathcal{H}$ with K_{i_k} every time a_k appears as an argument.

Fig. 5. Implementation of Simulator

4.4 Security of Disperse

Security of our construction function arises from one-wayness of Disperse. We explicitly show a simulator that simulates perfectly any given λ-bounded adversary $\mathcal{A}$, provided that a number of bad queries made by an adversary does not exceed ℓ^e. This bound is violated only with negligible probability, and therefore we claim our simulator fails with negligible probability as well.

Theorem 3 (Security). *For every ℓ^d-regular $(\ell^e, (1-\eta)\ell)$-disperser $\mathcal{G}_\sigma$, $\eta \leqslant p$ and $q = 2^{o(\ell^{1-e})n}$, and $\mathbf{H}_\infty(D) = pn\ell$, function $\mathsf{Disperse}_{\mathcal{G}_\sigma}$ is $\left(\lambda + \ell^e(\log q + n), 2^{-n((p-\eta-\lambda)\ell) + \ell^e(\log q + \log \ell)}\right)$-secure* kdf.

Proof. Let $X \in \{0,1\}^{\ell n}$ be a random variable of min-entropy at least $p\ell n$. We need to construct a simulator $\mathcal{S}$ such that

$$|\Pr(\text{real}_{\mathcal{Z},\mathcal{A}}(n, \text{Disperse}_{g_\sigma}, X) = 1) - \Pr(\text{ideal}_{\mathcal{Z},\mathcal{S}}(n, \ell n) = 1)| \leq \varepsilon(n),$$

Implementation of $\mathcal{S}$.

Setup phase:

1. A mock random variable D is sampled from the same distribution as X. An efficient data structure **OracleQueryList** for the on-the-fly storage of random oracle $\mathcal{H}$ queries is prepared.
2. Adversary $\mathcal{A}$ is initialized and given an access to a leakage oracle $\Omega(X_{\text{Mock}}, Y' \leftarrow \text{Disperse}_{g_\sigma}(X_{\text{Mock}}, \mathcal{H}\{X_{\text{Mock}} \xrightarrow{g_\sigma} Y\}))$.

Execution phase:

3. Every time $\mathcal{S}$ communicates with $\mathcal{Z}$, she performs the following steps:
   a) performs getIndices leakage:

---

getIndices leakage

Result The list indices containing pairs (i, v_i) of an index i and a result v_i of $\mathcal{A}$'s bad random oracle query (cf. Definition 3) conducted during its communication with an environment $\mathcal{Z}$ on the key $\text{Disperse}_{g_\sigma}(X_{\text{Mock}}, \mathcal{H}\{X_{\text{Mock}} \xrightarrow{g_\sigma} Y\})$ before sending the next message back to $\mathcal{Z}$.

Description of the function Just simulate the behaviour of $\mathcal{A}$ and check whether random oracle queries are bad or not.

Complexity Leakage: $|\text{indices}| \cdot (\log q + n)$, time: the same as $\mathcal{A}$ operation

---

   b) simulates the behaviour of $\mathcal{A}$ with the following recipe for answering leakage and random oracle queries:

How to reply to leakage and random oracle queries?

Random oracle queries If the index i appears in one of the pairs in the list indices leaked above then return v_i otherwise look up **OracleQueryList** and answer with a value from there or a random element drawn from U_n. In any case, add the whole query to **OracleQueryList**.

Leakage queries We answer a leakage oracle query f described by a circuit containing $\Omega(X_{\text{Mock}}, \mathcal{H})$ queries by the same circuit containing $\Omega(X_{\text{Mock}}, \mathcal{H}\{X_{\text{Mock}} \xrightarrow{g_\sigma} Y\})$ instead. Note that in order to substitute all bad queries of $\mathcal{H}$ by $\mathcal{H}\{X_{\text{Mock}} \xrightarrow{g_\sigma} Y\}$), we just need to access X_{Mock}, $\mathcal{H}$ and $\Omega(Y)$ which are all given to $\mathcal{S}$.

Complexity Leakage: same as $\mathcal{A}$'s, time: same as $\mathcal{A}$'s up to time necessary for **OracleQueryList** look ups. Bounded by $\lambda - \ell^e \cdot (\log q + n)$.

---

   c) if the total leakage equal to $\lambda + |\text{indices}| \cdot (\log q + n)$ exceeds $\lambda + \ell^e \cdot (\log q + n)$ then terminate with $\bot$;
   d) returns the message prepared by $\mathcal{A}$.

Fig. 6. Implementation of $\mathcal{S}$

where $\varepsilon(n) = 2^{-n((p-\eta-\lambda)\ell)+\ell^e(\log q+\log \ell)}$. On the high level we aim at simulating the behaviour of $\mathcal{A}$ on a mock randomness $X_{\text{Mock}} \in \{0,1\}^{\ell n}$ distributed equally as X pretending that the result of $\mathsf{Disperse}_{\mathcal{G}_\sigma}(X_{\text{Mock}}, \mathcal{H})$ is equal to the randomness Y that the environment obtains in the ideal scenario. The precise construction of $\mathcal{S} \in \mathbf{TM}_{\lambda+\ell^e(\log q+n)}^{\Omega(Y)}$ for $Y \sim U_{nl}$ simulating execution of $\mathcal{A} \in \mathbf{TM}_\lambda^{\Omega(X)}$ is given in Fig. 6.

To finish the proof we need the following claims.

Claim. The randomness Y equals

$$Y' \leftarrow \mathsf{Disperse}_{\mathcal{G}_\sigma}(X_{\text{Mock}}, \mathcal{H}\{X_{\text{Mock}} \xrightarrow{\mathcal{G}_\sigma} Y\}),$$

executed on mock randomness $(X_{\text{Mock}}, \mathcal{H})$. Furthermore, transcript of communication between $\mathcal{S}$ and $\mathcal{Z}$ does not differ from a transcript between $\mathcal{A}$ and $\mathcal{Z}$.

Proof. Firstly, observe that the key Y is equal to

$$\mathsf{Disperse}_{\mathcal{G}_\sigma}(X_{\text{Mock}}, \mathcal{H}\{X_{\text{Mock}} \xrightarrow{\mathcal{G}_\sigma} Y\})$$

(by definition of $\mathcal{H}\{X_{\text{Mock}} \xrightarrow{\mathcal{G}_\sigma} Y\}$) and therefore the input of $\mathcal{Z}$ in $\mathsf{ideal}_{\mathcal{Z},\mathcal{S}}(n, n\ell)$ is equal to input in $\mathsf{real}_{\mathcal{Z},\mathcal{A}}(n, \mathsf{kdf}, X_{\text{Mock}})$. Moreover, all the messages send by $\mathcal{S}$ are in fact produced the adversary $\mathcal{A}$ and therefore the only difference is that the leakage and random oracle queries of $\mathcal{A}$ are not processed honestly but simulated by means of leakage of $\mathcal{S}$ described in steps (3a) and (3b) in Fig. 6.

Claim (Simulation's correctness). The simulation above is faithful (i.e., $\mathcal{S}$ works the same as corresponding $\mathcal{A}$) unless $\bot$ is returned in part (3c) of simulation. This occurs with probability $\varepsilon = \Pr(|\mathsf{indices}_\mathcal{A}| > \ell^e) = 2^{-n((p-\eta-\lambda)\ell)+\ell^e(\log q+\log \ell)}$ and therefore $\Pr(\mathcal{A} \text{ is faithfully simulated}) = 1 - \Pr(|\mathsf{indices}_\mathcal{A}| > \ell^e) = 1 - \varepsilon$.

Proof. Proof has been omitted due to a page limit.

Acknowledgments. Michal Zajac and Maciej Zdanowicz would like to thank the National Science Centre for their support in form of the grant PRELUDIUM 7 no. UMO-2014/13/N/ST6/03029.

References

1. Alwen, J., Dodis, Y., Naor, M., Segev, G., Walfish, S., Wichs, D.: Public-key encryption in the bounded-retrieval model. In: Gilbert, H. (ed.) EUROCRYPT 2010. LNCS, vol. 6110, pp. 113–134. Springer, Heidelberg (2010). doi:10.1007/978-3-642-13190-5_6
2. Alwen, J., Dodis, Y., Wichs, D.: Leakage-resilient public-key cryptography in the bounded-retrieval model. In: Halevi, S. (ed.) CRYPTO 2009. LNCS, vol. 5677, pp. 36–54. Springer, Heidelberg (2009). doi:10.1007/978-3-642-03356-8_3
3. Barak, B., Dodis, Y., Krawczyk, H., Pereira, O., Pietrzak, K., Standaert, F.-X., Yu, Y.: Leftover hash lemma, revisited. In: Rogaway, P. (ed.) CRYPTO 2011. LNCS, vol. 6841, pp. 1–20. Springer, Heidelberg (2011). doi:10.1007/978-3-642-22792-9_1

4. Cash, D., Ding, Y.Z., Dodis, Y., Lee, W., Lipton, R., Walfish, S.: Intrusion-resilient key exchange in the bounded retrieval model. In: Vadhan, S.P. (ed.) TCC 2007. LNCS, vol. 4392, pp. 479–498. Springer, Heidelberg (2007). doi:10.1007/978-3-540-70936-7_26

5. Crescenzo, G., Lipton, R., Walfish, S.: Perfectly secure password protocols in the bounded retrieval model. In: Halevi, S., Rabin, T. (eds.) TCC 2006. LNCS, vol. 3876, pp. 225–244. Springer, Heidelberg (2006). doi:10.1007/11681878_12

6. Dodis, Y., Reyzin, L., Smith, A.: Fuzzy extractors: how to generate strong keys from biometrics and other noisy data. In: Cachin, C., Camenisch, J.L. (eds.) EUROCRYPT 2004. LNCS, vol. 3027, pp. 523–540. Springer, Heidelberg (2004). doi:10.1007/978-3-540-24676-3_31

7. Dodis, Y., Yu, Y.: Overcoming weak expectations. In: Sahai, A. (ed.) TCC 2013. LNCS, vol. 7785, pp. 1–22. Springer, Heidelberg (2013). doi:10.1007/978-3-642-36594-2_1

8. Dziembowski, S.: Intrusion-resilience via the bounded-storage model. In: Halevi, S., Rabin, T. (eds.) TCC 2006. LNCS, vol. 3876, pp. 207–224. Springer, Heidelberg (2006). doi:10.1007/11681878_11

9. Dziembowski, S., Pietrzak, K.: Intrusion-resilient secret sharing. In: 48th Annual Symposium on Foundations of Computer Science, pp. 227–237. IEEE Computer Society Press, Providence, USA, 20–23 October 2007

10. Håstad, J., Impagliazzo, R., Levin, L.A., Luby, M.: A pseudorandom generator from any one-way function. SIAM J. Comput. 28(4), 1364–1396 (1999)

11. Merkle, R.C.: Secrecy, authentication, and public key systems. Ph.D. thesis, Stanford University, Stanford, CA, USA, aAI8001972 (1979)

12. Nisan, N., Zuckerman, D.: Randomness is linear in space. J. Comput. Syst. Sci. 52(1), 43–52 (1996). http://dx.doi.org/10.1006/jcss.1996.0004

13. Radhakrishnan, J., Ta-Shma, A.: Bounds for dispersers, extractors, and depth-two superconcentrators. SIAM J. Discrete Math. 13, 2–24 (2000)

14. Vadhan, S.P.: Constructing locally computable extractors and cryptosystems in the bounded-storage model. J. Cryptology 17(1), 43–77 (2004)

Leakage-Resilient IND-CCA KEM from the Extractable Hash Proofs with Indistinguishability Obfuscation

Wenpan Jing[1,2(✉)], Xianhui Lu[1,2,3], and Bao Li[1,2,3]

[1] Data Assurance and Communication Security Research Center,
Chinese Academy of Sciences, Beijing, China
jingwenpan@iie.ac.cn
[2] State Key Laboratory of Information Security,
Institute of Information Engineering, Chinese Academy of Sciences, Beijing, China
[3] University of Chinese Academy of Sciences, Beijing, China

Abstract. Leakage-resilient cryptography requires that a crypto-system remain provably secure even if the attacker gets additional information about the internal states, which is usually the secret key in the scenario of public key encryption.

In this paper, we propose a solution to achieve leakage resilience CCA for key encapsulation mechanisms firstly based on the all-but-one extractable hash proof system in the bounded leakage model, where to the best of our knowledge, previous leakage resilient public key encryption schemes are mostly based on the Cramer-Shoup's universal hash proof system and its variations. The main technique we employ is the indistinguishability obfuscation. Specifically, we use the obfuscated decryption program as the secret key to deal with the leakage.

Although our schemes can tolerate a considerably good amount of leakage, the tolerated rate of leakage (defined as the ratio of leakage-amount to key size) is quite unsatisfactory because we use the whole obfuscated program as the secret key.

Keywords: Public key encryption · Leakage-resilience · Key-encapsulation mechanism · Hash-proof system · Indistinguishability obfuscation

1 Introduction

1.1 Background

Leakage-resilient cryptography was initiated by Dziembowski *et al.* in 2008 [2], due to the emergence of new attacks which were not considered in previous

This work is supported the by the National Natural Science Foundation of China (No. 61572495, No. 61272534, and No. 61379137) and the National Basic Research Program of China (973 project) (No.2013CB338002).

© Springer International Publishing AG 2017
K. Chen et al. (Eds.): Inscrypt 2016, LNCS 10143, pp. 291–308, 2017.
DOI: 10.1007/978-3-319-54705-3_18

security models. These new attacks can lead to the exposure of the secret internal states. For example, the side-channel attacks [7–9] can reveal internal states of a cryptography system through physical measurements such as power consuming, electric radiation, computing time and heat radiation; and the memory attacks such as cold boot attacks, can directly obtain the secret keys which are stored on a computing device and are not erased properly. Leakage-resilient cryptography maintains provable security while partial internal states get leaked by all means.

Here we are interested in the leakage-resilient public-key encryption schemes, more specifically the key encapsulation mechanisms (KEM) in the bounded leakage model. It is required that standard security goals like *indistinguishability against chosen plaintext attacks/chosen ciphertext attacks* (IND-CPA/CCA) should not be compromised while the adversary additionally gets several bits of information about the secret key during various stages of the attack. The bounded leakage model is considered to be a simple and general model and has been widely studied [3,5,10,12]. In this model, the adversary is assumed to be able to adaptively access a leakage oracle to learn the information about the secret key sk before the challenge ciphertext is given. It queries the leakage oracle with an efficiently computable function f of its own choice, and gets $f(sk)$ as the answer. The only restriction of this leakage oracle is that the total length of its outputs should not be greater than l bits, which is also known as "the bound of leakage". (See Sect. 2.5 for a formal definition.)

Consider most of the KEM schemes that achieves leakage-resilient IND-CPA/IND-CCA (IND-lrCPA/IND-lrCCA) security [3,5,10,12]. Their leakage-resilience property all comes from the fact that in these schemes while the public key is given, the secret key is not uniquely decided. In another word, the secret key has sufficient entropy. Therefore, though there is a few bits of leakage, through a randomness extraction, the scheme can still be IND-CPA/IND-CCA secure.

If a KEM with its secret key fixed by the public key can be improved to achieve leakage-resilience is an interesting problem. We intend to give a positive answer to this problem with the help of indistinguishable obfuscation.

1.2 Warm up

As a warm up, we would like to further introduce how does a KEM based on *universal hash proof system* (UHPS), whose secret key has entropy conditioned on the public key, achieve leakage-resilience. Then we explain why it is difficult for a KEM with its secret key fixed by the public key to resist leakage.

We briefly review the UHPS, which was introduced by Cramer and Shoup in [11]. A UHPS is usually built on the hardness of subset membership problems, which is a type of decisional problems. An UHPS consists of three algorithms, (Param, Priv, Pub). The underlying subset membership problem is specified by a language $\mathcal{C}$ and its subset $\mathcal{V}$, and by assumption it is infeasible to decide whether an instance $x \in \mathcal{C}$ is from $\mathcal{V}$ or $\mathcal{C} \backslash \mathcal{V}$. In Param a pair of public/secret key (pk, sk) is generated, where pk is computed from sk via a projective map, thus various sk's may be cast to one pk. The private evaluation algorithm Priv computes the hash value of $x \in \mathcal{C}$ with sk. And the public evaluation algorithm computes the hash value of $x \in \mathcal{V}$ with its witness w and pk. It is required that $\mathsf{Pub}(pk, x, w) = \mathsf{Priv}(sk, x)$. That is, the hash value of an instance $x \in \mathcal{V}$ is determined by the public key and its witness, and it is called the *projective property* of UHPS. However, for an instance $x' \in \mathcal{C}\backslash\mathcal{V}$ (without witness), its hash value $\mathsf{Priv}(sk, x')$ should be statistically close to uniform conditioned on pk and x', and it is called the *1-universal property*.

We now explain why it is convenient to obtain leakage resilience from UHPS. The leakage-resilient KEM based on the UHPS was firstly constructed by Naor et al. in the bounded leakage model [3]. In the security proof of the KEM from UHPS, a simulator receives an instance $x \in \mathcal{C}$ of the underlying subset membership problem and wants to use the ability of an adversary in the leakage model to decide whether it is from $\mathcal{V}$ or $\mathcal{C}\backslash\mathcal{V}$. The simulator starts by running Param and getting the (pk, sk) pair. Since it owns sk, it can naturally answer the leakage queries. Besides, the leakage-resilient property is achieved due to the *1-universal property* property. Essentially, since sk is not uniquely decided by pk, and the *1-universal property* property guarantees that there is information entropy in the hash value of an instance $x' \in \mathcal{C}\backslash\mathcal{V}$. Though the leakage of sk will result in an entropy decrease of the hash value, which will appear as the encapsulated key k, a universal hash function ext can be applied as a randomness extractor to extract the remaining entropy and produce a new encapsulated key $\mathsf{ext}(k, d)$ (where d is the random seed of ext) that is statistically close to a uniformly random string. A series of works are done to improve the efficiency of leakage-resilience from UHPS [10, 12] and minimize the underlying assumption [5].

However, obtaining leakage resilience from a KEM with its secret key fixed by the public key is difficult to accomplish. First of all, since the secret key is uniquely decided by the public key, which means that there is no information entropy in the encapsulated key. Therefore the IND-CPA security will be compromised by even one bit of the leakage. Secondly, the simulator in the security proof answers the decryption query with a trapdoor related to the underlying hard problem. Thus it does not possess the real secret key as the simulator in the UHPS. As a result, in the security model with leakage, it can not answer the leakage query about the secret key properly.

1.3   Main Idea

We observe that the indistinguishability obfuscation can somewhat provide the leakage resilient property. Therefore, with an indistinguishability obfuscation, even the secret key has no entropy conditioned on the public key, the scheme might still be leakage resilient.

The origin of the indistinguishability obfuscator is "program obfuscation", which aims to make computer programs "unintelligible" while preserving their functionality. An idealistic notion called virtual black-box (VBB) obfuscation was brought out by Barak et al. in 2001 [18]. VBB asks that an obfuscated program be no more useful than a black box implementing the program. A less intuitive yet achievable notion of indistinguishability obfuscation was then proposed [17]. Informally, an indistinguishability obfuscator provides obfuscation of any two equal-sized programs that are functionally identical. The obfuscated programs are functionally equal to the original programs and are computationally indistinguishable from each other [16] (one may refer to Definition 3 for detail).

First of all, we find that if we let the obfuscated decryption program $\Psi_{\mathsf{Dec}_{sk}}$ (we denote the program, or circuit, that implements the algorithm $\mathsf{Dec}_{sk}(\cdot)$ as $\Psi_{\mathsf{Dec}_{sk}}$) be the new secret key. Then as long as we can construct a simulated decryption program $\Psi_{\mathsf{Dec}^*_{sk^*}}$ (we denote the program, or circuit, that implements the algorithm $\mathsf{Dec}^*_{sk^*}(\cdot)$ as $\Psi_{\mathsf{Dec}^*_{sk^*}}$) which is functionally indistinguishable with $\Psi_{\mathsf{Dec}_{sk}}$, we can answer the leakage query with the obfuscation of $\Psi_{\mathsf{Dec}^*_{sk^*}}$. The difference between a real life execution and a simulated environment will not be detected by any PPT distinguisher.

The leakage-resilience property being brought out by the indistinguishability obfuscation can be explained by the intuition idea of VBB on another perspective. Imagine a VBB $\mathcal{VBB}$ applied on the decryption program $\Psi_{\mathsf{Dec}_{sk}}$ and let $\mathcal{VBB}(\Psi_{\mathsf{Dec}_{sk}})$ be the new secret key. The adversary can only get $f(\mathcal{VBB}(\Psi_{\mathsf{Dec}_{sk}}))$ instead of $f(sk)$ through its leakage query. Then as long as the adversary does not get enough information of $\mathcal{VBB}(\Psi_{\mathsf{Dec}_{sk}})$ that helps it to recover the whole algorithm, thus gives it the ability to decrypt the challenge ciphertext by itself, the leakage oracle only provides the adversary no more help than a decryption oracle, which it already has. We conjecture that any IND-CCA public-key encryption scheme with its decryption program been obfuscated can leak a large ratio of the obfuscated decryption program and still be secure. Unfortunately, the existing realizable definition of obfuscation (namely indistinguishability obfuscation, differing-inputs obfuscation, *etc.*) seems insufficient for a precise analysis for its effect on resisting leakage.

However, there is a main technical difficulty while applying the indistinguishability obfuscator on the decryption program. For most of the existing IND-CCA KEM, the real life decryption algorithm $\mathsf{Dec}_{sk}(\cdot)$ and the simulated decryption algorithm $\mathsf{Dec}^*_{sk^*}(\cdot)$ are just computationally indistinguishable. However, we need the programs to be obfuscated functionally identical, namely the algorithms have to outputs exactly the same value for almost all of the inputs.

We further find that the KEM based on the extractable EHPS can achieve the above requirements through some modification. Firstly introduced by Wee in [15], EHPS and its richer version, all-but-one EHPS (ABO-EHPS), play important roles in constructing IND-CCA secure KEMs (without leakage). Moreover, unlike UHPS whose security are based on decisional assumptions, EHPS is built from the hardness of search problems (namely computational problems), which are weaker in assumption thus stronger in security. Therefore, finding a way to obtaining leakage-resilience from the EHPS framework itself is an interesting and valuable problem.

1.4   Our Contributions

We propose a general construction of IND-lrCCA KEM from ABO-EHPS. As we explained previously, we should conquer two major problems to achieve this goal: the simulator can not answer the leakage query, for it does not have the real secret key; and there is no information entropy in the encapsulated key. Our results are obtained by applying an indistinguishability obfuscator, on the decryption program to deal with the leakage query and protect the secret key. More specifically, we use the whole obfuscated decryption program as the new secret key and answer the leakage query with it.

As we mentioned above, we need the real life decryption algorithm $\mathsf{Dec}_{sk}(\cdot)$ and the simulated decryption algorithm $\mathsf{Dec}^*_{sk^*}(\cdot)$ to statistically output the same value for all the inputs, in order to be able to apply the indistinguishability obfuscator on the programs $\Psi_{\mathsf{Dec}_{sk}}$ and $\Psi_{\mathsf{Dec}^*_{sk^*}}$. We make two modifications on the KEM based on ABO-EHPS proposed by Wee [15] to achieve this goal.

For an IND-CCA KEM based on ABO-EHPS as in [15], the secret key sk is uniquely decided by the public key. There is an internal state "tag", which is usually generated by a target collision resistant hash function (TCR) from a ciphertext. In the simulated proof of the scheme, the decryption algorithm uses an sk^* generated from a trapdoor to decrypt all the ciphertexts whose tag is unequal to the tag generated from the challenge ciphertext, denoted as tag^*.

We first define a secret key deduce mode, in which sk^* can be deduced from sk with the help of a trapdoor. Therefore, for the ciphertext with $tag \neq tag^*$, both $\mathsf{Dec}_{sk}(\cdot)$ and $\mathsf{Dec}^*_{sk^*}(\cdot)$ provides exact the same output. Note that the secret key deduce mode shares the same public key with the real life execution. This is quite different from the keys generated in an ABO mode, which only provide public keys statistically indistinguishable from the public keys generated in a real life execution. The sk^* generated in the ABO mode cannot let $\mathsf{Dec}^*_{sk^*}(\cdot)$ give the same outputs on the same inputs as $\mathsf{Dec}_{sk}(\cdot)$, since they do not share the same public key.

Secondly, since a TCR only ensures that it is computationally hard to find another ciphertext whose tag equals tag^*, while actually there might exist a lot of ciphertexts whose tag equals tag^*. Obviously $\mathsf{Dec}_{sk}(\cdot)$ can provide decryptions to these ciphertext while $\mathsf{Dec}^*_{sk^*}(\cdot)$ can not. In order to let $\mathsf{Dec}_{sk}(\cdot)$ and $\mathsf{Dec}^*_{sk^*}(\cdot)$ be statistically equal, we require an injective map from the ciphertexts to the tags, and store a decryption for the challenge ciphertext in $\mathsf{Dec}^*_{sk^*}(\cdot)$.

To sum up, in this paper, we give a positive answer to achieving leakage resilient security for a KEM whose secret key has no entropy conditioned on the public key. We give the first proposal of applying the indistinguishability obfuscation on an IND-CCA KEM based on ABO-EHPS to achieve provable IND-lrCCA security.

Compared with the schemes based on UHPS, we use weaker assumptions. However the shortcoming on efficiency is obvious. Although our schemes can tolerate a considerably good amount of leakage, the tolerated rate of leakage (defined as the ratio of leakage-amount to key size) is quite unsatisfactory. Compared with the framework in [5], we achieve IND-lrCCA security in the bounded leakage model while the framework in [5] achieves only IND-lrCPA security in the same model. Efficiency of both frameworks are unsatisfactory.

Nevertheless, we believe that our work is with more theoretical significance than practical significance. It is worth to mention that Dana Dachman-Soled *et al.* also build a leakage-resilient public-key encryption from obfuscation concurrently and independently with our work [24], and their construction are based on the deniable public-key encryption scheme of [16].

1.5   Organization

We give necessary preliminaries in Sect. 2. In Sect. 3, we give our general construction of IND-lrCCA KEM from ABO-EHPS. We also present a concrete instance in this framework in Sect. 4 for easier understanding. Section 5 is the conclusion.

2   Preliminary

2.1   Notations and Assumptions

Let λ denote the security parameter. For a distribution or random variable X, we write $x \leftarrow X$ to denote the operation of sampling a random x according to X. For a set S, we write $s \leftarrow S$ to denote sampling s uniformly and randomly from S. For distributions X and Y, $X \equiv Y$ means that X and Y are identically distributed, $X =_s Y$ means that they are statistically close, and $X =_c Y$ means that they are computationally indistinguishable.

2.2   One-Way Relation

A binary relation R_{pp}, where pp is efficiently samplable public parameter, is one-way if:

- With overwhelming probability for the public parameter pp and for all $c \in \mathcal{C}$, there exists at most one ω such that $(c, \omega) \in \mathsf{R}_{pp}$;
- There is an efficiently computable generator G such that $G(\omega)$ is pseudo-random even against an adversary that gets pp, c and oracle access to R_{pp}, where there is a efficiently computable algorithm $\mathsf{SampR}_{pp}(\cdot)$ such that $(c, \omega) \leftarrow \mathsf{SampR}_{pp}(r)$ for a randomly chosen $r \in \mathcal{R}$. (We will also refer to G as extracting hard-core bits from ω.).

Definition 1. *Consider a family of groups $\mathbb{G}$ of a large prime order p. The public parameter $pp = (g, g^\alpha)$ for a random $g \leftarrow \mathbb{G}$ and a random $\alpha \leftarrow \mathbb{Z}_p$. A Diffie-Hellman (DH) Relation is:*

$$\mathsf{R}_{pp}^{dh} = \{(c, \omega) \in \mathbb{G} \times \mathbb{G} : \omega = c^\alpha\}$$

Obviously, with pp and c, there is only one ω such that $\omega = c^a$. There is efficient sampling algorithm $\mathsf{SampR}_{pp}(r)$ outputs $(g^r, (g^\alpha)^r)$. We give the function G to obtain hard-core bits for R_{pp}^{dh} under the bilinear DDH (BDDH) assumption.

A bilinear map $\hat{e} : \mathbb{G}_1 \times \mathbb{G}_1 \to \mathbb{G}_2$, where $\mathbb{G}_1$ and $\mathbb{G}_2$ are two groups of prime order p, satisfies the following properties [23]:

- Bilinear: A map $\hat{e} : \mathbb{G}_1 \times \mathbb{G}_1 \to \mathbb{G}_2$ is bilinear if $\hat{e}(aP, bQ) = \hat{e}(P,Q)^{ab}$ for all $P, Q \in \mathbb{G}_1$ and all $a, b \in \mathbb{Z}$.
- Non-degenerate: The map does not send all pairs in $\mathbb{G}_1 \times \mathbb{G}_1$ to the identity in $\mathbb{G}_2$. Observe that since $\mathbb{G}_1, \mathbb{G}_2$ are groups of prime order, this implies that if P is a generater of $\mathbb{G}_1$ then $\hat{e}(P, P)$ is a generator of $\mathbb{G}_2$.
- Computable: There is an efficient algorithm to compute $\hat{e}(P, P)$ for any $P, Q \in \mathbb{G}_1$.

The Bilinear DDH (BDDH) assumption asserts that:

$$(g, g^a, g^b, g^c, u) =_c (g, g^a, g^b, g^c, \hat{e}(g,g)^{abc})$$

where g, g^a, g^b, g^c are random element in $\mathbb{G}_1$ and u is a random element in $\mathbb{G}_2$.

Set $pp = (g, g^\alpha, g^\gamma)$, we may extract a linear number of hard-core bits from ω using [15]:

$$G_{pp}^{bddh}(\omega) = \hat{e}(\omega, g^\gamma)$$

2.3   Randomness Extractors

The statistical distance of random variables X and Y:

$$SD(X, Y) = \frac{1}{2} \sum_{\omega \in \Omega} |Pr[X = \omega] - Pr[Y = \omega]|$$

The min-entropy of a random variable X is defined as:

$$H_\infty(X) = -\log(max_{\omega \in \Omega} Pr[X = \omega])$$

And the average min-entropy of variable X conditioned on a variable Y is defined as:

$$\widetilde{H}_\infty(X|Y) = -\log(E_{y \leftarrow Y}[2^{-H_\infty(X|Y=y)}])$$

Lemma 1. *Let X, Y and Z be random variables. If Y has at most 2^r possible values, then*

$$\widetilde{H}_\infty(X|(Y,Z)) \geq \widetilde{H}_\infty(X|Z) - r \qquad (1)$$

Definition 2. *An efficient function $Ext : \mathcal{X} \times \mathcal{S} \to \mathcal{Y}$ is a (v, ε)-extractor if for all random variables X, Z such that $X \in \mathcal{X}$ and $\widetilde{H}_\infty(X|Z) \geq v$, we have*

$$SD((Z, S, Ext(X, S)), (Z, S, Y)) \leq \varepsilon$$

where S and Y are uniformly and independently distributed over $\mathcal{S}$ and $\mathcal{Y}$ respectively.

According to the left-over hash lemma, we have:

Lemma 2. *A universal family of hash functions $\mathcal{H} = \{h_s : \mathcal{X} \to \mathcal{Y}\}_{S \in \mathcal{S}}$ can be used as (v, ε)-extractor for any $v \geq \log |\mathcal{Y}| + 2\log(1/\varepsilon)$.*

2.4   Indistinguishability Obfuscator

Definition 3 [16]. *A uniform PPT machine iO is called an indistinguishability obfuscator for a circuit class $\mathcal{C}_\lambda$, if the following conditions are satisfied:*

- *For all security parameters $\lambda \in \mathbb{N}$, for all $C \in \mathcal{C}_\lambda$, for all inputs x, we have that*

$$Pr[C'(x) = C(x) : C' \leftarrow i\mathcal{O}(\lambda, C)] = 1.$$

- *For any (not necessarily uniform) PPT adversaries Samp, D, there exists a negligible function ρ such that the following holds:*
  if:

$$\Pr[\forall x, C_0(x) = C_1(x) : (C_0, C_1, \sigma) \leftarrow \mathsf{Samp}(1^\lambda)] \geq 1 - \rho(\lambda),$$

then:

$$|\Pr[D(\sigma, i\mathcal{O}(\lambda, C_0)) = 1 : (C_0, C_1, \sigma) \leftarrow \mathsf{Samp}(1^\lambda)]$$
$$- \Pr[D(\sigma, i\mathcal{O}(\lambda, C_1)) = 1 : (C_0, C_1, \sigma) \leftarrow \mathsf{Samp}(1^\lambda)]|$$
$$\leq \rho(\lambda)$$

Note that although attacks on the general indistinguishability obfuscators of [17] have occurred lately, the idea of indistinguishability obfuscators still works, and we are optimistic for new mending and new constructions to come up soon.

2.5   IND-lrCCA KEM

The leakage of the secret key in real life is described by allowing the adversary to query a leakage oracle Leakage(SK). It takes as input a function $f : \mathcal{SK}_\lambda \rightarrow \{0,1\}^*$ and outputs $f(SK)$. $\mathcal{A}$ is an l-key-leakage adversary if the sum of output length of all functions that $\mathcal{A}$ submits to the leakage oracle is at most l bits.

Our definition of l-leakage-resilient IND-CCA key encapsulation mechanism follows [3,5], which allows leakage queries only after the key generation phase and before the challenge is given.

Definition 4. *A key encapsulation mechanism KEM = (KeyGen, Encap, Decap) is l-leakage-resilient chosen-ciphertext secure, if for any PPT l-key-leakage adversary $\mathcal{A} = (\mathcal{A}_1, \mathcal{A}_2)$, we have:*

$$|\Pr[\mathsf{Exp}_{\mathsf{KEM},\mathcal{A}}^{IND-lrCCA}(\lambda) = 1] - \frac{1}{2}| \leq negl(\lambda)$$

where $\mathsf{Exp}_{\mathsf{KEM},\mathcal{A}}^{IND-lrCCA}(\lambda)$ defined as below:

1. $(SK, PK) \leftarrow \mathsf{KeyGen}(1^\lambda)$, $(k_0^*, c^*) \leftarrow \mathsf{Encap}_{PK}(1^\lambda)$, $k_1^* \leftarrow \mathcal{K}$.
2. $\sigma \leftarrow \mathcal{A}_1^{\mathsf{Leakage}(SK), \mathsf{Decap}_{SK}(\cdot)}(PK)$.
3. $b \leftarrow \{0,1\}$, $b' \leftarrow \mathcal{A}_2^{\mathsf{Decap}_{SK}(\cdot)}(PK, c^*, k_b^*, \sigma)$.
4. *If $b = b'$, return 1; else return 0.*

3   A General Construction of IND-lrCCA KEM from EHPS

Our ABO-EHPS with a *secret key deduce mode* mainly follows the ABO-EHPS in [15] with a few modifications to enable the usage of indistinguishable obfuscation. In the secret key deduce mode, for every sk and any tag^*, a corresponding sk^* that works like the sk^* in the ABO mode is produced. This will not compromise the generality of ABO-EHPS since all existing schemes in this framework can provide algorithms to meet this requirement. Further more, we need an injective mapping $\mathcal{C} \to \mathcal{T}$, where $\mathcal{C}$ and $\mathcal{T}$ are the space of the ciphertexts and the tags respectively, to generate the tags in the ABO-EHPS. In this section, we first give the description of our ABO-EHPS, then give our construction of IND-lrCCA KEM from this ABO-EHPS.

3.1   All-But-One Extractable Hash Proofs

An extractable hash proof system is based on a one-way relation R_{pp}. Consider a family of hash functions $\mathsf{H}_{pk}(tag, \cdot)$, which is indexed by a public key pk, and takes a tag as an additional input. An ABO-EHPS with the secret key deduce mode for a one-way relation R_{pp} is a tuple of algorithms satisfying the following properties with overwhelming probability over λ:

$$\mathsf{ABO - EHPS} = (\mathsf{SetupExt}, \mathsf{SetupABO}, \mathsf{Pub}, \mathsf{Ext}, \mathsf{Ext}^*, \mathsf{Priv}, \mathsf{DD})$$

- PUBLIC EVALUATION.
  For all pk, tag, and $(c, \omega) \leftarrow \mathsf{SampR}_{pp}(r)$, there is an algorithm Pub such that:

  $$\mathsf{Pub}(pk, tag, r) = \mathsf{H}_{pk}(tag, c),$$

  where $\mathsf{SampR}_{pp}(r)$ takes a randomness r and outputs an instance $(c, \omega) \in \mathsf{R}_{pp}$.
- EXTRACTION MODE.
  For all $(pk, sk) \leftarrow \mathsf{SetupExt}(pp)$ and all (tag, c, π), there is:

  $$\pi = \mathsf{H}_{pk}(tag, c) \iff (c, \mathsf{Ext}(sk, tag, c, \pi)) \in \mathsf{R}_{pp}$$

- ALL-BUT-ONE MODE.
  For all $(pk^*, sk^*) \leftarrow \mathsf{SetupABO}(pp, tag^*)$, all tag^*, and all $(c, \omega) \in \mathsf{R}_{pp}$, there is

  $$\mathsf{Priv}(sk^*, tag^*, c) = \mathsf{H}_{pk^*}(tag^*, c)$$

  In addition, for all $tag \neq tag^*$ and all (c, π):

  $$\pi = \mathsf{H}_{pk^*}(tag, c) \iff (c, \mathsf{Ext}^*(sk^*, tag^*, tag, c, \pi)) \in \mathsf{R}_{pp}$$

- SECRET-KEY DEDUCE MODE.
  For all $(pk, sk) \leftarrow \mathsf{SetupExt}(pp)$ and all tag^*, there is an algorithm with auxiliary input aux such that $sk^* \leftarrow \mathsf{DD}(sk, tag^*, aux)$.

For all $(c, \omega) \in \mathsf{R}_{pp}$, there is

$$\mathsf{Priv}(sk^*, tag^*, c) = \mathsf{H}_{pk}(tag^*, c)$$

For all $tag \neq tag^*$, there is:

$$\mathsf{Ext}^*(sk^*, tag^*, tag, c, \pi) = \mathsf{Ext}(sk, tag, c, \pi).$$

- INDISTINGUISHABILITY.
  For all tag^*, the first outputs of $\mathsf{SetupABO}(pp, tag^*)$ and $\mathsf{SetupExt}(pp)$ (namely pk and pk^*) are statistically indistinguishable.

3.2 Constructing IND-lrCCA KEM from ABO-EHPS

Informally, a KEM based on the ABO-EHPS works as follows. In the real-life encapsulation, $\mathsf{SetupExt}$ is used to generate the key pair (pk, sk). The sender uses $\mathsf{SampR}(r)$ in the public evaluation mode to sample a pair $(c, \omega) \in \mathsf{R}_{pp}$, then let c be the encapsulation of $k = G(\omega)$. A variable $\pi = \mathsf{Pub}(pk, tag, r)$ which is used to prove the validity of the ciphertext is also output by the sender with a tag tag to ensure the CCA security. The receiver uses the program $\mathsf{Ext}(sk, tag, c, \pi)$ in the extraction mode to extract ω and verifies if $(c, \omega) \in \mathsf{R}_{pp}$.[1] Finally, it gets the encapsulated key as $k = G(\omega)$.

   In the simulation of the security proof, the challenger decides its challenge c^* and the correspondence tag tag^* according to the hard problem first and then uses $\mathsf{SetupABO}(pp, tag^*)$ to generate a key pair (pk^*, sk^*), where pk^* is statistically indistinguishable with the public keys generated in the real life and sk^* contains a trapdoor to enable the simulator to provide the decryption for all the valid ciphertext whose tag is unequal with tag^*. Then the algorithm Priv is used to generate the supposed validity proof π^* for c^*.

   As in the security definition of IND-lrCCA KEM, a leakage oracle for the secret key should be provided to the adversary. However, the simulated challenger does not have the real life secret key as we described above. Thus, the original KEM challenger can not answer the leakage query. To solve this problem, we employ an indistinguishability obfuscator $i\mathcal{O}$ on the decryption program $\Psi_{\mathsf{Dec}_{sk}}$ and view the whole obfuscated program as the new secret key SK. Correspondingly, the secret key used by the challenger is $SK^* = i\mathcal{O}(\Psi_{\mathsf{Dec}^*_{sk^*}})$ and the

---

[1] Note that there is $(c, \omega) \in \mathsf{R}_{pp}$ if and only if $\pi = \mathsf{H}_{pk}(tag, c)$. However, if the ω output by Ext satisfies the one-way relation R_{pp} might not be easily and publicly verified in a general way. Actually, the verification algorithm has to be designed according to concrete relations and assumptions. The same thing happens with the function G which extracts the hardcore bits from ω. Although one can always use some general hardcore bits such as Goldreich-Levin hardcore, there might be other functions that extracts the hardcore bits more efficiently under concrete assumptions. The output length of function G directly affects the design of a concrete scheme under this general framework since the overall length of the encapsulated keys has to be sufficient for the DEM.

leakage query is answered with $f(SK^*)$. According to the property of $i\mathcal{O}$, as long as the leakage is not big enough to help the adversary uses SK or SK^* to decrypt the challenge ciphertext, the adversary cannot tell the difference between SK and SK^*.

There are some details need to be noticed while applying the indistinguishability obfuscation. For an IND-CCA secure KEM based on ABO-EHPS as we described above, the intermediate variable tag is usually generated from c by a target collision resistant hash function (TCR). In the security reduction, the challenger is able to decrypt all the legitimate ciphertext whose tag is different with tag^*, and rejects all the decryption queries with tags equal to tag^* from the adversary. However, when we use the indistinguishable obfuscator, the indistinguishable obfuscator requires the programs statistically produce the same output with any input. The TCR just ensures that a computationally bounded adversary will query $tag = tag^*$ with negligible probability, where in fact, there might exist a lot of ciphertexts with their tags equals to tag^*, and in these point the simulated decryption algorithm $\mathsf{Dec}^*_{sk^*}$ can not give a proper answer as Dec_{sk} does. To solve this problem, we need an injective mapping $\mathcal{C} \to \mathcal{T}$ (where $\mathcal{C}$ and $\mathcal{T}$ refers to the domains of the ciphertexts and the tags respectively); moreover, when the challenge ciphertext is queried, we can provide an answer by storing a fixed answer in the simulated decryption program in advance. Then we have that the output of $\mathsf{Dec}^*_{sk^*}(\cdot)$ is statistically close to that of $\mathsf{Dec}_{sk}(\cdot)$ with exactly all the inputs. To be noted, it may not be easy to find the injective mapping in some concrete schemes under various intractability assumptions. Therefore, our framework only suits for those assumptions which are easy to construct the injective mapping. In fact, finding this kind of injective mapping for a concrete intractability assumption is an interesting problem *per se*.

Finally, we apply a randomness-extractor to extract the remained randomness in SK^* after the leakage, and provide an IND-lrCCA secure KEM.

The formal construction and detailed security proof is as follows.

Starting from an ABO-EHPS with the secret key deduce mode for a one-way relation R_{pp}, along with an injective mapping $\mathsf{INJ} : \mathcal{C} \to \mathcal{T}$, we present our IND-lrCCA KEM as follows:

$\mathsf{KEM} = (\mathsf{Gen}, \mathsf{Encap}, \mathsf{Decap})$

- $\mathsf{Gen}(pp)$: apply $\mathsf{SetupExt}(pp)$ to generate (pk, sk) and outputs $PK = pk$ and $SK = i\mathcal{O}(\Psi_{\mathsf{Dec}_{sk}})$. The algorithm Dec_{sk} takes (c, π) as input. It computes $tag = \mathsf{INJ}(c)$ and $\omega = \mathsf{Ext}(sk, tag, c, \pi)$. Finally, if $(c, \omega) \in \mathsf{R}_{pp}$ it outputs $k = G(\omega)$.
- $\mathsf{Encap}_{PK}(pp)$: sample $(c, \omega) \leftarrow \mathsf{SampR}_{pp}(r)$, and compute $tag = \mathsf{INJ}(c)$, $\pi = \mathsf{Pub}(PK, tag, r)$, let $d \leftarrow U_d$, $k = G(\omega)$, compute $e = \mathsf{ext}(k, d)$. Output $(e, (c, \pi, d))$.
- $\mathsf{Decap}_{SK}(c, \pi, d)$: uses SK to get the encapsulated string k, then return $e = \mathsf{ext}(k, d)$.

Theorem 1. *If R_{pp} is a one-way relation, INJ is an injective mapping from $\mathcal{C}$ to $\mathcal{T}$, then the above construction of KEM is IND-lrCCA secure.*

Proof. We give a sequence of hybrid experiments and prove that the KEM leakage adversary's advantage must be computational indistinguishable between each successive ones, where the first hybrid corresponds to the original IND-lrCCA KEM security game as Definition 4, and the adversary has no advantage in the final game.

1. Hyb0:
   (a) $(SK, PK) \leftarrow \mathsf{Gen}(pp)$, $(e_0^*, C^*) \leftarrow \mathsf{Encap}_{PK}(pp)$, where $C^* = (c^*, \pi^*, d^*)$; $e_1^* \leftarrow \{0,1\}^m$.
   (b) $\sigma \leftarrow \mathcal{A}_1^{\mathsf{Leakage}(SK),\mathsf{Decap}_{SK}(\cdot)}(PK)$.
   (c) $b \leftarrow \{0,1\}$, $b' \leftarrow \mathcal{A}_2^{\mathsf{Decap}_{SK}(\cdot)}(PK, C^*, e_b^*, \sigma)$.
   We have:

   $$\mathsf{Adv}_{\mathcal{A}=\{\mathcal{A}_1,\mathcal{A}_2\}}^{\mathsf{Hyb0}} = |\Pr[b = b'] - 1/2|$$

2. Hyb1: Hyb1 is the same as Hyb0, except for the key generation step. We have (pk, sk) the same as Hyb0, and set $sk^* \leftarrow DD(sk, tag^*)$ and $SK^* = i\mathcal{O}(\Psi_{\mathsf{Dec}_{sk^*, tag^*, W}^*})$, where $(c^*, \omega^*) \leftarrow \mathsf{SampR}_{pp}(r)$, $tag^* = \mathsf{INJ}(c^*)$, $\pi^* = \mathsf{Pub}(PK, tag^*, r)$, $W = G(\omega^*)$.
   The algorithm $\mathsf{Dec}_{sk^*, tag^*, W}^*$ takes (c, π, d) as input, computes $tag = \mathsf{INJ}(c)$. If $tag \neq tag^*$, it runs $\mathsf{Ext}^*(sk^*, tag^*, tag, c, \pi)$ to get ω and verifies if $(c, \omega) \in \mathsf{R}_{pp}$. If $tag = tag^*$ and $(c, \pi) = (c^*, \pi^*)$, it outputs $k = W$. Otherwise, the algorithm Dec^* outputs $k = G(\omega)$.

3. Hyb2: In the key generation step, let $(c^*, \omega^*) \leftarrow \mathsf{SampR}_{pp}(r)$, $tag^* = \mathsf{INJ}(c^*)$, and $W = G(\omega^*)$.
   Then call $\mathsf{SetupABO}(pp, tag^*)$ to get (pk^*, sk^*).
   Outputs (PK, SK) such that $PK = pk^*$, and
   $SK = i\mathcal{O}(\Psi_{\mathsf{Dec}_{sk^*, tag^*, W}^*})$. Moreover, compute $\pi^* = \mathsf{Pub}(PK, tag^*, r)$, and the challenge ciphertext is $C^* = (c^*, \pi^*, d)$.

4. Hyb3: Hyb3 is the same as Hyb2 except for the decapsulation for the challenge is a randomly chosen string: $W \leftarrow \{0,1\}^n$ and $\pi^* = \mathsf{Priv}(sk^*, tag^*, c^*)$.

- We prove that Hyb0 and Hyb1 are indistinguishable for any PPT leakage adversary according to the property of $i\mathcal{O}$.

We firstly prove that:

$$\Pr[\forall (c, \pi) : \mathsf{Dec}_{sk}(c, \pi) = \mathsf{Dec}_{sk^*, tag^*, W}^*(c, \pi)] \geq 1 - negl(\lambda)$$

First of all, the public keys in Hyb0 and Hyb1 are the same, therefore the same decapsulation for a $C = (c, \pi)$ such that $tag \neq tag^*$ is output according to the property of the algorithm $\mathsf{Ext}^*(sk^*, tag^*, tag, c, \pi)$.

Secondly, if (c^*, π^*) is queried, correct answer can also be given in Hyb1 because the $W = G(\omega^*)$, such that $(c^*, \omega^*) \in \mathsf{R}_{pp}(r)$, is previously stored. (Although (c^*, π^*) is computationally with negligible probability to be queried, according to the Definition 3 of $i\mathcal{O}$, both programs should be statistically indistinguishable in all of the inputs).

At last, the probability that there is a valid (c', π') such that $c' \neq c^*$ and $tag' = tag^*$ is negligible, because INJ is an injective mapping.

To sum up, we have:

$$\Pr[\forall(c, \pi) : \mathsf{Dec}_{sk}(c, \pi) = \mathsf{Dec}_{sk^*, tag^*, W}(c, \pi)] \geq 1 - negl_1(\lambda)$$

According to the property of indistinguishability obfuscator $i\mathcal{O}$ in Definition 3, there is

$$|\Pr[\mathcal{D}(SK) = 1] - \Pr[\mathcal{D}(SK^*) = 1]| \leq negl_1(\lambda)$$

for any PPT distinguisher $\mathcal{D}$. In another word, the leakage query answered with SK and SK^* is indistinguishable for any PPT adversary.

Therefore, Hyb0 and Hyb1 are computationally indistinguishable for any PPT leakage adversary. We have:

$$\mathsf{Adv}_{\mathcal{A}}^{\mathsf{Hyb0}} - \mathsf{Adv}_{\mathcal{A}}^{\mathsf{Hyb1}} \leq negl_1(\lambda).$$

- We argue that the advantages of any adversary in Hyb1 and Hyb2 are computational indistinguishable. First of all, according to the indistinguishable property of ABO-EHPS, the public keys generated by $\mathsf{SetupExt}(pp)$ and $\mathsf{SetupABO}(pp, tag^*)$ are indistinguishable for any tag^*. That is public keys output in Hyb0 and Hyb2 are statistically indistinguishable. Moreover, since the secret key sk^* in Hyb1 is generated via $(pk, sk) \leftarrow \mathsf{SetupExt}(pp)$ in Hyb0, and the sk^* is computed by $sk^* \leftarrow \mathsf{DD}(sk, tag^*)$, the public keys in Hyb0 and Hyb1 are the same. Therefore, we have the public keys in Hyb1 are statistically indistinguishable with the public keys in Hyb2, and both hybrids provides the same decryption.

Therefore, we have that for any adversary:

$$\mathsf{Adv}_{\mathcal{A}}^{\mathsf{Hyb1}} - \mathsf{Adv}_{\mathcal{A}}^{\mathsf{Hyb2}} \leq negl_2(\lambda).$$

- We first prove that the adversary's advantage in Hyb3 is negligible and an adversary's advantages in Hyb2 and Hyb3 are indistinguishable.

For Hyb3, e_0 is extracted from a random string $W \leftarrow \{0, 1\}^n$ and there is $e_1 \leftarrow \{0, 1\}^m$, none of them is related with c^*. Therefore, as long as W in the obfuscated program $i\mathcal{O}(\Psi_{\mathsf{Dec}_{sk^*, tag^*, W}})$ is not leaked completely, after the randomness extraction, $e_0 = \mathsf{ext}(W, d)$ is statistically indistinguishable with e_1. we have:

$$\mathsf{Adv}_{\mathcal{A}}^{\mathsf{Hyb3}} \leq negl_3(\lambda).$$

where $negl_3(\lambda)$ is decided by the distance between the output of the randomness extractor and a uniformly distributed string.

As for the leakage part, since W is a randomly chosen string from $\{0, 1\}^{n(\lambda)}$, The entropy in it is $\widetilde{H}_\infty(W|PK) = n(\lambda)$. After l bits of leakage, according to Lemma 1, we have:

$$\widetilde{H}_\infty(W|(PK, f(SK^*))) \geq n(\lambda) - l.$$

As long as $n(\lambda) - l \geq m + 2\log(1/\epsilon)$, according to Lemma 2 and Definition 2, there is a universal hash function to be applied as a $(n - l, \epsilon)$-extractor ext such that outputs m bits of pseudo-randomness e. There is:

$$SD((PK, U_d, e), (PK, U_d, U_m)) \leq \epsilon$$

Suppose the size of the obfuscated program is s, the leakage rate of this scheme is l/s.

Furthermore, assume that there exists a PPT adversary $\mathcal{A}$, whose advantages in Hyb2 and Hyb3 are distinguishable, then we have that $\mathcal{A}$'s advantage in Hyb2 is non-negligible, which contradicts the one-wayness of R_{pp} or the pseudorandom of $G(\cdot)$. (This part of security proof is the same as the security proof of IND-CCA KEM in [15].)

Hence there is

$$\mathsf{Adv}_{\mathcal{A}}^{\mathsf{Hyb2}} - \mathsf{Adv}_{\mathcal{A}}^{\mathsf{Hyb3}} \leq negl_4(\lambda).$$

To sum up, we have

$$\mathsf{Adv}_{\mathcal{A}}^{\mathsf{Hyb0}} \leq negl_1(\lambda) + negl_2(\lambda) + negl_3(\lambda) + negl_4(\lambda)$$

The length $n(\lambda)$ of the output of the function $G(\cdot)$ may not be long enough for the randomness extraction (at least logarithm of λ). For example, the output of $G(\cdot)$ may only be a hardcore bit. However, according to [12], with a polynomial parallel independent execution of above scheme, there will be enough bits for the randomness extraction and the CCA security will not be compromised. The numbers of the parallel will only affects the total amount of leakage and the leakage rate will not be changed.

4   Instance: IND-lrCCA KEM Based on BDDH Assumption

In this section, we present an instance for our IND-lrCCA KEM. We give our concrete IND-lrCCA KEM based on BDDH assumption for simplicity, since [22] already give an efficiently computable injective mapping from $\mathbb{G}$ to $\mathbb{Z}_p$, where $\mathbb{G}$ is a cyclic group of prime order p, and since the function $G(\cdot)$, which extracts hardcore bits, has a linear output under BDDH assumption as we introduced in the preliminary section. Note that instances can also be given under the GHDH assumption [14], for the BDDH assumption can be viewed as a special case of the GHDH assumption.

We first give our ABO-EHPS with the secret key deduce mode, which is a simple modification of the instance of ABO-EHPS in [15] for the DH relation. Then we present the IND-lrCCA KEM based on the BDDH assumption. Apart from the modification made in order to suit the use of $i\mathcal{O}$ as we explained above, our KEM also differs from it in [15] on the setting of parameters and the way of decryption, just in order to make the instance suits the general framework better.

4.1 ABO-EHPS with the Secret-Key Deduce Mode for the DH Relation Based on BDDH Assumption

Let g be the generator of a group $\mathbb{G}$ with prime order p. Set the public parameters $pp = (g, g^\alpha)$, where there is a trapdoor $\alpha \in \mathbb{Z}_p$, the tag space $\mathcal{T} = \mathbb{Z}_p$, $\mathsf{SampR}_{pp}(r) = (c, \omega) = (g^r, g^{\alpha r})$ where $r \in \mathbb{Z}_p$ and $\mathsf{H}_{pk}(tag, c) = (g^{\alpha \cdot tag} \cdot pk)^r$ where $c = g^r$, we give the $\mathsf{ABO} - \mathsf{EHPS}_{pp}^{dh}$ with the secret-key deduce algorithm as follows.

- $\mathsf{SetupExt}(pp)$: choose $sk \in \mathbb{Z}_p$, compute $pk = g^{sk}$, output (pk, sk).
- $\mathsf{SetupABO}(pp, tag^*)$: choose $sk^* \in \mathbb{Z}_p$, set $pk^* = g^{sk^*} \cdot (g^\alpha)^{-tag^*}$.
- $\mathsf{Pub}(pk, tag, r) = (g^{\alpha \cdot tag} \cdot pk)^r$.
- $\mathsf{Ext}(sk, tag, c, \pi) = (\pi \cdot c^{-sk})^{\frac{1}{tag}}$.
- $\mathsf{Ext}^*(sk^*, tag^*, tag, c, \pi) = (\pi \cdot c^{-sk^*})^{\frac{1}{tag - tag^*}}$.
- $\mathsf{Priv}(sk^*, tag^*, c) = c^{sk^*}$.
- $\mathsf{DD}(sk, tag^*, \alpha) = sk + \alpha \cdot tag^*$.

We now show that $\mathsf{ABO} - \mathsf{EHPS}_{pp}^{dh}$ is an ABO-EHPS with the secret-key deduce mode for R_{dh}.

- EXTRACTION MODE. For all $(pk, sk) \leftarrow \mathsf{SetupExt}(pp)$ and all (tag, c, π), there is:

$$\pi = \mathsf{H}_{pk}(tag, c) = (g^{\alpha \cdot tag} \cdot pk)^r = g^{tag \cdot \alpha \cdot r + sk \cdot r};$$

$$\mathsf{Ext}(sk, tag, c, \pi) = (\pi \cdot c^{-sk})^{\frac{1}{tag}} = \{g^{tag \cdot \alpha \cdot r + sk \cdot r} \cdot g^{-sk \cdot r}\}^{\frac{1}{tag}} = g^{\alpha r}$$

- ALL-BUT-ONE MODE.
  1. For all $(pk^*, sk^*) \leftarrow \mathsf{SetupABO}(pp, tag^*)$, all tag^*, and all $(c, \omega) \in \mathsf{R}_{pp}$, there is:

$$\mathsf{H}_{pk^*}(tag^*, c) = (g^{\alpha \cdot tag^*} \cdot pk^*)^r = g^{sk^* \cdot r} = c^{sk^*} = \mathsf{Priv}(sk^*, tag^*, c)$$

  2. For all $tag \neq tag^*$ and all (c, π), there is:

$$\pi = \mathsf{H}_{pk^*}(tag, c) = (g^{\alpha \cdot tag} \cdot pk^*)^r = g^{tag \cdot \alpha \cdot r + (sk^* - \alpha \cdot tag^*) \cdot r};$$

$$\mathsf{Ext}^*(sk^*, tag^*, tag, c, \pi) = (\pi \cdot c^{-sk^*})^{\frac{1}{tag - tag^*}} = g^{\alpha r \cdot (tag - tag^*) \cdot \frac{1}{tag - tag^*}} = g^{\alpha r}$$

- SECRET-KEY DEDUCE MODE. For all $(pk, sk) \leftarrow \mathsf{SetupExt}(pp)$ and all tag^*, there is: $sk^* = \mathsf{DD}(sk, tag^*, \alpha) = sk + \alpha \cdot tag^*$.
  1. For all $tag \neq tag^*$, there is:

$$\pi = \mathsf{H}_{pk}(tag, c) = (g^{\alpha \cdot tag} \cdot pk)^r = g^{tag \cdot \alpha \cdot r + sk \cdot r};$$

$$Ext^* = \mathsf{Ext}^*(sk^*, tag^*, tag, c, \pi) = (\pi \cdot c^{-sk^*})^{\frac{1}{tag - tag^*}}$$

$$= g^{[(tag \cdot \alpha \cdot r + sk \cdot r) - sk^* \cdot r] \cdot \frac{1}{tag - tag^*}} = g^{[(tag \cdot \alpha \cdot r + sk \cdot r) - (sk + \alpha \cdot tag^*) \cdot r] \cdot \frac{1}{tag - tag^*}}$$

$$= g^{\alpha r \cdot (tag - tag^*) \cdot \frac{1}{tag - tag^*}} = g^{\alpha r}$$

2. For all $(c, \omega) \in R_{pp}$, there is:

$$\mathsf{Priv}(sk^*, tag^*, c) = c^{sk^*} = c^{sk + \alpha \cdot tag^*} = g^{(sk + \alpha \cdot tag^*) \cdot r} = \mathsf{H}_{pk}(tag^*, c)$$

- INDISTINGUISHABILITY. Since both sk and sk^* are randomly chosen from $\mathbb{Z}_p$, pk and pk^* are statistically indistinguishable.

4.2   IND-lrCCA KEM Based on the BDDH Assumption

Starting from $\mathsf{ABO} - \mathsf{EHPS}_{pp}^{dh}$ for a one-way relation R_{pp}^{dh}, two groups $\mathbb{G}_1$ and $\mathbb{G}_2$ of prime order p, where there is a bilinear mapping $\hat{e} : \mathbb{G}_1 \times \mathbb{G}_1 \to \mathbb{G}_2$, and an injective mapping $\mathbb{G}_1 \to \mathbb{Z}_p$, we present our IND-lrCCA KEM based on BDDH assumption as follows.

Set the public parameters to be $pp = (g, u, v)$, where g is the generator of $\mathbb{G}$, $u = g^\alpha$, $v = g^\gamma$ and there is a trapdoor $sp = (\alpha, \gamma)$ such that $\alpha, \gamma \in \mathbb{Z}_p$. Let the hardcore extracting function $G = \hat{e}(\omega, v)$. We have:

- $\mathsf{Gen}(pp)$: Apply $\mathsf{SetupExt}(pp)$ to generate (pk, sk), randomly and outputs $PK = pk$ and $SK = i\mathcal{O}(\Psi_{\mathsf{Dec}_{sk}})$.
  The algorithm Dec_{sk} takes (c, π) as input. It computes $tag = \mathsf{INJ}(c)$ and verifies if $\hat{e}(g, \pi) = \hat{e}(c, u^{tag} \cdot PK)$. If the validity test passes, it computes $\omega = \mathsf{Ext}(sk, tag, c, \pi)$ and outputs $k = \hat{e}(\omega, v)$; otherwise, it outputs "$\perp$".
- $\mathsf{Encap}_{pk}(pp)$: Sample $(c, \omega) \leftarrow \mathsf{SampR}_{pp}(r)$, where $c = g^r$ and $\omega = u^r$, Then compute $tag = \mathsf{INJ}(c)$, $\pi = \mathsf{Pub}(PK, tag, r)$. Let $d \leftarrow U_d$, $k = \hat{e}(\omega, v)$, compute $e = \mathsf{ext}(k, d)$. Output $(e, (c, \pi, d))$.
- $\mathsf{Decap}_{SK}(c, \pi, d)$: Uses SK to get the encapsulated string k, then return $e = \mathsf{ext}(k, d)$.

Note that our instance is presented in the way that completely fits the general framework. Therefore, efficiency is not the primary concern. One can always view u as a part of the public keys, and include α as a part of the secret keys to simplify the decryption process as in [15].

References

1. Alwen, J., Dodis, Y., Wichs, D.: Leakage-resilient public-key cryptography in the bounded-retrieval model. In: Halevi, S. (ed.) CRYPTO 2009. LNCS, vol. 5677, pp. 36–54. Springer, Heidelberg (2009). doi:10.1007/978-3-642-03356-8_3
2. Dziembowski, S., Pietrzak, K.: Leakage-resilient cryptography. In: FOCS 2008, pp. 293–302. IEEE Computer Society, Los Alamitos (2008)
3. Naor, M., Segev, G.: Public-key cryptosystems resilient to key leakage. In: Halevi, S. (ed.) CRYPTO 2009. LNCS, vol. 5677, pp. 18–35. Springer, Heidelberg (2009). doi:10.1007/978-3-642-03356-8_2
4. Dodis, Y., Haralambiev, K., Lopez-Alt, A., Wichs, D.: Cryptography against continuous memory attacks. In: 51st Annual IEEE Symposium on FOCS 2010, pp. 511–520. IEEE (2010)

5. Hazay, C., López-Alt, A., Wee, H., Wichs, D.: Leakage-resilient cryptography from minimal assumptions. In: Johansson, T., Nguyen, P.Q. (eds.) EUROCRYPT 2013. LNCS, vol. 7881, pp. 160–176. Springer, Heidelberg (2013). doi:10.1007/978-3-642-38348-9_10

6. Kiltz, E., Pietrzak, K.: Leakage resilient ElGamal encryption. In: Abe, M. (ed.) ASIACRYPT 2010. LNCS, vol. 6477, pp. 595–612. Springer, Heidelberg (2010). doi:10.1007/978-3-642-17373-8_34

7. Kocher, P.C.: Timing attacks on implementations of Diffie-Hellman, RSA, DSS, and other systems. In: Koblitz, N. (ed.) CRYPTO 1996. LNCS, vol. 1109, pp. 104–113. Springer, Heidelberg (1996). doi:10.1007/3-540-68697-5_9

8. Kocher, P., Jaffe, J., Jun, B.: Differential power analysis. In: Wiener, M. (ed.) CRYPTO 1999. LNCS, vol. 1666, pp. 388–397. Springer, Heidelberg (1999). doi:10.1007/3-540-48405-1_25

9. Quisquater, J.-J., Samyde, D.: ElectroMagnetic Analysis (EMA): measures and counter-measures for smart cards. In: Attali, I., Jensen, T. (eds.) E-smart 2001. LNCS, vol. 2140, pp. 200–210. Springer, Heidelberg (2001). doi:10.1007/3-540-45418-7_17

10. Qin, B., Liu, S.: Leakage-resilient chosen-ciphertext secure public-key encryption from hash proof system and one-time lossy filter. In: Sako, K., Sarkar, P. (eds.) ASIACRYPT 2013. LNCS, vol. 8270, pp. 381–400. Springer, Heidelberg (2013). doi:10.1007/978-3-642-42045-0_20

11. Cramer, R., Shoup, V.: Universal hash proofs and a paradigm for adaptive chosen ciphertext secure public-key encryption. In: Knudsen, L.R. (ed.) EUROCRYPT 2002. LNCS, vol. 2332, pp. 45–64. Springer, Heidelberg (2002). doi:10.1007/3-540-46035-7_4

12. Liu, S., Weng, J., Zhao, Y.: Efficient public key cryptosystem resilient to key leakage chosen ciphertext attacks. In: Dawson, E. (ed.) CT-RSA 2013. LNCS, vol. 7779, pp. 84–100. Springer, Heidelberg (2013). doi:10.1007/978-3-642-36095-4_6

13. Dodis, Y., Reyzin, L., Smith, A.: Fuzzy extractors: how to generate strong keys from biometrics and other noisy data. In: Cachin, C., Camenisch, J.L. (eds.) EUROCRYPT 2004. LNCS, vol. 3027, pp. 523–540. Springer, Heidelberg (2004). doi:10.1007/978-3-540-24676-3_31

14. Kiltz, E.: Chosen-ciphertext secure key-encapsulation based on gap hashed Diffie-Hellman. In: Okamoto, T., Wang, X. (eds.) PKC 2007. LNCS, vol. 4450, pp. 282–297. Springer, Heidelberg (2007). doi:10.1007/978-3-540-71677-8_19

15. Wee, H.: Efficient chosen-ciphertext security via extractable hash proofs. In: Rabin, T. (ed.) CRYPTO 2010. LNCS, vol. 6223, pp. 314–332. Springer, Heidelberg (2010). doi:10.1007/978-3-642-14623-7_17

16. Sahai, A., Waters, B.: How to use indistinguishability obfuscation: deniable encryption, and more. In: STOC 2014, pp. 475–484 (2014)

17. Garg, S., Gentry, C., Halevi, S., Raykova, M., Sahai, A., Waters, B.: Candidate indistinguishability obfuscation and functional encryption for all circuits. In: FOCS 2013. pp. 40–49. IEEE Computer Society, Los Alamitos (2013)

18. Barak, B., Goldreich, O., Impagliazzo, R., Rudich, S., Sahai, A., Vadhan, S., Yang, K.: On the (im)possibility of obfuscating programs. In: Kilian, J. (ed.) CRYPTO 2001. LNCS, vol. 2139, pp. 1–18. Springer, Heidelberg (2001). doi:10.1007/3-540-44647-8_1

19. Boyle, E., Chung, K.-M., Pass, R.: On extractability obfuscation. In: Lindell, Y. (ed.) TCC 2014. LNCS, vol. 8349, pp. 52–73. Springer, Heidelberg (2014). doi:10.1007/978-3-642-54242-8_3

20. Cramer, R., Shoup, V.: A practical public key cryptosystem provably secure against adaptive chosen ciphertext attack. In: Krawczyk, H. (ed.) CRYPTO 1998. LNCS, vol. 1462, pp. 13–25. Springer, Heidelberg (1998). doi:10.1007/BFb0055717

21. Cramer, R., Shoup, V.: Design and analysis of practical public-key encryption schemes secure against adaptive chosen ciphertext attack. SIAM J. Comput. **33**(1), 167–226 (2004)

22. Boyen, X., Mei, Q., Waters, B.: Direct chosen ciphertext security from identity-based techniques. In: CCS 2005, pp. 320–329. ACM, New York (2005)

23. Boneh, D., Franklin, M.: Identity-based encryption from the weil pairing. SIAM J. Comput. **32**(3), 586–615 (2003)

24. Dachman-Soled, D., Dov Gordon, S., Liu, F.-H., O'Neill, A., Zhou, H.-S.: Leakage-resilient public-key encryption from obfuscation. In: Cheng, C.-M., Chung, K.-M., Persiano, G., Yang, B.-Y. (eds.) PKC 2016. LNCS, vol. 9615, pp. 101–128. Springer, Heidelberg (2016). doi:10.1007/978-3-662-49387-8_5

Codes for Detection of Limited View Algebraic Tampering

Fuchun Lin[(⊠)], Reihaneh Safavi-Naini, and Pengwei Wang

Department of Computer Science, University of Calgary, Calgary, Canada
fuchun.lin@ucalgary.ca

Abstract. Tamper resilient cryptography has recently gained attention, and novel coding solutions have been proposed. One such solutions is Tamper Detection (TD) codes that are used to detect tampering with a codeword when the tampering function belongs to a specified family of functions. We consider TD codes when the class of functions consists of functions where the adversary first selects a subset of size pn of the codeword components to *see*, and then uses this view to choose a noise vector that will be added (algebraically) to the codeword (n is the codeword length). We show it is impossible to construct codes that protect against tampering of all functions in this class. By removing the set of *bad* functions from the class, we obtain a subset of this family for which tamper detection codes exist, and give a construction of tamper detection codes for this subset. We discuss our results and directions for future work.

1 Introduction

Detection of adversarial tampering with the message is an important security goal that is traditionally provided using Message Authentication Codes (MAC) [5]. MAC is a shared secret key primitive and provides protection against unlimited adversarial tampering with the codeword: the adversary can see the codeword and arbitrarily change it. Detection of adversarial tampering when tampering is restricted to a constant fraction of the code vector has been studied using error detection codes in Hamming model [18]. In these codes the adversary sees the whole codeword and arbitrarily modifies a fraction of it. Randomized coding for protection against a wider class of tampering functions and without requiring a secret key, has recently received considerable attention [4,7,19,20]. Algebraic Manipulation Detection (AMD) codes [19] provide protection for the coded message against *algebraic tampering* when the adversary is *oblivious to the codeword*: the adversary, without seeing the codeword, adds an arbitrary tampering vector to the codeword. The obliviousness of the adversary has been relaxed in the followup works which allow some level of leakage of the codeword [4,6], before the error vector is constructed.

Tamper Detection (TD) codes, first informally introduced in [9,16] and formalized in [7], have a different protection goal: here the goal is to protect against *tampering of the codeword and not the message*. That is, one needs to detect tampering even if the message stays unchanged.

© Springer International Publishing AG 2017
K. Chen et al. (Eds.): Inscrypt 2016, LNCS 10143, pp. 309–320, 2017.
DOI: 10.1007/978-3-319-54705-3_19

A TD code is defined with respect to a class of tampering functions $\mathcal{F}$ and can detect any modification of a *codeword* when modification is by a function $f \in \mathcal{F}$. A codeword can be seen as a virtual box that holds the message and tampering with the box, even if the message remains intact must be detected with high probability.

It has been shown [7] that TD codes can not exist if $\mathcal{F}$ contains functions with "many fixed points" or functions with "low entropy" output. Assume the codeword is an n-bit string. Then a tampering function is a function from $\{0,1\}^n$ to $\{0,1\}^n$. A *fixed point* of a tampering function f is a point $\mathbf{x}$ that satisfies $f(\mathbf{x}) = \mathbf{x}$. The *output entropy* of a function is the min-entropy of the function output when a uniform distribution is used on the domain. A fixed point of a function f cannot be protected against tampering by the function simply because it is unaffected by the function. Also, for low entropy functions, there are many input strings being mapped to a single output string and cause a high detection error if that output string is a valid codeword. A small set of "many fixed points" functions or "low entropy" output functions are enough to make TD codes impossible. On the other hand, by excluding these cases, there is always a TD code if the function family $\mathcal{F}$ is sufficiently smaller than the set of all possible functions ($\log\log|\mathcal{F}| < n$). Efficiency of TD codes is measured by their *rate* k/n where k is the number of information bits. This existence result uses a probabilistic argument and the TD codes obtained achieve rate $1 - \frac{\log\log|\mathcal{F}|}{n}$, approximately. See Sect. 2 for more details.

Our work. We consider q-ary TD codes (tampering functions are functions from $\mathbb{F}_q^n$ to $\mathbb{F}_q^n$) for a special class $\mathcal{F}_\rho^{add}$ of tampering functions that we call *Limited View Algebraic Tampering (LVAT)* family, capturing an adversary that can choose their tampering vector after observing a fraction of the codeword. That is, for a constant $0 \le \rho \le 1$, the adversary uses their view of a subset of ρn components of the codeword, to construct a noise vector that is added (component-wise) to the codeword, and the goal is detection of tampering. The LVAT functions extend tampering functions of algebraic manipulation codes considered in [19], where the adversary obliviously adds a noise vector to the codeword. Each LVAT function $f_{S,g} \in \mathcal{F}_\rho^{add}$ is specified by two parameters S and g, where $S \subset [n]$ is a subset of size ρn, and a function $g : \mathbb{F}_q^{\rho n} \to \mathbb{F}_q^n$. In Sect. 3, we study the two properties of functions that are important in the context of tamper detection, that is the number of fixed points and their output entropy. We will show that $\mathcal{F}_\rho^{add}$ does not contain "low entropy" functions, but does contain functions that have "many fixed points". In Lemma 4 we prove that, for a constant ϕ where $0 \le \phi \le 1$, the detection failure of a TD code for the subclass of LVAT functions that has $\phi \cdot q^n$ fixed points is at least ϕ.

We define the function class $\mathcal{F}_{\rho,\phi}^{add}$ that is obtained from $\mathcal{F}_\rho^{add}$ by excluding all functions that have at least $\phi \cdot q^n$ fixed points. In Sect. 4, we define a (ρ, ϕ, δ)-LVAT-TD code as a TD code with error (detection failure) probability δ for the class $\mathcal{F}_{\rho,\phi}^{add}$ and give a construction for these codes and derive the detection error probability and rate of these codes.

Related work. The relation of the results in this work to existing results are summarized as follows.

- Same coding goal, different adversary: Traditional error detection codes encode a message so that error in transmission is detected. Since deterministic codes are used to encode the message, the coding goal is also detecting change of codeword, same as TD codes. Traditional models of error detection consider Shannon probabilistic model [1] where the error is due to a probabilistic process, or Hamming adversarial model [18] where the error is chosen by the adversary with the limitation that the weight of the error vector is bounded. In this latter case, the adversary's error is constructed after seeing the codeword.
- Different coding goal, same adversary: In Algebraic Manipulation Detection [19] the adversary is oblivious to the codeword, but there is no restriction on the weight of the error. This model was first motivated in the context of robust secret sharing and has found numerous other applications. The model is later extended to the case where the codeword is partially leaked to the adversary [4,6]. The main difference between [4,6] is the type of allowed leakage. The adversary model considered in [4] is exactly the same as considered in this work. But the coding goal of this line of works has been detection of tampering with the message.
- Special case of NMC: In non-malleable codes [20] the adversary's corruption is defined by a family of functions, and the protection is by using the concept of "non-malleability" which includes error detection as a special case. This is a general model with numerous followup work (just to name a few [3,9, 10,16,21]). In tamper detection [7] the goal is to detect *tampering with the codeword* and this is even if the message stays intact. This coding goal implies non-malleability. Here also the adversary's tampering is defined by a class of functions. We can say the codes obtained here are also non-malleable codes with respect to LVAT functions.
- More Generally: In this paper we consider tamper detection for a specific function family that we call Limited-View Algebraic Tampering (LVAT) where the tampering is by adding an error vector to the codeword, and the choice of the error is after observing a fraction of the codeword components. The observed components is the leakage of the codeword to the adversary that will enable them to choose their best error vector. A more general form of this class is when the adversary's error vector that is chosen after their observation, is a vector with limited support that affects only a ρ' fraction of components of the codeword. This class of functions was considered in [15] where the goal of protection is recovering the message and privacy [17]. A rate bound and a construction that achieves the rate upper bound was given also. Other models of adversarial errors with the goal of message recovery is given in [11,13,14,22].

2   Preliminary

We begin with a brief description of the notations. Calligraphy letters $\mathcal{X}$ denote sets and their corresponding capital letters denote the cardinality, $|\mathcal{X}| = X$.

Boldface letters $\mathbf{x}$ denote vectors. $\mathbf{x}_{|S}$ denotes the sub-vector of $\mathbf{x}$ consisting of the components specified by the index set S. $[n]$ denotes $\{1, 2, \cdots, n\}$. A capital boldface letter $\mathbf{X}$ denotes a random variable, and $\mathbf{X} \leftarrow \mathcal{X}$ denotes sampling of the variable from the set $\mathcal{X}$, with $\mathbf{X} \overset{\$}{\leftarrow} \mathcal{X}$ denoting a uniform distribution in sampling. The statistical distance between $\mathbf{X}$ and $\mathbf{Y}$ that are both defined over the set $\mathcal{W}$, is defined as,

$$\mathsf{SD}(\mathbf{X}, \mathbf{Y}) \triangleq \frac{1}{2} \sum_{\mathbf{w} \in \mathcal{W}} |\mathsf{Pr}[\mathbf{X} = \mathbf{w}] - \mathsf{Pr}[\mathbf{Y} = \mathbf{w}]|.$$

We say $\mathbf{X}$ and $\mathbf{Y}$ are δ-close if $\mathsf{SD}(\mathbf{X}, \mathbf{Y}) \leq \delta$. The *min-entropy* $\mathsf{H}_\infty(\mathbf{X})$ of a random variable $\mathbf{X} \leftarrow \mathcal{X}$ is

$$\mathsf{H}_\infty(\mathbf{X}) = -\log \max_{\mathbf{x} \in \mathcal{X}} \mathsf{Pr}[\mathbf{X} = \mathbf{x}].$$

All codes studied in this paper are *randomized codes*. A *coding scheme* is a randomized code that satisfies the correctness property, namely, a codeword is always decoded to its corresponding message. On the other hand, any vector that is not a codeword of any message is decoded to a symbol $\perp$ that denotes detection.

Definition 1. *An (n, k)-coding scheme consists of two functions: a randomized encoding function $Enc : \mathbb{F}_q^k \rightarrow \mathbb{F}_q^n$, and deterministic decoding function $Dec : \mathbb{F}_q^n \rightarrow \mathbb{F}_q^k \cup \{\perp\}$, where $\perp$ denotes detection, satisfying $Pr[Dec(Enc(\mathbf{m})) = \mathbf{m}] = 1$, for any $\mathbf{m} \in \mathbb{F}_q^k$. Here probability is taken over the randomness of the encoding algorithm.*

Wiretap II model [12] considers a scenario where Alice wants to send messages to Bob over a reliable channel that is eavesdropped by an adversary, Eve. The adversary can read a fraction ρ of the transmitted codeword components, and is allowed to choose any subset of her choice. A wiretap II code provides information-theoretic secrecy for message transmission against this adversary.

Definition 2. *A (ρ, ε) wiretap II code, or (ρ, ε)-WtII code for short, is an (n, k)-coding scheme that satisfies the following privacy property. For any $\mathbf{m}_0, \mathbf{m}_1 \in \mathbb{F}_q^k$, any $S \subset [n]$ of size $|S| \leq n\rho$,*

$$\mathsf{SD}(Enc(\mathbf{m}_0)_{|S}; Enc(\mathbf{m}_1)_{|S}) \leq \varepsilon. \tag{1}$$

The above definition of security is in line with [15] and is stronger than the original definition [12], and also the definition in [2]. When $\varepsilon = 0$ is achieved in (1), the distribution of any ρ fraction of the codeword components is independent of the message. This is achieved, for example, by the following construction, which is one of the two building blocks in our construction.

Lemma 1 [12]. *Let $G_{(n-k) \times n}$ be a generator matrix of an $[n, n-k, k+1]$ MDS code over $\mathbb{F}_q$. Append k rows to G such that the obtained matrix $\begin{bmatrix} G \\ \tilde{G} \end{bmatrix}$ is of full rank. Define the encoder $WtIIenc$ as follows.*

$$WtIIenc(\mathbf{m}) = [\mathbf{r}, \mathbf{m}] \begin{bmatrix} G \\ \tilde{G} \end{bmatrix}, \quad \text{where } \mathbf{r} \xleftarrow{\$} \mathbb{F}_q^{n-k}.$$

The decoder $WtIIdec$ uses a parity-check matrix of the MDS code to "remove the randomness $\mathbf{r}$" and then maps the syndrome back to the message. ($WtIIenc$, $WtIIdec$) gives a $(\frac{n-k}{n}, 0)$-WtII code.

Algebraic Manipulation Detection (AMD) codes [19] detect change of message with high probability against an adversary that can construct a constant error vector of any Hamming weight and add it to the codeword. On one hand, the error vector is not constrained in terms of Hamming weight. On the other hand, one can think of the adversary as being oblivious to the codeword, since the error vector (being a constant vector) does not depend on the codeword.

Definition 3 [19]. *An (M, G, δ)-Algebraic Manipulation Detection code, or (M, G, δ)-AMD code for short, is a probabilistic encoding map $Enc : \mathcal{M} \to \mathcal{G}$ from a set $\mathcal{M}$ of size M to an (additive) group $\mathcal{G}$ of order G, together with a (deterministic) decoding function $Dec : \mathcal{G} \to \mathcal{M} \bigcup \{\perp\}$ such that $Dec(Enc(\mathbf{m})) = \mathbf{m}$ with probability 1 for any $\mathbf{m} \in \mathcal{M}$. The security of an AMD code requires that for any $\mathbf{m} \in \mathcal{M}$, $\Delta \in \mathcal{G}$, $\Pr[Dec(Enc(\mathbf{m}) + \Delta) \notin \{\mathbf{m}, \perp\}] \leq \delta$.*

The following construction only incurs $2 \log q$ bits overhead and has detection error as small as $\delta = \frac{d+1}{q}$, where the message is a d-tuple over $\mathbb{F}_q$. We will use it as a building block in our construction in Sect. 4.

Lemma 2 [19]: *Let $\mathbb{F}_q$ be a field of size q and characteristic p, and let d be any integer such that $d + 2$ is not divisible by p. Define the encoding function,*

$$AMDenc : \mathbb{F}_q^d \to \mathbb{F}_q^d \times \mathbb{F}_q \times \mathbb{F}_q, \mathbf{m} \mapsto (\mathbf{m}, r, f(r, \mathbf{m})),$$

where $f(r, \mathbf{m}) = r^{d+2} + \sum_{i=1}^{d} m_i r^i$. The decoding function $AMDdec$ verifies $(\mathbf{m}, r, t)$ by comparing t and $f(r, \mathbf{m})$. It outputs $\mathbf{m}$ if $t = f(r, \mathbf{m})$ and $\perp$, otherwise. $(AMDenc, AMDdec)$ gives a $(q^d, q^{d+2}, \frac{d+1}{q})$-AMD code.

Tamper Detection (TD) code [7] provides detection of change of codeword. It was implicitly introduced in [9, 16], and later explicitly defined in [7].

Definition 4 (Tamper Detection (TD) code) [7][1]. *Let (Enc, Dec) be an (n, k)-coding scheme and let $\mathcal{F}$ be a family of functions of the form $f : \mathbb{F}_q^n \to \mathbb{F}_q^n$. We say that (Enc, Dec) is a $(\mathcal{F}, \delta)$-TD code if for any function $f \in \mathcal{F}$ and any message $\mathbf{m} \in \mathbb{F}_q^k$, we have $\Pr[Dec(f(Enc(\mathbf{m}))) \neq \perp] \leq \delta$, where the probability is over the randomness of the encoder.*

---

[1] The study in [7, 9, 16] are specific to $q = 2$.

Remark 1. The construction in Lemma 2 satisfies $\Pr[\text{AMDdec}(\text{AMDenc}(\mathbf{m}) + \Delta) \neq \perp] \leq \frac{d+1}{q}$, for any $\Delta \neq \mathbf{0}$. This means that $(\text{AMDenc}, \text{AMDdec})$ is also an $(\mathcal{F}, \frac{d+1}{q})$-TD code with respect to $\mathcal{F} = \{f(\mathbf{x}) = \mathbf{x} + \Delta | \Delta \in \mathbb{F}_q^{d+2} \setminus \{0^{d+2}\}\}$.

According to the definition of a coding scheme (see Definition 1), we have $\Pr[\text{Dec}(\text{Enc}(\mathbf{m})) = \mathbf{m}] = 1$. Let $f_{ID} : \mathbb{F}_q^n \to \mathbb{F}_q^n : \mathbf{x} \mapsto \mathbf{x}$ be the identity function. If the class of tampering functions $\mathcal{F}$ in Definition 4 includes the identity function, then the detection failure δ should satisfy the following.

$$\delta \geq \Pr[\text{Dec}(f_{ID}(\text{Enc}(\mathbf{m}))) \neq \perp] \geq \Pr[\text{Dec}(f_{ID}(\text{Enc}(\mathbf{m}))) = \mathbf{m}] = 1.$$

More generally, for a function $f : \mathbb{F}_q^n \to \mathbb{F}_q^n$, an n-tuple $\mathbf{x}' \in \mathbb{F}_q^n$ is called a *fixed point* of f if $f(\mathbf{x}') = \mathbf{x}'$. When the random variable $\text{Enc}(\mathbf{m})$ takes values in the fixed points of f, $\text{Dec}(f(\text{Enc}(\mathbf{m}))) = \mathbf{m} \neq \perp$ will inevitably occur. So functions that have fixed points need special attention when considering TD codes. There is another type of functions that also need special attention. Let $f_c : \mathbb{F}_q^n \to \mathbb{F}_q^n : \mathbf{x} \mapsto \mathbf{c}$ be the constant function that takes any n-tuple to a constant n-tuple $\mathbf{c}$. For an (n, k)-coding scheme (Enc, Dec) such that $\mathbf{c} \in \text{Supp}(\text{Enc}(\mathbf{m}_0))$ for a particular message $\mathbf{m}_0$, we always have $\text{Dec}(f_c(\text{Enc}(\mathbf{m}))) = \mathbf{m}_0 \neq \perp$ for any message $\mathbf{m}$. More generally, for a function $f : \mathbb{F}_q^n \to \mathbb{F}_q^n$, the quantity $\log |\{f(\mathbf{x}) | \mathbf{x} \in \mathbb{F}_q^n\}|$ is called the *output entropy* of f. Constant functions have zero output entropy.

Definition 5 [7,9]. *For a function $f : \mathbb{F}_q^n \to \mathbb{F}_q^n$, we define the following two properties.*

- *f is a ϕ-few fixed points function if $\frac{|\{\mathbf{x} \in \mathbb{F}_q^n | f(\mathbf{x}) = \mathbf{x}\}|}{q^n} \leq \phi$;*
- *f is a μ-entropy function if $\log |\{f(\mathbf{x}) | \mathbf{x} \in \mathbb{F}_q^n\}| = \mu$.*

Remark 2. It is shown in [8] (restricted to $q = 2$) that small classes of functions with either "many fixed points" or "low entropy" output can be constructed such that TD codes are impossible. In particular, for $\mu \leq k$, they showed a family $\mathcal{F}$ of μ-entropy, 0-few fixed points functions of size $(2^n)^{2^\mu}$ such that there does not exist any (n, k)-coding scheme that is a TD code with respect to $\mathcal{F}$, and for any ϕ, there is a family $\mathcal{F}$ of ϕ-few fixed points, n-entropy functions of size 2^n such that no $(\mathcal{F}, \phi)$-TD code exists. On the other hand, for any function family $\mathcal{F}$ of ϕ-few fixed points and μ-entropy functions of size $\log \log |\mathcal{F}| < n$, a probabilistic construction was given that yielded a $(\mathcal{F}, \delta)$-TD code with high probability, provided that $\phi \leq \frac{\delta}{4}$ and μ is lower-bounded by a quantity determined by δ, $\log \log |\mathcal{F}|$ and the message size of the coding scheme. Moreover, the rate of the code is $\frac{k}{n} \approx 1 - \frac{\log \log |\mathcal{F}|}{n}$.

3   Limited-View Algebraic Tampering

Let $\mathcal{S}^{[n\rho]}$ be the set of all subsets of $[n]$ of size $n\rho$. Let $\mathcal{M}(\mathbb{F}_q^{n\rho}, \mathbb{F}_q^n)$ denote the set of all functions from $\mathbb{F}_q^{n\rho}$ to $\mathbb{F}_q^n$, namely, $\mathcal{M}(\mathbb{F}_q^{n\rho}, \mathbb{F}_q^n) := \{g : \mathbb{F}_q^{n\rho} \to \mathbb{F}_q^n\}$.

Definition 6 (LVAT) [4]. *The set $\mathcal{F}_\rho^{add}$ of Limited-View Algebraic Tampering (LVAT) functions are defined as follows.*

$$\mathcal{F}_\rho^{add} = \left\{ f_{S,g} : \mathbb{F}_q^n \to \mathbb{F}_q^n | S \in \mathcal{S}^{[n\rho]}, g \in \mathcal{M}(\mathbb{F}_q^{n\rho}, \mathbb{F}_q^n) \right\}, \tag{2}$$

where $f_{S,g}(\mathbf{x}) = \mathbf{x} + g(\mathbf{x}_{|S})$ for $\mathbf{x} \in \mathbb{F}_q^n$.

A *tampering strategy* $f_{S,g}$ of the limited-view algebraic adversary is described by a *reading set* $S \subset [n]$ and a function $g : \mathbb{F}_q^{n\rho} \to \mathbb{F}_q^n$. The set S specifies the components that the adversary chooses to read (observe). The function $g : \mathbb{F}_q^{n\rho} \to \mathbb{F}_q^n$ expresses the details of the tampering: if the $n\rho$ positions of the codeword take value $\mathbf{a}$, the offset $g(\mathbf{a}) \in \mathbb{F}_q^n$ is added to the codeword. See Fig. 1 for an example of $f_{S,g} \in \mathcal{F}_{\frac{1}{2}}^{add}$. $\mathcal{F}_\rho^{add}$ characterizes the limited-view algebraic adversary in the sense that if a coding scheme guarantees δ-security for all tampering strategies in $\mathcal{F}_\rho^{add}$, then it guarantees δ-security against the limited-view algebraic adversary.

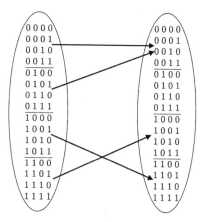

Fig. 1. An example of $f_{S,g} \in \mathcal{F}_{\frac{1}{2}}^{add}$ (assuming $q = 2$ and $n = 4$) with $S = \{1, 2\} \subset [4]$ and g defined by $g(00) = (0000), g(01) = g(10) = g(11) = (0100)$.

Before we consider tamper detection with respect to $\mathcal{F}_\rho^{add}$, we prove the following properties of LVAT functions.

Lemma 3. *For any $f_{S,g} \in \mathcal{F}_\rho^{add}$,*

- $|\{\mathbf{x} \in \mathbb{F}_q^n | f_{S,g}(\mathbf{x}) = \mathbf{x}\}| = |\{\mathbf{a} | g(\mathbf{a}) = 0^n\}| \cdot q^{n(1-\rho)}$;
- $\log |\{f_{S,g}(\mathbf{x}) | \mathbf{x} \in \mathbb{F}_q^n\}| \geq n(1 - \rho) \log q$.

Proof. Let $\mathcal{X}_S^{\mathbf{a}}$ denote the set of n-tuples, whose value at S is $\mathbf{a}$, namely, $\mathcal{X}_S^{\mathbf{a}} = \{\mathbf{x} \in \mathbb{F}_q^n | \mathbf{x}_{|S} = \mathbf{a}\}$. We observe that adding an n-tuple $\mathbf{y}$ to $\mathcal{X}_S^{\mathbf{a}}$ yields $\mathcal{X}_S^{\mathbf{b}}$, where $\mathbf{b} = \mathbf{a} + \mathbf{y}_{|S}$. As illustrated in Fig. 1, applying $f_{S,g}$ to $\mathbf{x} \in \mathcal{X}_S^{\mathbf{a}}$ is by definition adding $g(\mathbf{a})$ to it, hence turning it into an n-tuple in $\mathcal{X}_S^{\mathbf{b}}$, where $\mathbf{b} = \mathbf{a} + g(\mathbf{a})_{|S}$. We will simply write $f_{S,g}(\mathcal{X}_S^{\mathbf{a}}) = \mathcal{X}_S^{\mathbf{b}}$.

– Consider each subset $\mathcal{X}_S^{\mathbf{a}}$. For any $\mathbf{x} \in \mathcal{X}_S^{\mathbf{a}}$, $f_{S,g}(\mathbf{x}) = \mathbf{x} + g(\mathbf{a}) = \mathbf{x}$ if and only if $g(\mathbf{a}) = 0^n$, in which case every vector in $\mathcal{X}_S^{\mathbf{a}}$ is a fixed point of $f_{S,g}$. So the total number of fixed points of $f_{S,g}$ is given by $q^{n(1-\rho)} \cdot |\{\mathbf{a}|g(\mathbf{a}) = 0^n\}|$.

– Consider two subsets $\mathcal{X}_S^{\mathbf{a}}$ and $\mathcal{X}_S^{\mathbf{b}}$. We have $f_{S,g}(\mathcal{X}_S^{\mathbf{a}}) = f_{S,g}(\mathcal{X}_S^{\mathbf{b}})$ if and only if $\mathbf{a} + g(\mathbf{a})_{|S} = \mathbf{b} + g(\mathbf{b})_{|S}$. Once this happens, the range of $f_{S,g}$ is strictly smaller than $\mathbb{F}_q^n$. In the extreme case when $\mathbf{a} + g(\mathbf{a})_{|S} = \mathbf{c}$ for all $\mathbf{a} \in \mathbb{F}_q^{n\rho}$, the range of $f_{S,g}$ is $\mathcal{X}_S^{\mathbf{c}}$ and $\log |\{f_{S,g}(\mathbf{x})|\mathbf{x} \in \mathbb{F}_q^n\}| = n(1-\rho)\log q$. This is obviously the smallest value $\log |\{f_{S,g}(\mathbf{x})|\mathbf{x} \in \mathbb{F}_q^n\}|$ can get. The bound then follows.

Remark 3. As recalled in Remark 2, the impossibility result of [8] with respect to low entropy functions was shown for $\mu \leq k \log q$. Lemma 3 shows that the entropy of any function in $\mathcal{F}_\rho^{add}$ is at least $n(1-\rho)\log q$. So as long as the coding scheme has rate less than $1 - \rho$, namely, $n(1-\rho) > k$, we do not need to consider whether that particular attack applies here. But on the other hand, the number of fixed points is not bounded and could, in the worst case, be as big as q^n. In fact, the number of fixed points of a function $f_{S,g} \in \mathcal{F}_\rho^{add}$ for any ρ is q^n if the function g is defined such that $|\{\mathbf{a}|g(\mathbf{a}) = 0^n\}| = q^{n\rho}$.

In the sequel, we impose a bound on the number of fixed points and restrict ourselves to a subset of $\mathcal{F}_\rho^{add}$.

Definition 7. *Let $\phi = \frac{i}{q^{n\rho}}$, where $i = 0, 1, \cdots, q^{n\rho}$. The set $\mathcal{F}_{\rho,\phi}^{add}$ is the subset of $\mathcal{F}_\rho^{add}$ that contains the tampering functions that have less than $\phi \cdot q^n$ fixed points.*

The following Lemma shows that if a class of tampering functions can fix a ϕ fraction of the space $\mathbb{F}_q^n$, then the detection failure can not be made smaller than ϕ.

Lemma 4. *Let $\phi = \frac{i}{q^{n\rho}}$, where $i = 0, 1, \cdots, q^{n\rho}$. Let $\mathcal{F}$ be the subset of $\mathcal{F}_\rho^{add}$ that contains all the functions with $\phi \cdot q^n$ fixed points, namely,*

$$\mathcal{F} = \{f_{S,g} \in \mathcal{F}_\rho^{add} | f_{S,g} \text{ has } \phi \cdot q^n \text{ fixed points}\}.$$

If an (n,k)-coding scheme (Enc, Dec) is an $(\mathcal{F}, \delta)$-TD code, then $\delta \geq \phi$.

Proof. We need to show that given any (n,k)-coding scheme (Enc, Dec), there is a message $\mathbf{m}$, for which we can find a tampering function $f_{S,g} \in \mathcal{F}$ (by specifying the choice of S and g) such that $\Pr[\text{Dec}(f_{S,g}(\text{Enc}(\mathbf{m}))) \neq \bot] \geq \phi$. In fact, we can show this for any particular message $\mathbf{m}$ and any particular $S \subset [n]$.

Let $\mathbf{X} = \text{Enc}(\mathbf{m})$ be the random variable that is associated to the randomized codeword of a particular message $\mathbf{m}$. Let $\mathbf{Y} = \mathbf{X}_{|S}$ be the random variable that is associated to the sub-vector of $\mathbf{X}$, for a particular $S \subset [n]$ of size $n\rho$. Apparently, $\mathbf{Y}$ is a random variable over $\mathbb{F}_q^{n\rho}$. Here we consider all vectors in $\mathbb{F}_q^{n\rho}$, namely, we assume $\Pr[\mathbf{Y} = \mathbf{y}] = 0$, when $\mathbf{y} \in \mathbb{F}_q^{n\rho} \backslash \text{Supp}(\mathbf{Y})$. Let $D_\phi(\mathbf{Y})$ be a subset of $\mathbb{F}_q^{n\rho}$ of size $\phi \cdot q^{n\rho}$ that contains the "more likely" values of $\mathbf{Y}$, namely, start with the value of $\mathbf{Y}$ that has the highest probability and go all the way down till the $\phi \cdot q^{n\rho}$'th value is added into the set. By construction, we obviously have $\Pr[\mathbf{Y} \in D_\phi(\mathbf{Y})] \geq \phi$. We use it to define a function g as follows.

$$g(\mathbf{a}) = \begin{cases} 0^n, \mathbf{a} \in D_\phi(\mathbf{Y}) \subset \mathbb{F}_q^{n\rho}; \\ 1^n, \text{ otherwise.} \end{cases}$$

According to Lemma 3, the number of fixed points of $f_{S,g}$ is $q^{n(1-\rho)} \cdot |D_\phi(\mathbf{Y})| = \phi \cdot q^n$. So we have $f_{S,g} \in \mathcal{F}$. Finally, by the way g is defined, we have

$$\Pr[\text{Dec}(f_{S,g}(\text{Enc}(\mathbf{m}))) \neq \bot] \geq \Pr[\text{Dec}(f_{S,g}(\text{Enc}(\mathbf{m}))) = \mathbf{m}] \geq \Pr[\mathbf{Y} \in D_\phi(\mathbf{Y})],$$

which concludes the proof.

4   Limited-View Algebraic Tampering TD Codes

Definition 8 $((\rho, \phi, \delta)$**-LVAT-TD code**$)$. *Let* $\phi = \frac{i}{q^{n\rho}}$, *where* $i = 0, 1, \cdots, q^{n\rho}$. *An* (n, k)-*coding scheme (Enc, Dec) is called a* (ρ, ϕ, δ)-*LVAT-TD code if it is a* $(\mathcal{F}_{\rho,\phi}^{add}, \delta)$-*TD code, namely, if for any message* $\mathbf{m} \in \mathbb{F}_q^k$ *and any* $f \in \mathcal{F}_{\rho,\phi}^{add}$, $\Pr[\text{Dec}(f(\text{Enc}(\mathbf{m}))) \neq \bot] \leq \delta$.

Remark 4. Lemma 4 implies that (ρ, ϕ, δ)-LVAT-TD codes can only exist for $\phi < \delta$.

Code Construction

Theorem 1. *Let* $(WtIIenc, WtIIdec)$ *be the linear* $(\rho, 0)$-*WtII code in Lemma 1 with encoder* $WtIIenc : \mathbb{F}_q^{k+2} \to \mathbb{F}_q^n$. *Let* $(AMDenc, AMDdec)$ *be the* $(q^k, q^{k+2}, \frac{k+1}{q})$-*AMD code in Lemma 2. Then* (Enc, Dec) *defined as follows is a* $(\rho, \phi, \phi + \frac{k+1}{q})$-*LVAT-TD code.*

$$\begin{cases} Enc(\mathbf{m}) = WtIIenc(AMDenc(\mathbf{m})); \\ Dec(\mathbf{x}) = AMDdec(WtIIdec(\mathbf{x})). \end{cases}$$

The rate of the (n, k)-*coding scheme* (Enc, Dec) *is* $1 - \rho - \frac{2}{n}$.

Proof. Since both AMDenc and WtIIenc are randomised encoders, in this proof we write the randomness of a randomized encoder explicitly. Let I denote the randomness of AMDenc and let J denote the randomness of WtIIenc. As illustrated in Fig. 2, a message $\mathbf{m}$ is first encoded into an AMD codeword $A_{\mathbf{m}}^I = $ AMDenc$(\mathbf{m}, I)$. The AMD codeword $A_{\mathbf{m}}^I$ is then further encoded into a WtII codeword, which is the final $(\rho, \phi, \phi + \frac{k+1}{q})$-LVAT-TD codeword: WtIIenc$(A_{\mathbf{m}}^I, J)$. According to (1), SD $\left(\text{WtIIenc}(A_{\mathbf{m}}^{i_1}, J)_{|S}; \text{WtIIenc}(A_{\mathbf{m}}^{i_2}, J)_{|S}\right) = 0$. This says that $A_{\mathbf{m}}^I$ and Enc$(\mathbf{m})_{|S}$ are independent, in particular, I and Enc$(\mathbf{m})_{|S}$ are independent. According to Definition 8, to show that (Enc, Dec) is a $(\rho, \phi, \phi + \frac{k+1}{q})$-LVAT-TD code, we need to show that for any message $\mathbf{m}$, and any $f_{S,g} \in \mathcal{F}_{\rho,\phi}^{add}$,

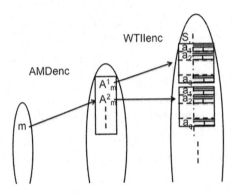

Fig. 2. WtII∘AMD construction

$\Pr[\text{Dec}(f_{S,g}(\text{Enc}(\mathbf{m})))\neq\perp] \leq \phi + \frac{k+1}{q}$, where the probability is over the randomness $(\mathbf{I}, \mathbf{J})$ of the encoder Enc. We show this in two steps.

Step 1. In this step, we assume that $\text{Enc}(\mathbf{m})_{|S} = \mathbf{a}$ has occurred and bound the failure probability of (Enc, Dec) under this condition. We compute

$$\Pr[\text{Dec}(f_{S,g}(\text{Enc}(\mathbf{m})))\neq\perp|(\text{Enc}(\mathbf{m})_{|S} = \mathbf{a})]$$
$$= \Pr[\text{Dec}(\text{Enc}(\mathbf{m}) + g(\mathbf{a}))\neq\perp|(\text{Enc}(\mathbf{m})_{|S} = \mathbf{a})]$$
$$= \Pr[\text{AMDdec}(\text{WtIIdec}(\text{WtIIenc}(\text{AMDenc}(\mathbf{m}, \mathbf{I}), \mathbf{J})$$
$$+ g(\mathbf{a})))\neq\perp|(\text{Enc}(\mathbf{m})_{|S} = \mathbf{a})]$$
$$= \Pr[\text{AMDdec}(\text{AMDenc}(\mathbf{m}, \mathbf{I}) + \text{WtIIdec}(g(\mathbf{a})))\neq\perp$$
$$|(\text{Enc}(\mathbf{m})_{|S} = \mathbf{a})]$$
$$= \Pr[\text{AMDdec}(\text{AMDenc}(\mathbf{m}, \mathbf{I}) + \text{WtIIdec}(g(\mathbf{a})))\neq\perp],$$

where the third equality follows from the linearity of (WtIIenc, WtIIdec) and the last equality follows from the fact that $\mathbf{I}$ and $\text{Enc}(\mathbf{m})_{|S}$ are independent discussed in the beginning of the proof. Now if $g(\mathbf{a}) = 0^n$, we have

$$\Pr[\text{AMDdec}(\text{AMDenc}(\mathbf{m}, \mathbf{I}) + \text{WtIIdec}(g(\mathbf{a}))) \neq\perp] = 1,$$

since $\text{AMDdec}(\text{AMDenc}(\mathbf{m}, \mathbf{I}) + \text{WtIIdec}(g(\mathbf{a}))) = \text{AMDdec}(\text{AMDenc}(\mathbf{m}, \mathbf{I})) = \mathbf{m}$. If otherwise $g(\mathbf{a}) \neq 0^n$, we have

$$\Pr[\text{AMDdec}(\text{AMDenc}(\mathbf{m}, \mathbf{I}) + \text{WtIIdec}(g(\mathbf{a}))) \neq\perp] \leq \frac{k+1}{q},$$

since (AMDenc, AMDdec) in fact "achieves tamper detection" (See Remark 1).

Step 2. In this step, we conclude the proof by showing

$$\Pr[\text{Dec}(f_{S,g}(\text{Enc}(\mathbf{m})))\neq\perp]$$
$$= \sum_{\mathbf{a}} \Pr[\text{Enc}(\mathbf{m})_{|S} = \mathbf{a}] \cdot \Pr[\text{Dec}(f_{S,g}(\text{Enc}(\mathbf{m})))\neq\perp$$
$$|(\text{Enc}(\mathbf{m})_{|S} = \mathbf{a})]$$
$$\leq \sum_{\mathbf{a}:g(\mathbf{a})=0^n} \Pr[\text{Enc}(\mathbf{m})_{|S} = \mathbf{a}] \cdot 1$$
$$+ \sum_{\mathbf{a}:g(\mathbf{a})\neq0^n} \Pr[\text{Enc}(\mathbf{m})_{|S} = \mathbf{a}] \cdot \frac{k+1}{q}$$
$$< \phi q^{n\rho} \cdot \frac{1}{q^{n\rho}} \cdot 1 + \frac{k+1}{q}$$
$$= \phi + \frac{k+1}{q},$$

where the first inequality follows from **Step 1.** and the following property of $(\rho, 0)$-WtII code: for any $A \in \mathbb{F}_q^{k+2}$, $\Pr[\mathrm{WtIIenc}(A)_{|S} = \mathbf{a}] = \frac{1}{q^{n\rho}}$ for any $\mathbf{a} \in \mathbb{F}_q^{n\rho}$. The rate of these $(\rho, \phi, \phi + \frac{k+1}{q})$-LVAT-TD codes is computed as follows.

$$R = \frac{k}{n} = \frac{(1-\rho)n - 2}{n} = 1 - \rho - \frac{2}{n}.$$

5   Concluding Remarks

We studied TD codes for a class of functions that we called LVAT function family. We first showed that the functions that have many fixed points have to be excluded from the set in order to have a small detection failure. We then gave a construction of tamper detection codes with respect to the remaining functions in the family.

LVAT family naturally arises when the codeword is partially leaked to the adversary and this information is used to choose the noise vector that is added to the codeword. We assumed leakage is in the form of the components of the codeword. An interesting open question is to consider codes when leakage is through an arbitrary function, with the restriction that the remaining entropy in the codeword remains sufficiently high. Another open question is construction of TD codes for LVAT family over binary alphabet.

References

1. Shannon, C.E.: A mathematical theory of communication. Bell Syst. Techn. J. **27**, 379–423, 623–656 (1948)
2. Cheraghchi, M., Didier, F., Shokrollahi, A.: Invertible extractors and wiretap protocols. IEEE Trans. Inf. Theory **58**(2), 1254–1274 (2012)
3. Aggarwal, D., Dodis, Y., Lovett, S.: Non-malleable codes from additive combinatorics. In Shmoys, D.B. (ed.) 46th ACM STOC, pp. 774–783. ACM Press, New York, 31 May–3 June 2014
4. Lin, F., Safavi-Naini, R., Wang, P.: Detecting algebraic manipulation in leaky storage systems. In: Nascimento, A.C.A., Barreto, P. (eds.) ICITS 2016. LNCS, vol. 10015, pp. 129–150. Springer, Cham (2016). doi:10.1007/978-3-319-49175-2_7
5. Simmons, G.J.: Authentication theory/coding theory. In: Blakley, G.R., Chaum, D. (eds.) CRYPTO 1984. LNCS, vol. 196, pp. 411–431. Springer, Heidelberg (1985). doi:10.1007/3-540-39568-7_32
6. Ahmadi, H., Safavi-Naini, R.: Detection of algebraic manipulation in the presence of leakage. In: Padró, C. (ed.) ICITS 2013. LNCS, vol. 8317, pp. 238–258. Springer, Cham (2014). doi:10.1007/978-3-319-04268-8_14
7. Jafargholi, Z., Wichs, D.: Tamper detection and continuous non-malleable codes. In: Dodis, Y., Nielsen, J.B. (eds.) TCC 2015. LNCS, vol. 9014, pp. 451–480. Springer, Heidelberg (2015). doi:10.1007/978-3-662-46494-6_19
8. Jafargholi, Z., Wichs, D.: Tamper Detection and Continuous Non-malleable Codes [full version] (2015). http://eprint.iacr.org/2014/956
9. Cheraghchi, M., Guruswami, V.: Capacity of non-malleable codes. In: Naor, M. (ed.) ITCS 2014, pp. 155–168. ACM, Princeton, 12–14 January 2014

10. Cheraghchi, M., Guruswami, V.: Non-malleable coding against bit-wise and split-state tampering. In: Lindell, Y. (ed.) TCC 2014. LNCS, vol. 8349, pp. 440–464. Springer, Heidelberg (2014). doi:10.1007/978-3-642-54242-8_19

11. Langberg, M.: Oblivious communication channels and their capacity. IEEE Trans. Inf. Theory **54**(1), 424–429 (2008)

12. Ozarow, L.H., Wyner, A.D.: Wire-tap channel II. At & T Bell Lab. Techn. J. **63**(10), 2135–2157 (1984)

13. Wang, P., Safavi-Naini, R., Lin, F.: Erasure adversarial wiretap channels. In: 53rd Annual Allerton Conference on Communication, Control, and Computing (2015)

14. Wang, P., Safavi-Naini, R.: Limited view adversary codes: bounds, constructions and applications. In: ICITS 2015, pp. 214–235 (2015)

15. Wang, P., Safavi-Naini, R.: A model for adversarial wiretap channels. IEEE Trans. Inf. Theory **62**(2) (2016)

16. Faust, S., Mukherjee, P., Venturi, D., Wichs, D.: Efficient non-malleable codes and key-derivation for poly-size tampering circuits. In: Nguyen, P.Q., Oswald, E. (eds.) EUROCRYPT 2014. LNCS, vol. 8441, pp. 111–128. Springer, Heidelberg (2014). doi:10.1007/978-3-642-55220-5_7

17. Safavi-Naini, R., Wang, P.: Codes for limited view adversarial channels. In: IEEE International Symposium on Information Theory (ISIT), pp. 266–270 (2013)

18. Hamming, R.W.: Error detecting and error correcting codes. Bell Syst. Techn. J. **29**, 147–160 (1950)

19. Cramer, R., Dodis, Y., Fehr, S., Padró, C., Wichs, D.: Detection of algebraic manipulation with applications to robust secret sharing and fuzzy extractors. In: Smart, N. (ed.) EUROCRYPT 2008. LNCS, vol. 4965, pp. 471–488. Springer, Heidelberg (2008). doi:10.1007/978-3-540-78967-3_27

20. Dziembowski, S., Pietrzak, K., Wichs, D.: Non-malleable codes. In: ICS, pp. 434–452 (2010)

21. Dziembowski, S., Kazana, T., Obremski, M.: Non-malleable codes from two-source extractors. In: Canetti, R., Garay, J.A. (eds.) CRYPTO 2013. LNCS, vol. 8043, pp. 239–257. Springer, Heidelberg (2013). doi:10.1007/978-3-642-40084-1_14

22. Guruswami, V., Smith, A.: Codes for computationally simple channels: explicit constructions with optimal rate. In: FOCS, pp. 723–732 (2010)

Post-quantum Cryptography

On Fast Calculation of Addition Chains for Isogeny-Based Cryptography

Brian Koziel[1]([⊠]), Reza Azarderakhsh[2], David Jao[3], and Mehran Mozaffari-Kermani[4]

[1] Texas Instruments, Dallas, USA
kozielbrian@gmail.com
[2] CEECS Department and I-SENSE FAU, Boca Raton, USA
razarderakhsh@fau.edu
[3] C&O Department, University of Waterloo, Waterloo, Canada
djao@uwaterloo.ca
[4] EME Department, RIT, Rochester, USA
mmkeme@rit.edu

Abstract. Addition chain calculations play a critical role in determining the efficiency of cryptosystems based on isogenies on elliptic curves. However, finding a minimal length addition chain is not easy; a generalized version of the problem, in which one must find a chain that simultaneously forms each of a sequence of values, is NP-complete. For the special primes used in such cryptosystems, finding fast addition chains for finite field arithmetic such as inversion and square root is also not easy. In this paper, we investigate the shape of smooth isogeny primes and propose new methods to calculate fast addition chains. Further, we also provide techniques to reduce the temporary register consumption of these large exponentials, applicable to both software and hardware implementations utilizing addition chains. Lastly, we utilize our procedures to compare multiple isogeny primes by the complexity of the addition chains.

Keywords: Addition chains · Post-quantum cryptography · Isogeny-based cryptosystems · Finite field

1 Introduction

An addition chain can be thought of as a sequence of integers starting from 1 to some number n, where each number is a sum of any two previous integers in the sequence. For finite fields, operations such as exponentiations, inversions, or square roots can be performed efficiently by utilizing an optimal addition chain, the smallest such addition chain sequence to reach n. In particular, fast exponentiation and inversion are paramount to the performance of scalar point multiplication in elliptic curve cryptography (ECC), pairings in pairing-based cryptosystems, and computing isogenies in the quantum-resistant isogeny-based cryptosystems [1].

K. Chen et al. (Eds.): Inscrypt 2016, LNCS 10143, pp. 323–342, 2017.
DOI: 10.1007/978-3-319-54705-3_20

There are several popular families of primes for fast computation of addition chains used in public key cryptography including Mersenne primes [2], Crandall primes [2], and Solinas primes [3]. Generally, these primes have a special form with most of the prime featuring all '1's. This speeds up most finite-field arithmetic tremendously and also produces extremely fast addition chains through the use of a regular chain of squaring and multiplying by $2^s - 1$ for increasing values of s. Similarly, binary extension fields can take advantage of the Itoh-Tsujii [4] method to compute the large exponential for inversion which also utilizes towering values of $2^s - 1$, typically found in hardware implementations.

None of the above primes can be utilized for post-quantum cryptography based on isogenies on elliptic curves, primarily because the curves generated from these primes do not have many isogenies that are fast to compute. Therefore, in [1], a special shape of primes called smooth isogeny primes is presented that produce curves of smooth shape for fast isogeny computations. These are of the form $p = \ell_A^a \ell_B^b f \pm 1$, where ℓ_A and ℓ_B are relatively small primes, a and b are positive integers, and f is a small cofactor to make the number prime. Most primes of this form appear in the general prime category. However, if $\ell_A = 2$, then the second half of the prime is either all '1's in the case that the prime is minus 1 or all '0's in the case that the prime is plus 1. The all '0's form is much faster in terms of speed as it just requires squarings, but the all '1's pattern is still a regular structure that can take advantage of long chains of '1', similar to Solinas or Mersenne primes. If $\ell \neq 2$, then a basic windowing technique should be used, similar to the general primes. A majority of the known software [5–8] and hardware [9,10] implementations do not consider calculating fast addition chains, which can improve inversion and square root computations essentially for free.

Motivation. Current isogeny-based cryptography requires many exponentiations through the use of inversions and square roots. Many finite field inversions are required as points must be recovered from scalar point multiplications to compute isogenies between curves. Finite field square roots have also been introduced to create a basis for key compression [7,11]. For example, in the supersingular isogeny Diffie-Hellman key exchange protocol [6] with key compression [7], approximately 844 finite field inversions and 56 finite field square roots for 85-bit quantum security level were counted through test runs. Interestingly, [8] revised the SIDH formula to only require a constant 4 finite field inversions, making constant-time implementations feasible. Addition chains perform large exponentiations efficiently and in a constant set of operations. Thus, they prove both security and speed to exponentiations used in the inversion and square root operations.

In this paper, we study addition chains for primes used in post-quantum cryptography based on isogenies on supersingular elliptic curves. This cryptosystem resembles ECC with its use of point multiplications, but also provides quantum resistance by walking large degree isogeny graphs [1]. Our goal is to improve the speed and efficiency of addition chains used in isogeny-based cryptography so that implementation of this post-quantum scheme can be practical. Our contributions can be itemized as follows:

- We analyze the shape of smooth isogeny primes, which are applicable to post-quantum cryptography based on isogenies on supersingular elliptic curves, and present several methods to design fast addition chains.
- We present a hybrid windowing method to optimize inversion for primes of the form $2^a \ell_B^b f \pm 1$.
- We present a windowing method with a subtraction to optimize computation of square root exponentials for $2^a \ell_B^b f - 1$.
- We introduce techniques to minimize the number of intermediate values that are stored for an addition chain.
- We present empirical results of our techniques on a few smooth isogeny primes.

2 Background of Addition Chains

In this section, we review basic concepts of addition chains, their computations, and a metric to compare them. All notations used in this paper are summarized in Table 1.

Table 1. Notations used in this paper

Notation	Definition
$\mathbb{Z}$	The set of integers
$\mathbb{F}_{p^n}$	A finite field of size p^n
m	Power of 2 to represent families of special primes
k	Iterating over k bits at a time (as in k-ary method)
c	Optimal power of 2 for use in Hybrid Windowing Method
I, M, S, A	Inversion, Multiplication, Squaring, and Addition in $\mathbb{F}_p$
$\tilde{I}, \tilde{M}, \tilde{S}, \tilde{A}$	Inversion, Multiplication, Squaring, and Addition in $\mathbb{F}_{p^2}$

2.1 Addition Chains

We formally introduce addition chains with the following definitions. We point the reader to [12] for an in-depth explanation of addition chains.

Definition 1. *An addition chain is a sequence of integers $(a_0, a_1, \ldots, a_r)$ with $a_0 = 1$ and $a_r = n$, such that $a_i = a_j + a_k$ for any $j, k < i$.*

Definition 2. *An addition chain is optimal if its length is the smallest among all possible addition chains.*

Algorithm 1. k-ary Precomputation

Input: n, k, c
Output: $c_i = c^i \bmod n$, with $i = 0 \ldots 2^k - 1$
1. $c_0 = 1$
2. for i from 1 to $2^k - 1$ do
3. $c_i = (c_{i-1} \times c) \bmod n$
4.   return c_i
5. end for

Algorithm 2. k-ary Exponentiation Method

Input: A, $c_i = c^i (i = 0 \ldots 2^k - 1)$, $d = d_{b-1} d_{b-2} \ldots d_1 d_0)_{2^k}$
Output: A^d
1. for i from $b - 1$ downto 0 do
2. $A = A^{2^k}$
3. $A = A \times c_{d_i}$
4. end for
5. return A

We are interested in finding optimal or almost optimal addition chains. It has not been formally proven that finding an optimal addition chain is NP-complete, but finding the optimal addition chain sequence for multiple numbers is believed to be NP-complete.

Essentially, addition chains can be thought of as sums of preceding values in the sequence. This is analogous to exponentiation because multiplying two numbers with the same base is the same as adding the two exponentials, e.g. $x^i \times x^j = x^{i+j}$.

Definition 3. *A Brauer chain [13] is an addition chain that always uses the previous value for the next one. In other words, it is a sequence of integers* $(a_0, a_1, \ldots, a_r)$ *with* $a_0 = 1$ *and* $a_r = n$, *such that* $a_i = a_j + a_{i-1}$.

Brauer chains utilize a stipulation that forces one of the inputs to be the previous value. This greatly reduces the number of possible combinations for addition chains. Several algorithms produce optimal Brauer chains, but unfortunately, these are typically not optimal among all addition chains. We point the readers to [13] for more analysis of Brauer chains. The general goal of Brauer chains is to precompute values and then use an accumulator to square and multiply these precomputed values.

2.2 Computations of Addition Chains

k-**Ary Method.** The binary method is among the simplest addition chains, that iterates over bits of an exponential with the square-and-multiply technique. However, this is part of a broader family, the k-ary method, which is also a form of a Brauer chain. The k-ary method iterates over k bits at a time by repeatedly performing k squarings followed by a multiplication with precomputed values. Algorithm 1 lists the precomputation phase and Algorithm 2 lists the iterative square-and-multiply method.

As an example, for $k = 5$ over a 512-bit exponential, there are approximately 511 squarings and 103 multiplications. Furthermore, at most 30 values must be precomputed for the general case, for a grand total of 511 squarings and 133 multiplications.

Windowing Method. The sliding windowing method, presented in works such as [14–17], optimizes the k-ary method by breaking the exponential into specific windows up to a maximum of k bits. Efficient addition chain sequences are generated to satisfy each of these windows using methods such as Lucas chains, halving, approximation, and division. After that, these windows are applied when it is its turn as the exponential is squared many times. The main advantage of this over the standard k-ary method is that addition chain sequences are used to generate only the necessary windows efficiently to reduce the total number of multiplications and squarings.

2.3   Comparison of Addition Chains

For our purposes, we compare addition chains by the number of squarings and multiplications for the exponentiation, as well as the number of temporary registers that must be stored when implemented in hardware or software. For instance, it is interesting that the basic square-and-multiply, or binary method, requires many more multiplications than the windowing method for the general case, but only requires 2 registers. Indeed, this is among the slowest addition chains, but it is among the most space-efficient. For some implementations, squarings are faster than multiplications. For our purposes, we will also try to optimize for the relationship $S = 0.8M$.

2.4   Finite Field Inversion and Square Root

We are interested in using fast addition chains to compute the exponentiations needed by inversion and square root in $\mathbb{F}_{p^2}$. For any $A \in \mathbb{F}_p$, finite field inversion computes a value $B = A^{-1}$ such that $A \cdot B = 1$, where $B \in \mathbb{F}_p$. This can be computed using Fermat's little theorem, which holds that $A^{-1} = A^{p-2}$. Addition chains can be used to efficiently evaluate these large powers in a constant set of operations, to protect against timing attacks and simple power analysis attacks. Conversely, the extended Euclidean algorithm could be applied to obtain the inversion with a smaller time complexity, but at the cost of revealing some information about the operand.

For any $A \in \mathbb{F}_p$, finite field square root computes a value $B = A^{1/2}$ such that $B \cdot B = A$ where $B \in \mathbb{F}_p$. It should be noted that $-B \in \mathbb{F}_p$ is also a square root because $-B \cdot -B = A$ where $-B \in \mathbb{F}_p$. We utilize the approach given by [18] over even extension fields. The square root operation utilizes multiple exponentiations, $\frac{p-3}{4}$, $\frac{p-1}{2}$, and p in the case that $p \equiv 3 \bmod 4$ and $\frac{p-1}{4}$, $\frac{p-1}{2}$, and p in the case that $p \equiv 1 \bmod 4$. Notably, if $p \equiv 1 \bmod 4$ then there is an additional square root operation that is extremely expensive. The exponentiation by p in $\mathbb{F}_{p^2}$ is special in that it can be performed using the Frobenius operator [18], which only requires a finite field negation. This is shown in Eq. 1. Consider an element, a, in $\mathbb{F}_{p^2}$ is represented as a_0 and a_1, where $a_0, a_1 \in \mathbb{F}_p$ and a_1 is the most significant element.

$$a^p = (a_0, a_1)^p = (a_0, -a_1) \qquad (1)$$

In general, inversion requires a single exponentiation in $\mathbb{F}_p$ and the square root requires one or two exponentiations in $\mathbb{F}_{p^2}$. We refer the reader to [18] and the Appendix for a longer discussion of inversion and the square root in even extension fields.

3 Supersingular Isogeny Cryptosystems

This section serves as a brief review of supersingular isogeny theory and its application as a cryptosystem. We point the reader to [1,19] for a much more in-depth look at isogeny theory.

Isogeny-based cryptography relies on the difficulty to compute isogenies between elliptic curves. An isogeny between two elliptic curves, E_1 and E_2, is defined as a morphism $\phi : E_1 \to E_2$ such that $\phi(O) = O$ [19]. Essentially, this is a non-constant rational map between these two curves that preserves the null point. We are particularly interested in supersingular curves. The endomorphism ring of a curve is defined as as the ring of all isogenies from a curve to itself, under point addition and functional composition. A curve is considered supersingular if it features a endomorphism ring with $\mathbb{Z}$-rank equal to 4. Supersingular curves can be defined over $\mathbb{F}_{p^2}$ or $\mathbb{F}_p$. Therefore, a common field that includes all isogenous curves is $\mathbb{F}_{p^2}$. Supersingular curves have the property that for every prime $\ell \neq p$, there exist $\ell + 1$ isogenies of degree ℓ from a base curve. An isogeny can be computed over a kernel, κ, such that $\phi : E \to E/\langle \kappa \rangle$ by using Vélu's formulas [20].

The supersingular isogeny Diffie-Hellman (SIDH) key exchange protocol, for instance, operates similar to the standard Elliptic Curve Diffie-Hellman version. In this case, Alice and Bob both have private keys to perform a double point multiplication that spans the entire isogeny space. They compute isogenies over the agreed upon bases with their double point multiplication result as the kernel. They exchange these applied isogenies and perform a second set of double point multiplications and isogeny computations, to arrive on curves with the same j-invariant [1].

Key compression and decompression have been introduced for this key exchange protocol in [7]. In this revised protocol, each party deterministically creates a shared torsion basis, which is used to reconstruct some public information that was originally intended to be exchanged over a public channel in the standard protocol. The algorithms related to SIDH key compression were also

---

Algorithm 3. Efficient Generation of Primes of the Form $2^a 3^b f - 1$

Output: Smooth isogeny primes of the form $2^a 3^b f - 1$
1. Define powers a and b for a balanced isogeny graph
2. Define a higher bound F on f
3. Define $\Pi = \prod_{i=1}^{k} p_i < F$, where p_i is a prime greater than 2 and 3 and Π is maximized
  3a. e.g. $\Pi = 5 \times 7 \times 11 \cdots$
4. Define the generator $g = (2^a 3^b)^{-1} \bmod \Pi$
5. While looking for primes, do
  6. Select some c_0 in $\mathbb{F}_\Pi^*$ //Must be coprime to each p_i
  7. While $(c_j \neq c_0)$, do //Test all candidates in cyclic sub-group for iteration j
    7a. Define $f = g + c \bmod \Pi$
    7b. Test if $p = 2^a 3^b f - 1$ is prime
    7c. $c_{j+1} = 3 \times c_j$ //Multiplication by 2 could also be used here
8. Return all valid primes p

---

recently improved in both speed and compression rate in [11]. An SIDH public key can be compressed to approximately $\frac{7}{2} \log p$ bytes [11].

How SIDH uses exponentiations. The SIDH protocol and compression were mentioned because they both use finite field inversions and square roots. Based on the new "projective" isogeny formulas presented in [8], 4 inversions are required for the SIDH protocol, far fewer than the original "affine" isogeny formulas. These inversions are necessary to recover the final curve coefficients, basis points, and j-invariant in the SIDH algorithm. The strong compression algorithm in [7] deterministically finds coordinates that can be used as a torsion basis. One essential part to finding a torsion basis is ensuring that the points have the right order, which utilizes square roots in the curve equation to recover y-coordinates. It performs the square root at each iteration until it finds points that have the correct order.

Isogeny-based cryptosystems use primes of the form $\ell_A^a \ell_B^b \cdot f \pm 1$ where ℓ_A and ℓ_B are small primes, a and b are positive integers, and f is a small cofactor to make the number prime. This prime is used to define a supersingular elliptic curve, $E(\mathbb{F}_q)$ where $q = p^2$. In the literature, the fastest known isogeny computations are over $\ell_A = 2$ and $\ell_B = 3$, presented in [8]. For secure primes of this form, we want the relative size of ℓ_A^a and ℓ_B^b to be approximately equal for balanced isogeny graphs. Furthermore, these primes can fit nicely for software applications by making the size of the prime as close to a multiple of 32. Lastly, the quantum security under these schemes was shown to be approximately the number of bits divided by 6 in [1].

Efficiently Finding Smooth Isogeny Primes. From the prime number theorem in arithmetic progressions in [21], it can be shown that the density of such smooth isogeny primes is sufficient. A brute force approach could be used by testing all values of f, but we adapted the methods of [22] to greatly reduce the number of prime candidates of smooth isogeny forms. Algorithm 3 demonstrates the approach for primes of the form $2^a 3^b f - 1$, but simple changes to the generator in the algorithm make it applicable to other smooth isogeny primes. The algorithm ensures that all primes that are tested are already coprime to the product of all small primes used, Π. We further note that each candidate is coprime to 2 and 3 in our example.

4   Fast Exponentiations for Smooth Isogeny Primes

In this section, we evaluate the structure of exponentiations for inversion and square root for smooth isogeny primes of the form $\ell_A^a \ell_B^b \cdot f \pm 1$ where ℓ_A and ℓ_B are small primes, a and b are positive integers, and f is a small cofactor to make the number prime. We break this prime form into the following families: $2^a \ell_B^b f - 1$, $2^a \ell_B^b f + 1$, and general smooth isogeny primes. Figure 1 summarizes our observations based on the addition chains method we found to be most effective.

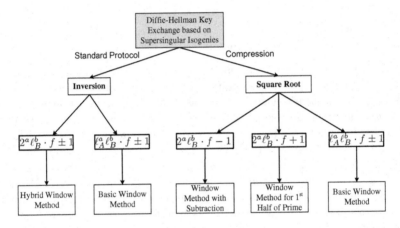

Fig. 1. Taxonomy of addition chains for smooth isogeny prime families

4.1 $2^a \ell_B^b f - 1$ - Taking Advantage of the Least Significant Half of the Prime

We introduce this family as a set of smooth isogeny primes that have the least signficant bits all set to '1'. Notably, these primes satisfy the Montgomery friendly property [23] to speed up Montgomery reduction [24]. Otherwise, it is essential to note that there will be many more factors of 2 than ℓ_B in the shape of the prime, so primes of this form are $p \equiv 3 \bmod 4$, equating to faster square root operations.

Proposition 1. *Very fast addition chains can be generated for primes of the form $2^a \ell_B^b f - 1$ by using an adaptation of the windowing method for the most significant half of the exponentials and precomputing a large value $2^c - 1$ for the least significant half.*

Algorithm 4. Hybrid windowing method for primes of the form $2^a \ell_B^b f - 1$.

Input: Smooth Isogeny prime of form $2^a \ell_B^b f - 1$
Output: Fast Addition Chains for $p - 2, \frac{p-3}{4}, p,$ and $\frac{p-1}{2}$
1. Split first half of prime into various max-sized windows
  1a. The best choice of window size varies based on the prime
2. Include an additional $2^c - 1$, such that c makes a large window of all '1's
that minimizes the number of multiplication windows for the second half of the
prime as well as minimizing the number of multiplications to generate
3. Determine good addition sequences to generate the windows
  3a. Add additional stored values if necessary
4. Slightly alter choice of c and multiplications to finish the addition chain between
$p - 2, \frac{p-3}{4}, p,$ and $\frac{p-1}{2}$

Proposition 1 is straightforward as the first half of primes of this form appear
random and the second half is all '1's. For inversion, we are interested in fast
addition chains for $p - 2$. For the square root, we want fast addition chains for
$\frac{p-3}{4}$ and $\frac{p-1}{2}$. Luckily, for primes of the form $2^a \ell_B^b f - 1$, only the last few bits of
these exponentials are different. Thus, fast addition chains are extremely similar
among these exponentiations. We present the general procedure in Algorithm 4.

As Algorithm 4 shows, the general procedure starts by dividing up the first
half of the prime. The size of the window depends on the shape of the first
half of the prime, but is typically more than 7 bits for primes of this family of
size 512-bits or larger. After the windows have been found, the addition chain
sequences are constructed to encapsulate each of these windows. [14] provides
one such algorithm to make addition chain sequences to generate these windows.
However, we complete the sequence by using our own pivot judging, which we
found to be very effective. This method determines which number acts as the
best pivot. We judged potential candidates based on:

- Number of newly connected elements with the inclusion of the pivot
- Cost to generate the pivot value based on existing values (doubles are scored
  higher)
- Among high scoring pivots, the uniqueness of the connected elements are
  valued

Based on these criteria and the abundance of windows available, relatively few
additional pivot values were added to complete the addition sequence. Our
judging criteria prioritized values that could be obtained through squarings
rather than multiplications, to reduce the total complexity of the addition chain
sequence. Since all windows were found as odd numbers, starting and ending
with a '1', primarily even values were added to finalize the addition sequence.

For the second half of the prime (a long chain of '1's), we require a high
value $2^c - 1$. Typically, this value will be a few bits larger than the large window
at the beginning of the exponential. The value $2^c - 1$ essentially acts as a very
large window for the structured second half of the prime. This value generally fits

nicely into the number of '1's at the end. The idea is to raise the value of c so that there are fewer windows on the second half of the prime. Indeed, larger values of $2^c - 1$ require more intermediate squarings and perhaps multiplications, but could reduce even more multiplications for the remaining windows. We consider this a "hybrid" windowing method because there are different strategies for the first and second half of the prime.

4.2 $2^a \ell_B^b f - 1$ - An Illustrative Example - $2^{253} 3^{161} 7 - 1$

As an example of a prime in this field, we point to the prime for 85-bit quantum security presented in [1]. We want to create fast addition chains for inversion, or $2^{253} 3^{161} 7 - 3$. From the above strategy, we start by taking windows of the prime. We are looking at approximately 256 bits for this prime, so a max window size of about 7–10 bits is sufficient. In Fig. 2, we use a max window of size 8, which was found to be the fastest addition chain based on our model. It was determined that the optimal value of c was 13, or $2^{13} - 1 = 8191$, which required only a single squaring and multiplication to reach and will complete the second half of the prime in 19 windows. Larger values of c would have required more multiplications and squarings, while not reducing the number of final windows enough to make it worth it. Table 2 illustrates the cost breakdown of various parts of the exponentiation for inversion.

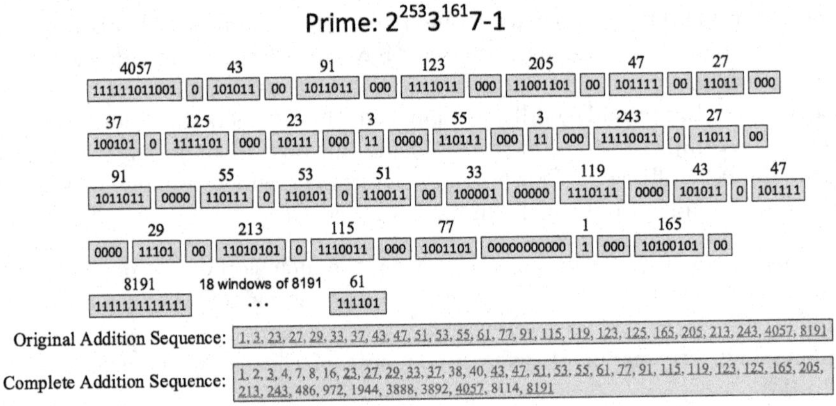

Fig. 2. Hybrid windowing method for $2^a \ell_B^b f - 1$

Table 2. Breakdown of costs for addition chains for $2^{253} 3^{161} 7 - 3$

Operation	Cost
Window generation	$28M + 9S$
Applying windows 1st half	$28M + 245S$
Applying windows 2nd half	$20M + 254S$
Total	$76M + 508S$

4.3 $2^a \ell_B^b f - 1$ - Why Use Constant-Time Square Roots?

Proposition 2. *For a non-constant time implementation of the square root, fast inversion algorithms such as the extended Euclidean algorithm can be used to produce negative values to greatly reduce the number of multiplications in an exponentiation.*

To demonstrate Proposition 2, we point to the fact that key compression and decompression, which require the square root, only reconstruct information that would be transmitted over a public channel. Thus, as long as a fast inversion produces an addition chain requiring far fewer multiplications, its use may be justified. Typically, addition-subtraction chains are used for scalar point multiplication operations where the negative of a point is easy to obtain, such as in [25]. But the requirement of constant time for security in compression and decompression is not necessary and addition chains can benefit as a result.

As an example to this proposition, let us consider $p = 4091 = 111111111011_2$. We want to take the square root of an element, x, in $\mathbb{F}_{p^2}$ in a fast non-constant time fashion, so we produce the inverse, x^{-1}, using the Extended Euclidean Algorithm (EEA). For the first exponentiation, $x^{\frac{p-3}{4}}$, the exponential is $1111111110_2 = 2^{10} - 2 = 10000000000_2 - 10_2$. A standard binary method would require $8M + 9S$, but a standard binary method with the second representation would require $1I + 1M + 11S$. Thus, in the general case, if $I < 7M - 2S$, then the addition-subtraction chain method is faster. This serves as a toy example to show a possible way to speed up the square root exponentiations, and is also key to the non-adjacent form method (NAF) form of exponentiation [17]. The NAF method does not necessarily mesh well with computing fast windows for addition chains because it typically iterates over single digits at a time and diminishes positive windows instead of growing them. However, it may provide far fewer multiplications for extremely long chains of '1's, which are prominent in square root exponentiations in the $2^a \ell_B^b f - 1$ family.

4.4 $2^a \ell_B^b f - 1$ - Addition-Subtraction Chains to Speed up Square Roots

Proposition 3. *Representing the exponentials used in square roots as $e - 1$ with a final subtraction likely produces much faster addition chains.*

Proposition 3 alludes to using an addition-subtraction chain for fast exponentiation. The long chain of '1's in the least significant half of the exponentials can be avoided by using -1, or the original value's inverse. Let us consider exponentiating by p, for instance. This value can be rewritten as $p = (p + 1) - 1$. Thus, we can assume that we are exponentiating $2^a \ell_B^b f$, which has the second half all '0's. After we have found that exponential, we multiply by the inverse of the element and the exponentiation is complete.

For our example in Sect. 4.2, the second half of the prime required 1 extra squaring and 22 extra multiplications to generate and apply the final windows.

Algorithm 5. Windowing method with a subtraction $2^a \ell_B^b f - 1$.

Input: Smooth Isogeny prime of form $2^a \ell_B^b f - 1$
Output: Fast Addition Chains for $\frac{p-3}{4}$, p, and $\frac{p-1}{2}$
1. Add '1' to the prime to cancel out all of the second half of the prime
2. Split first half of result into various max-sized windows
   2a. The best choice of window size varies based on the prime
3. Determine small addition sequences to generate the windows
   3a. Add additional stored values if necessary
4. Perform a fast inversion using a method such as EEA
5. Perform a subtraction by multiplying by the inverse
6. Slightly alter final multiplications to finish the chains for $\frac{p-3}{4}$, p, and $\frac{p-1}{2}$

We are essentially replacing this cost with a multiplication by the inverse. Thus, this method is faster if $\tilde{I} < \tilde{S} + 21\tilde{M}$ for this case. This may seem farfetched. However, in practice we have seen the ratio $\tilde{I} \approx 5\tilde{M}$ for 512-bit numbers in ARMv7 devices. This demonstrates that using a single subtraction at the end of the addition chain saves the cost of $\tilde{S} + 16\tilde{M}$ in this case, most likely even more for larger prime sizes.

4.5 $2^a \ell_B^b \cdot f + 1$ Family

The $2^a \ell_B^b \cdot f + 1$ family features a prime shape with a long string of '0's. Thus, this can take advantage of a regular shape as well. Inversions within this family can be performed with the hybrid windowing method and the square root exponentiations feature a second half of the prime that is all '0's.

Exponentiation by $p - 2$. The inversion exponentiation is similar to that of the $2^a \ell_B^b \cdot f - 1$ family, as the final half of the exponentation is all '1's. Thus, the hybrid windowing method is also valid for the $2^a \ell_B^b \cdot f + 1$ family and generates fast addition chains for these inversions.

Fast Exponentiations for Square Roots. This family has primes that are of the form $p \equiv 1 \mod 4$. Thus, the exponentials $\frac{p-1}{4}$, $\frac{p-1}{2}$, and p are used in the square root process. This means that the windowing method can be used for the first half of these primes and the second half is simply squarings since it is all '0's. This exponentiation is similar to that of the addition-subtraction chains used in $2^a \ell_B^b \cdot f - 1$, but without the need to compute a fast inverse. However, these fast square root exponentations do not make up for the fact that an extremely expensive square root [18] in the field $\mathbb{F}_p$ must be performed. Thus, this family is not necessarily a good fit for key compression and decompression.

4.6   General Smooth Isogeny Family

The binary representation of digits used in today's processors means that the representation of other "general" smooth isogeny primes will appear pseudorandom since there are no powers of 2. The general isogeny primes can further be classified based on their form of their square root functions. The two classifications are $p \equiv 3 \bmod 4$ or $p \equiv 1 \bmod 4$. Clearly, these are the two groupings because otherwise the number would not be prime. In either case, the inversion and square root exponentiations can be determined efficiently by using the windowing method over the entire prime. The exponentiations for the square root are slightly different in the two groupings, and the $p = 3 \bmod 4$ general prime is clearly faster as it does not require a square root operation in $\mathbb{F}_p$ in addition to the exponentiations.

5 Proposed Technique to Reduce Temporary Registers

In the previous sections, we have not considered the impact of storing intermediate addition chain windows. Here, we propose new techniques that reduce the number of intermediate values needed, while preserving the speed of the addition chains. In software and hardware implementations of inversion, the intermediate storage must be accounted for. This can make a large difference in embedded devices that are limited by the number of values that can be stored. Fast addition chains typically require many more temporary values than something like the binary method, but careful planning can be used to minimize the impact on a register file, for instance. We summarize our observations in Algorithm 6.

Algorithm 6. Minimizing register usage in windowing method

Input: Addition chain sequence based on the windowing method
Output: Efficient paths to perform the exponentiation with a reduced number of registers
1. Based on the addition sequence, generate a short path from 1 to the value of the first window
2. Remove values that are stored in registers based on the following criteria:
  2a. If a register has been used and is no longer required to make a path to other windows
  2b. If a separate register contains the value of a register multiplied by 2
3. As the windows are being applied, they can be performed by multiplying their factors directly instead of multiplying to a separate register.

5.1 New Techniques

Proposition 4. *Temporary registers can be reduced by creating a short path to reach the first window that involves other windows. The steps along the path that are also windows must be used as registers.*

Proposition 4 leads to a few different techniques to reduce the total number of registers:

Proposition 5. *The windows used in an addition chain do not have to be generated at the start. They only need to be generated in the order that they appear with the windowing method. Thus, after a window is used with no remaining dependencies, its register can be replaced.*

Proposition 5 is simple to see. So long as we can create the first window efficiently, we can recreate the other windows efficiently at a later time. The order of the windows is relevant. In addition, any window that is used twice must be stored as a temporary register so that the cost of generating it is not experienced twice. For example, let us consider we have windows in the order 9, 11, 9, 6, 4, 5. The optimal addition sequence for this toy example is 1, 2, 4, 5, 6, 9, and 11. The shortest addition sequence for the first window is 1, 2, 4, 5, and 9. In reality, we only have to store values for 2, 4, 5, 9, and an accumulator. The other values that are not stored can be recreated from each of these. For instance, $6 = 2 + 4$ and $11 = 2 + 9$. The register holding 9 can also be freed after the second 9 window is applied. There are no more dependencies on it within the window sequence. Likewise, the register holding 2 can be freed after applying the window of 6, and the register holding 4 can be freed after applying the window of 4.

Proposition 6. *New windows can be recreated from pre-existing windows using addition chains at no cost to the complexity of the exponentiation.*

Proposition 6 shows that only the absolutely necessary windows must be stored and that the others can be recreated from multiplications. In the toy example above, we can recreate the windows that are not included by adding the factors to generate the window in sequence. For instance, if we have a window of 11, we would multiply the accumulator by 9 and then multiply it by 2. Alternatively, one could use a temporary register to hold the product of 9 and 2, and then multiply that to the accumulator. In the end, this window costs 2 multiplications to use in the addition chain. Thus, storing the window to a temporary register wastes a register unless the window appears more than once. In our example, 5 and 9 appear twice in the sequence of windows, so a register must hold these values to prevent recreating the window multiple times. There is no reason to store 6 because it is only used once and is not necessary to generate any other windows.

5.2   An Illustrative Example - $2^{253}3^{161}7 - 1$

We demonstrate these techniques with our example in Sect. 4.2. Originally, this example requires 32 registers since there are 24 windows, 7 intermediate values necessary to complete the addition sequence, and a single register for the accumulator. However, it is worth noting that based on the order of the windows and above propositions, we can reduce the number of registers significantly.

One optimization that we can do is to reach our first window with as few steps as possible. 4057 can be reached in with 21 registers by using the addition chain sequence 1, 2, 3, 4, 7, 8, 16, 23, 27, 29, 37, 38, 40, 77, 115, 123, 125, 165,

205, 243, and an accumulator to perform the other squarings and multiplications up to 4057. The intermediate values must be saved as they are windows that will be used later. Unfortunately, the windows for 43 and 91 occur at the beginning of the exponential sequence and occur multiple times, thus registers must be used to store these as well. 43 requires one step and 91 requires 51, thus 3 additional registers are required. From there, all of the other windows can be reached within a single step. As windows are used in the exponentiation and are not needed to generate other values, these registers can be freed and reused for other windows. Technically, these new windows do not necessarily need to be stored since they can be factored to two of the existing windows, as noted in Proposition 6. Based on data dependency within the window order, 3 additional registers are used. Using these techniques, 5 temporary registers can be saved and 27 registers are required in total.

One more strategy is to free the start of the sequence as their values are used. Indeed, after 47 is obtained, 1, 7, 8, and 16 can each be removed. The rest of the sequence is obtainable. One interesting note is that 1 is not needed since 2 can serve as its window, but after one more squaring. Another interesting use of this technique is that 213 can be applied as a window in two multiplications, even if 8 is not available. One cycle before the window's turn, the factor 4 is multiplied to the accumulator. The accumulator is squared and multiplied with 205, to achieve $213 = 4 \times 2 + 205$. The data dependency technique can also remove 38 and 40 after 243 has been generated since they are not used in any other windows. Thus, we further reduce the register count from 32 at the start to 21, reducing the register usage by 34%.

6   Comparison of Methods

Using the above techniques, we demonstrate the reduced complexity of our method over a standard windowing method in Table 3. We used a Jetson TK1 development board with the GNU Multiprecision (GMP) Library version 6.1.0 to test our addition chain strategies. We used Karatsuba-optimized methods for arithmetic in $\mathbb{F}_{p^2}$ and GMP for arithmetic in $\mathbb{F}_p$. The timing result represents

Table 3. Comparison of addition chains for square root exponentiation by $p = 2^{253}3^{161}7 - 1$

Method	Window size	$\#\tilde{I}$	$\#\tilde{M}$	$\#\tilde{S}$	Time (μs)	#Registers
Binary	1	0	380	511	2.978	2
K-ary	2	0	224	511	2.435	4
K-ary	4	0	141	511	2.076	16
Standard window	8	0	87	508	1.877	20
Hybrid window	8	0	76	508	1.804	21
Window with a subtraction	8	1	56	508	1.751	21

Table 4. Comparison of addition chains for smooth isogeny primes p_{512}

Exponentiation	#I	#M	#S	Window addition sequence length	#Registers	Max window size	c
$p = 2^{253}3^{161}7 - 1$							
$p - 2$	0	75	508	31	21	8	13
$\frac{p-1}{2}$	1	56	505	31	21	8	-
$p = 2^{254}3^{158}71 + 1$							
$p - 2$	0	79	514	32	19	7	14
$\frac{p-1}{2}$	0	58	507	32	19	7	-
$p = 5^{108}7^{89}732 + 1$							
$p - 2$	0	99	505	55	28	10	-
$\frac{p-1}{2}$	0	99	504	55	28	10	-
$p = 5^{108}7^{90}102 + 1$							
$p - 2$	0	106	508	54	24	8	-
$\frac{p-1}{2}$	0	106	507	54	24	8	-

the cost of performing the exponential $p = 2^{253}3^{161}7 - 1$ over $\mathbb{F}_{p^2}$, designed for a square root. The k-ary method is presented in Algorithms 1 and 2. Our hybrid windowing method reduces the total number of multiplications needed by approximately 13% over a standard windowing method. Furthermore, our windowing method with a subtraction reduces the total number of multiplications by 36% at the cost of a fast inversion. The new methods are optimizations of the windowing strategy, applicable to special isogeny primes of the form $2^a \ell_B^b \cdot f \pm 1$. These optimizations require only a single register over the standard windowing method, but speed up the exponentiation by 3.9% for the hybrid windowing method and 6.8% for the window with a subtraction. Interestingly, the relative ratio of inversion over multiplication in $\mathbb{F}_{p^2}$, $\tilde{I}/\tilde{M}$, was found to be approximately 5 for the Jetson TK1. Thus, the window with a subtraction method reduced the cost of the square root exponentiation by approximately 15 multiplications in $\mathbb{F}_{p^2}$ for 512-bit primes.

We also apply the technique to the three major families with 512 bit primes in Table 4. These results show that the square root exponentiations are faster with the form $p = 2^a \ell_B^b \cdot f + 1$ because a fast inversion is not needed as the least half of the prime is already all '0's. We also compare primes of the form $2^a \ell_B^b \cdot f - 1$ in Table 5. For these two tables, exponentiation by $p - 2$ is for inversion and in $\mathbb{F}_p$ and exponentiation by $\frac{p-1}{2}$ is for the square root and in $\mathbb{F}_{p^2}$. Typically, the total number of registers appeared to be directly related to the max window size and addition sequence to generate the windows. Smaller window sizes required fewer steps to reach the first window and required fewer numbers for the remaining steps. It is also interesting that the optimal max window size did not necessarily scale with the prime size. Generally, windows of size 7–10 appeared the best for our results. These window sizes fit well for these sizes because many of the

Table 5. Comparison of addition chains for smooth isogeny primes of different sizes

Exponentiation	#I	#M	#S	Window addition sequence length	#Registers	Max window size	c
$p_{512} = 2^{253}3^{161}7 - 1$							
$p - 2$	0	76	508	31	21	8	13
$\frac{p-1}{2}$	1	56	506	31	21	8	-
$p_{768} = 2^{379}3^{239}497 - 1$							
$p - 2$	0	108	770	49	26	9	16
$\frac{p-1}{2}$	1	84	762	49	27	9	-
$p_{1024} = 2^{509}3^{320}107 - 1$							
$p - 2$	0	134	1029	52	28	8	18
$\frac{p-1}{2}$	1	102	1020	52	29	8	-

windows could be generated quickly and there were only additional windows as the max window size got larger. In contrast, the value of c in $2^c - 1$ did appear to scale with the size of the prime. This is to be expected as greater values of c required typically an additional squaring and multiplication, but saved many window multiplications at the end of the prime.

7   Conclusion

Overall, this paper investigated fast and efficient addition chains for smooth isogeny primes used in the supersingular isogeny Diffie-Hellman scheme. The hybrid windowing method produces fast addition chains for inversion for the $2^a \ell_B^b \cdot f \pm 1$ families by taking advantage of the semi-regular structure of $p - 2$. Other primes used in the scheme can use the basic windowing method, but typically require more multiplications. Square root exponentials can also benefit from a fast inversion for $2^a \ell_B^b \cdot f - 1$ or simply from having half of the exponential being zero for $2^a \ell_B^b \cdot f + 1$. The applications of inversions and square roots for isogeny-based cryptography necessitate the need for fast addition chains for fast and secure exponentiations. The hybrid and subtraction windowing methods find addition chains that feature reduced numbers of multiplications and squarings at an insignificant cost to temporary storage, which can be valuable to both the speed and size of ECC over prime curves.

Acknowledgment. The authors would like to thank the reviewers for their constructive comments. This material is based upon work supported by the NSF CNS-1464118 and NIST 60NANB16D246 awards.

A Appendix

A.1 Addition Chains for Inversion

Finite-field inversion finds some A^{-1} such that $A \cdot A^{-1} = 1$, where $A, A^{-1} \in \mathbb{F}_p$. This can be computed using Fermat's little theorem, which shows that $A^{-1} = A^{p-2}$. Addition chains can be used to efficiently evaluate these large powers in a constant set of operations, to protect against timing attacks and simple power analysis attacks.

Isogeny-based cryptosystems operate in $\mathbb{F}_{p^2}$, so the inversion in $\mathbb{F}_p$ must be extended as such. We use Eq. 2 to perform the inversions in $\mathbb{F}_{p^2}$ with irreducible modulus $x^2 + 1$ (assuming -1 is not a quadratic residue in $\mathbb{F}_p$). We note that an element, a, in $\mathbb{F}_{p^2}$ is represented as a_0 and a_1, where $a_0, a_1 \in \mathbb{F}_p$ and a_1 is the most significant element.

$$a^{-1} = (a_0, a_1)^{-1} = (a_0 \times (a_0^2 + a_1^2)^{-1}, -a_1 \times (a_0^2 + a_1^2)^{-1}) \qquad (2)$$

Fast non-constant time inversion. Inversion by Fermat's little theorem is accomplished in constant-time, but it is still slow compared to algorithms such as the Extended Euclidean Algorithm (EEA) and Kaliski's almost inverse. In fact, EEA has a significantly lower time complexity of $O(\log^2 n)$ compared to $O(\log^3 n)$ for Fermat's little theorem. EEA uses a greatest common divisor algorithm to compute the modular inverse of elements a and b with respect to each other, $ax + by = \gcd(a, b)$. We present this alternative for inversion because it makes an inversion term much quicker to compute, which can be used for the square root exponentiations. For our sample implementation, the GMP library incorporates EEA for fast inversion.

A.2 Fast Computation of Square Root

The finite-field square root finds some $A^{1/2}$ such that $A^{1/2} \cdot A^{1/2} = A$, where $A, A^{1/2} \in \mathbb{F}_p$. For the case that $p \equiv 3 \bmod 4$, which is true for primes of the form $2^a 3^b f - 1$, Shank's algorithm can be used to retrieve the square root of the quadratic residue by exponentiating the value by $\frac{p+1}{4}$. However, unlike inversion, not all elements in a prime field have a square root. Thus, there is also a check on the result that if its square and product by the original element is -1, then the square root does not exist.

For the case $p \equiv 1 \bmod 4$, there is also an additional square root operation in $\mathbb{F}_p$. Typically, the method to recover the square root in this case is based on the Tonelli-Shanks algorithm demonstrated in works such as [26]. We will not go into the specifics of this square root operation, but the extra overhead for the full square root is significant compared to the case $p \equiv 3 \bmod 4$.

Square roots in $\mathbb{F}_{p^2}$ are trickier than inversion. For the square root in this extension field, we refer to [18], which extends Shank's algorithm for even extension fields. In this work, Algorithms 9 and 10 contain the square root computation over even extension fields when $p \equiv 3 \bmod 4$ when $p \equiv 1 \bmod 4$, respectively.

References

1. Jao, D., Feo, L.: Towards quantum-resistant cryptosystems from supersingular elliptic curve isogenies. In: Yang, B.-Y. (ed.) PQCrypto 2011. LNCS, vol. 7071, pp. 19–34. Springer, Heidelberg (2011). doi:10.1007/978-3-642-25405-5_2
2. Crandall, R., Pomerance, C.: Prime Numbers: A Computational Perspective, 2nd edn. Springer, New York (2005)
3. Solinas, J.A.: Generalized Mersenne Numbers. Technical report, University of Waterloo (1999)
4. Itoh, T., Tsujii, S.: A fast algorithm for computing multiplicative inverses in $GF(2^m)$ using normal bases. Inf. Comput. **78**(3), 171–177 (1988)
5. Koziel, B., Jalali, A., Azarderakhsh, R., Jao, D., Mozaffari-Kermani, M.: NEON-SIDH: efficient implementation of supersingular isogeny Diffie-Hellman key exchange protocol on ARM. In: 15th International Conference on Cryptology and Network Security, CANS 2016 (2016)
6. De Feo, L., Jao, D., Plut, J.: Towards quantum-resistant cryptosystems from super-singular elliptic curve isogenies. J. Math. Crypt. **8**(3), 209–247 (2014)
7. Azarderakhsh, R., Jao, D., Kalach, K., Koziel, B., Leonardi, C.: Key compression for isogeny-based cryptosystems. In: Proceedings of the 3rd ACM International Workshop on ASIA Public-Key Cryptography, AsiaPKC 2016, pp. 1–10. ACM, New York (2016)
8. Costello, C., Longa, P., Naehrig, M.: Efficient algorithms for supersingular isogeny Diffie-Hellman. In: Robshaw, M., Katz, J. (eds.) CRYPTO 2016. LNCS, vol. 9814, pp. 572–601. Springer, Heidelberg (2016). doi:10.1007/978-3-662-53018-4_21
9. Koziel, B., Azarderakhsh, R., Mozaffari-Kermani, M., Jao, D.: Post-Quantum Cryptography on FPGA Based on Isogenies on Elliptic Curves. Cryptology ePrint Archive, Report 2016/672 (2016). http://eprint.iacr.org/2016/672
10. Koziel, B., Azarderakhsh, R., Mozaffari-Kermani, M.: Fast hardware architectures for supersingular isogeny Diffie-Hellman key exchange on FPGA. In: Dunkelman, O., Sanadhya, S.K. (eds.) INDOCRYPT 2016. LNCS, vol. 10095, pp. 191–206. Springer, Cham (2016). doi:10.1007/978-3-319-49890-4_11
11. Costello, C., Jao, D., Longa, P., Naehrig, M., Renes, J., Urbanik, D.: Efficient Compression of SIDH Public Keys. Cryptology ePrint Archive, Report 2016/963 (2016). http://eprint.iacr.org/2016/963
12. Knuth, D.E.: The Art of Computer Programming, vol. 2, 3rd edn. Addison-Wesley Longman Publishing Co., Inc., Boston (1997)
13. Brauer, A.: On addition chains. Bull. Am. Math. Soc. **45**(10), 736–739 (1939)
14. Bos, J., Coster, M.: Addition chain heuristics. In: Brassard, G. (ed.) CRYPTO 1989. LNCS, vol. 435, pp. 400–407. Springer, New York (1990). doi:10.1007/0-387-34805-0_37
15. Koc, Ç.K.: Analysis of sliding window techniques for exponentiation. Comput. Math. Appl. **30**, 17–24 (1995)
16. Gordon, D.M.: A survey of fast exponentiation methods. J. Algorithms **27**(1), 129–146 (1998)
17. Möller, B.: Improved techniques for fast exponentiation. In: Lee, P.J., Lim, C.H. (eds.) ICISC 2002. LNCS, vol. 2587, pp. 298–312. Springer, Heidelberg (2003). doi:10.1007/3-540-36552-4_21
18. Adj, G., Rodríguez-Henríquez, F.: Square Root Computation Over Even Extension Fields. Cryptology ePrint Archive, Report 2012/685 (2012). http://eprint.iacr.org/

19. Silverman, J.H.: The Arithmetic of Elliptic Curves. GTM, vol. 106. Springer, New York (1992)
20. Vélu, J.: Isogénies entre courbes elliptiques. Comptes Rendus de l'Académie des Sciences Paris Séries A-B **273**, A238–A241 (1971)
21. Lagarias, J., Odlyzko, A.: Effective versions of the chebotarev density theorem. In: Algebraic Number Fields: L-functions and Galois Properties. Symposium Proceedings of the University of Durham, pp. 409–464 (1975)
22. Joye, M., Paillier, P., Vaudenay, S.: Efficient generation of prime numbers. In: Koç, Ç.K., Paar, C. (eds.) CHES 2000. LNCS, vol. 1965, pp. 340–354. Springer, Heidelberg (2000). doi:10.1007/3-540-44499-8_27
23. Gueron, S., Krasnov, V.: Fast prime field elliptic-curve cryptography with 256-bit primes. J. Cryptogr. Eng. **5**(2), 141–151 (2014)
24. Montgomery, P.L.: Modular multiplication without trial division. Math. Comput. **44**(170), 519–521 (1985)
25. Oswald, E., Aigner, M.: Randomized addition-subtraction chains as a countermeasure against power attacks. In: Koç, Ç.K., Naccache, D., Paar, C. (eds.) CHES 2001. LNCS, vol. 2162, pp. 39–50. Springer, Heidelberg (2001). doi:10.1007/3-540-44709-1_5
26. Muller, S.: On the computation of square roots in finite fields. Des. Cod. Cryptogr. **31**(3), 301–312 (2004)

A Linear Algebra Attack on the Non-commuting Cryptography Class Based on Matrix Power Function

Jinhui Liu[1,2], Huanguo Zhang[1,2(✉)], and Jianwei Jia[1,2]

[1] Computer School of Wuhan University, Wuhan 430072, Hubei, China
{jh.liu,liss,jjwwhu}@whu.edu.cn
[2] Key Laboratory of Aerospace Information Security
and Trusted Computing Ministry of Education, Wuhan 430072, Hubei, China

Abstract. Advances in quantum computers threaten to break public key cryptosystems such as RSA, ECC, and EIGamal on the hardness of factoring or taking a discrete logarithm, while no quantum algorithms are found to solve certain mathematical problems on non-commutative algebraic structures until now. Under this background, a non-commuting cryptography class based on matrix power function has been given. In this paper we show that the non-commuting cryptography class based on MPF is vulnerable to a linear algebra attack which only requires polynomial time to achieve the equivalent keys respectively. In addition, we conduct an analysis on the flaws in this schemes and propose an improved scheme that remedies the weakness of their schemes.

Keywords: Cryptography · Post-quantum computational cryptography · Cryptanalysis · Asymmetric cipher · Matrix power function

1 Introduction

Most public key cryptosystems used today rely on the assumed difficulty of either factorization or computing discrete logarithms. Many experts believe that public-key cryptosystems on noncommutative algebraic structures used today have the potential to resist known quantum algorithms attacks which motivate researchers to develop a new family of cryptosystems that can resist quantum computers attacks and that are more efficient in terms of computation. In recent years, cryptographers have been making efforts in the area of post-quantum computational cryptography [1–6]. There also are some alternative quantum-resistant public key cryptosystems from other mathematically intractable problems, such as NPC problem [7–13].

Before going into details we would like to mention that nonabelian algebraic structures has already been used in a cryptographic context. We refer to [5,6] for a general introduction to non-commutative cryptography. In this paper we study a non-commutative cryptography class based on matrix power function

© Springer International Publishing AG 2017
K. Chen et al. (Eds.): Inscrypt 2016, LNCS 10143, pp. 343–354, 2017.
DOI: 10.1007/978-3-319-54705-3_21

problem proposed in [14–16]. The novelty of launching such attacks on the non-commuting cryptography class which have the potential to resist known quantum algorithms attacks is that we can obtain the equivalent keys from an associated public key with significant probability in a reasonable time.

There are many cryptography which are broken by some linear algebra attack [5,12,17]. Because these schemes have some weak keys by using some linear algebra knowledge. Our main results are that the non-commutative cryptography class is vulnerable to a linear algebra attack based on the probable occurrence of weak keys in the generation process. Then we analyze the basic rationale for the linear algebra attack and show corresponding algorithmic description and efficiency analysis. We also propose an improved scheme that remedies the weakness of their schemes.

The rest of this paper is organised as follows. Section 2 reviews necessary material for this paper. Section 3 gives an overview on the asymmetric cipher scheme based on MPF proposed in [14–16]. Section 4 proposes an attack method, and shows corresponding algorithmic description and efficiency analysis respectively. In Sect. 5, the modified scheme and the security analysis are proposed. At the end, Sect. 6 provides some concluding remarks and discusses possible lines of future work.

2   Preliminaries

Here, we have a quick review of necessary material for this paper.

Throughout in this paper, we use the following notations. q is a power of prime. $\mathbb{F}_q$ is a finite field of order q.

$GL_k(\mathbb{F}_q)$ is a set of $k \times k$ invertible matrices of $\mathbb{F}_q$-entries. $M_k(\mathbb{F}_q)$ is a set of $k \times k$ matrices of $\mathbb{F}_q$-entries. $I_k \in GL_k(\mathbb{F}_q)$ is the identity matrix. For a matrix A, A^T is the transpose of A.

For $A = (a_{ij})_{k_1 \times k_1} \in M_{k_1}(\mathbb{F}_q)$, and $B = (b_{ij})_{k_2 \times k_2} \in M_{k_2}(\mathbb{F}_q)$, $\overrightarrow{A} = (a_{ij}) \in \mathbb{F}_q^{1 \times k_1^2}$,

$$A \otimes B = \begin{pmatrix} a_{11}B & \cdots & a_{1k_1}B \\ \vdots & \ddots & \vdots \\ a_{k_1 1}B & \cdots & a_{k_1 k_1}B \end{pmatrix}.$$

Proposition 1. *The Kronecker product "$\otimes$" has the following simple properties:*

$$(A \otimes B) \otimes C = A \otimes (B \otimes C), A \otimes (B + C) = (A \otimes B) + (A \otimes C),$$
$$(A \otimes B)^T = A^T \otimes B^T, (A \otimes B)(C \otimes D) = AC \otimes BD.$$

Proposition 2. *Stacking the row of a matrix into one long row vector "$\overrightarrow{\cdot}$" has the following simple properties:*

$$\overrightarrow{\alpha A + \beta B} = \alpha \overrightarrow{A} + \beta \overrightarrow{B}, (\overrightarrow{AX})^T = (A \otimes I)(\overrightarrow{X})^T,$$
$$(\overrightarrow{XB})^T = (I \otimes B^T)(\overrightarrow{X})^T, (\overrightarrow{ACB})^T = (A \otimes B^T)(\overrightarrow{C})^T.$$

Define 1 (one-sided Matrix Power Function). *Let matrix* $Q = (q_{ij})_{n \times n}$ *powered by matrix* $Y = (y_{ij})_{n \times n}$ *from the right be a matrix* $C = (C_{ij})_{n \times n}$ *and matrix* Q *powered by matrix* $X = (x_{ij})_{n \times n}$ *from the left be a matrix* $D = (d_{ij})_{n \times n}$, *i.e.,*

$$C = Q^Y, D = {}^X Q$$

where elements of C *are computed by the formula* $C_{ij} = \prod_{k=1}^{n} q_{ik}^{y_{kj}}$, *elements of* D *are computed by the formula* $d_{ij} = \prod_{k=1}^{n} q_{kj}^{x_{ik}}$.

Define 2 (two-sided Matrix Power Function or MPF). *Denoting the result matrix by* $E = (e_{ij})_{n \times n}$ *we have the following MPF definition*

$$E = {}^X Q^Y.$$

The elements e_{ij} *are then computed in a following way:*

$$
\begin{cases}
q_{11}^{x_{11} y_{11}} \cdots q_{m1}^{x_{1m} y_{11}} q_{12}^{x_{11} y_{21}} \cdots q_{m2}^{x_{1m} y_{21}} \cdots q_{mm}^{x_{1m} y_{m1}} = e_{11} \\
q_{11}^{x_{11} y_{12}} \cdots q_{m1}^{x_{1m} y_{12}} q_{12}^{x_{11} y_{22}} \cdots q_{m2}^{x_{1m} y_{22}} \cdots q_{mm}^{x_{1m} y_{m2}} = e_{12} \\
\vdots \\
q_{11}^{x_{m1} y_{1m}} \cdots q_{m1}^{x_{mm} y_{1m}} q_{12}^{x_{m1} y_{2m}} \cdots q_{m2}^{x_{mm} y_{2m}} \cdots q_{mm}^{x_{mm} y_{mm}} = e_{mm}
\end{cases}
\tag{1}
$$

where $X = (x_{ij})_{n \times n}$ *and* $Y = (y_{ij})_{n \times n}$.

Define 3 (Matrix MQ problem). *Suppose that matrix* Q *is defined over some cyclic group* G *and the generator* g *of the group* G *is given and due to Fermat's theorem. A discrete logarithm with the base of this generator of* $E = {}^X Q^Y$ *can be applied to* E, Q *to obtain*

$$ld_g E = ld_g^X Q^Y = X ld_g Q Y = XTY,$$

where $ld_g E$ *and* $ld_g Q$ *mean,* $T = ld_g Q$. *So, suppose that* T *and* $ld_g E$ *are given, find matrices* X *and* Y *which is called matrix MQ problem.*

This problem is similar to well known NP-complete problem, namely multivariate quadratic (MQ) problem. In [14,16,17], they made a conjecture that the matrix MQ problem is a candidate one-way function since its inversion is related with the solution of known multivariate quadratic problem which is NP-complete over any field.

3   Description of Asymmetric Cipher Class

In this section, we briefly review the asymmetric cipher of non-commuting cryptography class based on matrix power function proposed by Sakalauskas et al. as follows.

3.1   The Asymmetric Cipher 1

The asymmetric cipher 1 given in [14] can be summarized as follows:

At first, the common setting on the public parameters of the proposed schemes are given by $< M_L, M_R, \mathcal{P}_L, \mathcal{P}_R, \mathcal{P}, \mathbb{M}_n(\mathbb{F}_q) >$, where let $\mathcal{P} = \{p_i()\}$ be a set of all polynomials over $\mathbb{F}_q$, subsets $\mathcal{P}_L \subseteq \mathcal{R}, \mathcal{P}_R \subseteq \mathcal{R}$ are generated by matrices M_L and M_R respectively, i.e., $\mathcal{P}_L = \{p_i(M_L)\}, \mathcal{P}_R = \{p_i(M_R)\}$. It is evident, that all matrices in $\mathcal{P}_L$ and all matrices in $\mathcal{P}_R$ are commuting. All matrices are numbers in finite field $\mathbb{F}_q$.

Now, the key agreement protocol using matrix power functions is described as follows.

KeyGen: Alice and Bob agree on publicly available matrix $Q \in \mathbb{M}_n(\mathbb{F}_q)$.

(1) Alice chooses at random secret matrices $X \in \mathcal{P}_L, Y \in \mathcal{P}_R$, calculates

$$A = {}^X Q^Y,$$

then sends A to Bob.

(2) Bob chooses randomly matrices $U \in \mathcal{P}_L, V \in \mathcal{P}_R$ and calculates

$$B = {}^U Q^V$$

and sends B to Alice.

(3) Both parties compute the following common secret key

$$K = {}^X B^Y = {}^{XU} Q^{VY} = {}^{UX} Q^{YV} = {}^U A^V.$$

3.2   The Asymmetric Cipher 2

The asymmetric cipher 2 given in [15, 16] can be summarized as follows:

At first, the common setting on the public parameters of the proposed schemes are given by $< Q, A, \mathbb{M}_S, \mathbb{M}_R >$, where

(1) $\mathbb{M}_S$ and $\mathbb{M}_R$ are a matrix semigroup and a matrix ring respectively;
(2) Matrix Q is selected from platform semigroup $\mathbb{M}_S$ and matrix A is selected from power ring $\mathbb{M}_R$.

Now, the encryption protocol is described as follows.

KeyGen: Alice randomly selects a non-singular matrix $X \in \mathbb{M}_R$ and a polynomial $\mathbf{P}_U$. Calculate $U = \mathbf{P}_U(A)$, $XAX^{-1} = B$ and ${}^X Q^U = E$. Output (B, E) as the public key pair and (U, X) as the private key pair.

Enc: Input the public key pair (B, E) and the message M. Bob chooses a non-singular matrix $Y \in \mathbb{M}_R$ and a polynomial $\mathbf{P}_V$.

(1) Bob computes $V = \mathbf{P}_V(A)$, and $\mathbf{P}_V(B) = XVX^{-1}$.

(2) He raises matrix $E =^X Q^U$ to the obtained power matrix XVX^{-1} on the left and obtains $^{XV}Q^U$. He also raises the power matrix Y on the right and obtains $K =^{XV} Q^{UY}$.

(3) He computes $C = K \oplus M$, where $\oplus$ is bitwise sum modulo 2 of all entries of matrices K and M.

(4) Bob sends $(C, D = Y^{-1}AY, F =^V Q^Y)$ to Alice.

Dec: (1) Alice computes $\mathbf{P}_U(Y^{-1}AY) = Y^{-1}UY$. Then Alice raises the matrix F to the power X on the left, raises matrix F to the obtained power matrix $Y^{-1}UY$ on the right and obtains the same encryption key $K =^{XV} Q^{UY}$.

(2) Alice decrypts the ciphertext C using encryption key K and the message $M = K \oplus C = K \oplus K \oplus M$ is obtained.

4   The Linear Algebra Attack

This section attempts to attack the non-commuting cryptography class based on MPF mentioned above. The attack makes use of the elementary tools and this is intended to show the structural vulnerabilities of asymmetric cipher of non-commuting cryptography class based on matrix power function.

4.1   Attack on the Asymmetric Cipher 1

Suppose an attacker $\mathcal{A}$ is observing the asymmetric cipher protocol, he is then able to get the information: (M_L, M_R, A, B, Q). He searches for a pair of matrices (X, Y) such that

$$\begin{cases} A =^X Q^Y; \\ XM_L = M_L X; \\ YM_R = M_R Y, \end{cases} \qquad (2)$$

then the proposed scheme have always had weakness. It remains to analyze the asymmetric cipher, which can be concluded as follows.

Proposition 3. *If an adversary can find matrices $\widetilde{X}, \widetilde{Y}$ satisfying the Eq. (2), then the asymmetric cipher 1 can be broken.*

Proof. If an adversary can find matrices $\widetilde{X}, \widetilde{Y}$ satisfying the Eq. (2), then the asymmetric cipher 1 based on matrix power function may be summarized as follows.

According to $\widetilde{X}M_L = M_L\widetilde{X}, \widetilde{Y}M_R = M_R\widetilde{Y}$ and $U \in \mathcal{P}_L, V \in \mathcal{P}_R$, then $\widetilde{X}U = U\widetilde{X}, \widetilde{Y}V = V\widetilde{Y}$.

Thus

$$\begin{aligned}
{}^{\tilde{X}}B^{\tilde{Y}} &= {}^{\tilde{X}}\left({}^{U}Q^{V}\right)^{\tilde{Y}} \\
&= {}^{\tilde{X}U}Q^{V\tilde{Y}} \\
&= {}^{U\tilde{X}}Q^{\tilde{Y}V} \\
&= {}^{U}\left({}^{\tilde{X}}Q^{\tilde{Y}}\right)^{V} \\
&= {}^{U}A^{V} \\
&= K.
\end{aligned} \tag{3}$$

This completes the proof.

4.2 Attack on the Asymmetric Cipher 2

This section attempts to attack the asymmetric cipher 2. For each $n \times n$ matrix $A \in \mathbb{M}_n(\mathbb{F}_q)$ with entries over $\mathbb{F}_q$, the characteristic polynomial $f_A(x)$ is defined to be

$$f_A(x) = det(xI_n - A) = a_n x^n + a_{n-1}x^{n-1} + \cdots + a_1 x + a_0,$$

where $a_i \in \mathbb{F}_q$. $f_A(x)$ tells us that A^n can be linearly represented by the set $\mathcal{B} = \{I, A, \cdots, A^{n-1}\}$. For the matrix A, there exists a corresponding minimum polynomial $f_{minA}(x)$ such that $f_{minA}(A) = O$. We know that $f_{minA}(x) \mid f_A(x)$, thus for any $k \in \mathbb{Z}$ and each $n \times n$ matrix A, A^k can also be linearly represented by the set $\mathcal{B}$.

If we could find any pair of matrices (X, U, Y) such that

$$\begin{cases}
XAX^{-1} = B; \\
Y^{-1}AY = D; \\
{}^{X}Q^{U} = E; \\
U = \sum\limits_{i=0}^{n-1} a_i A^i.
\end{cases} \tag{4}$$

then the proposed scheme 2 is always had weakness. It remains to analyze the asymmetric cipher 2, which can be concluded as follows.

Proposition 4. *If an adversary can find matrices X, Y, U satisfying the Eq. (4), then the asymmetric cipher 2 can be broken.*

Proof. If an adversary can find matrices $\tilde{X}, \tilde{Y}, \tilde{U}$ satisfying the Eq. (4), then the asymmetric cipher of non-commuting cryptography class based on matrix power function may be summarized as follows.

Let $\widetilde{U} = \mathbf{P}_{\widetilde{U}}(A), \widetilde{Y}^{-1}\widetilde{U}\widetilde{Y} = \mathbf{P}_{\widetilde{U}}(\widetilde{Y}^{-1}A\widetilde{Y}) = \mathbf{P}_{\widetilde{U}}(D) = \mathbf{P}_{\widetilde{U}}(Y^{-1}AY) = Y^{-1}\widetilde{U}Y$, the adversary calculates encryption key $\widetilde{K}$,

$$
\begin{aligned}
\widetilde{K} &=^{\widetilde{X}} F^{\mathbf{P}_{\widetilde{U}}(D)} \\
&=^{\widetilde{X}V} Q^{(Y\mathbf{P}_{\widetilde{U}}(D))} \\
&=^{\widetilde{X}V} Q^{(\mathbf{P}_{\widetilde{U}}(YDY^{-1})Y)} \\
&=^{(\widetilde{X}V)} Q^{(\mathbf{P}_{\widetilde{U}}(A)Y)} (using\ Y^{-1}AY = D) \\
&=^{(\widetilde{X}\mathbf{P}_V(A))} Q^{\widetilde{U}Y} \\
&=^{(\mathbf{P}_V(\widetilde{X}A\widetilde{X}^{-1})\widetilde{X})} Q^{\widetilde{U}Y} \\
&=^{(\mathbf{P}_V(B)\widetilde{X})} Q^{\widetilde{U}Y} (using\ XAX^{-1} = B) \\
&=^{\mathbf{P}_V(B)} (^{\widetilde{X}}Q^{\widetilde{U}})^Y \\
&=^{\mathbf{P}_V(B)} E^Y \\
&= K
\end{aligned}
\tag{5}
$$

So the message $M = \widetilde{K} \oplus C = K \oplus C$ is obtained by the attacker.

4.3   Algorithmic Description and Efficiency Analysis

The Asymmetric Cipher 1. Recall the matrix Eq. (2) over $\mathbb{F}_q$ and matrix Q is defined over some cyclic group $G = \mathbb{F}_q$ and the generator g of the group G is given and due to Fermat's theorem. A discrete logarithm with the base of this generator of $A =^X Q^Y$ can be applied to A, Q to obtain

$$
ld_g A = ld_g^X Q^Y = Xld_g QY = XTY = E,
$$

where $E = ld_g A$ and $ld_g Q$ mean, $T = ld_g Q$. If the matrix X is an inverse matrix, then the matrix Eq. (2) is actually to solve multivariate linear equations as follows:

$$
\begin{cases}
X^{-1}E = TY; \\
X^{-1}M_L = M_L X^{-1}; \\
Y M_R = M_R Y.
\end{cases}
\tag{6}
$$

He can easily get the following results by Proposition 2

$$
WN^T = 0
\tag{7}
$$

where

$$
W = \begin{pmatrix} I_n \otimes E^T & -T \otimes I_n \\ M_L \otimes I_n - I_n \otimes M_L^T & 0 \\ 0 & M_R \otimes I_n - I_n \otimes M_R^T \end{pmatrix}_{3n^2 \times 2n^2}, \quad N = \left(\overrightarrow{X^{-1}}, \overrightarrow{Y} \right),
$$

$\overrightarrow{X^{-1}}, \overrightarrow{Y}$ are the stretch of the matrices X^{-1}, Y and $det(X^{-1}) \neq 0, det(Y) \neq 0$, $\otimes$ represents the Kronecker product, I_n is the $n \times n$ identity, 0 is the matrix with all zero elements.

The method to calculate a matrix pair $\widetilde{X^{-1}}, \widetilde{Y}$ of (7) is shown in Algorithm 1. Formally, the key recovery attack can be described by Algorithm 1. It takes as input matrices (M_L, M_R, A, Q) and outputs equivalent keys $\widetilde{X^{-1}}, \widetilde{Y}$.

Algorithm 1. Recovering equivalent keys for any given public key

Input: Matrices $(M_L, M_R, A, Q,)$
Output: Equivalent keys $\widetilde{X^{-1}}, \widetilde{Y}$
1: Compute discrete logarithms of matrices A and Q respectively
2: By employing the method of Gauss elimination to solve the homogeneous linear equations in the $2n^2$ entries of the unknown vector N: $WN^T = 0$
3: Fix a basis for the solution space and transform vectors $\overrightarrow{X^{-1}}^T, \overrightarrow{Y}^T$ to matrices $\widetilde{X^{-1}}, \widetilde{Y}$ respectively. Pick random solution matrix $\widetilde{X^{-1}}$ until $\widetilde{X^{-1}}$ is invertible
4: Compute $\widetilde{X^{-1}}^{-1} = \widetilde{X}$
5: Return $\widetilde{X}, \widetilde{Y}$.

Combining the above discussions together, let us give a performance evaluation on Algorithm 1. Since the classical techniques for matrix multiplication/inversion in $\mathbb{Z}_q$ take about $\mathcal{O}(n^\omega log^2 q)$ bit operations, where the best known algorithm of the product of two $n \times n$ matrices requires $\mathcal{O}(n^\omega)(\omega = 2.3755)$ $\mathbb{Z}_q$ operations and each $\mathbb{Z}_q$ operation needs $\mathcal{O}(log^2 q)$ bit operations [17–20]. Suppose that the rank of a $3n^2 \times 2n^2$ coefficient matrix W is r. By employing the method of Gauss elimination we know that $0 < r \leq 2n^2$. If $r = 2n^2$, then the matrix W has full column rank, i.e. $N = 0$. We know that there is at least a solution to the Eq. (6), namely: the private keys, thus $0 < r < 2n^2$. Then, it remains to analyze the complexity of the Algorithm 1, which can be concluded in Table 1.

Table 1. Computation cost of Algorithm 1

Comp. content	Comp. cost	Explanation
$E = ld_g A, T = ld_g Q$	$\mathcal{O}(2n^2 q)$	Discrete logarithms of two matrices
$WN^T = 0$	$\mathcal{O}(3n^2 \cdot (2n^2)^{\omega-1} log^2 q)$	$3n^2$ equations in $2n^2$ variables
Invertible $\widetilde{X^{-1}}, \widetilde{Y}$	$\mathcal{O}(3n^2(2n^2 - r)^{\omega-1} log^2 q)$	A linear combination of solution space
$\widetilde{X^{-1}}^{-1}$	$\mathcal{O}(n^\omega log^2 q)$	1 inversion

There are an invertible solution to the Eq. (7), namely: the private keys X and Y. Thus, to generate one random elements $\widetilde{X^{-1}}, \widetilde{Y}$, one takes a linear combination of a basis of the solution space respectively. The number of free variables of the matrix Eq. (7) are $2n^2 - r$, then the total expected running time of step 2 is $3n^2(2n^2 - r)^{\omega-1} \leq n^2 \cdot (2n^2)^{\omega-1}$. On one hand, for any $n \times n$ matrix A over

$\mathbb{F}_q$, the number of rank r_0 is $\dfrac{q^{r_0(r_0-1)/2}\displaystyle\prod_{i=n-r_0+1}^{n}(q^i-1)^2}{\displaystyle\prod_{i=1}^{r_0}(q^i-1)}$, thus the probability of A

of rank n is $\dfrac{q^{n(n-1)/2}\displaystyle\prod_{i=1}^{n}(q^i-1)}{q^{n^2}}$. On the other hand, the probability that random solution matrices X and Y are invertible may be assumed arbitrarily close to $1-\frac{n}{q}(q>n)$ [5]. Now, if we neglect small constant factors, then the key recovery attack against asymmetric cipher 1 based on MPF can be finished with the bit complexity of $\mathcal{O}(n^{2\omega}log^2q)$.

The Asymmetric Cipher 2. We eliminate U of (4) as follows:

$$\begin{cases} AX^{-1}=X^{-1}B; \\ AY=YD; \\ M(\sum_{i=0}^{n-1}a_iA^i)=X^{-1}N \end{cases} \tag{8}$$

where M and N are discrete logarithms of matrices Q and E respectively, i.e. $M=ld_gQ$ and $N=ld_gE$, and $det(X^{-1})\neq 0, det(Y)\neq 0$.

By Proposition 2, we can easily get the following results.

$$\begin{cases} (A\otimes I_n-I_n\otimes B^T)\overrightarrow{X^{-1}T}=0; \\ (A\otimes I_n-I_n\otimes D^T)\overrightarrow{Y}^T=0; \\ (I_n\otimes N^T)\overrightarrow{X^{-1}T}-\left(\overrightarrow{MA^0T}\ \cdots\ \overrightarrow{MA^{n-1}T}\right)\begin{pmatrix} a_0 \\ \vdots \\ a_{n-1} \end{pmatrix}=0. \end{cases} \tag{9}$$

where $\overrightarrow{X^{-1}},\overrightarrow{Y},\overrightarrow{U}$ are the stretch of the matrices X^{-1},Y,U, $\otimes$ represents the Kronecker product, I_n is the $n\times n$ identity. Let

$$L=\begin{pmatrix} A\otimes I_n-I_n\otimes B^T & 0 & 0 \\ 0 & A\otimes I_n-I_n\otimes D^T & 0 \\ (I_n\otimes N^T) & 0 & -m \end{pmatrix}_{3n^2\times(2n^2+n)},$$

$$W=\left(\overrightarrow{X^{-1}}\ \overrightarrow{Y}\ \overrightarrow{a}\right)_{1\times(2n^2+n)},$$

where $m=\left(\overrightarrow{MA^0T}\ \cdots\ \overrightarrow{MA^{n-1}T}\right),\ a=\begin{pmatrix} a_0 \\ \vdots \\ a_{n-1} \end{pmatrix}.$

Suppose that the rank of a $4n^2\times(2n^2+n)$ coefficient matrix L is r. By employing the method of Gauss elimination we know that $0<r\leq 2n^2+n$. If $r=2n^2+n$, then the matrix L has full column rank, i.e. $W=0$. We know that there is at least a solution X,Y,U to the Eq. (9), namely: the private keys, thus

$0 < r < 2n^2 + n$. Then the method to calculate matrices $\widetilde{X}, \widetilde{Y}, \widetilde{U}$ is shown in Algorithm 2. It takes as input matrices (Q, A, B, D) and outputs equivalent keys $\widetilde{X}, \widetilde{Y}, \widetilde{U}$.

Algorithm 2. Recovering equivalent keys for any given public key

---

Input: Matrices (Q, A, B, D)

Output: Equivalent keys $\widetilde{X}, \widetilde{Y}, \widetilde{U}$

Step 1: Compute discrete logarithms M, N of matrices Q and E respectively

Step 2: Solve homogeneous linear equations in the $2n^2 + n$ entries of W respectively $LW^T = 0$

Step 3: Fix a basis for the solution space and transform vectors $\overrightarrow{X^{-1T}}, \overrightarrow{Y}^T$ to matrices X^{-1}, Y respectively. Pick the matrices $\widetilde{X^{-1}}, \widetilde{Y}$ until $\widetilde{X^{-1}}$ and $\widetilde{Y}$ are invertible and obtain the vector a

Step 4: Compute $U = \sum\limits_{i=0}^{n-1} a_i A^i$

Step 5: Compute the inverse matrix $\widetilde{X^{-1}}^{-1}$

Step 6: Return $\widetilde{X}, \widetilde{Y}, \widetilde{U}$.

Then, it remains to analyze the complexity of the Algorithm 2, which can be concluded in Table 2.

Table 2. Computation cost of Algorithm 2

Comp. content	Comp. cost	Explanation
$LW^T = 0$	$\mathcal{O}(4n^2 \cdot (2n^2 + n)^{\omega-1} log^2 q)$	$4n^2$ equations in $2n^2 + n$ variables
Solutions $\widetilde{X^{-1}}, \widetilde{Y}$	$\mathcal{O}(4n^2(2n^2 + n - r)^{\omega-1} log^2 q)$	A linear combination of solution space
$U = \sum\limits_{i=0}^{n-1} a_i A^i$	$\mathcal{O}((n-2)n^\omega log^2 q)$	$n-2$ multiplication
$\widetilde{X^{-1}}^{-1}$	$\mathcal{O}(n^\omega log^2 q)$	1 inversion

Thus, to generate random elements $\widetilde{X}, \widetilde{Y}$, one takes a linear combination of a basis of the solution space respectively. The number of free variables of the matrix Eq. (9) are $3n^2 - r$, then the total expected running time of step 2 is about $(2n^2 + n - r)^{\omega-1} \le (2n^2 + n)^{\omega-1}$. Now, if we neglect small constant factors, then the key recovery attack against asymmetric cipher based on MPF can be finished with the complexity of $\mathcal{O}(n^{2\omega} log^2 q)$. The recommended maximal parameters are given as follows: $n = 15, m = 141$, then the total bit complexity of asymmetric cipher 2 based on MPF is about $2^{24.2}$.

5   Improvement of the Non-commuting Cryptography Class Based on a MPF Problem

Our improved scheme uses the non-commuting cryptography class based on matrix power function, which relies on the solution of a multivariate polynomial system of equations. We provide two improvement methods in the following.

5.1 Improvement 1

In the two scheme above, it is known that even the solution of a multivariate quadratic polynomial system of equations over any field is an NP-complete problem. Hence, the security of the proposed improved scheme is also based on the solution of a system of multivariate equations, which is a hard problem.

If we cannot compute discrete logarithms M of the matrix Q or discrete logarithms N of the matrix E by designing parameters, then we also can propose an improved scheme that can protect against key recovery attack.

5.2 Improvement 2

When neither a pair of matrix (X, Y) nor a pair of matrix (U, V) is an invertible matrix, the key recovery attack fails, as mentioned in Sect. 4 and Ref. [12], where $A =^X Q^Y, B =^U Q^V$. We therefore can propose an improved scheme that can protect against key recovery attack.

6 Conclusions

We have showed that two asymmetric ciphers based on MPF are insecure in the sense that an attacker, who is able to solve the linear equations with high efficiency over a given general linear group, is able to break asymmetric cipher schemes. The question, whether there exists groups on which an asymmetric cipher scheme based on MPF is secure, remains open. When studying asymmetric cipher based on MPF on other groups the considerations of the previous section must be taken into account. How to use several nonabelian algebraic structures make a public-key cryptosystem, which has the potential to resist known quantum algorithms attacks, also remains open.

Acknowledgments. We want to thank the anonymous reviewers for their comments which helped to improve the paper. This work is supported by the National Natural Science Foundation of China (Grant Nos. 61303212, 61170080), the State Key Program of National Natural Science of China(Grant Nos. 61332019, U1135004), the Major Research Plan of the National Natural Science Foundation of China (Grant No. 91018008), the Hubei Natural Science Foundation of China (Grant Nos. 2011CDB453, 2014CFB440).

References

1. Takagi, T.: Post-quantum cryptography. In: Proceedings of PQCrypto 2016, Fukuoka, Japan, pp. 1–245 (2016)
2. Faugere, J.C., Perret, L., De Portzamparc, F.: Algebraic attack against variants of McEliece with Goppa polynomial of a special form. In: Proceedings of Asiacrypt 2014, Kaoshiung, Taiwan, pp. 21–41 (2014)
3. Armknecht, F., Gagliardoni, T., Katzenbeisser, S., Peter, A.: General impossibility of group homomorphic encryption in the quantum world. In: Proceedings of Public Key Cryptography 2014, Buenos Aires, Argentina, pp. 556–573 (2014)

4. Mao, S.W., Zhang, H.G., Wu, W.Q., et al.: A resistant quantum key exchange protocol and its corresponding encryption scheme. China Commun. **11**(9), 131–141 (2014)

5. Tsaban, B.: Polynomial-time solutions of computational problems in noncommutative algebraic cryptography. J. Cryptology **28**(3), 601–622 (2015)

6. Zhang, H.G., Liu, J.H., Jia, J.W., et al.: A survey on applications of matrix decomposition in cryptography. J. Cryptologic Res. **1**(4), 341–357 (2014)

7. Lyubashevsky, V., Prest, T.: Quadratic time, linear space algorithms for gram-schmidt orthogonalization and gaussian sampling in structured lattices. In: Oswald, E., Fischlin, M. (eds.) EUROCRYPT 2015. LNCS, vol. 9056, pp. 789–815. Springer, Heidelberg (2015). doi:10.1007/978-3-662-46800-5_30

8. Wang, H.Z., Zhang, H.G., Wang, Z.Y., et al.: Extended multivariate public key cryptosystems with secure encryption function. Sci. China Inf. Sci. **6**, 1161–1171 (2011)

9. Ling, S., Phan, D.H., Stehlé, D., Steinfeld, R.: Hardness of k-LWE and applications in traitor tracing. In: Garay, J.A., Gennaro, R. (eds.) CRYPTO 2014. LNCS, vol. 8616, pp. 315–334. Springer, Heidelberg (2014). doi:10.1007/978-3-662-44371-2_18

10. Gaborit, P.: Proceedings of PQCrypto 2013, Limoges, France, pp. 1–200 (2013)

11. Braun, J., Buchmann, J., Mullan, C., Wiesmaier, A.: Long term confidentiality: a survey. Des. Codes Crypt. **71**(3), 459–478 (2014)

12. Liu, J.H., Zhang, H.G., Jia, J.W., et al.: Cryptanalysis of an asymmetric cipher protocol using a matrix decomposition problem. Sci. China Inf. Sci. **59**(5), 1–11 (2016)

13. Zhang, H.G., Han, W.B., Lai, X.J., et al.: Survey on cyberspace security. Sci. China Inf. Sci. **58**(110101), 1–43 (2015)

14. Sakalauskas, E., Listopadskis, N., Tvarijonas, P.: Key agreement protocol (KAP) based on matrix power function. Advanced Studies in Software and Knowledge, Engineering, pp. 92–96 (2008)

15. Mihalkovich, A., Sakalauskas, E., Venckauskas, A.: New asymmetric cipher based on matrix power function and its implementation in microprocessors efficiency investigation. Elektronika ir Elektrotechnika **19**(10), 119–122 (2013)

16. Mihalkovich, A., Sakalauskas, E.: Asymmetric cipher based on MPF and its security parameters evaluation. In: Proceedings of the Lithuanian Mathematical Society, Series A, vol. 52, pp. 72–77 (2012)

17. Liu, J.H., Zhang, H.G., Jia, J.W., et al.: Cryptanalysis of HKKS key exchange protocols. Chin. J. Comput. **39**(3), 516–528 (2016)

18. Liu, M.J., Chen, J.Z.: Improved linear attacks on the Chinese block cipher standard. J. Comput. Sci. Technol. **29**(6), 1123–1133 (2014)

19. Gashkov, S.B., Sergeev, I.S.: Complexity of computation in finite fields. J. Math. Sci. **191**(5), 661–685 (2013)

20. Zhao, J.Y., Wang, M.Q., Wen, L.: Improved linear cryptanalysis of CAST-256. J. Comput. Sci. Technol. **29**(6), 1134–1139 (2014)

Commitment and Protocol

Partial Bits Exposure Attacks on a New Commitment Scheme Based on the Zagier Polynomial

Xiaona Zhang[1,2,3] and Li-Ping Wang[1,2(✉)]

[1] State Key Laboratory of Information Security,
Institute of Information Engineering, Chinese Academy of Sciences, Beijing, China
wangliping@iie.ac.cn
[2] Data Assurance and Communications Security Research Center,
Chinese Academy of Sciences, Beijing, China
[3] University of Chinese Academy of Sciences, Beijing, China

Abstract. In Asiacrypt'14, Boneh et al. built a new statistically hiding and computationally binding commitment scheme based on the collision-resistant property of the Zagier polynomial $f_{zag}(x,y) = x^7 + 3y^7$. In this paper, we describe several types of partial bits exposure attacks on this new commitment, that is, the most significant bits exposure attack, the least significant bits exposure attack and the middle parts exposure attack. Besides, we study the partial bits exposure attack on the situation that a message is committed twice. We mainly use the famous Coppersmith's method in our analyses.

Keywords: Bivariate polynomials · Collision-resistant · Cryptographic commitments · Lattices · LLL algorithm · Coppersmith's method

1 Introduction

Commitment schemes play an important role as a primitive in cryptographic protocols. They can be used to construct secure multi-party computation [1], anonymous Bitcoin transactions [2], digital signatures [3,4], zero-knowledge proofs and arguments [5,6], electronic auctions, e-voting systems and threshold cryptography. In a commitment scheme, a player can commit to a secret value S by publishing a commitment C without revealing anything about the secret S, which is called the hiding property. The player can later open C to reveal S in a way verifiable by anyone else, i.e., the commitment value is binding to the committer in the sense that the player can't open C to any other value than S to cheat on the receiver.

In Crypto'97, Okamoto et al. [5] presented the first efficient integer commitment scheme and also suggested an efficient multiplication protocol. Later several related works are inspired. Prior works have derived statistically hiding commitment schemes based on the discrete log problem [7], the Paillier crypto system [8], the RSA problem [9], pseudo-random generators [10,11], and some specific harness assumptions such as the availability of collision-free hash functions [12].

© Springer International Publishing AG 2017
K. Chen et al. (Eds.): Inscrypt 2016, LNCS 10143, pp. 357–366, 2017.
DOI: 10.1007/978-3-319-54705-3_22

Verifying the correctness of opening a commitment in these schemes calls for expensive modular exponentiations or elliptic curve scalar multiplications.

Low-degree collision-resistant bivariate polynomials are very useful, which gives rise to very efficient instantiations of a number of cryptographic primitives. The Zagier polynomial $f_{zag}(x,y) = x^7 + 3y^7$, produced by Don Zagier [13], is conjectured to possess this nice property. Boneh et al. [14] did comprehensive research on the properties of the Zagier polynomial. Based on its algebraic collision-resistant property, they designed a new statistically hiding and computationally binding commitment scheme, a conceptually simple cryptographic accumulator, and an efficient chameleon hash function.

Boneh et al.'s commitment scheme can be briefly described as follows. N is a public parameter, which is an RSA modulus of unknown factorization. To commit to a value $m \in \mathbb{Z}_N^*$, where $\mathbb{Z}_N^* = \{x \in \mathbb{Z}_N : gcd(x,N) = 1\}$, the committer samples a random blinding value r from $\mathbb{Z}_N^*$ and computes the value of $f(m,r) = m^7 + 3r^7 \mod N$ at the point (m,r). Verifying an opening in this commitment scheme requires just a few modular multiplications [14].

In his seminal work [15,16] in 1996, Coppersmith described polynomial time algorithms for finding small roots of univariate modular polynomials as well as bivariate integer polynomials based on lattice basis reduction. The essence of Coppersmith's method is to find integer linear combinations of polynomials which share a common root modulo some integer such that the derived polynomials have small coefficients. Thus one may obtain several polynomials that possess the desired root over integers and then find the desired root using standard root finding algorithms. Howgrave-Graham [17] reformulated Coppersmith's method in a simpler way which has been widely adopted by researches for cryptanalysis.

Recently, side-channel attack is becoming a power tool in cryptanalysis by exploiting the leakage of some kind of information from the cryptosystem during its execution [18–21]. In this paper, we use the leakage information of the message m and the blinding value r, which can be obtained via side-channel methods, to consider several types of partial bits exposure attack on Boneh et al.'s new commitment scheme by applying Coppersmith's method so that the whole information m can be recovered. Then, we study how one can recover a message when the message is committed twice and the attacker gets access to the approximates of the random numbers r_1 and r_2.

The rest of this paper is organized as follows. In Sect. 2, we recall some preliminaries. In Sect. 3, we present our attacks on this new commitment scheme. And experimental results are also involved. Section 4 is some conclusions.

2   Preliminaries

2.1   Lattices

Let $\mathbf{b_1}, \ldots, \mathbf{b_\omega}$ be linear independent row vectors in $\mathbb{R}^n$, and a lattice $\mathcal{L}$ spanned by them is

$$\mathcal{L} = \{\sum_{i=1}^{\omega} k_i \mathbf{b_i} \mid k_i \in \mathbb{Z}\},$$

where $\{\mathbf{b_1}, \ldots, \mathbf{b_\omega}\}$ is a basis of $\mathcal{L}$ and $B = [\mathbf{b_1}^T, \ldots, \mathbf{b_\omega}^T]^T$ is the corresponding basis matrix. The dimension and determinant of $\mathcal{L}$ are respectively

$$\dim(\mathcal{L}) = \omega, \text{ and } \det(\mathcal{L}) = \sqrt{\det(BB^T)}.$$

A lattice can be represented by different bases. Different bases would have different computational cost and lead to different results when solving problems relevant to lattices, even if the involved algorithms are exactly the same. Thus, one always wants to find the bases satisfying some certain constraints, and it would be much easier to solve the problems by using these specific bases as the input. The process of choosing such a basis is called lattice basis reduction, and the corresponding basis is called a reduced basis. The criteria for a reduced basis varies from different requirements of problems.

Reduced basis vectors possess much elegant properties, like short norms and the property of being approximate orthogonal to each other. Thus, calculating a reduced basis of a given lattice is always a hot topic. In 1982, Lenstra, Lenstra and Loyáze proposed the distinguished LLL-algorithm [22] that can find vectors in polynomial time whose norm is small enough to satisfy the following condition.

Lemma 1 ([22]). *Let $\mathcal{L}$ be a lattice. In polynomial time, the LLL algorithm outputs reduced basis vectors $\mathbf{v_1}, \ldots, \mathbf{v_\omega}$ that satisfy*

$$\|\mathbf{v_1}\| \leq \|\mathbf{v_2}\| \leq \cdots \leq \|\mathbf{v_i}\| \leq 2^{\frac{\omega(\omega-1)}{4(\omega+1-i)}} \det(\mathcal{L})^{\frac{1}{\omega+1-i}}, 1 \leq i \leq \omega.$$

2.2 Finding Small Roots

Coppersmith gave rigorous methods for extracting small roots of modular univariate polynomials and bivariate integer polynomials. These methods can be heuristically extended to multivariate cases. Howgrave-Graham reformulated Coppersmith' s ideas of finding modular roots in [17], of which we use the following lemma.

Lemma 2 ([17]). *Let $g(x_1, x_2) \in \mathbb{Z}[x_1, x_2]$ be an integer polynomial that consists of at most ω nonzero monomials. Define the norm of $g(x_1, x_2) := \sum b_{i_1,i_2} x_1^{i_1} x_2^{i_2}$ as the Euclidean norm of its coefficient vector, namely,*

$$\|g(x_1, x_2)\| = \sqrt{\sum b_{i_1,i_2}^2}.$$

Suppose that

1. $g(x_1^{(0)}, x_2^{(0)}) = 0 \pmod{N}$, for $|x_1^{(0)}| < X_1$, $|x_2^{(0)}| < X_2$;
2. $\|g(X_1 x_1, X_2 x_2)\| < \frac{N}{\sqrt{\omega}}$.

Then $g(x_1^{(0)}, x_2^{(0)}) = 0$ holds over integers.

Combining Howgrave-Graham's lemma with the LLL algorithm, one can deduce that the equations of the polynomials corresponding to the shortest i reduced basis vectors hold over integers under the following condition

$$2^{\frac{\omega(\omega-1)}{4(\omega+1-i)}} \det(\mathcal{L})^{\frac{1}{\omega+1-i}} < \frac{N}{\sqrt{\omega}}.$$

Neglecting the low order terms which are independent on N, the above condition can be simplified as

$$\det(\mathcal{L}) < N^{\omega+1-i}. \tag{1}$$

After obtaining enough equations over integers, one can extract the shared roots by either resultant computation or Gröbner basis technique.

We need the following assumption through our analyses, which is widely adopted in previous works.

Assumption 1. *The polynomials corresponding to the first n LLL-reduced vectors are algebraically independent.*

2.3 Boneh et al.'s New Commitment Scheme Based on the Zagier Polynomial

Boneh et al.'s commitment scheme uses the following assumption.

Assumption 2. *The Zagier polynomial $f_{zag}(x,y) = x^7 + 3y^7 \in \mathbb{Z}[x,y]$ is collision resistant.*

This commitment scheme consists of only one public parameter, an RSA modulus N, for which its factorization is unknown. To commit to a value $m \in \mathbb{Z}_N^*$, the committer computes the value of $f_{zag}(m,r) \bmod N$ where r is a random blinding value sampled from $\mathbb{Z}_N^*$.

The construction of this commitment scheme is as follows.

Setup(λ) $\rightarrow N$. N is an RSA modulus, the product of two random $\lambda-$bit primes p and q satisfying that $\gcd(\phi(N),7) = 1$, where $\phi(N)$ is the Euler's totient function of N. The commitment space $\mathcal{C}$ is $\mathbb{Z}_N$. The message space $\mathcal{M}$ and the space of blinding values $\mathcal{R}$ are $\mathbb{Z}_N^*$.

Commit(m) $\rightarrow (c,r)$. Choose a random blinding value $r \leftarrow \mathbb{Z}_N^*$ and set

$$c = m^7 + 3r^7 \bmod N. \tag{2}$$

Return r as the commitment secret.

Open(c,m,r) $\rightarrow \{0,1\}$. Output "1" if $m,r \in \mathbb{Z}_N^*$ and $c = m^7 + 3r^7 \bmod N$. Output "0" otherwise.

3 Attacks on the New Commitment Scheme

In this section, we discuss our main attacks on this commitment scheme.

3.1 MSBs Exposure Attack on Boneh et al.'s New Commitment Scheme

First, we describe the most significant bits exposure attack on this scheme.

We consider the following situation. When an attacker gets access to the most significant bits of the message m and the random number r by some methods, for example, side-channel attacks, which means that the approximations of m and r can be derived. Our task is to recover the whole knowledge of m and r.

Set $m = A + x$ and $r = B + y$, where A and B are the approximations to m and r, and x and y are the error terms. Suppose that $|x| \leq X = N^{\alpha_1}$, $|y| \leq Y = N^{\alpha_2}$. We have

$$c = (A + x)^7 + 3(B + y)^7 \bmod N.$$

Then, this problem can be transformed into finding the small roots of the following bivariate modular polynomial

$$f(x, y) = (A + x)^7 + 3(B + y)^7 - c \bmod N. \qquad (3)$$

We use Coppersmith's idea to solve this polynomial equation. Choose a proper integer n and construct the shifting polynomials as follows,

$$g^1_{k,i,j}(x, y) = y^j f^k N^{n-k}, \ k = 0, ..., n; \ i = 0; \ j = 0, ..., 7(n - k),$$

and

$$g^2_{k,i,j}(x, y) = x^i y^j f^k N^{n-k}, \ k = 0, ..., n - 1; \ i = 1, ..., 6; \ j = 0, ..., 7(n - k - 1).$$

Use the coefficient vectors of $g^1(xX, yY)$ and $g^2(xX, yY)$ to build a lattice $\mathcal{L}$, and arrange them according to the lexicographical order of $\{k, i, j\}$, so that each polynomial introduces one and only one new monomial. Thus, we can obtain a lower triangular lattice, whose determinant can be easily calculated as $\det(\mathcal{L}) = X^{S_X} Y^{S_Y} N^{S_N}$ as well as its dimension ω, where

$$S_X = \sum_{k=0}^{n} \sum_{j=0}^{7(n-k)} 7k + \sum_{k=0}^{n-1} \sum_{i=0}^{6} \sum_{j=0}^{7(n-k-1)} (i + 7k) = \frac{7}{6} n(49n^2 - 42n + 17) = \frac{343}{6} n^3 + o(n^3),$$

$$S_Y = \sum_{k=0}^{n} \sum_{j=0}^{7(n-k)} j + \sum_{k=0}^{n-1} \sum_{i=0}^{6} \sum_{j=0}^{7(n-k-1)} j = \frac{7}{6} n(49n^2 - 42n + 17) = \frac{343}{6} n^3 + o(n^3),$$

$$S_N = \sum_{k=0}^{n} \sum_{j=0}^{7(n-k)} (n - k) + \sum_{k=0}^{n-1} \sum_{i=0}^{6} \sum_{j=0}^{7(n-k-1)} (n - k) = \frac{7}{3} n(7n^2 + 3n - 4) = \frac{49}{3} n^3 + o(n^3),$$

$$\omega = \sum_{k=0}^{n} \sum_{j=0}^{7(n-k)} 1 + \sum_{k=0}^{n-1} \sum_{i=0}^{6} \sum_{j=0}^{7(n-k-1)} 1 = \frac{1}{2}(49n^2 - 21n + 2) = \frac{49}{2} n^2 + o(n^2),$$

Put these values into (1), we obtain

$$XY < N^{\frac{1}{7}}.$$

Since $X = N^{\alpha_1}, Y = N^{\alpha_2}$, the above condition can be written as

$$\alpha_1 + \alpha_2 < \frac{1}{7}.$$

3.2   LSBs Exposure Attack on the New Commitment Scheme

Here we analyze the case when the least significant bits of m and r are leaked.

In this situation, we assume that $m = m_1 R + m_2$ and $r = r_1 S + r_2$, where m_2 and r_2 refer to the leaked least significant parts, R and S represent the sizes of m_2 and r_2 respectively, that is, if m_2 is l bit long, we take $R = 2^l$. The value for S is set analogously. So m_1 and r_1 are the unknown high parts. Define

$$f_{lsb}(x, y) = (Rx + m_2)^7 + 3(Sy + r_2)^7 - c \bmod N,$$

where x and y represent the unknown parts m_1 and r_1. It is easy to get that $(x_0, y_0) = (m_1, r_1)$ is a root of $f_{lsb}(x, y) \equiv 0 \bmod N$. This polynomial possesses the same structure with (3), except for different coefficient settings. We omit the detailed calculations and directly give the derived bounds for the unknowns, that is, $XY < N^{1/7}$.

Set $R = N^{\beta_1}$ and $S = N^{\beta_2}$, according to the relation $\frac{(m-m_1)(r-r_1)}{RS} < N^{1/7}$, and we obtain that $N^{\beta_1+\beta_2} > \frac{(m-m_1)(r-r_1)}{N^{1/7}}$. Since m and r are of the same size as N, we can recover the whole information of m and r when

$$\beta_1 + \beta_2 > \frac{13}{7}.$$

3.3   Middle Bits Exposure Attack on the New Commitment Scheme

In this subsection, we discuss the case when the middle parts of m and r are leaked. We write $m = m_{2,1} + \hat{m}R_1 + m_{2,2}R_2$ and $r = r_{2,1} + \hat{r}S_1 + r_{2,2}S_2$, where $m_{2,1}$ and $r_{2,1}$ are the unknown least significant parts, $\hat{m}$ and $\hat{r}$ correspond to the leaked middle bits, R_1 and S_1 mark the scales of $m_{2,1}$ and $r_{2,1}$ respectively. For example, $R_1 = 2^{\lceil \log_2 m_{2,1} \rceil}$, $S_1 = 2^{\lceil \log_2 r_{2,1} \rceil}$, $m_{2,2}$ and $r_{2,2}$ represent the unknown high bits, and R_2 and S_2 mark the ending points of the leaked parts, that is $R_2 = 2^{\lceil Log_2(m_{2,1}+\hat{m}R_1) \rceil}$, $S_2 = 2^{\lceil Log_2(r_{2,1}+\hat{r}S_1) \rceil}$.

According to (2), we get that $c = (m_{2,1} + \hat{m}R_1 + m_{2,2}R_2)^7 + 3(r_{2,1} + \hat{r}S_1 + r_{2,2}S_2)^7 \bmod N$. Thus, the problem of attacking this commitment scheme can be reduced to solving the following four variable polynomial equation.

$$f(x, y, z, w) = (x + R_2 y + \hat{m}R_1)^7 + 3(z + S_2 w + \hat{r}S_1)^7 - c \bmod N.$$

It is obvious that $(x_0 = m_{2,1}, y_0 = m_{2,2}, z_0 = r_{2,1}, w_0 = r_{2,2})$ is a root of the above equation.

It is difficult to derive a general formula for the shifting polynomials which share the same roots modulo N^n with $f(x, y, z, w) \bmod N$, where n is a positive integer. Here we only use the knowledge of $f(x, y, z, w)$ to build a lattice $\hat{\mathcal{L}}$ and compute a rough bound on the solvable value ranges of x, y, z and w. Construct the following polynomials, which share the same root with $f(x, y, z, w) \equiv 0 \bmod N$,

$$\hat{g}_{i_1, i_2, i_3, i_4}(x, y, z, w) = x^{i_1} y^{i_2} z^{i_3} w^{i_4} N,$$

where $x^{i_1} y^{i_2} z^{i_3} w^{i_4} \in f(x, y, z, w)$ and $x^{i_1} y^{i_2} z^{i_3} w^{i_4} \neq w^7$.

Use the coefficient vectors of $\hat{g}_{i_1, i_2, i_3, i_4}(xX, yY, zZ, wW)$ and $f(xX, yY, zZ, wW)$ as a basis to build the lattice $\hat{\mathcal{L}}$, where X, Y, Z and W are the upper bounds of x, y, z and w. Notice that all monomials that belong to $f(x, y, z, w)$ are included in $\hat{g}_{i_1, i_2, i_3, i_4}(x, y, z, w)$ except for w^7, which will be introduced by $f(x, y, z, w)$ itself. Arranging polynomials $\hat{g}_{i_1, i_2, i_3, i_4}(xX, yY, zZ, wW)$ in front of the polynomial $f(xX, yY, zZ, wW)$, we get a lower triangular lattice with a dimension $\omega(\hat{\mathcal{L}}) = 71$, which is computed by counting the monomials of $f(x, y, z, w)$. The determinant of $\hat{\mathcal{L}}$ can also be easily calculated as $det(\hat{\mathcal{L}}) = (XYZW)^{84} N^{70}$. Put these values into (1), and we can obtain the constraints for x, y, z and w, that is $XYZW < N^{1/84}$. Set $X = N^{\gamma_1}, Y = N^{\gamma_2}, Z = N^{\gamma_3}, W = N^{\gamma_4}$, then the above condition can be written as

$$\gamma_1 + \gamma_2 + \gamma_3 + \gamma_4 < \frac{1}{84}.$$

3.4   Attack on the Twice Committed Message

In this subsection, we study the side channel attack on the case when a message is committed twice. Assuming that c_1 and c_2 are two commitments of a same message m, that is, $c_1 = m^7 + 3r_1^7 \bmod N$ and $c_2 = m^7 + 3r_2^7 \bmod N$, we get that $c_2 - c_1 = 3(r_2^7 - r_1^7) \bmod N$. Once an attacker gets the approximates of r_1 and r_2, that is, $r_2 = \hat{A} + x$, $r_1 = \hat{B} + y$, we show that the whole knowledge of r_1 and r_2 can be recovered, and so the message m can be obtained.

Construct a bivariate polynomial

$$\hat{f}(x, y) = 3(x + \hat{A})^7 - 3(y + \hat{B})^7 + \hat{c} \bmod N.$$

We have that $(x_0, y_0) = (r_2 - \hat{A}, r_1 - \hat{B})$ is a root of the above polynomial equation $\hat{f}(x, y) \equiv 0 \bmod N$ for a constant $\hat{c} = (c_1 - c_2)$. This polynomial is also of the same structure as (3) except for some different coefficient settings. Thus, we directly put the analysis result here and omit detailed calculation steps. That is, we can recover the message m from the approximates of r_1 and r_2 when the approximation error terms satisfy $XY < N^{1/7}$, where X and Y represents the upper bounds of x and y. Set $X = N^{\eta_1}, Y = N^{\eta_2}$, and the above constraints can be written as

$$\eta_1 + \eta_2 < \frac{1}{7}.$$

3.5 Experimental Results

The following Tables 1, 2 and 3 display some experimental data performed to verify our analyses. These tests are done in Magma on a PC with Intel (R) Core(TM) Quad CPU (3.20 GHz, 4.00 GB RAM, Windows 10).

Table 1. Experimental data for the MSBs exposure attack

N (bits)	n	dim	α_1	α_2	LLL (seconds)	Gröbner (seconds)
256	2	78	1/40	1/40	16.703	9.625
512	2	78	1/40	1/40	90.797	25.766
1024	2	78	1/40	1/40	430.281	84.094
2048	2	78	1/40	1/40	2201.031	251.484

Table 2. Experimental data for the LSBs exposure attack

N (bits)	n	dim	β_1	β_2	LLL (seconds)	Gröbner (seconds)
256	2	78	55/56	55/56	197.357	10.719
512	2	78	55/56	55/56	56.609	33.500
1024	2	78	55/56	55/56	202.938	104.328
2048	2	78	55/56	55/56	804.156	275.484

Table 3. Experimental data for the attack in Sect. 3.4

N (bits)	n	dim	η_1	η_2	LLL (seconds)	Gröbner (seconds)
256	2	78	1/40	1/40	23.328	8.938
512	2	78	1/40	1/40	103.422	27.969
1024	2	78	1/39	1/39	445.297	87.766
2048	2	78	1/39	1/39	2184.906	275.891

In our problems, the polynomials involved are $7°$. And the dimensions of the lattices increases greatly as the parameter n goes larger, which makes the process of executing the LLL algorithm quite time-consuming. Taking into account the time performance, we set $n = 2$ in our experiments, however, which makes the experimental results not as good as the theoretical bounds.

4 Conclusion

In this paper, we proposed four kinds of partial bits exposure attacks on the newly proposed commitment scheme based on the Zagier polynomial, that is, the most significant bits exposure attack, the middle bits exposure attack, the least significant bits exposure attack, and the partial bits exposure attack on the twice committed message. All of our attacks can be reduced to solving a certain type of modular polynomial equation, whose small roots can then be extracted by applying the distinguished Coppersmith's root finding method. Our work are based on the background of side channel attacks.

Acknowledgements. During my visit to the University of California Irvine in 2015, Alice Silverberg et al. studied this new commitment scheme in their seminar, which drew my attention to this commitment scheme. We thank them for helpful conversations about this work. Our work was partially supported by the National Key Basic Research Program of China (2013CB834203).

References

1. Goldwasser, S., Micali, S., Rackoff, C.: The knowledge complexity of interactive proof systems. SIAM J. Comput. **18**(1), 186–208 (1989)
2. Miers, I., Garman, C., Green, M., Rubin, A.D.: Zerocoin: anonymous distributed e-cash from bitcoin. In: 2013 IEEE Symposium on Security and Privacy, SP 2013, Berkeley, 19–22 May 2013, pp. 397–411 (2013)
3. Al-saggaf, A.A., Ghouti, L.: Efficient abuse-free fair contract-signing protocol based on an ordinary crisp commitment scheme. IET Inf. Secur. **9**(1), 50–58 (2015)
4. Gritti, C., Susilo, W., Plantard, T.: Logarithmic size ring signatures without random oracles. IET Inf. Secur. **10**(1), 1–7 (2016)
5. Fujisaki, E., Okamoto, T.: Statistical zero knowledge protocols to prove modular polynomial relations. In: 17th Annual International Cryptology Conference on Advances in Cryptology - CRYPTO 1997, Santa Barbara, California, USA, 17–21 August 1997, pp. 16–30 (1997)
6. Haitner, I., Nguyen, M., Ong, S.J., Reingold, O., Vadhan, S.P.: Statistically hiding commitments and statistical zero-knowledge arguments from any one-way function. SIAM J. Comput. **39**(3), 1153–1218 (2009)
7. Pedersen, T.P.: Non-interactive and information-theoretic secure verifiable secret sharing. In: Proceedings of 11th Annual International Cryptology Conference on Advances in Cryptology - CRYPTO 1991, Santa Barbara, California, USA, 11–15 August 1991, pp. 129–140 (1991)
8. Catalano, D., Gennaro, R., Howgrave-Graham, N., Nguyen, P.Q.: Paillier's cryptosystem revisited. In: Proceedings of the 8th ACM Conference on Computer and Communications Security, CCS 2001, Philadelphia, Pennsylvania, USA, 6–8 November 2001, pp. 206–214 (2001)
9. Ateniese, G., de Medeiros, B.: Identity-based chameleon hash and applications. In: 8th International Conference on Financial Cryptography, FC 2004, Revised Papers, Key West, FL, USA, 9–12 February 2004, pp. 164–180 (2004)
10. Naor, M.: Bit commitment using pseudo-randomness. In: Proceedings of 9th Annual International Cryptology Conference on Advances in Cryptology - CRYPTO 1989, Santa Barbara, California, USA, 20–24 August 1989, pp. 128–136 (1989)
11. Kim, S.G.: Adaptive cryptographic protocol for fair exchange of secrets using pseudo-random-sequence generator. J. Digital Contents Soc. **8**(4), 631–637 (2007)

12. Halevi, S., Micali, S.: Practical and provably-secure commitment schemes from collision-free hashing. In: Proceedings of 16th Annual International Cryptology Conference on Advances in Cryptology - CRYPTO 1996, Santa Barbara, California, USA, 18–22 August 1996, pp. 201–215 (1996)

13. Cornelissen, G.: Stockage diophantien et hypothse abc gnralise. Comptes Rendus de l'Acadmie des Sciences - Series I - Mathematics **328**(1), 3–8 (1999)

14. Boneh, D., Corrigan-Gibbs, H.: Bivariate polynomials modulo composites and their applications. In: Proceedings of 20th International Conference on the Theory and Application of Cryptology and Information Security on Advances in Cryptology - ASIACRYPT 2014, Part I, Kaoshiung, Taiwan, R.O.C., 7–11 December 2014, pp. 42–62 (2014)

15. Coppersmith, D.: Finding a small root of a univariate modular equation. In: Proceeding of International Conference on the Theory and Application of Cryptographic Techniques Advances in Cryptology - EUROCRYPT 1996, Saragossa, Spain, 12–16 May 1996, pp. 155–165 (1996)

16. Coppersmith, D.: Finding a small root of a bivariate integer equation; factoring with high bits known. In: Proceeding of International Conference on the Theory and Application of Cryptographic Techniques Advances in Cryptology - EUROCRYPT 1996, Saragossa, Spain, 12–16 May 1996, pp. 178–189 (1996)

17. Howgrave-Graham, N.: Finding small roots of univariate modular equations revisited. In: Darnell, M. (ed.) Cryptography and Coding 1997. LNCS, vol. 1355, pp. 131–142. Springer, Heidelberg (1997). doi:10.1007/BFb0024458

18. Ambrose, J.A., Ragel, R.G., Parameswaran, S., Ignjatovic, A.: Multiprocessor information concealment architecture to prevent power analysis-based side channel attacks. IET Comput. Digital Tech. **5**(1), 1–15 (2011)

19. Karakoyunlu, D., Gürkaynak, F.K., Sunar, B., Leblebici, Y.: Efficient and side-channel-aware implementations of elliptic curve cryptosystems over prime fields. IET Inf. Secur. **4**(1), 30–43 (2010)

20. Marchand, C., Francq, J.: Low-level implementation and side-channel detection of stealthy hardware trojans on field programmable gate arrays. IET Comput. Digital Tech. **8**(6), 246–255 (2014)

21. Vaquie, B., Tiran, S., Maurine, P.: Secure D flip-flop against side channel attacks. IET Circ. Dev. Syst. **6**(5), 347–354 (2012)

22. Lenstra, A.K., Lenstra, H.W., Lovász, L.: Factoring polynomials with rational coefficients. Mathematische Annalen **261**(4), 515–534 (1982)

Key Predistribution Schemes Using Bent Functions in Distributed Sensor Networks

Deepak Kumar Dalai[1(✉)] and Pinaki Sarkar[2]

[1] School of Mathematical Sciences,
National Institute of Science Education and Research (HBNI),
Bhubaneswar 752 050, Odisha, India
deepak@niser.ac.in
[2] Department of Computer Science and Automation,
Indian Institute of Science, Bangalore, Karnataka, India
pinakisark@csa.iisc.ernet.in

Abstract. Key management is an essential functionality for developing secure cryptosystems; particularly for implementations to low cost devices of a Distributed Sensor Networks (DSN)–a prototype of Internet of Things (IoT). Low cost leads to constraints in various resources of constituent devices of a IoT (e.g., sensors of a DSN); thereby restricting implementations of computationally heavy public key cryptosystems. This leads to adaptation of the novel key predistribution trick in symmetric key platform to efficiently tackle the problem of key management for these resource starved networks. After a few initial proposals based on random graphs, most key predistribution schemes (KPS) use deterministic (combinatorial) approaches to assure essential design properties. Combinatorial designs like a $(v, b, r, k)-$configuration which forms a $\mu(v, b, r, k)-$CID are effective schemes to design KPS [20]. In this paper, we use bent Boolean functions to generate four combinatorial designs for the purpose of designing deterministic KPS. Of particular interest are our later (two) schemes that are constructed over Dillon's bent Boolean function. Effectiveness of our solutions in term of crucial metrics in comparison to prominent schemes has been theoretically established.

Keywords: Bent functions · Partial spread · Combinatorial designs · Key predistribution scheme(s) · Internet of Things · Distributed Sensor Networks

1 Introduction

Distributed (Wireless) Sensor Networks (DSN) are regarded as revolutionary information gathering systems owing to their easy deployment and flexible topology. They are decentralized with numerous low-cost identical resource starved wireless devices, called sensors or nodes, that deal with sensory data. They are considered as a nice prototype of Internet of Things (IoT) which is a sophisticated concept that aims to connect our world more than we ever thought possible. This has boosted the study of such distributed networks in modern times.

© Springer International Publishing AG 2017
K. Chen et al. (Eds.): Inscrypt 2016, LNCS 10143, pp. 367–385, 2017.
DOI: 10.1007/978-3-319-54705-3_23

Prominent scientific applications of IoT are smart homes, smart cities, smart grids, smart water networks, agriculture, health-care, etc. Of particular interest are applications of DSN to networks where security is a premium. For instance, security may be essential for certain sensitive scientific and military networks that are meant for (i) military surveillance, (ii) force protection.arenas, (iii) self healing minefields, and so on. Primary tasks of devices of an IoT in any such application are to collect information from their surrounding, process and forward them to other devices. Depending on specific applications, they may be further required to (i) track and/or classify an object, (ii) determine parametric value(s) of a given location, etc. These sensitive task for such critical applications create the necessity of security of message communication among the resource starved devices of these useful low cost networks.

1.1 Type of Cryptosystem: Key Predistribution Schemes (KPS)

Constraints in resources of constituent ordinary devices of any IoT (like sensors of DSN) make us opt for symmetric key cryptosystems (SKC) over their public key counterparts while designing security protocols for such networks. SKC require both the sender and receiver to possess the same encryption–decryption key before message exchange. Standard online key exchange techniques that involve public parameters are generally avoided due to their heavy computations.

One can think of two trivial key distribution techniques. First is to assign a single key for entire network devices. Second is to think of assigning pairwise distinct (symmetric) keys for every pair of devices. Former method is completely vulnerable to single point failure (compromise of even *one* sensor reveals this single system key). Whereas, the second strategy overloads the memory of each sensor, since $\mathcal{N} - 1$ keys are required to be stored per sensor for a network of size $\mathcal{N}$. This is particularly impractical for large networks (i.e., large value of $\mathcal{N}$).

Treating a node (or a few) as Trusted Authority (TA) is risky. This also makes the network prone to single point failure.[1] Thereby schemes like Kerberos [18] are avoided while designing secure key management schemes for DSN.

These facts emphasizes the importance of employing an adequate key management scheme for such networks. This stalemate situation was wittily overcome in 2002 by Eschenauer and Gligor by introducing the concept of *key predistribution* that involves applications of SKC to sensor networks. Any key predistribution scheme (KPS) primarily execute the following steps:

– Prior to deployment of the network, *keys* are preloaded into sensors to form their *key rings or key chains* from the key pool. *Key pool* is the collection of all network keys. Each sensor is preloaded with a subset of keys from this pool to form its *key ring* or *key chain*. Each system key is marked with an unique identifier *(key id)*. These key id are used during key establishment.

---

[1] Capture of this authority (sensor) acting as a TA makes the system vulnerable.

- These preloaded keys are *established* by a two steps process, given below:
  - *(i) Shared key discovery phase*: establishes shared common key(s) among participant nodes. This may be achieved by broadcasting the key ids of all keys contained in a node. On receiving each other's key ids, the sensors tally them to trace their mutual shared key id(s), hence common shared key(s).
  - *(ii) Path key establishment phase*: establishes an optimized path key between a pair of nodes that do not share a common key. This process involves intermediate nodes. Refer to common intersection designs in Sect. 3.

Depending on whether the above processes are probabilistic or deterministic, such schemes are classified into two types: (a) *random* and (b) *deterministic*. Sections 2.1 and 2.2 present a brief overview of individual type of schemes.

1.2 Our Contribution and Paper Organization

Observing the significant advantages of deterministic KPS during key management for low cost distributed networks, we set out to propose four such schemes. Our proposals uses Bent Boolean functions that have been well studied combinatorially. However, we are not aware of any KPS constructed using these functions. After a brief literature survey on KPS in Sect. 2, we present preliminaries of Boolean functions in Sect. 3 that are needed for our work. Two simple schemes are first proposed in Sect. 4. These proposal have certain weaknesses, but can be useful for certain constructions. Section 5 presents our main schemes that adhere to the desirable criteria set out in Sect. 2.4. We analyze our later schemes in terms of various performance metrics set out in Sect. 6; thereby establish their efficiency in comparison to prominent existing proposals. We summarize our work in Sect. 8 while stating related future research directions.

2 Key Predistribution Schemes (KPS): A Brief Survey

This section presents a state-of-the art survey of prominent KPS. We split survey into three stage: (i) random KPS, (ii) deterministic KPS, and (iii) advantages of the later type over former. Thereby, we justify our proposals of four new deterministic KPS that adhere to the design criteria set out in Sect. 2.4.

2.1 Random Key Predistribution Schemes (RKPS)

First generation KPS rely on random graph theory pioneered by Erdős and Rényi [14] to preload (symmetric) cryptographic keys into sensors. Therefore, key rings are formed randomly. This leads to probabilistic key sharing and establishment. Later is achieved by either broadcast of key ids or *challenge and response* (refer to [15, Sect. 2.1]). Earlier, Blom proposed the first key distribution scheme [4] in public key settings meant for resourceful ad hoc networks. Blom's schemes uses pairs of public-private matrices for key distribution. Blom's scheme cannot be applied to resource constraint sensor networks due to its heavy memory requirement to store huge vectors. Several researchers use variants of Blom's scheme to propose both random and deterministic KPS for DSN. Çamptepe and Yener [7] provides an excellent survey of such random KPS.

2.2 Deterministic Key Predistribution Schemes (DKPS)

Deterministic KPS were proposed simultaneously by Çamtepe and Yener [6], Lee and Stinson [20] and Wei and Wu [28] in 2004. Wei and Wu [28] combines subset-based schemes with existing key distribution schemes such as [4] to obtain multiple key spaces. Çamtepe and Yener [6] exploits combinatorial designs like symmetric Balanced Incomplete Block Designs (BIBD), generalized quadrangles and projective planes. The scheme of Lee and Stinson [21] uses quadratic equation solving and can be viewed as a *scalable extension* of their later proposal using Transversal Design $(TD(k, p))$ [20]. Their work [20] further summarizes the necessary conditions for a combinatorial design to yield a deterministic KPS. Certain KPS exploit special structures like Reed Solomon code based KPS [25] that permit alternate combinatorial description [1,11,22]. In the same light, we show our schemes derived from Bent functions, particularly of Dillon types, can yield nice combinatorial properties meant for designing deterministic KPS.

2.3 Advantages of Deterministic KPS (Over Random Ones)

Deterministic schemes have certain advantages over their random counterparts. For instance, a desired property of a randomized scheme may occur only with a certain probability whereas they can be proven to hold in a deterministic scheme (refer to [20–22]). This led to proposals of numerous deterministic KPS using various combinatorial tricks. Further the predictable nature of these combinatorial structures has been efficiently exploited to address design weaknesses of certain prominent schemes. For instance [1,11] primarily address the connectivity aspect of [25] by deterministic and random approaches respectively.

Contrary to these observations, Ruj and Pal [24] state that random graph models are well suited for 'scalability' and 'resilience'. Thereby they justify their proposals of random graph based preferential attachment models with degree bounds. They design various network using their model. All of their designs suffers from highly skewed load distribution, poor connectivity and resiliency; and hence, are inappropriate for (distributed) IoT applications.

In fact, sensitive IoT applications require protocols to yield equal distribution of tasks among peers. Moreover, to reduce hops and hence potential risks from node capture, it is more important to have connected networks that can not be guaranteed by random schemes. Therefore to secure IoT networks, we opt for deterministic protocols that assure predictable (high) connectivity; despite most of them having restricted scaling operations. This is a major area of study for most (deterministic) KPS proposals, including ours (recalled in Sect. 8).

Observe that the structure of the combinatorial objects used to design deterministic KPS can not directly model network of any specified size $\mathcal{N}$. Usually, such structures result in designs having a specific pattern in the number of resultant blocks; viz. a prime power or 2^n, $s2^m$ (like ours), etc. Since $\mathcal{N}$ can be any number, a standard strategy is to consider the least prime power (or power of 2 here) that is greater than the network size (i.e., $p^n \geq \mathcal{N}$ or 2^n, $s2^m \geq \mathcal{N}$ for ours). Then $\mathcal{N}$ subset are randomly selected to form the key rings of the resultant network nodes. Bose et al. [3] speculate that random removal of blocks may have a disadvantageous affect on the underlying design properties and hence become an issue of concern.

Fortunately, this claim of Bose et al. has been successfully challenged by Henry et al. [16]. Through practical experiments, they establish that random removal of key rings of a combinatorial KPS has negligible effect on underlying (crucial) design properties with overwhelming probability. This work reestablishes the importance of combinatorial schemes. An updated study of KPS based on combinatorial schemes can be traced in [22] and the references therein.

2.4 KPS for DSN (IoT in General): Desirable Design Criteria

Devices of an IoT (for instance, sensors of a DSN) are highly prone to damage and/or physical capture. This is a crucial consideration while designing any KPS. Primary objectives of any KPS is to ensure that the resulting network:

1. has less number of keys per node, i.e., sizes of individual key rings are less;
2. have large *node support*, i.e., support large number of network nodes;
3. has good (ideally full secure) connectivity. *Secure connectivity* or simply *connectivity* is the ratio of number of (secure) links in eventual network to all possible links. A pair of nodes are said to be connected by a (secure) link if there exists at least one secret key between them;
4. is *resilient* against adversarial attacks. A prevailing method adopted in most existing works [6,19,20,22] is to show that the standard resiliency coefficient $\mathtt{fail}(t)$ is minimized. This work will follow suit. The quantifier $\mathtt{fail}(t)$ measures the ratio of links broken after compromise of t sensors to the total number of links in the remaining network. Notationally:

$$\mathtt{fail}(t) = \frac{\text{Number of links broken when } t \text{ nodes are compromised}}{\text{total links among uncompromised nodes of remaining network}}.$$

Ideally, a KPS should have small key rings, and yet support large number of nodes with appreciable resiliency, scalability and connectivity. However, renowned scientists proved the impossibility of constructing a 'perfect KPS' that meet all these criteria [20–22]. This motivates continual research to propose adequate designs that are robust for specific applications.

3 Preliminary

In this section we introduce the definitions and notations which will be used to describe the schemes presented in this paper.

3.1   Combinatorial Set Systems and KPS

There have been several papers that have used combinatorial design technique on the basic idea presented in [15]. The use of different combinatorial designs was primarily presented in paper [19,20] for having deterministic KPS. After then there are several KPS based on combinatorial designs have been proposed. A survey on KPS in WSN are available by Chen and Chao [9]. Recently, Paterson and Stinson have unified the combinatorial design techniques by partially balanced t−design [22]. The same paper has listed the important schemes based on combinatorial designs with proper references.

Let $\mathcal{X}$ be a finite set. The elements of $\mathcal{X}$ are called varieties. Each subset of $\mathcal{X}$ is termed as a block. Consider $\mathcal{A}$ to be a collection of blocks of $\mathcal{X}$. Then the pair $(\mathcal{X}, \mathcal{A})$ is said to be a *set system or, a design*. $(\mathcal{X}, \mathcal{A})$ is regular (of degree r) if each point is contained in r blocks. $(\mathcal{X}, \mathcal{A})$ is uniform (of rank k) if all blocks have the same size, say k.

Further, a design $(\mathcal{X}, \mathcal{A})$ is said to form a $(v, b, r, k) − 1 − design$ if

− $|\mathcal{X}| = v$ and $|\mathcal{A}| = b$;
− $(\mathcal{X}, \mathcal{A})$ is regular of degree r and uniform of rank k.

A $(v, b, r, k) − 1 −$design forms a $(v, b, r, k) − configuration$ if any arbitrary pair of blocks intersect in *at most* one point. Moreover, if any pairs of varieties occur in exactly λ block, then a $(v, b, r, k) − 1 −$design forms a $(v, b, r, k, \lambda) −$BIBD (Balanced Incomplete Block Designs). These designs can be used to construct various KPS(see [20]) by mapping:

1. the v *varieties* of $|\mathcal{X}|$ to the set of keys in the scheme (i.e., *key pool*),
2. b to the number of nodes in the system (i.e., *network size*),
3. k to the number of keys per node (i.e., *size of key rings*), and
4. r to the number of nodes sharing a key (i.e., *degree of the resultant KPS*).

Target is to construct KPS with identical burden on each sensor. This leads to opting for design with uniform rank (k) and regular degree (r); so that every *key ring* is of equal size (k) and same number of nodes (r) share each key for the resultant network.

A (v, b, r, k)−configuration $(\mathcal{X}, \mathcal{A})$ is said to form a $\mu − common\ intersection\ design(CID)$ in case:

$$|\{A_\alpha \in \mathcal{A} : A_i \cap A_\alpha \neq \emptyset \text{ and } A_j \cap A_\alpha \neq \emptyset\}| \geq \mu \text{ whenever } A_i \cap A_j = \emptyset, \ \forall\ i \neq j.$$

That is, if two nodes A_i and A_j do not share any key then there are at least μ other nodes which share keys with both A_i and A_j. In this case, the nodes A_i and A_j can communicate via another node which share keys with both A_i and A_j. It is important to construct design that maximize the value of μ.

3.2   Bent Boolean Functions

Boolean function is a very interesting entity in the study of cryptography, coding theory and combinatorics. The book by Cusick and Stănică [10] can enlighten

the reader about the significance of Boolean functions in the study of cryptography. We denote by $\mathbb{F}_2$ the finite field of two elements set $\{0, 1\}$ with the usual
operations $+$ (XOR) and $\cdot$ (AND). Denote V_n be the $n-$dimensional vector space
$\mathbb{F}_2^n$ over $\mathbb{F}_2$ and $\mathbf{0}$ is the zero vector in V_n. A *Boolean function* on n variables is
a mapping from V_n into $\mathbb{F}_2$ and define B_n as the set of all $n-$variable Boolean
functions. One of the standard representation of a Boolean function $f \in B_n$ is
by the output column of its *truth table* in an order of input vectors, i.e., a binary
string of length 2^n,

$$f = [f(0, \cdots, 0, 0), f(0, \cdots, 0, 1), f(0, \cdots, 1, 0), \cdots, f(1, \ldots, 1, 1)].$$

The *support set* of f is defined as $\Omega_f = \{v \in V_n : f(v) = 1\}$. The *Hamming*
weight (in short, *weight*) of $f \in B_n$ is denoted as $\mathsf{wt}(f) = |\Omega_f|$. A Boolean
function $f \in B_n$ is called *balanced* if $\mathsf{wt}(f) = 2^{n-1}$.

A Boolean function can be represented as a multivariate polynomial over $\mathbb{F}_2$,
called the *algebraic normal form* (ANF), as

$$f(x_1, \cdots, x_n) = a_0 + \sum_{1 \leq i \leq n} a_i x_i + \sum_{1 \leq i < j \leq n} a_{i,j} x_i x_j + \cdots + a_{1,2,\cdots,n} x_1 x_2 \cdots x_n,$$

where the coefficients $a_0, a_i, a_{i,j}, \cdots, a_{1,2,\ldots,n} \in \mathbb{F}_2$. The *algebraic degree* (in
short, *degree*), $\deg(f)$, is the number of variables in the highest order term with
non zero coefficient. A Boolean function f is *affine* if the $\deg(f) \leq 1$ and the set
of all affine functions is denoted by A_n.

The *Walsh transform* of $f \in B_n$ is an integer valued function from V_n which
is defined as

$$W_f(\omega) = \sum_{x \in V_n} (-1)^{f(x) + x \cdot \omega}, \text{ for any } \omega \in V_n.$$

The conservation law of the Walsh spectral values of the $n-$variable Boolean
functions, i.e., $\sum_{\omega \in V_n} (W_f(\omega))^2 = 2^{2n}$, is known as Parseval's equality. The *non-*
linearity of $f \in B_n$ is given by $\min\{d(f, l) : l \in A_n\}$ where the distance function
$d(f, g) = |\{v \in V_n : f(v) \neq g(v)\}| = \mathsf{wt}(f + g)$. The nonlinearity of f can be rep-
resented in terms of its Walsh spectra as $nl(f) = 2^{n-1} - \frac{1}{2} \max_{\omega \in V_n} |W_f(\omega)|$. A
function $f \in B_n$ achieves the maximum nonlinearity if and only if $W_f(\omega) = \pm 2^{\frac{n}{2}}$,
for all $\omega \in V_n$ and the nonlinearity is $2^{n-1} - 2^{\frac{n}{2}-1}$. The functions achieving this
value of nonlinearity are called *bent Boolean functions* and they exist only when
n is even [23]. Note that, through out this paper, we call as bent function in
stead of bent Boolean function.

Note 1. Since we are constructing KPS from the bent functions $f \in B_n$ and
underlying Cayley graph is connected, we always consider $n = 2m \geq 4$ is an
even positive integer in the rest part of this paper.

The weight of a bent function is $2^{n-1} - 2^{m-1}$ (unbalanced) and the algebraic
degree of a bent function is at most m for $n \geq 4$. This class of functions are very
important in the literature of cryptography, coding theory and combinatorics.
We refer [26, Sect. 4.3] for the study about the involvement of bent functions in
combinatorial set designs.

Dillon's Bent Function: Partial spreads play fundamental role in this construction of bent functions. A *partial spread* Σ of order s in V_n is a set of pairwise supplementary $m-$dimensional subspaces $E_1, E_2, \cdots, E_s$ of V_n i.e., $E_i \cap E_j = \{0\}$ for all $1 \leq i < j \leq s$. A Boolean function $f \in B_n$ is called in $\mathcal{PS}^+$ if $\Omega_f = \cup_{i=1}^s E_i$ where $s = 2^{m-1} + 1$ and in $\mathcal{PS}^-$ if $\Omega_f = \cup_{i=1}^s E_i^*$ where $s = 2^{m-1}$ and $E_i^* = E_i \setminus \{0\}$. Dillon proposed bent functions in following theorem.

Theorem 1 [12,13]. *The functions from $\mathcal{PS}^+$ or, $\mathcal{PS}^-$ are bent.*

A partial spread Σ is a *spread* if $\cup_{i=1}^s E_i = V_n$, in which case $|\Sigma| = 2^m + 1$. Therefore, from a given spread Σ each of the $\binom{2^m+1}{2^{m-1}+1}$ or, $\binom{2^m+1}{2^{m-1}}$ choices of $2^{m-1} + 1$ (respectively, 2^{m-1}) members of Σ provides a bent function from $\mathcal{PS}^+$ (respectively, $\mathcal{PS}^-$). Recently, the bent functions from partial spreads are restudied using pre-quasifields in the papers [8,17,27].

3.3 Strongly Regular Graph

A graph Γ consists of a finite set V of vertices and an edge set E is a 2$-$element multi-subset of V. We denote edges $\{u, v\}$ as (u, v). The edges of the form (v, v) are called loop. The graphs without loops are called simple graphs. For a vertex $v \in V$, the neighbor of v is defined as $N(v) = \{u : (v, u) \in E\}$ i.e., the set of vertices adjacent to v. The degree of a vertex $v \in V$ is $|N(v)|$ and it is denoted as $\deg(v)$. A graph Γ is regular of degree r (or, $r-$regular) if the degree of each vertex of Γ is r. A *strongly regular graph* with parameters (n, r, λ, μ) (or, $\text{srg}(n, r, \lambda, \mu)$) is a $r-$regular graph with additional property that for each pair of vertices $u, v \in V$, $|N(u) \cap N(v)|$ is equal to λ, μ if u, v are adjacent, respectively, nonadjacent. We refer the draft [5] by Cameron for a detailed study on strongly regular graphs.

3.4 Cayley Graph of Boolean Function and Block Graph of Set Design

Given a Boolean function $f \in B_n$, the *Cayley graph* Γ_f is defined with vertex set Ω_f and edge set E_f as defined

$$E_f = \{(u, v) : u + v \in \Omega_f \text{ i.e., } f(u + v) = 1\}.$$

The graph Γ_f is a regular graph of degree $\text{wt}(f)$. The graph Γ_f is connected if and only if the subspace generated by Ω_f is V_n i.e., $< \Omega_f >= V_n$. If Γ_f is disconnected then the vertex sets of connected components are the cosets of $< \Omega_f >$. We refer [2,10] for detailed study of Cayley graph of Boolean functions.

For $n \geq 4$ and $f \in B_n$ is bent, it can be shown that $< \Omega_f >= V_n$ and hence, Γ_f is connected.

Theorem 2 [10, Theorem 8.7, 8.10]. *A Boolean function $f \in B_n$ ($n = 2m \geq 4$ and even) is bent if and only if its associated Cayley graph Γ_f is strongly regular graph of degree $\text{wt}(f) = 2^{n-1} \pm 2^{m-1}$ and $\lambda = \mu = 2^{n-2} \pm 2^{m-1}$ respectively.*

The *block graph* $\Gamma_{\mathcal{A}}$ of the set design $(\mathcal{X}, \mathcal{A})$ is defined with the vertex set $\mathcal{A}$ and edge set $E_{\mathcal{A}} = \{(A, B) : A, B \in \mathcal{A} \text{ and } A \cap B \neq \emptyset\}$.

4   Bent Boolean Functions and KPS

In this section we present the trivial construction of KPS from bent functions by connecting the support set of bent functions with combinatorial set designs.

Lemma 1 [13]. *A Boolean function $f \in B_n$ is bent if and only if Ω_f is a $(2^n, 2^{n-1} \pm 2^{m-1}, 2^{n-2} \pm 2^{m-1})$ difference set [2] in V_n.*

For any $f \in B_n$ and $v \in V_n$, define the translation $v + \Omega_f = \{v + x : x \in \Omega_f\}$. Then define, $\text{Dev}(\Omega_f) = \{v + \Omega_f : v \in V_n\}$. Now, connecting Lemma 1 with [26, Theorem 3.8], we have

Theorem 3. *If $f \in B_n$ is bent, then $(V_n, Dev(\Omega_f))$ is a symmetric $(2^n, 2^{n-1} \pm 2^{m-1}, 2^{n-2} \pm 2^{m-1})-BIBD$, where $b = v = 2^n$ and $r = k = 2^{n-1} \pm 2^{m-1}$. Therefore, if $f \in B_n$ is bent, then $(V_n, Dev(\Omega_f))$ is a $(2^n, 2^n, 2^{n-1} \pm 2^{m-1}, 2^{n-1} \pm 2^{m-1}) - 1-design.*$

As per the combinatorial construction in [20, Sect. 2], we have a KPS with 2^n nodes, each node containing $2^{n-1} \pm 2^{m-1}$ keys and each key is hold by $2^{n-1} \pm 2^{m-1}$ nodes. Since it is a symmetric BIBD each pair of nodes contain exactly $2^{n-2} \pm 2^{m-1}$ common keys.

Now we shall describe to have KPS with 2^{n+1} nodes (where $n + 1 = 2m + 1$ is odd) from a bent function $f \in B_n$. From another characterization of bent functions due to Dillon [12,13] *a Boolean function f is bent if and only if for any nonzero vector $y \in V_n$ its derivative $D_y(f(x)) = f(x) + f(x + y)$ is balanced*, we have the following type of difference set:

Lemma 2 [12,13]. *A Boolean function $f \in B_n$ is a bent function if and only if the set $\Delta_f = \{(x, f(x)) | x \in V_n\}$ is a $(2^{n+1}, 2^n, 2^{n-1})$ difference set in V_{n+1}.*

Now, again connecting Lemma 2 with [26, Theorem 3.8], we have the following scheme with $b = v = 2^{n+1}$ and $r = k = 2^n$.

Theorem 4. *If $f \in B_n$ is a bent function, then $(V_{n+1}, Dev(\Delta_f))$ is a symmetric $(2^{n+1}, 2^{n+1}, 2^n, 2^n, 2^{n-1})-BIBD$. Therefore, if $f \in B_n$ is a bent function, then $(V_{n+1}, Dev(\Delta_f))$ is a $(2^{n+1}, 2^{n+1}, 2^n, 2^n) - 1-design.*$

By the combinatorial construction in [20, Sect. 2], we have a KPS with 2^{n+1} nodes where each node contains 2^n keys and each key is held by 2^n nodes. Since it is a symmetric BIBD each pair of nodes contain exactly 2^{n-1} common keys.

Remark 1. The above schemes are completely connected. The main disadvantage in both the schemes is storage requirement. In both the cases the number of keys

---

[2] The definition of *difference set* can be found in the book by Stinson [26].

need to be stored at each node is $O(2^n)$, which is same as order of the number of nodes. Hence the schemes may not be preferred for practical applications. We presented the schemes for the shake of theoretical interest. However, in the following section we shall describe another key pre-distribution schemes from a class of bent functions where the number of keys in each block is order of square root of the number of blocks. In fact most prominent protocols [6, 19–21, 25] aim to achieve a same ratio. These design typically burden each sensor with q keys to support a network of size $\mathcal{N} = q^2$ where $q = p^r$ is a prime power [1, 22].

5   KPS from Dillon's Bent Functions

Let f be a bent function from $\mathcal{PS}^+$ or $\mathcal{PS}^-$ where $\Sigma = \{E_1, E_2, \cdots, E_s\}$ be the partial spread in V_n. Therefore, if

1. $f \in \mathcal{PS}^+$ then $s = 2^{m-1}+1$, $\Omega_f = \cup_{i=1}^s E_i$ and $\mathsf{wt}(f) = 2^m(2^{m-1}+1)-2^{m-1} = 2^{2m-1} + 2^{m-1} = 2^{n-1} + 2^{m-1}$.
2. $f \in \mathcal{PS}^-$ then $s = 2^{m-1}$, $\Omega_f = \cup_{i=1}^s E_i^*$ and $\mathsf{wt}(f) = (2^m - 1)2^{m-1} = 2^{2m-1} - 2^{m-1} = 2^{n-1} - 2^{m-1}$.

Let denote and fix $\overline{E}_i$ be a supplementary subspace of E_i in V_n (i.e., their direct sum $E_i \oplus \overline{E}_i = V_n$ and $E_i \cap \overline{E}_i = \{\mathbf{0}\}$). Note that the subspaces E_i's in a partial spread are pairwise supplementary. So, any $E_j, j \neq i$ can be chosen as $\overline{E}_i$. Consider the set system $(\mathcal{X}, \mathcal{A})$ such that $\mathcal{X} = V_n$ and and the set of blocks $\mathcal{A} = \{\alpha + E_i : \alpha \in \overline{E}_i \text{ and } 1 \leq i \leq s\}$ i.e., set of all cosets of E_i's.

Theorem 5. *The set design $(\mathcal{X}, \mathcal{A})$ is a $\mu(2^n, s2^m, s, 2^m)-CID$ where $\mu = (s - 1)2^m$.*

Proof. Here $v = |\mathcal{X}| = 2^n$. Consider two blocks $\alpha + E_i$ and $\beta + E_j$. Now we have the following cases.

1. If $i = j$, then
   (a) $\alpha + E_i = \beta + E_j$ if $\alpha = \beta$ or,
   (b) $(\alpha + E_i) \cap (\beta + E_j) = \emptyset$ if $\alpha \neq \beta$.
2. If $i \neq j$, then we shall show that $|(\alpha + E_i) \cap (\beta + E_j)| = 1$. Since E_i and E_j are supplementary to each other, the element $\alpha + \beta \in V_n$ can be uniquely expressed as $u + v$ where $u \in E_i$ and $v \in E_j$. That is, $\alpha + \beta = u + v$ which implies, $\alpha + u = \beta + v$ is the unique element in $(\alpha + E_i) \cap (\beta + E_j)$.

Therefore, the number of blocks i.e., the number of cosets is $b = s2^m$ and each block contains $k = 2^m$ elements. Given a subspace $E_i, i \in \{1, 2, \cdots, s\}$, each element $u \in V_n$ belongs to exactly one coset of E_i. So, each $u \in V_n$ belongs to exactly s many blocks in $\mathcal{A}$. The set design $(\mathcal{X}, \mathcal{A})$ is regular with $r = s$. Here, every two distinct blocks intersect each other by at most one element which implies that $(\mathcal{X}, \mathcal{A})$ is a $(2^n, s2^m, s, 2^m)-$configuration.

We see that two blocks $\alpha + E_i$ and $\beta + E_j$ does not intersect iff $i = j$ and $\alpha \neq \beta$ i.e., both are distinct cosets of same subspace E_i. For the case of non intersecting blocks $\alpha + E_i$ and $\beta + E_i$, $\alpha \neq \beta$, both blocks intersect all other blocks of the form $\gamma + E_j$ where $j \neq i$. Since there are $\mu = (s - 1)2^m$ such blocks $\gamma + E_j$ in $\mathcal{A}$, $(\mathcal{X}, \mathcal{A})$ is a $(s - 1)2^m(2^n, s2^m, s, 2^m)-$CID. □

It also can easily be checked that the block graph of $(\mathcal{X}, \mathcal{A})$ is a strongly regular graph with parameters $(n = s2^m, r = (s-1)2^m, \lambda = (s-2)2^m, \mu = (s-1)2^m)$. In the study of finite geometry, the varieties together with the blocks (i.e., cosets) form the points and lines of an affine plane. Two non-parallel lines (i.e., $\alpha + E_i$ and $\beta + E_j$ for $i \neq j$) intersect at one point.

Example 1. This example is from a simple bent function $f(x_1, x_2, x_3, x_4) = 1 + x_1 x_2 + x_3 x_4 \in B_4$. Let represent each vector by its integer value. Hence, $\Omega_f = \{0, 1, 2, 4, 5, 6, 8, 9, 10, 15\} = E_1 \cup E_2 \cup E_3$ where $E_1 = \{0, 1, 4, 5\}, E_2 = \{0, 2, 8, 10\}$ and $E_3 = \{0, 6, 9, 15\}$. So, the scheme $(\mathcal{X}, \mathcal{A})$, where $\mathcal{X} = V_4$ and $\mathcal{A} = \{E_1, 2+E_1, 8+E_1, 10+E_1, E_2, 1+E_2, 4+E_2, 5+E_2, E_3, 1+E_3, 2+E_3, 3+E_3\}$, is a $8(16, 12, 3, 4)-$CID.

Example 2. Dillon studied a subclass denoted $\mathcal{PS}_{ap}$ of $\mathcal{PS}^-$ to construct a class of bent functions which can be presented in explicit form. Here, we consider $\mathbb{F}_{2^n}$ as a vector space V_n and identified with $\mathbb{F}_{2^m} \times \mathbb{F}_{2^m}$. The partial spread class $\mathcal{PS}_{ap}$ consists of the functions f on $\mathbb{F}_{2^m} \times \mathbb{F}_{2^m}$ of the form $f(x, y) = g(xy^{2^m-2})$ where g is a balanced function on $\mathbb{F}_{2^m}$ with $g(0) = 0$. For $a \in \mathbb{F}_2^m$, define the subspace $E_a = \{(ax, x) : x \in \mathbb{F}_2^m\}$ of dimension m. For $(ax, x) \in E_a, f(ax, x) = g(ax.x^{2^m-2}) = g(ax^{2^m-1})$ i.e., $f(ax, x) = g(a)$ when $x \neq \mathbf{0}$ and 0 when $x = \mathbf{0}$. Since g is balanced, $\Sigma = \{E_a : a \in \Omega_g\}$ forms a partial spread in $\mathbb{F}_{2^n}$ and f is a bent function from $\mathcal{PS}^-$.

Let $(\mathcal{Y}, \mathcal{B})$ be the dual design of $(\mathcal{X}, \mathcal{A})$. Then $\mathcal{Y} = \mathcal{A}$ i.e., the set of all cosets of E_i's and $\mathcal{B} = \{Z_v : v \in V_n\}$ where $Z_v = \{A : v \in A$ and $A \in \mathcal{A}\}$ i.e., set of cosets containing v. Now we have the following design.

Lemma 3. *The dual design $(\mathcal{Y}, \mathcal{B})$ of $(\mathcal{X}, \mathcal{A})$ is a $(s2^m, 2^n, 2^m, s)-$configuration.*

Proof. Here $v = |\mathcal{Y}| = s2^m$ and $b = |\mathcal{B}| = 2^n$. Since each $v \in V_n$ belongs to s cosets, the rank of each Z_v in $\mathcal{B}$ is $k = |Z_v| = s$. Moreover, as each coset contains 2^m vectors of V_n, a coset is contained in 2^m many Z_v's for each v in that coset i.e., degree of each block is $r = 2^m$.

To complete the proof we need to show that $(\mathcal{Y}, \mathcal{B})$ is a configuration i.e., $|Z_u \cap Z_v| \leq 1$ for distinct $u, v \in V_n$. That is, we need to show that every distinct pair $u, v \in V_n$ belongs to at most one coset. Let $u, v \in (\alpha + E_i) \cap (\beta + E_j)$. It is clear that $i \neq j$. Then $u = \alpha + w_1 = \beta + z_1$ and $v = \alpha + w_2 = \beta + z_2$ for some $w_1, w_2 \in E_i$ and $z_1, z_2 \in E_j$. So, $\alpha + \beta = w_1 + z_1 = w_2 + z_2$. Since E_i and E_j are supplementary to each other, $w_1 = w_2$ and $z_1 = z_2$. That is, $u = v$. $\square$

Lemma 4. *The block graph $\Gamma_\mathcal{B}$ of the set design $(\mathcal{Y}, \mathcal{B})$ is isomorphic to the Cayley graph Γ_f of $f \in B_n$ from $\mathcal{PS}^+$ or $\mathcal{PS}^-$ with the partial spread $\Sigma = \{E_1, E_2, \cdots, E_s\}$.*

Proof. The correspondence between the vertex set $\mathcal{B}$ of $\Gamma_\mathcal{B}$ and vertex set V_n of Γ_f is from Z_v to v. (Z_u, Z_v) is an edge in $\Gamma_\mathcal{B}$ iff there is a coset $A \in \mathcal{A}$ such that $u, v \in A$ iff there is a subspace E_i such that $u + v \in E_i$ iff (u, v) is an edge in Γ_f. $\square$

As the Cayley graph Γ_f is a strongly regular graph with $\lambda = \mu = 2^{n-2} \pm 2^{m-1}$ [from Theorem 2], we have the following design.

Theorem 6. *The set design* $(\mathcal{Y}, \mathcal{B})$ *is a* $\mu(s2^m, 2^n, 2^m, s) - CID$ *where*

$$\mu = \begin{cases} 2^{n-2} + 2^{m-1} & if\ s = 2^{m-1} + 1 \\ 2^{n-2} - 2^{m-1} & if\ s = 2^{m-1}. \end{cases}$$

Example 3. We return to Example 1 and identify the cosets in $\mathcal{A}$ as $L_1, L_2, \cdots, L_{12}$ in the order the cosets written in $\mathcal{A}$. Here, the scheme $(\mathcal{Y}, \mathcal{B})$, where $\mathcal{Y} = \{L_1, L_2, \cdots, L_{12}\}$ and $\mathcal{B} = \{Z_v : v \in B_4\}$ and $Z_v = \{i : v \in L_i, 1 \le i \le 12\}$, is a $6(12, 16, 4, 3) - CID$.

In this section we presented constructions with number of nodes (i.e., b) 2^{n-1} and $2^{n-1} + 2^m$ in Theorem 5 and 2^n in Theorem 6. In both the cases, the number of keys need to be stored is $O(2^m)$ i.e., order of square root of number of nodes. These schemes has storage space advantage over the trivial schemes presented in previous section.

6   Analysis of the Schemes: Comparative Study

There are various metrics that evaluate different performance and security aspects of a KPS for a wireless sensor network. We analyze our schemes (described in Sect. 5) on the basis of four of these metrics. For the remaining party of the paper, we denote the schemes proposed in Theorem 5 and 6 by $(\mathcal{X}, \mathcal{A})$ and $(\mathcal{Y}, \mathcal{B})$ respectively.

6.1   Key-Node Ratio $(\sigma(n))$

The *key-node ratio* is defined as $\sigma = \frac{k}{b}$. This ratio provides idea about the storage requirement of the scheme at each node with respect to the total number of nodes. The value of σ closer zero implies lesser amount of memory required for key storage at each node. In our constructions, both the schemes $(\mathcal{X}, \mathcal{A})$ and $(\mathcal{Y}, \mathcal{B})$ have key-node ratio $\sigma(n) = O(2^{-m}) = O(2^{-\frac{n}{2}})$.

6.2   Key Establishment and Time Complexity

In this subsection, we discuss about the process of key establishment between two nodes and time complexity of the process. There are two ways of key establishment. One is shared key discovery if two nodes have a common key and other is path key agreement by two hops if there is no common key between two nodes. In the later case, both the nodes has to find a common neighbor node with whom they discover their share key and establish connection between them. Here, we will discuss about the key establishment process of both the schemes presented in Sect. 5.

KPS Using the Set Design $(\mathcal{X}, \mathcal{A})$: In this scheme the key establishment is done using the node id. Let $\beta_i^1, \beta_i^2, \cdots, \beta_i^m$ be a basis set of the subspace E_i for $1 \leq i \leq s$. Then, the node $\alpha + E_i$ can be identified by the node id $(\alpha, \beta_i^1, \beta_i^2, \cdots, \beta_i^m)$. When the node $\alpha + E_i$ wants for key establishment with another node $\beta + E_j$, then they can follow the following arguments to discover the common key.

Step 1: The nodes $\alpha + E_i$ and $\beta + E_j$ compare the last m vectors (i.e., basis vectors) in their node id. If they are same then follow Step 3 otherwise follow Step 2.

Step 2: In this case, the $E_i \neq E_j$ i.e., they share a common key. Let the common key is $\alpha + u = \beta + v$ where $u \in E_i$ and $v \in E_j$. Now we need to find u and v in terms of the basis vectors of E_i and E_j respectively. Here, $\alpha + \beta = u + v \in V_n$. Since E_i and E_j are supplementary subspaces in V_n, $\alpha + \beta$ can be uniquely expressed as a linear combination of the basis vectors of E_i and E_j. Let $\alpha + \beta = (b_1 \beta_i^1 + \cdots + b_m \beta_i^m) + (b_{m+1} \beta_j^1 + \cdots + b_n \beta_j^m)$, where $b_i \in \mathbb{F}_2$. That is, $\alpha + b_1 \beta_i^1 + \cdots + b_m \beta_i^m = \beta + b_{m+1} \beta_j^1 + \cdots + b_n \beta_j^m$. Hence, the common key is $\alpha + b_1 \beta_i^1 + \cdots + b_m \beta_i^m = \beta + b_{m+1} \beta_j^1 + \cdots + b_n \beta_j^m \in E_i \cap E_j$. The time complexity in this step is the time complexity to express $\alpha + \beta$ in terms of the basis vectors in a basis i.e., $O(n^3)$.

Step 3: In this case, the $E_i = E_j$ i.e., they do not share any common key. In this case, they have to establish connection through another node with whom they share a key. That is, they have to find a node $\gamma + E_k$ where $k \neq i$. The probability of finding such a node using a random pick up is $\frac{s-1}{s}$ which is very high. Since both $\alpha + E_i$ and $\beta + E_j$ share a key with $\gamma + E_k$, each one do the same process described in Step 2 with $\gamma + E_k$ to discover their common key. After then $\alpha + E_i$ and $\beta + E_j$ can establish connection through $\gamma + E_k$. Hence, in step the time complexity is $O(n^3)$.

Therefore, each node needs $(m+1)*n = O(n^2)$ bits of memory for their identification and the time complexity to discover the common key(s) for the connection establishment is $O(n^3)$. Here, the nodes have to broadcast only node id i.e., $O(n^2)$ bits instead of all (i.e., $O(2^m)$ many) key ids as many other KPS.

KPS Using the Set Design $(\mathcal{Y}, \mathcal{B})$: Let f be the bent function used for this scheme, where $\Omega_f = \cup_{i=1}^s E_i$. In this scheme two distinct nodes Z_u, Z_v share a common key if and only if $u + v \in \Omega_f$. It seems that the node id computation technique to find common key will not work for this scheme.

The common key can be found by comparing all the key ids (in an order). When two nodes Z_u and Z_v wants to establish connection, they need to search for common key id by linear comparison of their key ids which takes $O(s)$ time complexity. If the common key is found then it is done. Otherwise they have to communicate through another node Z_w where both have common key. Since they have $\mu = 2^{n-2} \pm 2^{m-1}$ common neighbors Z_w, the probability of finding such Z_w is $\frac{\mu}{2^n} \approx \frac{1}{4}$. After finding such common neighbor Z_w, both Z_u and Z_v discover their common key with Z_w by linear comparisons which takes $O(s)$ time complexity. The key establishment process of the scheme $(\mathcal{Y}, \mathcal{B})$ is very slow in comparison with the earlier scheme $(\mathcal{X}, \mathcal{A})$.

6.3   Resiliency(fail(t))

We prove our scheme is well equipped to perform against adversarial attacks. To this end, we establish that a standard resiliency metric fail(t) is minimized. This is prevalent method adopted by most existing works [1,6,19,20,22]. The quantifier fail(t) measures the probability that a random link between two sensors is broken due to the compromise of t other random nodes not in the link. Notationally:

$$\text{fail}(t) = \frac{\text{No. of links broken when } t \text{ nodes are compromised}}{\text{No. of links among uncompromised nodes of remaining network}}.$$

Theorem 7 is due to Lee and Stinson in [20, Sect. 8] provides the formula to compute fail(t) for any $(v, b, r, k)-$ configuration.

Theorem 7. *For any $(v, b, r, k)-$configuration, the value of the metric* fail(t) *on random compromise of t nodes is given by:*

$$\text{fail}(t) = 1 - \left(\frac{b - r}{b - 2}\right)^t. \tag{1}$$

Corollaries 1 and 2 are immediate outcomes of substituting in Eq. 1, the values of b and r, that our design achieves.

Corollary 1. *The value of the resilience metric* fail(t) *for the set system* $(\mathcal{X}, \mathcal{A})$, *which is a* $(2^n, s2^m, s, 2^m)-$configuration *is:*

$$\text{fail}(t) = 1 - \left(\frac{s2^m - s}{s2^m - 2}\right)^t.$$

In particular,

$$\text{fail}(1) = \frac{s - 2}{s2^m - 2} \approx 2^{-m}.$$

Corollary 2. *The value of the resilience metric* fail(t) *for the set system* $(\mathcal{Y}, \mathcal{B})$, *which is a* $(s2^m, 2^n, 2^m, s)-$configuration *is:*

$$\text{fail}(t) = 1 - \left(\frac{2^n - 2^m}{2^n - 2}\right)^t.$$

In particular,

$$\text{fail}(1) = \frac{2^m - 2}{2^n - 2} \approx 2^{-m}.$$

In both the schemes, the metric fail(1) $= O(2^{-m})$ i.e., if a node N is compromised, then the probability that a link (which is not incident with N) fails is $O(2^{-m})$. For example, if $n = 10$ (i.e., there are approximately 2^{10} many nodes) then the value fail(1) ≈ 0.03.

6.4   Connectivity

We say two blocks in a set system are connected by e−link (or, are at a distance e) if the shortest path between them in the block graph includes e edges. Hence, we define the metric connectivity (or, connection probability) p_e of the network to be the probability that two nodes (placed in physical neighborhood) are connected by e−links for a fixed e.

Observe that the value of e for a μ−CID with $\mu > 1$ is either 1 (if they share a key) or 2 (if they do not share a key). Theorems 5 and 6 states that $\mu = (s-1)2^m$ and $\mu = 2^{n-2} \pm 2^{m-1}$ for the schemes based on $(\mathcal{X}, \mathcal{A})$ and its dual $(\mathcal{Y}, \mathcal{B})$.

The formulae for p_1 and p_2 are provided in [20, Sect. 6], which are being formally restated in the following theorem. Let η denote the number of nodes in the intersection of the physical neighborhood of two given nodes.

Theorem 8. *The connection probabilities of a $\mu(v,b,r,k)$-CID are given by*

$$p_1 = \frac{k(r-1)}{b-1} \text{ and } p_2 \approx (1-p_1) \times \left(1 - \left(\frac{b-\mu-2}{b-2}\right)^\eta\right).$$

Following two corollaries are immediate outcome for our schemes by substituting the values of b, r, k and λ in Theorem 8.

Corollary 3. *The value of the connectivities for the set system $(\mathcal{X}, \mathcal{A})$, which is a $(s-1)2^m(2^n, s2^m, s, 2^m)$−CID, are*

$$p_1 \approx 1 - \frac{1}{s} \text{ and } p_2 \approx \frac{s^\eta - 1}{s^{\eta+1}}.$$

Proof. Now putting the value of $b = s2^m, r = s, k = 2^m$ and $\mu = (s-1)2^m$ in p_1 and p_2, we have

$$p_1 = \frac{2^m(s-1)}{s2^m-1} = \frac{s2^m-2^m}{s2^m-1} = 1 - \frac{2^m-1}{s2^m-1} \approx 1 - \frac{1}{s},$$

$$\text{and } p_2 \approx \frac{1}{s}\left(1 - \left(\frac{s2^m-(s-1)2^m-2}{s2^m-2}\right)^\eta\right) = \frac{1}{s}\left(1 - \left(\frac{2^m-2}{s2^m-2}\right)^\eta\right)$$

$$\approx \frac{1}{s}\left(1 - \frac{1}{s^\eta}\right) = \frac{s^\eta-1}{s^{\eta+1}}.$$
$\square$

Corollary 4. *The value of the connectivities for the set system $(\mathcal{Y}, \mathcal{B})$, which is a $\mu(s2^m, 2^n, 2^m, s)$−CID, are*

$$p_1 \approx \frac{1}{2} \pm \frac{1}{2^{m+1}} \text{ and } p_2 = (1-p_1)\left(1 - \left(\frac{3}{4}\right)^\eta\right).$$

Proof. Now putting the value of $b = 2^n, r = 2^m, k = s, \mu = 2^{n-2} \pm 2^{m-1}$ and $s = 2^{m-1}+1$ or, 2^{m-1} for p_1 and p_2, we have

$$p_1 = \frac{s(2^m-1)}{2^n-1} \approx \frac{2^{n-1} \pm 2^{m-1}}{2^n-1} \approx \frac{1}{2} \pm \frac{2^{m-1}}{2^n-1} \approx \frac{1}{2} \pm \frac{1}{2^{m+1}},$$

$$\text{and } p_2 \approx (1-p_1)\left(1 - \left(\frac{2^n-(2^{n-2} \pm 2^{m-1})-2}{2^n-2}\right)^\eta\right) \approx (1-p_1)\left(1 - \left(\frac{3}{4}\right)^\eta\right).$$
$\square$

Remark 2. From the above analysis of our schemes, it is evident that the scheme based on $(\mathcal{X}, \mathcal{A})$ outperforms the scheme based its dual $(\mathcal{Y}, \mathcal{B})$ in terms of the time complexity and the amount of broadcasted data during the key establishment. Moreover, our former scheme out scores our later scheme in providing better connectivity for similar storage and resiliency factor.

7 Comparative Study

This section presents a comparative study of our Dillon type schemes, $(\mathcal{X}, \mathcal{A})$ and $(\mathcal{Y}, \mathcal{B})$, with prominent existing works with respect to resilience and network scaling. Performance of our schemes with respect to other metric like storage connectivity, etc. has been discuss in Sect. 6 (refer to Remarks 1 and 2).

7.1 Connectivity and Resiliency Tradeoff

There have been several proposals for deterministic key predistribution schemes for wireless sensor networks based on various types of combinatorial structures such as designs and codes. The paper [22] proposes a general framework by unifying those structures into a new design, termed as "partially balanced t-designs(PBtD)". Although, our schemes falls into $2 - (v, k, \lambda_0 = b, \lambda_1 = r)$−PBtD as a configuration, their generalization does not consider μ−CIDs. Hence, being a μ−CID, our schemes do not classify as PBtD by their description [22]. There are few comparison tables of different schemes are provided in [22]. In the following, we take data of $\mathrm{TD}(t, k, n)$ with intersection threshold $\eta = 1$ from the paper [22] along with other designs to compare with our schemes.

Let consider the number of nodes in all the compared scheme is $\mathcal{N}$. Now we will compare the asymptotic behavior of metrics p_1, $\mathtt{fail}(1)$ and the ratio $\rho = \frac{p_1}{\mathtt{fail}(1)}$. It is desirable that the ratio ρ be as large as possible. The comparison is displayed in Table 1.

From this comparison table it is clear that the asymptotic behavior of the ratio ρ of our scheme $(\mathcal{X}, \mathcal{A})$ is similar or better than all other schemes except the scheme $\mathrm{TD}(3,k,q)$, $k = q$ and Merging Block (MB) design of [1]. The later has significantly less (merging) block support (halved). Moreover, in our scheme $(\mathcal{X}, \mathcal{A})$, the shared key discovery is done with time complexity $O((\log N)^3)$ and the amount of data need to be broadcasted is $O((\log N)^2)$. This is an added advantage over most KPS that require key id comparisons for key discovery including our dual scheme $(\mathcal{Y}, \mathcal{B})$.

7.2 Scalability Comparison

Our Dillon type schemes, $(\mathcal{X}, \mathcal{A})$ and $(\mathcal{Y}, \mathcal{B})$ can support large networks. This is because the choice n and respectively m and/or s are unbounded in theory. This may help in scaling networks designed by our schemes (prefix large values).

Scalability, otherwise is a major challenge in most deterministic KPS. For instance the schemes [6, 19–21, 25] have restricted scaling. This owes to the fact

Table 1. Comparison of asymptotic behavior of different schemes.

Scheme	No. of nodes	p_1	fail(1)	$\rho = \frac{p_1}{\text{fail}(1)}$
$(\mathcal{X}, \mathcal{A})$	$\mathcal{N} = s2^m \approx 2^{n-1}$	$1 - \frac{1}{s} = 1 - \frac{1}{\sqrt{\mathcal{N}/2}}$	$\approx \frac{1}{\sqrt{2\mathcal{N}}}$	$\approx \sqrt{2\mathcal{N}} - 2$
$(\mathcal{Y}, \mathcal{B})$	$\mathcal{N} = 2^n$	$\frac{1}{2} \pm \frac{1}{2^{m+1}} = \frac{1}{2} \pm \frac{1}{2\sqrt{\mathcal{N}}}$	$\approx \frac{1}{\sqrt{\mathcal{N}}}$	$\approx \frac{\sqrt{\mathcal{N}} \pm 1}{2}$
$TD(2,k,q)$, $k = cn$ [22]	$\mathcal{N} = q^2$	c	$\approx 1/\sqrt{\mathcal{N}}$	$\approx c\sqrt{\mathcal{N}}$
$TD(3,k,q)$, $k = cq, c < 1$ [22]	$\mathcal{N} = q^3$	$c(2-c)/2$	$2(1-c)/\mathcal{N}^{1/3}$	$\frac{c(2-c)^2}{4(1-c)}\mathcal{N}^{1/3}$
$TD(3,k,q)$, $k = q$ [22]	$\mathcal{N} = q^3$	$1/2$	$\approx 5/\mathcal{N}^{2/3}$	$\approx \mathcal{N}^{2/3}/10$
Symmetric BIBD of [6]	$\mathcal{N} = q^2 + q + 1$	1	$\approx 1/\sqrt{\mathcal{N}}$	$\approx \sqrt{\mathcal{N}}$
RS code based design of [25]	$\mathcal{N} = q^2$	$\frac{q-1}{q+1}$	$\frac{q-2}{q^2-2} \approx 1/\sqrt{\mathcal{N}}$	$\approx \sqrt{\mathcal{N}}$
MB designs of [1] for $TD(2,k,q)$ or RS code	$\mathcal{N} = q^2/2$	1	$\frac{q/2-2}{q^2/2-2} \approx 1/\sqrt{2\mathcal{N}}$	$\approx \sqrt{2\mathcal{N}}$

that key establishment for these network require general solutions of polynomials. Therefore, the complexity of the key establishment process increases with increment in degree of these polynomials. The hallmark Abel-Ruffini theorem states that (general) algebraic solutions of quintic polynomials in not possible. Random schemes can scalable arbitrarily [24]; at the expense of desirable parameters like connectivity, resilience, storage (key-node ratio), etc. Therefore, we opt deterministic schemes while designing KPS [22]. Also refer to Sect. 2.3.

8   Conclusion and Future Work

Realizing the need of deterministic KPS with desirable properties (set out in Sect. 2.4) to address the problem of key management in low cost networks, we propose four such schemes. Our schemes are constructed using bent functions. Of particular interest are the later two schemes whose block graphs are dual to each other. These schemes are based on Dillon's bent functions, also known as partial spreads. Rigorous analysis show that our first proposal is better suited to design KPS as compared to its dual and other prominent existing protocols.

Both our proposed block designs suffers from lack of full connectivity. Though the generic computations in Sect. 6.4 establish that the connectivity of our both schemes is good (either direct or 1−hop path connectivity), it is preferable to have full connectivity or at least a deterministic path in case of 1−hop connectivity. The sophisticated MB designs of [1,11] establishes a deterministic 1−hop connectivity for the Reed Solomon code based KPS [25]. These heavily design dependent works can certainly open the doors for future research by considering similar constructions over our schemes in place of [25].

Acknowledgement. This work was accomplished during Dr. Pinaki Sarkar's tenure as a post doctoral fellow at Indian Institute of Science (IISc), Bangalore. The author would like to cordially thank Defense Research Development Organization (DRDO), India for funding his post doctoral research program at IISc, Bangalore.

References

1. Bag, S., Dhar, A., Sarkar, P.: 100% connectivity for location aware code based KPD in clustered WSN: merging blocks. In: Gollmann, D., Freiling, F.C. (eds.) ISC 2012. LNCS, vol. 7483, pp. 136–150. Springer, Heidelberg (2012). doi:10.1007/978-3-642-33383-5_9
2. Bernasconi, A., Codenotti, B.: Spectral analysis of boolean functions as a graph eigenvalue problem. IEEE Trans. Comput. **48**(3), 345–351 (1999)
3. Bose, M., Dey, A., Mukerjee, R.: Key predistribution schemes for distributed sensor networks via block designs. Des. Codes Crypt. **67**(1), 111–136 (2013)
4. Blom, R.: An optimal class of symmetric key generation systems. In: Beth, T., Cot, N., Ingemarsson, I. (eds.) EUROCRYPT 1984. LNCS, vol. 209, pp. 335–338. Springer, Heidelberg (1985). doi:10.1007/3-540-39757-4_22
5. Cameron, P.J.: Strongly regular graphs. Preprint (2001). http://designtheory.org/library/preprints/srg.pdf
6. Çamtepe, S.A., Yener, B.: Combinatorial design of key distribution mechanisms for wireless sensor networks. In: Samarati, P., Ryan, P., Gollmann, D., Molva, R. (eds.) ESORICS 2004. LNCS, vol. 3193, pp. 293–308. Springer, Heidelberg (2004). doi:10.1007/978-3-540-30108-0_18
7. Çamtepe, S.A., Yener, B.: Key Distribution Mechanisms for Wireless Sensor Networks: a Survey. Technical report. Rensselaer Polytechnic Institute (2005)
8. Carlet, C.: More ps and h-like bent functions (2015). http://eprint.iacr.org/2015/168
9. Chen, C.Y., Chao, H.C.: A survey of key predistribution in wireless sensor networks. Secur. Commun. Netw. (2011)
10. Cusick, T.W., Stănică, P.: Cryptographic Boolean Functions and Applications. Academic Press, Elsevier (2009)
11. Dhar, A., Sarkar, P.: Full Communication in a Wireless Sensor Network by Merging Blocks of a Key Predistribution Using Reed Solomon Code (2011)
12. Dillon, J.F.: A survey of bent functions. NSA Tech. J., 191–215, 1972
13. Dillon, J.F.: Elementary Hadamard Difference sets. Ph.D thesis, University of Maryland (1974)
14. Erdős, P., Rényi, A.: On the evolution of random graphs. In: Publication of the Mathematical Institute of the Hungarian Academy of Sciences, pp. 17–61 (1960)
15. Eschenauer, L., Gligor, V.: A key-management scheme for distributed sensor networks. In: 9th ACM Conference on Computer and Communications Security, pp. 41–47. ACM Press, New York (2002)
16. Henry, K., Paterson, M.B., Stinson, D.R.: Practical approaches to varying network size in combinatorial key predistribution schemes. In: Lange, T., Lauter, K., Lisoněk, P. (eds.) SAC 2013. LNCS, vol. 8282, pp. 89–117. Springer, Heidelberg (2014). doi:10.1007/978-3-662-43414-7_5
17. Kantor, W.M.: Bent functions and spreads (2005). http://pages.uoregon.edu/kantor/PAPERS/Bent+spreadsFinal.pdf
18. Steiner, J.G., Neuman, B.C., Schiller, J.I.: Kerberos: an authentication service for open network systems. In: USENIX Winter, pp. 191–202 (1988)

19. Lee, J., Stinson, D.R.: Deterministic key predistribution schemes for distributed sensor networks. In: Handschuh, H., Hasan, M.A. (eds.) SAC 2004. LNCS, vol. 3357, pp. 294–307. Springer, Heidelberg (2004). doi:10.1007/978-3-540-30564-4_21

20. Lee, J., Stinson, D.R.: A combinatorial approach to key predistribution for distributed sensor networks. In: IEEE Wireless Communications and Networking Conference, WCNC 2005, pp. 1200–1205 (2005)

21. Lee, J., Stinson, D.R.: On the construction of practical key predistribution schemes for distributed sensor networks using combinatorial designs. ACM Trans. Inf. Syst. Secur. **11**(2), 1–35 (2008)

22. Paterson, M.B., Stinson, D.R.: A unified approach to combinatorial key predistribution schemes for sensor networks. Des. Codes Crypt. **71**(3), 433–457 (2014)

23. Rothaus, O.S.: On bent functions. J. Comb. Theo. Ser. A **20**, 300–305 (1976)

24. Ruj, S., Pal, A.: Preferential attachment model with degree bound and its application to key predistribution in WSN. In: 30th IEEE International Conference on Advanced Information Networking and Applications, AINA 2016, Crans-Montana, Switzerland, 23–25, pp. 677–683, March 2016

25. Ruj, S., Roy, B.K.: Key predistribution schemes using codes in wireless sensor networks. In: 4th International Conference on Information Security and Cryptology, Inscrypt 2008, Beijing, China, December 14–17, Revised Selected Papers, pp. 275–288 (2008)

26. Stinson, D.R., Designs, C.: Constructions and Analysis. Springer, New York (2003)

27. Wu, B.: PS bent functions constructed from finite pre-quasifield spreads (2013). http://arxiv.org/pdf/1308.3355.pdf

28. Wei, R., Wu, J.: Product Construction of Key Distribution Schemes for Sensor Networks. In: Handschuh, H., Hasan, M.A. (eds.) SAC 2004. LNCS, vol. 3357, pp. 280–293. Springer, Heidelberg (2004). doi:10.1007/978-3-540-30564-4_20

One-Round Cross-Domain Group Key Exchange Protocol in the Standard Model

Xiao Lan[1,4], Jing Xu[2(✉)], Hui Guo[3], and Zhenfeng Zhang[2]

[1] State Key Laboratory of Information Security,
Institute of Information Engineering, Chinese Academy of Sciences, Beijing, China
lanxiao@iie.ac.cn
[2] Trusted Computing and Information Assurance Laboratory,
Institute of Software, Chinese Academy of Sciences, Beijing, China
{xujing,zfzhang}@tca.iscas.ac.cn
[3] State Key Laboratory of Cryptology, Beijing, China
sklcguohui@163.com
[4] University of Chinese Academy of Sciences, Beijing, China

Abstract. Cross-domain group key exchange protocols enable participants from different domains, even with various cryptographic settings and system parameters, to establish a common secret session key. In prior cross-domain key exchange works, only the case of two communication parties is considered, and the two parties are required to adopt a common cryptographic setting (e.g., identity-based setting) or shared parameters (e.g., algebraic group), which is not suitable for group data sharing in many cross-domain interoperability scenarios. In this paper, we present the first one-round cross-domain group key exchange protocol, and by using indistinguishability obfuscation as the main tool, we prove our construction can achieve the desired security properties in the standard model. It is especially attractive for our protocol that existing PKIs can be used and all participants do not have to accommodate any other peers (even do not need to know other peers' algebraic settings) to agree on the session key.

Keywords: Group key exchange protocol · Cross-domain · Interoperability · Indistinguishability obfuscation · Standard model

1 Introduction

Secure group communication is an increasingly popular research area and has received much attention in modern collaborative and distributed applications such as distributed social networks, peer-to-peer file sharing, and cloud computing. Group key exchange protocols are fundamental to secure communication among a group of users. In a group key exchange protocol, a group of users are allowed to communicate over an untrusted, open network to agree on a common secret session key and thereafter, they can securely exchange messages using this shared key.

© Springer International Publishing AG 2017
K. Chen et al. (Eds.): Inscrypt 2016, LNCS 10143, pp. 386–400, 2017.
DOI: 10.1007/978-3-319-54705-3_24

With the popularity of group data sharing in distributed networks, cross-domain group key exchange protocols have become the basis of securely connecting distributed multi-domain systems. Each domain environment would have its own users and resources within specific trust domain, however, since diverse type of requirements can be made by the users, which may not be offered by one single domain system, one domain system has to request another domain system or multiple domain systems. Therefore, the demand of cooperative work in multiple domains, i.e., cross-domain interoperability, is rising. Nonetheless, cross-domain group key exchange protocols are hard to design for its complexity in system deployment and user operation, all of which need large amount computation and resource consumption. In particular, there are many differences in the design between cross-domain authenticated group key exchange protocol and two-party key exchange protocol. First, the users' structure is more complex: in two-party case, users are on equal status, while in the group case, users are usually in the ring structure, tree structure, or line structure; second, the parameters setting is more universal: in two-party case, the same cryptographic setting is used, while in the group case, the users may be in various algebraic settings; third, the round of the protocol is more dynamic: the two-party case usually has constant round, while in the group case, the round is closely linked with the group structure and size, usually increasing with the group size.

Over the past several years, many solutions to group key exchange protocols have been proposed [1–13]. However, all of these constructions require all participants to adopt a common cryptographic setting and shared parameters. In practical applications, the common scheme and parameter requirements can be a large barrier when entities coming from different settings wish to communicate with each other. Taking an example of signature, existing users have already established signing keys and algorithms which are entrenched in an existing public key infrastructure. The changing and re-certifying of one's public keys may bring much resource consumption and make the user store many suits of keys, which absolutely results in complexity of operation. Aiming at tackling the challenges above, we propose a one-round cross-domain group key exchange protocol which removes the complex group structure, and most of all, it allows group members to come from different cryptographic settings (e.g., identity-based setting, certificate-based setting) and use different signature schemes (e.g., RSA, ECDSA).

1.1 Related Work

Group Key Exchange Protocol. Burmester et al. [4] proposed an efficient and practical group key exchange protocol, in which the number of the communication rounds is constant when broadcast messages are allowed, however, there is no security proof for it. Later, Bresson et al. [7] introduced a formal security model for group key exchange protocols based on the Bellare and Rogaway model [14] and proposed the first provably secure protocol in this setting. Users in their protocol communicate in a ring structure, and only after receiving messages from his predecessor, the user can produce his own message. Unfortunately, the essence of their communication structure makes their protocol quite impractical for large groups due to the number of communication rounds linear in the number of group users. In 2003, Katz and Yung [10] analyzed Burmester's protocol [4], who also proposed the first constant round and fully scalable authenticated group key exchange protocol which is provably secure in the standard model. Besides this, there are some identity-based group key exchange protocols [2,5,13], using the identity information in place of public keys to provide authentication. Recently, Boneh and Zhandry [15] constructed the first multi-party non-interactive key exchange protocol requiring trusted setup based on indistinguishability obfuscation, and gave the formal security proof in the static and semi-static models, however, their protocol does not consider entity authentication, and moreover the group session key is generated only by group users' public keys, which makes the session key static and fixed.

Cross-Domain Key Exchange Protocol. Chen et al. [16] introduced the concept of two-party cross-domain communication and proposed an ID-based protocol that allows two parties to communicate through different domains. In 2005, McCullagh et al. [17] proposed a more efficient cross-domain two-party construction. However, both of constructions [16,17] require all parties from different domains adopt the common group parameter. Ustaoğlu [18] also proposed a collection of integrating protocols which support interoperability between two different cryptographic settings, but their protocols still require that the participants use parameters from the same algebraic group. Later, Guo et al. [19] proposed a two-party key exchange protocol where one entity is certificate-based and the other one is identity-based, and the parameters of both entities may come from different groups. Recently, Chen et al. [20] proposed a cross-domain four-party password-based authenticated key exchange protocol in a scenario that two cross-domain clients establish secure communication through their servers, which is a nice work but needs the client share password with its server. In summary, it seems that no existing solutions can perfectly support cross-domain group key exchange while not changing participants' existing cryptographic settings.

Obfuscation and Its Security. Obfuscation was first rigorously defined and studied by Barak et al. [21]. Roughly speaking, obfuscation security requires an obfuscated version $\mathcal{O}(P)$ of a program P to behave like a virtual black box (VBB) in the sense that anything one can compute given $\mathcal{O}(P)$, one could also compute from the input-output behavior of the program P. However, it has been known that it is impossible to realize it in general. This leads to an alternative and weaker notion called indistinguishability obfuscation ($i\mathcal{O}$), which requires that if two programs of the same size compute the same function, then their obfuscations should be indistinguishable. In 2013, Garg et al. [22] (known as GGH13) proposed the first candidate construction of an efficient $i\mathcal{O}$ for all circuits. Since their breakthrough result, an extremely large number of uses for $i\mathcal{O}$ in cryptography have been found, not only in obtaining classical cryptographic primitives, but also in reaching new possibilities. Subsequently, several other candidate $i\mathcal{O}$ schemes have been proposed, and almost all known schemes rely on multilinear maps. Unfortunately, there have been several attacks [23–25] on multilinear maps that exploit extra information revealed by the zero-test procedure. However, known attacks exploit the correlations among ring elements, and these correlations are much harder to leverage in the case where only "highest-level" zero-encodings can be obtained, which is the case for known obfuscation candidates. Therefore, such attacks are not applicable to candidate $i\mathcal{O}$ schemes. The only known attacks against obfuscation schemes are the recent annihilation attacks of Miles et al. [25]. However, not all the obfuscation candidates are broken by the annihilation attacks. Recently, Garg, Mukherjee et al. [26] gave a beautiful new candidate $i\mathcal{O}$ construction, using a new variant of the GGH13 multilinear map candidate, and proved its security in the weak multilinear map model assuming an explicit PRF in NC^1. Concurrently, Lin [27] also proposed a construction of $i\mathcal{O}$ from a simple assumption (joint-SXDH assumption) on prime-order graded encodings.

1.2   Technical Contributions

Cross-domain group key exchange (CDGKE) protocols are fundamental building blocks for securing communication over public, insecure cross-domain networks. In this paper, we propose the first universal cross-domain group key exchange protocol. In a universal cross-domain group key exchange protocol, users coming from different domains (with various cryptographic settings and system parameters) communicate over an insecure public network and establish a common secret session key.

Our primary challenge is how to create a way to make all the participants have the uniform computation even though they are coming from different settings, and then hide the computation result from the outsiders. Inspired by Boneh and Zhandry's multiparty non-interactive key exchange scheme [15], we use indistinguishability obfuscation as the main tool. The essential idea is the following: the global agreed domain parameter consists of an obfuscated program for a constrained pseudorandom function PRF which requires to operate the verification of signature, and each user P_i generates a signature on the message x_i chosen randomly using its own signature scheme and broadcasts it. By running the global agreed domain parameter program, each user in the group can independently evaluate the obfuscated program to obtain the shared session key, which is the PRF output evaluated at the concatenation of the message x_i. However, such an approach fails because a signature can be replayed by an adversary. To prevent such attacks, we require the random value s_i used for generating the message x_i also as the input of the obfuscated program.

Compared to existing constructions, our protocol has a number of advantages: (i) It is optimal in terms of round complexity, which is a central measure of efficiency for any interactive protocol; (ii) Each participant neither needs to change or re-certify his public keys, nor holds many suites of keys; (iii) Each participant in the group may use different signature scheme (e.g., BLS, RSA, ECDSA, or FS-IBS) even in various algebraic settings (e.g., using RSA in different modulo), which is more suitable for cross-domain setting; (iv) Each participant does not need to know the exact identity of any other participant, only the identifier in the group; (v) The group session key is different in each protocol execution even though the group users are not changed; (vi) It is provably secure in the standard model. It is also worth noting that since our protocol is built from a generic indistinguishability obfuscation mechanism other than secure multilinear maps, it may eventually depend on a weaker complexity assumption.

2   Preliminaries

In this section we start by briefly recalling the definitions of different cryptographic primitives essential for our study. Let $x \leftarrow S$ denote a uniformly random element drawn from the set S and λ the security parameter.

2.1   Indistinguishability Obfuscation

Definition 1 (Indistinguishability Obfuscation [22]). An *indistinguishability obfuscator $i\mathcal{O}$* for a circuit class $\mathcal{C}_\lambda$ is a probabilistic polynomial time (PPT) algorithm satisfying the following conditions:

- $i\mathcal{O}(\lambda, C)$ preserves the functionality of C. That is, for any $C \in \mathcal{C}_\lambda$, if we compute $C' = i\mathcal{O}(\lambda, C)$, then $C'(x) = C(x)$ for all inputs x.
- For any λ and any two circuits $C_0, C_1 \in \mathcal{C}_\lambda$ with the same functionality, the circuits $i\mathcal{O}(\lambda, C_0)$ and $i\mathcal{O}(\lambda, C_1)$ are indistinguishable. More precisely, for all pairs of PPT adversaries $(Samp, D)$ there exists a negligible function α such that, if

$$\Pr[\forall x, C_0(x) = C_1(x) : (C_0, C_1, \tau) \leftarrow Samp(\lambda)] > 1 - \alpha(\lambda),$$

then

$$|\Pr[D(\tau, i\mathcal{O}(\lambda, C_0)) = 1] - \Pr[D(\tau, i\mathcal{O}(\lambda, C_1)) = 1]| < \alpha(\lambda).$$

In this paper, we will make use of such indistinguishability obfuscators for all polynomial-size circuits.

Definition 2 (Indistinguishability Obfuscation for P/poly). A uniform PPT machine $i\mathcal{O}$ is called an indistinguishability obfuscator for P/*poly* if the following holds: Let $\mathcal{C}_\lambda$ be the class of circuits of size at most λ, Then $i\mathcal{O}$ is an indistinguishability obfuscator for the class $\{\mathcal{C}_\lambda\}$.

2.2   Constrained Pseudorandom Functions

A pseudorandom function (PRF) [28] is a function PRF: $\mathcal{K} \times \mathcal{X} \rightarrow \mathcal{Y}$ where $\text{PRF}(k, \cdot)$ is indistinguishable from a random function for a randomly chosen key k. Following Boneh and Waters [29], we recall the definition of constrained pseudorandom function[1].

---

[1] The Boneh and Waters's construction for the class of circuit-constrained PRFs [29] is based on the multilinear maps, however, to the best of our knowledge, there does

Definition 3 (Constrained Pseudorandom Function [29]). A PRF $F: \mathcal{K} \times \mathcal{X} \to \mathcal{Y}$ is said to be *constrained* with respect to a set system $\mathcal{S} \subseteq 2^{\mathcal{X}}$ if there is an additional key space $\mathcal{K}_\mathcal{C}$ and two additional algorithms:

- $F.constrain(k, S)$: On input a PRF key $k \in \mathcal{K}$ and the description of a set $S \in \mathcal{S}$ (so that $S \subseteq \mathcal{X}$), the algorithm outputs a constrained key $k_S \in \mathcal{K}_\mathcal{C}$.
- $F.eval(k_S, x)$: On input $k_S \in \mathcal{K}_\mathcal{C}$ and $x \in \mathcal{X}$, the algorithm outputs

$$F.eval(k_S, x) = \begin{cases} F(k, x) & \text{if } x \in S \\ \bot & \text{otherwise} \end{cases}$$

For ease of presentation, we use $F(k_S, x)$ to represent $F.eval(k_S, x)$.

Security. Intuitively, we require that even after obtaining several constrained keys, no polynomial time adversary can distinguish a truly random string from the PRF evaluation at a point not queried. This intuition can be formalized by the following security game between a challenger and an adversary $\mathcal{A}$.

Let $F : \mathcal{K} \times \mathcal{X} \to \mathcal{Y}$ be a constrained PRF with respect to a set system $\mathcal{S} \subseteq 2^{\mathcal{X}}$. The security game consists of three phases:

Setup Phase. The challenger chooses a random key $K \leftarrow \mathcal{K}$ and a random bit $b \leftarrow \{0, 1\}$.

Query Phase. In this phase, $\mathcal{A}$ is allowed to ask for the following queries:

- Evaluation Query: On input $x \in \mathcal{X}$, it returns $F(K, x)$.
- Key Query: On input $S \in \mathcal{S}$, it returns $F.constrain(K, S)$.
- Challenge Query: $\mathcal{A}$ sends $x \in \mathcal{X}$ as a challenge query. If $b = 0$, the challenger outputs $F(K, x)$; else, the challenger outputs a random element $y \leftarrow \mathcal{Y}$.

Guess Phase. $\mathcal{A}$ outputs a guess b' of b.

Let $E \subseteq \mathcal{X}$ be the set of evaluation queries, $C \subseteq \mathcal{S}$ be the set of constrained key queries and $Z \subseteq \mathcal{X}$ the set of challenge queries. $\mathcal{A}$ wins if $b = b'$ and $E \cap Z = \phi$ and $C \cap Z = \phi$. The advantage of $\mathcal{A}$ is defined to be $\text{Adv}_\mathcal{A}^F(\lambda) = |\text{Pr}[\mathcal{A} \text{ wins}] - 1/2|$.

Definition 4. The PRF F is a secure constrained PRF with respect to $\mathcal{S}$ if for all probabilistic polynomial time adversaries $\mathcal{A}$, $\text{Adv}_\mathcal{A}^F(\lambda)$ is negligible in λ.

2.3 Signature Scheme

A digital signature scheme is a triple $SIG = (Sig.Gen, Sig.Sign, Sig.Verify)$, consisting of a key generation algorithm $(pk, sk) \leftarrow Sig.Gen(1^\lambda)$ generating a public verification key pk and a private signing key sk on input of security parameter λ, signing algorithm $\sigma \leftarrow Sig.Sign(sk; m)$ generating a signature for message m, and verification algorithm $Sig.Verify(pk; m, \sigma)$ returning 1 if σ is a valid signature for m under key pk, and 0 otherwise.

---

not exist any negative result on its security, and the attack [24] on multilinear maps is not applicable to it.

Correctness. For all $\lambda \in \mathbb{N}$, $(pk, sk) \leftarrow Sig.Gen(1^\lambda)$, message $m \in \mathcal{M}(\lambda)$, we require that $Sig.Verify(pk; m, Sig.Sign(sk; m)) = 1$.

Security. Consider the following security experiment (defined by [30]) played between a challenger $\mathcal{C}$ and an adversary $\mathcal{A}$.

1. The challenger generates a public/private key pair $(pk, sk) \leftarrow Sig.Gen(1^\lambda)$, the adversary receives pk as input.
2. The adversary may query arbitrary messages m_i to the challenger. The challenger replies to each query with a signature $\sigma_i = Sig.Sign(sk; m_i)$. Here i is an index, ranging between $1 \le i \le q$ for some $q \in \mathbb{N}$. Queries can be made adaptively.
3. Eventually, the adversary outputs a message/signature pair (m^*, σ^*).

Definition 5 (Secure Signatures [30]). We say that SIG is *existentially unforgeable under adaptive chosen-message attacks* (EUF-CMA), if for all adversaries $\mathcal{A}$, there exists a negligible function negl such that

$$\Pr[(m^*, \sigma^*) \leftarrow \mathcal{A}^{\mathcal{C}}(1^\lambda, pk) \quad such \quad that$$
$$Sig.Verify(pk; \sigma^*, m^*) = 1 \wedge m^* \notin \{m_1, \ldots, m_q\}] \le \mathsf{negl}(\lambda).$$

3   Security Model

In this section, we briefly recall the formal security model for group key exchange protocols as presented in [10] (which is based on the model by Bresson [9]).

Parties and initialization. In a group key exchange protocol, we assume for simplicity a fixed, polynomial-size set $\mathcal{P} = \{P_1, \ldots, P_l\}$ of potential parties. Any subset of $\mathcal{P}$ may decide at any point to establish a session key, and we do not assume that these subsets are always the same size or always include the same participants. There are two different types of party: $\mathcal{CP}$ (certification based party) and $\mathcal{IP}$ (identity based party). Before the protocol is run for the first time, an initialization phase occurs. For each participant $P_i \in \mathcal{CP}$, it runs an algorithm $\mathcal{G}_i(1^\lambda)$ to generate public/private keys (PK_i, SK_i), where each P_i may be from different cryptographic settings (e.g., finite field, elliptic curve, or RSA). For each $P_i \in \mathcal{IP}$, the public key PK_i is its own identity ID_i and the private key SK_i is generated by its private key generator (PKG). Each player P_i stores SK_i, and the public key PK_i is known by all participants (and is also known by the adversary).

Adversary model. We denote instance i of user P as π_P^i. A given instance may be used only once. Each instance π_P^i has associated with it the variables acc_P^i, sid_P^i, pid_P^i, sk_P^i with the following semantics:

- acc_P^i: 0/1-valued variable which is set to be 1 by π_P^i upon normal termination of the session and 0 otherwise.
- sid_P^i: session identity for instance π_P^i, which is a protocol-specified function of all communication sent and received by π_P^i.

- pid_P^i: partner identity for instance π_P^i, which consists of the identities of the players in the group with whom π_P^i intends to establish a session key (including P itself).
- sk_P^i: session key after the execution of the protocol by π_P^i.

During the execution of the protocol, an adversary $\mathcal{A}$ could interact with protocol participants via several oracle queries, which model adversary's possible attacks in the real execution. All possible oracle queries are listed in the following:

- $\text{Send}(\pi_P^i, m)$: This query is used to simulate active attacks, in which the adversary may tamper with the message being sent over the public channel. It returns the message that the user instance π_P^i would generate upon receipt of message m.
- $\text{Execute}(\pi_{P_1}^{i_1}, \ldots, \pi_{P_n}^{i_n})$: This query models passive attacks in which the attacker eavesdrops on honest executions among the user instances $\pi_{P_1}^{i_1}, \ldots, \pi_{P_n}^{i_n}$. It returns the messages that were exchanged during an honest execution of the protocol.
- $\text{Reveal}(\pi_P^i)$: This query models the possibility that an adversary gets the session key. It returns to the adversary the session key sk_P^i of the user instance π_P^i.
- $\text{Corrupt}(P)$: This query returns the long-term secret key of player P.
- $\text{Test}(\pi_P^i)$: This query tries to capture the adversary's ability to tell apart a real session key from a random one. It returns the session key for instance π_P^i if $b = 1$ or a random number of the same size if $b = 0$. This query is called only once.

Partnering. Two instances π_P^i and $\pi_{P'}^j$ are said to be partnered if and only if (1) $\text{pid}_P^i = \text{pid}_{P'}^j$, (2) $\text{sid}_P^i = \text{sid}_{P'}^j$, and (3) $\text{acc}_P^i = \text{acc}_{P'}^j = 1$.

Freshness. We say an instance π_P^i is *fresh* if none of the following conditions hold:

(1) the adversary queries $\text{Reveal}(\pi_P^i)$ or $\text{Reveal}(\pi_{P'}^j)$, where $\pi_{P'}^j$ is partnered with π_P^i;
(2) the adversary queries $\text{Corrupt}(V)$ (with $V \in \text{pid}_P^i$) before a query of the form $\text{Send}(\pi_{P'}^j, *)$, where $P' \in \text{pid}_P^i$.

Correctness. The correctness of group key exchange protocol requires that, whenever two instances π_P^i and $\pi_{P'}^j$ are partnered, both instances should hold the same non-null session key.

Security. For any adversary $\mathcal{A}$, let $Succ(\mathcal{A})$ be the event that $\mathcal{A}$ makes a single Test query directed to some fresh instance π_P^i at the end of a protocol Π and correctly guesses the bit b used in the Test query. The advantage of $\mathcal{A}$ in violating the semantic security of the protocol Π is defined as:

$$\text{Adv}_\Pi(\mathcal{A}) = |2\Pr[Succ(\mathcal{A})] - 1|.$$

Definition 6. We say a group key exchange protocol Π is selectively secure if, for any PPT adversary $\mathcal{A}$ satisfying the following properties, $\mathsf{Adv}_\Pi(\mathcal{A})$ is negligible:

– $\mathcal{A}$ commits to a set $\hat{S}$ of users at the beginning of the security game.
– Test query must be on a subset S of $\hat{S}$.

4   One-Round Cross-Domain Group Key Exchange Protocol

In this section we present our construction of a one-round cross-domain group key exchange protocol.

4.1   Protocol Description

The idea of our cross-domain group key exchange (CDGKE) protocol is the following: In the setup phase, a trusted third party chooses a key K for a constrained pseudorandom function PRF and publishes an obfuscated program for the PRF as the global agreed domain parameter. In the group key exchange phase, each participant P_i broadcasts a signature σ_i of the random x_i generated by P_i using his own signature scheme. The shared session key will be the function PRF evaluated at the concatenation of the identity P_i and x_i. However, to make the session key shared only among legal participants, the knowledge of a seed s will be required to operate an obfuscated program for PRF. More precisely, each participant generates a seed s_i and computes $x_i = PRG(s_i)$, where PRG is a pseudorandom generator. In this way, all users can compute the session key, but anyone else without the corresponding private key or seed, will therefore be unable to compute the session key.

A formal description of our protocol appears in Fig. 1.

4.2   Correctness and Security

The correctness is obvious by inspection. For security, we have the following theorem.

Theorem 1. Let $PRG : \{0,1\}^\lambda \to \{0,1\}^{2\lambda}$ be a secure pseudorandom generator, let F be a secure constrained PRF, let SIG_i ($i \in \{1, 2, \cdots, n\}$) be a signature scheme that is existentially unforgeable under adaptive chosen-message attacks, and let $i\mathcal{O}$ be a secure indistinguishability obfuscator. Then, the protocol in Fig. 1 is a secure group key exchange protocol.

Proof. Fix a PPT adversary $\mathcal{A}$ attacking the cross-domain group key exchange protocol. We use a hybrid argument to bound the advantage of $\mathcal{A}$. We define a sequence of experiments $\mathbf{Hyb}_0, \cdots, \mathbf{Hyb}_3$, and denote the advantage of adversary $\mathcal{A}$ in experiment $\mathbf{Hyb}_i$ as:

$$\mathrm{Adv}_i(\mathcal{A}) \overset{\mathrm{def}}{=} |2 \cdot \Pr[\mathcal{A} \text{ succeeds in } \mathbf{Hyb}_i] - 1|.$$

Protocol

Consider an execution of the protocol among participants $P_1, \cdots, P_n$ belonging to different security domains and wishing to establish a common session key. Let F be a pseudorandom function, PRG be a pseudorandom generator, and iO be a program indistinguishability obfuscator.

Global Agreed Domain Parameter: A trusted third party chooses a random key K to obtain an instance of a pseudorandom function F, builds the program P_{CDGKE} in Fig. 2, and then outputs $P_{iO} = iO(P_{CDGKE})$ as the global agreed domain parameter.

Setup: Build the global agreed domain parameter and publish it. Each participant P_i chooses his own signature scheme $SIG_i = (SIG_i.Gen, SIG_i.Sign, SIG_i.Verify)$, runs the key generation algorithm $SIG_i.Gen$ on input 1^λ to obtain a public/private key pair (pk_i, sk_i) (i.e., $(pk_i, sk_i) \leftarrow SIG_i.Gen(1^\lambda)$), where $\lambda \in \mathbb{N}$ is a security parameter.

Round 1: Each participant P_i proceeds as:

1. Choose s_i randomly, compute $x_i = PRG(s_i)$, and generate the signature $\sigma_i = SIG_i.Sign(sk_i; x_i || P_1 || \cdots || P_n)$.
2. Broadcast $m_i = (P_i, S_i, pk_i, x_i, \sigma_i)$.

Key Generation: Each participant P_i runs P_{iO} on $(m_1, m_2, \cdots, m_n, i, s_i)$ to obtain the session key SK or $\perp$.

Fig. 1. An honest execution of the cross-domain group key exchange protocol

---

Inputs: $m_1, m_2, \cdots, m_n, i, s_i$
Constants: F key K

if $x_i \neq PRG(s_i)$ **then**
        Output $\perp$
else if there exists $j \leq n$ such that $SIG_j.Verify(pk_j; x_j || P_1 || \cdots || P_n, \sigma_j) = 0$ **then**
        Output $\perp$
else Output $F(K, x_1, x_2, \ldots, x_n, P_1, P_2, \ldots, P_n)$

Fig. 2. The program P_{CDGKE}

We bound the difference between the adversary's advantage in successive experiments, and then bound the adversary's advantage in the final experiment. Finally, combining all the above results, we get the desired bound on $Adv_0(\mathcal{A})$, the adversary's advantage when attacking the real protocol.

Experiment Hyb$_0$. This is the original experiment with respect to a given polynomial-time adversary $\mathcal{A}$, in which $\mathcal{A}$ commits to a set $\hat{S} = \{\hat{P}_1, \hat{P}_2, \cdots, \hat{P}_n\}$ and interacts with the real protocol as defined in Sect. 3.

Experiment Hyb$_1$. This experiment is different from **Hyb$_0$** only in that it is aborted and the adversary does not succeed if the following event **Forge** occurs.

Forge: Let **Forge** be the event that, the adversary makes send query of the form $\mathsf{Send}(\pi_P^i, m)$ such that the message m contains a new, valid message/signature pair with respect to the public key pk_U of some user U before querying Corrupt(U).

Lemma 1. $|Adv_1(\mathcal{A}) - Adv_0(\mathcal{A})| < negl(\lambda)$.

Proof. Assuming that the event **Forge** occurs, we can construct an algorithm $\mathcal{F}$ which outputs, with a non-negligible probability, a forgery against a signature scheme SIG_i for some $i \in \{1, 2, \cdots, n\}$ as follows.

The given public key PK is assigned to one of the n participants. All other parties are initialized as normal according to the protocol. All queries to the parties can be easily answered by following the protocol specification since all secret keys are known, except for the private key corresponding to the public key of the forgery attack game. In the latter case the signing oracle that is available as part of the chosen message attack can be used to simulate the answers. If **Forge** occurs against an instance who holds PK, $\mathcal{F}$ halts and outputs the message/signature pair generated by $\mathcal{A}$ as its forgery. Otherwise, $\mathcal{F}$ halts and outputs a failure indication.

The success probability of $\mathcal{F}$ is exactly $\Pr[\textbf{Forge}]/n$. Then, the lemma follows by noticing that the signature scheme SIG_i ($i \in \{1, 2, \cdots, n\}$) is existentially unforgeable under adaptive chosen-message attacks.

Experiment Hyb$_2$. In this experiment, for $P_i \in \hat{S}$, we will choose random $x_i \in \{0, 1\}^{2\lambda}$ instead of generating them from PRG. The security of PRG yields the lemma 2.

Lemma 2. $|Adv_2(\mathcal{A}) - Adv_1(\mathcal{A})| < negl(\lambda)$.

Experiment Hyb$_3$. Replace the $F(\cdot)$ in P_{CDGKE} by a constrained pseudo-random function $F^C(\cdot)$, arriving at the program P'_{CDGKE} given in Fig. 3. The constrained set C is defined as $C = \{(x_1, x_2, \ldots, x_n, P_1, P_2, \ldots, P_n) : \text{there exists some } P_j \text{ (and respective } x_j) \text{ that is not contained in the set } \hat{S}\}$.

Inputs: $m_1, m_2, \cdots, m_n, i, s_i$
Constants: Constrained F key K_C

  if $x_i \neq PRG(s_i)$ **then**
    Output $\perp$
  else if there exists $j \leq n$ such that $SIG_j.Verify(pk_j; x_j||P_1||\cdots||P_n, \sigma_j) = 0$ **then**
    Output $\perp$
  else Output $F^C(K_C, x_1, x_2, \ldots, x_n, P_1, P_2, \ldots, P_n)$

Fig. 3. The program P'_{CDGKE}

Lemma 3. $|Adv_3(\mathcal{A}) - Adv_2(\mathcal{A})| < negl(\lambda)$.

Proof. Note that with overwhelming probability, none of x_i (the corresponding $P_i \in \hat{S}$) in Experiment Hyb$_2$ has a pre-image under PRG. Therefore, with overwhelming probability, there is no input to P_{CDGKE} that will cause F to be evaluated on points of the form $(\hat{x}_1, \hat{x}_2, \ldots, \hat{x}_n, \hat{P}_1, \hat{P}_2, \ldots, \hat{P}_n)$, where $\hat{P}_i \in \hat{S}$. We can conclude that the modified program P'_{CDGKE} has the same functionality with the original program P_{CDGKE}. Then based on the property of indistinguishability obfuscation, it is easy to see that the experiments Hyb$_2$ and Hyb$_3$ are computationally indistinguishable. Thus, security of $i\mathcal{O}$ yields the lemma.

Bounding the advantage in Hyb$_3$. We reduce the non-negligible advantage of the adversary $\mathcal{A}$ in the experiment **Hyb$_3$** to the security of the constrained PRF presented above. We construct a PRF adversary $\mathcal{B}$ that breaks the security of F as a constrained PRF as follows: adversary $\mathcal{B}$ simulates the entire experiment for $\mathcal{A}$. In response to Execute query, $\mathcal{B}$ computes the signature of m_i with correct private key sk_i exactly as in experiment Hyb$_3$. In response to Reveal query, $\mathcal{B}$ also queries its PRF oracle and thus always reveals the correct session key. At the end of the experiment, for a test query, $\mathcal{B}$ makes a real-or-random challenge query for the constrained function F^C as defined above. One can easily see that, $\mathcal{B}$ is given a real PRF or a random value, then its simulation is performed exactly as in experiment Hyb$_3$. Thus, the advantage of $\mathcal{B}$ is exactly Adv$_3(\mathcal{A})$. It conflicts with the security of the constrained PRF. Thus the advantage of the adversary $\mathcal{A}$ in this experiment is negligible.

4.3 Comparison with Related Protocols

The core of our protocol is an obfuscation program, therefore, any polynomial-time bounded indistinguishability obfuscation candidates (e.g., [26,27]) can be adopted to instantiate our scheme. In this subsection, we compare our protocol with Katz *et al.*'s protocol [10], Neupane *et al.*'s protcol [12], Ustaoğlu's protocol [18], and Guo *et al.*'s protocol [19] from many respects. Table 1 summarizes the comparison results[2].

In Table 1, both Katz *et al.*'s protocol [10] and Neupane *et al.*'s protocol [12] are group key exchange protocols proven to be secure in the standard model. However, their constructions require all participants to adopt a common cryptographic setting and shared parameters, which means that cross-domain interaction is not supported. Both Ustaoğlu's protocol [18] and Guo *et al.*'s protocol [19] are two-party key exchange protocols supporting cross-domain interaction. However, as the authors commented, the protocol in [18] requires the participants to use parameters from the same algebraic group and the protocol in [19] requires one party being identity-based and the other one being certificate-based, which means that the involved cryptographic setting is not universal. Meanwhile,

---

[2] Since our protocol is universal, the concrete computation & communication complexity relies on the instantiated schemes, and we omit it in the comparison.

Table 1. Comparison of related protocols

Protocol	Type	Communication rounds	Cross-domain support?	Universal?	Standard model?
Protocol in [10]	Group	3	✗	✗	✓
Protocol in [12]	Group	2	✗	✗	✓
Protocol in [18]	2-Party	2	✓	✗	✗
Protocol in [19]	2-Party	3	✓	✗	✗
Our protocol	Group	1	✓	✓	✓

our protocol is a group key exchange protocol supporting cross-domain interaction. Moreover, the participants may come from various cryptographic settings (universal) and do not need anything special to generate the shared session key.

In summary, our protocol only has one round, and supports cross-domain interaction from different cryptographic settings, and it is proven secure in the standard model. To the best of our knowledge, there is no cross-domain group key exchange protocol (until this work) whose security directly relies on standard model and does not need to use the same algebraic setting and shared parameters.

5   Conclusion

In this paper, we investigate cross-domain group key exchange protocol for interoperability scenarios. Our main contribution is to propose the first one-round group key exchange protocol which supports participants coming from different domains. Besides, different signature schemes and different system parameters can be used, which is more flexible and more suitable for interoperability scenarios. We also prove that our protocol can achieve the desired security goals in the standard model. It remains an open problem to further reduce the computational costs of group participants, whilst maintaining its optimal communication round.

Acknowledgments. We want to thank the anonymous reviewers for their comments which helped to improve the paper. This work was supported by the National Grand Fundamental Research (973) Program of China under Grant 2013CB338003, and the National Natural Science Foundation of China (NSFC) under Grants U1536205 and 61572485.

References

1. Ingemarsson, I., Tang, D.T., Wong, C.K.: A conference key distribution system. IEEE Trans. Inf. Theory **28**(5), 714–720 (1982)
2. Koyama, K., Ohta, K.: Identity-based conference key distribution systems. In: Pomerance, C. (ed.) CRYPTO 1987. LNCS, vol. 293, pp. 175–184. Springer, Heidelberg (1988). doi:10.1007/3-540-48184-2_13
3. Steer, D.G., Strawczynski, L., Diffie, W., Wiener, M.: A secure audio teleconference system. In: Goldwasser, S. (ed.) CRYPTO 1988. LNCS, vol. 403, pp. 520–528. Springer, New York (1990). doi:10.1007/0-387-34799-2_37
4. Burmester, M., Desmedt, Y.: A secure and efficient conference key distribution system. In: Santis, A. (ed.) EUROCRYPT 1994. LNCS, vol. 950, pp. 275–286. Springer, Heidelberg (1995). doi:10.1007/BFb0053443
5. Saeednia, S., Safavi-Naini, R.: Efficient identity-based conference key distribution protocols. In: Boyd, C., Dawson, E. (eds.) ACISP 1998. LNCS, vol. 1438, pp. 320–331. Springer, Heidelberg (1998). doi:10.1007/BFb0053744
6. Tzeng, W.-G., Tzeng, Z.-J.: Round-efficient conference key agreement protocols with provable security. In: Okamoto, T. (ed.) ASIACRYPT 2000. LNCS, vol. 1976, pp. 614–627. Springer, Heidelberg (2000). doi:10.1007/3-540-44448-3_47
7. Bresson, E., Chevassut, O., Pointcheval, D., Quisquater, J.J.: Provably authenticated group diffie-hellman key exchange. In: CCS 2001, pp. 255–264. ACM (2001)
8. Bresson, E., Chevassut, O., Pointcheval, D.: Provably authenticated group diffie-hellman key exchange — the dynamic case. In: Boyd, C. (ed.) ASIACRYPT 2001. LNCS, vol. 2248, pp. 290–309. Springer, Heidelberg (2001). doi:10.1007/3-540-45682-1_18
9. Bresson, E., Chevassut, O., Pointcheval, D.: Dynamic group diffie-hellman key exchange under standard assumptions. In: Knudsen, L.R. (ed.) EUROCRYPT 2002. LNCS, vol. 2332, pp. 321–336. Springer, Heidelberg (2002). doi:10.1007/3-540-46035-7_21
10. Katz, J., Yung, M.: Scalable protocols for authenticated group key exchange. In: Boneh, D. (ed.) CRYPTO 2003. LNCS, vol. 2729, pp. 110–125. Springer, Heidelberg (2003). doi:10.1007/978-3-540-45146-4_7
11. Burmester, M., Desmedt, Y.: A secure and scalable group key exchange system. Inf. Process Lett. (IPL) **94**(3), 137–143 (2005)
12. Neupane, K., Steinwandt, R.: Communication-efficient 2-round group key establishment from pairings. In: Kiayias, A. (ed.) CT-RSA 2011. LNCS, vol. 6558, pp. 65–76. Springer, Heidelberg (2011). doi:10.1007/978-3-642-19074-2_5
13. Arifi, M., Gardeshi, M., Farash, M.S.: A new efficient authenticated id-based group key agreement protocol. Cryptology ePrint Archive: Report 2012/395 (2012)
14. Bellare, M., Rogaway, P.: Entity authentication and key distribution. In: Stinson, D.R. (ed.) CRYPTO 1993. LNCS, vol. 773, pp. 232–249. Springer, Heidelberg (1994). doi:10.1007/3-540-48329-2_21
15. Boneh, D., Zhandry, M.: Multiparty key exchange, efficient traitor tracing, and more from indistinguishability obfuscation. In: Garay, J.A., Gennaro, R. (eds.) CRYPTO 2014. LNCS, vol. 8616, pp. 480–499. Springer, Heidelberg (2014). doi:10.1007/978-3-662-44371-2_27
16. Chen, L., Kudla, C.: Identity based authenticated key agreement protocols from pairings. In: CSFW 2003, pp. 219–233. IEEE Computer Society (2003)
17. McCullagh, N., Barreto, P.S.L.M.: A new two-party identity-based authenticated key agreement. In: Menezes, A. (ed.) CT-RSA 2005. LNCS, vol. 3376, pp. 262–274. Springer, Heidelberg (2005). doi:10.1007/978-3-540-30574-3_18

18. Ustaoğlu, B.: Integrating identity-based and certificate-based authenticated key exchange protocols. Int. J. Inf. Secur. **10**(4), 201–212 (2011)

19. Guo, Y., Zhang, Z.: Authenticated key exchange with entities from different settings and varied groups. In: Takagi, T., Wang, G., Qin, Z., Jiang, S., Yu, Y. (eds.) ProvSec 2012. LNCS, vol. 7496, pp. 276–287. Springer, Heidelberg (2012). doi:10.1007/978-3-642-33272-2_18

20. Chen, L., Lim, H.W., Yang, G.: Cross-domain password-based authenticated key exchange revisited. ACM Trans. Inf. Syst. Secur. (TISSEC) **15:16**(4), 1–15:32 (2014)

21. Barak, B., Goldreich, O., Impagliazzo, R., Rudich, S., Sahai, A., Vadhan, S., Yang, K.: On the (im) possibility of obfuscating programs. In: Kilian, J. (ed.) CRYPTO 2001. LNCS, vol. 2139, pp. 1–18. Springer, Heidelberg (2001)

22. Garg, S., Gentry, C., Halevi, S., Raykova, M., Sahai, A., Waters, B.: Candidate indistinguishability obfuscation and functional encryption for all circuits. In: FOCS 2013, pp. 40–49. IEEE (2013)

23. Garg, S., Gentry, C., Halevi, S.: Candidate multilinear maps from ideal lattices. In: Johansson, T., Nguyen, P.Q. (eds.) EUROCRYPT 2013. LNCS, vol. 7881, pp. 1–17. Springer, Heidelberg (2013). doi:10.1007/978-3-642-38348-9_1

24. Hu, Y., Jia, H.: Cryptanalysis of GGH map. In: Fischlin, M., Coron, J.-S. (eds.) EUROCRYPT 2016. LNCS, vol. 9665, pp. 537–565. Springer, Heidelberg (2016). doi:10.1007/978-3-662-49890-3_21

25. Miles, E., Sahai, A., Zhandry, M.: Annihilation attacks for multilinear maps: cryptanalysis of indistinguishability obfuscation over GGH13. In: Robshaw, M., Katz, J. (eds.) CRYPTO 2016. LNCS, vol. 9815, pp. 629–658. Springer, Heidelberg (2016). doi:10.1007/978-3-662-53008-5_22

26. Garg, S., Mukherjee, P., Srinivasan, A.: Obfuscation without the vulnerabilities of multilinear maps. Cryptology ePrint Archive: Report 2016/390 (2016)

27. Lin, H., Vaikuntanathan, V.: Indistinguishability obfuscation from DDH-like assumptions on constant-degree graded encodings. In: FOCS 2016, pp. 11–20. IEEE (2016)

28. Goldreich, O., Goldwasser, S., Micali, S.: How to construct random functions. J. ACM (JACM) **33**(4), 792–807 (1986)

29. Boneh, D., Waters, B.: Constrained pseudorandom functions and their applications. In: Sako, K., Sarkar, P. (eds.) ASIACRYPT 2013. LNCS, vol. 8270, pp. 280–300. Springer, Heidelberg (2013). doi:10.1007/978-3-642-42045-0_15

30. Goldwasser, S., Micali, S., Rivest, R.L.: A digital signature scheme secure against adaptive chosen-message attacks. SIAM J. Comput. **17**(2), 281–308 (1988)

Elliptic Curves

On Constructing Parameterized Families of Pairing-Friendly Elliptic Curves with $\rho = 1$

Meng Zhang[1], Zhi Hu[2], and Maozhi Xu[1(✉)]

[1] LMAM, School of Mathematical Sciences, Peking University,
Beijing 100871, People's Republic of China
{menglucky,mzxu}@pku.edu.cn
[2] School of Mathematics and Statistics, Central South University,
Changsha 410083, People's Republic of China
huzhi_math@csu.edu.cn

Abstract. The problem of constructing pairing-friendly elliptic curves is the key ingredients for implementing pairing-based cryptographic systems. In this paper, we aim at constructing such curves with $\rho = 1$. By offering a more generalized concept "parameterized families", we propose a method for constructing parameterized families of pairing-friendly elliptic curves which can naturally include many existent (and even more new) families of curves without exhaustive survey. We demonstrate the utility of the method by constructing concrete parameterized family in the cases of embedding degree 3, 4 and 6. An interesting result is proved that all the possible quadratic families of pairing-friendly elliptic curves of desired embedding degrees satisfying $\rho = 1$ have been covered in our parameterized families. As a by-product, we also revisit the supersingular elliptic curves from a new perspective.

Keywords: Elliptic curves · Pairing based cryptography · Cyclotomic polynomials · Parameterized families

1 Introduction

Bilinear pairings on elliptic curves, such as Tate pairing, Weil pairing and their variations, have drawn much attention in cryptography for the past decades. For one thing, bilinear pairings on curves can be used for translating the elliptic curve discrete logarithm problem (a.k.a ECDLP) to discrete logarithm problem (a.k.a DLP) in a multiplicative group of some finite field, and thus reduce the computational complexity of ECDLP on desired curves. Two representative examples are the Frey-Rück (FR) reduction [5] or the Menezes-Okamoto-Vanstone (MOV) attack [11]. For another, numerous schemes in identity based cryptography now are built based on some bilinear maps, where the using of bilinear pairing on elliptic curves has become a common and standardized approach to instantiate such special maps. Suggested pairing-based cryptographic protocols include the well known one-round three-way key exchange by Joux [9], ID based encryption by Boneh and Franklin [3], ID-based signatures by Paterson [13], and so on.

© Springer International Publishing AG 2017
K. Chen et al. (Eds.): Inscrypt 2016, LNCS 10143, pp. 403–415, 2017.
DOI: 10.1007/978-3-319-54705-3_25

Suppose E is an elliptic curve defined over some finite field $\mathbb{F}_q$, and P is a base point with prime order r dividing $\#E(\mathbb{F}_q)$. Let k be the embedding degree with respect to r, i.e., the smallest positive integer such that $r|q^k - 1$. The so called bilinear pairing on $E/\mathbb{F}_q$ can reduce the discrete logarithm problem in the group $\langle P \rangle \subset E(\mathbb{F}_q)$ to the same problem in $\mathbb{F}_{q^k}^*$. It should be noted that not every elliptic curve facilitates efficiently computable bilinear pairings. Parameters (q, k, r) should be chosen such that the DLP is infeasible both in $\langle P \rangle$ and in $\mathbb{F}_{q^k}^*$, while the arithmetic in $\mathbb{F}_{q^k}$ is feasible. Elliptic curves which satisfy these properties are named as pairing-friendly curves [4].

Efficient constructions of pairing friendly elliptic curves have been studied in several literatures, most of which can be referred to the exhaustive survey by Freeman et al. [4]. As shown by Balasubramanian and Koblitz [2], the embedding degree k of a random elliptic curve could be expected around r, which implies that the pairing friendly curves are very rare [15]. Though families of such curves have been introduced, it still needs further work on exploring more curves which provides efficient pairing computation for cryptographic application in different scenarios.

In this work, we further investigate the construction of pairing-friendly curves with $\rho = \frac{\log q}{\log r} \approx 1$. By defining a more generalized concept "parameterized families", we present a method for constructing parameterized families of pairing-friendly elliptic curves which helps us to discover many pairing-friendly families of curves and also rediscover known families. We apply it to the case of $\phi(k) = 2$ and prove all quadratic families of curves satisfying $\rho = 1$ can be obtained from parameterized families. As a by-product, we rediscover the supersingular elliptic curves from a new perspective.

The paper is organized as follows: In Sect. 2 we briefly describe the concept of pairing-friendly curves. We introduce the new strategy and algorithm for constructing parameterized families of pairing-friendly elliptic curves in Sect. 3 and apply the new algorithm to construct parameterized families of pairing-friendly curves with $\phi(k) = 2$ in Sect. 4. Finally, we conclude the paper in Sect. 5.

2   Pairing Friendly Curves

In this section we recall some basic knowledge about pairing friendly elliptic curves. As defined in [4], an elliptic curve E over $\mathbb{F}_q$ is said to be *pairing friendly* if there is a prime r with $r|E(\mathbb{F}_q)$ and the ratio $\rho = \frac{\log q}{\log r} \leq 2$, while the embedding degree k with respect to r satisfies $k \leq \frac{\log r}{8}$.

We also use the same notations as [4,14] to define a family of curves. An irreducible polynomial $f(x) \in \mathbb{Q}(x)$ is said to be *prime representative* if $f(x)$ has positive leading coefficient, and the set $S(f) = \{f(x) \in \mathbb{Z} : x \in \mathbb{Z}\}$ satisfies that $|S(f)| > 1$ and $\gcd(S(f)) = 1$. Based on the complex multiplication (a.k.a. CM) method for generating elliptic curves [1], we now introduce the triple $(q(x), t(x), r(x))$ in $\mathbb{Q}(x)$ which represents a family of elliptic curves with the embedding degree (with respect to r) k and the CM discriminant D:

1. $q(x) = p(x)^d$ for some $d \geq 1$ and $q(x)$ is irreducible and prime representative;
2. $r(x) = c \cdot r'(x)$ with $c \in Z, c \geq 1$ and $r'(x)$ is irreducible and prime representative;
3. $q(x) + 1 - t(x) = h(x)r(x)$ for some $h(x) \in \mathbb{Q}(x)$;
4. $r(x) | \phi_k(t(x) - 1)$, where ϕ_k is the k-th cyclotomic polynomial;
5. The CM equation $4q(x) - t(x)^2 = Dy^2$ has infinitely many integer solutions (x, y).

For a family $(q(x), t(x), r(x))$, we can also use the definition of the ratio ρ in [4] as

$$\rho(q, t, r) = \lim_{x \to \infty} \frac{\log q}{\log r} = \frac{\deg q(x)}{\deg r(x)}.$$

If the CM equation in (5) has a set of integer solutions (x_0, y_0) with both of $q(x_0)$ and $r'(x_0)$ are primes, then we are able to construct curves E over $\mathbb{F}_{q(x_0)}$ via the CM method, where $E(\mathbb{F}_{q(x_0)})$ has a subgroup of order $r'(x_0)$ and the embedding degree k with respect to $r'(x_0)$.

3   Construction of Parameterized Families of Pairing Friendly Curves

3.1   Factorization of Cyclotomic Polynomial

When constructing pairing-friendly elliptic curves, one of ideas is to find factorization of cyclotomic polynomial. If $\Phi_k(q(x))$ is reducible with a factor $r(x)$ of degree $\phi(k)$ for some $q(x) \in \mathbb{Q}[x]$ and $q(x)$ represents a prime number or power of a prime number, then there exists an elliptic curve defined over $\mathbb{F}_{q(x)}$ and it is possible to find a family of elliptic curve $(q(x), r(x), t(x))$ with embedding degree k.

However, such factorizations are rare. The pioneer work of finding factorizations is due to Galbraith, Mckee, and Valenca [6] who provide a criterion for quadratic polynomial $q(x)$ to give a factorization of $\Phi_k(q(x))$. Tanaka and Nakamula [14] generalize $q(x)$ to arbitrary degree and offer a method which converts the problem of finding a suitable $q(x)$ to solving an equation system.

Lemma 1. *Let $q(x) \in \mathbb{Q}[x]$. Then the polynomial $\Phi_k(q(x))$ has an irreducible factor of degree $\phi(k)$ if and only if the equation $q(z) = \xi_k$ has a solution in $\mathbb{Q}(\xi_k)$.*

Proof. Refer to Lemma 5.1 in [6].

In order to introduce our idea, we generalize the definition of families of pairing-friendly elliptic curves as follows, where the coefficients of desired polynomials are taken into account.

Definition 1 (parameterized families of pairing-friendly elliptic curves). *Let the denotations be the same as those in Sect. 2, a parameterized family of pairing-friendly elliptic curves is given by the following triple*

$$(q(x, a_0, a_1, ..., a_n), t(x, a_0, a_1, ..., a_n), r(x, a_0, a_1, ..., a_n)),$$

where $a_0, a_1, ..., a_n \in \mathbb{Q}$.

It is easy to see when $a_0, a_1, ..., a_n$ are substituted by concrete rational values, a family of pairing-friendly elliptic curves tends to be obtained.

3.2   Strategy for Constructing Parameterized Families

We propose our strategy to construct parameterized families of desired curves as follows: Given a parameterized polynomial $q(x, a_0, ..., a_n)$ in $\mathbb{Q}[x, a_0, ..., a_n]$, if we could obtain a degree $\phi(k)$ irreducible factor of $\Phi_k(q(x, a_0, ..., a_n))$ via the factorization of cyclotomic polynomials as above, then it follows a parameterized expression of $r(x, a_0, ..., a_n)$. Note that $t(x, a_0, ..., a_n) = q(x, a_0, ..., a_n) + 1 - h \cdot r(x, a_0, ..., a_n)$, and therefore we get a potential family $(q(x, a_0, ..., a_n), h \cdot r(x, a_0, ..., a_n), t(x, a_0, ..., a_n))$. Moreover, the conditions of Hasse-Weil Bound and CM equation should also be satisfied for the tripe (q, t, r), which can be achieved by solving corresponding equations with regard to $h, a_0, ..., a_n$.

The key step of the above strategy is to find appropriate $q(x, a_0, ..., a_n)$, of which the solution can be derived from the method proposed by Tanaka and Nakamula [14].

Let $\Phi_k(x)$ be the kth cyclotomic polynomial, then we can construct $\mathbb{Q}(\xi_k)$ as $\mathbb{Q}(\xi_k) = \mathbb{Q}[x]/\Phi_k(x)$, thus $\xi_k = x$, and thereby the condition in Lemma 1 can be rewritten as $q(a(x)) \equiv x \bmod \Phi_k(x)$ for some $a(x) \in \mathbb{Q}[x]$. It is a necessary and sufficient condition for $q(x)$ such that $\Phi_k(q(x))$ has a factor of degree $\phi(k)$. Moreover, since we concentrate on constructing families of pairing-friendly elliptic curves with $\rho(q, r, t) = 1$, the degree of $q(x)$ should also be set as $\phi(k)$.

Let $q(x) = \sum_{i=0}^{\phi(k)} q_i x^i$, $a(x) = \sum_{i=0}^{\phi(k)-1} a_i x^i$ and set $v(x)$ to be the polynomial of degree $< \phi(k)$ such that $v(x) \equiv q(a(x)) (\bmod \Phi_k(x))$, then $v(x)$ can be computed as $v(x) = \sum_{i=0}^{\phi(k)-1} \sum_{j=0}^{\phi(k)} q_j v_{ij} x^i$, where v_{ij} is a combination of $a_0, ..., a_{\phi(k)-1}$.

Taking $a_0, ..., a_{\phi(k)-1}$ as indeterminate coefficients, we get an equation system

$$V \begin{pmatrix} q_0 \\ q_1 \\ q_2 \\ \vdots \\ q_{\phi(k)} \end{pmatrix} = \begin{pmatrix} 0 \\ 1 \\ 0 \\ \vdots \\ 0 \end{pmatrix} \qquad (1)$$

where $V = (v_{ij})$ is a $\phi(k) \times (\phi(k) + 1)$ matrix.

Unfortunately, the Eq. (1) is an over-determined equation system. To deal with this problem, we divide V into two parts as $V = (V_1, V_2)$, where V_1 is a

$\phi(k) \times \phi(k)$ matrix and V_2 is a $\phi(k) \times 1$ vector. Adding $q_{\phi(k)}$ as an indeterminate coefficient, we get a new equation system

$$V_1 \begin{pmatrix} q_0 \\ q_1 \\ q_2 \\ \vdots \\ q_{\phi(k)-1} \end{pmatrix} = \begin{pmatrix} 0 \\ 1 \\ 0 \\ \vdots \\ 0 \end{pmatrix} - q_{\phi(k)} \cdot V_2 \tag{2}$$

If the Eq. (2) has a solution in $\mathbb{Q}[q_{\phi(k)}, a_0, a_1, ..., a_{\phi(k)-1}]$, then a parameterized expression of $q(x, q_{\phi(k)}, a_0, a_1, ..., a_{\phi(k)-1})$ for $\Phi_k(q)$ admitting an irreducible factor of degree $\phi(k)$ has been obtained.

3.3   Algorithm for Generating Parameterized Families with $\rho = 1$

The method of generating the parameterized expression of q is summarized below as Algorithm 1.

Algorithm 1. Generating the parameterized expression of q

Input: Embedding degree k.

Output: the parameterized expression of $q(x, q_{\phi(k)}, a_0, a_1, ..., a_{\phi(k)-1})$ such that $\Phi_k(q)$ has an irreducible factor of degree $\phi(k)$.

1. Construct the Equation (2)
2. Solve Equation (2) in $\mathbb{Q}[q_{\phi(k)}, a_0, a_1, ..., a_{\phi(k)-1}]$:
3.   If it has no solution, then there is no family, exit;
4.   Otherwise, go to step 5.
5. Construct the parameterized expression $q(x, q_{\phi(k)}, a_0, a_1, ..., a_{\phi(k)-1})$ by substituting each solution into coefficients of x. It has the form as

$$q(x, q_{\phi(k)}, a_0, a_1, ..., a_{\phi(k)-1}) = q_{\phi(k)} x^{\phi(k)} + \sum_{i=0}^{\phi(k)-1} f_i(q_{\phi(k)}, a_0, a_1, ..., a_{\phi(k)-1}) x^i.$$

The method of generating the parameterized families with $\rho = 1$ is summarized in Algorithm 2.

Remark 1. Freeman et al. in [4] concluded that if $f(x) = 4q(x) - t(x)^2$ is a square-free polynomial of degree at least 3, then there will be only a finite number of integer solutions to the equation $Dy^2 = f(x)$. So in step 5 of Algorithm 2, if the degree of x in $f(x, q_{\phi(k)}, a_0, a_1, ..., a_{\phi(k)-1})$ is less than 3, the condition of CM equation is thought to be satisfied.

Algorithm 2. Generating the parameterized families with $\rho = 1$

Input: $q(x, q_{\phi(k)}, a_0, a_1, ..., a_{\phi(k)-1})$ and embedding degree k.
Output:The parameterized families of pairing-friendly elliptic curves with $\rho = 1$.
1. See $\Phi_k(q(x, q_{\phi(k)}, a_0, a_1, ..., a_{\phi(k)-1})$ as a polynomial with regard to x. Factor it and get all irreducible factors $r((x, q_{\phi(k)}, a_0, a_1, ..., a_{\phi(k)-1})$ of degree $\phi(k)$.
2. For each pair of $q((x, q_{\phi(k)}, a_0, a_1, ..., a_{\phi(k)-1}), r(x, q_{\phi(k)}, a_0, a_1, ..., a_{\phi(k)-1}))$:
3. Compute

$$t(x, q_{\phi(k)}, a_0, ..., a_{\phi(k)-1}) = q(x, q_{\phi(k)}, a_0, ..., a_{\phi(k)-1}) + 1 - h \cdot r(x, q_{\phi(k)}, a_0, ..., a_{\phi(k)-1})$$

where $h \in \mathbb{Q}$ is a cofactor;
4. If degree of x in $t(x, q_{\phi(k)}, a_0, a_1, ..., a_{\phi(k)-1})$ is less than or equal to half the degree of x in $q(x, q_{\phi(k)}, a_0, a_1, ..., a_{\phi(k)-1})$, the triple (u, t, r) satisfies the Hasse-Weil Bound.
5. Computer CM equation $f(x, q_{\phi(k)}, a_0, a_1, ..., a_{\phi(k)-1}) = 4q - t^2$. If the degree of x in $f(x, q_{\phi(k)}, a_0, a_1, ..., a_{\phi(k)-1})$ is less than 3, then the triple $(q, t, h \cdot r)$ is a parameterized family of pairing-friendly elliptic curves with $\rho = 1$.

4   Parameterized Families for $\phi(k) = 2$

Miyaji, Nakabayashi and Takano [12] presented explicit families of prime orders of ordinary elliptic curves with $\phi(k) = 2$ (a.k.a MNT curves). In this section, we construct the parameterized families and prove that our results can cover all families of curves satisfying $\rho = 1$. we generalise the MNT argument to allow for cofactors.

As a result, MNT families can be viewed as a special case of our parameterized families. We also revisit the supersingular elliptic curves from a new perspective.

4.1   The Case $k = 3$

When the embedding degree k equals to 3, then $\phi_3(x) = x^2 + x + 1$, we have $\mathbb{Q}(\xi_3) = \mathbb{Q}[x]/(x^2 + x + 1)$ and $\xi_3 = x$.

Let $q(x) = q_2 x^2 + q_1 x + q_0$ and $a(x) = a_1 x + a_0 \in \mathbb{Q}(\xi_3)$, we have

$$q(a(x)) = q(a_1 x + a_0) \equiv x \bmod (x^2 + x + 1) \tag{3}$$

Using Algorithm 1, we get the unique parameterized expression of $q(x, q_2, a_0, a_1)$:

$$q = q_2 x^2 + q_1 x + q_0$$
$$= q_2 x^2 - \frac{2q_2 a_1 a_0 - q_2 a_1^2 - 1}{a_1} x + \frac{q_2 a_1 a_0^2 - a_0 q_2 a_1^2 + q_2 a_1^3 - a_0}{a_1}.$$

Factoring $\Phi_3(q(x, q_2, a_0, a_1))$, we get

$$\Phi_3(q(x, q_2, a_0, a_1)) = \frac{1}{a_1^2} r_1(x, q_2, a_0, a_1) \cdot r_2(x, q_2, a_0, a_1),$$

where

$$r_1(x, q_2, a_0, a_1) = x^2 - (2a_0 - a_1)x + a_0^2 - a_0a_1 + a_1^2,$$
$$r_2(x, q_2, a_0, a_1) = q_2^2 a_1^2 x^2 - 2a_0 a_1^2 q_2^2 x + 2a_1 q_2 x + a_1^3 q_2^2 x + q_2^2 a_1^2 a_0^2 - 2q_2 a_1 a_0$$
$$- a_0 q_2^2 a_1^3 + q_2 a_1^2 + q_2^2 a_1^4 + 1.$$

We have the following result:

Theorem 1. *All quadratic families of pairing-friendly elliptic curves with $k = 3$ satisfying $\rho = 1$ must have the form as:*

$$
\begin{cases}
q(x, q_2, a_0, a_1) = q_2 x^2 - \dfrac{2q_2 a_1 a_0 - q_2 a_1^2 - 1}{a_1} x + \dfrac{q_2 a_1 a_0^2 - a_0 q_2 a_1^2 + q_2 a_1^3 - a_0}{a_1} \\[2mm]
r(x, q_2, a_0, a_1) = h_1(x^2 - (2a_0 - a_1)x + a_0^2 - a_0 a_1 + a_1^2) \quad or \\[1mm]
\qquad\qquad = h_2(q_2^2 a_1^2 x^2 - 2a_0 a_1^2 q_2^2 x + 2a_1 q_2 x + a_1^3 q_2^2 x + q_2^2 a_1^2 a_0^2 - \\[1mm]
\qquad\qquad\quad 2q_2 a_1 a_0 - a_0 q_2^2 a_1^3 + q_2 a_1^2 + q_2^2 a_1^4 + 1) \\[1mm]
t(x, q_2, a_0, a_1) = q(x, q_2, a_0, a_1) + 1 - r(x, q_2, a_0, a_1)
\end{cases}
$$

where the degree of x in $t(x, q_2, a_0, a_1)$ is 1.

Proof. Suppose $(q(x), r(x), t(x))$ is an arbitrary quadratic family of pairing-friendly elliptic curves with $k = 3$ and $\rho = 1$, then $r(x)$ is an irreducible factor of $\Phi_3(q(x))$ and the degree of $q(x)$ and $r(x)$ is 2. By Lemma 1, $q(x)$ must satisfy the Eq. (3). Since $q(x, q_2, a_0, a_1)$ is the unique solution of Eq. (3), $q(x)$ can be expressed by $q(x, q_2, a_0, a_1)$.

Curves on $\mathbb{F}_{q^n}$. We discuss the conditions of curves with embedding degree $k = 3$ on extension field $\mathbb{F}_{q^n}$ where $n > 0$.

Apparently, in this case, $q(x, q_2, a_0, a_1) = q_2 x^2$, so we have

$$
\begin{cases}
q_0 = \dfrac{q_2 a_1 a_0^2 - a_0 q_2 a_1^2 + q_2 a_1^3 - a_0}{a_1} = 0, \\[3mm]
q_1 = -\dfrac{2q_2 a_1 a_0 - q_2 a_1^2 - 1}{a_1} = 0.
\end{cases}
$$

Solving the equation, we get 2 solutions:

$$\{a_0 = a_1, a_1 = a_1, q_2 = \frac{1}{a_1^2}\}, \quad \{a_0 = -a_1, a_1 = a_1, q_2 = -\frac{1}{3a_1^2}\}.$$

Since $q_2 > 0$ must be satisfied, $q(x)$ has the unique form $q(x) = x^2$. Factoring $\Phi_3(q(x))$, we obtain

$$\Phi_3(x^2) = (x^2 + x + 1)(x^2 - x + 1),$$

And thus

$$q = p^{2m}, r = q \pm \sqrt{q} + 1, t = \mp\sqrt{q},$$

where p is a prime. This is exactly the only kind of supersingular elliptic curves with embedding degree 3 [4, Sect. 3.3].

Curves on $\mathbb{F}_q$. According to Theroem 1, all quadratic families of pairing-friendly elliptic curves can be obtained by changing values of q_2, a_1 and a_0.

We list some examples as below:

- $q_2 = 12, a_1 = \frac{1}{6}, a_0 = \frac{1}{3}$.
  This family can be computed as

$$\begin{cases} q(x) =12x^2 - 1, \\ r(x) =h_1(x^2 - \dfrac{1}{2}x + \dfrac{1}{12}) \quad or \\ \qquad =h_2(4x^2 + 2l + \dfrac{1}{3}), \\ t(x) =q(x) + 1 - r(x). \end{cases}$$

In order to satisfy Hasse-Weil Bound, set $h_1 = 12, h_2 = 3$, then

$$\begin{cases} q(x) =12x^2 - 1, \\ r(x) =12x^2 \pm 6x + 1, \\ t(x) = \mp 6x - 1. \end{cases}$$

This is just the family of MNT curves [12].

- $q_2 = 8, a_1 = \frac{1}{2}, a_0 = \frac{1}{4}$.
  This family can be written as

$$\begin{cases} q(x) =8x^2 + 2x + 1 \\ r(x) =h_1(x^2 + \dfrac{3}{16}) \quad or \\ \qquad =h_2(16x^2 + 8x + 4) \\ t(x) =q(x) + 1 - r(x) \end{cases}$$

For the condition of Hasse-Weil Bound, h_2 is set to be $\frac{1}{2}$, then

$$\begin{cases} q(x) =8x^2 + 2x + 1, \\ r(x) =2(4x^2 + 2x + 1), \\ t(x) = -2x. \end{cases}$$

4.2   The Case $k = 4$

If $k = 4$, then $\phi_4(x) = x^2 + 1$, we have $\mathbb{Q}(\xi_4) = \mathbb{Q}[x]/(x^2 + 1)$ and $\xi_4 = x$.
Let $q(x) = q_2x^2 + q_1x + q_0$ and $a(x) = a_1x + a_0 \in \mathbb{Q}(\xi_4)$, we have

$$q(a(x)) = q(a_1x + a_0) \equiv x \bmod (x^2 + 1). \tag{4}$$

Using Algorithm 1, we get the unique solution of $q(x, q_2, a_0, a_1)$ as:

$$q = q_2 x^2 + q_1 x + q_0$$

$$= q_2 x^2 - \frac{2 q_2 a_1 a_0 - 1}{a_1} x + \frac{q_2 a_1 a_0^2 + q_2 a_1^3 - a_0}{a_1}.$$

Factoring $\Phi_4(q(x, q_2, a_1, a_0))$, we get

$$\Phi_4(q(x, q_2, a_1, a_0)) = \frac{1}{a_1^2} r_1(x, q_2, a_1, a_0) r_2(x, q_2, a_1, a_0),$$

where

$$r_1(x, q_2, a_1, a_0) = x^2 - 2a_0 x + a_0^2 + a_1^2,$$
$$r_2(x, q_2, a_1, a_0) = q_2^2 a_1^2 x^2 - 2 a_0 a_1^2 q_2^2 x + 2 a_1 q_2 x + q_2^2 a_1^2 a_0^2 - 2 q_2 a_1 a_0 + q_2^2 a_1^4 + 1.$$

Similarly with the case $k = 3$, we obtain the following result.

Theorem 2. *All quadratic families of pairing-friendly elliptic curves with $k = 4$ satisfying $\rho = 1$ must have the form as:*

$$\begin{cases} q(x, q_2, a_0, a_1) = q_2 x^2 - \dfrac{2 q_2 a_1 a_0 - 1}{a_1} x + \dfrac{q_2 a_1 a_0^2 + q_2 a_1^3 - a_0}{a_1}, \\ r(x, q_2, a_0, a_1) = h_1(x^2 - 2a_0 x + a_0^2 + a_1^2) \quad or \\ \qquad\qquad = h_2(q_2^2 a_1^2 x^2 - 2 a_0 a_1^2 q_2^2 x + 2 a_1 q_2 x + q_2^2 a_1^2 a_0^2 - 2 q_2 a_1 a_0 + q_2^2 a_1^4 + 1), \\ t(x, q_2, a_0, a_1) = q(x, q_2, a_0, a_1) + 1 - r(x, q_2, a_0, a_1). \end{cases}$$

where the degree of x in $t(x, q_2, a_0, a_1)$ is 1.

Curves on $\mathbb{F}_{q^n}$. We also explore the conditions of curves with embedding degree $k = 4$ on extension field $\mathbb{F}_{q^n}$ where $n > 0$.

In this case, $q(x, q_2, a_0, a_1) = q_2 x^2$. So we have

$$\begin{cases} q_0 = \dfrac{q_2 a_1 a_0^2 + q_2 a_1^3 - a_0}{a_1} = 0, \\ q_1 = \dfrac{2 q_2 a_1 a_0 - 1}{a_1} = 0. \end{cases}$$

Solving the equation, we get 2 solutions:

$$\{a_0 = a_1, a_1 = a_1, q_2 = \frac{1}{2a_1^2}\}, \quad \{a_0 = -a_1, a_1 = a_1, q_2 = -\frac{1}{2a_1^2}\}.$$

Since $q_2 > 0$ must be satisfied, $q(x)$ has the unique form $q(x) = 2x^2$. Factoring $\Phi_3(q(x))$, we get

$$\Phi_4(2x^2) = (2x^2 + 2x + 1)(2x^2 - 2x + 1).$$

It is only of interest when $x = 2^m$ is a power of 2. Given $q = 2^{2m+1}$, we obtain

$$q = 2^{2m+1}, r = q \pm \sqrt{2q} + 1, t = \mp\sqrt{2q}.$$

This is exactly the only kind of supersingular elliptic curves with embedding degree 4 [4, Sect. 3.4].

Curves on $\mathbb{F}_q$. According to Theorem 2, all quadratic families of pairing-friendly elliptic curves can be obtained by choosing proper values of q_2, a_1 and a_0.

We list some examples as following:

- $q_2 = 1, a_1 = 1, a_0 = 0$.
  For the condition of Hasse-Weil Bound, we set $h_1 = 1, h_2 = 1$ and obtain the family

$$\begin{cases} q(x) = x^2 + x + 1, \\ r(x) = x^2 + 1 \quad or \\ \quad = x^2 + 2x + 2, \\ t(x) = x + 1 \quad or \\ \quad = -x. \end{cases}$$

This also belongs to the family of the MNT curves [12].
- $q_2 = 8, a_1 = \frac{1}{2}, a_0 = -\frac{1}{4}$.
  We get the family by setting $h_2 = \frac{1}{2}$, then

$$\begin{cases} q(x) = 8x^2 + 6x + 3, \\ r(x) = 4(2x^2 + 2x + 1), \\ t(x) = -2x. \end{cases}$$

4.3 The Case $k = 6$

If $k = 6$, write $\phi_6(x) = x^2 - x + 1$, then we have $\mathbb{Q}(\xi_6) = \mathbb{Q}[x]/(x^2 - x + 1)$ and $\xi_6 = x$.

Let $q(x) = q_2 x^2 + q_1 x + q_0$ and $a(x) = a_1 x + a_0 \in \mathbb{Q}(\xi_3)$, we obtain

$$q(a(x)) = q(a_1 x + a_0) \equiv x \mod (x^2 - x + 1). \tag{5}$$

Using Algorithm 1, we get the unique parameterized expression of $q(x, q_2, a_0, a_1)$ as

$$q = q_2 x^2 + q_1 x + q_0$$
$$= q_2 x^2 - \frac{2q_2 a_1 a_0 + q_2 a_1^2 - 1}{a_1} x + \frac{q_2 a_1 a_0^2 + a_0 q_2 a_1^2 - a_0 + q_2 a_1^3}{a_1}.$$

We factor $\Phi_6(q(x, q_2, a_0, a_1))$ as

$$\Phi_6(q(x)) = \frac{1}{a_1^2} r_1(x) r_2(x),$$

where

$$r_1(x) = x^2 - (2a_0 + a_1)x + a_0^2 + a_0a_1 + a_1^2,$$
$$r_2(x) = q_2^2 a_1^2 x^2 - 2a_0 a_1^2 q_2^2 x + 2a_1 q_2 x - a_1^3 q_2^2 x + q_2^2 a_1^2 a_0^2 - 2q_2 a_1 a_0 + a_0 q_2^2 a_1^3$$
$$- q_2 a_1^2 + q_2^2 a_1^4 + 1.$$

It follows that

Theorem 3. *All quadratic families of pairing-friendly elliptic curves with $k = 6$ satisfying $\rho = 1$ must have the form as:*

$$
\begin{cases}
q(x, q_2, a_0, a_1) = q_2 x^2 - \dfrac{2q_2 a_1 a_0 + q_2 a_1^2 - 1}{a_1} x + \dfrac{q_2 a_1 a_0^2 + a_0 q_2 a_1^2 - a_0 + q_2 a_1^3}{a_1}, \\
r(x, q_2, a_0, a_1) = h_1(x^2 - (2a_0 + a_1)x + a_0^2 + a_0 a_1 + a_1^2) \quad or \\
\qquad = h_2(q_2^2 a_1^2 x^2 - 2a_0 a_1^2 q_2^2 x + 2a_1 q_2 x - a_1^3 q_2^2 x + q_2^2 a_1^2 a_0^2 - 2q_2 a_1 a_0 \\
\qquad\quad + a_0 q_2^2 a_1^3 - q_2 a_1^2 + q_2^2 a_1^4 + 1, \\
t(x, q_2, a_0, a_1) = q(x, q_2, a_0, a_1) + 1 - r(x, q_2, a_0, a_1),
\end{cases}
$$

where the degree of x in $t(x, q_2, a_0, a_1)$ is 1.

Curves on $\mathbb{F}_{q^n}$. We find the conditions of curves with embedding degree $k = 6$ on extension field $\mathbb{F}_{q^n}$ where $n > 0$.

Apparently $q(x) = q_2 x^2$, so we have

$$
\begin{cases}
q_0 = \dfrac{q_2 a_1 a_0^2 + a_0 q_2 a_1^2 - a_0 + q_2 a_1^3}{a_1} = 0, \\
q_1 = -\dfrac{2q_2 a_1 a_0 + q_2 a_1^2 - 1}{a_1} = 0.
\end{cases}
$$

Solving the equation, we obtain 2 solutions as

$$\{a_0 = -a_1, a_1 = a_1, q_2 = -\frac{1}{a_1^2}\}, \quad \{a_0 = a_1, a_1 = a_1, q_2 = \frac{1}{3a_1^2}\}.$$

Since $q_2 > 0$ must be satisfied, $q(x)$ has the unique form $q(x) = \frac{1}{3}x^2$, then $\Phi_6(q(x))$ has the following factorization as

$$\Phi_6(\frac{1}{3}x^2) = \frac{1}{9}(x^2 + 3x + 3)(x^2 - 3x + 3)$$
$$= (\frac{1}{3}x^2 + x + 1)(\frac{1}{3}x^2 - x + 1).$$

It is only of interest when $l = 3^m$ is a power of 3, giving $q = 3^{2m-1}$, we obtain

$$q = 3^{2m-1}, r = q \pm \sqrt{3q} + 1, t = \mp\sqrt{3q}.$$

This is exactly the only kind of supersingular elliptic curves with embedding degree 6 [4, Sec. 3.5].

Curves on $\mathbb{F}_q$. All quadratic families of pairing-friendly elliptic curves in this situation can be obtained by iterating all possible values of q_2, a_1 and a_0. Some examples of this kind are listed as follows:

- $q_2 = 4, a_0 = 0, a_1 = \frac{1}{2}$.
  This tripe lies in the family of MNT curves [12], since

$$\begin{cases} q(x) = 4x^2 + 1, \\ r(x) = 4x^2 \pm 2x + 1, \\ t(x) = \mp 2x + 1. \end{cases}$$

  where $h_1 = 4, h_2 = 1$.
- $q_2 = 16, a_1 = \frac{1}{2}, a_0 = -\frac{1}{2}$.
  Set $h_1 = 16$, then the family in this case is

$$\begin{cases} q(x) = 16x^2 + 10x + 5, \\ r(x) = 4(4x^2 + 2x + 1), \\ t(x) = 2x + 2. \end{cases}$$

4.4 Cryptographic Perspectives

The above constructions are mainly in a mathematical fashion. The results derived from our parameterized method naturally covered families of ordinary/supersingular elliptic curves with desired embedding degrees and ρ-value (as summarized in [4]). It should be noted that not all of these families of paring friendly curves are applicable for cryptography.

For one thing, elliptic curves with low embedding degrees and ρ-values are desirable in order to speed up arithmetic on the elliptic curve [4]. Since for our parameterized families of curves the ρ-values are approximate to 1 and the embedding degrees are no more than 6, the required field arithmetic for pairing evaluation would also be very efficient.

For another, pairing friendly curves defined over finite fields with characteristic 2 and 3 are considered to be not safe now in cryptographic applications, since the progress in function fields sieve method [10] makes the DLP in the multiplicative group of $\mathbb{F}_{2^n}$ or $\mathbb{F}_{3^n}$ less complex, which implies that the corresponding ECDLP on desired elliptic curves would be vulnerable to MOV/FR attack. Practical attack implementations have been exploited in several literatures [7,8]. Thus, we should avoid to choose such curves for building up pairing based crypto-systems.

5 Conclusion

In this work, we presented a new strategy to construct pairing-friendly elliptic curves. The utility of such method has been illustrated by constructing parameterized families of pairing-friendly elliptic curves of embedding degrees 3, 4 and 6. It is also shown in all these 3 cases, our results can cover all the quadratic families. We hope this method would also serve as an inspiration to explore more pairing friendly elliptic curves with higher embedding degrees.

Acknowledgments. The authors would like to thank the anonymous reviewers for their helpful comments and suggestions. Meng Zhang and Maozhi Xu were partially supported by the Natural Science Foundation of China (Grants No. 61272499, 61472016 and 61672059), Zhi Hu was partially supported by the Natural Science Foundation of China (Grant No. 61602526).

References

1. Atkin, A.O.L., Morain, F.: Elliptic curves and primality proving. Math. Comput. **61**(203), 29–68 (1997)
2. Balasubramanian, R., Koblitz, N.: The improbability that an elliptic curve has subexponential discrete log problem under the Menezes-Okamoto-Vanstone algorithm. J. Crypt. **11**(2), 141–145 (1998)
3. Dan, B., Franklin, M.: Identity-based encryption from the Weil pairing. SIAM J. Comput. **32**(3), 213–229 (2003)
4. Freeman, D., Scott, M., Teske, E.: A taxonomy of pairing-friendly elliptic curves. J. Crypt. **23**(2), 224–280 (2010)
5. Frey, G., Rück, H.: A remark concerning m-divisibility and the discrete logarithm in the divisor class group of curves. Math. Comput. **62**, 865–874 (1994)
6. Galbraith, S.D., Mckee, J.F., Valena, P.C.: Ordinary abelian varieties having small embedding degree. Finite Fields Appl. **13**(4), 800–814 (2007)
7. Granger, R., Kleinjung, T., Zumbrägel, J.: Breaking '128-bit secure' supersingular binary curves. In: Garay, J.A., Gennaro, R. (eds.) CRYPTO 2014. LNCS, vol. 8617, pp. 126–145. Springer, Heidelberg (2014). doi:10.1007/978-3-662-44381-1_8
8. Hayashi, T., Shimoyama, T., Shinohara, N., Takagi, T.: Breaking pairing-based cryptosystems using η_T pairing over GF($3^9$7). In: Wang, X., Sako, K. (eds.) ASIACRYPT 2012. LNCS, vol. 7658, pp. 43–60. Springer, Heidelberg (2012). doi:10.1007/978-3-642-34961-4_5
9. Joux, A.: A one round protocol for tripartite Diffie-Hellman. J. Crypt. **17**(4), 385–393 (2006)
10. Joux, A., Pierrot, C.: Technical history of discrete logarithms in small characteristic finite fields - the road from subexponential to quasi-polynomial complexity. Des. Codes Crypt. **78**(1), 73–85 (2016)
11. Menezes, A.J., Okamoto, T., Vanstone, S.A.: Reducing elliptic curve logarithms to logarithms in a finite field. IEEE Trans. Inf. Theor. **39**(5), 1639–1646 (1993)
12. Miyaji, A., Nakabayashi, M., Takano, S.: New explicit conditions of elliptic curve traces for FR-reductions. IEICE Trans. Fundam. Electron. Commun. Comput. Sci. **84**(5), 1234–1243 (2001)
13. Paterson, K.: ID-based signatures from pairings on elliptic curves. Electron. Lett. **38**, 1025–1026 (2002)
14. Tanaka, S., Nakamula, K.: Constructing pairing-friendly elliptic curves using factorization of cyclotomic polynomials. In: Galbraith, S.D., Paterson, K.G. (eds.) Pairing 2008. LNCS, vol. 5209, pp. 136–145. Springer, Heidelberg (2008). doi:10.1007/978-3-540-85538-5_10
15. Urroz, J.J., Shparlinski, I.E.: On the number of isogeny classes of pairing-friendly elliptic curves and statistics of MNT curves. Math. Comput. **81**(278), 1093–1110 (2012)

Constructing Isogenies on Extended Jacobi Quartic Curves

Xiu Xu[1,2,3], Wei Yu[1,2(✉)], Kunpeng Wang[1,2,3], and Xiaoyang He[1,2,3]

[1] State Key Laboratory of Information Security,
Institute of Information Engineering, Chinese Academy of Sciences,
Beijing, China
yuwei_1_yw@163.com, xuxiu@iie.ac.cn
[2] Data Assurance and Communication Security Research Center,
Chinese Academy of Sciences, Beijing, China
[3] University of Chinese Academy of Sciences, Beijing, China

Abstract. Isogenies are widely used in elliptic curves. Since Moody and Shumow [20] proposed isogenies on Edwards and Huff curves analogues of Vélu's formulas, they have pointed out a new way to construct isogenies. However, hardly any isogeny on Jacobi quartic curves has been designed, this paper extends their work to construct isogenies on extended Jacobi quartic curves for the first time including a 2-isogeny and a generalized l-isogeny for any odd l as well as an improved l-isogeny. This paper also estimates the time complexity of the improved l-isogeny. If the constants are carefully chosen, the Jacobi quartic isogeny is about to catch up with Huff isogeny.

Keywords: Elliptic curves · Isogeny · Extended Jacobi quartic curves · Vélu's formulas

1 Introduction

Since the elliptic curve was first put forward by Miller and Koblitz [1,2], it has shown a boom for its highest security in one bit. Isogenies play an important role in elliptic curves as a special structure, especially in some relevant computational problems. Brier and Joye [3] justified that most curves recommended in cryptographic standards can be mapped to a curve $y^2 = x^3 + ax + b$ with parameter $a = -3$ by an isogeny of small degree. One of these problems is that if given the kernel of an isogeny, how to determine the rational functions forming the isogeny. Tate [4] put forward the theorem stating that two elliptic curves are isogenous over a finite field $\mathbb{F}_q$ if and only if they have the same number of $\mathbb{F}_q$-points. Therefore, many algorithms to count the number of points on an elliptic

This work is supported in part by National Research Foundation of China under Grant No. 61502487, 61272040, and in part by National Basic Research Program of China (973) under Grant No. 2013CB338001.

K. Chen et al. (Eds.): Inscrypt 2016, LNCS 10143, pp. 416–427, 2017.
DOI: 10.1007/978-3-319-54705-3_26

curve are raised, such as Schoof's idea [5]. Galbraith [6] described a probabilistic algorithm for counting the isogeny, known that two curves defined over the same finite field have the same rational points. Galbraith, et al. also proposed a low storage algorithm for constructing isogenies between ordinary elliptic curves in [7] and gave an improvement by modifying the pseudorandom walk so that lower-degree isogenies can be used more frequently in [8]. With the development of quantum algorithms, David Jao, et al. [9] described a quantum algorithm for computing an isogeny between any two supersingular elliptic curves, and they also presented quantum-resistant public cryptosystems based on supersingular elliptic curves isogenies in [10].

In an algebraic view, isogenies of elliptic curves are independent of the specific model chosen for the curve. However, for computational aspects the model chosen for the curve matters a lot. So there is a need to carry out more research on isogenies for different models of elliptic curves. Jacobi quartic curves [11,12] are acknowledged for efficient arithmetics in regard to their group law and immunity to side channel attacks. This form produces the fastest unified addition formula for curves of even order. Later, many researchers improved this operation [13–15]. But we can hardly find any isogenies on Jacobi quartic curves after a careful survey. Hence, it is essential to construct one isogeny on this model and it is just what this paper will do.

The principal operation in elliptic curves is scalar multiplication and it is also the most time-consuming. Scalar multiplication is to compute kP where k is an integer and P is a rational point on an elliptic curve. A large number of methods have been raised to speed up this calculation. The significant application of isogenies is to compute scalar multiplication efficiently. If there is an l-isogeny φ on an elliptic curve, then we have a product expression $[l] = \hat{\varphi}\varphi$. The complexity to directly evaluate $[l]P$ is $O(l^2)$, since the $[l]$ map has degree l^2. But the existence of an l-isogeny yields an improvement to $O(l)$ theoretically. Galbraith, Lin and Scott [16] gave a universal construction combining Frobenius expansion and l-isogeny, quadratic twists of curves in particular. They made full use of the property of efficiently computable endomorphisms on a large class of curves. GLS method has opened up new opportunities for GLV [17]. A speedup of up to 50% was reached in GLV. In [18] scalar multiplication 2P and 3P are computed by suitable isogeny decompositions with the fastest speed for specific curves. Subsequently, Dustin Moody [19] quintupled points on curves using 5-isogenies. He also pointed out that it is unlikely to be more efficient than other methods using l-isogenies to compute the multiplication by l map (if l larger than 5).

Dustin Moody and Daniel Shumow [20] proposed isogenies on Edwards and Huff curves based on Vélu formulas [21]. Vélu formulas work in an additive form, which is different from our multiplicative form about point coordinates. The method of coordinate multiplication seems to be available for all kinds of elliptic curve forms. This paper not only constructs a 2-isogeny on extended Jacobi quartic curves for the first time, but also a general l-isogeny for any odd l. We give a detailed proof about the isogenies and their properties. Since there exist efficient alternative addition formulas, we attempt to construct a faster isogeny relatively. We also estimate the time complexity and compare it with Edwards and Huff curves.

The rest of this paper is structured as follows. Section 2 reviews the preliminaries of how Vélu's formulas work and some properties of the extended Jacobi quartic curves. Section 3 constructs a 2-isogeny on extended Jacobi quartic curves by mapping to and from Weierstrass form. Section 4 constructs isogenies of any odd degree and demonstrates the theorem in detail. Section 5 analyzes the advantages and drawbacks about the isogeny we obtain in Sect. 4 and then presents a more efficient formula with a brief estimate about the computation complexity. Finally, we draw our conclusions and discuss avenues for future work.

2   Preliminaries

2.1   Vélu's Formulas

Vélu [21] provided a method to construct explicit isogenies between Weierstrass curves. Vélu's formulas give explicit isogenies if given the kernel, but only take effect for curves in Weierstrass form. Let $E : y^2 = x^3 + ax + b$ be an elliptic curve in short Weierstrass form for simplicity. Next we describe Vélu's formulas briefly, where we adopt the notations in [20] for the most part. An isogeny $\varphi : E_1 \to E_2$ over field K may be expressed by rational functions

$$\varphi(x, y) = \left(\frac{\varphi_1(x, y)}{\psi^2(x, y)}, \frac{\varphi_2(x, y)}{\psi^3(x, y)} \right),$$

where φ_1, φ_2 and ψ are rational functions over K. Vélu told how to explicitly find the rational functions of an isogeny with kernel F.

For any $P = (x_P, y_P)$ on E, define

$$\varphi(P) = \begin{cases} \infty & P \in F \\ \left(x_P + \sum_{Q \in F - \infty} (x_{P+Q} - x_Q), y_P + \sum_{Q \in F - \infty} (y_{P+Q} - y_Q) \right) & P \notin F \end{cases}$$

In order to present the formulas with rational functions, Vélu partitioned F into two sets F^+ and F^- such that $F = F^+ \cup F^-$. In this way, $P \in F^+$ if and only if $-P \in F^-$. Then the l-isogeny $\varphi : E_1 \to E_2$ is defined as

$$(x, y) \mapsto$$

$$\left(x + \sum_{P \in F^+} \left(\frac{v_P}{x - x_P} - \frac{u_P}{(x - x_P)^2} \right), y - \sum_{P \in F^+} \left(\frac{2u_P * y}{(x - x_P)^3} + v_P \frac{y - y_P - g_P^x * g_P^y}{(x - x_P)^2} \right) \right)$$

where

$$v = \sum_{P \in F^+} v_P, v_P = 2g_P^x, g_P^x = 3x_P^2 + a;$$

$$w = \sum_{P \in F^+} u_P + x_P * v_P, u_P = (g_P^y)^2, g_P^y = -2y_P.$$

Here, let $g = x^3 + ax + b - y^2$. g_P^x and g_P^y represent the partial derivatives of g at point P, respectively.

There is another method to show the isogeny φ written by its kernel polynomial [22]. The additive form is utilized in Vélu's formulas, by which inspiration may be sparked. One may ask if multiplicative form is reasonable here. That's just what we will have a try later on.

2.2 Extended Jacobi Quartic Curves

Suppose K is a finite field of characteristic greater than 2, an extended Jacobi quartic curve can be defined as

$$E_{J,d,a} : y^2 = dx^4 + 2ax^2 + 1$$

where $a, d \in K$ with $\Delta = 256d(a^2 - d)^2 \neq 0$ [11]. All elliptic curves with a point of order 2 can be represented in this form. The j-invariant of this curve is given by $64d^{-1}(a^2 - d)^{-2}(a^2 + 3d)^3 \in K$. The identity element is $(0, 1)$ and the negative of a point (x, y) is $(-x, y)$. The point $(0, -1)$ has order 2. The addition formula [11] is defined by

$$(x_1, y_1) + (x_2, y_2) = (x_3, y_3).$$

$$x_3 = \frac{x_1 y_2 + x_2 y_1}{1 - dx_1^2 x_2^2},$$

$$y_3 = \frac{(y_1 y_2 + 2ax_1 x_2)(1 + dx_1^2 x_2^2) + 2dx_1 x_2(x_1^2 + x_2^2)}{(1 - dx_1^2 x_2^2)^2}.$$

This formula can prevent SPA-like attacks. Suppose that a Weierstrass elliptic curve has a point of order 2, then there is a birational equivalence from a curve in extended Jacobi quartic form to a curve in Weierstrass form. The map is

$$\phi : E_{J,d,a} \rightarrow E_1$$

$$(x, y) \mapsto \left(\frac{2y + 2}{x^2} + 2a, \frac{4y + 4}{x^3} + \frac{4a}{x}\right), \tag{1}$$

and the inversion is

$$\phi^{-1} : E_1 \rightarrow E_{J,d,a}$$

$$(x, y) \mapsto \left(\frac{2x}{y}, \frac{2(x - 2a)x^2}{y^2} - 1\right).$$

After the birational transform, the equation becomes $E_1 : y^2 = x^3 - 4ax^2 + (4a^2 - 4d)x$. We can easily see that $\phi \circ \phi^{-1} = id_{E_1}$ and $\phi^{-1} \circ \phi = id_{E_{J,d,a}}$. But the map ϕ is regular at all points except $(0, -1)$ and $(0, 1)$ corresponding to ∞. However, in [23] it is successful to change ϕ to map all points except $(0, 1)$. Then alternative maps are defined

$$\phi' : E_{J,d,a} \to E_1$$

$$(x,y) \mapsto \left(\frac{2dx^2 + 2a(1+y)}{y-1}, \frac{4a(dx^2+2a) - 4d(1-y)}{(1-y)^2} x \right). \qquad (2)$$

$$\phi'^{-1} : E_1 \to E_{J,d,a},$$

$$(x,y) \mapsto \left(\frac{2y}{(x-2a)^2 - 4d}, \frac{x^2 - 4(a^2-d)}{(x-2a)^2 - 4d} \right).$$

They seem to be a little more complicated to express than the former birational transform.

3   2-Isogeny on Extended Jacobi Quartic Curves

Although Vélu's formulas are intended for odd prime isogeny, when $l = 2$ it is still available for some kind of forms. Then 2-isogeny on the extended Jacobi quartic curve is constructed as follows.

Theorem 1. *Suppose that $E_{J,d,a}$ is the extended Jacobi quartic curve defined over field K, then there is a 2-isogeny φ from $E_{J,d,a}$ to $E_{J,4a^2-4d,-2a}$, given by*

$$\varphi(x,y) = (X(x,y), Y(x,y)),$$

where

$$X(x,y) = \frac{2x(y+1+x^2)}{(y+1+ax^2)^2 - (a^2-d)x^4},$$

$$Y(x,y) = 4\frac{(y+1+ax^2)^3 + (4a^2-4d)(y+1+ax^2)x^4}{((y+1+ax^2)^2 - (a^2-d)x^4)^2} - 1.$$

Proof. First, let ϕ_1 be the birational transform from $E_{J,d,a}$ to a Weierstrass curve E_1 given in (1) which is easier to perform by comparison with (2). Even though it is not regular at $(0,-1)$, we make sacrifices. Then the equation becomes $E_1 : y^2 = x^3 - 4ax^2 + (4a^2 - 4d)x$. Then it is easy to see that $(0,0)$ is the point with order two. By using Vélu's formulas, we get a 2-isogeny ϕ_2 defined as

$$\phi_2 : E_1 \to E_2$$

$$(x,y) \mapsto \left(x + \frac{4a^2 - 4d}{x}, y\frac{x^2 - (4a^2-4d)}{x^2} \right),$$

where E_2 is $y^2 = x^3 - 4ax^2 - (16a^2 - 16d)x + 16a(4a^2 - 4d)$. When only considering the field K itself instead of its algebraic closure $\bar{K}$, there is a unique point $(4a,0)$ of order 2. With the purpose to map E_2 to an extended Jacobi quartic curve, we make use of a linear transform ϕ_3. Then we get a curve E_3 in a similar form to E_1. The linear transform ϕ_3 is performed as

$$\phi_3 : E_2 \to E_3$$

$$(x,y) \mapsto (x - 4a, y),$$

where E_3 is $y^2 = x^3 + 8ax^2 + 16dx$. Since every $v^2 = u^3 + a_2u^2 + a_4u$ is birationally equivalent over K as $E_{Q,(a_2^2-4a_4)/16,-a_2/4}$ [23],

$$\phi_4 : E_3 \to E_{J,\hat{d},\hat{a}}$$

$$(x,y) \mapsto (2\frac{x}{y}, 2(x+4a)\frac{x^2}{y^2} - 1),$$

then we get $E_{J,\hat{d},\hat{a}} : y^2 = \hat{d}x^4 + 2\hat{a}x^2 + 1$, with $\hat{d} = 4a^2 - 4d, \hat{a} = -2a$.

Finally, we compose all the maps above and get the 2-isogenies from $E_{J,d,a}$ to $E_{J,\hat{d},\hat{a}}$. Besides, if we consider the algebraic closure field $\bar{K}$, we can find two more points of order 2 of E_2 and then there are the other two linear transforms. If so, we can obtain the other two 2-isogenies by using the similar way. Here, we omit the detailed description.

4   General l-isogeny on Extended Jacobi Quartic Curves

Theorem 2. *Suppose that F is a subgroup of the extended Jacobi quartic curve $E_{J,d,a}$ with the odd order $l = 2s + 1$, and points*

$$G = \{(0,1), (\pm\alpha_1, \beta_1), ..., (\pm\alpha_s, \beta_s)\}.$$

For any point $P = (x_P, y_P)$ on $E_{J,d,a}$, define

$$\psi(P) = \left(x_P \prod_{Q \in G-(0,1)} \frac{x_{P+Q}}{x_Q}, y_P \prod_{Q \in G-(0,1)} \frac{y_{P+Q}}{y_Q} \right).$$

Then ψ is an l-isogeny, with kernel G, from the curve $E_{J,d,a}$ to the curve $E_{J,\hat{d},\hat{a}}$ with $\hat{a} = a + \sum_{i=1}^{s} \lambda_i$ and $\hat{d} = \mu - 4(a + \sum_{i=1}^{s} \lambda_i)\gamma$ where $\lambda_i = 2d\alpha_i^2 + 2a - \left(\frac{2a\alpha_i + 2d\alpha_i^3}{\beta_i}\right)^2 + 4d\alpha_i, \mu = d + \sum_{i=1}^{s}(4a\lambda_i + \lambda_i^2) + \sum_{j=1, j\neq i}^{s} \sum_{i=1}^{s} 4\lambda_i\lambda_j$ and $\gamma = \sum_{i=1}^{s}(d\alpha_i^2 + 2a - \frac{\beta_i}{\alpha_i^2})$. The coordinate maps are given by

$$\psi(x,y) = (X(x,y), Y(x,y)),$$

where

$$X(x,y) = (-1)^s \frac{x}{A^2} \prod_{i=1}^{s} \frac{\beta_i^2 x^2 - \alpha_i^2 y^2}{1 - d\alpha_i^2 x^2},$$

$$Y(x,y) = \frac{y}{B^2} \prod_{i=1}^{s} \frac{\beta_i^2 y^2 (1 + d\alpha_i^2 x^2)^2 - ((2a\alpha_i + 2d\alpha_i^3)x + (2ad\alpha_i^3 + 2d\alpha_i)x^3)^2}{(1 - d\alpha_i x^2)^4},$$

with $A = \prod_{i=1}^{s} \alpha_i$ and $B = \prod_{i=1}^{s} \beta_i$.

Proof. First, we must show that G is just the kernel of ψ. On the one hand, as it is to see that $\psi(0,1) = (0,1)$ and $\psi(\pm\alpha_i, \beta_i) = (0,1)$, so $G \subseteq ker(\psi)$. On the other hand, if any $P \in ker(\psi)$, i.e. $\psi(P) = (0,1)$ which means that there are some $Q \in G$ such that $x_{P+Q} = 0, y_{P+Q} = 1$. y_{P+Q} is not equal to -1 here because $P \in ker(\psi)$ and $Q \in G \subseteq ker(\psi)$, as a result of which we must have $P + Q \in ker(\psi)$, i.e. $x_{P+Q} = 0, y_{P+Q} = 1$. After that, $P = \pm Q \in G$. So we get $ker(\psi) \subseteq G$ and hence $ker(\psi) = G$. Subsequently, it 's natural to derive the coordinate maps according to the addition law.

Next, $\hat{d}$ and $\hat{a}$ remain to be derived in the image curve $Y^2 = \hat{d}X^4 + 2\hat{a}X^2 + 1$, where X and Y are just the functions of coordinates above. We adopt the similar method as [20]. Considering the function

$$G(x,y) = \hat{d}X(x,y)^4 + 2\hat{a}X(x,y)^2 + 1 - Y(x,y)^2,$$

we are supposed to solve for $\hat{d}$ and $\hat{a}$. If $G(x,y)$ is identically zero, we can conclude that the codomain curve is really an extended Jacobi quartic curve.

We can check that $\psi(0,-1) = (0,-1)$. $\psi(0,1) = (0,1)$ which has been verified above. That is to say points $(0,1)$ and $(0,-1)$ are preserved by the coordinate maps. What's more, on the domain curve $E_{J,d,a}$, the two points are the only two leading to the x-coordinate equal to 0. That is the same to $E_{J,\hat{d},\hat{a}}$. We can prove that the two points are nonsingular, namely simple zeros. We know the representations of X and Y as rational functions of x and y as well as $G(x,y)$. Calculating the partial derivatives of $G(x,y)$, we have

$$G_x(x,y) = 2X \cdot X_x + 2Y \cdot Y_x - \hat{d}(2X \cdot X_x \cdot Y^2 + 2Y \cdot Y_x \cdot X^2),$$

$$G_y(x,y) = 2X \cdot X_y + 2Y \cdot Y_y - \hat{d}(2X \cdot X_y \cdot Y^2 + 2Y \cdot Y_y \cdot X^2).$$

For convenience, let X and Y denote $X(x,y)$ and $Y(x,y)$ respectively. When $(x,y) = (0,1)$, then $G_x(0,1) = 2Y_x(0,1)$ and $G_y(0,1) = 2Y_y(0,1)$. Let

$$T_i = \frac{\beta_i^2 y^2 (1 + d\alpha_i^2 x^2)^2 - ((2a\alpha_i + 2d\alpha_i^3)x + (2ad\alpha_i^3 + 2d\alpha_i)x^3)^2}{(1 - d\alpha_i x^2)^4},$$

$T_i(0,1) = T_i(0,-1) = \beta_i^2$. Here T_i represents the rational function $T_i(x,y)$. By the chain rule, it is convenient to gain the derivatives of product of multiple functions.

$$Y_x(0,1) = \frac{1}{B^2}(T_{1_x} \prod_{i=2}^{s} \beta_i^2 + T_{2_x} \prod_{i=1, i\neq 2}^{s} \beta_i^2 + \cdots + T_{s_x} \prod_{i=1}^{s-1} \beta_i^2)$$

$$= \sum_{i=1}^{s} \frac{T_{i_x}}{\beta_i^2}.$$

where $T_{i_x}(0,1) = 0$. Therefore, $Y_x(0,1) = 0$ and so that $G_x(0,1) = 0$. Similarly,

$$Y_y(0,1) = \frac{1}{B^2} \prod_{i=1}^{s} T_i + \frac{1}{B^2}(T_{1_y} \prod_{i=2}^{s} \beta_i^2 + T_{2_y} \prod_{i=1, i \neq 2}^{s} \beta_i^2 + \cdots + T_{s_y} \prod_{i=1}^{s-1} \beta_i^2)$$

$$= 1 + \sum_{i=1}^{s} \frac{T_{i_y}}{\beta_i^2},$$

where $T_{i_y}(0,1) = 2\beta_i^2$. Therefore, $Y_y(0,1) = 1 + 2s$ and so that $G_y(0,1) = 2 + 4s$. G_x and G_y are not zero at point $(0,1)$ at the same time. Hence, it's verified that $G(x,y)$ has simple zero at point $(0,1)$. We can conclude that $G(x,y)$ also has simple zero at point $(0,-1)$ in the same way.

With the purpose to solve for $\hat{d}$ and $\hat{a}$, we present X and Y as power series at $x = 0$. Since y^2 can be replaced by $dx^4 + 2ax^2 + 1$, $X(x,y)$ and $Y(x,y)$ becomes rational functions about only one variable x.

$$X(x) = x \prod_{i=1}^{s} (1 + (d\alpha_i^2 + 2a - \frac{\beta_i}{\alpha_i^2})x^2 + O(x^4)), \tag{3}$$

$$Y(x) = y \prod_{i=1}^{s} (1 + \lambda_i x^2 + O(x^4)), \tag{4}$$

Then

$$X(x)^2 = x^2 + 2 \sum_{i=1}^{s} (d\alpha_i^2 + 2a - \frac{\beta_i}{\alpha_i^2})x^4 + O(x^8),$$

$$X(x)^4 = x^4 + O(x^8),$$

$$Y(x)^2 = 1 + (2a + 2 \sum_{i=1}^{s} \lambda_i)x^2 + \mu x^4 + O(x^8),$$

where $O(x^n)$ represents all the terms of power equal or greater than n, $\lambda_i = 2d\alpha_i^2 + 2a - \left(\frac{2a\alpha_i + 2d\alpha_i^3}{\beta_i}\right)^2 + 4d\alpha_i$ and $\mu = d + \sum_{i=1}^{s}(4a\lambda_i + \lambda_i^2) + \sum_{j=1, j \neq i}^{s} \sum_{i=1}^{s} 4\lambda_i \lambda_j$. Substituting these into $G(x,y)$ and then we call it $G'(x)$,

$$G'(x) = (2\hat{a} - 2a - 2 \sum_{i=1}^{s} \lambda_i)x^2 + (\hat{d} + 4\hat{a}\gamma - \mu)x^4 + o(x^8),$$

with $\gamma = \sum_{i=1}^{s}(d\alpha_i^2 + 2a - \frac{\beta_i}{\alpha_i^2})$. However, when we consider the divisors of $\hat{d}X^4 + 2\hat{a}X^2$ and $1 - Y^2$, we find that both of them have zeros of order 2 at $(0,1)$ and $(0,-1)$. So $G'(x)$ has a zero of order 2. Nevertheless we have verified before that $(0,1)$ is a simple zero, which is a contradiction. $G'(x)$ has to be identically zero. Therefore, the coefficients of x^2 and x^4 need to be zero. Based on above, we can easily obtain one choice about $\hat{d}$ and $\hat{a}$. The map we have defined is really an isogeny from an extended Jacobi quartic curve to another extended Jacobi quartic curve.

Solve the equation set

$$\begin{cases} 2\hat{a} - 2a - 2\sum_{i=1}^{s} \lambda_i = 0 \\ \hat{d} + 4\hat{a}\gamma - \mu = 0 \end{cases}$$

and then get $\hat{a} = a + \sum_{i=1}^{s} \lambda_i$ and $\hat{d} = \mu - 4(a + \sum_{i=1}^{s} \lambda_i)\gamma$. It completes the proof.

5   Analysis and Improvement

One important property deserving to figure out is that the isogeny we have defined is normalized. If the isogeny ψ is normalized, the pullback of the invariant differential must be equal to the invariant differential on the curve $E_{J,\hat{d},\hat{a}}$. Let $\psi(x,y) = (X(x,y), Y(x,y))$, then

$$\frac{X_x \partial x}{2Y} = \frac{c\partial x}{2y}$$

for some constant c. The equation implies

$$X_x = \frac{cY}{y}.$$

According to (3) and (4), we derive

$$X_x = 1 + o((x^2)),$$

$$\frac{cY}{y} = c\prod_{i=1}^{s}(1 + \lambda_i x^2 + o(x^4)).$$

The constant item of $\frac{cY}{y}$ must be 1, so $c = 1$. Hence, the isogeny ψ is normalized.

Reviewing the l-isogeny we have constructed above, it's not difficult to find a drawback that the computation is a little complex. Even though the computation of Jacobi quartic curve is not as efficient as Edwards and Huff curves, we still would like to find a faster formula. Hisil, et al. [12] provided some new efficient arithmetic on Jacobi quartic curves. New addition formulas are achieved by Jacobi quartic functions.

From Lemma 2.1, 2.2 and 2.3 in [12], let $a, d, x_1, y_1, x_2, y_2 \in K$ such that $d(a^2 - d) \neq 0$. Assume that d is non-square, then $1 - dx_1^2x_2^2 \neq 0$. Assume that $P = (x_1, y_1)$ and $Q = (x_2, y_2)$ on $E_{J,d,a}$ and $P \neq Q$. Then $x_1y_2 - y_1x_2 \neq 0$. We have a new choice to compute $(x_3, y_3) = (x_1, y_1) + (x_2, y_2)$.

$$x_3 = \frac{x_1^2 - x_2^2}{x_1y_2 - y_1x_2},$$

$$y_3 = \frac{x_1y_1(2 + 2ax_2^2 - y_2^2) - x_2y_2(2 + 2ax_1^2 - y_1^2)}{(x_1y_2 - y_1x_2)(1 - dx_2^2x_2^2)}.$$

Utilizing these addition formulas, we construct another l-isogeny analogues of Vélu's formulas with more constant terms and no one quartic term. The symbols below inherit those in the last section. We sacrifice some points in G. When $P \in G$, denote $\psi(P)$ by ∞.

For any P, define

$$
\varphi(P) = \begin{cases} \infty & P \in G \\ \left(x_P \prod_{Q \in G-(0,1)} \frac{x_{P+Q}}{x_Q}, y_P \prod_{Q \in G-(0,1)} \frac{y_{P+Q}}{y_Q} \right) & P \notin G \end{cases}
$$

When $P \notin G$, the coordinate maps are given by

$$
\psi(x,y) = (X(x,y), Y(x,y)),
$$

where

$$
X(x,y) = (-1)^s \frac{x}{A^2} \prod_{i=1}^{s} \frac{(x^2 - \alpha_i^2)^2}{\beta_i^2 x^2 - \alpha_i^2 y^2},
$$

$$
Y(x,y) = \frac{y}{B^2} \prod_{i=1}^{s} \frac{x^2 y^2 (2 + 2a\alpha_i^2 - \beta_i^2)^2 - \alpha_i^2 \beta_i^2 (2 + 2ax^2 - y^2)^2}{(\beta_i^2 x^2 - \alpha_i^2 y^2)(1 - d\alpha_i^2 x^2)^2}.
$$

We leave out the proof here. If readers want to know more about it, the proof of Theorem 1 is a reference.

Next we give a brief evaluation about the computation complexity. In this paper, M stands for a field multiplication, S for a field squaring, C for a multiplication by a curve constant and I for a field inversion. S is about 0.8 M in most time. Since additions cost much less than squaring and multiplication, we omit its cost here. It's reasonable to some extend.

At first, computing x^2, y^2 and $x^2 y^2$ cost $2S + M$. As $dx^4 = y^2 - 2ax^2 - 1$, we get x^4 by computing $2ax^2$ and another one multiplication by a constant. Computing $\prod_{i=1}^{s}(x^2 - \alpha_i^2)^2$ which is equal to $\prod_{i=1}^{s} x^4 + \alpha_i^4 - 2\alpha_i^2 x^2$ amounts to $sC + (s-1)M$. Computing $\prod_{i=1}^{s} \beta_i^2 x^2 - \alpha_i^2 y^2$ costs $2sC + (s-1)M$, the same as $\prod_{i=1}^{s} 1 + d^2 \alpha_i^4 x^4 - 2d\alpha_i^2 x^2$. It is essential to compute $(2 + 2a\alpha_i^2 - \beta_i^2)^2$ before computing $x^2 y^2 (2 + 2a\alpha_i^2 - \beta_i^2)^2$ for s times. We have to compute another squaring unavoidably. That is $(2 + 2ax^2 - y^2)^2$. Then computing $\alpha_i^2 \beta_i^2 (2 + 2ax^2 - y^2)^2$ costs sC. The first items of both X and Y cannot be left out, which cost $2(C+M)$. In the affine space, inversions of $\prod_{i=1}^{s} \beta_i^2 x^2 - \alpha_i^2 y^2$ and $\prod_{i=1}^{s} 1 + d^2 \alpha_i^4 x^4 - 2d\alpha_i^2 x^2$ amount to $2I$, after which $3M$ is needed. Therefore, the total cost is $(4s+2)M + 3S + (7s+4)C + 2I$. In the projective space, the inversion can be avoided. If the constants are carefully chosen, the cost of C can be decreased greatly.

There is no doubt that the isogenies derived in this paper can be used to perform efficient scalar multiplication. The projective weighted coordinates or even a redundant representation of points may help a lot. So far, only [24] has given explicit formulas for the i-th multiple of a point on Jacobi quartic curves. [24] made use of the division polynomial, but didn't give an evaluation of the computation complexity. Since the division polynomials are recursive, they seem to be quite complex intuitively. Another advantage of the isogenies in this paper is that the construction is very flexible, as it relies on the addition formulas. If a more efficient addition formula is found, a more efficient isogeny can correspondingly take place. Although Jacobi quartic is not as fast as Edwards and Huff curves generally, it prevents SPA-like attacks. [20] gives an estimate of the Edwards isogeny in $(3s + 1)M + 2S + 3sC + I$ and the Huff isogeny in $(4S - 2)M + 2S + 2sC + 2I$. If the constants are carefully chosen, the Jacobi quartic isogeny is about to catch up with Huff isogeny. Dustin Moody and Daniel Shumow have compared Edwards and Huff curves with Weierstrass curves by experiments in [20], as it is not easy to estimate the time complexity of Weierstrass curves explicitly. They showed that isogenies on Edwards and Huff curves are considerably faster than Vélu's Formulas on Weierstrass curves (Table 1).

Table 1. Theoretic time cost of different curves

Curve	Cost
Edwards	$(3s + 1)M + 2S + 3sC + I$
Huff	$(4s - 2)M + 2S + 2sC + 2I$
Jacobi quartic	$(4s + 2)M + 3S + (7s + 4)C + 2I$

6 Conclusion

In this paper we extend the results in [20] to Jacobi quartic curves and accompany our routine with a robust proof of the validity of the isogenies. Based on different addition formulas we construct two kinds of isogenies and the latter one is more efficient. We stress that this is the first time to construct isogenies on Jacobi quartic curves and one could speed up the computation by many other methods. Our method to compute the isogeny costs $(4s + 2)M + 3S + (7s + 4)C + 2I$. Ultimately, the crucial future work is to accelerate the scalar multiplication by isogenies to obtain the n-th multiple of a point on the fly at little cost.

References

1. Koblitz, N.: Elliptic curve cryptosystems. Math. Comput. **48**(177), 203–209 (1987)
2. Miller, V.S.: Use of elliptic curves in cryptography. In: Williams, H.C. (ed.) CRYPTO 1985. LNCS, vol. 218, pp. 417–426. Springer, Heidelberg (1986). doi:10.1007/3-540-39799-X_31
3. Brier, E., Joye, M.: Fast point multiplication on elliptic curves through isogenies. In: Fossorier, M., Høholdt, T., Poli, A. (eds.) AAECC 2003. LNCS, vol. 2643, pp. 43–50. Springer, Heidelberg (2003). doi:10.1007/3-540-44828-4_6
4. Tate, J.: Endomorphisms of abelian varieties over finite field. Ivent. Math. **2**(2), 134–144 (1966)
5. Schoof, R.: Elliptic curves over finite field and the computation of square roots mod p. Math. Comp. **44**(170), 483–494 (1985)

6. Galbraith, S.D.: Constructing isogenies between elliptic curves over finite fields. J. Comput. Math. **2**, 118–138 (1999)
7. Gaudry, P., Hess, F., Smart, N.P.: Constructive and destructive facets of Weil descent on elliptic curves. J. Cryptology **15**(1), 19–46 (2002)
8. Galbraith, S., Stolbunov, A.: Improved algorithm for the isogeny problem for ordinary elliptic curves. Appl. Algebra Eng. Commun. Comput. **24**(2), 107–131 (2013)
9. Biasse, J.-F., Jao, D., Sankar, A.: A quantum algorithm for computing isogenies between supersingular elliptic curves. In: Meier, W., Mukhopadhyay, D. (eds.) INDOCRYPT 2014. LNCS, vol. 8885, pp. 428–442. Springer, Cham (2014). doi:10. 1007/978-3-319-13039-2_25
10. Jao, D., Feo, L.: Towards quantum-resistant cryptosystems from supersingular elliptic curve isogenies. In: Yang, B.-Y. (ed.) PQCrypto 2011. LNCS, vol. 7071, pp. 19–34. Springer, Heidelberg (2011). doi:10.1007/978-3-642-25405-5_2
11. Billet, O., Joye, M.: The jacobi model of an elliptic curve and side-channel analysis. In: Fossorier, M., Høholdt, T., Poli, A. (eds.) AAECC 2003. LNCS, vol. 2643, pp. 34–42. Springer, Heidelberg (2003). doi:10.1007/3-540-44828-4_5
12. Hisil, H., Wong, K.K.-H., Carter, G., Dawson, E.: Jacobi quartic curves revisited. In: Boyd, C., González Nieto, J. (eds.) ACISP 2009. LNCS, vol. 5594, pp. 452–468. Springer, Heidelberg (2009). doi:10.1007/978-3-642-02620-1_31
13. Duquesne, S.: Improving the arithmetic of elliptic curves in the Jacobi model. Inf. Process. Lett. **104**(3), 101–105 (2007)
14. Hisil, H., Carter, G., Dawson, E.: New formulae for efficient elliptic curve arithmetic. In: Srinathan, K., Rangan, C.P., Yung, M. (eds.) INDOCRYPT 2007. LNCS, vol. 4859, pp. 138–151. Springer, Heidelberg (2007). doi:10.1007/ 978-3-540-77026-8_11
15. Hisil, H., Wong, K.K.H., Carter, G., Dawson, E.: Faster group operations on elliptic curves. AISC 2009, vol. 98, pp. 7–20 (2009)
16. Galbraith, S.D., Lin, X., Scott, M.: Endomorphisms for faster elliptic curve cryptography on a large class of curves. In: Joux, A. (ed.) EUROCRYPT 2009. LNCS, vol. 5479, pp. 518–535. Springer, Heidelberg (2009). doi:10.1007/ 978-3-642-01001-9_30
17. Gallant, R.P., Lambert, R.J., Vanstone, S.A.: Faster point multiplication on elliptic curves with efficient endomorphisms. In: Kilian, J. (ed.) CRYPTO 2001. LNCS, vol. 2139, pp. 190–200. Springer, Heidelberg (2001). doi:10.1007/3-540-44647-8_11
18. Doche, C., Icart, T., Kohel, D.R.: Efficient scalar multiplication by isogeny decompositions. In: Yung, M., Dodis, Y., Kiayias, A., Malkin, T. (eds.) PKC 2006. LNCS, vol. 3958, pp. 191–206. Springer, Heidelberg (2006). doi:10.1007/11745853_13
19. Moody, D.: Using 5-isogenies to quintuple points on elliptic curves. Inf. Process. Lett. **111**, 314–317 (2011)
20. Moody, D., Shumow, D.: Analogues of Vélu's formulas for isogenies on alternate models of elliptic curves. Math. Comp. **85**(300), 1929–1951 (2016)
21. Vélu, J.: Isogénied entre courbes elliptiques. C.R. Acad. Sc. Paris Série A. **273**, 238–241 (1971)
22. Kohel, D.: Endomorphism rings of elliptic curves over finite fields. PhD thesis, University of California at Berkeley (1996)
23. Hisil, H.: Elliptic curves, group law, and efficient computation. PhD thesis, Queensland University of Technology (2010)
24. Moody, D.: Divison polynomials for alternate models of elliptic curves. IACR Cryptology ePrint Archive **2010**, 630 (2010)

Security and Implementation

Cyber-Attacks on Remote State Estimation in Industrial Control System: A Game-Based Framework

Cong Chen[1,2(✉)] and Dongdai Lin[1]

[1] State Key Laboratory of Information Security,
Institute of Information Engineering, Chinese Academy of Sciences,
Beijing 100093, China
{chencong,ddlin}@iie.ac.cn
[2] University of Chinese Academy of Sciences, Beijing 100093, China

Abstract. Recently, the security of Industrial Control Systems (ICSs) is widely concerned all over the world. In this paper, the security issues in remote state estimation process of ICSs will be considered. The communication channel between sensor nodes and the remote state estimator may be maliciously interfaced and manipulated by the internal or external attacker. With resources constraints for both the sensor and the attacker side, the interactive decision making process of whether to send or receive data packets or not for estimation process and whether to launch an attack on some data packets or not for an attacker are studied in this paper. A game theory based framework is formulated in the paper and it has been proved that a Nash equilibrium of the final pay-off arbitration game is existed. For the practical computation convenience, an on-line updating algorithm is proposed. What's more, the simulation of the game-based framework described in this paper is demonstrated to verify the validity and efficiency of this framework. The experimental results have shown that the game-based framework could improve performance of the decision making and estimation process and mitigate the impact of the attack. It may provide a novel and feasible approach to protect the state estimation process and improve the intrusion tolerance in ICSs.

Keywords: ICS · Critical infrastructures · False data injection · Remote state estimation · Game theory · Nash equilibrium

1 Introduction

Nowadays, Industrial Control Systems (ICSs) are ubiquitously applied in various industrial control processes, especially national critical infrastructures as electric power generation, transmission and distribution, chemical production, oil and gas, refining and water desalination [1,2]. Industrial control systems are computer-controlled systems that manage industrial processes automatically in the physical world. These systems include Distributed Control Systems (DCS),

© Springer International Publishing AG 2017
K. Chen et al. (Eds.): Inscrypt 2016, LNCS 10143, pp. 431–450, 2017.
DOI: 10.1007/978-3-319-54705-3_27

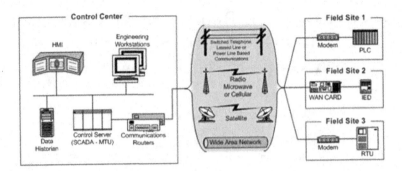

Fig. 1. Structure of SCADA.

Supervisory Control and Data Acquisition systems (SCADA), Programmable Logic Controllers (PLC), and devices such as remote telemetry units (RTU), smart meters, and intelligent field instruments including remotely programmable valves and intelligent electronic relays [2,3]. In [3], the classical structure of a SCADA system is given as showing in Fig. 1.

As hearts of critical infrastructure in industrial processes, ICSs are the key drivers of sensing, monitoring, control and management. While sharing basic constructs with Information Technology (IT) business systems, ICSs are technically, administratively, and functionally more complex and unique than business IT systems. Such systems increasingly rely on remote operations via local area networks or the Internet, which are enabled by software with limited security protections. Cyber attacks on such systems can lead to devastating effects on the functionality of national critical infrastructures. As a consequence, ICSs are inviting targets for adversaries attempting to disable critical infrastructure through cyber attacks. Therefore, the security of ICS has attracted considerable interest from both academic and industrial communities in the past few years.

In the past, ICSs were mainly conceived as isolated systems. While, with the ever growing demand of both highly ubiquitous computing services and location-independent access to Information and Communication Technology (ICT) resources, they are more and more connected to all kinds of desktop and business computing systems (DBCS) [4] and often to the Internet.

The increasing connection with Internet, kinds of applications and various terminals units brings threats to the ICSs of cyber-attacks from adversaries around the world. The threat and possible disastrous consequence of cyber attacks on ICSs has been demonstrated by the Stuxnet worm in 2011. The Stuxnet worm is a sophisticated malware specially designed to sabotage ICSs. It exploited several previously unknown vulnerabilities in the Windows operating system and Siemens STEP 7 software to target specific control systems appearing in uranium enrichment facilities [1,5–7].

Moreover, information security methods, such as authentication, access control, and message integrity, appear inadequate for a satisfactory protection of ICSs. Indeed, these security methods do not exploit the compatibility of the measurements with the underlying physical process or the control mechanism, and they are therefore ineffective against insider attacks targeting the physical dynamics [8].

A. Related Work

ICSs, however, suffer from specific vulnerabilities which do not affect classical control systems, and for which appropriate detection and identification techniques need to be developed. For instance, the reliance on communication networks and standard communication protocols to transmit measurements and manipulation packets increases the possibility of intentional and worst case attacks against physical plants. The challenges here at hand include data integrity, data veracity and trustworthiness, and resources availability. The vulnerabilities analysis of ICSs to external attacks has received increasing attention in recent years [2,8]. The general approach has been to study the effect of specific attacks against particular systems. For instance, deception and denial of service (DoS) attacks against a networked control system are defined in [9]. Deception attacks compromise the integrity of control packets of measurements, while DoS attacks refer to compromising the availability of resources by, for instance, jamming the communication channels. As specific deception attacks in the context of static estimators, false data injection attacks against static estimators are introduced in [10]. Stealthy deception attacks against SCADA system are introduced in [11]. Reply attacks and covert attacks effect are introduced in [12,13] respectively.

Clark A. et al. in [1] proposed a proactive defense framework against Stuxnet. Commands from the system operator to the PLC are authenticated using a randomized set of cryptographic keys. It leverages cryptographic analysis and control and game-theoretic methods to quantify the impact of malicious commands on the performance of physical plants. The works in [14,15] studies the timing of DoS in the term of attackers. Considering the vulnerabilities of stale data in ICSs, properly timed DoS could drive the system to unsafe states. By attacking sensor and controller signals, the attacker can manipulate the process at will. Similarly, Heng Zhang et al. in [16] studies the optimal DoS attack schedule in Wireless Networked Control System (WNCS). The optimal jamming attack schedule is proposed to maximize the attack effect on the control system. Also, centralized and distributed monitors are proposed to detect and identify the attacks in Cyber-physical Systems(CPSs) by Pasqualetti F. et al. in [17]. Krotofil M. et al. in [18] investigated a set of lightweight real-time algorithms for spoofing sensor signals directly at the microcontroller of the field device. The data veracity detection toke the form of plausibility and consistency checks with the help of the correlation entropy in a cluster of related sensors.

However, these works have focused only on one side, i.e., the attacker or the defender. If attackers have knowledge of system parameters, then both defender and attacker may involve in an interactive decision making process. To handle these issues, some researchers proposed the game-theory approach [19–23]. In the similar fashion, Li Y. et al. in [24,25] introduced zero-sum game approaches to optimize the decision process both for the jamming attacker and the remote state estimator in CPSs. The existence of optimal solutions, i.e., Nash equilibrium of zero-sum game, in the decision process is proved and illustrated in numerical examples.

B. Summary of Results and Organization

Obviously, compromising devices or transmission channel used to monitor or control an industrial system is a necessary prerequisite for launching a cyber-physical attack aimed at disrupting the physical process. As far as know, there isn't any relative researches on the game-based framework for decision making process in deception attacks in ICSs. This paper presents an analytical game theory approach to analyzing and mitigating the efficacy of a special deception attack, namely false data injection attack, on remote state estimation in ICSs. The main contributions can be summarized as follows:

(1) Propose a game-based framework to a special kind of deception attack - false data attack. The game framework is based on the final pay-off arbitration model.
(2) A practical updating algorithm is proposed to apply the game based framework into the practical situation and update the framework on-line.
(3) Simulation of the proposed game-based framework is executed. Experimental results shown verification of the validity and efficacy of this framework to the false data injection attack.

The reminder of the paper is organized as follows. In Sect. 2, we present the models and problem formulation. In Sect. 3, we introduce some basic properties of system performance under arbitrary false data injection attacks under game-theory framework. We construct game-theory framework and analyze the system performance. In Sect. 4, dynamic update of the game theory action is illustrated. In Sect. 5, numerical examples are shown to demonstrate the effectiveness of the proposed framework. Finally, Sect. 6 concludes this paper.

Notations: Z denotes the set of all integers and N the set of all positive integers. R is the set of all real numbers. R^n is the n-dimensional Euclidean space. S_+^n (and S_{++}^n) is the set of n by n positive semi-definite matrices (and positive definite matrices). When $X \in S_+^n$ (and S_{++}^n), we write $X \geq 0$ (and $X > 0$). $X \geq Y$ if $X - Y \in S_+^n$. $Tr(\cdot)$ is the trace of a matrix. The superscript $'$ stands for transposition. For functions $f, f1, f2$ with appropriate domains, $f1f2(x)$ stands for the function composition $f1(f2(x))$, and $f^n(x) \triangleq f(f^{n-1}(x))$, where $n \in N$ and with $f^0(x) \triangleq x$. δ_{ij} is discrete-time Dirac delta function, i.e., δ_{ij} equals to 1 when $i = j$ and 0 otherwise. The notation $P[\cdot]$ refers to probability and $E[\cdot]$ to expectation. $T!$ stands for the factorial of T. We write C_M^T for $\binom{T}{M} = T!/(M!(T-M)!)$.

2   Problem Analysis

2.1   System Model

In this paper, a general discrete linear time-invariant(LTI) control process is considered, which is described by the following state space expression:

$$x_{k+1} = Ax_k + w_k$$
$$y_k = Cx_k + v_k \tag{1}$$

where $k \in N, x_k \in R^{n_x}$ is the control process state vector at time k, $y_k \in R^{n_y}$ is the measurement taken by the sensor, $w_k \in R^{n_x}$ and $v_k \in R^{n_y}$ are zero-mean i.i.d. Gaussian noises with $E[w_k w_j'] = \delta_{kj} Q(Q \geq 0)$. $E[v_k v_j'] = \delta_{kj} R(R > 0)$, $E[w_k v_j'] = 0, \forall j, k \in N$. The pair (A, C) is assumed to be observable and $(A, Q^{1/2})$ controllable.

2.2   Attack Model

In this paper, a kind of special deception attack - false data injection attack is considered. With the knowledge of the system configuration and the historical transportation on the communication channel, the attacker can systematically generate and inject malicious measurements which will mislead the state estimation process without being detected by any of the exiting techniques for bad measurements detection as shown in [10]. For realistic scenarios, the attacker is either constrained to some specific sensor measurements or limited in the resources required to launch attack on sensor measurements or communication channels.

Let z_a represent the vector of observed measurements that may contain malicious data. z_a can be represented as $z_a = z + a$, where $z = (z_1, ..., z_m)^T$ is the vector of original measurements and $a = (a_1, ..., a_m)^T$ is the malicious data added to the original measurements. Attack vector is denoted as a. The i-th element a_i being non-zero means that the attacker compromises the i-th measurements, and then replaces its original measurements z_i with a phoney measurement $z_i + a_i$. The attacker can choose any non-zero arbitrary vector as the attack vector a, and then construct the malicious measurements $z_a = z + a$. Let $\hat{x}_k^a$ and $\hat{x}_k$ denote the estimate of x_k using the malicious measurements z_a and the original measurements z, respectively. $\hat{x}_k^a$ can be represented as $\hat{x}_k + c$, where c is a non-zero vector of length n. Note that c reflects the estimation error injected by the attacker. The attack model can be described as:

$$\hat{x}_k = \begin{cases} \hat{x}_k^a, & \text{if an attack vector arrives} \\ \hat{x}_k, & \text{otherwise} \end{cases} \tag{2}$$

where $\hat{x}_k^a$ is the an attack on k-th state variable at this moment with the attacking vector z_a.

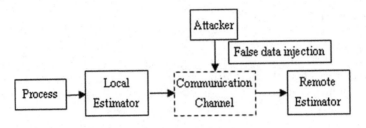

Fig. 2. Security issue of state estimation.

2.3   Local State Estimation

Here, the security issue of state estimation is considered as depicted in Fig. 2. The on-board processors equipped on the sensors can be used to significantly improve system performance [26]. State estimator is widely used to ensure the safety and economy of operation in ICS. Essentially, state estimation is a process which uses real-time redundant measurements to improve data accuracy and automatically excluded from the error message caused by random interference. For state estimation, e.g. in power system, measurements are usually the values that can be observed by sensors easily, such as line power flow, power injection, voltage magnitudes etc., while the state variables are usually complex phasor voltages which cannot be measured conveniently. Its objective is to find estimates of states that are best fit to the corresponding measurements.

For local state estimation, at each time k, the sensor first estimate the state x_k based on all the measurements it collects from the field up to time k and then transmits its local estimate to the remote estimator. Let $\hat{x}_k^s$ and P_k^s as the sensor's local Minimum Mean-Squares Error (MMSE) estimate of the state x_k and the corresponding estimation error covariance. They are given by the following functions and could be calculated by a Kalman filter.

$$\hat{x}_k^s = E[x_k | y_1, y_2, ..., y_k] \tag{3}$$

$$P_k^s = E[(x_k - \hat{x}_k^s)(x_k - \hat{x}_k^s)' | y_1, y_2, ..., y_k] \tag{4}$$

For notational case, the following functions are introduced: $h, \tilde{g} : S_+^n \to S_+^n$ as

$$h(X) \triangleq AXA' + Q$$
$$\tilde{g}(X) \triangleq X - XC'[CXC' + R]_{-1}CX \tag{5}$$

It is well-known that under suitable conditions the estimation error covariance of the Kalman filter converges to a unique value from any initial condition, thus the local estimation error covariance p_k^s will converge to a steady-state. Generally (similar assumptions can be found in [27,28]), the Kalman filter at the sensor side is assumed that it has entered the steady state and the subsequent discussion could be simplified by setting

$$P_k^s = \overline{P}, k \geq 1 \tag{6}$$

As discussed in [29], $\overline{P}$ is the steady-state error covariance, which is the unique positive semi-definite solution of $\tilde{g} \circ h(X) = X$.

2.4   Remote State Estimation

Remote state estimation process in networked control systems has been well studied recent years. In the similar fashion with the local state estimation process, let $\hat{x}_k$ and P_k denote as the remote state estimator's MMSE state estimate and the corresponding error covariance. Here, $\hat{x}_k$ can be calculated as following: once the sensor's local estimate packet arrives, the remote state estimator synchronizes its own estimate with the sensor's $\hat{x}_k^s$; otherwise, the remote state estimator just predicts its estimate $\hat{x}_k$ based on its previous optimal estimate [28].

$$\hat{x}_k = \begin{cases} \hat{x}_k^s, & \text{if } \hat{x}_k^s \text{ arrives} \\ A\hat{x}_{k-1}, & \text{otherwise} \end{cases} \tag{7}$$

Correspondingly, the remote state estimation error covariance P_k can be calculated as:

$$P_k = \begin{cases} \overline{P}, & \text{if } \hat{x}_k^s \text{ arrives} \\ h(P_{k-1}), & \text{otherwise} \end{cases} \tag{8}$$

The remote state estimator is assumed that it knows the system parameters A, C, Q, R. Thus the expected state estimation error covariance can be easily written as:

$$E[P_k] = p_k\overline{P} + (1 - p_k)(E[P_{k-1}]) \tag{9}$$

where p_k is denoted as the possibility for remote estimator receiving data packets from sensor nodes. $p_k = 0$ means the remote state estimator didn't received data packets, otherwise, the remote state estimator received data packets successfully.

2.5   Communication Channel

As described in [10], typical false data injection attack can inject malicious measurements into the data transportation process between components in networked control systems i.e. ICSs without being detected by existing fault detection mechanisms. As described previously, the attacker is assumed to be able to manipulate the measurements or inject false data into the data transportation process between sensors and remote state estimator, which may mislead the state estimation process and drive the system into undesired situations (see Fig. 2).

In practice, for both sensors and attackers, energy and source constraint is a natural concern, which affects the state estimation performance and attacking policies. Here, let m denotes the total number of sensors, $M(M \leq m)$ denotes the total number of the state estimate that are accepted by remote state estimator successfully at each time k, $N(N \leq m)$ denotes the total state estimate that attacker could compromise or manipulate at each time k. Within a given time horizon $t \in [0, T]$, the attacker can launch false date attack for $k_a(k_a \leq T)$ times at most. To encompass energy limitations, we will assume that, at each sampling time the sensor can send the data packet at most times to the remote estimator, while the attacker can launch false data injection attack at most times.

Thus, the sensor's data-sending strategy at each sampling time is denoted as:

$$\theta_S \triangleq \{\gamma_1, \gamma_2, ..., \gamma_m\} \tag{10}$$

where $\gamma_i = 1$ for $i = 1, 2, ..., m$ means that the k-th sensor's data packet is received by remote state estimator at a certain sampling time, otherwise $\gamma_i = 0$ for $i = 1, 2, ..., m$. Consequently, we have the following constraint:

$$\sum_{i=1}^{m} \leq M \tag{11}$$

Similarly, the attacker's strategy is denoted as:

$$\theta_A \triangleq \{\lambda_1, \lambda_2, ..., \lambda_m\} \tag{12}$$

where $\lambda_i = 1$ for $i = 1, 2, ..., m$ means that the attacker launches a false data injection attack on the k-th sensor's data packet, otherwise $\lambda_i = 0$ for $i = 1, 2, ..., m$. The associated constraint is

$$\sum_{i=1}^{m} \leq N \tag{13}$$

In practical communication systems, packet dropouts may occur due to different reasons, including signal degradation, channel fading and channel congestion. However, we assume the communication dropout probability of data packet from the sensor arrives at the remote estimator is 0 all the time to simplify the simulation and explanation. As noted above, the strategies of the sensor and the attacker at every sampling time are assumed to be θ_S and θ_A respectively.

2.6   Main Problem

The quality of the state estimation process during a certain time horizon $[0, T]$ is quantified by the trace of error covariance as proposed in [24]. It is the cost function as following function:

$$J_\alpha(T) \triangleq \alpha \frac{1}{T} \sum_{k=1}^{T} Tr(E[P_k]) + (1 - \alpha)Tr(E[P_T]) \tag{14}$$

where $\alpha = 1$ or 0, corresponding to the overall performance and terminal performance, respectively. Here, overall state estimation performance is considered, namely let $\alpha = 1$, the cost function is simplified as:

$$J_\alpha(T) \triangleq \frac{1}{T} \sum_{k=1}^{T} Tr(E[P_k]) \tag{15}$$

In term of the sensor's side, the goal of the decision maker is to minimize the cost function $J_\alpha(T)$ in (15). Oppositely, the goal of the attacker is to maximize the $J_\alpha(T)$. So, the objective function of sensor's side is obtained as:

$$J_S(\theta_S) \triangleq -J_\alpha(T) \tag{16}$$

while the objective function of attacker's side is obtained as:

$$J_A(\theta_A) \triangleq J_\alpha(T) \tag{17}$$

Thus, the objective function of sensor and attacker are simplified since the objective of sensor is opposite to the one of attacker. The goal of the both sides is to maximize the objective functions. Here, θ_S and θ_A are defined in (10) and (12).

The optimal strategies for both sides subjecting to the constrains described in (11) and (13) are the solutions of the optimal problems based on the above analysis. Since getting more measurements always benefits for improving the performance for both sides, it is not difficult to show that the optimal strategies for both sides remain the same if (11) and (13) are changed to $\sum_{i=1}^{m} = M$ and $\sum_{i=1}^{m} = N$, respectively.

Thus, the optimization problem is obtained as following for the sensor's side:

$$\max_{\theta_S}\{J_S(\theta_S)\}$$
$$s.t. \sum_{i=1}^{m} = M \tag{18}$$

In the similar fashion, for the attacker's side:

$$\max_{\theta_A}\{J_A(\theta_A)\}$$
$$s.t. \sum_{i=1}^{m} = N \tag{19}$$

where θ_S and θ_A are same as the definition in (10) and (12).

3   Game-Based Framework

In this section, the decision making processes of both the sensor side and the attacker side are demonstrated in a game-theory framework based on the optimization problems, i.e.(18) and (19). Here, the decision maker on sensor side and the one on the attacker side are considered as the two players of a final pay-off arbitration game model. The details of this game model and the decision making process are discussed below.

3.1   Final Pay-Off Arbitration Framework

Farber developed a model of final-offer arbitration trying to solve the wage disputes of firms or unions in 1980 [30]. The two major forms of arbitration are conventional and final-offer arbitration. In final-offer arbitration medel, the two sides make wage offers and then the arbitrator picks one of the offers as the settlement. In conventional arbitration model, in contrast, the arbitrator is free to impose any wage as the settlement. Here, the former model would be taken into consideration.

So far, relative researches in the existing literature mainly focus on only one side with energy or resource constraint. In this paper, for the case with constraints for both sides, i.e., $M \leq m$ and $N \leq m$, those cannot be used. For there may be kinds of different strategies for both sides, the problem will be investigated from a game-theoretic view adopting the following definitions according to the final pay-off arbitration model:

(1) *Player:* there are two players: the sensor and the attacker.
(2) *Action:* θ_S for the sensor and θ_A for the attacker.
(3) *Payoff:* $J_S(\theta_S)$ for the sensor and $J_A(\theta_A)$ for the attacker.

In the final pay-off arbitration model, there is an arbitrator in the arbitration process. For the situation in this paper, the arbitration is between the local state estimate and the state estimate calculated upon the historical data. The local state estimate is generated by sensors and transferred to remote estimator through the communication channel. The remote state estimator acts as the arbitrator during the arbitration process in this game model. The output of the arbitration process will be accepted as the system's present state estimate by the remote state estimator, according to which the controllers regulate and control the system's performance.

3.2   Nash Equilibrium

In game theory, Nash equilibrium is a state that no single player wants to deviate [30]. If in a game, each player has chosen a strategy and no player can benefit by changing his own strategy while the other players keep theirs unchanged, then the current strategy of both sides constitutes a Nash equilibrium. Nash defined a mixed strategy Nash Equilibrium for any game with a finite set of strategies and proved that at least one mixed strategy Nash equilibrium must exist in such a game in [31].

As proved in [31], for any game with a finite set of strategies, there exists at least one mixed strategy Nash equilibrium in the game.

3.3   Existence of Nash Equilibrium

To analyze the Nash equilibrium of the game between the sensor and the attacker, the number of all the pure strategies need to be taken into account first. For the sensor, the number of pure strategies P is $P = C_m^M = \binom{m}{M}$, which are denoted as $\theta_S^{prue}(1), \theta_S^{prue}(2),...,\theta_S^{prue}(T)$. Correspondingly, the mixed strategies can be denoted as: $\theta_S^{mixed}(\pi_1, \pi_2, ..., \pi_P) = \theta_S^{prue}(p)$ with $\pi_p, p = 1, 2, ..., P$, where π_p is the probability of $\theta_S^{prue}(p)$ and $\sum_{p=1}^{P} \pi_p = 1, \pi_p \in [0,1]$.

In the same way, for the attacker, the number of pure strategies Q is $Q = C_m^N = \binom{m}{N}$, which are denoted as $\theta_A^{prue}(1), \theta_A^{prue}(2),...,\theta_A^{prue}(T)$. Correspondingly, the mixed strategies can be denoted as: $\theta_A^{mixed}(\pi_1, \pi_2, ..., \pi_Q) = \theta_A^{prue}(q)$ with π_q, $q = 1, 2, ..., Q$, where π_q is the probability of $\theta_A^{prue}(q)$ and $\sum_{q=1}^{Q} \pi_q = 1, \pi_q \in [0,1]$.

Different combinations of π_p and π_q constitute different mixed strategies for both the sensor and the attacker, respectively. Obviously, that the number of pure strategies is finite, there are infinitely many mixed strategies for each side.

It has been proved in [27] that a Nash equilibrium exists for the considered two-player zero-sum game between the sensor and the attacker. The optimal strategies for each side are denoted as $\theta_S^\star$ and $\theta_A^\star$, respectively. By giving the optimal strategy $\theta_A^\star$ chosen by the attacker, the optimal strategy for the sensor is the one that maximizes its objective function $J_S(\theta_S)$ as described in (18), i.e., $J_S(\theta_S^\star|\theta_A^\star) \geq J_S(\theta_S|\theta_A^\star), \forall \theta_S$. For the attacker, a similar conclusion is obtained, i.e., $J_A(\theta_A^\star|\theta_S^\star) \geq J_A(\theta_A|\theta_S^\star), \forall \theta_A$. Since the payoff functions are objective functions for each sides respectively, the optimal strategies for the sensor and the attacker constitute a Nash equilibrium of this game naturally.

4   Update of the Game Theory Action

Though the decisions are chosen randomly on both sides in the game investigated in the last section, all decisions are made before the initial time of the system. Anyway, it can just be regarded as a off-line schedule. In some practical situations, both sides may be able to monitor the performance of the opponent and renew their choices at each sampling time according to the practical status of the system. For example, after the attacker launches a attack, the system server may be able to detect and identify the abnormality and inform the responsive sensors about that [17], through which the sensors and the state estimation process could do some corresponding adjustment, i.e. abandon the abnormal measurements or refuse the relevant suspicious sensor's data uploading mission. The attacker can also detect whether the data packet is accepted or not based on the system status. Thus, though each side can not be sure about the next decision of their opponent, they can still make prediction on the opponent's future action through the system's present performance and therefore narrow the scope of their opponent's action sets.

For this situation, based on the observation on the past action of opponents, a new game with new constrains will be considered at each time step for both the sensor and the attacker during the whole time horizon T. At each time step, let $\theta_S^\star(T, M, N, \Phi_0)$ denotes the optimal mixed strategies for the sensor and $\theta_A^\star(T, M, N, \Phi_0)$ denotes the one for attacker with parameters of T, M, N, Φ_0. Here, T is the time-horizon, M and N are the resource constraints of sensor and attacker respectively, and $\Phi_0 = \overline{P}$ is the expected initial remote state estimate error covariance. $\theta_S^\star(T, M, N, \Phi_0)$ and $\theta_A^\star(T, M, N, \Phi_0)$ is calculated at each time and contain the action sequences for the whole time-horizon of each side respectively, but only the first step will be kept as the initial parameters of the next time step at both sides. Moving to the next step, the parameters, e.g., system outcomes, constraints and time-horizon, are updated, and thus the game, decision and constraints will be renewed continually.

To update the whole decision making process at each time step for each sides in the game-based framework, a recursive algorithm is proposed here as showing in Algorithm 1. Following this algorithm, both sides are able to involve in the decision making process of the game-based framework described above with the time varying, resource constrains and any initial states.

Algorithm 1. Game updating for both sides

Initialize: $\overline{x}_S$, $\theta_S^\star(T, M, N, \Phi_0)$ and $\theta_A^\star(T, M, N, \Phi_0)$.

1. Game begins with the initial parameters;
2. **for** $t = 1 : T$ **do**
3. Solve for $\theta_S^\star(T, M, N, \Phi_0)$ and $\theta_A^\star(T, M, N, \Phi_0)$;
4. Employ the actions of $\theta_S^\star(T, M, N, \Phi_0)$ and $\theta_A^\star(T, M, N, \Phi_0)$ designed for the first time step for the new game as the action of the current time step t;
5. Each side observe the action taken by the opponent at time step t;
6. **if** $\gamma = 1$ **then**
7. $M = M - 1$;
8. **else**
9. $M = M$;
10. **end if**
11. **if** $\lambda = 1$ **then**
12. $N = N - 1$;
13. **else**
14. $N = N$;
15. **end if**
16. $T = T - 1$;
17. $\Phi_0 = E[P_t]$;
18. **end for**

Example: Suppose such s situation in a time horizon $T = 5$ and the constraint for both side are $M = 2$ and $N = 1$ when $m = 3$. At time step $k = 1$, sensor side send data packet by a strategy $\theta_S^{t=1}$ chosen from its strategy set which includes the pure strategies $\theta_S = \{1, 0, 0\}$, $\{0, 1, 0\}$, $\{0, 0, 1\}$ and the mixed strategies proportionally consisting of them. As the mixed strategies for the the sensor side is chosen from proportional combination of the pure strategies $\{1, 1, 0\}$, $\{1, 0, 1\}$ and $\{0, 1, 1\}$, the sensor's strategy can be deduced by the attacker side according to the observe the action taken by the opponent after the time step $t = 1$. Thus the attacker side could make corresponding adjustment to his next strategy.

The similar mechanism also happened at the sensor's side. By this accumulative process, both sides of the game could make good use of their resources and make optimal decisions at each step t.

5   Example and Simulation Analysis

To verify the validity and efficiency of this game-based decision making framework, simulation experiment is employed in this section.

Consider a LTI control process with Gaussian White Noise which is similar to function (3) as following:

$$
\begin{aligned}
x_{t+1} &= Ax_t + Bu_t + w_t \\
y_t &= Cx_t + Du_t + v_t
\end{aligned}
\tag{20}
$$

with parameters as following:

$$
A = \begin{bmatrix} 1.1269 & -0.4940 & 0.1129 \\ 1.0000 & 0 & 0 \end{bmatrix}
\tag{21}
$$

$$
B = \begin{bmatrix} -0.3832 \\ 0.5919 \\ 0.5191 \end{bmatrix}
\tag{22}
$$

$$
C = \begin{bmatrix} 1 & 0 & 0 \end{bmatrix}
\tag{23}
$$

$$
D = \begin{bmatrix} 0 \\ 0 \\ 0 \end{bmatrix}
\tag{24}
$$

where, $t \in [0, T]$ is the time horizon, $u_t = sin(t/5)$ is the input of the system, $w_k \in R^{n_x}$ and $v_k \in R^{n_y}$ are Gaussian White Noise with error covariances of $Q = 1$ and $R = 1$ respectively, which are generated and mixed into the system by the function $awgn(\cdot)$ provided by MATLAB. In this system, the number of system state x is $m = 3$, the number of system output y is 1, the constrains for both sides are $M = 2$ and $N = 3$, respectively. Both the local and remote state estimator are standard Kalman filters as described in [29]. The attacker takes an action of random false data injection on state estimate which will be represented by a sequence of random values generated by an algorithm based on the observation of the system's previous states.

In the following simulation results, the attack moments denoted as set kat where $kat = [8, 24, 31, 42, 92]$, and the responding sequence number of attacked sensors are denoted as Ka where $Ka(kat) = [1, 3, 3, 3, 1]$. Actually, both kat and Ka are generated randomly in the practical. According to the calculation of the ranks of the pair (A, C) and $(A, Q^{1/2})$ respectively, it is confirmed that (A, C) and $(A, Q^{1/2})$ are nonsingular and the system is controllable and observable. When the data packet $\hat{x}_k^s$ is arriving through the communication channel, the remote state estimator will arbitrate between $\hat{x}_k^s$ and the expected state value $\bar{x}$, which is obtained by learning on the communication channel or receiving from the local state estimation.

Figure 3 shows the comparison of the states time-changing curve during the time window T of the original system with and without Gaussian White Noise w_k and v_k. Here in Fig. 3, the states of original system without noise are x_s. x_v are the states of the same system with Gaussian White Noises.

Figure 4 shows the comparison of the outputs time-changing curve during the time window T of the system with and without Gaussian White Noise w_k and v_k in the same situation described in Fig. 3. Here in Fig. 4, the output of original system without noise is ys. yv is the output of the same system with Gaussian White Noises.

According to Figs. 3 and 4, it is easy to figure that the system performance, i.e., xs and ys, driven by the input ut can follow the expected performance well, i.e., xv and yv.

Figure 5 shows the comparison of the states time-changing curve during the time window T of the above system with the state estimator. Here, the xs and xv are states same as they are described in Fig. 3, and xf are the results of the state estimation process.

Figure 6 shows the comparison of the outputs time-changing curve during the time window T of the above system with the state estimator in the same situation described in Fig. 5. Here in Fig. 6, ys and yv are outputs same as they are described in Fig. 4, and ye is the output of the system with state estimation.

Figure 7 shows the comparison of the states time-changing curve during the time window T of the above system and the same system applying the game

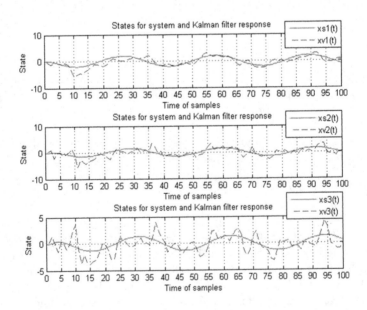

Fig. 3. States of the original system with and without Noise.

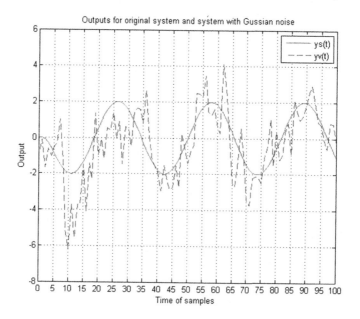

Fig. 4. Outputs of the original system with and without Noise.

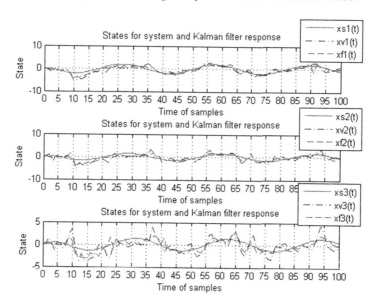

Fig. 5. States of the above system with state estimator.

framework under the false data injection attack on the state estimate. Here, the original system state are xs, the states of system with attack obtained from the communication channel are xle. $\overline{x}$ are the expected states of the system, which equal to states estimate xre as shown in the Fig. 7. Xcf are the results of the

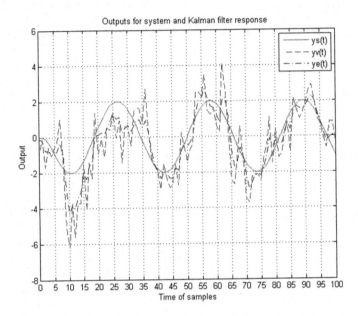

Fig. 6. Outputs of the above system with state estimator.

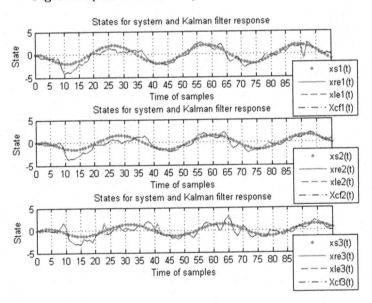

Fig. 7. States of the above system under attack. (Color figure online)

arbitration process of the game-based decision making framework in the same situation, which are accepted by the remote state estimator and then employed by the controllers of the system into the adjustment of the control process.

Obviously, applying the game framework into the system described above, the states estimation process could be improved and the attacking effectiveness could be relieved as shown in Fig. 7.

According to the simulation experiment and corresponding to the time steps $kat = [8, 24, 31, 42, 92]$, the state estimate received by remote state estimation generated by local estimation process are as shown by green line in Fig. 7: $xre = [-1.1710, 1.6322, 0.5043, 1.5360, -1.2311]$; the expected state estimate $\overline{x} = x_{le}$ received by calculation based on previous measurement are as shown by red line in Fig. 7: $xle = [-0.3228, -0.9031, -0.2526, -0.1653, 2.0693]$; the final state outputs of the final pay-off arbitration game process is denoted as x_{cf}, which are shown by blue line in Fig. 7: $xcf = [-0.3228, -0.9031, -0.2526, -0.1653, 2.0693]$.

Figure 8 shows the overall estimation error covariance trace time-varying during the time window T. The system state estimation error covariance trace Trs of the steady state is $Trs = 2.5150$. While in the same time window T, the corresponding remote state estimation error covariance trace at the attack moments $kat = [8, 24, 31, 42, 92]$ are denoted as $Trat$, where $Trat(kat) = [2.5175, 2.6783, 2.5213, 2.5942, 2.6792]$, corresponding to the attack moments $kat = [8, 24, 31, 42, 92]$, respectively. It is easy to figure that the traces of the attack moments are higher than the stable state without any attack. So the result of the decision making process accepts the state estimate value with smaller error covariance trace Trs at each time step, meaning that the calculated state estimation values are kept as the output of the decision making process of the game-base framework in this simulation experiment.

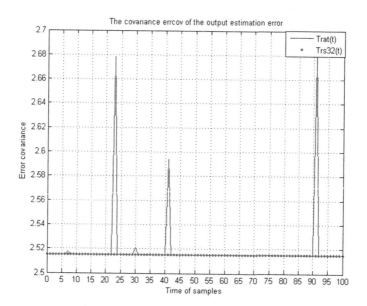

Fig. 8. Estimation error covariances of the above system under attacker.

Obviously, by applying the final pay-off arbitration game-based framework in the decision making process for the remote state estimator, performance of the same system under false data attack, i.e., xle, has been improved and the attack impact on the remote state estimate has been relieved, i.e., Xcf.

6   Conclusion

The former ICSs with poor security mechanism are feeble and vulnerable to malicious attacks from internal system and external network. As the new kind of sophisticated attack, which is called APT including Stuxnet and Flames, targets the ICSs and there are no effective strategies to detect and defense them up to now, the ICSs need to be able to relieved the attack impact of certain degree to keep plants work as normal and to minimize the loss and harm caused by the malicious action.

A situation where a game-based framework under a kind of special deception attack - false data injection attack on the remote estimator in the ICSs has been studied in this paper. The attack is carried out by manipulating the data packet on the communication channel between sensors and remote state estimator. To improve the system control performance and mitigate the attack impact on the state estimation process in the ICSs, the final pay-off arbitration game-based decision making framework is applied.

To verify the validity and efficiency of this game-based decision making framework, a simulation experiment is employed. Simulation of a discrete LTI control process applying the game framework mentioned above has been done in MATLAB software. Experimental results have shown that the final pay-off arbitration game-based decision making framework could relief the impact of the false data injection attack on the remote state estimator and improve the state estimation performance of the ICSs.

In our future work, the other game frameworks applying into the similar attacking situations aiming at the ICSs would be our interests. What's more, the objective functions used to improve the system performance and find the Nash equilibrium on both the attacker and sensor sides will be studied at the same time.

Acknowledgement. The authors would like to thank anonymous reviewers for considerate and helpful comments. The work described in this paper is supported by National Natural Science Foundation of China (61379139) and the "Strategic Priority Research Program" of the Chinese Academy of Sciences, Grant No. XDA06010701.

References

1. Clark, A., Zhu, C., Poovendran, R., Başar, T.: An impact-aware defense against stuxnet. In: 2013 American Control Conference, pp. 4140–4147. IEEE (2013)
2. Cheminod, M., Durante, L., Valenzano, A.: Review of security issues in industrial networks. IEEE Trans. Ind. Inf. **9**(1), 277–293 (2013)

3. Stouffer, K., Falco, J., Scarfone, K.: Guide to industrial control systems (ics) security. NIST Spec. Publ. **800**(82), 16 (2011)
4. Sahli, N., Benmohamed, M., Bourennane, E.-B.: Security for industrial automation and control systems. In: Conception et Production Intégrées/Integrated Desing and Production (CPI 2013), pp. 40–46 (2013)
5. Byres, E., Ginter, A., Langill, J.: How stuxnet spreads-a study of infection paths in best practice systems. Tofino Security, white paper (2011)
6. Falliere, N., Murchu, L.O., Chien, E.: W32. stuxnet dossier. White Paper Symantec Corp. Secur. Response **5**, 6 (2011)
7. Albright, D., Brannan, P., Walrond, C.: Did Stuxnet Take Out 1,000 Centrifuges at the Natanz Enrichment Plant? Institute for Science and International Security (2010)
8. Slay, J., Miller, M.: Lessons learned from the maroochy water breach. In: Goetz, E., Shenoi, S. (eds.) ICCIP 2007. IFIP, vol. 253, pp. 73–82. Springer, Boston (2008). doi:10.1007/978-0-387-75462-8_6
9. Amin, S., Cárdenas, A.A., Shankar Sastry, S.: Safe and secure networked control systems under denial-of-service attacks. In: Majumdar, R., Tabuada, P. (eds.) HSCC 2009. LNCS, vol. 5469, pp. 31–45. Springer, Heidelberg (2009). doi:10.1007/978-3-642-00602-9_3
10. Liu, Y., Ning, P., Reiter, M.K.: False data injection attacks against state estimation in electric power grids. ACM Trans. Inf. Syst. Secur. (TISSEC) **14**(1), 13 (2011)
11. Teixeira, A., Amin, S., Sandberg, H., Johansson, K.H., Shankar Sastry, S.: Cyber security analysis of state estimators in electric power systems. In: 49th IEEE Conference on Decision and Control (CDC), pp. 5991–5998. IEEE (2010)
12. Mo, Y., Sinopoli, B.: Secure control against replay attacks. In: 47th Annual Allerton Conference on Communication, Control, and Computing, Allerton 2009, pp. 911–918. IEEE (2009)
13. Smith, R.S.: A decoupled feedback structure for covertly appropriating networked control systems. IFAC Proc. **44**(1), 90–95 (2011)
14. Krotofil, M., Cárdenas, A.A.: Is this a good time?: deciding when to launch attacks on process control systems. In: Proceedings of the 3rd International Conference on High Confidence Networked Systems, pp. 65–66. ACM (2014)
15. Krotofil, M., Cardenas, A., Larsen, J., Gollmann, D.: Vulnerabilities of cyber-physical systems to stale data-determining the optimal time to launch attacks. Int. J. Crit. Infrastruct. Prot. **7**(4), 213–232 (2014)
16. Zhang, H., Cheng, P., Shi, L., Chen, J.: Optimal dos attack scheduling in wireless networked control system. IEEE Trans. Control Syst. Technol. **24**(3), 843–852 (2016)
17. Pasqualetti, F., Dörfler, F., Bullo, F.: Attack detection and identification in cyber-physical systems. IEEE Trans. Autom. Control **58**(11), 2715–2729 (2013)
18. Krotofil, M., Larsen, J., Gollmann, D.: The process matters: ensuring data veracity in cyber-physical systems. In: Proceedings of the 10th ACM Symposium on Information, Computer and Communications Security, pp. 133–144. ACM (2015)
19. Bhattacharya, S., Başar, T.: Game-theoretic analysis of an aerial jamming attack on a uav communication network. In: Proceedings of the 2010 American Control Conference, pp. 818–823. IEEE (2010)
20. Roy, S., Ellis, C., Shiva, S., Dasgupta, D., Shandilya, V., Wu, Q.: A survey of game theory as applied to network security. In: 43rd Hawaii International Conference on System Sciences (HICSS), pp. 1–10. IEEE (2010)
21. Kashyap, A., Basar, T., Srikant, R.: Correlated jamming on mimo gaussian fading channels. IEEE Trans. Inf. Theor. **50**(9), 2119–2123 (2004)

22. Gupta, A., Langbort, C., Başar, T.: Optimal control in the presence of an intelligent jammer with limited actions. In: 49th IEEE Conference on Decision and Control (CDC), pp. 1096–1101. IEEE (2010)

23. Agah, A., Das, S.K., Basu, K.: A game theory based approach for security in wireless sensor networks. In: IEEE International Conference on Performance, Computing, and Communications, pp. 259–263. IEEE (2004)

24. Li, Y., Shi, L., Cheng, P., Chen, J., Quevedo, D.E.: Jamming attacks on remote state estimation in cyber-physical systems: a game-theoretic approach. IEEE Trans. Autom. Control **60**(10), 2831–2836 (2015)

25. Li, Y., Quevedo, D.E., Dey, S., Shi, L.: Sinr-based dos attack on remote state estimation: a game-theoretic approach. IEEE Trans. Control Netw. Syst. (2016). doi:10.1109/TCNS.2016.2549640

26. Hovareshti, P., Gupta, V., Baras, J.S.: Sensor scheduling using smart sensors. In: 46th IEEE Conference on Decision and Control, pp. 494–499. IEEE (2007)

27. Li, Y., Shi, L., Cheng, P., Chen, J., Quevedo, D.E.: Jamming attack on cyber-physical systems: a game-theoretic approach. In: IEEE 3rd Annual International Conference on Cyber Technology in Automation, Control and Intelligent Systems (CYBER), pp. 252–257. IEEE (2013)

28. Shi, L., Epstein, M., Murray, R.M.: Kalman filtering over a packet-dropping network: a probabilistic perspective. IEEE Trans. Autom. Control **55**(3), 594–604 (2010)

29. Anderson, B.D.O., Moore, J.B.: Optimal filtering. Courier Corporation (2012)

30. Gibbons, R.: A primer in game theory. Harvester Wheatsheaf (1992)

31. Nash, J.: Non-cooperative games. Ann. Math. **54**, 286–295 (1951)

Secure Collaborative Outsourced k-Nearest Neighbor Classification with Multiple Owners in Cloud Environment

Hong Rong[✉], Huimei Wang, Jian Liu, Wei Wu, Jialu Hao, and Ming Xian

State Key Laboratory of Complex Electromagnetic Environment Effects on Electronics and Information System, National University of Defense Technology, Changsha, China
r.hong_nudt@hotmail.com, freshcdwhm@163.com, goodwuwei18@163.com, haojialupb@163.com, ljabc730@gmail.com, qwertmingx@tom.com

Abstract. With the advent of big data era, it's becoming an increasing trend for different clients lack of computational resources to cooperate in outsourcing data mining tasks to cloud service providers in order to produce maximum value of the joint database. Generally, the outsourced data contributed by clients should be encrypted under different keys owing to security concerns. Unfortunately, existing privacy-preserving outsourcing protocols are either restricted to a single key setting or quite inefficient due to frequent server-client interactions, making the deployment far from practical. In this paper, we focus on outsourced k-Nearest Neighbor (kNN) classification over encrypted data under multiple keys, and propose a set of secure building blocks and the Secure Collaborative Outsourced kNN (SCOkNN) protocol. Theoretical analysis shows that the proposed protocol protects the confidentiality of data from data owners, privacy of query, and access patterns in the semi-honest model with negligible computation and communication costs. Experimental evaluation also demonstrates its practicability and efficiency.

Keywords: Big data · Cloud computing · Privacy-preserving data mining · K-nearest neighbor classification · Multiple owners

1 Introduction

With an inevitable trend on rapid growth of the volume and variety of data captured by organizations, outsourcing both data and data mining tasks to cloud service providers to reduce management costs and improve efficiency becomes a natural solution. As the concerns of data security and privacy are also on the rise, clients intend to encrypt their data before outsourcing to protect data confidentiality from unauthorized access. Therefore, the secure outsourcing protocol should not only guarantee the accuracy of target computation, but also preserves privacy of users' data, query, as well as access patterns.

In this paper, we focus on the problem of securely processing k-Nearest Neighbor (kNN) queries in the cloud. kNN algorithm identifies the k points nearest to

© Springer International Publishing AG 2017
K. Chen et al. (Eds.): Inscrypt 2016, LNCS 10143, pp. 451–471, 2017.
DOI: 10.1007/978-3-319-54705-3_28

a query point in a given database according to some distance measurements like Minkowski or Euclidean distance, and classifies the query based on the majority classifications of the neighboring points. Particularly, we consider a more practical scenario that the federal databases in the cloud are contributed by multiple data owners, and the cloud servers process kNN queries over the encrypted database in a collaborative way, which may maximize the benefit of big data.

Most existing works [1–4] on outsourced kNN computation were based on a single data owner situation. F. Li *et al.* [5] first considered multiple distrusted owners and used kernel density estimation instead of kNN to prevent distance-learning attacks. These methods require that data owners encrypt their datasets under the cloud server's public key which is also used to encrypt queries. However, this single key setting faces two problems in multi-user scenario: (1) The compromised server or key leakage may jeopardize the privacy of all clients' data. (2) The cloud storage cannot function properly, since data owners don't possess the private key for decryption. Therefore, generating and utilizing different keys for different owners proves to be essential in this model. Recently, [6] leveraged the two independent decryption mechanisms of BCP cryptosystem to convert ciphertexts under different keys, which also incurs heavy interactions between servers. To reduce the costs, [7,8] proposed two schemes for outsourced computation based on ElGamal encryption. But its additive scheme needs solving discrete logarithm which is considered to be computationally intractable, while its multiplicative scheme may reveal partial privacy under the two-server model. As a consequence, it still remains unsolved to efficiently and securely perform outsourced kNN tasks over distributed datasets from multiple owners.

Main Contributions. In this paper, we propose a set of privacy-preserving building blocks and Secure Collaborative Outsourced kNN (SCOkNN) protocol that allows data owners to encrypt data with their own keys while the cloud servers can perform kNN over the encrypted federate datasets. To the best of our knowledge, there's no prior work that addresses outsourced kNN problem under multiple keys setting. The main contributions of this work are three-fold:

- Our protocol is able to process ciphertexts under multiple keys by re-encryption technique, and returns the correct kNN class label for a given query. In the meantime, it meets the privacy requirements that none of the following should be revealed to the cloud servers or other participants: (1) contents of joint datasets or any intermediate results; (2) query and its response; (3) encrypted records corresponding to the majority class label. Thus, our protocol protects the data privacy, query privacy, and access patterns from unauthorized access via open channel.
- We emphasize that the data owners or querists are not required to involve in any kNN computations after uploading their encrypted dataset or query record to the cloud. They are allowed to obtain the uploaded dataset from cloud storage or final result with their own keys. Moreover, the usage of separate keys lowers down the risks of key leakage as well as eavesdropping attacks.

– Theoretical analysis demonstrates that the proposed schemes execute kNN computation correctly, and they're secure under the standard semi-honest model, with lower computational and communication complexity compared with similar works. Extensive experiments on real datasets also show its significant improvements in efficiency.

The rest of the paper is organized as follows. Our system model and threat model are described in Sect. 2. In Sect. 3, we briefly introduce proxy re-encryption techniques. The design details of privacy-preserving building blocks and corresponding SCOkNN protocol are presented in Sect. 4. Then, we evaluate the performance of our schemes in Sect. 5, and we review the related work regarding outsourced privacy-preserving kNN computation in Sect. 6. Finally, we summarize the paper and outline future work in Sect. 7.

2 Problem Statement

In this section, we formally describe our system model, threat model and design objectives.

2.1 System Model

In our system model depicted in Fig. 1, there are n data owners $U_1, ..., U_n$ who hold their own database $D_1, ..., D_n$ along with their respective public/private key pairs, denoted as $pk_1/sk_1, ..., pk_n/sk_n$. The database D_i has l_i records with $m+1$ attributes for $i \in [1, n]$, in which the $(m+1)^{th}$ attribute contains corresponding class label of that record. For simplicity, we assume l_i has the equal length l. There's also an authorized querist Q with a kNN query $q = <q_1, ..., q_m>$ and key pair pk_Q/sk_Q. The cloud environments are composed of two servers, namely C_1 and C_2. Let $t^i_{j,h}$ denote the hth attribute value of record t^i_j of D_i for $h \in [1, m]$ and $j \in [1, l]$. Initially, U_i encrypts each attribute $t^i_{j,h}$ with pk_i and acquires $\mathsf{Enc}_{pk_i}(D_i)$ denoted by D'_i as well, which is then uploaded to C_1 for storage and

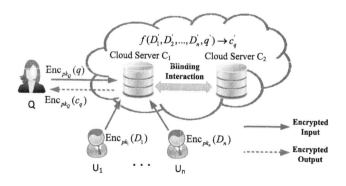

Fig. 1. System Model

kNN classification. Q uses pk_Q to compute $\mathsf{Enc}_{pk_Q}(q)$ denoted by q', which is then submitted to C_1. After C_1 obtains the joint encrypted databases, it begins to evaluate over the kNN function $f(D'_1, ..., D'_n, q') = c'_q$ together with C_2 through cryptographic protocols, where c'_q denotes the encrypted class label for q. Finally, the encrypted result is returned to Q under its public key.

Our system model is appropriate and applicable for the following two reasons. On one hand, to protect confidentiality of users' data, it is essential for data owners and querists to encrypt their data before outsourcing. Besides, the encryptions are conducted by using their own keys, which reduces the risks of secret key disclosure and being intercepted by other owners or compromised cloud servers (e.g., private key leakage in single-key model may endanger data privacy of all participants [9]). This is also consistent with the security demands of real world application. On the other hand, two non-colluding servers to perform privacy-preserving computations is commonly used to eliminate users' interactions [10], and previous work [11] has proven that a non-interactive solution is impossible to implement under traditional single server model. Furthermore, two servers may belong to different cloud providers, generally driven by different business model and competing relationship (e.g., Google Compute Engine and Amazon EC2), thus lowering down the chances of collusion attacks.

2.2 Threat Model

As Fig. 1 shows, our threat model primarily includes cloud servers, data owners and querist, communication channel.

(1) Servers: The two cloud servers are assumed to be semi-honest, which means that each server will follow the protocol, but may try to analyze user's inputs, intermediate results, as well as outputs in order to infer sensitive information. We also assume the servers have background knowledge of the distribution of owners' data.

(2) Data owners and querists: They are assumed to be semi-honest clients of outsourced kNN service. They can cooperate with other participants for the sake of collaborative data mining, meanwhile they may attempt to gather others' private information. Besides, their online periods are relatively short and non-deterministic.

(3) Channel: Communication channel is supposed to be open and insecure. Adversary may launch eavesdropping attacks and infer additional information from intercepted data.

2.3 Design Objectives

Given the model above, our design should achieve the following objectives:

- **Correctness.** If the clients and cloud servers both follow the designed protocol, the returned result should be decrypted to a correct class label for the specific kNN query.

- **Confidentiality**. During the outsourced computation process, nothing regarding the content of data owners' datasets, query record, kNN result, or access patterns should be revealed and conjectured by the cloud servers, or other parties.
- **Efficiency**. Due to the users' insufficient computation scalability, their participation should be minimized, while the major workload should be completed at servers' side at an appealing rate.

3   Preliminaries

Proxy Re-Encryption (PRE) is a useful primitive introduced by Blaze, Bleumer and Strauss [12]. In a PRE system, a proxy is given a re-encryption key $rk_{i \to j}$ so that it can transform a ciphertext under public key pk_i into a ciphertext of the same plaintext under another user's public key pk_j. The proxy, however, learns nothing in terms of the corresponding plaintext. Only by transform those ciphertexts into ones under a unified key can the servers conduct any arithmetic operations.

In this work, we use the classic bidirectional PRE scheme in [12] because ciphertext conversion from two directions (i.e., user-to-server and server-to-user) is required. The scheme is constructed on ElGamal cryptosystem, which is secure against chosen-plaintext attacks (CPA). It consists of the following five algorithms [13,14]:

- KeyGen($\mathbb{G}, p, g$) $\to \{pk_i, sk_i\}$: Let $\mathbb{G}$ be a multiplicative cyclic group of an order of p, and g be a generator of $\mathbb{G}$. U_i uses this key generation algorithm to generate a key pair $sk_i = a \in Z_p^*$ and $pk_i = g^a \in \mathbb{G}$.
- ReKeyGen(sk_i, sk_j) $\to \{rk_{i \to j}\}$: The re-encryption key generation algorithm takes two private keys sk_i and sk_j as inputs, and outputs a re-encryption key $rk_{i \to j} = sk_j / sk_i \in \mathbb{Z}_p^*$. Here, it is required that $i \neq j$ in that there's no point to re-encrypt oneself's ciphertext.
- Enc(pk_i, b) $\to \{CT_i\}$: The encryption algorithm takes a public key pk_i and a message $b \in \mathcal{M}$ as inputs. It outputs an ciphertext $CT_i = (b \cdot g^r, pk_i^r)$ under pk_i. Here, $\mathcal{M}$ denotes the message space, and r is a random number generated from $\mathbb{Z}_p^*$. Let the notion $r \in_R \mathbb{Z}_p^*$ denote the random number generation.
- ReEnc($rk_{i \to j}, CT_i$)$\to \{CT_j\}$: The re-encryption algorithm takes a re-encryption key $rk_{i \to j}$ and an original ciphertext CT_i as inputs, and outputs a transformed ciphertext $CT_j = (b \cdot g^r, (pk_i^r)^{rk_{i \to j}})$ under pk_j.
- Dec(sk_i, CT_i) $\to \{m\}$: The decryption algorithm takes a private key sk_i and an original or converted ciphertext CT_i under public key pk_i. It outputs a plaintext message $b \leftarrow b \cdot g^r / ((pk_i^r)^{1/sk_i})$.

Moreover, ElGamal encryption has multiplicatively homomorphic property over ciphertexts. More specifically, we have

$$\mathsf{Enc}_{pk}(b_1) \times \mathsf{Enc}_{pk}(b_2) = \mathsf{Enc}_{pk}(b_1 \cdot b_2), \tag{1}$$

$$\mathsf{Enc}_{pk}(b_1)^\alpha = \mathsf{Enc}_{pk}(b_1^\alpha), \text{ where } \alpha \in \mathbb{Z}_p. \tag{2}$$

Here, "$\cdot$" denotes the multiplication operation in the plaintext domain while "$\times$" denotes the multiplication operation in the ciphertext domain.

4   Secure Collaborative Outsourced kNN Scheme

In this section, we first give an overview of our outsourced privacy-preserving kNN protocol with multiple owners under corresponding keys. Then, we present the design details of building blocks and complete protocol. And the security and complexity of the proposed scheme are further analyzed.

4.1   Overview

With the assumption of two semi-honest, but non-colluding servers, the basic idea of our SCOkNN scheme is to utilize the ciphertext conversion property of PRE. Initially, the server C_1 runs a setup operation and distributes the system public parameters, based on which $U_i (i \in [1, n])$, Q and C_2 generate their respective public and private key pairs. After this, both servers and clients jointly generate the re-encryption keys via key distribution protocol. After U_i's encrypted dataset under pk_i are uploaded to the cloud, C_1 transforms all the ciphertexts into encryptions under a unified key (C_2's key). Let D'_{joint} denote the combination of the ultimate converted datasets. When Q submits its encrypted query q' to cloud, C_1 begins to conduct ciphertext transformation. And then, kNN classification can feasibly be performed through a set of cryptographic subprotocols. The final class label under the unified key should be converted back to the ciphertext under Q's public key. Finally, Q retrieves the encrypted output with its private key. Note that the outsourced kNN computation part is conducted with no interactions of data owners and queriest whatsoever.

4.2   Privacy-Preserving Building Blocks

During privacy-preserving kNN outsourcing, the cloud servers need to initialize encryption keys and then perform a lot of basic operations over ciphertexts, including multiplication, addition, distance computation, comparison, as well as computing the majority class. They are regarded as privacy-preserving building blocks of SCOkNN protocol, which are presented as follows:

1. The Key Initialization (KI) Protocol: At first, the server C_1 runs a setup process that initializes the ElGamal cryptosystem and distributes system parameters to the other participants. Each party generates its key pairs by KeyGen($\mathbb{G}, p, g$), including U_i's (pk_i, sk_i), Q's (pk_Q, sk_Q) and C_2's unified key (pk_u, sk_u). For simplicity, we treat Q as $(n + 1)^{th}$ data owner, but this does not affect the security. C_1 computes $n + 1$ re-encryption keys for each user through secure interactions with U_i, Q, and C_2. C_1 first generates $r_i \in_R \mathbb{Z}_p^*$, and distributes it to U_i; after that, U_i computes r_i/sk_i and sends it to C_2 who obtains $r_i/sk_i \cdot sk_u$ and returns it to C_1; thus, C_1 gets re-encryption key by $r_i/sk_i \cdot sk_u \cdot r_i^{-1}$. The overall communication is protected by secure protocol like SSL. Note that C_2 cannot know the secret keys of U_i or Q during execution of this protocol because they're blinded by random number r_i.

2. The Secure Multiplication (SM) Protocol: Given that C_1 holds private inputs $(\mathsf{Enc}_{pk_u}(a), \mathsf{Enc}_{pk_u}(b))$ and C_2 holds the secret key sk_u, the goal of this protocol is to compute the encryption of multiplication of a and b (i.e., $\mathsf{Enc}_{pk_u}(a \cdot b)$). Since ElGamal encryption is multiplicatively homomorphic, the multiplication over the two ciphertexts can be performed by C_1 independently as follows.

$$\mathsf{Enc}_{pk_u}(a \cdot b) = \mathsf{Enc}_{pk_u}(a) \times \mathsf{Enc}_{pk_u}(b)$$
$$= ((a \cdot b) \cdot g^{r_a + r_b}, g^{(r_a + r_b) \cdot sk_u}), \tag{3}$$

where r_a, r_b are random numbers in $\mathbb{Z}_p^*$. According to the security of ElGamal scheme, SM protocol is semantic secure.

3. The Secure Addition (SA) Protocol: Assume that C_1 with private inputs $(\mathsf{Enc}_{pk_u}(a), \mathsf{Enc}_{pk_u}(b))$, and C_2 with sk_u. The goal of this protocol is to compute the encrypted addition of a and b (i.e., $\mathsf{Enc}_{pk_u}(a + b)$) as output to C_1. As the encryption system is not additively homomorphic, it requires interactions between C_1 and C_2.

The first scheme to address addition over ciphertexts under multiple keys using ElGamal-based PRE was proposed by B. Wang, et al. in their works [7,8]. Their scheme under two-server model works like this: C_1 uses a random factor r to blind the input ciphertexts by performing $\mathsf{Enc}_{pk_u}(ra) \leftarrow \mathsf{Enc}_{pk_u}(a) \times \mathsf{Enc}_{pk_u}(r)$, and $\mathsf{Enc}_{pk_u}(rb) \leftarrow \mathsf{Enc}_{pk_u}(b) \times \mathsf{Enc}_{pk_u}(r)$. Then, C_2 decrypts those blinded ciphertexts, and computes $ra + rb$, the encryption of which is sent back to C_1. The blinding factor is removed through $\mathsf{Enc}_{pk_u}(a+b) \leftarrow \mathsf{Enc}_{pk_u}(ra + rb) \times \mathsf{Enc}_{pk_u}(r^{-1})$ by C_1. During the process, a, b, ra, rb are not directly revealed to both servers. However, C_2 may compute ratio of inputs by $a/b \leftarrow ra/rb$. This information can be used to distinguish ra and rb if the knowledge of data distribution is known to C_2. To avoid leaking the input ratio, they adopted the third server to enhance security [7].

Similar with [8], our SA protocol is also based on ElGamal cryptosystem under two-server model, whereas we assume the adversary may possess the knowledge of data owners' data distribution. Hence, none of a, b, $a + b$, or a/b should be revealed to cloud servers to protect privacy.

Our solution utilizes a kind of blinding technique, denoted by Blind. $\mathsf{Blind}(C, r)$ is an operation that randomizes c_1 of ciphertext C by multiplying random value r so that the plaintext b is blinded by r, where $C = (c_1, c_2)$, $c_1 = bg^{r'}$, $r, b \in \mathbb{G}$, and $r' \in Z_p^*$. This operation only requires one multiplication over $\mathbb{G}$. The overall steps of SA are presented in Algorithm 1.

First, C_1 generates random numbers: r_1, r_2 from $\mathbb{Z}$, r_3, r_4 from $\mathbb{G}$, while ensuring the relation: $r_1 + r_2 \equiv 2 \bmod H$, where H is used to generate $\mathbb{G}$. Then, C_1 computes an encrypted set L, in which $L_1 = \mathsf{SM}(\mathsf{Enc}_{pk_u}(a), \mathsf{Enc}_{pk_u}(b))$, $L_2 = \mathsf{Blind}(\mathsf{Enc}_{pk_u}(a)^2, r_3)$, $L_3 = \mathsf{Blind}(L_1, r_1 \cdot r_3)$, $L_4 = \mathsf{Blind}(\mathsf{Enc}_{pk_u}(b)^2, r_4)$, $L_5 = \mathsf{Blind}(L_1, r_2 \cdot r_4)$. Based on Eq. (1), we can infer that $L_1 = \mathsf{Enc}_{pk_u}(a \cdot b)$. Based on Eq. (2), it can be verified that $L_2 = \mathsf{Enc}_{pk_u}(a^2 \cdot r_3)$, $L_3 = \mathsf{Enc}_{pk_u}(r_1 \cdot r_3 \cdot a \cdot b)$, $L_4 = \mathsf{Enc}_{pk_u}(b^2 \cdot r_4)$, $L_5 = \mathsf{Enc}_{pk_u}(r_2 \cdot r_4 \cdot a \cdot b)$. The two sets $\{L_2, L_3\}$, $\{L_4, L_5\}$ are sent to C_2.

Upon receiving L, C_2 begins to decrypt those ciphertexts by sk_u, denoted by L'. Let S be the sum set between L'_2 and L'_3, L'_4 and L'_5. C_2 calculates S and encrypts it as S' which is returned back to C_1. Then, C_1 removes the blinding factors r_3, r_4 via Blind operation with the multiplicative inverses of them, meanwhile randomizing the ciphertexts again with another random r_5. Thus, C_1 obtains the encryptions of $r_5 \cdot a^2 + r_1 \cdot r_5 \cdot a \cdot b$, and $r_5 \cdot b^2 + r_2 \cdot r_5 \cdot a \cdot b$, denoted by α_1 and α_2, respectively, which are sent to C_2 for further processing. Afterwards, C_2 decrypts α_1, α_2 and computes their sum, denoted as λ. Before transmitting to C_1, C_2 encrypts it using pk_u. In the end, C_1 can get the encrypted value of $a + b$ by blinding with r_5^{-1} and exponentiating with 2^{-1}. The correctness can be proven as follows:

$$
\begin{aligned}
\mathsf{Blind}(\lambda', r_5^{-1})^{2^{-1}} &= \mathsf{Enc}_{pk_u}(r_5^{-1}(r_5 a^2 + r_1 r_5 ab + r_2 r_5 ab + r_5 b^2))^{2^{-1}} \\
&= \mathsf{Enc}_{pk_u}(a^2 + (r_1 + r_2)ab + b^2)^{2^{-1}} \\
&= \mathsf{Enc}_{pk_u}((a+b)^2)^{2^{-1}} \\
&= \mathsf{Enc}_{pk_u}(a+b).
\end{aligned}
\tag{4}
$$

Security Analysis of SA. The security of SA protocol is discussed based on "Real-vs.-Ideal" framework [15]. Under this framework, we need to show that SA is secure against both adversary $\mathcal{A}_{C_1}^{\mathrm{SH}}$ corrupting C_1 and $\mathcal{A}_{C_2}^{\mathrm{SH}}$ corrupting C_2.

(1) Security Against Cloud Server C_1: During SA protocol, the inputs of C_1 are $\mathsf{Enc}_{pk_u}(a)$, $\mathsf{Enc}_{pk_u}(b)$, S', and λ', all of which are encrypted under pk_u. So without decryption key sk_u, C_1 can only obtain the encryption form of inputs and outputs. By the semantic security of the ElGamal encryption scheme, the encrypted data C_1 stores are indistinguishable from encryptions of random values simulated by $\mathcal{F}^{\mathrm{SH}}$ in the ideal world. We have the following

$$
\mathrm{Ideal}_{f, \mathcal{F}^{\mathrm{SH}}}(\mathsf{Enc}_{pk_u}(b_i)) \overset{c}{=} \mathrm{Real}_{\mathrm{SA}, \mathcal{A}_{C_1}^{\mathrm{SH}}}(\mathsf{Enc}_{pk_u}(b_i)),
\tag{5}
$$

where $i \in \{1, 2\}$. Thereby, no privacy leakage to $\mathcal{A}_{C_1}^{\mathrm{SH}}$ is guaranteed.

(2) Security Against Cloud Server C_2: Since C_2 has the secret key sk_u, it can get the intermediate results: $r_3 a^2, r_1 r_3 ab, r_4 b^2, r_2 r_4 ab$ in the first round of computation. However, C_2 cannot obtain either a, b or $a+b$, because they are blinded by the C_1's generated random numbers. Although C_2 can compute $a/r_1 b \leftarrow L'_2/L'_3$, $b/r_2 a \leftarrow L'_4/L'_5$, and also has the knowledge of $r_1 + r_2 \equiv 2 \bmod H$, it's not sufficient to infer a/b in that $r_1 + r_2 = 2 + xH$, where $x \in \mathbb{Z}$. Without knowing x, C_2 cannot setup enough equations to obtain a/b. During the second round, C_2 obtains $r_5 a^2 + r_1 r_5 ab$ and $r_5 b^2 + r_2 r_5 ab$ by decryption under sk_u. These two messages are randomized by r_1, r_2, r_5. We can build a simulator $\mathcal{F}^{\mathrm{SH}}$ in the ideal world that uses random values as inputs, and executes the protocol for C_2's part. As long as C_2 does not know the blinding factors, $\mathcal{A}_{C_2}$ is not able to distinguish from the real world and the ideal world. We have the following

$$
\mathrm{Ideal}_{f, \mathcal{F}^{\mathrm{SH}}}(\mathsf{Enc}_{pk_u}(r_i b_i^2)) \overset{c}{=} \mathrm{Real}_{\mathrm{SA}, \mathcal{A}_{C_2}^{\mathrm{SH}}}(\mathsf{Enc}_{pk_u}(r_i b_i^2)),
\tag{6}
$$

where $i \in \{1, 2\}$. Thereby, no privacy leakage to $\mathcal{A}_{C_2}^{\mathrm{SH}}$ is guaranteed.

Algorithm 1. $\mathsf{SA}(\mathsf{Enc}_{pk_u}(a), \mathsf{Enc}_{pk_u}(b)) \rightarrow \mathsf{Enc}_{pk_u}(a+b)$

Require: C_1 has $\mathsf{Enc}_{pk_u}(a)$ and $\mathsf{Enc}_{pk_u}(b)$; C_2 has sk_u.

C_1:

1. Generate random numbers $r_1, r_2 \in_R \mathbb{Z}$, $r_3, r_4 \in_R \mathbb{G}$, where $r_1 + r_2 \equiv 2 \bmod H$, and H is used to generate the multiplicative cyclic group $\mathbb{G}$;
2. Compute $L_1 \leftarrow \mathsf{SM}(\mathsf{Enc}_{pk_u}(a), \mathsf{Enc}_{pk_u}(b))$;
3. Compute $L_2 \leftarrow \mathsf{Blind}(\mathsf{Enc}_{pk_u}(a)^2, r_3)$;
4. Compute $L_3 \leftarrow \mathsf{Blind}(L_1, r_1 \cdot r_3)$;
5. Compute $L_4 \leftarrow \mathsf{Blind}(\mathsf{Enc}_{pk_u}(b)^2, r_4)$;
6. Compute $L_5 \leftarrow \mathsf{Blind}(L_1, r_2 \cdot r_4)$;
7. Send $\{L_2, L_3\}, \{L_4, L_5\}$ to C_2;

C_2:

1. Receive encrypted results $\{L_2, L_3\}, \{L_4, L_5\}$ from C_1;
2. Decrypt: $L_i' \leftarrow \mathsf{Dec}(sk_u, L_i)$, for $i = 2, 3, 4, 5$;
3. Compute $S_1 \leftarrow L_2' + L_3'$;
4. Compute $S_2 \leftarrow L_4' + L_5'$;
5. Encrypt: $S_i' \leftarrow \mathsf{Enc}(pk_u, S_i)$, for $i = 1, 2$;
6. Send S' to C_1;

C_1:

1. Receive encrypted set S' from C_2;
2. Generate random number $r_5 \in_R \mathbb{G}$;
3. Compute $\alpha_1 \leftarrow \mathsf{Blind}(S_1', r_3^{-1} \cdot r_5)$;
4. Compute $\alpha_2 \leftarrow \mathsf{Blind}(S_2', r_4^{-1} \cdot r_5)$;
5. Send α_1, α_2 to C_2;

C_2:

1. Receive α_1, α_2 from C_1;
2. Decrypt: $\alpha_i' \leftarrow \mathsf{Dec}(sk_u, \alpha_i)$, for $i = 1, 2$;
3. Compute $\lambda \leftarrow \alpha_1' + \alpha_2'$;
4. Encrypt: $\lambda' \leftarrow \mathsf{Enc}(pk_u, \lambda)$;
5. Send λ' to C_1;

C_1:

1. Receive λ' from C_2;
2. Compute $\mathsf{Enc}_{pk_u}(a+b) \leftarrow \mathsf{Blind}(\lambda', r_5^{-1})^{2^{-1}}$;

---

4. The Secure Squared Distance (SSD) Protocol: Given that C_1 holds private inputs $(\mathsf{Enc}_{pk_u}(A), \mathsf{Enc}_{pk_u}(B))$ and C_2 holds the secret key sk_u, the goal of this protocol is to compute the encryption of squared distance between A and B, where A, B are two m-dimension vectors with the form: $\mathsf{Enc}_{pk_u}(A) = <\mathsf{Enc}_{pk_u}(a_1), ..., \mathsf{Enc}_{pk_u}(a_m) >$ and $\mathsf{Enc}_{pk_u}(B) = < \mathsf{Enc}_{pk_u}(b_1), ..., \mathsf{Enc}_{pk_u}(b_m) >$. In this paper, we only consider the Euclidean Distance. So the goal of this protocol is to compute $\mathsf{Enc}_{pk_u}(\sum_{i=1}^{m}(a_i - b_i)^2)$. First, the servers compute the difference between the elements of vectors by SA protocol. Then the differences are squared by C_1 running SM. The final result is calculated by adding the squared differences via SA. The main steps involved in SSD are shown in Algorithm 2.

Security Analysis of SSD. SSD protocol is performed through execution of SM and SA. According to the Composition Theorem for the semi-honest model [15], this protocol does not reveal any privacy about inputs and outputs as long as SM and SA are secure, which have been illustrated before.

Algorithm 2. SSD($\mathsf{Enc}_{pk_u}(A), \mathsf{Enc}_{pk_u}(B)$) $\rightarrow$ $\mathsf{Enc}_{pk_u}(|A - B|^2)$

Require: C_1 has $\mathsf{Enc}_{pk_u}(A) =< \mathsf{Enc}_{pk_u}(a_1), ..., \mathsf{Enc}_{pk_u}(a_m) >$ and $\mathsf{Enc}_{pk_u}(B) =< \mathsf{Enc}_{pk_u}(b_1), ..., \mathsf{Enc}_{pk_u}(b_m) >$; C_2 has sk_u.

C_1 and C_2, **for** $i = 1$ to m **do:**

    1. Compute $\mathsf{Enc}_{pk_u}(-b_i) \leftarrow \mathsf{Blind}(\mathsf{Enc}_{pk_u}(b_i), -1)$;

    2. Compute $\mathsf{Enc}_{pk_u}(a_i - b_i) \leftarrow \mathsf{SA}(\mathsf{Enc}_{pk_u}(a_i), \mathsf{Enc}_{pk_u}(-b_i))$;

C_1, **for** $i = 1$ to m **do:**

    1. Compute $\mathsf{Enc}_{pk_u}((a_i - b_i)^2) \leftarrow \mathsf{SM}(\mathsf{Enc}_{pk_u}(a_i - b_i), \mathsf{Enc}_{pk_u}(a_i - b_i))$;

C_1 and C_2:

    1. Initialize $\mathsf{Enc}_{pk_u}(|A - B|^2) \leftarrow \mathsf{Enc}_{pk_u}(0)$;

    2. **for** $i = 1$ to m **do:**

        – Compute $\mathsf{Enc}_{pk_u}(|A - B|^2) \leftarrow \mathsf{SA}(\mathsf{Enc}_{pk_u}(|A - B|^2), \mathsf{Enc}_{pk_u}((a_i - b_i)^2))$;

---

5. The Secure Minimum between 2 Numbers (SM2N) Protocol: Given that C_1 holds private inputs ($\mathsf{Enc}_{pk_u}(a), \mathsf{Enc}_{pk_u}(b)$) and C_2 holds the secret key sk_u, the goal of this protocol is to compute the encryption of minimum from the two inputs. The main idea of this protocol is to compute the sign of difference between inputs. In most practical applications, the size of plaintext is far smaller than the key size. Let ζ be the size of key size, and ε denote the maximum size of our plaintext. The max value and the min value we can express are $2^\varepsilon - 1$ and $-2^\varepsilon + 1$. Likewise, the max difference between two values is $2^{\varepsilon+1} - 2$ while the min difference can be $-2^{\varepsilon+1} + 2$. During modular computation in $\mathbb{G}$, the negative value is in the range $[\gamma - 2^{\varepsilon+1} + 2, \gamma - 1]$, where γ is the group modulus. C_1 computes the encrypted difference and generates a random number r to blind the difference. To ensure there's no integer overflow, the size of r should be chosen as the following:

$$|r| \in_R [1, \log(\gamma - 2^{\varepsilon+1} + 1) - 64]. \tag{7}$$

The complete steps are presented in Algorithm 3.

Security Analysis of SM2N. This protocol utilizes SA to compute the difference of inputs, which is blinded by a random number r. Hence, C_2 cannot know the exact difference of distances during kNN computation apart from the sign of that value, denoted by σ. Since the max value of γ can be $2^\varsigma - 1$ and $\varepsilon \ll \zeta$, the random number r is large enough to guarantee security. In the end, C_1 outputs the minimum ciphertext based on σ. Note that the transmitted σ should be protected by SSL protocol. Combined with security discussion mentioned earlier, SM2N does not disclose any privacy of user's data.

Algorithm 3. $\text{SM2N}(\text{Enc}_{pk_u}(a), \text{Enc}_{pk_u}(b)) \rightarrow \text{Enc}_{pk_u}(\min(a,b))$

Require: C_1 has $\text{Enc}_{pk_u}(a), \text{Enc}_{pk_u}(b)$; C_2 has sk_u.

C_1:

1. Compute $\text{Enc}_{pk_u}(-b) \leftarrow \text{Blind}(\text{Enc}_{pk_u}(b), -1)$;
2. Compute $\text{Enc}_{pk_u}(a-b) \leftarrow \text{SA}(\text{Enc}_{pk_u}(a), \text{Enc}_{pk_u}(-b))$ with C_2;
3. Generate a random number $r \in_R \mathbb{G}$ that satisfies the Eq. (7);
4. Send $\text{Enc}_{pk_u}(r(a-b))$ to C_2;

C_2:

1. Initialize $\sigma \leftarrow 0$;
2. **if** $\text{Dec}(sk_u, \text{Enc}_{pk_u}(r(a-b))) > 0$ **then** $\sigma \leftarrow 1$;
3. Send σ to C_1 via SSL protocol;

C_1:

1. Initialize $\text{Enc}_{pk_u}(\min(a,b)) \leftarrow \text{Enc}_{pk_u}(a)$;
2. **if** $\sigma == 1$ **then** $\text{Enc}_{pk_u}(\min(a,b)) \leftarrow \text{Enc}_{pk_u}(b)$;

---

6. The Secure Minimum in n Numbers (SMnN) Protocol: Assume that C_1 with inputs $(\text{Enc}_{pk_u}(d_1),..., \text{Enc}_{pk_u}(d_n))$ interacts with C_2 securely compute minimum from n inputs. The main goal of the SMnN protocol is to compute $\text{Enc}_{pk_u}(d_{min})$) and its corresponding index without revealing any information about d_i to C_1 and C_2. Here, d_{min} denotes the minimum value of inputs, i.e., $d_{min} = \min(d_1,...,d_n)$. Since we already have constructed secure comparison protocol–SM2N, SMnN is designed based on SM2N as the building block, and any generic sort algorithm can be applied to SMnN. Considering the efficiency, we implement heap sort algorithm to compute the encrypted minimum value, the complexity of which is $O(\log n)$. Due to space limitations, the complete presentation of SMnN is omitted. Furthermore, no exact information of input data is disclosed to C_1 and C_2 during SMnN, because SM2N is a privacy-preserving protocol and the security of SMnN depends on SM2N.

7. The Secure Major Class Computation (SMCC) Protocol: C_1 with $< \mathsf{Enc}_{pk_u}(c'_1), ..., \mathsf{Enc}_{pk_u}(c'_k) >$, and C_2 securely compute major class label. Recall that k is number of nearest points. We also assume that C_1 knows the encrypted vector of each class label, i.e., $< \mathsf{Enc}_{pk_u}(c_1), ..., \mathsf{Enc}_{pk_u}(c_\theta) >$, where θ is number of class labels. Here, c'_i denotes the class label of ith closest neighbor to query q for $1 \leq i \leq k$, while c_j denotes the unique class label in the joint database for $1 \leq j \leq \theta$. Obviously, $c'_i \in \{c_1, ..., c_\theta\}$. During the SMCC protocol, the output $\mathsf{Enc}_{pk_u}(c_{major})$ is revealed only to C_1 whereas neither c'_i nor c_j is revealed to C_1 and C_2. Besides, C_1 does not know which data record corresponds to $\mathsf{Enc}_{pk_u}(c_{major})$.

The overall steps involved in the SMCC protocol are shown in Algorithm 4. In the beginning, C_1 generates a permutation function π, which is used to disorder the arrangement of encrypted vector of class labels denoted by Θ. Then, C_1 and C_2 cooperate to compute such a matrix S that the element $S_{i,j} = \mathsf{Enc}_{pk_u}(c'_i - c_j)$, for $1 \leq i \leq k$ and $1 \leq j \leq \theta$. C_1 later obtains S' by randomizing each element of S with a random value r_j. After receiving S', C_2 decrypts every component of the matrix and computes the frequencies. It can be easily observed that the row S'_i must contains merely one encryption of 0 and $\theta - 1$ encryptions of random values based on the fact $c'_i \in \{c_1, ..., c_\theta\}$. Therefore, C_2 calculates a frequency vector fr, the element of which corresponds to the frequency of that class. After that, the index of most frequent class in Λ is computed, and C_2 returns C_1 an encrypted vector CL in which the frequent index is the ciphertext of 1 and the rest are ciphertexts of 0. Upon receiving CL, C_1 reorders it through the inverse of π and computes the encrypted scalar product between CL' and Θ. Obviously, the scalar product result is the final encryption of majority class label because the only desired element is left after component-wise multiplication of $< c_1, ..., c_\theta >$ and $< 0, ..., 1_{major}, ..., 0 >$.

Security Analysis of SMCC. During the first round computation of C_1, its inputs $\{\Theta, \Theta'\}$ and processed results $\{\Lambda, S'\}$ are all encrypted under C_2's private key. During the second round computation of C_1, the input CL and final result $\mathsf{Enc}_{pk_u}(c_{major})$ are also encrypted values. Due to security of ElGamal cryptosystem and SM, SA sub-protocols, these ciphertexts are computationally indistinguishable from random numbers in $\mathbb{G}$. During the computation of C_2, even though C_2 can attain the frequencies of each class label, it infers neither the exact class label values nor the index corresponds to which class, in that $S'_{i,j}$ are randomized by r_j and the column order of S' is altered by π. Therefore, we can build a simulator in the ideal world that is computationally indistinguishable from SMCC based on [15]. In other words, SMCC does not disclose anything about the class labels. Additionally, as fr is only known to C_2, the record of actual majority class is oblivious to C_1. So the query access patterns are hidden.

Algorithm 4. $\text{SMCC}(\Theta, \Theta') \rightarrow \text{Enc}_{pk_u}(c_{major})$

Require: C_1 has $\Theta =< \text{Enc}_{pk_u}(c_1), \text{Enc}_{pk_u}(c_2), ..., \text{Enc}_{pk_u}(c_\theta) >$ and $\Theta' =< \text{Enc}_{pk_u}(c'_1), \text{Enc}_{pk_u}(c'_2), ..., \text{Enc}_{pk_u}(c'_k) >$; C_2 has sk_u.

C_1:

1. Generate a permutation function π;
2. Compute $\Lambda \leftarrow \pi(\Theta)$;
3. **for** $i = 1$ to k **do**:

   - Compute $P_i \leftarrow \text{Blind}(\text{Enc}_{pk_u}(c'_i), -1)$;
   - **for** $j = 1$ to θ **do**:

     • Compute $S_{i,j} \leftarrow \text{SA}(\Lambda[j], P_i)$ with C_2;
     • C_1 generates a random number $r_j \in_R \mathbb{G}$;
     • C_1 computes $S'_{i,j} \leftarrow \text{Blind}(S_{i,j}, r_j)$;

4. Send S' to C_2;

C_2 **for** $j = 1$ to θ **do**:

1. **for** $i = 1$ to k **do**:

   - **if** $\text{Dec}(sk_u, S'_{i,j}) == 0$ **then** $fr_j \leftarrow fr_j + 1$; //Initial $fr_j \leftarrow 0$;

2. **for** $j = 2$ to θ **do**:

   - **if** $fr_{max} < fr_j$ **then**:

     • $\varrho \leftarrow j$; $fr_{max} \leftarrow fr_j$; //Initial $fr_{max} \leftarrow fr_1$ and $\varrho \leftarrow 1$

3. Compute an encrypted vector CL, where $CL[i] \leftarrow \text{Enc}_{pk_u}(1)$, for $i = \varrho$; otherwise, $CL[i] \leftarrow \text{Enc}_{pk_u}(0)$, for $i \neq \varrho$ and $1 \leq i \leq \theta$;
4. Send CL to C_1;

C_1:

1. Compute $CL' \leftarrow \pi^{-1}(CL)$;
2. Compute $V_i \leftarrow \text{SM}(CL[i], \Theta[i])$, for $1 \leq i \leq \theta$;
3. Initialize $\text{Enc}_{pk_u}(c_{major}) \leftarrow \text{Enc}_{pk_u}(0)$;
4. Compute $\text{Enc}_{pk_u}(c_{major}) \leftarrow \text{SA}(V_i, \text{Enc}_{pk_u}(c_{major}))$ with C_2, for $1 \leq i \leq \theta$;

4.3 The Complete Protocol of SCOkNN

On the basis of the privacy-preserving building blocks described above, we discuss the SCOkNN protocol in cloud environments with multiple data owners who have realistic demands for collaborative data mining. This protocol handles kNN queries over the joint database in a privacy-preserving manner while still guaranteeing U_i's ($i \in [1, n]$) necessary rights to retrieve and decrypt encrypted data locally like using cloud storage. More specifically, the total process of SCOkNN comprises of four phases, that is, Secure Data Outsourcing Phase, kNN Query

Phase, Outsourced kNN Classification Phase, and Result Retrieval Phase, the major steps of which are shown in Algorithm 5.

During Secure Data Outsourcing Phase, to begin with, data owner $U_i (i \in [1, n])$, querist Q, and cloud servers C_1, C_2 jointly run KI protocol in order to generate their own key pairs and re-encryption keys. Then, U_i encrypts its databset D_i component-wise with its public key pk_i, where $D_i = \{t^i_{j,h} | i \in [1, n], j \in [1, l], h \in [1, m + 1]\}$ and $t^i_{j,m+1}$ denotes the class label for j^{th} record of that databset. We assume that the sizes of all owners' databsets are the same, denoted by l. With its own public key, U_i encrypts D_i by running $\mathsf{Enc}_{pk_i}(D_i) = \{\mathsf{Enc}(pk_i, t^i_{j,h}) | j \in [1, l], h \in [1, m + 1]\}$, and uploads them to C_1. Upon receiving all data owners' data, C_1 re-encrypts the ciphertexts under multiple keys by leveraging PRE technique long with $\{rk_{i \mapsto u} | i \in [1, n]\}$. At the end of the protocol execution, C_1 gets the merged encrypted dataset under pk_u. We use D_{mer}, D'_{mer} to denote this joint dataset and its encrypted form respectively, where $D'_{mer} = \{t'_{i,j} | i \in [1, nl], j \in [1, m + 1]\}$.

During kNN Query Phase, suppose Q intends to know the kNN class of its query q over the federal database. In the first place, Q submits its identity ID_Q and q' to C_1. Here, q should be encrypted component-wise, but we express it as $q' = \mathsf{Enc}_{pk_Q}(q)$ to be intuitive. C_1 then checks whether Q is an authorized party. After successful identification, q' is then transformed into encryption under pk_u using its re-encryption key. Let q'_u denote the transformed ciphertext of q. After this, C_1 activates the kNN computation procedures.

During Outsourced kNN Classification Phase, first of all, C_1 and C_2 compute the encryptions of squared distances between all records of D_{mer} and q via SSD protocol. Let E denote the encryption vector, where $E = < d'_1, ..., d'_{ln} >$, $d'_i = \mathsf{Enc}_{pk_u}(d_i)$, and $d_i = |t_i - q|^2$ for $1 \leq i \leq ln$. After that, the top k smallest values in $\{d'_1, ..., d'_{ln}\}$ are selected by conducting SMnN protocol. More specifically, when C_1 computes the first minimum value d'_{ν_1} and its corresponding index ν_1, $\mathsf{Enc}_{pk_u}(d_{\nu_1})$ is removed from E. Likewise, the top kNN index set denoted by $V = \{\nu_1, ..., \nu_k\}$ can be computed in an iterative fashion. Based on V, C_1 is able to pick the recordings of encrypted kNN class label. As mentioned before, we use c'_i to denote $t_{i,m+1}$ for $i \in V$. Hence, C_1 gets Θ' as the encrypted class set of k closest records. With Θ and Θ' as inputs, C_1 computes the ciphertext of majority class among Θ' through cooperation with C_2 using SMCC protocol. The output of this step is $\mathsf{Enc}_{pk_u}(c_q)$, where c_q is the class label for q. Last but not least, C_1 transforms $\mathsf{Enc}_{pk_u}(c_q)$ to $\mathsf{Enc}_{pk_Q}(c_q)$ (also denoted by c'_q) with re-encryption key $rk^{-1}_{Q \mapsto u}$.

During Result Retrieval Phase, the final encrypted result c'_q under public key pk_Q is transferred back to Q from C_1. Finally, Q retrieves the desired class label by decrypting c'_q using its private key sk_Q.

Security Analysis of SCOkNN. According to Composition Theorem [15], if every step of SCOkNN is secure, then we can prove that the complete protocol is secure. The security of SCOkNN under semi-honest model is defined as follows.

Algorithm 5. $\text{SCOkNN}(D_1, ..., D_n, q, \kappa) \rightarrow c_q$

Require: U_i holds its dataset D_i where $i \in [1, n]$; Q holds its query q; C_1 has security parameter κ.

{**Secure Data Outsourcing Phase**}

1. C_1, C_2, and U_i (for $1 \leq i \leq n$) run $\text{KI}(\kappa)$ protocol interactively to generate their own public/private key pairs and re-encryption keys;
2. U_i, **for** $i = 1$ to n **do**:

   - Compute $D'_i \leftarrow \{\text{Enc}_{pk_i}(t^i_{j,h}) | j \in [1, l], h \in [1, m + 1]\}$;
   - Upload D'_i to C_1;

3. C_1:

   - Compute $D'_{mer} \leftarrow \{\text{ReEnc}(rk_{i \mapsto u}, D'_i) | i \in [1, n]\}$;

{**kNN Query Phase**}
Q:

1. Submit its identity ID_Q and encrypted query q' to C_1, where $q' \leftarrow \text{Enc}_{pk_Q}(q)$;

C_1:

1. Authenticate Q's identity, **if** Q is not authorized **then** abort;
2. Compute $q'_u \leftarrow \text{ReEnc}(rk_{Q \mapsto u}, q')$;

{**Outsourced kNN Classification Phase**}
C_1 and C_2:

1. **for** $i = 1$ to ln **do**:

   - Compute $d'_i \leftarrow \text{SSD}(D'_{mer}[i], q'_u)$;
   - Compute $E \leftarrow E \cup \{d'_i\}$; //Initial $E \leftarrow \emptyset$

2. **for** $i = 1$ to k **do**:

   - Compute $\nu_i \leftarrow \text{SMnN}(E)$;
   - Compute $V \leftarrow V \cup \{\nu_i\}$; //Initial $V \leftarrow \emptyset$
   - Compute $\Theta' \leftarrow \Theta' \cup \{t'_{\nu_i, m+1}\}$; //Initial $\Theta' \leftarrow \emptyset$
   - Compute $E \leftarrow \{d'_1, ..., d'_{\nu_i - 1}\} \cup \{d'_{\nu_i + 1}, ..., d'_{ln}\}$;

3. Compute $\text{Enc}_{pk_u}(c_q) \leftarrow \text{SMCC}(\Theta, \Theta')$;
4. Compute $c'_q \leftarrow \text{ReEnc}(rk^{-1}_{Q \mapsto u}, \text{Enc}_{pk_u}(c_q))$, and send it to Q;

{**Result Retrieval Phase**}
Q:

1. Receive c'_q from C_1;
2. Compute $c_q \leftarrow \text{Dec}(sk_Q, c'_q)$;

Theorem 1. *During the execution of the SCOkNN protocol, no privacy regarding the inputs of data owners and querist, the final output or the access pattern are revealed to cloud servers or other participants as long as ElGamal cryptosystem is semantically secure, and blinding factors are randomly selected.*

Proof. First of all, during the Secure Data Outsourcing phase, the key distribution protocol KI ensures every party has its own key without being known by anyone else. We stress that due to the encryption of $D_i(i \in [1, n])$ and by semantic security of the ElGamal cryptosystem, U_i's dataset D_i is protected from other data owners $U_j(j \neq i)$, C_1, C_2 and Q. Furthermore, C_1 cannot get anything private by the re-encryption technique. Similarly, Q's submitted query q is unknown to all the other parities in the kNN Query Phase. During the Outsourced kNN Classification Phase, C_1 and C_2 cooperate to compute the encryptions of the squared Euclidean distances, minimum values and major class label via SSD, SMnN and SMCC protocols as building blocks, which have been proven secure in previous section. SMCC protocol also preserves the access pattern for the given query. Then, the output is re-encrypted by C_1, which can only be decrypted by the Q. In the last phase, the class label is encrypted under pk_Q, so nothing is revealed to other parties owing to the security of encryption scheme. Supposing one of the participants is corrupted by semi-honest adversary $\mathcal{A}$, we can build a simulator $\mathcal{F}$ to simulate the view of $\mathcal{A}$ in the ideal world. Since all sub-protocols are secure under the threat model, $\mathcal{A}$ cannot distinguish the real world from ideal world, which means no privacy regarding any party's input and output are revealed. We also stress that SCOkNN is secure against eavesdropping attacks, because each party holds its own key for encryption, and the corrupted party's secret key cannot be used to decrypt other parties' ciphertexts. Based on the above discussions, our solution protects confidentiality of joint database, queries, as well as query access pattern.   □

Complexity Analysis of SCOkNN. Let Exp, Mult denote operations of exponentiation, multiplication, respectively. Let N denote the size of the joint datasets, i.e., $N = nl$. ElGamal cryptosystem requires $2\text{Exp} + 1\text{Mult}$ to encrypt one plaintext, and $1\text{Exp} + 1\text{Mult}$ for corresponding decryption. The computation cost and communication overhead of the proposed building blocks are presented in Table 1. Recall that m, n, k, θ denote the number of attributes, the number of records, the closest neighbor counts, and the number of different class labels, respectively.

The outsourced computation invokes SSD N times, SMnN k times, and SMCC once. Since exponentiation calculation accounts for the primary cost and $m, k, \theta \ll N$, the overall computation complexity for cloud is bounded by $O(mN)$ while communication complexity is bounded by $O(mN|\mathbb{G}|)$. PPkNN protocol constructed based on Paillier cryptosystem in work [4] is most similar with ours. Unlike other kNN outsourcing protocols which requires frequent client-server interactions [2], PPkNN also protects the privacy of inputs and outputs without clients' participation. The computation complexity of PPkNN is bounded by $O(kpN \log N)$, where p is referred to as value size in bits while

Table 1. Computation and communication overhead of building blocks

Sub-protocol	Computation overhead	Communication overhead
SM	2Mult	–
SA	15Exp + 20Mult	$18|\mathbb{G}|$
SSD	$30m$Exp + $42m$Mult	$36m|\mathbb{G}|$
SM2N	16Exp + 23Mult	$21|\mathbb{G}|$
SMnN	$\log n(16$Exp + 23Mult$)$	$21\log n|\mathbb{G}|$
SMCC	$(16k\theta + 17\theta)$Exp + $(2k\theta + 23\theta)$Mult	$20\theta(k+1)|\mathbb{G}|$

Table 2. Complexity comparison between SCOkNN and PPkNN [4]

Algorithm	SCOkNN	PPkNN
Computation	$O(mN)$	$O(kpN \log N)$
Communication	$O(mN|\mathbb{G}|)$	$O(kpN \log N|\mathbb{G}|)$

the communication complexity is bounded by $O(kpN \log N|\mathbb{G}|)$. As shown in Table 2, it's apparent that our scheme incurs much less computation time and communication overhead for $m \ll N$. The reason is that in order to compare two ciphertexts securely, PPkNN should decompose every ciphertext into form of encrypted bits by complex bit-decomposition protocol, the time complexity of which is $O(pN)$. By the way, PPkNN only works in single-key scenario.

5 Experimental Results

In this section, we analyze and evaluate the performance of our schemes for outsourced kNN classification under multiple keys in cloud environment and compare our work with similar methods.

5.1 Settings and Implementation

The experiments of SCOkNN are performed on two non-colluding servers, which have identical configurations which are Intel Xeon E5-2620 @ 2.10 GHz with 8 GB RAM running CentOS 6.5. We implement a proof-of-concept version of the proposed protocols and PPkNN [4] in C++ using the Crypto++5.6.3 library.

Our experiments are performed on real dataset–Wine Quality dataset from the UCI Machine Learning Repository [16], with 12 attributes, and 11 class labels. These records are evenly distributed among 10 data owners. The key size of the encryption scheme is chosen to be 1024 bits.

5.2 Empirical Analysis

We evaluate the performance of our protocols based on the parameters: the count of nearest neighbors (k) and the outsourced database size (N).

We choose k varying from 5 to 25 and N from 500 to 2500. Each data owner's encrypted dataset is outsourced to the simulated server for collaborative kNN computation. The query is chosen from the entire instances randomly for each test. Each client takes about 3.426 s to encrypt its data during SCOkNN, whereas for PPkNN a client spends 7.632 s to encrypt the same amount of data. Then we consider to evaluate the performance during Outsourced kNN Classification Phase. The results presented in the following are averaged over 100 repeated tests.

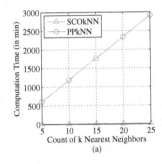 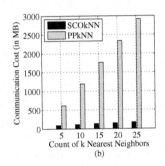

Fig. 2. Cloud computation time and communication cost for varying count of nearest neighbors

First, we assess the computation time and communication overhead of cloud servers with varying number of nearest neighbors. The outsourced database includes 1599 records. From Fig. 2(a), it can be observed that the computation cost for servers grows linearly with k, and our proposed protocol runs several orders faster than PPkNN scheme. For example, when $k = 5$, it takes PPkNN 610.2 min to process outsourced kNN while it only requires 10.16 min for SCOkNN. So our speedup rate is about 60 times. Moreover, the cost growth of SCOkNN is not as sharp as that of PPkNN. The hug gap is mainly caused by expensive bit-decomposition operations during comparison in PPkNN, which drags down the entire performance while we apply blinding technique in SA and SM2N sub-protocols to boost speed.

Figure 2(b) shows the communication overhead increases with the growth of k. The reason is that the larger k is, the more comparisons are required. As we mentioned earlier, both schemes take heavy interactions for cloud servers to compare two ciphertexts. We can easily see that the traffic caused by PPkNN mounts up much more rapidly, which produces approximately 16 times more network flow than ours. The latency of SCOkNN is relatively small compared to computation. For instance, when $k = 25$, the communication cost is 173 MB whose delay is 1.45 s for 1 Gbps bandwidth, accounting for 0.13% of outsourced computation cost.

Next, we evaluate the scalability of our solution. The dataset is randomly picked from wine-quality dataset. As shown in Fig. 3(a) and (b), both the cloud

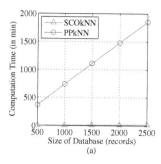 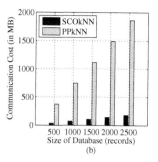

Fig. 3. Cloud computation time and communication cost for varying size of database with $k = 10$

computation time and communication cost increase linearly with the size of outsourced database. For adding every 500 instances with 12 attributes, the growth for computational and communication overhead of SCOkNN increase by 3.77 min and 36 MB, respectively. As for PPkNN, the costs are 370 min and 373 MB. It's apparent that SCOkNN is significantly more efficient due to optimization techniques used in privacy-preserving primitives.

6   Related Work

In this section, we review the existing outsourced privacy-preserving kNN approaches under different models.

Single-key outsourced model. This model assumes the data are encrypted and outsourced in the cloud while all the participants share the same key. Most recent methods have been proposed based on this assumption. Distance-Recoverable Encryption (DRE) is the straightforward solution, but it's not secure against level-2 or level-3 attacks [1]. Wong *et al.* [1] suggested preserving a special type of scalar product instead of distance to find kNN, whereas their scheme is not secure enough to resist against key leakage. B. K. Samanthula *et al.* [4] proposed PPkNN protocol by utilizing Paillier Cryptosystem's additively homomorphic property and proposed a set of generic primitives to perform Secure Multiplication, Secure Squared Euclidean Distance, Secure Bit-Decomposition, Secure Minimum, Secure Bit-OR, etc., based on which the outsourced kNN protocol was proposed. Their approach is similar with ours and it also protects the confidentiality of data, query and access patterns, whereas their methods have high computation and communication overhead caused by heavy server-server interactions. In order to compare two encrypted distances, PPkNN invokes bit-decomposition for every ciphertext and then used bit operations to compute the encrypted minimum. However, our simple strategy works more efficient in practice. Based on practical observations, the single-key model faces two potential security risks: key leakage and eavesdropping attacks. Once the private key is revealed, then all clients' data can be decrypted by the adversary, including the query record and class label. Moreover, if the corrupted server is able to sniff the network, any data encrypted may be accessed illegally.

Multiple-key outsourced model. This model supposes different parties hold their respective keys, hence mitigating the single-key risks. Recently, paper [6] shed light upon multiple-key computation issues, and made use of the two independent decryption mechanisms of BCP cryptosystem to transform ciphertexts, while moving the workload of users' interactive decryptions to the non-colluding servers. Following this, B. Wang et al. [7,8] made further improvements in efficiency by using ElGamal-based PRE scheme, by proposing a new method to compute addition over ciphertexts with the assumption that the cloud servers do not have knowledge of data distribution as we explain in SA protocol of Sect. 4.2. Collaborative outsourced data mining with multi-owner was studied in [17]. They utilized multiplicative transformation to encrypt data, which is more efficient than public-key encryption. Nevertheless, their approaches directly reveal the secret matrix of data owner to data user, with a strong security assumption on the trust in users. Our previous work [18] proposed a scheme to compute outsourced scalar product under multiple keys, and its secure addition protocol was achieved by inserting ciphertexts of random numbers, but the corrupted server may guess the ratio of inputs with a small probability. Therefore, current solutions are not secure and efficient to address kNN outsourcing problems.

7   Conclusion

In this paper, we focused on the outsourced kNN classification scenario where multiple data owners encrypt data with their own keys, by proposing an efficient privacy-preserving solution based on PRE scheme, called SCOkNN for short. With a prevalent security model of two semi-honest but non-colluding servers in cloud environments, our scheme does not require any user interactions during the outsourcing period. Theoretical analysis show that the proposed protocols ensure the confidentiality of data, kNN query, query result and access patterns with small costs produced by the servers. We also highlight the efficiency of our protocols by performing experiments under different parameter settings with similar work. However, SCOkNN was only tested over a small-size dataset, and its performance is not so excellent to be adopted in processing big data, so we plan to investigate more secure and faster solutions as our future work.

References

1. Wong, W.K., Cheung, D.W., Kao, B., Mamoulis, N.: Secure kNN computation on encrypted database. In: SIGMOD, pp. 139–152 (2009)
2. Xu, H., Guo, S., Chen, K.: Building confidential and efficient query services in the cloud with RASP data perturbation. IEEE Trans. Knowl. Data Eng. **26**(2), 322–335 (2014)

3. Elmehdwi, Y., Samanthula, B.K., Jiang, W.: Secure k-nearest neighbor query over encrypted data in outsourced environments. In: ICDE, pp. 664–675 (2014)
4. Samanthula, B.K., Elmehdwi, Y., Jiang, W.: K-nearest neighbor classification over semantically secure encrypted relational data. IEEE Trans. Knowl. Data Eng. **27**(5), 1–14 (2015)
5. Li, F., Shin, R., Paxson, V.: Exploring privacy preservation in outsourced K-nearest neighbors with multiple data owners. In: CCSW 2015, pp. 53–64 (2015)
6. Peter, A., Tews, E., Katzenbeisser, S.: Efficiently outsourcing multiparty computation under multiple keys. IEEE Trans. Inf. Forensics Secur. **8**(12), 2046–2058 (2013)
7. Wang, B., Li, M., Chow, S.S.M., Li, H.: Computing encrypted cloud data efficiently under multiple keys. In: 4th International Workshop on Security and Privacy in Cloud Computing, pp. 504–513 (2013)
8. Wang, B., Li, M., Chow, S.S.M., Li, H.: A tale of two clouds: computing on data encrypted under multiple keys. In: IEEE CNS, pp. 337–345 (2014)
9. Zhu, Y., Xu, R., Takagi, T.: Secure k-NN computation on encrypted cloud data without sharing key with query users. In: ACM Cloud Computing, pp. 55–60 (2013)
10. Chow, S.S.M., Lee, J.H., Strauss, M.: Two-party computation model for privacy-preserving queries over distributed databases. In: NDSS (2009)
11. Van, M.D., Juels, A.: On the impossibility of cryptography alone for privacy-preserving cloud computing. In: HotSec 2010, pp. 1–8 (2010)
12. Blaze, M., Bleumer, G., Strauss, M.: Divertible protocols and atomic proxy cryptography. In: Nyberg, K. (ed.) EUROCRYPT 1998. LNCS, vol. 1403, pp. 127–144. Springer, Heidelberg (1998). doi:10.1007/BFb0054122
13. Weng, J., Deng, R.H., Liu, S., Chen, K.: Chosen-ciphertext secure bidirectional proxy re-encryption schemes without pairings. Inf. Sci. **180**, 5077–5089 (2010)
14. Canetti, R., Hohenberger, S.: Chosen-ciphertext secure proxy re-encrytpion. In: CCS 2007, pp. 185–194 (2007)
15. Goldreich, O.: The Foundations of Cryptography: Volume 2, Basic Applications, pp. 600–759. Cambridge University Press, Cambridge (2004)
16. Cortez, P., Cerdeira, A., Almeida, F., Matos, T., Reis, J.: The UCI Machine Learning Repository. http://archive.ics.uci.edu/ml/datasets/Wine+Quality
17. Huang, Y., Lu, Q., Xiong, Y.: Collaborative outsourced data mining for secure cloud computing. J. Netw. **9**(10), 2655–2664 (2014)
18. Rong, H., Wang, H., Huang, K., Liu, J., Xian, M.: Privacy-preserving scalar product computation in cloud environments under multiple keys. In: Yin, H., Gao, Y., Li, B., Zhang, D., Yang, M., Li, Y., Klawonn, F., Tallón-Ballesteros, A.J. (eds.) IDEAL 2016. LNCS, vol. 9937, pp. 248–258. Springer, Cham (2016). doi:10.1007/978-3-319-46257-8_27

Video Steganalysis Based on Centralized Error Detection in Spatial Domain

Yu Wang[1,2]([⊠]), Yun Cao[1,2], and Xianfeng Zhao[1,2]

[1] State Key Laboratory of Information Security,
Institute of Information Engineering, Chinese Academy of Sciences,
Beijing 100093, China
{wangyu9078,caoyun,zhaoxianfeng}@iie.ac.cn
[2] School of Cyber Security, University of Chinese Academy of Sciences,
Beijing 100093, China

Abstract. This paper presents a novel steganalytic method for detection of quantized DCT-based video steganography. First, the modification on the partially decoded quantized coefficients is modeled. Then the influence of the embedding operation on spatial domain is illustrated, which takes the form of the centralization of errors within each corresponding spatial pixel block. Finally, based on this fact, a 36-dimension feature set is extracted and used for classification. Experiments are carried out on videos corrupted by various quantized DCT-based steganography methods and encoded by various motion estimation methods. Performance results demonstrate the effectiveness of our scheme.

Keywords: Video steganalysis · DCT · H.264/AVC · Intra-frame distortion drift

1 Introduction

Steganography is the art and science of data hiding, the purpose of which is to hide the presence of covert data within innocent-looking media, called cover media, such as digital video, image and audio, etc. Facilitated by the booming of H.264/advance video coding (AVC) [1], digital video has become a carrier object provided with inherent advantages. Consequently, this fact has also drawn more researchers in the area of video steganalysis which is to detect the presence of hidden messages.

H.264/AVC is a hybrid video coding standard which provides many different venues for data hiding. The secret message can be embedded into intra prediction mode assignment, block partition type, motion vector, quantization parameter and discrete cosine transform (DCT) coefficients, etc. Compared with the others, the venue of DCT coefficients is a superb choice considering all associated factor. Several researches on watermarking and data hiding based on H.264/AVC have been published [2–6]. However, video steganographic methods using DCT coefficients can not be as mature as image steganography. One of

© Springer International Publishing AG 2017
K. Chen et al. (Eds.): Inscrypt 2016, LNCS 10143, pp. 472–483, 2017.
DOI: 10.1007/978-3-319-54705-3_29

the most important reasons is that the intra-prediction of H.264/AVC includes many heuristic schemes that cannot recover the data exactly [7]. That means all of mentioned approaches could not handle the intra-frame distortion drift of H.264/AVC except [8,9]. Ma et al. [8] proposed a data hiding algorithm by justifying paired-coefficients to prevent intra-frame distortion drift. Lin et al. [9] further considered Ma's work and proposed a novel algorithm to achieve a higher payload.

To cope with the abuse of steganography, video steganalysis has attracted much attention recently. Budhia et al. [10] presented a video steganalytic method exploiting the temporal statistical visibility to detect the presence of additive Gaussian spread-spectrum watermarks in a video sequence. Pankajakshan et al. [11] proposed a new blind steganalysis scheme for which features extracted from the residual frames after spatio-temporal prediction. Furthermore, Da et al. [12] presented a new steganalysis scheme utilizing the temporal and the spatial correlation. A new video steganalysis detecting spread spectrum data hiding schemes was proposed by Zarmehi et al. [13]. The schemes [10–13] are more effective for detecting these steganalytic methods using raw video. Liu et al. [14] proposed a scheme based on Markov and joint distribution features in the DCT and DWT transform domains. Similarly, a novel steganalysis is proposed exploiting the spatial-temporal correlation between adjacent frames by Zhao et al. [15]. Absolute central moments, skewness, kurtosis and Markov features are extracted from the DCT domain which are only effective for detecting ones using spread-spectrum-based steganography [16]. Both [14,15] obtain features from DCT coefficients. In this study, we focus on detection of the embedded message into DCT coefficients using quantized DCT-based video steganographic methods.

A recent tread in DCT-based video steganographic methods of H.264/AVC is the one that prevents intra-frame distortion drift. To our knowledge, there was no existing video steganalysis that tried to detect the DCT-based perturbation in this category. So in this paper, we propose a steganalytic scheme against the DCT-based perturbation in intra frames of H.264/AVC. For comparison, another video steganalytic method is also achieved in the Sect. 4.

The rest of paper is structured as follows. In Sect. 2, the intra prediction process is briefly introduced, and we interpret that what causes the intra-frame distortion drift and how to prevent it. In Sect. 3, the centralized error residual (CER) features in intra frames are illustrated, and our proposed steganalytic scheme is described in details. Section 4 describes comparative experiments which are conducted mainly to prove the feasibility and validity. In Sect. 5, conclusion is drawn in the end.

2 Preliminaries

2.1 Intra-Frame Prediction in H.264

As a major departure from the previous coding standards, H.264 tries to remove the spatial redundancies existing within one single frame via intra prediction.

To minimize the prediction error, nine optional prediction modes for each 4×4 luminance blocks and four for each 16×16 luminance blocks are provided by H.264. 9 intra 4×4 prediction modes are illustrated in Fig. 1 and 4 intra 16×16 prediction modes are illustrated in Fig. 2. Each sample of the current block is calculated by the samples $A \sim M$.

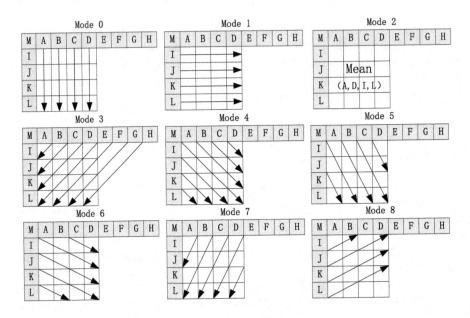

Fig. 1. Intra 4×4 prediction modes

Furthermore, We give a real 4×4 block as an example to illustrate how to get the residual matrix of this block, which is to be encoded. We assume that the current 4×4 luma block is recorded as $B_{i,j}$ and its four adjacent luma blocks are represented by $B_{i-1,j-1}$, $B_{i-1,j}$, $B_{i-1,j+1}$ and $B_{i,j-1}$, which is shown in Fig. 3. The samples of $a \sim p$ to be predicted are based on encoded and restructured samples $A \sim M$ corresponding to the selected prediction mode. R_i denotes the residual value of sample i, P_i^p denotes the predicted value of sample i and P_i denotes the value of sample i when $i \in a, b..., p$. The residual R_i of each sample is rational on condition that

$$R_i = P_i - P_i^p. \tag{1}$$

2.2   Error Caused by DCT-based Perturbation

Since I4PM is mainly used for characterizing the details which are less sensitive for human eyes, I4PM is much more appropriate for embedding than I16PM.

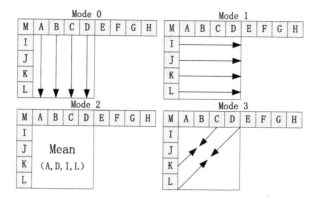

Fig. 2. Intra 16×16 prediction modes

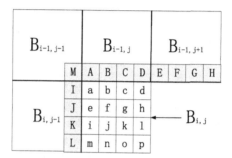

Fig. 3. The current 4×4 block and the reference pixels in the adjacent encoded blocks

Given a 4×4 intra block, the residual matrix of each block are denoted as $R \in \mathbb{R}^{4 \times 4}$. The quantized DCT coefficient matrix $\widetilde{Y}$ of R can be expressed as follows:

$$\widetilde{Y} = round[(C_f R C_f^T). \times PF./Q] \tag{2}$$

where $C_f = \begin{pmatrix} 1 & 1 & 1 & 1 \\ 2 & 1 & -1 & -2 \\ 1 & -1 & -1 & 1 \\ 1 & -2 & 2 & -1 \end{pmatrix}$, $PF = \begin{pmatrix} a^2 & \frac{ab}{2} & a^2 & \frac{ab}{2} \\ \frac{ab}{2} & \frac{b^2}{4} & \frac{ab}{2} & \frac{b^2}{4} \\ a^2 & \frac{ab}{2} & a^2 & \frac{ab}{2} \\ \frac{ab}{2} & \frac{b^2}{4} & \frac{ab}{2} & \frac{b^2}{4} \end{pmatrix}$,

$a = \frac{1}{2}$, $b = \sqrt{\frac{2}{5}}$. $'.\times'$ denotes element by element product of two matrices and Q is the quantization step size determined by the quantization parameter(QP). The modified quantized DCT coefficient matrix $\widetilde{Y}'$ is defined as follows:

$$\widetilde{Y}' = \widetilde{Y} + \Delta \tag{3}$$

where Δ is the error matrix. In the decoding stage, the restructured residual matrix before embedding $R^{'} \in \mathbb{R}^{4 \times 4}$ can be calculated as follows:

$$R^{'} = C_i^T (\tilde{Y}. \times Q. \times IPF)C_i \tag{4}$$

where $C_i = \begin{pmatrix} 1 & 1 & 1 & 1 \\ 1 & \frac{1}{2} & -\frac{1}{2} & -1 \\ 1 & -1 & -1 & 1 \\ \frac{1}{2} & -1 & 1 & -\frac{1}{2} \end{pmatrix}$, $IPF = \begin{pmatrix} a^2 & ab & a^2 & ab \\ ab & b^2 & ab & b^2 \\ a^2 & ab & a^2 & ab \\ ab & b^2 & ab & b^2 \end{pmatrix}$.

Similarly, the restructured residual matrix after embedding $R^{''}$ is calculated as follows:

$$R^{''} = C_i^T (\tilde{Y}^{'}. \times Q. \times IPF)C_i \tag{5}$$

Since $R^{'}$ and $R^{''}$ are obtained, the error E of residuals between the original restructured block and perturbed restructured block is derived as

$$E = R^{''} - R^{'} \tag{6}$$

2.3 Distortion Drift and Counter Measures

As illustrated in Fig. 3, the residual values of $B_{i-1,j-1}$, $B_{i-1,j}$, $B_{i-1,j+1}$ and $B_{i,j-1}$ are perturbed artificially and the samples of $A \sim M$ which are utilized to calculate the predicted values of the samples $a \sim p$ could be perturbed too. Therefore, the error induced by the perturbation would propagate to $B_{i,j}$. Similarly, the perturbation of $B_{i,j}$ would further propagate to other blocks, i.e., the right block, the under block, the under and left (under-left) block, the under and right (under-right) block. It is called intra-frame distortion drift.

Actually, Ma et al. [8] has solved the error propagation problem. Based on the analysis of the relationship between the quantized DCT coefficients and the distortion incurred in residual values, they proposed to hide data into the paired-coefficients which can prevent the distortion drift effectively. The paired-coefficients are two quantized DCT coefficients which are manipulated to embed data in the current 4×4 luma block while no error incurred in the right-most line or the bottom line. As an extension of Ma's work, Lin et al. [9] added a new coefficient-pair to each block. Besides, more 4×4 luma blocks were exploited based on a new perturbation technique which changed quadruple coefficients simultaneously and achieved a higher payload. The new perturbed residual values indicated that no error incurred in the right-most line and the bottom line at the same time.

It is not complicated to get three patterns of E shown in Fig. 4. '*' denotes the perturbed sample, and the blank denotes the non-perturbed sample. According to Fig. 4, the perturbation of Pattern - 1 would not propagate to the right, under-right blocks and the perturbation of Pattern - 2 would not propagate to the under, under-left and under-right blocks. Also the perturbation of Pattern - 3 would not propagate to all adjacent blocks. Distortion drift can be prevented by different patterns corresponding to intra-frame prediction modes.

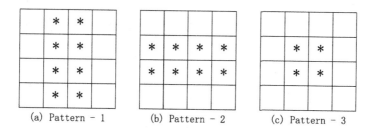

(a) Pattern – 1   (b) Pattern – 2   (c) Pattern – 3

Fig. 4. Three particular patterns of the error between original blocks and perturbed blocks

3 Proposed Steganalytic Scheme

3.1 The Centralized Error in Spatial Blocks

As described in Sect. 2, the intra-frame distortion drift can be prevented by paired-coefficients. Ma's and Lin's work achieve a new perturbation technique in intra frames without drift prevention which even can be exploited in real-time applications. However, the error which is prevented from propagating to next blocks shows some particular patterns. Following the derivation in Lin et al. [9] and doing further derivation, three particular patterns of the error can be derived as follows:

$$
\begin{bmatrix} 0 & 0 & 0 & 0 \\ 2T & 2T & 2T & 2T \\ 2T & 2T & 2T & 2T \\ 0 & 0 & 0 & 0 \end{bmatrix}
\begin{bmatrix} 0 & 2T & 2T & 0 \\ 0 & 2T & 2T & 0 \\ 0 & 2T & 2T & 0 \\ 0 & 2T & 2T & 0 \end{bmatrix}
\begin{bmatrix} 0 & 0 & 0 & 0 \\ 0 & 4T & 4T & 0 \\ 0 & 4T & 4T & 0 \\ 0 & 0 & 0 & 0 \end{bmatrix}
\tag{7}
$$

where $T \in \{-a^2, -ab, -b^2, 0, a^2, ab, b^2\} \times Q$.

Considering (1) and (6), we can get a new relationship which is seen in (8) with regard to E, P' and P''.

$$E = P'' - P'. \tag{8}$$

where P' denotes the restructured luminance values of sample matrix and P'' denotes the restructured perturbed luminance values of sample matrix. (8) indicates that the sample values are perturbed as the same as the residuals which are also satisfied with three patterns of (7). Four samples, i.e., a, d, m and p in one block are never perturbed and eight samples, i.e., b, c, e, h, i, l, n and o are sometimes perturbed. Four samples, i.e., f, g, j and k are always perturbed. In other words, the DCT-based perturbation of paired-coefficients causes the centralized error in spatial blocks when preventing the error from propagating to next blocks.

Taking the reference from Fig. 5 to illustrate the centralized error in spatial blocks, the dark circles represent the samples of f, g, j and k and the slightly dark circles represent the samples of b, c, e, h, i, l, n and o. The remaining samples of a, d, m and p are represented by the blank circles. The color depth embodies the perturbed extent, i.e., the color of sample deepens as the sample gets more perturbed.

a	b	c	d
e	f	g	h
i	j	k	l
m	n	o	p

Fig. 5. Samples of the centralized error in spatial blocks

The centralized error in spatial blocks indicates that intra-frame data-hiding algorithms without distortion drift prevents the drift at the expense of causing much more perturbation of the other positions of the block. Taking video spatial correlation between samples [17] into consideration, the centralized error is reliably an opportunity to detect the existing data hiding algorithms of intra-frame DCT-based perturbation without distortion drift.

3.2   CER Features

Our overall goal is to capture the different and fundamental types of dependencies among neighboring samples. The distinguishing features of intra-frame perturbed 4×4 blocks without distortion drift can be described precisely based on these dependencies.

In Fig. 5, Correlation between the horizontal, vertical and diagonal of two neighboring samples will be destroyed on condition that non-distortion drift perturbation emerges in intra-frame 4×4 blocks. Correlation with regard to the samples in blank circles is always wrecked because the samples in blank circles never change while neighboring samples are perturbed. However, the correlation between the samples in dark circles and slightly dark circles might maintain consistency on account of different patterns in Fig. 4. Fundamental dependencies is emerged at the residuals of neighboring samples and different residuals of neighboring samples promote the diversity of dependencies. Having acquaintance with that, we propose that the centralized error residual (CER) features should be exploited to represent these dependencies. There are four residuals are defined as follows:

$$R_h = P_{h1} - P_{h2} \tag{9}$$

where $(P_{h1}, P_{h2}) \in U_h = \{(b,a), (c,d), (n,m), (o,p)\}$. U_h^i denotes the i-th element of U_h when $1 \leq i \leq 4$.

$$R_v = P_{v1} - P_{v2} \tag{10}$$

where $(P_{v1}, P_{v2}) \in U_v = \{(e, a), (h, d), (i, m), (l, p)\}$. U_v^i denotes the i-th element of U_v when $1 \leq i \leq 4$.

$$R_d = P_{d1} - P_{d2} \tag{11}$$

where $(P_{d1}, P_{d2}) \in U_d = \{(f, a), (g, d), (j, m), (k, p)\}$. U_d^i denotes the i-th element of U_d when $1 \leq i \leq 4$.

$$R_m = max\{P_m - P_{m1}, P_m - P_{m2}\} \tag{12}$$

where $(P_m, P_{m1}, P_{m2}) \in U_m = \{(f, b, e), (g, c, h), (j, n, i), (k, o, l)\}$. U_m^i denotes the i-th element of U_m when $1 \leq i \leq 4$.

For given a group of pictures (GOP), N denotes the number of 4×4 intra blocks in the GOP. Here we utilize R_h, R_v, R_d and R_m. Four co-occurrence matrices C_h, C_v, C_d and C_m are set up as

$$C_h(j) = \frac{\sum_{n=1}^{N} \sum_{i=1}^{4} \delta(R_h = j, (P_{h1}, P_{h2}) = U_h^i)}{Z} \tag{13}$$

$$C_v(j) = \frac{\sum_{n=1}^{N} \sum_{i=1}^{4} \delta(R_v = j, (P_{v1}, P_{v2}) = U_v^i)}{Z} \tag{14}$$

$$C_d(j) = \frac{\sum_{n=1}^{N} \sum_{i=1}^{4} \delta(R_d = j, (P_{d1}, P_{d2}) = U_d^i)}{Z} \tag{15}$$

$$C_m(j) = \frac{\sum_{n=1}^{N} \sum_{i=1}^{4} \delta(R_m = j, (P_m, P_{m1}, P_{m2}) = U_m^i)}{Z} \tag{16}$$

where Z is the normalization factor and $\delta = 1$ if its arguments are satisfied. The four matrices processed using the range of j limited $[-4, +4]$ are constructed based on consecutive residuals of neighboring samples which represent the fundamental dependencies. The total CER features in co-occurrence matrices C_h, C_v, C_d and C_m are up to 36.

4   Comparative Experiments

4.1   Experimental Setup

All experiments in this section are carried out on a database containing 150 video subsequences of 480P in the YUV420 format. Each video are intercepted 500 frames as a source sequence which is further divided into 5 subsequences. Therefore, 150 subsequences intercepted by 30 videos are used for training and prediction. Randomly selecting 120 video subsequences for training, the rest subsequences are used for prediction. The experiment is repeated 5 times.

Aimed at data hiding in H.264 intra frames of non-distortion drift, our experiment implements two typical data hiding algorithms, i.e., Ma's [8] and Lin's [9] using open source encoder/decoder FFmpeg. Two methods are denoted as Alg_{Ma} and Alg_{Lin}. In order to compare the results of different application scenarios, the source sequences are compressed with different values of QP. Owing to simulating the real intra-frame data hiding, the GOP size of sequences is also configured as twelve.

As the DCT-based perturbation incurring in intra frames, Liu et al. [14] proposed a scheme of detecting information hiding in videos on the pairs of condition and joint distributions in the DCT domains. They utilize the best 468 features of expanding Markov and joint distribution features which are denoted as EMJD features to analyse the perturbation of DCT coefficients. For performance comparisons, EMJD features are tested as well.

4.2   Results and Analysis

True positive rate (TP) and True negative rate (TP) are utilized to evaluate the detection performance in our experiment. Based on the SVM classifier [18], classification model are constructed on the training sequences and predict the testing video sequences. The embedding intensity is measured based on the average perturbed block rate (APBR), which indicates the modification rate of available intra 4×4 blocks.

In Table 1, the performance results of detecting Alg_{Ma} and Alg_{Lin} are exhibited within the proposed CER features and the EMJD features. Based on the results of TP and TN, it is obvious to see that the proposed CER features perform much better than EMJD features. For detecting of Alg_{Ma}, the TP value of CER is up to 82.4% when APBR is 100%, but EMJD is only 70.2%. And for

Table 1. Performance comparison of different data hiding methods within EMJD and CER features (480 P, GOP Size = 12).

Methods	QP	APBR (%)	EMJD		CER	
			TP(%)	TN(%)	TP(%)	TN(%)
Alg_{Ma}	20	10	52.8	52.7	54.3	55.6
		25	54.0	52.5	69.1	70.6
		50	62.4	64.1	73.4	74.0
		100	65.2	68.1	80.1	81.4
	28	10	52.9	50.4	63.0	61.1
		25	57.9	60.7	71.0	73.2
		50	68.3	69.0	76.8	77.5
		100	70.2	71.7	82.4	84.5
Alg_{Lin}	20	10	54.3	53.1	64.2	66.1
		25	53.9	57.2	70.4	71.4
		50	64.8	66.7	77.4	80.3
		100	68.8	70.1	83.9	85.9
	28	10	55.9	56.4	63.3	69.2
		25	56.4	63.8	77.0	78.1
		50	68.1	70.4	83.1	85.2
		100	75.7	80.5	90.3	92.1

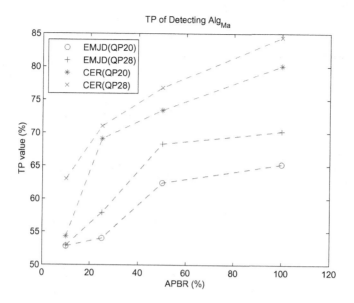

Fig. 6. Detection performance TP of Alg_{Ma} for QP 20 and 28 when steganalyzed with the proposed CER and EMJD

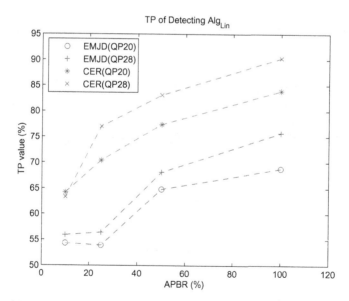

Fig. 7. Detection performance TP of Alg_{Lin} for QP 20 and 28 when steganalyzed with the proposed CER and EMJD

detecting of Alg_{Lin}, the TP value of CER is up to 90.3% when APBR is 100%, but EMJD is only 75.7%. Even when APBR is low and QP is low, CER features still perform better results. One more finding of the experiment is that the performance results of Alg_{Lin} are better than the results of Alg_{Ma}. Although APBR is the same value and sequences are of no difference, more intra 4×4 blocks can be perturbed by Lin's which also results in the better detection performance.

Figure 6 exhibits the TP results of Alg_{Ma} for QP 20 and 28 when steganalyzed with the proposed CER and EMJD. We can see that detection accuracy becomes higher as QP is higher. This is a result of high QP pricking up the perturbation of the positions in the block. Except for the correlation between accuracy and QP corresponding to Fig. 6, another finding is also shown in Fig. 7 that CER features can effectively detect the stego-objects when APBR is 25% but 50% for EMJD features.

5   Conclusion

This paper introduces a novel steganalytic method for detecting DCT-based perturbation in intra frames of H.264/AVC. Three particular patterns are presented to characterize the modification on the partially decoded quantized coefficients and the features which are interpreted as one-dimensional histograms of residuals, are extracted and used for classification. Since the algorithms of this category break the correlation of neighboring samples and even pricks up the perturbation of other positions in the blocks, CER features can be a good candidate for building practical detectors in steganalysis applications. Experiment results prove the feasibility and validity of our proposed features.

Acknowledgments. This work was supported by the NSFC under 61303259 and U1536105, National Key Technology R&D Program under 2014BAH41B01, Strategic Priority Research Program of CAS under XDA06030600, and Key Project of Institute of Information Engineering, CAS, under Y5Z0131201.

References

1. Marpe, D., Wiegand, T., Sullivan, G.J.: The H.264/MPEG4 advanced video coding standard and its applications. IEEE Commun. Mag. **44**(8), 134–143 (2006)
2. Guo-Zua, W., Wang, Y.-J., Hsu, W.-H.: Robust watermark embedding/detection algorithm for H.264 video. J. Electron. Imaging **14**(1), 013013 (2005)
3. Noorkami, M., Mersereau, R.M.: Compressed-domain video watermarking for H.264. In: IEEE International Conference on Image Processing 2005, vol. 2, pp. II–890. IEEE (2005)
4. Noorkami, M., Mersereau, R.M.: A framework for robust watermarking of H.264-encoded video with controllable detection performance. IEEE Trans. Inf. Forensics Secur. **2**(1), 14–23 (2007)
5. Gong, X., Lu, H.-M.: Towards fast and robust watermarking scheme for H.264 video. In: 2008 Tenth IEEE International Symposium on Multimedia, ISM 2008, pp. 649–653. IEEE (2008)

6. Wong, K.S., Tanaka, K., Takagi, K., Nakajima, Y.: Complete video quality-preserving data hiding. IEEE Trans. Circuits Syst. Video Technol. **19**(10), 1499–1512 (2009)
7. Kim, D.-W., Choi, Y.-G., Kim, H.-S., Yoo, J.-S., Choi, H.-J., Seo, Y.-H.: The problems in digital watermarking into intra-frames of H.264/AVC. Image Vis. Comput. **28**(8), 1220–1228 (2010)
8. Ma, X., Li, Z., Tu, H., Zhang, B.: A data hiding algorithm for H.264/AVC video streams without intra-frame distortion drift. IEEE Trans. Circuits Syst. Video Technol. **20**(10), 1320–1330 (2010)
9. Lin, T.-J., Chung, K.-L., Chang, P.-C., Huang, Y.-H., Liao, H.-Y.M., Fang, C.-Y.: An improved DCT-based perturbation scheme for high capacity data hiding in H.264/AVC intra frames. J. Syst. Softw. **86**(3), 604–614 (2013)
10. Budhia, U., Kundur, D., Zourntos, T.: Digital video steganalysis exploiting statistical visibility in the temporal domain. IEEE Trans. Inf. Forensics Secur. **1**(4), 502–516 (2006)
11. Pankajakshan, V., Ho, A.T.S.: Improving video steganalysis using temporal correlation. In: 2007 Third International Conference on Intelligent Information Hiding and Multimedia Signal Processing, IIHMSP 2007, vol. 1, pp. 287–290. IEEE (2007)
12. Da, T., Li, Z.T., Feng, B.: A video steganalysis algorithm for H.264/AVC based on the markov features. In: Huang, D.-S., Jo, K.-H., Hussain, A. (eds.) ICIC 2015. LNCS, vol. 9226, pp. 47–59. Springer, Cham (2015). doi:10.1007/978-3-319-22186-1_5
13. Zarmehi, N., Akhaee, M.A.: Digital video steganalysis toward spread spectrum data hiding. IET Image Proc. **10**(1), 1–8 (2016)
14. Liu, Q., Sung, A.H., Qiao, M.: Video steganalysis based on the expanded markov and joint distribution on the transform domains detecting MSU stegovideo. In: 2008 Seventh International Conference on Machine Learning and Applications, ICMLA 2008, pp. 671–674. IEEE (2008)
15. Zhao, H., Wang, H., Malik, H.: Steganalysis of youtube compressed video using high-order statistics in 3d DCT domain. In: 2012 Eighth International Conference on Intelligent Information Hiding and Multimedia Signal Processing (IIH-MSP), pp. 191–194. IEEE (2012)
16. Yen, S.-H., Chang, M.-C., Wang, C.-J.: A robust video watermarking scheme of H.264. In: 2009 Joint Conferences on Pervasive Computing (JCPC), pp. 155–160, December 2009
17. Fridrich, J., Kodovsky, J.: Rich models for steganalysis of digital images. IEEE Trans. Inf. Forensics Secur. **7**(3), 868–882 (2012)
18. Chang, C.-C., Lin, C.-J.: LIBSVM: a library for support vector machines. ACM Trans. Intell. Syst. Technol. (TIST) **2**(3), 42–50 (2011). 27

Log Your Car: Reliable Maintenance Services Record

Hafizah Mansor[✉], Konstantinos Markantonakis, Raja Naeem Akram, Keith Mayes, and Iakovos Gurulian

Information Security Group, Smart Card Centre, Royal Holloway, University of London, London, UK
{Hafizah.Mansor.2011,RajaNaeem.Akram.2008, Iakovos.Gurulian.2014}@live.rhul.ac.uk, {K.Markantonakis,Keith.Mayes}@rhul.ac.uk

Abstract. A maintenance services logging system is a useful tool for car owners to keep track of the car's condition and also can increase the market value of the car. Logging systems range from manual, paper-based, to automated, cloud-based systems. The automated process provides ease of use and availability of the records. A secure protocol is required to ensure that the workshop and service record are authentic, and hence the records are reliable. In this paper, we propose a secure protocol for automated maintenance services logging systems, through the use of a mobile application called AutoLOG. The multiple electronic control units (ECUs) used to support the connected and intelligent vehicle's technology are used to support the digital automated logging system. The car is the trusted entity that generates the log. The records are stored in an authorised mobile device and uploaded onto a cloud server to ensure availability. The proposed protocol is implemented to measure the performance and is formally analysed using Scyther and CasperFDR, with no known attack found.

1 Introduction

Maintenance services conducted are manually recorded by workshops. The services are either not recorded at all, or recorded in a logbook kept by the car owners. For reminder purposes, to notify the car owner of the next service date, a workshop may attach a sticker on the windshield. Recent use of mobile applications that have been introduced for car maintenance include a notification reminder for the next service date. However, other than the date of the next service, the type of maintenance repair, replacement or any other services might also be useful for the car owner to keep track of. The process of recording is manual, whereby the user has to manually enter the information using the mobile application. The logbook not only will keep the owner up-to-date on the health status of the car and avoid higher maintenance cost due to breakdowns, but it will also add value to the car, especially when the car is resold. The recent implementation which notifies the date of next service is available through the

© Springer International Publishing AG 2017
K. Chen et al. (Eds.): Inscrypt 2016, LNCS 10143, pp. 484–504, 2017.
DOI: 10.1007/978-3-319-54705-3_30

car dealer's cloud server [6]. When a car is being serviced by a car dealer, the details are uploaded onto the car dealer's server. When the next service date is nearing, the car owner will be contacted by the car dealer as a reminder.

An Electronic Control Unit (ECU) is a microcontroller that controls the operations of a car. In modern cars, there can be around 70 ECUs that control the overall operations of the vehicle [20]. Each ECU is responsible for different operations, such as body control, engine control and telematics. The different ECUs are connected within a car through networks such as Local Interconnect Network (LIN) [40], Controller Area Network (CAN) bus [22], FlexRay [25] and Media Oriented Systems Transport (MOST) [27]. The OBD-II (On-Board Diagnostic) port is a port that interfaces the outside world to the in-vehicle networks [41]. The port can be interfaced with a Wi-Fi, Bluetooth or serial connection using the ELM327 interface [17].

1.1   Problem Statement

The challenges in a maintenance services record system are to provide integrity, authenticity and reliability of the data. The process of recording the maintenance log is manual, and the car owner normally does not have access to the data, unless it is manually recorded in a logbook that he/she keeps. The car owner cannot validate the services being conducted but must trust the information provided by the workshop through the receipts or documents provided. Furthermore, it is inconvenient to keep these receipts and/or documents for all the records of maintenance services. Equally, a potential buyer does not have an assurance that the records in the maintenance log and the workshops who had performed the services are authentic.

1.2   Contribution

In this paper we propose a protocol for a secure automated process of recording the maintenance services for car maintenance. It ensures integrity of the data stored as well as the authenticity of the data and party conducting the service. The automated process ensures the maintenance data is available all the time to the car owner. The list of services/repairs conducted by the workshop is also validated. The protocol is not only useful to the car owners, but also benefits the garages, car sales organisations and vehicle manufacturers.

2   Maintenance Services Logging System

A maintenance logging system allows the car owner to keep the car's maintenance services record updated and hence can reduce the cost of maintenance by avoiding major car breakdowns. Other than that, it can also add value to the car when it is resold [10]. The potential buyer is assured that the car is in good condition as it is well maintained. The logging of the maintenance services also shows the party who conducted the services: for example, if it is conducted by a reliable and trusted workshop or car dealer.

2.1   Manual Maintenance Services Logging System

A manual maintenance services logging system is where the process of uploading and storing the records of the services is performed manually. The workshop will issue receipts to show the list of services performed, or enter this information on the car's physical logbook.

In a manual maintenance logging system, a malicious entity can:

(i)   Fake a signature to show that the service is conducted by a recognised dealer or workshop. If the process is manual and using a printed document, the document is stamped as a proof of signature. This stamp can be forged.
(ii) Fake a record to show that a service is conducted when it is not. Dates can easily be changed or faked.
(iii) Change the list of maintenance services conducted.

For a manual logging system, the manipulation could be conducted by the car dealer or the car owner. The purpose is to increase a car's value when reselling it [5,7]. The owner might also collude with a workshop to falsify the records. The car dealer might falsify the records themselves, or an untrustworthy workshop might falsify the list of conducted services, repairs or parts replaced to obtain a higher profit.

2.2   Automated Services Logging System

In this system, the process of recording and storing the log is automated, mainly operated by the workshop or car dealer. An automated process can ensure availability of data and ease of use. In the automated logging system, the potential storage locations are the electronic data logger, mobile devices or cloud server. The electronic data logger resides in the car and is connected to the CAN bus as one of the nodes. The mobile device is an external device (to the car), and it requires a connection to communicate with the in-vehicle network. The log could also be stored on a cloud server.

3   Proposed Solution

The framework is shown in Fig. 1. The mobile device gives both the graphical user interface (GUI) and the connectivity. The mobile application supporting our proposed protocol is called AutoLOG. The process starts with the workshops updating in the car log of the list of services conducted, the date the service was conducted and the next of date of service. In order to communicate with the car, the workshop uses a diagnostic tool (DT). The diagnostic tool will communicate with the car through its Central Communication Unit (CCU). The CCU is a type of Electronic Control Unit (ECU). It is the first node any external device will have to go through in order to communicate with other ECUs. The related sensors and/or ECU(s) for the service will validate the information given to the CCU by the DT. After the validation, the CCU will store the latest record of

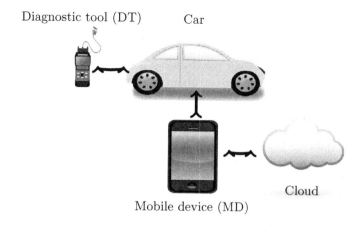

Fig. 1. Framework for the automated maintenance logging system

maintenance services. The mobile device will then retrieve this data from the CCU and upload the data to the cloud. This way, the records are always available on both the mobile device and the cloud. In case the mobile device is lost, the data is always available on the cloud. In this proposal, the trust foundation is moved from the workshop to the car's sensors and ECU nodes. The cloud server could be owned by the user, trusted third party, community or government body. The cloud ownership is out of the scope of this paper.

Our proposal is based on the EVITA project [19], which proposed an embedded Hardware Security Module (HSM) in the ECU to ensure secure communications for on-board system. As proposed in the EVITA project, each ECU has its own HSM. This suggests that any node communicating through the CAN bus is required to have access authorisation in order to send or receive messages. In our proposal, the mobile device and diagnostic tool act as a communicating node through the CAN bus, and so requires access authorisation. This avoids the issue of unauthorised access to the in-vehicle networks, especially the CAN bus. The assumption on our proposal is based on the capability of the sensors in the car to validate the services being performed. While this may not be available now in current implementations, future firmware updates may introduce a version of this work.

3.1   Related Work

There are many mobile applications available in the market that provide maintenance service logging systems [1–4,9]. However, these applications require manual information to be entered by the car owner. After a car is serviced or repaired, the information can either be keyed in, or a photo of the document is captured to be stored. The data can later be stored in the cloud, depending on the application feature. Some applications require a manual upload to the cloud, while other applications will store the data automatically to the chosen cloud server.

Another type of maintenance service logging system is the one provided by car dealers [6,11]. When a car is being serviced by a car dealer, details are uploaded onto the car dealer's server. When the next service date is nearing, the car owner will be contacted by the car dealer as a reminder.

A most recent development for car maintenance logging systems was introduced in "AUTObiography" by Motoriety [8]. This service logs the maintenance services record onto the cloud. Trusted workshops registered with Motoriety can use the service and will digitally sign the services conducted to be stored on the cloud. The data, or the "biography" of the car will then be available on the cloud, and can be passed from one owner to another. All the records are being managed by the service, can be retrieved by the car owners, and owners will get reminders for the next service date.

In the above-mentioned works, the trust is completely in the hands of the workshops. If an untrustworthy workshop fakes an item in the list of services conducted, nobody could prove this. On the other hand, a trustworthy workshop might mistakenly insert an item as a result of human error, since the process of recording and keying in the data is manual.

There are proposals for reminder notifications of the next service date [12,21]. There is also a system proposed using a passive radio frequency identification (RFID) device to detect the repairs/services being conducted [13].

Table 1 shows the added features of AutoLOG compared to other related works, which include manual and automated systems. AutoLOG, AUTObiography and a car dealer's cloud server provide automation, but the mobile applications do not [1–4,9]. Data ownership of the records belong to the car owner in AutoLOG, AUTObiography and the discussed mobile applications. However, the ownership of the records in a car dealer's cloud server belongs to the car dealer. Data availability is supported by all the works discussed including AutoLOG. However, since the uploading process is manual for these mobile applications, data availability depends on this manual process. Unlike other related works, in our proposal, we consider the capability of the ECUs to validate the services. Security is a feature provided by all three automated systems. The car owners have the flexibility to choose from a range of different workshops for AutoLOG, AUTObiography and the discussed mobile applications. However, in the car dealer's cloud server system, the options of workshops are limited to the ones appointed by the car manufacturers.

Table 1. Features of AutoLOG compared to other related works

Features	AutoLOG	AUTObiography	Mobile applications	Car dealer's cloud server
Automation	✔	✔	✘	✔
Data ownership	✔	✔	✔	✘
Data availability	✔	✔	✔	✔
Validation of services	✔	✘	✘	✘
Security	✔	✔	✘	✔
Options of workshops	✔	✔	✔	✘

The reason for not choosing TLS protocol for this application is because it is too much for CCU/ECU devices to cope with. The TLS protocol is bulky and has many implementation options. This will lead to more vulnerabilities. Our proposed protocol is very specific for this application, eliminating additional vulnerabilities. The TLS protocol is also slower in performance [38].

3.2   Threat Model

In the maintenance services logging system, assets to be protected are the read and write access authorisation and the authentication and integrity of the data. Potential attackers are untrustworthy workshops, owners and hackers with financial motivation, and potential buyers attempting to reduce the selling price. The two most likely threats are:

(i) Dishonest mechanic charges owner for a full service, but may have done little/nothing.
(ii) Owner changes service log to make the car more attractive to a buyer.

There are a number of possible attacks that could be performed in a digital maintenance logging system as follows:

(i) Denial of service (DoS) attack: to cause an availability issue, where data stored is not able to be retrieved, or data cannot be stored. Denying access of data to an authorised party is also a method of DoS.
(ii) Impersonation attack: to impersonate an authorised party to conduct further attacks, for example, an attacker impersonating an authorised workshop to log a record showing that the service is conducted by a certain trusted workshop.
(iii) Data manipulation attack: to change the list of the services, either by changing the data before or after the storage.
(iv) Replay attack: by replaying the same record of service to be stored on a different date to fake a record.

An additional assumption of the threat model in the digital automated system is the attacker cannot break well-established cryptographic algorithms.

3.3   Security Requirements

From the architecture, the security requirements can be elicited [26]. In general, a maintenance services logging system should satisfy the following security requirements:

- Integrity: The data stored should not be changed, modified or added to, to ensure that the record of the maintenance services integrity is protected.
- Authentication: Data authentication and data origin authentication should be in place. This is to ensure that the data comes from an authorised party (workshop and car) and the data itself is authentic.

– Non-repudiation: To ensure that the data stored by the workshop can be verified, i.e., the workshop cannot deny that the data stored originated from its diagnostic tool and services were conducted by the workshop or dealer.

– Freshness: To ensure no replay attack is possible, hence a record of services cannot be logged/replayed if it is not actually performed.

The records should not be linked to a car owner's personally identifiable information (PII). Hence, privacy is not a concern in the maintenance services record, unlike various other applications involving cyber-physical systems [39].

3.4 Protocol Goals

This section discusses the requirements of each party involved in the automated maintenance service log update.

(i) Car: The car requires authentication of the diagnostic tool, authentication of mobile device and data integrity of the information transferred from the diagnostic tool.

(ii) Mobile device (MD): The mobile device requires authentication of the car (CCU) and data integrity of the information transferred from the CCU.

(iii) Diagnostic tool (DT): The diagnostic tool requires authentication of the car (CCU).

3.5 Protocol Assumptions and Preconditions

Assumptions and preconditions on the successful use of AutoLOG are as follows.

1. The mobile application is installed on a mobile device and the cloud server is properly set up for the data to be stored.
2. The nonces generated (by DT, CCU and MD) should be random and not predictable.
3. The ECUs and sensors are equipped with the capability to validate the services being conducted on the car. For example, the sensor can validate the parameter given by the CCU, such as the serial ID of a new component. The proposal [13] could be used for this purpose. For a start, the firmware update status could be logged. Cars are now full of electronic modules that may require firmware updates. As part of the normal service, logging the status of all this firmware (which may then trigger updates) could be useful. So, when buying a second-hand car, not only does the potential buyer know it had a normal service on a particular date but also whether its IT/electronic systems have been "serviced" (kept up-to-date).
4. The cloud is securely managed. A user is authenticated to access the cloud server, and only authorised users have access to the data. However, even if an attacker is able to get access to the data in the cloud, the main concern is to protect the integrity of the data, which is provided by our protocol.
5. The data is always automatically transmitted to the phone and later to the cloud. If data is not updated after a certain time, the owner will be notified.

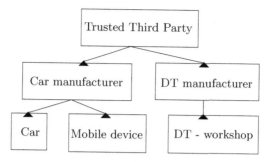

Fig. 2. Hierarchy for the key distribution

3.6   Protocol Key Distribution

Figure 2 shows the hierarchy for the key distribution. The hierarchy may be implemented for a specific car manufacturer. A car manufacturer may have a list of trusted workshops and diagnostic tool manufacturers. Each diagnostic tool of a workshop has its own set of public and private keys, one set for signature and one set for encryption. The digital certificates contain the public keys of the diagnostic tools, which tie the diagnostic tool to a workshop, and are available at a diagnostic tool manufacturer server, which is under a trusted third-party server. The cars and mobile devices are registered under the car manufacturer, which is also under the same trusted third-party server of the diagnostic tool manufacturer. Each CCU has its own set of public and private keys, which are pre-installed during manufacturing. These keys are updated by the car manufacturer. The mobile device needs to be registered to the car manufacturer in order to communicate with the car. After the AutoLOG application is installed on the mobile device, the registration of the mobile device via the AutoLOG application will enable the mobile device to communicate with the car. Based on the input parameters during registration, which include the Vehicle Identification Number (VIN), the car manufacturer will share a symmetric key, k_{ccu-md} of the CCU with the intended mobile device. Similarly, the diagnostic tool will acquire the public key of the CCU from the trusted third party. The CCU, which is the master ECU in the car, has the records of all ECUs. The records of ECUs include their IDs, the hash content of the firmware and their symmetric keys to communicate with the CCU, $k_{ccu-ecu}$. The keys are stored in the HSM for the car (CCU and ECUs) and the diagnostic tool. For the mobile device, the keys are stored in a secure memory for example on a secure element.

3.6.1   Protocol Description

To communicate with the car, the mobile device is connected to the OBD-II port via Wi-Fi or Bluetooth. Once connected, the mobile device will be authenticated, to determine whether it is authorised to retrieve the requested data. Once authenticated, the mobile device is connected to the CAN bus, and able to access the required data. The protocol notations are as shown in Table 2.

Table 2. Notations for the protocol

DT	Diagnostic tool
CCU	Central Communication Unit
MD	Mobile device
dt	ID of DT
ccu	ID of CCU
md	ID of MD
pk_x	Public key of x, x = DT or CCU
sk_x	Private key of x, x = DT or CCU
na, nb, nc, nd	Message Authentication Code (MAC) keys
ne, nf	AES keys
$k_{ccu-ecu}$	Symmetric key shared between CCU and ECU
k_{ccu-md}	Symmetric key shared between CCU and MD
ENC	Encryption using RSA
enc	Encryption using AES128
$sign$	Sign using RSA
MAC	HMAC using SHA256
$a\|\|b$	a concatenate with b
$a \oplus b$	a XOR b
$mile$	Mileage
$servicetype$	Type of service (basic, full or major)
$servicedate$	Date of service
$nextdate$	Next date of service
$serviceupdate$	Command to conduct the log update
$serviceupdatereq$	Command to obtain the log update
$validateservice$	Command to validate service from CCU to ECU
$serviceupdateready$	Response from CCU to acknowledge it is ready with updated data
$ackready$	Response from ECU to acknowledge it is ready for validation
ack	Acknowledgement
$s1, s2, s3$	List of services, repairs and/or updates conducted

The protocol, which is divided into three phases, is shown in Tables 3, 4 and 5. The first part (Table 3) shows the communication between the DT and CCU.

1. In the first message, the DT will send its ID, concatenated with update notification, $serviceupdate$, and a nonce, na. These parameters are signed with the DT's private key and encrypted with the CCU's public key. The digital signature is using signature with message recovery. The signature is then encrypted with the CCU's public key. The objective is to protect the secret nonce na, so that only the authorised CCU is able to obtain the value of na. The CCU will decrypt the message and verify the signature of the DT. From that, it will obtain the na, to be sent in the second message to the DT.

2. In the second message, the CCU will send its ID concatenated with the acknowledgment receipt of service update command and nonce na. It will be concatenated with its own generated nonce, nb. This message will be signed by its private key and encrypted with DT's public key. This signature is also using signature with message recovery and then encrypted with DT's public key in order to protect nb.

3. The DT will then decrypt the message to get the nonce nb. The nonces na and nb are used for MAC computation for the following messages between DT and CCU. The DT will then reply with all the required information, i.e. the maintenance type of service conducted (either basic, full or major), the service date, the next date of service to be conducted and the mileage reading, and concatenated with the MAC of all the parameters. The MAC is to ensure that the integrity of the data can be verified by the CCU.

4. The CCU will acknowledge the receipt of these parameters and concatenate it with the MAC.

5. Upon receiving the acknowledgment, the DT will send the list of services, repairs or updates conducted; in this example, they are $s1$, $s2$ and $s3$.

6. The next part is the communication between the CCU and the related ECU(s), as shown in Table 4. The CCU will validate the list of services, repairs and/or updates claimed by the DT. The related ECUs, equipped with sensors to verify the services/repairs/updates conducted, will respond accordingly. The CCU will send a command *validateservice* and a nonce nc, which is encrypted with $k_{ccu-ecu}$ to ensure only authorised ECU can read the nonce.

7. The ECU will decrypt the message to obtain the nonce nc. It will then send a message to acknowledge the receipt of nonce nc, and that it is prepared for the validation process, and will send its own generated nonce nd. This message is encrypted with the same $k_{ccu-ecu}$. The CCU will then decrypt the message in order to obtain the nonce nd. These nonces nc and nd are used for MAC computation for the following messages between CCU and corresponding ECU.

8. The CCU will send the list of services/repairs/updates conducted, concatenated with a MAC.

9. The ECU, after verifying the MAC received from the CCU, will validate each service/repair through its related sensors. After validating the list, it will send an acknowledgment of whether or not the validation is successful, concatenated with a MAC. If all items in the list are true, only the acknowledgment is sent with a MAC. Otherwise, the failed item is included in the message.

10. The last part of the protocol is where the mobile device retrieves the list of services/repairs/updates from the CCU. The mobile device will send a message containing its ID concatenated with a command of *serviceupdatereq* and a nonce ne, which is encrypted with a pre-shared symmetric key between the mobile device and CCU, k_{ccu-md}. The encryption is to ensure the confidentiality of the nonce ne. Only the authorised CCU will be able to decrypt the message and obtain ne.

11. The CCU will decrypt the message to get the nonce ne and then will reply with a message telling that a new service is available. If the service has already been retrieved before, it will send a different message to inform the MD. The message contains the ID of the mobile device, $serviceupdate$ reply, concatenated with nonce ne and its own generated nonce nf. They are encrypted with the pre-shared symmetric key between the mobile device and CCU, k_{ccu-md}. The nonces ne and nf are used for AES computation for the proceeding messages between the CCU and MD.

12. The MD will then decrypt the message to obtain the nonce nf and will then send an acknowledgment message to the CCU. This message is encrypted using the nonces as the key.

13. The CCU will then start sending the required service information to the MD, i.e., the maintenance type of service conducted (either basic, full or major), the service date and the next date of service to be conducted, the current mileage and the signature of this message. The signature is using signature with appendix. The signature is used to verify that the message originates from the CCU. The record transferred to the mobile device will not be able to be changed, because only the CCU has the private key to sign the message.

14. The MD, upon receiving these data, will be able to verify the origin of the message (i.e., CCU) by verifying the signature. It will then acknowledge the receipt of this message, in an encrypted message using AES128.

15. The CCU will next send the list of services/repairs/updates conducted. They are also appended with a signature for the same reason as in step 13, i.e. origin authentication and integrity protection.

16. Finally, the MD, upon receiving and storing these data, will send an acknowledgment encrypted using AES128 to the CCU. This will notify the CCU that the latest maintenance services record has been retrieved.

Table 3. DT-CCU update of services protocol

1.	DT	: $M1 = ccu\|\|serviceupdate\|\|na$
	DT → CCU	: $dt\|\|ENC_{pk_{ccu}}\{sign_{sk_{dt}}\{M1\}\}$
2.	CCU	: $M2 = dt\|\|ack\|\|na\|\|nb$
	CCU → DT	: $ccu\|\|ENC_{pk_{dt}}\{sign_{sk_{ccu}}\{M2\}\}$
3.	DT	: $M3 = ccu\|\|servicetype\|\|servicedate\|\|nextdate\|\|mile$
	DT→ CCU	: $dt\|\|M3\|\|MAC_{na\|\|nb}\{M3\}$
4.	CCU	: $M4 = dt\|\|ack$
	CCU → DT	: $ccu\|\|M4\|\|MAC_{na\|\|nb}\{M4\}$
5.	DT	: $M5 = s1\|\|s2\|\|s3$
	DT→ CCU	: $dt\|\|M5\|\|MAC_{na\|\|nb}\{M5\}$

Table 4. CCU-ECU validation of services protocol

6.	CCU	$: M6 = ecu \| validateservice \| nc$
	CCU $\rightarrow$ ECU	$: ccu \| enc_{k_{ccu-ecu}} \{M6\}$
7.	ECU	$: M7 = ccu \| ackready \| nc \| nd$
	ECU $\rightarrow$ CCU	$: ecu \| enc_{k_{ccu-ecu}} \{M7\}$
8.	CCU	$: M8 = ecu \| s1 \| s2 \| s3$
	CCU $\rightarrow$ ECU	$: ccu \| M8 \| MAC_{nc\|nd} \{M8\}$
9.	ECU	$: M9 = ccu \| ack$
	ECU $\rightarrow$ CCU	$: ecu \| M9 \| MAC_{nc\|nd} \{M9\}$

Table 5. MD-CCU request for services update protocol

10.	MD	$: M10 = serviceupdatereq \| ne$
	MD $\rightarrow$ CCU	$: md \| enc_{k_{ccu-md}} \{M10\}$
11.	CCU	$: M11 = md \| serviceupdate \| ne \| nf$
	CCU $\rightarrow$ MD	$: ccu \| enc_{k_{ccu-md}} \{M11\}$
12.	MD	$: M12 = ack$
	MD $\rightarrow$ CCU	$: md \| ccu \| enc_{(ne \oplus nf)} \{M12\}$
13.	CCU	$: M13 = servicetype \| servicedate \| nextdate \| mile$
	CCU $\rightarrow$ MD	$: ccu \| enc_{(ne \oplus nf)} \{M13\} \| sign_{sk_{ccu}} \{enc_{(ne \oplus nf)} \{M13\}\}$
14.	MD	$: M14 = ccu \| ack$
	MD $\rightarrow$ CCU	$: enc_{(ne \oplus nf)} \{M14\}$
15.	CCU	$: M15 = s1 \| s2 \| s3$
	CCU $\rightarrow$ MD	$: ccu \| enc_{(ne \oplus nf)} \{M15\} \| sign_{sk_{ccu}} \{enc_{(ne \oplus nf)} \{M15\}\}$
16.	MD	$: M16 = md \| ack$
	MD $\rightarrow$ CCU	$: enc_{(ne \oplus nf)} \{M16\}$

3.7   Security Analysis

The protocol is first analysed using informal analysis. Then, formal analysis is conducted using CasperFDR [24] and Scyther [16] tools to verify the protocol and provide indicative results.

3.7.1   Informal Analysis of the Protocol

Based on the threat model discussed in the previous section, the protocol addresses them accordingly.

Denial of service attack (DoS) could be conducted:

(i) by stealing the mobile device. If the mobile device is stolen, all the records are still available on the server. A stolen mobile device would not be able to tamper with the available stored data, because the data is signed by the car's CCU.

(ii) by disabling connectivity between mobile device and CCU to disable the update. Since the logging process is automated, once a mobile device is authenticated to the CCU, it will ask for an update every time they are connected. If the update is not conducted, the owner will be notified.

(iii) by introducing manual errors. However, the process may repeat and retry the update. The diagnostic tool will likely abort after a few attempts. A notification message will be prompted after a certain retry limit. An error could occur in normal use; however it could also be evidence of an attack. The data will always be consistent, as the mobile device will verify with the CCU whether the last data has been retrieved. If not, the CCU will retain the last record.

(iv) by causing the related ECUs/sensors to malfunction. During the second phase, i.e., the validation of the services, the ECU will acknowledge that the services are correctly being performed as given by the DT to the CCU in the previous phase. In this phase, all the related sensors will verify the correctness of the provided data. If any of the sensors fail, this will be displayed on the diagnostic transmission code (DTC, which is the error code) before the services is being performed. The faulty sensor should be fixed prior to updating the maintenance services logging system.

Impersonation of recognised workshop or dealer is prohibited with the use of digital signature to ensure only authorised DT can conduct the storing of information to CCU.

Data manipulation attack (change, deletion or insertion) could be conducted at three different stages:

(i) From the DT side: Digital signature is used to ensure that only authorised DT can sign the message required. Therefore, the message is authentic and comes from an authorised party, unless the private key is compromised.

(ii) After storing the information to the CCU, and during retrieval of data from CCU to the MD: The CCU only stores the last record of maintenance service conducted. This information is important to the car owner, in order to know the last service record. If the adversary wanted to modify or manipulate this one record, he/she needs to have the access to the CCU information, i.e., key to read and/or write to the specific memory address.

(iii) After storing the information in the mobile application or server: Fake records could be inserted to increase the car resale value. With this protocol, this is impossible because the record is protected by the CCU's signature to ensure its integrity is protected. The mileage can also prove the age of the car when the service is conducted.

Replay attack is not possible through the use of random nonces for each transaction.

The proposal also addresses all the security requirements discussed in Sect. 3.3, as follows:

- Integrity: The data stored could not be changed, modified or added. To ensure that the record of maintenance service is integrity protected, MAC and digital signatures are used.
- Authentication: Data authentication and data origin authentication should be in place. MAC is used to verify the data origin authentication.
- Non-repudiation: Digital signatures are used to ensure that the workshop and the car cannot deny their own data.
- Freshness: Freshness is verified by using nonces and the mileage reading.

3.7.2 Formal Analysis of the Protocol Using CasperFDR and Scyther Tools

The security requirements to be verified include confidentiality and authentication properties. Aliveness, agreement and synchronisation are part of the authentication property. Scyther is an automated tool for the verification of security protocols [16]. CasperFDR tool uses Communication Sequential Process (CSP) files to be analysed using Failure Divergence Refinement (FDR) [24]. CasperFDR and Scyther input scripts are as in link: CasperFDR and Scyther input scripts (https://www.dropbox.com/sh/ixqrynsxb6tfvr0/AAB0Q7ohHbcA9atE9O854ZWxa?dl=0). The protocol is modelled as follows. The DT knows the CCU, but does not know the MD. MD only communicates with the CCU and not with the DT.

The protocol security objectives are key confidentiality and internal (CCU-ECU) and external (DT-CCU and MD-CCU) authentication. From our Scyther and CasperFDR input scripts, the following security claims are made and verified.

(i) Confidentiality: To verify the confidentiality of the cryptographic keys. The key confidentiality includes confidentiality of secret nonce (na, nb, nc and nd: used as the MAC keys, and ne and nf: used as the AES keys), and all secret keys (sk_{dt}, sk_{ccu} and sk_{md}).
(ii) Authenticity: To verify the authenticity of all entities involved in the process (DT, CCU and MD). This includes agreement and aliveness tests as defined in [15,23]. In Scyther, additional authentication property, i.e., synchronisation is also verified. Synchronisation considers the content and ordering of the messages [15].

Analysis using CasperFDR. The security properties verified are secrecy, aliveness and agreement. The confidentiality property is to verify the secrecy of the nonces (na, nb, nc and nd) that are used as keys for MAC computations, and (ne and nf) that are used as keys for AES computations. The aliveness property is to verify the aliveness between DT and CCU, between CCU and ECU and between MD and CCU. The agreement property is to ensure the agreement of variables shared between DT and CCU (na and nb), between CCU and ECU (nc and nd)

and between MD and CCU (*ne* and *nf*). The threat model is that the attacker knows all the entities involved, i.e., the DT, CCU, ECU and MD, and their corresponding public keys. No known attack was found in the protocol.

The scripts are divided into three parts for the three different parts of the protocol. The full script for the first part (DT-CCU) can be found in link: CasperFDR input script (https://www.dropbox.com/s/mlvl33829kkppo4/maintenance.spl?dl=0). The script starts with #Free variables declaration, which declares all the variables used in the protocol. It is followed with the #Protocol description. This describes the messages being transmitted (in sequence) during the information passing from DT to CCU, which starts from service update notification (i.e., *1.a -> c:a,{{c,serviceupdate,na}{SK(a)}}{PK(c)}*). In *3. a -> c:a,c,service,mile,h(a,c,service,mile,na,nb)*, the list of services is passed from DT to CCU in clear text but appended with MAC of the message. It is the same in *5. a -> c:a,s1,s2,s3,h(s1,s2,s3,na,nb)*. Only DT and CCU can compute the MAC and verify them based on the shared keys in the previous message.

In the #Processes, all the involved entities in the protocol and their knowledge are declared. For example, *INITIATOR(a,c,serviceupdate,na,service,mile, s1,s2,s3) knows PK,SK(a)*, where a is the DT and c is the CCU.

The #Specification declares all the assertions made to verify the security properties. The confidentiality of na and nb are declared as Secret(a,na,[c]) and Secret(c,nb,[c]). As an authentication verification, the aliveness property between DT-CCU and the Agreement property between DT-CCU are verified.

The #Actual variables section describes the names of the actual agents, servers and the actual variables such as agent a is DT and agent c is CCU. In the #Functions section the public and secret keys are declared (symbolic PK,SK). The #System section again declares all the involved entities in the protocol and their knowledge, but with their actual names. For example, *INITIATOR(DT,CCU,Serviceupdate,Na,Service,Mile,S1,S2,S3)*.

The #Intruder Information declares the intruder X who has the knowledge of all the entities involved and their public keys, and its own public and secret keys, i.e., IntruderKnowledge=DT,CCU,X,PK.

All the specifications made are verified and no attack is found for all the assertions.

Analysis using Scyther. The security properties verified are secrecy, non-injective synchronisation, non-injective agreement and aliveness. The secrecy property is to verify the confidentiality of the nonces that are used as keys for MAC computations. The non-injective synchronisation property is to verify that parties know who they are communicating with, agree on the content of the messages and the order of the messages. The non-injective agreement is to verify that parties agreed on the content of the variables. The aliveness property is to verify that the intended communication partner (DT-CCU, CCU-ECU and MD-CCU) has executed some events. In Scyther, all the security properties are modelled in role-base. The properties are viewed from the local view of each role.

The full script for MD-CCU communication can be found in link: Scyther input scripts (https://www.dropbox.com/s/i1f9zax8d2ga549/AutoLOG_mdccu.spdl?dl=0). In this section, the discussion is about the third part of the protocol, i.e., between MD-CCU. The script starts with functions declarations (line 1–4). Then, we have macros of messages to make the script neat and easy to follow (line 8–14). Next, the events and claims are made for each role (MD: line 16–42 and CCU: line 44–69).

For example, for MD role, the examples of events are $send\_10(md, ccu, m10)$ and $recv\_11(ccu, md, m11)$, which means the MD sends the macro $m10$ to the CCU and later receives macro $m11$ from the CCU. Claims are the security properties to be verified. For example, for the MD role, $claim\_I3(md, SKR, ne)$ is for confidentiality. Authentication properties are verified through Agreement ($claim\_I6$ $(md, Weakagree)$, $claim\_I2(md, Niagree)$), Synchronisation ($claim\_I1(md, Nisynch)$), and Aliveness ($claim\_I4(md, Alive)$).

The default verification setup was used (i.e., five maximum number of runs, type-matching and to find best attack with ten maximum patterns per claim). The results for all the claims made are verified as "Ok" in the "Status" with "Verified" and "No attacks" in the "Comments". This means that no attack was found within the bounded or unbounded statespace; the security property has been successfully verified [14].

3.8 Protocol Implementation

The protocol was then implemented on a PIC32MZ Microchip microcontroller and an Android device to obtain indicative performance results.

3.8.1 Implementation Platform

Our approach of implementation is to observe the computation time on the DT, CCU, ECU and the mobile device separately. The mobile device communicates via Wi-Fi, while the DT, CCU and ECU via CAN bus. There is a Wi-Fi module connected to the CCU to receive the Wi-Fi messages from the mobile device and convert these messages into UART messages. There is another interface module between the Wi-Fi module and the CCU to translate UART messages into CAN messages and vice versa. The DT, CCU and ECU are simulated using a microcontroller with all the functions required to be an actual ECU with cryptographic engines. PIC32MZ2048ECM144 [37] is chosen as the implementation platform for all three components (DT, CCU and ECU). It is a 32 bit microcontroller with 2048 KB of flash and 512 KB of SRAM, and operates at 200 MHz clock. It supports CAN bus communication, as required in an ECU. The hardware cryptographic engines support the computation of cryptographic algorithms to produce faster performance. For the mobile device, the application protocol is loaded into a LG Nexus 5 with a Quad-core 2.3 GHz Krait 400 CPU running on Android 5.1. PIC18F4580 is used as the interface module to translate UART-CAN messages. PIC18F4580 [29] is an 8 bit microcontroller with 32 KB of flash and 256 bytes of RAM. It operates with a 16 MHz clock and supports CAN bus and UART communication. For the Wi-Fi module, the Wi-Fi G demo board [36] is used (Fig. 3).

Fig. 3. CCU's setup for communication with MD

3.8.2 Experiment Setup

For the DT, CCU and ECU setup, the simulation of the messages from and to each component uses the Microchip CAN bus analyser tool [31]. The tool can be used to observe the messages sent from the PIC32MZ microcontroller and also to send messages to it. On the PIC32MZ part, the PIC32MZ2048ECM144 starter kit [35] is connected to a CAN PICtail daughter board [32] through a starter kit adapter [34] and an I/O expansion board [30]. The CAN PICtail daughter board is then connected to the CAN bus analyser. The setup is shown in Fig. 4. The computation performance is measured based on cycle count given by MPLABX debugger.

For the interface module (using PIC18F4580), an additional CAN transceiver, MCP2551 [28], is connected to the PIC18. The interface module is then connected to MCP2200 breakout module [33] to observe the UART messages. The performance of communication is measured using an oscilloscope. The performance of Wi-Fi communication is measured using the "Inspector" feature from the internet browser.

All the protocol messages are in the data byte of the CAN message. The header of the CAN message is used in the same manner as in current implementation where it indicates what operation is to be handled. Based on the proposed protocol, the length of a message is more than eight bytes, hence, all the messages will need to be divided into more than one CAN message due to the limited number of bytes (8 bytes) of data per CAN message transmission. The messages are divided into three to eighteen messages to be transmitted via CAN.

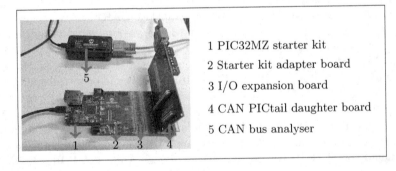

Fig. 4. Lab setup for DT, CCU and ECU through CAN bus communication

3.8.3   Performance Results

The computation and communication performance is as shown in Table 6. The communication includes the transfer of data from the Wi-Fi module to the middle interface module (via UART) and from the middle interface module to the CCU (via CAN). To the authors' knowledge, there is no related work that proposes an automated maintenance services logging system that we can compare the performance with. However, the total time for the protocol to complete is only about 883 ms. This shows that the protocol is efficient and practical for implementation. Although the computation time for AES and HMAC is faster using PIC32MZ as compared to the Android phone, the RSA computation is longer for PIC32MZ. This is because PIC32MZ has cryptographic engines for AES and HMAC which compute the algorithms at hardware level. Hence, this results in a faster computation time. The communication time is longer for the third part of the protocol, because the messages from the mobile device need to go through Wi-Fi, be converted to UART messages, then to CAN messages. It is the same for the communication from the CCU to mobile device, where the messages from the CCU are in CAN, then converted to UART, and later

Table 6. Protocol performance on LG Nexus 5 and PIC32MZ; for Protocol part I: A = DT, B = CCU, for Protocol part II: A = CCU, B = ECU, for Protocol part III: A = MD, B = CCU

Protocol part	Message	Time (ms)			
		Computation		Communication	Total time (ms)
		A	B		
I	1	53.041	52.691	1.825	107.557
	2	52.680	53.012	1.825	107.517
	3	0.102	0.086	0.859	1.046
	4	0.084	0.079	0.752	0.915
	5	0.077	0.086	0.752	0.914
II	6	0.099	0.050	0.537	0.686
	7	0.039	0.083	0.537	0.659
	8	0.103	0.083	0.859	1.045
	9	0.083	0.078	0.537	0.697
III	10	0.605	0.049	57.627	58.280
	11	0.805	0.083	72.818	73.705
	12	0.382	0.036	50.031	50.450
	13	1.216	39.459	163.962	204.636
	14	0.231	0.031	34.841	35.103
	15	1.082	39.609	163.962	204.652
	16	0.199	0.030	34.841	35.069
Total					882.933

to Wi-Fi. The baud rates of communication are at 9600 bps for UART and at 1 Mbps for CAN. The communication time can be further improved if CAN FD [18] is used, where one message can contain up to 64 bytes of data, instead of just 8 bytes.

4   Conclusion

The automated logging of car maintenance services helps car owners to keep track of the car maintenance record and avoid major breakdowns that can contribute to large costs. Having a secure protocol to conduct the automated logging can ensure that no records can be faked or modified. This will not only help the owner during the ownership of the car but also during car reselling, by increasing value of the car's price through showing that the car has been well maintained. The use of a mobile device gives a user interface as well as connectivity for the car, and thus helps the widespread use of this application since not all cars have connectivity and/or user interface. The proposed protocol provides integrity, authenticity and reliability of the data. It is also efficient and practically implementable.

References

1. aCar - Car Management, Mileage. https://play.google.com/store/apps/details?id=com.zonewalker.acar.pro. Accessed 22 Oct 2016
2. Auto Care. https://itunes.apple.com/gb/app/auto-care-free-car-maintenance/id576958809?mt=8. Accessed 22 Oct 2016
3. AUTOsist. https://itunes.apple.com/gb/app/autosist-car-motorcycle-vehicle/id897916520?mt=8. Accessed 22 Oct 2016
4. Car Minder. https://itunes.apple.com/us/app/car-minder-plus-car-maintenance/id310809791?mt=8. Accessed 22 Oct 2016
5. Fake Car Service Histories Spot One In 8 Easy Steps. https://www.onlinespyshop.co.uk/blog/tips-guides/fake-car-service-histories-spot-one-in-8-easy-steps/. Accessed 22 Oct 2016
6. Ford's Vehicle Repair and Service. http://www.ford.co.uk/OwnerServices/VehicleServiceandRepair/ServicingyourFord/VehicleServicing. Accessed 22 Oct 2016
7. How to Spot a Fake Service History. http://www.autoexpress.co.uk/car-news/58853/how-spot-a-fake-service-history. Accessed 22 Oct 2016
8. Motoriety. http://motoriety.co.uk/. Accessed 22 Oct 2016
9. My Cars. https://play.google.com/store/apps/details?id=com.aguirre.android.mycar.activity. Accessed 22 Oct 2016
10. The Value of a Full Service History. http://www.telegraph.co.uk/cars/advice/the-value-of-a-full-service-history/. Accessed 22 Oct 2016
11. Toyota Service History. http://www.toyota.com/owners/parts-service/history. Accessed 22 Oct 2016
12. Amouzegar, F., Patel, A.: Vehicle maintenance notification system using RFID technology. Int. J. Comput. Theor. Eng. 5(2), 312 (2013)

13. Boss, G.J., Finn, P.G., II Rick, A.H., O'Connell, B.M., Seaman, J.W., Walker, K.R.: Tracking Vehicle Maintenance using Sensor Detection, US Patent 8,311,698, November 2012
14. Cremers, C.: Scyther User Manual, draft edition, February 2014
15. Cremers, C., Mauw, S.: Operational Semantics and Verification of Security Protocols. Springer, Heidelberg (2012)
16. Cremers, C.J.F.: The scyther tool: verification, falsification, and analysis of security protocols. In: Gupta, A., Malik, S. (eds.) CAV 2008. LNCS, vol. 5123, pp. 414–418. Springer, Heidelberg (2008). doi:10.1007/978-3-540-70545-1_38
17. ELM Electronics. ELM327L. https://www.elmelectronics.com/wp-content/uploads/2016/07/ELM327L_Data_Sheet.pdf. Accessed 22 Oct 2016
18. Hartwich, F.: CAN with Flexible Data Rate (2012)
19. Henniger, O.: EVITA: E-Safety Vehicle Intrusion Protected Applications. Technical report, EVITA (2011)
20. Henniger, O., Apvrille, L., Fuchs, A., Roudier, Y., Ruddle, A., Weyl, B.: Security requirements for automotive on-board networks. In: 2009 9th International Conference on Intelligent Transport Systems Telecommunications (ITST), pp. 641–646. IEEE (2009)
21. Hiraoka, H., Iwanami, N., Fujii, Y., Seya, T., Ishizuka, H.: Network agents for life cycle support of mechanical parts. In: 2003 3rd International Symposium on Environmentally Conscious Design and Inverse Manufacturing, EcoDesign 2003, pp. 61–64. IEEE (2003)
22. Road vehicles – Controller Area Network (CAN) – part 1: Data link layer and physical signalling. Standard, International Organization for Standardization, February 2013
23. Lowe, G.: A hierarchy of authentication specifications. In: Proceedings of the 10th Computer Security Foundations Workshop, pp. 31–43. IEEE (1997)
24. Lowe, G.: Casper: a compiler for the analysis of security protocols. J. Comput. Secur. 6(1), 53–84 (1998)
25. Makowitz, R., Temple, C.: FlexRay- a communication network for automotive control systems. In: 2006 IEEE International Workshop on Factory Communication Systems, pp. 207–212 (2006)
26. Mavropoulos, O., Mouratidis, H., Fish, A., Panaousis, E., Kalloniatis, C.: APPARATUS: reasoning about security requirements in the internet of things. In: Krogstie, J., Mouratidis, H., Su, J. (eds.) CAiSE 2016. LNBIP, vol. 249, pp. 219–230. Springer, Heidelberg (2016). doi:10.1007/978-3-319-39564-7_21
27. Media Oriented Systems Transport Specifications (2006)
28. Microchip. High-Speed CAN Transceiver (2003). http://ww1.microchip.com/downloads/en/devicedoc/21667d.pdf. Accessed 22 Oct 2016
29. Microchip. PIC18F2480/2580/4480/4580 Data Sheet (2007). http://ww1.microchip.com/downloads/en/DeviceDoc/39637c.pdf. Accessed 22 Oct 2016
30. Microchip. Starter Kit I/O Expansion Board Information Sheet (2010). http://ww1.microchip.com/downloads/en/DeviceDoc/51950A.pdf. Accessed 22 Oct 2016
31. Microchip. CAN BUS Analyzer Users Guide (2011). http://ww1.microchip.com/downloads/en/DeviceDoc/51848B.pdf. Accessed 22 Oct 2016
32. Microchip. CAN/LIN/J2602 PICtail (Plus) Daughter Board Users Guide (2011). http://ww1.microchip.com/downloads/en/DeviceDoc/70319B.pdf. Accessed 22 Oct 2016
33. Microchip. MCP2200 Breakout Module User's Guide (2012). http://ww1.microchip.com/downloads/en/DeviceDoc/52064A.pdf. Accessed 22 Oct 2016

34. Microchip. PIC32MZ Embedded Connectivity (EC) Adapter Board Information Sheet (2013). http://ww1.microchip.com/downloads/en/DeviceDoc/50002199A.pdf. Accessed 22 Oct 2016
35. Microchip. PIC32MZ Embedded Connectivity (EC) Starter Kit Users Guide (2013). http://ww1.microchip.com/downloads/en/DeviceDoc/70005147A.pdf. Accessed 22 Oct 2016
36. Microchip. Wi-Fi G Demo Board Users Guide (2013). http://ww1.microchip.com/downloads/en/DeviceDoc/50002147A.pdf. Accessed 22 Oct 2016
37. Microchip. PIC32MZ Embedded Connectivity (EC) Family (2015). http://ww1.microchip.com/downloads/en/DeviceDoc/60001191F.pdf. Accessed 22 Oct 2016
38. Miranda, P., Siekkinen, M., Waris, H.: TLS and energy consumption on a mobile device: a measurement study. In: 2011 IEEE Symposium on Computers and Communications (ISCC), pp. 983–989. IEEE (2011)
39. Petroulakis, N.E., Askoxylakis, I.G., Traganitis, A., Spanoudakis, G.: A privacy-level model of user-centric cyber-physical systems. In: Marinos, L., Askoxylakis, I. (eds.) HAS 2013. LNCS, vol. 8030, pp. 338–347. Springer, Heidelberg (2013). doi:10.1007/978-3-642-39345-7_36
40. Ruff, M.: Evolution of local interconnect network (LIN) solutions. In: 2003 IEEE 58th Vehicular Technology Conference, VTC 2003-Fall, vol. 5, pp. 3382–3389. IEEE (2003)
41. SAE J1962 Revised APR2002. Standard, SAE Vehicle Electrical and Electronics Diagnostics Systems Standards Committee, April 2002

Provably Secure Fair Mutual Private Set Intersection Cardinality Utilizing Bloom Filter

Sumit Kumar Debnath[✉] and Ratna Dutta

Department of Mathematics, Indian Institute of Technology Kharagpur,
Kharagpur 721302, India
sd.iitkgp@gmail.com, ratna@maths.iitkgp.ernet.in

Abstract. The availability of electronic information is necessary in our everyday life. Progressively, often, data needs to be shared among the unreliable entities. In this field, one interesting and common problem occurs when two parties want to secretly determine the intersection or cardinality of intersection of their respective private sets. PSI or its variants are ideal to solve the aforementioned problems. Existing solutions of mPSI and mPSI-CA mainly use trusted third party to achieve fairness. However, in real life, the unconditional trust is fraught with security risks as the trusted third party may be unfaithful or corrupted. As a consequence, construction of an efficient mPSI-CA preserving fairness remains a challenging problem. In this paper, we address this issue by employing an off-line third party, called arbiter, who is assumed to be semi-trusted in the sense that he does not have access to the private information of the entities while he will follow the protocol honestly. In this work, we design a construction of *fair* and *efficient* mPSI-CA utilizing *Bloom filter*. Our mPSI-CA is proven to be secure in the random oracle model (ROM) and achieves *linear* communication and computation overheads. A concrete security analysis is provided in *malicious* environments under the Decisional Diffie-Hellman (DDH) assumption.

Keywords: mPSI-CA · Malicious adversary · Fairness · Semi-trusted arbiter · Bloom filter

1 Introduction

Nowadays, there are many realistic modern scenarios where electronic information is increasingly often shared among mutually dishonest parties. Let us consider some real-life scenarios where private data needs to be shared:

1. Program chairs of a conference may wish to determine that none of the submitted papers are also under review in other conferences or journals, while at the same time they are not allowed to reveal papers in submission.
2. Two different health organizations want to know the number of common villagers who are suffering from a particular disease in a village. None of the organizations will disclose their list of suspects to other. Note that revealing the name of the suspects may create an impact on patient's mind.

© Springer International Publishing AG 2017
K. Chen et al. (Eds.): Inscrypt 2016, LNCS 10143, pp. 505–525, 2017.
DOI: 10.1007/978-3-319-54705-3_31

To address associated security and privacy issues in the aforementioned scenarios, we need some strong cryptographic techniques, such as Private Set Intersection (PSI). In PSI, two parties want to learn the intersection of their respective private sets, while they also want to prevent the other party from finding out anything more about their own sets except the elements of the intersection. According to the functionality, PSI can be divided into the following two classes: (i) *one-way PSI*, where the functionality enables only one of the two parties to learn the intersection and the other party to receive nothing and (ii) *two-way or mutual PSI*, where the functionality enables both the parties to receive the intersection. In several applicative scenarios (see Example 2), the entities wish to learn only the cardinality of the intersection rather than the intersection of their private data sets. This cardinality version of PSI is known as PSI-CA. Similar to PSI, PSI-CA can be divided into two classes: one-way PSI-CA and two-way or mutual PSI-CA (mPSI-CA).

The primary challenge in designing mPSI-CA is its efficiency. Achieving fairness is another crucial fact for mPSI-CA. Fairness guarantees that on completion of the protocol, if one of the entities receives the cardinality of the intersection then the other should also receive that. By using a fully trusted third party, easily fairness can be achieved. However, in real life, existence of such fully trusted third party seems to be impossible as the party may be compromised or dishonest.

Related Works: Agrawal et al. [1] introduced the concept of PSI relying on commutative encryption and attains linear complexity. Following this a number of one-way PSI protocols were proposed in [14, 19, 20, 22, 23, 26, 27]. The first one-way PSI-CA dates back to the work of Agrawal et al. [1]. After that a sequence of one-way PSI-CAs were presented in [12, 14, 15, 20]. Kissner and Song [25] combined oblivious polynomial evaluation (OPE) with additively homomorphic encryption (AHE) to design the first mPSI protocol which can support more than two players in the communication system. In the subsequent years, a variety of mPSI protocols were proposed in [10, 13, 16–18, 24].

mPSI-CA: The concept of OPE based mPSI-CA was introduced by Kissner and Song [25]. More than two players can participate in their construction. Fairness is not considered in this work. Later, Camenisch and Zaverucha [10] introduced a fair mPSI-CA protocol for certified sets relying on OPE. Recently, the authors of [16] proposed the first fair optimistic mPSI-CA protocol over prime order group with linear complexity.

Our Results: In this paper, we are aiming to design *fair* and *efficient* mPSI-CA protocol instead of one-way PSI-CA. We utilize Bloom filter as building blocks of our construction. We integrate distributed ElGamal encryption [6], Cramer-Shoup cryptosystem [11] and blend zero-knowledge proofs for discrete logarithm together with zero-knowledge argument for shuffle to build the proposed mPSI-CA. Our scheme is proven to be secure in the ROM [3] against *malicious* adversaries with *linear* complexity under the DDH assumption. In mPSI-CA, *fairness* is a major concern as it ensures that the intersection is received either by both the participants or none on completion of the protocol. We emphasize that *fairness* is achieved in our construction using an optimistic fair exchange by using an off-line third party, called arbiter who is assumed to be semi-trusted. The arbiter is semi-trusted in the sense that he cannot get access to the private information of the participants but follows the protocol honestly. As far as we are aware of, there is only one fair mPSI-CA [16] with *linear* complexity over *prime* order group. The authors of [16] proposed that their construction of mPSI-CA is secure against malicious adversaries. However, it seems to us that their scheme does not remain secure when the participants behave maliciously. In the efficiency section, we will discuss about this in detail. On a more positive note, our protocol requires only 4 rounds whilst the mPSI-CA of [16] requires 5 rounds. Apart from [16], there are two existing mPSI-CA protocols [10,25], both of which use composite order group and attain quadratic computational overhead. Fairness is not considered in [25]. The authors of [10] pointed out that their construction of mPSI-CA can be modified to achieve fairness using an optimistic fair exchange scheme where a trusted third party certifies the inputs. However, they have not given any construction of that and their approach of attaining fairness does not work in general cases where inputs are not certified by a trusted authority. This is because forcing the participants to use the same inputs in two different instances is practically infeasible in real life applications.

2   Preliminaries

Throughout the paper, the notations κ, $a \leftarrow A$, $x \hookleftarrow X$ and $\{\mathcal{X}_t\}_{t \in \mathcal{N}} \equiv^c \{\mathcal{Y}_t\}_{t \in \mathcal{N}}$ are respectively used to represent "security parameter", "a is output of the procedure A", "variable x is chosen uniformly at random from set X" and "the distribution ensemble $\{\mathcal{X}_t\}_{t \in \mathcal{N}}$ is computationally indistinguishable from the distribution ensemble $\{\mathcal{Y}_t\}_{t \in \mathcal{N}}$". Formally, $\{\mathcal{X}_t\}_{t \in \mathcal{N}} \equiv^c \{\mathcal{Y}_t\}_{t \in \mathcal{N}}$ means for all probabilistic polynomial time (PPT) distinguisher $\mathcal{Z}$, there exists a negligible function $\epsilon(t)$ such that $|Pr_{x \leftarrow \mathcal{X}_t}[\mathcal{Z}(x) = 1] - Pr_{x \leftarrow \mathcal{Y}_t}[\mathcal{Z}(x) = 1]| \leq \epsilon(t)$. A function $\epsilon : \mathbb{N} \to \mathbb{R}$ is said to be a negligible function of κ if for each constant $c > 0$, we have $\epsilon(\kappa) = o(\kappa^{-c})$ for all sufficiently large κ.

Definition 1 Functionality: *A functionality $\mathcal{F}_\Pi$, computed by two parties A and B with inputs X_A and X_B respectively by running a protocol Π, is defined as $\mathcal{F}_\Pi : X_A \times X_B \to Y_A \times Y_B$, where Y_A and Y_B are the outputs of A and B respectively on completion of the protocol Π between A and B.*

Definition 2 Decisional Diffie-Hellman (DDH) Assumption [5]**:** *Let the algorithm gGen generate a modulus n and a generator g of a multiplicative group $\mathbb{G}$ of order n on the input 1^κ. Suppose $a, b, c \hookleftarrow \mathbb{Z}_n$. Then the DDH assumption states that no PPT algorithm $\mathcal{A}$ can distinguish between the two distributions $\langle g^a, g^b, g^{ab} \rangle$ and $\langle g^a, g^b, g^c \rangle$ i.e., $|Prob[\mathcal{A}(g, g^a, g^b, g^{ab}) = 1] - Pr[\mathcal{A}(g, g^a, g^b, g^c) = 1]|$ is negligible function of κ.*

2.1   Security Model

Informally, the basic security requirements of any multi-party protocol are

(a) *Correctness.* At the end of the protocol an honest party should receive the correct output.
(b) *Privacy.* After completion of the protocol, no party should learn more than its prescribe output.
(c) *Fairness.* A dishonest party should receive its output if and only if the honest party also receives its output.

In this work, we focus on the *malicious* model where the adversary can behave arbitrarily. A protocol is said to be secure if any adversary in the real protocol can be simulated by an adversary in the ideal world. The security framework of mPSI-CA is formally described below following [18].

The real world: The protocol has three participants – party A, party B and an arbiter Ar. All the participants have knowledge about the public parameters of the protocol mPSI-CA, the functionality $\mathcal{F}_{\mathsf{mPSI}-CA} : ((X, |Y|), (Y, |X|)) \rightarrow (|X \cap Y|, |X \cap Y|)$, the security parameter κ, Ar's public key pk_{Ar} and other cryptographic parameters such as hash functions to be used. Party A has a private input X, party B has a private input Y and Ar has an input $\in \{\circ, \perp\}$, where $\perp$ stands for "nothing". The real world adversary $\mathcal{C}$ can corrupt upto two parties in the protocol and can behave arbitrarily. At the end of the protocol execution, an honest party outputs whatever prescribed in the protocol, a corrupted party outputs nothing, and an adversary outputs its view which consists of the transcripts available to the adversary. The joint output of $A, B, Ar, \mathcal{C}$ in the real world is denoted by $\mathsf{REAL}_{\mathsf{mPSI}-CA,\mathcal{C}}(X, Y)$.

The ideal process: In the ideal process, there is an incorruptible trusted party T who can compute the ideal functionality $\mathcal{F}_{\mathsf{mPSI}-CA}$ and parties $\overline{A}, \overline{B}$ and $\overline{Ar}$. Party $\overline{A}$ has input X, $\overline{B}$ has input Y and $\overline{Ar}$ has an input $\in \{\circ, \perp\}$. The interaction is as follows:

(i) $\overline{A}$ sends $\overline{X}$ or $\perp$ to T, following it $\overline{B}$ sends $\overline{Y}$ or $\perp$ to T; and then $\overline{Ar}$ sends two messages $b_A \in (\{\circ, \perp\} \cup X_A)$ and $b_B \in (\{\circ, \perp\} \cup Y_B)$ to T, where $X_A = Y_B = \mathbb{N} \cup \{0\}$, set of non-negative integers. The inputs $\overline{X}$ and $\overline{Y}$ may be different from X and Y respectively if the party is malicious.

(ii) T sends private delayed output to $\overline{A}$ and $\overline{B}$. T's reply to $\overline{A}$(resp. $\overline{B}$) depends on $\overline{A}$ and $\overline{B}$'s messages and b_A(resp. b_B). Response of T to $\overline{A}$(resp. $\overline{B}$) is as follows:

   (a) If b_A(resp. b_B) = $\circ$, and T has received $\overline{X} \neq \perp$ from $\overline{A}$ and $\overline{Y} \neq \perp$ from $\overline{B}$, then T sends $|\overline{X} \cap \overline{Y}|$ to $\overline{A}$(resp. $\overline{B}$).
   (b) Else if b_A(resp. b_B) = $\circ$, but T has received $\perp$ from either $\overline{A}$ or $\overline{B}$, then T sends $\perp$ to $\overline{A}$(resp. $\overline{B}$).
   (c) Else b_A(resp. b_B) $\neq \circ$, then T sends b_A(resp. b_B) to $\overline{A}$(resp. $\overline{B}$).

In the ideal process, if $\overline{A}$, $\overline{B}$ and $\overline{Ar}$ are honest then they behave as follows: $\overline{A}$ and $\overline{B}$ send their inputs to T and $\overline{Ar}$ sends $b_A = \circ$ and $b_B = \circ$. The ideal process simulator $\mathcal{SIM}$ gets the inputs of the corrupted parties and may replace them and gets T's response to corrupted parties. The joint output of $\overline{A}, \overline{B}, \overline{Ar}, \mathcal{SIM}$ in the ideal process is denoted by $\mathsf{IDEAL}_{\mathcal{F}_{\mathsf{mPSI-CA}}, \mathcal{SIM}}(X, Y)$. The security definition in terms of simulatability is

Definition 3. Simulatability: *Let the functionality of* $\mathsf{mPSI} - CA$ *be* $\mathcal{F}_{\mathsf{mPSI}-CA} : ((X, |Y|), (Y, |X|)) \rightarrow (|X \cap Y|, |X \cap Y|)$. *Then the protocol* $\mathsf{mPSI\text{-}CA}$ *is said to securely compute* $\mathcal{F}_{\mathsf{mPSI}-CA}$ *in malicious model if for every real world adversary* $\mathcal{C}$, *there exists an ideal world adversary* $\mathcal{SIM}$ *such that the joint distribution of all outputs of the ideal world is computationally indistinguishable from the outputs in the real world, i.e.,* $\mathsf{IDEAL}_{\mathcal{F}_{\mathsf{mPSI}-CA}, \mathcal{SIM}}(X, Y) \equiv^c \mathsf{REAL}_{\mathsf{mPSI}-CA, \mathcal{C}}(X, Y)$.

2.2 Homomorphic Encryption [7]

We describe below the distributed ElGamal encryption [6] which is *multiplicatively* homomorphic encryption scheme and semantically secure provided DDH problem is hard in underlying group. The distributed ElGamal encryption $\mathcal{DEL} = (\mathcal{DEL}.\mathsf{Setup}, \mathcal{DEL}.\mathsf{KGen}, \mathcal{DEL}.\mathsf{Enc}, \mathcal{DEL}.\mathsf{Dec})$ is executed between two parties A_1 and A_2 as follows:

(par) $\longleftarrow \mathcal{DEL}.\mathsf{Setup}(1^\kappa)$. On input 1^κ, a trusted third party outputs a public parameter $\mathsf{par} = (p, q, g)$, where p, q are primes such that q divides $p - 1$ and g is a generator of the unique cyclic subgroup $\mathbb{G}$ of $\mathbb{Z}_p^*$ of order q.

$(pk, sk) \longleftarrow \mathcal{DEL}.\mathsf{KGen}(\mathsf{par})$. Each participant $A_i, i = 1, 2$ selects $a_i \longleftarrow \mathbb{Z}_q$, publishes $epk_{A_i} = y_{A_i} = g^{a_i}$ and keeps $esk_{A_i} = a_i$ as secret to itself. Then, each of A_1, A_2 publishes the public key for the $\mathcal{DEL}$ as $pk = h = g^{a_1+a_2}$, while the secret key for $\mathcal{DEL}$ is $sk = a_1 + a_2$. Note that sk is not known to anyone under the hardness of DLP in $\mathbb{G}$.

$(\mathsf{dE}_{pk}(m)) \longleftarrow \mathcal{DEL}.\mathsf{Enc}(m, pk, \mathsf{par}, r)$. Encryptor encrypts a message $m \in \mathbb{G}$ using public key $pk = h = g^{a_1+a_2}$ and computes the ciphertext tuple $\mathsf{dE}_{pk}(m) = (\alpha, \beta) = (g^r, mh^r)$, where $r \longleftarrow \mathbb{Z}_q$.

$(m \vee \perp) \longleftarrow \mathcal{DEL}.\mathsf{Dec}(\mathsf{dE}_{pk}(m), a_1, a_2)$. Given a ciphertext $\mathsf{dE}_{pk}(m) = (\alpha, \beta) = (g^r, mh^r)$, each participant A_i publishes $\alpha_i = \alpha^{a_i}$ and proves the correctness of the proof $\mathsf{PoK}\{a_i | y_{A_i} = g^{a_i} \wedge \alpha_i = \alpha^{a_i}\}$ to A_j, where $i, j \in \{1, 2\}$ and $i \neq j$. If proofs are valid, then each of A_1, A_2 recovers the message m as $\frac{\beta}{\alpha_1 \alpha_2} = \frac{\beta}{(\alpha)^{(a_1+a_2)}} = \frac{mh^r}{g^{r(a_1+a_2)}} = \frac{mh^r}{h^r} = m$; otherwise outputs $\perp$.

2.3 Verifiable Encryption [7]

We describe below a CCA2-secure verifiable encryption scheme $\mathcal{VE} = (\mathcal{VE}.\mathsf{Setup}, \mathcal{VE}.\mathsf{KGen}, \mathcal{VE}.\mathsf{Enc}, \mathcal{VE}.\mathsf{Dec})$ which is a variant of Cramer-Shoup cryptosystem [11] over prime order group [18].

(ppar) $\longleftarrow$ $\mathcal{VE}$.Setup(1^κ). On input 1^κ, a trusted third party outputs a public parameter ppar $= (\text{par}, \widehat{g}, \mathcal{H})$, where par $= (p, q, g)$, p, q are primes such that q divides $p - 1$ and g, $\widehat{g}$ are generators of the unique cyclic subgroup $\mathbb{G}$ of $\mathbb{Z}_p^*$ of order q, $\mathcal{H} : \{0, 1\}^* \to \mathbb{Z}_q$ is an one-way hash function.

(vpk_U, vsk_U) $\longleftarrow$ $\mathcal{VE}$.KGen(par, $\widehat{g}, U$). User U chooses $u_1, u_2, v_1, v_2, w_1 \hookleftarrow \mathbb{Z}_q$, computes $a = g^{u_1}\widehat{g}^{u_2}, b = g^{v_1}\widehat{g}^{v_2}$, $c = g^{w_1}$, publishes $vpk_U = (a, b, c)$ as his public key and keeps $vsk_U = (u_1, u_2, v_1, v_2, w_1)$ secret to itself.

(v$\mathsf{E}_{vpk_U}(m)$) $\longleftarrow$ $\mathcal{VE}$.Enc($m, vpk_U, \text{ppar}, z, L, \mathcal{H}$). To encrypt a message $m \in \mathbb{G}$ using public key $vpk_U = (a, b, c)$, encryptor picks $z \hookleftarrow \mathbb{Z}_q$, sets $e_1 = g^z, e_2 = \widehat{g}^z, e_3 = c^z m$, uses a label $L \in \{0, 1\}^*$ which is computed using some information that are available to both encryptor and decryptor, computes $\rho = \mathcal{H}(e_1, e_2, e_3, L)$, sets $e_4 = a^z b^{z\rho}$, and computes the ciphertext v$\mathsf{E}_{vpk_U}(m) = (e_1, e_2, e_3, e_4)$.

($m \vee \perp$) $\longleftarrow$ $\mathcal{VE}$.Dec(v$\mathsf{E}_{vpk_U}(m), vsk_U, L, \mathcal{H}$). Decryptor U, on receiving ciphertext v$\mathsf{E}_{vpk_U}(m) = (e_1, e_2, e_3, e_4)$, computes $\rho = \mathcal{H}(e_1, e_2, e_3, L)$ and then verifies $e_1^{u_1} e_2^{u_2}(e_1^{v_1} e_2^{v_2})^\rho = e_4$ using secret key $vsk_U = (u_1, u_2, v_1, v_2, w_1)$. If the verification succeeds, then he recovers the message m by computing $e_3/(e_1)^{w_1} = c^z m/g^{zw_1} = g^{zw_1} m/g^{zw_1} = m$; otherwise outputs $\perp$.

2.4   Bloom Filter [4]

Bloom filter (BF) is a data structure that represents a set $X = \{s_1, s_2, ..., s_v\}$ of v elements by an array of m bits and uses k independent hash functions $H = \{h_1, ..., h_k\}$ with $h_i : \{0, 1\}^* \to \{1, ..., m\}$ for $i = 1, ..., k$ to insert elements or to check the presence of an element. Let $\mathsf{BF}_X \in \{0, 1\}^m$ represent a Bloom filter for the set X and $\mathsf{BF}_X[i]$ represents the bit at the index i in BF_X. We describe below a variant of Bloom filter [4] that performs following three operations:

Initialization: Set 1 to all the bits of an m-bit array, which is an empty Bloom filter with no element in that array.

Add(s): To add an element $s \in X \subseteq \{0, 1\}^*$ into a Bloom filter, s is hashed with the k hash functions $\{h_1, ..., h_k\}$ to get k indices $h_1(s), ..., h_k(s)$. Set 0 to the indices $h_1(s), ..., h_k(s)$ of the Bloom filter. Each $s \in X$ needs to be added to get $\mathsf{BF}_X \in \{0, 1\}^m$.

Check($\hat{s}$): To check if an element $\hat{s}$ belongs to X or not, $\hat{s}$ is hashed with the k hash functions $\{h_1, ..., h_k\}$ to get k indices $h_1(\hat{s}), ..., h_k(\hat{s})$. Now if atleast one of $\mathsf{BF}_X[h_1(\hat{s})], ..., \mathsf{BF}_X[h_k(\hat{s})]$ is 1 then $\hat{s}$ is not in X, otherwise $\hat{s}$ is *probably* in X.

Bloom filter allows false positives whereby an element that has not been inserted in the filter can mistakenly pass the set membership test. This happens when an element $\hat{s}$ does not belong to X but $\mathsf{BF}_X[h_i(\hat{s})] = 0$ for all $i = 1, ..., k$. On the contrary, Bloom filter never yields a false negative i.e., an element that has been inserted in the filter will always pass the test. This is because if $\hat{s}$ belongs to X, then each of $\mathsf{BF}_X[h_1(\hat{s})], ..., \mathsf{BF}_X[h_k(\hat{s})]$ is 0.

Theorem 1 [19]. *Given the number v of elements to be added and a desired maximum false positive rate $\frac{1}{2^k}$, the optimal size m of the Bloom filter is $m = \frac{vk}{\ln 2}$.*

2.5   Zero-Knowledge Proof of Knowledge [2]

Zero-Knowledge proof [2] is a two-party protocol, where prover ($\mathcal{P}$) wants to convince the verifier ($\mathcal{V}$) about the truth of the claim that he knows some secret values, and the verifier wants to check that the claim is true. A zero-knowledge proof protocol π for relation R should satisfy the following three properties:

(a) *Completeness.* Completeness, also known as *proof of knowledge*, means that an honest prover convinces the verifier that he knows the secret values.
(b) *Soundness.* Soundness indicates that a cheating prover, who does not know the actual secret values, will succeed to convince the verifier with negligible probability. In other words, if the success-probability of the prover is non-negligible, then there exists a *knowledge extractor* that can extract the secret values.
(c) *Zero-knowledge.* Zero-knowledge ensures that the verifier does not obtain any useful information about the secret values of the prover.

Zero-Knowledge Proof for Discrete Logarithm [9]: We follow the notations introduced by [8] for the various zero-knowledge proofs of knowledge of discrete logarithms and proofs of validity of statements about discrete logarithms. We describe below a general construction of interactive zero-knowledge proofs of knowledge, denoted by $\pi = \mathsf{PoK}\{(\alpha_1, ..., \alpha_l) | \bigwedge_{i=1}^{M} X_i = f_i(\alpha_1, ..., \alpha_l)\}$, where the prover $\mathcal{P}$ wants to prove the knowledge of $(\alpha_1, ..., \alpha_l)$ to the verifier $\mathcal{V}$ by sending the commitments to $X_i = f_i(\alpha_1, ..., \alpha_l), i = 1, ..., M$ such that extracting $(\alpha_1, ..., \alpha_l)$ from $X_1, ..., X_M$ is infeasible for anyone. For each $i = 1, ..., M$, f_i is publicly computable linear function from $\mathcal{X}^l$ to $\mathcal{Y}$, where $\mathcal{X}$ is *additive* set and $\mathcal{Y}$ is *multiplicative* set. This proof system satisfies soundness property under the hardness of DDH assumption. For verification process see [16].

Lemma 1. *If Exp is the total number of exponentiations computed and GE is the total number of group elements sent for verification of the proof system π, then: (a) $Exp = M + 2\sum_{i=1}^{M}$ (number of exponentiations to compute X_i), and (b) $GE = M + l + 1$.*

Zero-Knowledge Argument for Shuffle [21]: We briefly discuss the zero-knowledge argument for shuffle of [21] which we use in our mPSI-CA. Let p, q be two primes such that q divide $p - 1$, $\mathbb{G}$ be a subgroup of $\mathbb{Z}_p^*$ of order q, $g_0(\neq 1)$ be an element of $\mathbb{G}$, $x \leftarrow \mathbb{Z}_q$ be a private key and $m_0 = g_0^x \bmod p$ be a public key used for re-encryption in shuffling. Let $\{\tau_u\}_{u=-4}^{v}$ be $v + 5$ elements of $\mathbb{G}$ that are uniformly and randomly generated so that neither $\mathcal{P}$ nor $\mathcal{V}$ can generate non-trivial integers $a, \{a_u\}_{u=-4}^{v}$ satisfying $g_0^a \prod_{u=-4}^{v} \tau_u^{a_u} \equiv 1 \bmod p$ with non-negligible probability.

The prover $\mathcal{P}$ chooses $\{A_{0i} \leftarrow \mathbb{Z}_q\}_{i=1}^{v}$ and a permutation matrix $(A_{ji})_{j,i=1,...,v}$ of order $v \times v$ corresponding to a permutation $\phi \in \Sigma_v$, where Σ_v denotes the set of all possible permutations over the set $\{1, ..., v\}$ and the permutation matrix $(A_{ji})_{j,i=1,...,v}$ is defined as $A_{ji} = 1 \bmod q$ if $\phi(j) = i, 0$ otherwise.

The prover $\mathcal{P}$ shuffles v ElGamal ciphertexts $\{(g_i, m_i)\}_{i=1}^{v}$, yielding ciphertexts $\{(g_i', m_i')\}_{i=1}^{v}$ as

$$(g_i', m_i') = \left(\prod_{u=0}^{v} g_u^{A_{ui}}, \prod_{u=0}^{v} m_u^{A_{ui}} \right) = (g_0^{A_{0i}} g_{\phi^{-1}(i)}, m_0^{A_{0i}} m_{\phi^{-1}(i)}) \bmod p. \quad (1)$$

The zero-knowledge argument of [21] for the correctness of a shuffle is denoted by $\widehat{\pi} = \mathsf{PoKArg}\{(\phi \in \Sigma_v, A_{01}, ..., A_{0v} \in \mathbb{Z}_q) | \{(g_i', m_i') = (g_0^{A_{0i}} g_{\phi^{-1}(i)}, m_0^{A_{0i}} m_{\phi^{-1}(i)})\}_{i=1}^{v}\}$. The prover $\mathcal{P}$ wants to prove the knowledge of the permutation $\phi \in \Sigma_v$ and randomness $\{A_{0i} \in \mathbb{Z}_q\}_{i=1}^{v}$ to the verifier $\mathcal{V}$ such that Eq. 1 holds for each $i = 1, ..., v$. Note that decryption of the ciphertexts (g_i', m_i') and $(g_{\phi^{-1}(i)}, m_{\phi^{-1}(i)})$ give same message. This proof system satisfies soundness property under the hardness of DDH assumption. For verification process see [21].

Lemma 2. *If Exp is the total number of exponentiations computed and GE is the total number of group elements sent for verification of the proof system represented by $\widehat{\pi}$, then (a) $Exp = 15v + 22$, (b) $GE = 4v + 16$. In particular, commitment generation requires $9v + 12$ Exp and verification process requires $6v + 10$ Exp.*

For the distributed ElGamal encryption $\mathcal{DEL}$ presented in the Sect. 2.2, the zero-knowledge argument for shuffle will be of the form $\mathsf{PoKArg}\{(\phi \in \Sigma_v, \rho_1, ..., \rho_v \in \mathbb{Z}_q) | \{C_i' = C_{\phi^{-1}(i)} \mathcal{DEL}.\mathsf{Enc}(g^0, pk, \mathsf{par}, \rho_i)\}_{i=1}^{v}\}$, where ciphertexts $\{C_i = (g_i, m_i)\}_{i=1}^{v}$ are shuffled to $\{C_i' = (g_i', m_i')\}_{i=1}^{v}$.

3   Protocol

Our mPSI-CA protocol consists of three algorithms: (I) Setup, (II) procedure mPSI-CA and (III) procedure Dispute Resolution. It involves two parties A and B together with an arbiter Ar. In the Setup phase, a trusted third party generates the global parameter and each of parties A, B and Ar generate their public/secret key pair. The procedure mPSI-CA is executed between the parties A and B with respective input sets $X = \{x_1, ..., x_v\} \subset \{0,1\}^*$ and $Y = \{y_1, ..., y_w\} \subset \{0,1\}^*$ to compute $|X \cap Y|$, the cardinality of the set intersection. A high level overview of this process is given in Fig. 2. Finally, in the procedure Dispute Resolution, the arbiter Ar takes part only when a corrupted player prematurely aborts the procedure mPSI-CA and resolves the dispute without knowing the private information of the parties A and B.

(I) **Setup.** The Setup algorithm is represented by Fig. 1.
Note that a session identity sid is agreed by the parties A, B and Ar before involving in the procedure mPSI-CA.

(II) **procedure mPSI-CA.** This is a four round procedure executed between the parties A and B. We describe the steps below.

Setup(1^κ) – We use the distributed ElGamal encryption $\mathcal{DEL}$ and the verifiable encryption $\mathcal{VE}$ over prime order group as described in the sections 2.2 and 2.3.

- A trusted third party generates $\mathsf{ppar} = (\mathsf{par}, \hat{g}, \mathcal{H}) \leftarrow \mathcal{VE}.\mathsf{Setup}(1^\kappa)$, where $\mathsf{par} = (p, q, g)$, selects Bloom filter parameters $\{m, k, H\}$, chooses $\tau_i, \iota_j \hookleftarrow \mathbb{G}$ for $i = -4, ..., m; j = -4, ..., w$, where $\mathbb{G} = <g>$ is the cyclic subgroup of $\mathbb{Z}_p^*$ of order q. Finally, the trusted third party publishes all these as global parameter gpar i.e., $\mathsf{gpar} = (\mathsf{ppar}, m, k, H, \{\tau_i\}_{i=-4}^m, \{\iota_j\}_{j=-4}^w)$. Note that $\{\tau_i\}_{i=-4}^m, \{\iota_j\}_{j=-4}^w$ are to be used in zero-knowledge arguments for shuffle of the procedure mPSI-CA.
- Each of the parties A, B generates
$$(epk_A, esk_A) \leftarrow \mathcal{DEL}.\mathsf{KGen}(\mathsf{par}), esk_A = a_1 \hookleftarrow \mathbb{Z}_q, epk_A = y_A = g^{a_1},$$
$$(epk_B, esk_B) \leftarrow \mathcal{DEL}.\mathsf{KGen}(\mathsf{par}), esk_B = a_2 \hookleftarrow \mathbb{Z}_q, epk_B = y_B = g^{a_2}.$$
They publish their respective public keys y_A, y_B through the trusted third party who acts as the certifying authority in this case. Parties A, and B keeps the respective secret keys esk_A, esk_B secret to themselves.

- The off-line arbiter Ar generates
$$(vpk_{Ar} = (a, b, c), vsk_{Ar} = (u_1, u_2, v_1, v_2, w_1)) \leftarrow \mathcal{VE}.\mathsf{KGen}(\mathsf{par}, \hat{g}),$$
where $u_1, u_2, v_1, v_2, w_1 \hookleftarrow \mathbb{Z}_q$ and $a = g^{u_1}\hat{g}^{u_2}, b = g^{v_1}\hat{g}^{v_2}, c = g^{w_1}$, and then publishes the public key vpk_{Ar} through the trusted third party who works as the certifying authority in this case also.
- Let $pk = h = (epk_A)(epk_B) = g^{a_1 + a_2}$ and $sk = a_1 + a_2$. Then (pk, sk) pair serves as the public-secret key pair for $\mathcal{DEL}$. Note that the secret key $sk = a_1 + a_2$ for $\mathcal{DEL}$ is not known to anyone. However, the public key pk for $\mathcal{DEL}$ is publicly computable from epk_A and epk_B.

Fig. 1. Setup algorithm of our mPSI-CA

Step 1. The party A proceeds as follows:
  (i) constructs a Bloom filer BF_X of his private set X following the procedure defined in Sect. 2.4; using k independent hash functions $\{h_1, ..., h_k\}$, where $h_i : \{0, 1\}^* \to \{1, ..., m\}$ for $i = 1, ..., k$;
  (ii) for $i = 1, ..., m$, encrypts each of $g^{b_i} = g^{\mathsf{BF}_X[i]}$ using the public key pk to get $C_i = (c_i, d_i) \leftarrow \mathcal{DEL}.\mathsf{Enc}(g^{b_i}, pk, \mathsf{par}, r_{b_i})$, where $c_i = g^{r_{b_i}}, d_i = g^{b_i}h^{r_{b_i}}$;
  (iii) generates a proof $\pi_1 = \mathsf{PoK}\{r_{b_1}, ..., r_{b_m} | \bigwedge_{i=1}^m (c_i = g^{r_{b_i}})\}$;
  (iv) sends $R_1 = \langle \{C_i\}_{i=1}^m, \pi_1 \rangle$ to the party B.
Step 2. On receiving $R_1 = \langle \{C_i\}_{i=1}^m, \pi_1 \rangle$ from A, the party B verifies the validity of the proof π_1 following the zero-knowledge proof for discrete logarithm (DL) described in Sect. 2.5. If the verification fails then B aborts. Otherwise, does the following:
  (i) chooses a random permutation ϕ from the set Σ_m of all possible permutations over the set $\{1, ..., m\}$, selects $\alpha_1, ..., \alpha_m \hookleftarrow \mathbb{Z}_q$ and computes
$$\overline{C}_i = C_{\phi^{-1}(i)}\mathcal{DEL}.\mathsf{Enc}(g^0, pk, \mathsf{par}, \alpha_i) = (c_{\phi^{-1}(i)}, d_{\phi^{-1}(i)})(g^{\alpha_i}, g^0 h^{\alpha_i}) = (c_i', d_i'),$$
  where $c_i' = c_{\phi^{-1}(i)}g^{\alpha_i}, d_i' = d_{\phi^{-1}(i)}h^{\alpha_i}$ for $i = 1, ..., m$;

(ii) for each $j = 1, ..., w$, constructs an m-bit string s_j (corresponding to $y_j \in Y$, B's input set) whose i-th bit $s_j^{(i)}$ is defined as follows

$$s_j^{(i)} = \begin{cases} 1, & \text{if } i \in \{\phi(h_1(y_j)), ..., \phi(h_k(y_j))\} \\ 0, & \text{elsewhere;} \end{cases}$$

(iii) chooses $k_1, ..., k_w \hookleftarrow \mathbb{Z}_q$ and uses $\{s_1, ..., s_w\}$ to compute for $j = 1, ..., w$

$$\nu_j = \prod_{i=1}^{m} (\overline{C}_i)^{s_j^{(i)}} = (\lambda_j, \delta_j), \text{ where } \lambda_j = \prod_{i=1}^{m} (c_i')^{s_j^{(i)}}, \delta_j = \prod_{i=1}^{m} (d_i')^{s_j^{(i)}},$$

$$\overline{y}_j = (\nu_j)^r = (\overline{c}_j, \overline{d}_j), \text{ where } \overline{c}_j = (\lambda_j)^{k_j}, \overline{d}_j = (\delta_j)^{k_j};$$

(iv) generates a label $L \in \{0,1\}^*$ using a session identity sid which has been agreed by all parities beforehand and the hash of past communication;

(v) selects $r_1, ..., r_w, z_1, ..., z_w \hookleftarrow \mathbb{Z}_q$, for $j = 1, ..., w$, computes $T_j = (\overline{c}_j)^{a_2} g^{r_j}$ and $\mathsf{vE}_{vpk_{Ar}}(g^{r_j}) = (t_{1j}, t_{2j}, t_{3j}, t_{4j}) \leftarrow \mathcal{VE}.\mathsf{Enc}(g^{r_j}, vpk_{Ar}, \mathsf{ppar}, z_j, L, \mathcal{H})$, where $t_{1j} = g^{z_j}, t_{2j} = (\widehat{g})^{z_j}, t_{3j} = c^{z_j} g^{r_j}, t_{4j} = a^{z_j} b^{z_j \rho_j}, \rho_j = \mathcal{H}(t_{1j}, t_{2j}, t_{3j}, L)$ and $vpk_{Ar} = (a, b, c)$ is the public key of the arbiter Ar;

(vi) generates the proofs $\pi_2, \widehat{\pi}_2$ as

$$\pi_2 = \mathsf{PoK}\{(a_2, r_1, ..., r_w, z_1, ..., z_w, k_1, ..., k_w) | (y_B = g^{a_2}) \bigwedge_{j=1}^{w} (t_{1j} = g^{z_j})(t_{2j} = (\widehat{g})^{z_j})$$

$$\bigwedge_{j=1}^{w} (t_{3j} = c^{z_j} g^{r_j})(t_{4j} = a^{z_j} b^{z_j \rho_j})(\overline{c}_j = (\lambda_j)^{k_j})(\overline{d}_j = (\delta_j)^{k_j})(T_j = (\overline{c}_j)^{a_2} g^{r_j})\},$$

$$\widehat{\pi}_2 = \mathsf{PoKArg}\{(\phi \in \Sigma_m, \alpha_1, ..., \alpha_m) | \{\overline{C}_i = C_{\phi^{-1}(i)} \mathcal{DEL}.\mathsf{Enc}(g^0, pk, \mathsf{par}, \alpha_i)\}_{i=1}^{m}\};$$

(v) sends $R_2 = \langle \{\overline{C}_i\}_{i=1}^{m}, \{\overline{y}_j, s_j, T_j, \mathsf{vE}_{vpk_{Ar}}(g^{r_j})\}_{j=1}^{w}, \pi_2, \widehat{\pi}_2 \rangle$ to A.

Note that the members of the set $\{g^{r_1}, ..., g^{r_w}\}$ are encrypted under the public key of the arbiter Ar in order to make sure that if B aborts prematurely then A will get the correct output by involving in the procedure Dispute Resolution.

Step 3. The party A, on receiving $R_2 = \langle \{\overline{C}_i\}_{i=1}^{m}, \{\overline{y}_j, s_j, T_j, \mathsf{vE}_{vpk_{Ar}}(g^{r_j})\}_{j=1}^{w},$

$\pi_2, \widehat{\pi}_2 \rangle$ from B, computes $\nu_j = \prod_{i=1}^{m} (\overline{C}_i)^{s_j^{(i)}} = (\lambda_j, \delta_j)$ for $j = 1, ..., w$. The party A then checks the validity of the proofs $\pi_2, \widehat{\pi}_2$ following the zero-knowledge proof for discrete logarithm and zero-knowledge proof of argument for shuffle as described in Sect. 2.5, and aborts if verification of atleast one of $\pi_2, \widehat{\pi}_2$ fails; otherwise, executes the following steps:

(i) chooses a random permutation $\psi \in \Sigma_w$, where Σ_w is the set of all possible permutations over the set $\{1, ..., w\}$, selects $\beta_1, ..., \beta_w \hookleftarrow \mathbb{Z}_q$ and computes $\mu_j = \nu_{\psi^{-1}(j)} \mathcal{DEL}.\mathsf{Enc}(g^0, pk, \mathsf{par}, \beta_j) = (\lambda_{\psi^{-1}(j)}, \delta_{\psi^{-1}(j)})(g^{\beta_j}, g^0 h^{\beta_j}) = (e_j, f_j)$ and $\overline{e}_j = (e_j)^{a_1}$, where $e_j = \lambda_{\psi^{-1}(j)} g^{\beta_j}, f_j = \delta_{\psi^{-1}(j)} h^{\beta_j}$ for each $j = 1, ..., w$;

(ii) generates the proofs $\pi_3 = \mathsf{PoK}\{(a_1) | (y_A = g^{a_1}) \bigwedge_{j=1}^{w} (\overline{e}_j = (e_j)^{a_1})\}$,

$\widehat{\pi}_3 = \mathsf{PoKArg}\{(\psi \in \Sigma_w, \beta_1, ..., \beta_w) | \{\mu_j = \nu_{\phi^{-1}(j)} \mathcal{DEL}.\mathsf{Enc}(g^0, pk,$
$\mathsf{par}, \beta_j)\}_{j=1}^{w}\};$

(iii) sends $R_3 = \langle \{\mu_j, (\overline{e}_j)\}_{j=1}^w, \pi_3, \widehat{\pi}_3 \rangle$ to B.

Step 4. On receiving $R_3 = \langle \{\mu_j, (\overline{e}_j)\}_{j=1}^w, \pi_3, \widehat{\pi}_3 \rangle$ from A, party B verifies the correctness of the proofs $\pi_3, \widehat{\pi}_3$. If atleast one of $\pi_3, \widehat{\pi}_3$ does not valid then B aborts, else executes the following steps

(i) sets $\mathsf{card} = 0$ and for $j = 1, ..., w$,

    (a) extracts $e_j, f_j, \overline{e}_j = (e_j)^{a_1}$ from $R_3 = \langle \{\mu_j = (e_j, f_j), (\overline{e}_j)\}_{j=1}^w, \pi_3, \widehat{\pi}_3 \rangle$, received from A in *Step* 3,

    (b) computes $(e_j)^{a_2}$ using secret key $esk_B = a_2$ and utilizes $(e_j)^{a_2}$ to compute $l_j = \frac{f_j}{(\overline{e}_j)(e_j)^{a_2}} = \frac{f_j}{(e_j)^{a_1}(e_j)^{a_2}}$,

    (c) increases card by 1 i.e., sets $\mathsf{card} = \mathsf{card} + 1$ if $l_j = 1$;

(ii) generates a zero-knowledge proof π_4 as

$$\pi_4 = \mathsf{PoK}\big\{(z_1, ..., z_w)| \wedge_{j=1}^w (t_{1j} = g^{z_j})(t_{2j} = \widehat{g}^{z_j})(t_{3j} = c^{z_j}g^{r_j})(t_{4j} = a^{z_j}b^{z_j\rho_j})\big\};$$

(iii) sends $R_4 = \langle \{g^{r_j}\}_{j=1}^w, \pi_4 \rangle$ to A and outputs card as the cardinality of $X \cap Y$. Note that B constructs the proof π_4 to prove that $g^{r_j} \in R_4$ was encrypted in *Step* 2 to generate $\mathsf{vE}_{vpk_{Ar}}(g^{r_j})$ for $j = 1, ..., w$ using Ar's public key.

Step 5. On receiving $R_4 = \langle \{g^{r_j}\}_{j=1}^w, \pi_4 \rangle$ from B, party A verifies the validity of the proof π_4. If the proof is valid then A proceeds as follows

(i) sets $\mathsf{card} = 0$ and for $j = 1, .., w$,

    (a) extracts $T_j, \overline{c}_j, \overline{d}_j$ from $R_2 = \langle \{\overline{C}_i\}_{i=1}^m, \{\overline{y}_j = (\overline{c}_j, \overline{d}_j), s_j, T_j, \mathsf{vE}_{vpk_{Ar}}(g^{r_j})\}_{j=1}^w, \pi_2, \widehat{\pi}_2 \rangle$, received from B in *Step* 2,

    (b) computes $\frac{T_j}{g^{r_j}} = \frac{(\overline{c}_j)^{a_2}g^{r_j}}{g^{r_j}} = (\overline{c}_j)^{a_2}$ and utilizes $(\overline{c}_j)^{a_2}$ to compute $l'_j = \frac{\overline{d}_j}{(\overline{c}_j)^{a_1}(\overline{c}_j)^{a_2}}$, where $esk_A = a_1$ is A's secret key,

    (c) increases card by 1 i.e., sets $\mathsf{card} = \mathsf{card} + 1$ if $l'_j = 1$;

(ii) finally, outputs card as the cardinality of $X \cap Y$.

If the verification of the proof π_4 does not succeed or B does not send $\{g^{r_1}, ..., g^{r_w}\}$ to A (i.e., B prematurely aborts) then A sends a dispute resolution request to the arbiter Ar.

(III) procedure Dispute Resolution. On receiving a dispute resolution request from A, the arbiter Ar who is an off-line semi-trusted third party interacts with A and B as follows:

Step 1. Party A sends all the messages sent and received in *Step* 1-2 of the mPSI-CA protocol to the arbiter Ar. As the session ID sid is known to Ar, on receiving the messages from A, the arbiter Ar computes the label L and verifies the consistency between messages and the label L. If the verification fails or if the transcript ends before the end of *Step* 2 of the procedure mPSI-CA then Ar aborts so that neither party gets any advantage. Otherwise, Ar continues with the following steps.

Step 2. As in *Step* 3 of the procedure mPSI-CA, A sends $R_3 = \langle \{\mu_j, (\overline{e}_j)\}_{j=1}^w, \pi_3, \widehat{\pi}_3 \rangle$ to Ar.

Step 3. On receiving $R_3 = \langle \{\mu_j, (\overline{e}_j)\}_{j=1}^w, \pi_3, \widehat{\pi}_3 \rangle$ from B, the arbiter Ar checks the validity of the proofs $\pi_3, \widehat{\pi}_3$. If atleast one the proofs does not valid then Ar aborts so that neither party gets any advantage. Otherwise, Ar decrypts each member of $\{\text{vE}_{vpk_{Ar}}(g^{r_1}), ..., \text{vE}_{vpk_{Ar}}(g^{r_w})\}$ using its secret key vsk_{Ar} and sends $\{g^{r_j}\}_{j=1}^w$ to A, thereby A can evaluate $|X \cap Y|$ using the similar technique as described in *Step* 5 of the procedure mPSI-CA. On the other hand, Ar forwards $\langle \{\mu_j, (\overline{e}_j)\}_{j=1}^w \rangle$ to B who in turn can execute $|X \cap Y|$ using the similar technique as explained in *Step* 4 of the procedure mPSI-CA.

4   Security

We present two cases to prove the security of mPSI-CA. In Case I, the adversary corrupts two of the three parties while in Case II, when the adversary corrupts only one of the three parties.

Theorem 2. *Suppose the encryption schemes $\mathcal{DEL}$ and $\mathcal{VE}$ are semantically secure, the associated proof protocols are zero knowledge proofs and zero-knowledge argument of proofs for shuffle. Then our proposed mPSI-CA presented in Sect. 3 is a secure computation protocol in ROM for the functionality $\mathcal{F}_{\text{mPSI}-CA} : ((X, |Y|), (Y, |X|)) \rightarrow (|X \cap Y|, |X \cap Y|)$ in the security model described in Sect. 2.1 except with negligible probability ϵ, where ϵ is the false positive rate of the Bloom filter BF_X.*

Proof. Let $\mathcal{C}$ be the real world adversary who breaks the security of our mPSI-CA protocol executed between two parties A and B with their respective private input sets X and Y; and an arbiter Ar. Suppose there be an incorruptible trusted party T, parties $\overline{A}, \overline{B}, \overline{Ar}$ and simulator $\mathcal{SIM}$ in the ideal process. In the real world, a trusted party generates the global parameter $\text{gpar} = (\text{ppar}, m, k, H, \{\tau_i\}_{i=-4}^m, \{\iota_j\}_{j=-4}^w)$ and certifies the public keys epk_A, epk_B, vpk_{Ar} of A, B, Ar respectively. On the other hand, simulator $\mathcal{SIM}$ performs these works in the ideal process. Let us denote $\text{REAL}_{\text{mPSI}-CA,\mathcal{C}}(X, Y)$ as the joint output of $A, B, Ar, \mathcal{C}$ in the real world and $\text{IDEAL}_{\mathcal{F}_{\text{mPSI}-CA},\mathcal{SIM}}(X, Y)$ as the joint output of $\overline{A}, \overline{B}, \overline{Ar}, \mathcal{SIM}$ in the ideal process.

Case I (When the adversary $\mathcal{C}$ corrupts two parties). There are three subcases – either (I) A and Ar are corrupted or (II) b and Ar are corrupted or (III) A and B are corrupted. We analyze each of these subcases below.

Subcase I (A and Ar are corrupted). Let us consider $\mathcal{Z}$ as a distinguisher to distinguish the real world from the ideal world. The distinguisher $\mathcal{Z}$ controls $\mathcal{C}$, feeds the input of the honest party B and observes B's output. We present a sequence of games $\mathbf{G}_0, ..., \mathbf{G}_4$ to prove indistinguishability of $\mathcal{Z}$'s views in the real world and in the ideal world. The view of the real world adversary $\mathcal{C}$ together with B's output constitutes $\mathcal{Z}$'s view in the real world. On the other hand, the view of the ideal world simulator $\mathcal{SIM}$ along with output of $\overline{B}$ forms $\mathcal{Z}$'s view in the ideal world. Here view of an entity means the transcripts available to it.

Common input: gpar, epk_A, epk_B, $pk = epk_A \cdot epk_B$, vpk_{Ar}

A's private input:
$X = \{x_1, ..., x_v\}, esk_A = a_1$

B's private input:
$Y = \{y_1, ..., y_w\}, esk_B = a_2$

constructs $\mathsf{BF}_X \in \{0,1\}^m$
$r_{b_1}, ..., r_{b_m} \leftarrowtail \mathbb{Z}_q$
for $i = 1, ..., m$,
  $C_i = (c_i, d_i) \leftarrow \mathcal{DEL}.\mathsf{Enc}(g^{b_i}, pk, \mathsf{par}, r_{b_i})$
$R_1 = \langle \{C_i\}_{i=1}^m, \pi_1 \rangle$

$\xrightarrow{\quad R_1 \quad}$ $\phi \leftarrowtail \Sigma_m$, $\alpha_1, ..., \alpha_m, k_1, ..., k_w \leftarrowtail \mathbb{Z}_q$
$r_1, ..., r_w, z_1, ..., z_w \leftarrowtail \mathbb{Z}_q$, for $i = 1, ..., m$,
$\overline{C}_i = C_{\phi^{-1}(i)} \mathcal{DEL}.\mathsf{Enc}(g^0, pk, \mathsf{par}, \alpha_i)$
for $j = 1, ..., w$, constructs m-bit string s_j as
$$s_j^{(i)} = \begin{cases} 1, & \text{if } i \in \{\phi(h_1(y_j)), ..., \phi(h_k(y_j))\} \\ 0, & \text{elsewhere;} \end{cases}$$
for $j = 1, ..., w$,
$\nu_j = \prod_{i=1}^m (\overline{C}_i)^{s_j^{(i)}} = (\lambda_j, \delta_j)$
$\overline{y}_j = (\nu_j)^{k_j} = (\overline{c}_j, \overline{d}_j), T_j = (\overline{c}_j)^{a_2} g^{r_j}$
$\mathsf{vE}_{vpk_{Ar}}(g^{r_j}) = (t_{1j}, t_{2j}, t_{3j}, t_{4j})$
$\leftarrow \mathcal{VE}.\mathsf{Enc}(g^{r_j}, vpk_{Ar}, \mathsf{ppar}, z_j, L, \mathcal{H})$

$\xleftarrow{\quad R_2 \quad}$ $R_2 = \langle \{\overline{C}_i\}_{i=1}^m, \{\overline{y}_j, s_j, T_j, \mathsf{vE}_{vpk_{Ar}}(g^{r_j})\}_{j=1}^w,$
$\pi_2, \widehat{\pi}_2 \rangle$

$\psi \in \Sigma_w, \beta_1, ..., \beta_w \leftarrowtail \mathbb{Z}_q$
for $j = 1, ..., w$,
$\nu_j = \prod_{i=1}^m (\overline{C}_i)^{s_j^{(i)}} = (\lambda_j, \delta_j)$
$\mu_j = (e_j, f_j)$
$= \nu_{\psi^{-1}(j)} \mathcal{DEL}.\mathsf{Enc}(g^0, pk, \mathsf{par}, \beta_j)$
$\overline{e}_j = (e_j)^{a_1}$
$R_3 = \langle \{\mu_j, (\overline{e}_j)\}_{j=1}^w, \pi_3, \widehat{\pi}_3 \rangle$

$\xrightarrow{\quad R_3 \quad}$ sets $\mathsf{card} = 0$ and for $j = 1, ..., w$,
$l_j = \frac{f_j}{(\overline{e}_j)(e_j)^{a_2}} = \frac{f_j}{(e_j)^{a_1}(e_j)^{a_2}}$
if $l_j = 1$, sets $\mathsf{card} = \mathsf{card} + 1$
outputs card as $|X \cap Y|$

$\xleftarrow{\quad R_4 \quad}$ $R_4 = \langle \{g^{r_j}\}_{j=1}^w, \pi_4 \rangle$

sets $\mathsf{card} = 0$ and for $j = 1, ..., w$,
$\frac{T_j}{g^{r_j}} = (\overline{c}_j)^{a_2}, l_j' = \frac{\overline{d}_j}{(\overline{c}_j)^{a_1}(\overline{c}_j)^{a_2}}$
if $l_j' = 1$ sets $\mathsf{card} = \mathsf{card} + 1$
outputs card as $|X \cap Y|$

Fig. 2. Communication flow of procedure mPSI-CA

We argue that $\mathcal{Z}$'s views in any two neighbouring game are indistinguishable. Let S_i be the simulator in $\mathbf{G}_i$ that simulates the honest party B and $\mathcal{Z}$ distinguishes the view of $\mathbf{G}_i$ from the view of the real protocol with the probability $Pr[\mathbf{G}_i]$ for $i = 0, ..., 4$.

$\mathbf{G}_0$: It corresponds to the real protocol, where the simulator S_0 has the full knowledge of B and interacts with $\mathcal{C}$. Hence, $Pr[\mathsf{REAL}_{\mathsf{mPSI}-CA,\mathcal{C}}(X, Y)] = Pr[\mathbf{G}_0]$.

$\mathbf{G}_1$: This game is same as $\mathbf{G}_0$ except the following:

(a) The simulator S_1 maintains a list X' and records all queries the adversary made to the random oracles, such as $h_1, ..., h_k$. Without loss of generality, we assume the adversary makes no more than $poly(\kappa)$ queries and stops at some point, where κ is security parameter.

(b) If the proof π_1 is valid then the simulator S_1 runs the extractor algorithm for π_1 with $\mathcal{C}$ to extract the exponents $\{r_{b_1}, ..., r_{b_m}\}$. These exponents r_{b_i} for $i = 1, ..., m$ are utilized by the simulator S_1 to compute $g^{b_i} = \frac{d_i}{h^{r_{b_i}}}$, where $d_i = g^{b_i} h^{r_{b_i}}$ is extracted from $C_i = (c_i, d_i)$ in the first round message $R_1 = \langle \{C_i\}_{i=1}^m, \pi_1 \rangle$ sent by the party A (i.e., $\mathcal{C}$) to B (i.e., S_1) and $h = epk_A \cdot epk_B = g^{a_1 + a_2}$. Note that $C_i = (c_i, d_i)$ is the encryption of $\mathsf{BF}_X[i]$ using distributed ElGamal encryption scheme under pk using randomness r_{b_i}. The simulator S_1 then extracts Bloom filter $\mathsf{BF}_X = \{b_1, ..., b_m\}$ for the set X by setting $\mathsf{BF}_X[i] = 0$ if $g^{b_i} = 1, 1$ otherwise for $i = 1, ..., m$.

(c) The simulator S_1 runs the check step of Bloom filter presented in Sect. 2.4 for membership check of each element in X' against BF_X. If the check is valid then the corresponding element is put in a set X''. Note that the set X'' is identical to the set X except with negligible probability ϵ.

The views of $\mathcal{Z}$ are indistinguishable in $\mathbf{G}_0$ and $\mathbf{G}_1$ by the simulation soundness property of π_1. Therefore, $|Pr[\mathbf{G}_1] - Pr[\mathbf{G}_0]| \leq \epsilon_1(\kappa)$, a negligible function.

$\mathbf{G}_2$: Note that in this game the simulator S_2 has the knowledge of A's input set $X = \{x_1, ..., x_v\}$ extracted as in $\mathbf{G}_1$, B's input set $Y = \{y_1, ..., y_w\}$ and secret key $esk_B = a_2$ of B. $\mathbf{G}_2$ is exactly same as $\mathbf{G}_1$ except the following:

(a) If the verifications of both the proofs $\pi_3, \widehat{\pi}_3$ succeed then S_2 outputs $|X \cap Y|$ as the final output of B using Y and the above extracted set X.

(b) If the verification of atleast one of the proofs $\pi_3, \widehat{\pi}_3$ fails or $\mathcal{C}$ aborts prematurely in the procedure mPSI-CA, then the following cases arise:
 - if $\mathcal{C}$ sends $\{\mu_j = (e_j, f_j), \overline{e}_j\}_{j=1}^w$ to S_2 in the procedure Dispute Resolution, then S_2 first sets $\mathsf{card} = 0$. For $j = 1, ..., w$, the simulator S_2 computes $(e_j)^{a_2}$ and utilizes it to compute $l_j = \frac{f_j}{(\overline{e}_j)(e_j)^{a_2}}$. The simulator S_2 increases card by 1 if $l_j = 1$, for $j = 1, ..., w$ and outputs card as the final output of B.
 - if $\mathcal{C}$ aborts in the procedure Dispute Resolution then S_2 outputs $\perp$ as the final output of B.

Clearly, $\mathcal{Z}$'s views in $\mathbf{G}_2$ and $\mathbf{G}_3$ are indistinguishable. Hence,

$$|Pr[\mathbf{G}_2] - Pr[\mathbf{G}_1]| \leq \epsilon_2(\kappa),$$ where $\epsilon_2(\kappa)$ is a negligible function.

$\mathbf{G}_3$: This game is identical to $\mathbf{G}_2$ except that S_3 simulating the honest party B does the following after extracting $X = \{x_1, ..., x_v\}$ as in $\mathbf{G}_1$:

(a) Computes $|X \cap Y|$ using the input set $Y = \{y_1, ..., y_w\}$ of B and constructs a set $Y' = \{y'_1, ..., y'_w\}$ by including $|X \cap Y|$ many random elements of X together with $w - |X \cap Y|$ many random elements chosen from $\{0, 1\}^* \setminus X$.

(b) Chooses a random permutation $\phi \in \Sigma_m$ over the set $\{1, ..., m\}$, selects $\alpha_1, ..., \alpha_m \hookleftarrow \mathbb{Z}_q$ and computes for each $i = 1, ..., m$,

$$\overline{C}_i = C_{\phi^{-1}(i)} \mathcal{DEL}.\mathsf{Enc}(g^0, pk, \mathsf{par}, \alpha_i) = (c_{\phi^{-1}(i)}, d_{\phi^{-1}(i)})(g^{\alpha_i}, g^0 h^{\alpha_i}) = (c'_i, d'_i),$$

where $c'_i = c_{\phi^{-1}(i)} g^{\alpha_i}, d'_i = d_{\phi^{-1}(i)} h^{\alpha_i}$.

(c) For each $j = 1, ..., w$, constructs an m-bit string s_j (corresponding to y'_j) whose i-th bit $s_j^{(i)}$ is defined as $s_j^{(i)} = \begin{cases} 1, & \text{if } i \in \{\phi(h_1(y'_j)), ..., \phi(h_k(y'_j))\} \\ 0, & \text{otherwise.} \end{cases}$

(d) Selects $k_j \hookleftarrow \mathbb{Z}_q$, computes $\nu_j = \prod_{i=1}^m (\overline{C}_i)^{s_j^{(i)}} = (\lambda_j, \delta_j)$ and $\overline{y}_j = (\overline{c}_j, \overline{d}_j)$, where $\overline{c}_j = (\lambda_j)^{k_j}, \overline{d}_j = (\delta_j)^{k_j}$ for $j = 1, ..., w$.

(e) Generates a label $L \in \{0, 1\}^*$ using a session ID which has been agreed by all parities beforehand and the hash of past communication, chooses $r_1, ..., r_w, z_1, ..., z_w \hookleftarrow \mathbb{Z}_q$ and computes $T_j = (\overline{c}_j)^{a_2} g^{r_j}$ and $\mathsf{vE}_{vpk_{Ar}}(g^{r_j}) = (t_{1j}, t_{2j}, t_{3j}, t_{4j}) \hookleftarrow \mathcal{VE}.\mathsf{Enc}(g^{r_j}, vpk_{Ar}, \mathsf{ppar}, z_j, L, \mathcal{H})$ for $j = 1, ..., w$.

(f) Finally, sends $\langle \{\overline{C}_i\}_{i=1}^m, \{\overline{y}_j, s_j, T_j, \mathsf{vE}_{vpk_{Ar}}(g^{r_j})\}_{j=1}^w \rangle$ to $\mathcal{C}$ and simulates $\pi_2, \widehat{\pi}_2$.

As the encryption schemes $\mathcal{DEL}$ and $\mathcal{VE}$ are semantically secure, the tuple $\langle \{\overline{C}_i\}_{i=1}^m, \{\overline{y}_j, s_j, T_j, \mathsf{vE}_{vpk_{Ar}}(g^{r_j})\}_{j=1}^w \rangle$ is identically distributed in $\mathbf{G}_3$ and $\mathbf{G}_2$. The zero-knowledge (simulatability) of $\pi_2, \widehat{\pi}_2$ and indistinguishability of the tuple $\langle \{\overline{C}_i\}_{i=1}^m, \{\overline{y}_j, s_j, T_j, \mathsf{vE}_{vpk_{Ar}}(g^{r_j})\}_{j=1}^w \rangle$ make the views of $\mathcal{Z}$ in $\mathbf{G}_2$ and $\mathbf{G}_3$ indistinguishable. Therefore, there exists a negligible function $\epsilon_3(\kappa)$ such that $|Pr[\mathbf{G}_3] - Pr[\mathbf{G}_2]| \leq \epsilon_3(\kappa)$.

$\mathbf{G}_4$: This game is analogous to $\mathbf{G}_3$ except that during the setup phase, the simulator S_4 in simulating B chooses $a_2 \hookleftarrow \mathbb{Z}_q$ and simulates π_4 as in *Step 4*. By the zero-knowledge (simulatability) of π_4, the views of $\mathcal{Z}$ in $\mathbf{G}_3$ and $\mathbf{G}_4$ are indistinguishable. Consequently, $|Pr[\mathbf{G}_4] - Pr[\mathbf{G}_3]| \leq \epsilon_4(\kappa)$, a negligible function.

Let us now construct the ideal world simulator $\mathcal{SIM}$ that uses $\mathcal{C}$ as subroutine, simulates the honest party B, controls $\overline{A}, \overline{Ar}$ and incorporates all steps from $\mathbf{G}_4$.

(i) First, $\mathcal{SIM}$ plays the role of trusted party and generates the global parameter $\mathsf{gpar} = (\mathsf{ppar}, m, k, H, \{\tau_i\}_{i=4}^m, \{\iota_j\}_{j=4}^w)$, where $\mathsf{ppar} = (\mathsf{par}, \widehat{g}, \mathcal{H})$. It then plays the role of honest party B by choosing $\overline{a}_2 \hookleftarrow \mathbb{Z}_q$ and publishing $g^{\overline{a}_2}$ as the public key $epk_B = y_B$. It also acts as a certifying authority to obtain respective public keys epk_A, vpk_{Ar} of A, Ar. Finally, $\mathcal{SIM}$ invokes $\mathcal{C}$.

(ii) $\mathcal{SIM}$ keeps records for all $poly(\kappa)$ queries the adversary made to the random oracles in a list X', where κ is security parameter.

(iii) On receiving $R_1 = \langle \{C_i\}_{i=1}^m, \pi_1 \rangle$ from $\mathcal{C}$, $\mathcal{SIM}$ verifies the proof π_1. If the verification fails, $\mathcal{SIM}$ instructs $\overline{A}$ to send $\perp$ to T, $\overline{Ar}$ to send $b_B = \circ$ to T and terminates the execution; otherwise, runs the extractor algorithm for π_1 with $\mathcal{C}$ to extract the exponents $\{r_{b_1}, ..., r_{b_m}\}$ and extracts the Bloom filter BF_X for the set X exactly in the same way as described in $\mathbf{G}_1$.

Similar to $\mathbf{G}_1$, $\mathcal{SIM}$ queries each element in X' against BF_X to construct a set X'' which is essentially X except with negligible probability ϵ. $\mathcal{SIM}$ then instructs $\overline{A}$ to send X to T, $\overline{Ar}$ to send $b_A = \circ$ to T and receives $|X \cap Y|$ from T.

(iv) As in $\mathbf{G}_3$, $\mathcal{SIM}$ constructs a set $Y' = \{y'_1, ..., y'_w\}$, computes
$$\overline{C}_i = (c'_i = c_{\phi^{-1}(i)} g^{\alpha_i}, d'_i = d_{\phi^{-1}(i)} h^{\alpha_i}), i = 1, ..., m$$
$$\nu_j = \prod_{i=1}^{m} (\overline{C}_i)^{s_j^{(i)}} = (\lambda_j, \delta_j) \text{ and } \overline{y}_j = (\overline{c}_j, \overline{d}_j) = ((\lambda_j)^{k_j}, (\delta_j)^{k_j}), j = 1, ..., w$$
$$T_j = (\overline{c}_j)^{\overline{a}_2} g^{r_j} \text{ and } \mathsf{vE}_{vpk_{Ar}}(g^{r_j}) = (t_{1j}, t_{2j}, t_{3j}, t_{4j}), j = 1, ..., w,$$
where $s_j^{(i)} = \begin{cases} 1, & \text{if } i \in \{\phi(h_1(y'_j)), ..., \phi(h_k(y'_j))\} \\ 0, & \text{otherwise,} \end{cases}$

$\phi \leftarrowtail \Sigma_m$ and $\alpha_1, ..., \alpha_m, k_1, ..., k_w, r_1, ..., r_w \leftarrowtail \mathbb{Z}_q$. It also simulates the proofs $\pi_2, \widehat{\pi}_2$ and sends $\langle \{\overline{C}_i\}_{i=1}^{m}, \{\overline{y}_j, s_j, T_j, \mathsf{vE}_{vpk_{Ar}}(g^{r_j})\}_{j=1}^{w} \rangle$ to $\mathcal{C}$. $\mathcal{SIM}$ then executes following steps according to $\mathcal{C}$'s reply.

(v) If $\mathcal{C}$ instructs A to send $\langle \{\mu_j, (\overline{e}_j)\}_{j=1}^{w}, \pi_3, \widehat{\pi}_3 \rangle$, then $\mathcal{SIM}$ verifies the validity of each of the proofs $\pi_3, \widehat{\pi}_3$. If the verifications of both the proofs succeed then $\mathcal{SIM}$ instructs $\overline{Ar}$ to send $b_B = \circ$. If verification of atleast one of the proofs fails or $\mathcal{C}$ instructs A to abort in the procedure mPSI-CA then the following cases arise:

- if $\mathcal{C}$ instructs Ar to send $\{\mu_j = (e_j, f_j), \overline{e}_j\}_{j=1}^{w}$ in the procedure Dispute Resolution, then as in $\mathbf{G}_2$, $\mathcal{SIM}$ computes $(e_j)^{a_2}$, utilizes it to compute $l_j = \frac{f_j}{(\overline{e}_j)(e_j)^{\overline{a}_2}}$ and sets card = card + 1 if $l_j = 1$ for $j = 1, ..., w$, where card is a count variable which is set 0 initially. Finally, $\mathcal{SIM}$ instructs $\overline{Ar}$ to send $b_B = \mathsf{card}$ to T, outputs whatever $\mathcal{C}$ outputs and terminates.

- if $\mathcal{C}$ instructs Ar to abort in the procedure Dispute Resolution, $\mathcal{SIM}$ instructs $\overline{Ar}$ to send $b_B = \perp$ to T, outputs whatever $\mathcal{C}$ outputs and terminates.

(vi) If $\mathcal{C}$ instructs both A and Ar to abort, then $\mathcal{SIM}$ instructs $\overline{Ar}$ to send $b_B = \perp$ to T, outputs whatever $\mathcal{C}$ outputs and terminates.

Note that the ideal world simulator $\mathcal{SIM}$ provides the real world adversary $\mathcal{C}$ exactly the same simulation as the simulator S_4 in $\mathbf{G}_4$. Therefore, we have $Pr[\mathsf{IDEAL}_{\mathcal{F}_{\mathsf{mPSI-CA}}, \mathcal{SIM}}(X, Y)] = Pr[\mathbf{G}_4]$; yielding $|Pr[\mathsf{IDEAL}_{\mathcal{F}_{\mathsf{mPSI-CA}}, \mathcal{SIM}}(X, Y)] - Pr[\mathsf{REAL}_{\mathsf{mPSI-CA}, \mathcal{C}}(X, Y)]| = |Pr[\mathbf{G}_4] - Pr[\mathbf{G}_0]| \leq \Sigma_{i=1}^{4}|Pr[\mathbf{G}_i] - Pr[\mathbf{G}_{i-1}]| \leq \Sigma_{i=1}^{4} \epsilon_i(\kappa) = \rho(\kappa)$, where $\rho(\kappa)$ is a negligible function.

Consequently, we have $\mathsf{IDEAL}_{\mathcal{F}_{\mathsf{mPSI-CA}}, \mathcal{SIM}}(X, Y) \equiv^c \mathsf{REAL}_{\mathsf{mPSI-CA}, \mathcal{C}}(X, Y)$.

Subcase II (*B* and *Ar* are corrupted). Let $\mathcal{Z}$ be a distinguisher who controls $\mathcal{C}$, feeds the input of the honest party A and also sees the output of B. Now we argue that $\mathcal{Z}$'s view in the real world ($\mathcal{C}$'s view + A's output) and its view in the ideal world ($\mathcal{SIM}$'s view + $\overline{A}$'s output) are indistinguishable, where the view of an entity consists of the transcripts available to it. Due to limited space we give only construction of the ideal world simulator $\mathcal{SIM}$ that uses $\mathcal{C}$ as subroutine, simulates the honest party A and controls $\overline{B}, \overline{Ar}$ and we will show the simulatability holds in this case.

(i) $\mathcal{SIM}$ first plays the role of trusted party by generating the global para-meter $\mathsf{gpar} = (\mathsf{ppar}, m, k, H, \{\tau_i\}_{i=-4}^m, \{\iota_j\}_{j=-4}^w)$, where $\mathsf{ppar} = (\mathsf{par}, \widehat{g}, \mathcal{H})$. It then simulates the honest party A by choosing $\overline{a}_1 \leftarrowtail \mathbb{Z}_q$ and publishing $g^{\overline{a}_1}$ as the public key $epk_A = y_A$. It also acts as a certifying authority to obtain public keys epk_B, vpk_{Ar} of B, Ar. $\mathcal{SIM}$ then invokes $\mathcal{C}$.

(ii) $\mathcal{SIM}$ constructs a Bloom filter $\mathsf{BF}_{X'}$ whose all entries are set as 0 and encrypts each of $g^{b_i} = g^{\mathsf{BF}_{X'}[i]} = g^0$ using public key $pk = epk_A \cdot epk_B$ to get the ciphertext $C_i \leftarrow \mathcal{DEL}.\mathsf{Enc}(g^{b_i}, pk, \mathsf{par}, r_{b_i})$ for $i = 1, ..., m$. $\mathcal{SIM}$ then simulates the proof π_1 and sends $\{C_1, ..., C_m\}$ to $\mathcal{C}$.

(iii) The simulator $\mathcal{SIM}$ maintains a list Y' by recording all the $poly(\kappa)$ queries the adversary made to the random oracles.

(iv) On receiving $R_2 = \left\langle \{\overline{C}_i\}_{i=1}^m, \{\overline{y}_j, s_j, T_j, \mathsf{vE}_{vpk_{Ar}}(g^{r_j})\}_{j=1}^w, \pi_2, \widehat{\pi}_2 \right\rangle$ from $\mathcal{C}$, $\mathcal{SIM}$ verifies each of the proofs $\pi_2, \widehat{\pi}_2$. If the verifications of atleast one of the proofs does not succeed then $\mathcal{SIM}$ instructs $\overline{B}$ to send $\perp$ to T, $\overline{Ar}$ to send $b_A = \circ$ to T and terminates the execution; otherwise, $\mathcal{SIM}$ runs the extractor algorithm for $\widehat{\pi}_2$ with $\mathcal{C}$ to extract the permutation $\phi \in \Sigma_m$. For each $y' \in Y'$, the simulator $\mathcal{SIM}$ constructs an m-bit string s whose i-th bit $s^{(i)}$ is defined as $s^{(i)} = \begin{cases} 1, & \text{if } i \in \{\phi(h_1(y')), ..., \phi(h_k(y'))\} \\ 0, & \text{otherwise} \end{cases}$ and checks that s is in $\{s_1, ..., s_w\}$ or not. If the check is valid then it includes y' in Y''. Note that the extracted set Y'' is identical to the set Y except with negligible probability ϵ. $\mathcal{SIM}$ then instructs $\overline{B}$ to send Y to T, $\overline{Ar}$ to send $b_B = \circ$ to T and receives $|X \cap Y|$ from T.

(v) $\mathcal{SIM}$ constructs a set $\widetilde{Y} = \{\widetilde{y}_1, ..., \widetilde{y}_w\}$ by including $|X \cap Y|$ many ciphertexts as $\mathsf{dE}_{pk}(0)$ together with $v - |X \cap Y|$ many random cipher-texts as $\mathsf{dE}_{pk}(r)$, where $r \leftarrowtail \mathbb{Z}_q$ and $r \neq 0$. Let $\widetilde{y}_j = (\widetilde{\lambda}_j, \widetilde{\delta}_j)$ for $j = 1, ..., w$. Then $\mathcal{SIM}$ chooses a random permutation $\psi \in \Sigma_w$ over the set $\{1, ..., w\}$, selects $\beta_1, ..., \beta_w \leftarrowtail \mathbb{Z}_q$ and computes for each $j = 1, ..., w$, $\mu_j = \widetilde{y}_{\psi^{-1}(j)} \mathcal{DEL}.\mathsf{Enc}(g^0, pk, \mathsf{par}, \beta_j) = (e_j, f_j)$ and $\overline{e}_j = (e_j)^{\overline{a}_1}$, where $e_j = \widetilde{\lambda}_{\psi^{-1}(j)} g^{\beta_j}, f_j = \widetilde{\delta}_{\psi^{-1}(j)} h^{\beta_j}$. $\mathcal{SIM}$ then simulates $\pi_3, \widehat{\pi}_3$, sends $\left\langle \{\mu_j, (\overline{e}_j)\}_{j=1}^w \right\rangle$ to $\mathcal{C}$ and executes following steps according to $\mathcal{C}$'s reply.

(vi) If $\mathcal{C}$ instructs B to send $\left\langle \{g^{r_j}\}_{j=1}^w, \pi_4 \right\rangle$, then $\mathcal{SIM}$ checks the validity of the proof π_4. If the verification succeeds then $\mathcal{SIM}$ instructs $\overline{Ar}$ to send $b_A = \circ$ to T. If verification fails or $\mathcal{C}$ instructs B to abort in the procedure mPSI-CA then the following cases arise:

- if $\mathcal{C}$ instructs Ar to send $\{g_1, ..., g_w\}$ in the procedure Dispute Resolution then the simulator $\mathcal{SIM}$ extracts $T_j, \overline{c}_j, \overline{d}_j$ from $R_2 = \left\langle \{\overline{C}_i\}_{i=1}^m, \{\overline{y}_j = (\overline{c}_j, \overline{d}_j), s_j, T_j, \mathsf{vE}_{vpk_{Ar}}(g^{r_j})\}_{j=1}^w, \pi_2, \widehat{\pi}_2 \right\rangle$, computes $\widehat{e}_j = \frac{T_j}{g_j}$ and uses $\widehat{e}_j$ to compute $l'_j = \frac{\overline{d}_j}{(\overline{c}_j)^{\overline{a}_1} \widehat{e}_j}$ for $j = 1, ..., w$. The simulator $\mathcal{SIM}$ then increases card by 1 if $l'_j = 1$ for $j = 1, ..., w$, where the count variable card is initially set as 0. Finally, $\mathcal{SIM}$ instructs $\overline{Ar}$ to send $b_A = $ card to T, outputs whatever $\mathcal{C}$ outputs and terminates.

     – if $\mathcal{C}$ instructs Ar to abort in dispute resolution protocol then $\mathcal{SIM}$ instructs $\overline{Ar}$ to send $b_A = \perp$ to T. $\mathcal{SIM}$ then outputs whatever $\mathcal{C}$ outputs and terminates.

(vii) If $\mathcal{C}$ instructs both B and Ar to abort, then $\mathcal{SIM}$ instructs $\overline{Ar}$ to send $b_A = \perp$ to T. Then outputs whatever $\mathcal{C}$ outputs and terminates.

The outputs of the honest parties A and $\overline{A}$ are always the same. All we need to check is whether $\mathcal{SIM}$'s view is indistinguishable from the view of $\mathcal{C}$. The differences between the simulation and the real executions are – $\mathcal{SIM}$ uses the Bloom filter $\mathsf{BF}_{X'}$ instead of BF_X to generate $\{C_i\}_{i=1}^m$ and $\widetilde{Y}$ instead of $\overline{Y}$ to generate $\{\mu_j, \overline{e}_j\}_{j=1}^w$. As the encryption scheme $\mathcal{DEL}$ is semantically secure, $\langle \{C_i\}_{i=1}^m, \{\mu_j, \overline{e}_j\}_{j=1}^w \rangle$ is identically distributed in the simulation and real executions. Thus the use of $\mathsf{BF}_{X'}$ and $\widetilde{Y}$ does not affect the distribution of the views of $\mathcal{SIM}$ and $\mathcal{C}$. Consequently, $\mathcal{Z}$'s view in the real world ($\mathcal{C}$'s view $+A$'s output) and its view in the ideal world ($\mathcal{SIM}$'s view $+ \overline{A}$'s output) are indistinguishable.

Subcase III (A and B are corrupted). This case is trivial as $\mathcal{C}$ has full knowledge of X and Y and the encryption scheme used by Ar is semantically secure. Therefore a simulator can always be constructed.

Case II (When the adversary $\mathcal{C}$ corrupts only one party). If only Ar is corrupted then Ar is not involved in the protocol as A and B are honest. Thus it is trivial to construct a simulator in this case. If only A or B is corrupted then the simulator can be constructed as in steps (i)–(iv) of the case when both A and Ar are corrupted or in steps (i)–(v) of the case when both B and Ar are corrupted. The only change in these cases is that $\overline{Ar}$ is honest and always sends $\circ$ to T.

5   Efficiency

The computation overhead of our mPSI-CA protocol is measured by modular exponentiation (Exp), modular inversion (Inv) and hash function evaluation (H). On the other hand, the number of group elements (GE) transmitted publicly by the users in our mPSI-CA protocol incurs the communication cost. The complexities of our mPSI-CA protocol are displayed in Table 1, where $\pi_1, \pi_2, \pi_3, \pi_4, \widehat{\pi}_2, \widehat{\pi}_3$ are associated interactive zero-knowledge proofs.

Note: In [16], the authors proposed a mPSI-CA protocol, where two parties A and B involve with their private sets $X = \{x_1, ..., x_v\}$ and $Y = \{y_1, ..., y_w\}$ respectively. On completion of the protocol, both of them learn the sets $\overline{X} = \{(gx_{\phi^{-1}(1)})^{rr'}, ..., (gx_{\phi^{-1}(v)})^{rr'}\}$, $\overline{Y} = \{(gy_{\psi^{-1}(1)})^{rr'}, ..., (gy_{\psi^{-1}(w)})^{rr'}\}$ and computes $|\overline{X} \cap \overline{Y}|$ which is actually $|X \cap Y|$.

    The authors of [16] claimed that their mPSI-CA is secure against malicious adversaries. However it seems to us that their scheme is no longer secure when the adversaries are malicious due to the following:

(i) Let the participant A behave maliciously and involve in the mPSI-CA protocol with the set $X' = \{x'_1, ..., x'_v\}$ instead of the private $X = \{x_1, ..., x_v\}$,

Table 1. Complexity of our mPSI-CA protocol

	Party A	Party B	Arbiter Ar	Total
Exp	$9m + 39w + 25$	$13m + 30w + 25$	$14w + 12$	$22m + 83w + 62$
GE	$9m + 22w + 38$	$5m + 25w + 20$	$5w + 1$	$14m + 52w + 59$
Inv	$2w$	w	w	$4w$
H	$v + w$	$2w$	w	$v + 4w$

GE = number of group elements, Exp = number of exponentiations, Inv = number of inversions, H = number of hash query, $m = \frac{kv}{\ln 2}$.

Table 2. Comparative summary of mutual PSI-CA protocols in malicious model

mPSI-CA Protocol	Adv. Model	Security Assumption	Comm. Cost	Comp. Cost	Fairness	Optimistic	Group Order	Arbiter
[25]	Mal	AHE	$O(v)$	$O(v^2)$	No	No	Composite	
[10]	Mal	Strong RSA	$O(w + v)$	$O(wv)$	Yes	Yes	composite	FT
Our	Mal	DDH	$O(w + v)$	$O(w + v)$	Yes	Yes	Prime	SH

AHE = Additively Homomorphic Encryption, FT = Fully Trusted, Mal = Malicious, DDH = Decisional Diffie-Hellman, v, w are the sizes of input sets.

where $x'_i = g^{(k-1)}x_i^k$ for some $k \hookleftarrow \mathbb{Z}_q^*$ and $i = 1, ..., v$. Then at the end of the protocol, both A and B learn the sets $\overline{X'} = \{(gx'_{\phi^{-1}(1)})^{rr'}, ..., (gx'_{\phi^{-1}(v)})^{rr'}\}$, $\overline{Y} = \{(gy_{\psi^{-1}(1)})^{rr'}, ..., (gy_{\psi^{-1}(w)})^{rr'}\}$. From these sets, B computes $|\overline{X'} \cap \overline{Y}|$ and outputs this as $|X \cap Y|$. However, $|\overline{X'} \cap \overline{Y}|$ is not actually $|X \cap Y|$ due to X'. Thus B does not get the correct cardinality. On the other hand, for each $i = 1, ..., v$, the malicious party A computes $(gx'_{\phi^{-1}(i)})^{rr'k^{-1}} = (gg^{(k-1)}x_{\phi^{-1}(i)}^k)^{rr'k^{-1}} = (g^k x_{\phi^{-1}(i)}^k)^{rr'k^{-1}} = (gx_{\phi^{-1}(i)})^{rr'}$. In other words, A extracts the set $\overline{X} = \{(gx_{\phi^{-1}(1)}),^{rr'} ..., (gx_{\phi^{-1}(v)})^{rr'}\}$. The party A then computes $|\overline{X} \cap \overline{Y}|$ which is actually $|X \cap Y|$.

(ii) Similarly, when B behaves maliciously, it can be shown that B gets the exact cardinality whereas A does not get the correct one.

We briefly summarize comparison of our mPSI-CA from prior works in Table 2.

6   Conclusion

In this paper, we have designed a fair optimistic mPSI-CA protocol attaining linear complexity overhead. We have utilized Bloom filter as building blocks of our scheme. The proposed mPSI-CA is provably secure under DDH assumption against malicious entities in ROM. Fairness of this protocol is achieved by using an off-line semi-trusted arbiter. Particularly, our mPSI-CA is more efficient than existing mPSI-CA protocols. To the best of our knowledge, our mPSI-CA is the *first fair* mPSI-CA that achieves *linear* complexity in the *malicious* environment.

References

1. Agrawal, R., Evfimievski, A., Srikant, R.: Information sharing across private databases. In: Proceedings of the 2003 ACM SIGMOD International Conference on Management of Data, pp. 86–97. ACM (2003)
2. Bellare, M., Goldreich, O.: On defining proofs of knowledge. In: Brickell, E.F. (ed.) CRYPTO 1992. LNCS, vol. 740, pp. 390–420. Springer, Heidelberg (1993). doi:10. 1007/3-540-48071-4_28
3. Bellare, M., Rogaway, P.: Random oracles are practical: a paradigm for designing efficient protocols. In: Proceedings of the 1st ACM Conference on Computer and Communications Security, pp. 62–73. ACM (1993)
4. Bloom, B.H.: Space/time trade-offs in hash coding with allowable errors. Commun. ACM **13**(7), 422–426 (1970)
5. Boneh, D.: The decision Diffie-Hellman problem. In: Buhler, J.P. (ed.) ANTS 1998. LNCS, vol. 1423, pp. 48–63. Springer, Heidelberg (1998). doi:10.1007/BFb0054851
6. Brandt, F.: Efficient cryptographic protocol design based on distributed El Gamal encryption. In: Won, D.H., Kim, S. (eds.) ICISC 2005. LNCS, vol. 3935, pp. 32–47. Springer, Heidelberg (2006). doi:10.1007/11734727_5
7. Camenisch, J., Shoup, V.: Practical verifiable encryption and decryption of discrete logarithms. In: Boneh, D. (ed.) CRYPTO 2003. LNCS, vol. 2729, pp. 126–144. Springer, Heidelberg (2003). doi:10.1007/978-3-540-45146-4_8
8. Camenisch, J., Stadler, M.: Efficient group signature schemes for large groups. In: Kaliski, B.S. (ed.) CRYPTO 1997. LNCS, vol. 1294, pp. 410–424. Springer, Heidelberg (1997). doi:10.1007/BFb0052252
9. Camenisch, J., Stadler, M.: Proof systems for general statements about discrete logarithms. Citeseer (1997)
10. Camenisch, J., Zaverucha, G.M.: Private intersection of certified sets. In: Dingledine, R., Golle, P. (eds.) FC 2009. LNCS, vol. 5628, pp. 108–127. Springer, Heidelberg (2009). doi:10.1007/978-3-642-03549-4_7
11. Cramer, R., Shoup, V.: A practical public key cryptosystem provably secure against adaptive chosen ciphertext attack. In: Krawczyk, H. (ed.) CRYPTO 1998. LNCS, vol. 1462, pp. 13–25. Springer, Heidelberg (1998). doi:10.1007/BFb0055717
12. Cristofaro, E., Gasti, P., Tsudik, G.: Fast and private computation of cardinality of set intersection and union. In: Pieprzyk, J., Sadeghi, A.-R., Manulis, M. (eds.) CANS 2012. LNCS, vol. 7712, pp. 218–231. Springer, Heidelberg (2012). doi:10. 1007/978-3-642-35404-5_17
13. Debnath, S.K., Dutta, R.: A fair and efficient mutual private set intersection protocol from a two-way oblivious pseudorandom function. In: Lee, J., Kim, J. (eds.) ICISC 2014. LNCS, vol. 8949, pp. 343–359. Springer, Cham (2015). doi:10.1007/ 978-3-319-15943-0_21
14. Debnath, S.K., Dutta, R.: Efficient private set intersection cardinality in the presence of malicious adversaries. In: Au, M.-H., Miyaji, A. (eds.) ProvSec 2015. LNCS, vol. 9451, pp. 326–339. Springer, Cham (2015). doi:10.1007/978-3-319-26059-4_18
15. Debnath, S.K., Dutta, R.: Secure and efficient private set intersection cardinality using bloom filter. In: Lopez, J., Mitchell, C.J. (eds.) ISC 2015. LNCS, vol. 9290, pp. 209–226. Springer, Cham (2015). doi:10.1007/978-3-319-23318-5_12
16. Debnath, S.K., Dutta, R.: Fair mPSI and mPSI-CA: Efficient constructions in prime order groups with security in the standard model against malicious adversary. IACR Cryptology ePrint Archive (2016)

17. Debnath, S.K., Dutta, R.: Towards fair mutual private set intersection with linear complexity. Secur. Commun. Netw. **9**(11), 1589–1612 (2016)
18. Dong, C., Chen, L., Camenisch, J., Russello, G.: Fair private set intersection with a semi-trusted arbiter. In: Wang, L., Shafiq, B. (eds.) DBSec 2013. LNCS, vol. 7964, pp. 128–144. Springer, Heidelberg (2013). doi:10.1007/978-3-642-39256-6_9
19. Dong, C., Chen, L., Wen, Z.: When private set intersection meets big data: an efficient and scalable protocol. In: Proceedings of the 2013 ACM SIGSAC Conference on Computer & Communications Security, pp. 789–800. ACM (2013)
20. Freedman, M.J., Hazay, C., Nissim, K., Pinkas, B.: Efficient set intersection with simulation-based security. J. Cryptology **29**(1), 115–155 (2016)
21. Furukawa, J.: Efficient and verifiable shuffling and shuffle-decryption. IEICE Trans. Fundam. Electron. Commun. Comput. Sci. **88**(1), 172–188 (2005)
22. Hazay, C.: Oblivious polynomial evaluation and secure set-intersection from algebraic prfs. IACR Cryptology ePrint Archive 2015, 4 (2015)
23. Huang, Y., Evans, D., Katz, J.: Private set intersection: are garbled circuits better than custom protocols. In: Network and Distributed System Security Symposium (NDSS), The Internet Society (2012)
24. Kim, M., Lee, H.T., Cheon, J.H.: Mutual private set intersection with linear complexity. In: Jung, S., Yung, M. (eds.) WISA 2011. LNCS, vol. 7115, pp. 219–231. Springer, Heidelberg (2012). doi:10.1007/978-3-642-27890-7_18
25. Kissner, L., Song, D.: Privacy-preserving set operations. In: Shoup, V. (ed.) CRYPTO 2005. LNCS, vol. 3621, pp. 241–257. Springer, Heidelberg (2005). doi:10.1007/11535218_15
26. Pinkas, B., Schneider, T., Segev, G., Zohner, M.: Phasing: private set intersection using permutation-based hashing. In: 24th USENIX Security Symposium (USENIX Security 2015), pp. 515–530 (2015)
27. Pinkas, B., Schneider, T., Zohner, M.: Faster private set intersection based on OT extension. In: USENIX Security, vol. 14, pp. 797–812 (2014)

Evaluating Entropy for True Random Number Generators: Efficient, Robust and Provably Secure

Maciej Skorski[✉]

University of Warsaw, Warsaw, Poland
maciej.skorski@mimuw.edu.pl

Abstract. Estimating entropy of randomness sources is a task of critical importance in the context of true random number generators, as feeding cryptographic applications with insufficient entropy is a serious real-world security risk. The challenge is to maximize accuracy and confidence under certain data models and resources constraints.

In this paper we analyze the performance of a simple collision-counting estimator, under the assumption that source outputs are independent but their distribution can change due to adversarial influences.

For n samples and confidence $1 - \epsilon$ we achieve the following features
(a) Efficiency: reads the stream in one-pass and uses constant memory (forward-only mode)
(b) Accuracy: estimates the amount of extractable bits with a relative error $O(n^{-\frac{1}{2}} \log(1/\epsilon))$ per sample, when the source outputs are i.i.d.
(c) Robustness: the same error when the source outputs are independent but the distribution changes up to $t = O(n^{\frac{1}{2}})$ times during runtime
We demonstrate that the estimator is accurate enough to adjust post-processing components dynamically, estimating entropy on the fly instead investigating it off-line. Our work thus continues the line of research on "testable random number generators" (originated by Bucii and Luzzi at CHES'05) combining it with the robustness against source changes (originated by Barak et al. at CHES'03).

Keywords: Online entropy estimators · Testable random number generators · True random number generators in changing environments

1 Introduction

1.1 Estimating Entropy for True Random Number Generators

True Random Number Generators (TRNGs) are devices that utilize some underlying physical process to generate bits that are statistically indistinguishable[1]

A full and updated version is available at ePrint (Report 2016/272).

M. Skorski—Supported by the National Science Center, Poland (2015/17/ N/ST6/03564).

[1] Which means closeness in the variational distance (distance ϵ smaller than 2^{-80} for practical applications).

K. Chen et al. (Eds.): Inscrypt 2016, LNCS 10143, pp. 526–541, 2017.
DOI: 10.1007/978-3-319-54705-3_32

from independent and unbiased bits (we call these indistinguishable bits truly random). Examples of such processes are radio noise [Haa], radiation [Wal], thermal noise [JK99] or noise from sensors in mobile devices [BKMS09,BS]. A typical TRNG consists of an entropy source, harvesting mechanism and a post-processing[2] component which reduces bias and correlations present in raw data [Sun09,TBK+]. In reality, outputs of available randomness sources are some-what unpredictable but biased, therefore the output quality depends critically on adjusting the post-processing part to the source. Basically, post-processing func-tions give provable guarantees on the output quality when fed with inputs of suf-ficiently high entropy (well known examples are universal hash functions [BST03] or the von Neumann extractor [vN51]). Therefore, to achieve the required qual-ity we need to estimate the entropy in the source. This requirement is not only a matter of provable security, but a serious practical concern as low entropy may lead to attacks on real-world applications [dRHG+99]. Recent examples are bugs in the Linux Random Number Generator on Debian distributions [GPR06] on Android distributions [KKHD14]. For this reason, entropy evaluation is con-sidered a necessary part of the developing designing process and is strongly recommended by standards [TBK+].

To formulate the problem more precisely, we assume without losing generality that the entropy source output is already digitized and forms a sequence of symbols $X_1, \ldots, X_n$ over a finite alphabet $\mathcal{X}$ (for example $\mathcal{X}$ may be the set of 10-bit strings), which are produced by repeating the generating procedure in consecutive time intervals. Keeping in mind that there are many entropy notions and not all of them are suitable for cryptographic purposes (such as generating random numbers) we can state the following problem

Problem: How to estimate the (cryptographically relevant) entropy of a stochastic process $X_1, X_2, \ldots, X_n$ over an alphabet $\mathcal{X}$?

The right entropy notion here is not the popular Shannon entropy, but the more conservative entropy notion called *min-entropy*. The theory of randomness extraction characterizes min-entropy as the measure of the amount of almost uniform bits that can be extracted (using best post-processing functions) from a given distribution [RW05,Sha11]. More specifically, the min-entropy is the negative logarithm of the likelihood of the most heavy element: if every outcome appears with probability at most 2^{-k} then we say that the distribution has k-bits of min-entropy.

Once we know how much entropy we have collected, we can tune the para-meters of the appropriate extractor (post-processing) function and produce an almost unbiased string. The task of estimating entropy is independent on a specific post-processing function. Different post-processing functions yield only different trade-offs between the input entropy and the output length and quality (also in memory and time resources consumed). What makes this problem hard

---

[2] Sometimes called also the conditioning component [TBK+], or an extractor in the theoretical literature.

is finding the right balance between the accuracy, sample complexity and the source model (in particular, utilize as few samples as possible).

1.2 Related Works

Standards like the most recent NIST recommendation [TBK+] suggest to approximate the min-entropy based on empirical frequencies plugged into the entropy formula and many independent samples. This approach is applied in works with focus on provable security [BST03, BKMS09, VSH11]. We note that this process requires a large amount of extra memory, namely one needs to compute the frequencies of all elements $x \in \mathcal{X}$. This costs $\Omega(|\mathcal{X}|)$ bits of memory, actually more if we want an entropy estimate with a small relative error δ. For this we need to keep the frequencies with a precision up to $\frac{\delta}{|\mathcal{X}|}$, which means $\Omega(|\mathcal{X}| \log \left(\frac{|\mathcal{X}|}{\delta}\right))$ bits. For 30-bit blocks this is more than 4 GB of memory (see Appendix A for a quantitative explanation).

In general, the "plug-in" estimator is not memory-efficient on small mobile or embedded devices [LRSV12]. The authors of the referenced work proposed to construct an estimator for Shannon entropy instead of min-entropy, which basically just quickly reads the stream and operates within a constant amount of memory. However, this is not provably secure except the case of stateless sources (producing i.i.d. symbols) as shown by a result called the Asymptotic Equipartition Property [Sha48, Ash90]. The price is a wide error margin which the best known bound is as large as $O(|\mathcal{X}|)$ [Hol06], which is more than 1000 bits for a source with only 10-bit outputs blocks.

1.3 Our Contributions

We analyze the simple estimator based on the idea of *collisions counting*, which operates in *constant memory*. Technically speaking, we estimate not the min-entropy but a slightly weaker notion called collision entropy, which turns out to be close enough. Using the technique called *entropy smoothing* (see Lemma 1) we can go back from collision entropy to be ϵ-close to min-entropy losing only $\log(1/\epsilon)$ bits where ϵ is the chosen security parameter, typically $\epsilon = 2^{-80}$. Moreover, for most popular post-processing functions based on universal hashing [BST03, VSH11] our estimate can be applied with no loss as if it was min-entropy, because universal hash functions work with collision entropy [HILL99]. The pseudocode of our estimator is given in Algorithm 1.

For this estimator, we prove the following key features:

(a) Convergence bounds: we give clear error bounds on the estimator convergence, depending on the chosen security level (output indistinguishability) and the number of samples. Namely, for n samples at confidence $1 - \epsilon$ we estimate the entropy per bit with a relative error $\delta = O\left(\sqrt{\frac{|\mathcal{X}| \log(1/\epsilon)}{n}}\right)$, for $n = \Omega(|\mathcal{X}| \log(1/\epsilon))$. Moreover, the alphabet size $|\mathcal{X}|$ can be replaced by

---

Algorithm 1. Collision Entropy Estimator

Data: independent samples $x_1, \ldots, x_n$ from X over an alphabet $\mathcal{X}$
Result: An estimation for the source collision entropy $H_2(X)$

1 $P \leftarrow 0$
2 **for** $i = 2, \ldots, n$ **do**
3   **if** $x_i = x_{i-1}$ **then**
4        $P \leftarrow P + 1$

5 $\hat{H} \leftarrow -\log_2\left(\frac{P}{n-1}\right)$
6 **return** $\hat{H}$

2^{H_2} where H_2 is the collision entropy rate (collision entropy per block) of the source. For more details, see Theorem 1.

(b) Provable security: using the estimate together with universal hash functions we extract all the entropy but $O\left(\sqrt{n 2^{H_2} |\mathcal{X}|}\right)$ bits (the result being at most $O(\epsilon)$-far from the uniform distribution). For more details, see Corollary 1.

(c) Efficiency: by definition, the estimator works in one pass and constant memory, being extremely efficient for long streams of data. This way we improve previous heuristic on on-line entropy estimation [LPR11] with an estimator even more efficient and, in addition, provably secure.

(d) Robustness in changing environments: we prove the convergence relaxing the i.i.d assumption. Namely, we require consecutive outputs to be independent but allow the source to "switch" its internal state t times, changing the output distribution ($t \ll n$). This result has two consequences: first, the estimator is robust against *environmental changes* (accidental or adversarial); second, it allows for estimating entropy in *production environments* (in real time) where distributions may be different than laboratory estimates. The importance of these features were discussed in CHES papers [BST03, BL05]. As for further applications, in Sect. 5 we show how to adapt our technique to estimate entropy of a source consisting of a few independent sources.

While it is straightforward to analyze the collision counting estimator for i.i.d. samples (see for example [Sko16]), our novel contribution is relaxing this assumption and proving robustness. See Table 1 for a brief overview of our contribution.

1.4 Source Model

The source must have a certain structure to allow for estimating entropy from samples with high accuracy and confidence (because we are interested in provable security) but on the other hand the model should be possibly general to cover a possibly large range of real-world applications. From a theoretical perspective, the most general approach is to model entropy sources by Markov chains of finite order [Mau92, TBK+]. This is, however, extremely inefficient in terms of the complexity/accuracy trade-off [TBK+]. In this work we adopt the common

Table 1. Our estimator compared to related works.

Estimator	Source model	Robustness	Adaptive	Prov. Sec.
[BST03]	Small family of sources	Entropy-preserving off-line changes	No	Yes
[BL05]	Independent binary	On-line changes to bias	Yes	Yes
[LRSV12]	i.i.d symbols	Fixed distribution	Yes	No
This paper	Independent symbols	Any on-line distribution changes	Yes	Yes

modeling approach, which assumes that the source outputs are i.i.d. [LRSV12, VSH11,BL05,BKMS09]. Our model is substantially stronger: we assume that the source distribution changes at most t times at arbitrarily chosen (for example by an adversary) moments. That is

- $X_1, X_2, \ldots, X_n$ are independent
- The number of indexes $= 1, \ldots, n$ such that $X_i \overset{d}{\neq} X_{i+1}$ is at most t

This model captures scenarios where environmental conditions change and influence the source during entropy harvesting.

1.5   Convergence Bounds

In the cryptographic literature, estimating entropy is typically not given a rigorous treatment. The newest NIST recommendation [TBK+] suggest to take $n \gg 10^6$ for empirical evaluations, which should be big enough to ensure convergences. Other works [VSH11] also evaluate entropy over huge data sets, like "overnight" samples. On the other hand our bounds show that, at least under our (relaxed) i.i.d. assumption, this number can be much smaller. In fact, we are able to estimate entropy in production environments, when we don't have much more data except what is necessary for extraction. This way we can make the statistical error small enough to not to affect provable security level we want to achieve (e.g. make the statistical error same as security $\epsilon = 2^{-80}$).

1.6   Efficiency and Provable Security

The work [LPR11] discusses an on-line entropy estimation technique for TRNGs by approximating the source Shannon Entropy, under the i.i.d. assumption. This is however not secure, as in this setting Shannon Entropy can be converted to min-entropy only with a huge entropy loss $O(|\mathcal{X}|\sqrt{n \log(1/\epsilon)})$ [Hol06]. Also, only asymptotic convergence was proven for the entropy estimator. Comparing to this work, we lose at most $\log(1/\epsilon)$ bits when converting to min-entropy (see Corollary 1) and provide a clear convergence bound with a loss at most $O(\sqrt{|\mathcal{X}|n \log(1/\epsilon)})$ for confidence $1 - \epsilon$. Also, we use less memory as [LPR11] need a sliding window with a variable size to further reduce the estimator bias.

1.7 Robustness in Changing Environments

In real world, devices that generate random numbers operate under varying environmental conditions and can be indirectly affected by a number of processes. The output distribution in the production environment may be different than during the testing stage. Examples may be temperature or voltage changes [BST03], or even different way the user is interacting with the device - for example, the quality of accelerometer-based TRNG depends on the "shaking pattern" [VSH11]. The issue becomes even more serious, where environmental parameters can be manipulated by a malicious adversary [BST03]. There are two ways to handle this issue: (a) trying to investigate all relevant factors during off-line tests, an provide a lower bound [VSH11] or (b) developing a design robust against changes in the entropy rate [BST03,BL05,LRSV12]. The second way seems to be more promising (and also more challenging) as addressing all factors that can influence the source is binded to a particular hardware and thus is not a generic approach. Moreover, the approach (a) is a passive way of solving the issue whereas (b) can be used to actively monitor the device behavior in production environments. More concretely, detecting a decrease in the entropy rate may be a trigger raising an attack alarm [BL05]. Lastly, we may want to use the robustness to handle multiple sources which contribute synchronously but independently to outputs blocks (for example, readings from all three accelerometer axes). A short example is discussed in Sect. 5.

1.8 Our Techniques

Our approach is based on using large deviation inequalities and some Jensen inequalities.

1.9 Organization

In Sect. 2 we provide necessary definitions and useful inequalities. The convergence of the entropy estimator is discussed in Sect. 3. Some further applications are explained in Sects. 4 and 5.

2 Preliminaries

2.1 Information-Theoretic Divergence Measures

Definition 1 (Variational (Statistical) Distance). *We say that discrete random variables X_1 and X_2, taking values in the same space, have the statistical distance at least ϵ if their probability mass functions are at most ϵ-away in terms of the ℓ_1 norm, that is*

$$\sum_x |\mathbf{P}_{X_1}(x) - \mathbf{P}_{X_2}(x)| \leqslant \epsilon.$$

2.2   Entropy Notions

Definition 2 (Min-Entropy). *The min-entropy of a random variable X is defined as* $\mathbf{H}_\infty(X) = \max_x \log \frac{1}{\mathbf{P}_X(x)}$.

Definition 3 (Collision-Entropy). *The collision-entropy of a random variable X is defined as* $\mathbf{H}_2(X) = -\log\left(\sum_x (\mathbf{P}_X(x))^2\right)$.

Definition 4 (Shannon-Entropy). *The Shannon-entropy of a random variable X is defined as* $\mathbf{H}(X) = -\sum_x \mathbf{P}_X(x) \log \mathbf{P}_X(x)$.

Definition 5 (Smooth Min-Entropy). *We say that X has k-bits of ϵ-smooth min-entropy if X is ϵ-close to Y such that* $\mathbf{H}_\infty(Y) \geqslant k$.

Lemma 1 (From collision to smooth min-entropy [Cac97]). *Suppose that $\mathbf{H}_2(X) \geqslant k$. Then* $\mathbf{H}_\infty^\epsilon(X) \geqslant k - \log(1/\epsilon)$.

2.3   Randomness Extractors

Extractors are functions which process weak sources into distributions that are close (in the information-theoretic sense) to the uniform distribution. In general, they need some amount of auxiliary randomness called *seed*. The seed is passed as an extra argument in the definition.

Definition 6 (Seeded extractors). *A deterministic function* $\mathrm{Ext} : \{0,1\}^n \times \{0,1\}^d \to \{0,1\}^k$ *is a (k, ϵ)-extractor for X if we have*

$$\mathrm{SD}\left(\mathrm{Ext}(X, U_d), U_d; U_k, U_d\right) \leqslant \epsilon$$

Remark 1 (Relaxing min-entropy for seeded extractors). The min-entropy required in the source can be relaxed at least in two ways:

(a) X needs to be only close to a distribution with entropy k
(b) The entropy notion can be collision entropy, instead of much more restrictive min-entropy.

Lemma 2 (A necessary conditions for extracting [Sha11]). *Suppose that Ext on input X outputs a distribution which is ϵ-close Let Ext be any function such that $\mathrm{SD}\left(\mathrm{Ext}(X, S); U_k | S\right) \leqslant \epsilon$. Then X is ϵ-close to a distribution of min-entropy at least k.*

Definition 7. *A family $\mathcal{H}$ of functions from n to m is called* universal, *if for a random member $H \in \mathcal{H}$ and every different $x, y \in \{0,1\}^n$ we have*

$$\Pr[H(x) = H(y)] = 2^{-m}.$$

Lemma 3 (Universal families are good extractors). *Suppose that $\mathbf{H}_2(X) \geqslant k + 2\log(1/\epsilon)$. Let $\mathcal{H}$ be a universal family of functions from n to m bits. For any $x \in \{0,1\}^n$ and $h \in \mathcal{H}$ define*

$$\mathrm{Ext}(x, h) = h(x)$$

Then we have

$$\mathrm{SD}\left(\mathrm{Ext}(X, H), H; U_k, H\right) \leqslant \epsilon$$

where H is a random element of $\mathcal{H}$.

2.4   Useful Inequalities

Lemma 4 (Jensen's Inequality). *Let I be an interval and $f : I \to \mathbb{R}$ be a convex function. Then we have*

$$\sum_{i=1}^{n} \alpha_i f(u_i) \geqslant f\left(\sum_{i=1}^{n} \alpha_i u_i\right)$$

for any numbers $u_1, \ldots, u_n \in I$ and non-negative weights $\alpha_1, \ldots, \alpha_n$ that sum up to 1.

Lemma 5 (Multiplicative Chernoff Bound [Che52]). *Let $X_1, \ldots, X_n$ be independent binary random variables. Define $\hat{p} = \frac{\sum_{i=1}^{n} X_i}{n}$. Then we have*

$$\Pr\left[\hat{p} \leqslant (1 - \delta)\mathbf{E}\hat{p}\right] \leqslant \exp\left(-np\delta^2/2\right)$$

for any positive number δ.

3   Main Result

Theorem 1 (The estimator convergence). *Let $X_1, \ldots, X_n$ be independent random variables over a finite domain $\mathcal{X}$. Suppose that the distribution of X_i changes at most t times when i goes from 1 to n. Then for any ϵ the output $\hat{H}$ of Algorithm 1 ran over $X_1, \ldots, X_n$ and the collision entropy rate $H_2 = \frac{1}{n}\mathbf{H}_2(X_1, \ldots, X_n)$ satisfy*

$$\mathbf{H}_2(X_1, \ldots, X_n) \geqslant (\hat{H} - \delta) \cdot n$$

with probability $1 - \epsilon$ where the relative error δ smaller than any of the two bounds below

$$\delta = \sqrt{\frac{2^{\hat{H}} \cdot 4\log(2/\epsilon)}{n}} + \frac{2^{\hat{H}} \cdot 4\log(2/\epsilon)}{n} + \frac{2^{\hat{H}} \cdot (t+1)}{n\ln 2} \qquad (1)$$

$$\delta = \sqrt{\frac{2^{H_2} \cdot 4\log(2/\epsilon)}{n}} + \frac{2^{H_2} \cdot (t+1)}{n\ln 2}. \qquad (2)$$

Corollary 1 (Provable security with any min-entropy extractor). *Let Ext be any (k, ϵ) extractor from X^n to $\{0,1\}^\ell$. Then the output of Ext on $X_1, \ldots, X_n$ is $O(\epsilon)$-close to the uniform distribution on $\{0,1\}^\ell$, provided that*

$$k \geqslant n\hat{H} - (n\delta + \log(1/\epsilon)).$$

were $\hat{H}$ and δ are as in Theorem 1. Moreover, for universal hash functions it's enough to assume

$$k \geqslant n\hat{H} - n\delta.$$

Proof. The proof follows immediately from the extractor definition and the conversion between smooth min-entropy and collision entropy (Lemma 1). For the extractor built on universal hash functions we simply use the fact that the assumption about k bits of min-entropy on input can be relaxed to k bits of collision entropy.

Remark 2. This corollary shows that our estimator can be coupled with any min-entropy extractor (post-processing function). The entropy loss is due to the estimation statistical error plus up to $\log(1/\epsilon)$ bits for conversion (not needed for universal hash functions). Note that typically we have $n \gg \log(1/\epsilon)$ and therefore $\log(1/\epsilon) \ll n\delta$. Thus the entropy loss in Corollary 1 equals $O(\delta n)$

Proof. (Proof of Theorem 1). Suppose that $X_1, \ldots, X_n$ are independent, and for some $t \in [0, T]$ there are numbers n_j satisfying

$$1 = n_0 < n_1 < n_2 \ldots < n_{t+1} = n + 1 \tag{3}$$

such that for every $j = 0 \ldots, t$ we have

$$\forall i \in \{n_j, \ldots, n_{j+1} - 1\} \quad X_i \overset{d}{=} Y_j.$$

This corresponds to the scenario where the distribution of the source is switched at moments $n_1, \ldots, n_t$. Let $\hat{p}_{col}^j$ be the collision probability estimate for samples X_i where $i = n_j, \ldots, n_{j+1} - 1$. That is

$$\hat{p}_{col}^j = \begin{cases} \frac{\sum_{n_j < i < n_{j+1}} \mathbf{1}_{\{X_i = X_{i-1}\}}}{n_{j+1} - n_j - 1}, & n_{j+1} - n_j > 1 \\ 0, & n_{j+1} - n_j = 1 \end{cases} \tag{4}$$

Note that

$$\mathbf{E}\left[\hat{p}_{col}^j\right] = p_{coll}^j \tag{5}$$

where $p_{coll}^j = CP(Y_j)$. Let p_{col} be the collision probability estimate, computed by the algorithm, over samples $X_1, \ldots, X_n$. In other words

$$\hat{p}_{col} = \frac{\sum_{i=1}^{n-1} \mathbf{1}_{\{X_i = X_{i+1}\}}}{n - 1} \tag{6}$$

Skipping in Eq. (6) these indexes i for which $i = n_j - 1$ for some j, and using Eq. (5) we obtain

$$\mathbf{E}\left[\hat{p}_{coll}\right] = \frac{1}{n-1} \sum_{i=n_j}^{n_{j+1}-1} \mathbf{E}\left[\mathbf{1}_{\{X_i = X_{i+1}\}}\right]$$

$$> \frac{1}{n-1} \sum_{j=0}^{t} \sum_{i=n_j}^{n_{j+1}-2} \mathbf{E}\left[\mathbf{1}_{\{X_i = X_{i+1}\}}\right]$$

$$= \frac{1}{n-1} \sum_{j=0}^{t} (n_{j+1} - n_j - 1)\, p_{coll}^j. \tag{7}$$

Note that thre random variables $Z_i = 1_{\{X_i=X_{i+1}\}}$ are not independent, so we cannot apply the Chernoff Bound directly. However, we can take advantage of the fact that the subsequences with odd and even indexes are independent. Define

$$I_1 = \{j : 1 \leqslant i \leqslant n - 1, \ j \equiv 1 \mod 2\}$$
$$I_2 = \{j : 1 \leqslant j \leqslant n - 1, \ j \equiv 0 \mod 2\}$$

The estimate in Eq. (6) can be expressed as a combination of estimates over the set I_1 and I_2, as follows

$$\hat{p}_{\text{col}} = \frac{|I_1|}{n-1} \cdot \hat{p}_1 + \frac{|I_2|}{n-1} \cdot \hat{p}_2 \tag{8}$$

where

$$\hat{p}_i = \frac{\sum_{i \in I_j} Z_i}{|I_j|}, \quad j = 1, 2.$$

By the Chernoff Bound applied separately to $\hat{p}_1$ and $\hat{p}_2$, we conclude that every of the following inequalities

$$\mathbf{E}\left[\hat{p}_1\right] \leqslant \hat{p}_1 + \sqrt{\frac{2\ln(2/\epsilon)\mathbf{E}\left[\hat{p}_1\right]}{|I_1|}}$$

$$\mathbf{E}\left[\hat{p}_2\right] \leqslant \hat{p}_2 + \sqrt{\frac{2\ln(2/\epsilon)\mathbf{E}\left[\hat{p}_2\right]}{|I_1|}}$$

holds with probability $1 - \frac{\epsilon}{2}$. By the union bound, they are satisfied simultaneously with probability at least $1-\epsilon$. Multiplying these inequalities by the weights $\frac{|I_j|}{n-1}$ for $j = 1, 2$ respectively, and using Eq. (8) we obtain

$$\mathbf{E}\hat{p}_{\text{col}} = \frac{|I_1|}{n-1} \cdot \mathbf{E}\left[\hat{p}_1\right] + \frac{|I_2|}{n-1} \cdot \mathbf{E}\left[\hat{p}_2\right]$$

$$\leqslant \frac{|I_1|}{n-1} \cdot \hat{p}_1 + \frac{|I_2|}{n-1} \cdot \hat{p}_2 + \left(\frac{|I_1|}{n-1} \cdot \sqrt{\frac{2\ln(2/\epsilon)\mathbf{E}\left[\hat{p}_1\right]}{|I_1|}} + \frac{|I_2|}{n-1} \cdot \sqrt{\frac{2\ln(2/\epsilon)\mathbf{E}\left[\hat{p}_2\right]}{|I_2|}}\right)$$

$$\leqslant \hat{p}_{\text{coll}} + \frac{\left(\sqrt{2\ln(2/\epsilon)|I_1|\mathbf{E}[\hat{p}_1]} + \sqrt{2\ln(2/\epsilon)|I_2|\mathbf{E}[\hat{p}_2]}\right)}{n-1}. \tag{9}$$

with probability $1 - \epsilon$. In order to simplify the rest of the proof, we use the following convention: from now all the inequalities hold with probability $1 - \epsilon$ unless stated otherwise. From Eq. (9), by applying the inequality $\sqrt{a} + \sqrt{b} \leqslant \sqrt{2(a+b)}$ (which follows by the Jensen inequality) and Eq. (8), we conclude that

$$\mathbf{E}\hat{p}_{\text{col}} \leqslant \hat{p}_{\text{coll}} + \frac{\sqrt{4\ln(2/\epsilon)(n-1)\mathbf{E}[\hat{p}_{\text{coll}}]}}{n-1}$$

$$= \hat{p}_{\text{coll}} + \sqrt{\frac{4\ln(2/\epsilon)\mathbf{E}[\hat{p}_{\text{coll}}]}{n-1}} \tag{10}$$

To make the right-hand side independent of the unknown parameter $\mathbf{E}\hat{p}_{\mathrm{col}}$ we rewrite Eq. (10) as

$$\left(\sqrt{\mathbf{E}\hat{p}_{\mathrm{col}}} - \sqrt{\frac{\ln(2/\epsilon)}{n-1}}\right)^2 \leqslant \hat{p}_{\mathrm{coll}} + \frac{\ln(2/\epsilon)}{n-1}$$

which implies

$$\mathbf{E}\hat{p}_{\mathrm{col}} \leqslant \left(\sqrt{\hat{p}_{\mathrm{coll}} + \frac{\ln(2/\epsilon)}{n-1}} + \sqrt{\frac{\ln(2/\epsilon)}{n-1}}\right)^2$$

$$= \hat{p}_{\mathrm{coll}} + \frac{2\ln(2/\epsilon)}{n-1} + 2\sqrt{\left(\hat{p}_{\mathrm{coll}} \cdot \frac{\ln(2/\epsilon)}{n-1}\right)^2 + \left(\frac{\ln(2/\epsilon)}{n-1}\right)^2}$$

$$\leqslant \hat{p}_{\mathrm{coll}} + \sqrt{\frac{4\hat{p}_{\mathrm{coll}}\ln(2/\epsilon)}{n-1}} + \frac{4\ln(2/\epsilon)}{n-1}. \qquad (11)$$

where the last line follows by the elementary inequality $\sqrt{a+b} \leqslant \sqrt{a} + \sqrt{b}$. Now, from Eqs. (7) and (11) it follows that

$$\frac{1}{n-1}\sum_{j=0}^{t}(n_{j+1} - n_j - 1)\,p_{\mathrm{coll}}^j \leqslant \hat{p}_{\mathrm{coll}} + \sqrt{\frac{4\hat{p}_{\mathrm{coll}}\ln(2/\epsilon)}{n-1}} + \frac{4\ln(2/\epsilon)}{n-1}$$

or, equivalently, that

$$\sum_{j=0}^{t}(n_{j+1} - n_j)\,p_{\mathrm{coll}}^j \leqslant (n-1)\hat{p}_{\mathrm{coll}} + \sqrt{4(n-1)\hat{p}_{\mathrm{coll}}\ln(2/\epsilon)} + 4\ln(2/\epsilon) + \sum_{j=0}^{t}p_{\mathrm{coll}}^j$$

Bounding p_{coll}^j by 1 on the right-hand side and dividing both sides by n we obtain

$$\sum_{j=0}^{t}\frac{(n_{j+1} - n_j)}{n}p_{\mathrm{coll}}^j \leqslant \frac{n-1}{n}\hat{p}_{\mathrm{coll}} + \sqrt{\frac{4(n-1)\hat{p}_{\mathrm{coll}}\ln(2/\epsilon)}{n^2}} + \frac{4\ln(2/\epsilon) + t + 1}{n}$$

$$\leqslant \hat{p}_{\mathrm{coll}} + \sqrt{\frac{4\hat{p}_{\mathrm{coll}}\ln(2/\epsilon)}{n}} + \frac{4\ln(2/\epsilon) + t + 1}{n} \qquad (12)$$

with probability $1 - \epsilon$. To derive a bound in terms of entropies, we rewrite the right-hand side in a relative-error form

$$\sum_{j=0}^{t}\frac{(n_{j+1} - n_j)}{n}p_{\mathrm{coll}}^j \leqslant \hat{p}_{\mathrm{coll}}\left(1 + \sqrt{\frac{4\ln(2/\epsilon)}{n\hat{p}_{\mathrm{coll}}}} + \frac{4\ln(2/\epsilon) + t + 1}{n\hat{p}_{\mathrm{coll}}}\right).$$

This inequality can be rewritten, by taking the logarithm of both sides, as

$$-\log\left(\sum_{j=0}^{t}\frac{(n_{j+1} - n_j)}{n}p_{\mathrm{coll}}^j\right) \geqslant -\log\hat{p}_{\mathrm{coll}} - \log\left(1 + \sqrt{\frac{4\ln(2/\epsilon)}{n\hat{p}_{\mathrm{coll}}}} + \frac{4\ln(2/\epsilon) + t + 1}{n\hat{p}_{\mathrm{coll}}}\right).$$

The right-hand side can be bounded in a simper way by the elementary inequality $\log(1 + u) \leqslant \frac{u}{\ln 2}$ valid for all $u > -1$. This gives us (with probability $1 - \epsilon$)

$$- \log \left(\sum_{j=0}^{t} \frac{(n_{j+1} - n_j)}{n} p_{\text{coll}}^j \right) \geqslant - \log \hat{p}_{\text{coll}} - \sqrt{\frac{4 \log(2/\epsilon)}{n \hat{p}_{\text{coll}}}} - \frac{4 \log(2/\epsilon) + \frac{t+1}{\ln 2}}{n \hat{p}_{\text{coll}}}$$

(13)

Consider now the left-hand side. By applying the Jensen Inequality to the convex function $u \to - \log u$, arguments $u_j = p_{\text{coll}}^j$ and weights $\alpha_j = \frac{n_{j+1} - n_j}{n}$ we obtain

$$\sum_{j=0}^{t} \frac{(n_{j+1} - n_j)}{n} \left(- \log \left(p_{\text{coll}}^j \right) \right) \geqslant - \log \left(\sum_{j=0}^{t} \frac{(n_{j+1} - n_j)}{n} p_{\text{coll}}^j \right)$$

$$\geqslant - \log \hat{p}_{\text{coll}} - \sqrt{\frac{4 \log(2/\epsilon)}{n \hat{p}_{\text{coll}}}} - \frac{4 \log(2/\epsilon) + \frac{t+1}{\ln 2}}{n \hat{p}_{\text{coll}}}.$$

(14)

Since $X_1, \ldots, X_n$ are independent, we have

$$\mathrm{CP}\,(X_1, \ldots, X_n) = \prod_{i=1}^{n} \mathrm{CP}(X_i)$$

$$= \prod_{j=0}^{t} \prod_{i=n_j}^{n_{j+1}-1} \mathrm{CP}(X_i)$$

$$= \prod_{j=0}^{t} \prod_{i=n_j}^{n_{j+1}-1} \mathrm{CP}(Y_j)$$

$$= \prod_{j=0}^{t} \left(p_{\text{coll}}^j \right)^{n_{j+1}-n_j},$$

and therefore the collision entropy per bit equals

$$- \frac{\log \mathrm{CP}\,(X_1, \ldots, X_n)}{n} = \sum_{j=0}^{t} \frac{n_{j+1} - n_j}{n} \cdot \left(- \log p_{\text{coll}}^j \right),$$

which combined with Eq. (14) finishes the proof. To obtain the second bound on δ, we simply skip the step just after Eq. (10) and proceed with the unknown parameter $\mathbf{E}\hat{p}_{\text{coll}}$.

4   Application to On-Line Estimation

Consider a source which outputs 10-bit samples. Suppose that the entropy rate is $r = \frac{2}{10}$. Suppose we want to generate a key of length $\ell = 256$ which is at most

$\epsilon = 2^{-112}$-far from the uniform distribution. If we use universal hashing then we need $\ell + 2\log(1/\epsilon)$ entropy bits, that is 480 entropy bits. This, we need at least 240 samples.

Suppose we have collected $n = 240$ samples and estimate the entropy rate at 0.2 by our algorithm. Taking the error into account, we conclude that we can generate $\ell = 120$ bits with security $\epsilon = 2^{-60}$. Thus, the quality goes down but our gain is provable security without assumptions on the entropy rate.

5   Application to Mixed Sources

Imagine a stream of data, where a few different independent sources contributes to every consecutive block. For example in [VSH11] the authors consider using an iPhone accelerometer as a source, which outputs readings from three axes X, Y and Z. The corresponding random process may be described as

$$V_1, V_2, \ldots, V_{3n} = X_1, Y_1, Z_1, X_2, Y_2, Z_2, \ldots, X_n, Y_n, Z_n$$

It can be seen that if in our collision counting estimator we compare $V_i = V_{i-3}$ instead of $V_i = V_{i-1}$ then we get a collision-entropy estimator with the same convergence bounds (up to a constant factor). Indeed, the random variables $Z_i = \mathbf{1}_{\{V_i = V_{i-3}\}}$ are all independent, and thus the estimator doesn't depend on the order. We can now imagine that the order is slightly different

$$V_{\sigma_1}, V_{\sigma_2}, \ldots, V_{\sigma_{3n}} = X_1, X_2, \ldots, X_n, Y_1, Y_2, \ldots, Y_n, Z_1, Z_2, \ldots, Z_n$$

which corresponds to $t = 2$ switches (the distribution changes two times). Therefore, our bounds apply.

6   Conclusion

We have shown that the simple collision-counting entropy estimator is (almost) as good as estimating min-entropy in terms of the number of extracted bits, but it is very efficient and robust against changing the source distribution. The assumption that consecutive outputs are independent is not that restrictive as it has been confirmed empirically and argued theoretically in previous works for many sources.

A   Inefficiency of Plugin Estimators

Let X be an m-bit distribution. Suppose that we want to estimate $\mathbf{P}_X$ from i.i.d samples $X_1, \ldots, X_n$, and use this estimate in the entropy formula. Let $\hat{X}$ be the random variable corresponding to the empirical distribution of n samples, that is

$$\forall x : \quad \Pr[\hat{X} = x] = \frac{1}{n} \sum_{i=1}^{n} \mathbf{1}_{\{X_i = x\}}.$$

We want to use the estimate

$$\mathbf{H}_\infty(X) \approx \mathbf{H}_\infty(\hat{X}).$$

Consider the case when X is uniform. Suppose that we want the absolute error to be at most γ, that is

$$\left| \mathbf{H}_\infty(X) - \mathbf{H}_\infty(\hat{X}) \right| \leqslant \gamma.$$

According to the min-entropy definition, this means that

$$\left| m + \max_x \log \left(\mathbf{P}_{\hat{X}}(x) \right) \right| \leqslant \gamma.$$

which is equivalent to

$$m - \gamma \leqslant \max_x \log \left(\mathbf{P}_{\hat{X}}(x) \right) \leqslant -m + \gamma.$$

In particular,

$$\forall x: \quad \mathbf{P}_{\hat{X}}(x) \leqslant 2^{-n+\gamma} = 2^\gamma \cdot \mathbf{P}_X(x).$$

This means that we need to estimate the probability mass function $\mathbf{P}_X(x)$ up to a relative error $\delta = 2^\gamma - 1$. According to the Chernoff Bound, with fixed x and n samples we get the error probability $\exp(-3\mathbf{P}_X(x)\delta^2) \leqslant \exp(-3 \cdot n2^{-m}\delta^2)$ for some c. Thus, to get the error term below ϵ, we need $\delta = O\left(\sqrt{2^m \log(1/\epsilon)/3n} \right)$. Even for a pretty weak bound $\gamma = 1$ (an error of 1 bit) we need $\delta = 1$ which means $n > 2^m \log(1/\epsilon)/3$ samples.

References

[Ash90]   Ash, R.B.: Information Theory. Dover Publications, New York (1990)
[BKMS09] Bouda, J., Krhovjak, J., Matyas, V., Svenda, P.: Towards true random number generation in mobile environments. In: Jøsang, A., Maseng, T., Knapskog, S.J. (eds.) NordSec 2009. LNCS, vol. 5838, pp. 179–189. Springer, Heidelberg (2009). doi:10.1007/978-3-642-04766-4_13
[BL05]   Bucci, M., Luzzi, R.: Design of testable random bit generators. In: Rao, J.R., Sunar, B. (eds.) CHES 2005. LNCS, vol. 3659, pp. 147–156. Springer, Heidelberg (2005). doi:10.1007/11545262_11
[BS]   Bedekar, N., Shee, C.: A novel approach to true random number generation in wearable computing environments using MEMS sensors. In: Lin, D., Yung, M., Zhou, J. (eds.) Inscrypt 2014. LNCS, vol. 8957, pp. 530–546. Springer, Cham (2015). doi:10.1007/978-3-319-16745-9_29
[BST03]   Barak, B., Shaltiel, R., Tromer, E.: True random number generators secure in a changing environment. In: Walter, C.D., Koç, Ç.K., Paar, C. (eds.) CHES 2003. LNCS, vol. 2779, pp. 166–180. Springer, Heidelberg (2003). doi:10.1007/978-3-540-45238-6_14

[Cac97] Cachin, C.: Smooth entropy and Rényi entropy. In: Fumy, W. (ed.) EURO-CRYPT 1997. LNCS, vol. 1233, pp. 193–208. Springer, Heidelberg (1997). doi:10.1007/3-540-69053-0_14

[Che52] Chernoff, H.: A measure of asymptotic efficiency for tests of a hypothesis based on the sum of observations. Ann. Math. Stat. **23**(4), 493–507 (1952)

[dRHG+99] de Raadt, T., Hallqvist, N., Grabowski, A., Keromytis, A.D., Provos, N.: Cryptography in OpenBSD: an overview. In: Proceedings of the Annual Conference on USENIX Annual Technical Conference, ATEC 1999, p. 33. USENIX Association, Berkeley (1999)

[GPR06] Gutterman, Z., Pinkas, B., Reinman, T.: Analysis of the linux random number generator. In: Proceedings of the 2006 IEEE Symposium on Security and Privacy, SP 2006, pp. 371–385. IEEE Computer Society, Washington, DC (2006)

[Haa] Haahr, M.: random.org homepage. Online; Accessed 01 Jul 2016

[HILL99] Hastad, J., Impagliazzo, R., Levin, L.A., Luby, M.: A pseudorandom generator from any one-way function. SIAM J. Comput. **28**(4), 1364–1396 (1999)

[Hol06] Holenstein, T.: Pseudorandom generators from one-way functions: a simple construction for any hardness. In: Halevi, S., Rabin, T. (eds.) TCC 2006. LNCS, vol. 3876, pp. 443–461. Springer, Heidelberg (2006). doi:10.1007/11681878_23

[JK99] Jun, B., Kocher, P.: The intel random number generator, white paper prepared for Intel corporation (1999)

[KKHD14] Kaplan, D., Kedmi, S., Hay, R., Dayan, A.: Attacking the linux prng on android: weaknesses in seeding of entropic pools and low boot-time entropy. In: 8th USENIX Workshop on Offensive Technologies (WOOT 2014). USENIX Association, San Diego (2014)

[LPR11] Lauradoux, C., Ponge, J., Röck, A.: Online Entropy Estimation for Non-Binary Sources and Applications on iPhone. Rapport de recherche, Inria, June 2011

[LRSV12] Lacharme, P., Röck, A., Strubel, V., Videau, M.: The linux pseudorandom number generator revisited. Cryptology ePrint Archive, Report 2012/251 (2012). http://eprint.iacr.org/

[Mau92] Maurer, U.: A universal statistical test for random bit generators. J. Cryptology **5**, 89–105 (1992)

[RW05] Renner, R., Wolf, S.: Simple and tight bounds for information reconciliation and privacy amplification. In: Roy, B. (ed.) ASIACRYPT 2005. LNCS, vol. 3788, pp. 199–216. Springer, Heidelberg (2005). doi:10.1007/11593447_11

[Sha48] Shannon, C.E.: A mathematical theory of communication. Bell Syst. Techn. J. **27** (1948)

[Sha11] Shaltiel, R.: An introduction to randomness extractors. In: Aceto, L., Henzinger, M., Sgall, J. (eds.) ICALP 2011. LNCS, vol. 6756, pp. 21–41. Springer, Heidelberg (2011). doi:10.1007/978-3-642-22012-8_2

[Sko16] Skórski, M.: Evaluating entropy sources for true random number generators by collision counting. In: Batten, L., Li, G. (eds.) ATIS 2016. CCIS, vol. 651, pp. 69–80. Springer, Singapore (2016). doi:10.1007/978-981-10-2741-3_6

[Sun09] Sunar, B.: True random number generators for cryptography. In: Koç, Ç.K. (ed.) Cryptographic Engineering, pp. 55–73. Springer, US (2009) (English)

[TBK+] Turan, M.S., Barker, E., Kelsey, J., McKay, K.A., Baish, M.L., Boyle, M.:

[vN51] von Neumann, J.: Various techniques used in connection with random digits. J. Res. Nat. Bur. Stand. **12**, 36–38 (1951)

[VSH11] Voris, J., Saxena, N., Halevi, T.: Accelerometers and randomness: perfect together. In: WiSec 2011, pp. 115–126. ACM (2011)

[Wal] Walker, J.: Hotbits homepage. Accessed 01 Jul 2016

Author Index

Printed in the United States
By Bookmasters